THE LIFE OF
KATHERINE MANSFIELD

THE LIFE OF
Katherine Mansfield

Antony Alpers

THE VIKING PRESS
NEW YORK

Library of Congress Cataloging in Publication Data
Alpers, Antony, 1919–
The life of Katherine Mansfield.
Bibliography: p.   Includes index.
1. Mansfield, Katherine, 1888–1923—Biography.
2. Authors, New Zealand—20th century—Biography.   I. Title.
PR9639.3.M258Z58   823'.9'12   79–12088
ISBN 0–670–42805–1

Printed in the United States of America
Set in CRT Janson

Page 466 constitutes an extension of the copyright page.

For George Whalley

Preface

This book replaces a youthful work of mine that was published in 1953, and is in no sense a revised edition. Except for one short scenic description and a few surviving sentences in the early chapters, it is a distinct and different biography, different for several reasons: it draws on more than twenty times as much material; it is freed from constraint in many directions; and it now combines, in a manner which presumably is rather unusual, personal information obtained from friends and contemporaries of its subject, and historical research done at a suitable distance in time. Perhaps in addition I myself have been better equipped this time to present a story which is so darkly tragic—and yet which even in its darkest places sparkles like the inside of a geode, thanks to the gaiety and wit of its central figure.

The previous biography, published as my own first book when Katherine Mansfield would have been only sixty-four, was written with assistance freely given by both of her husbands and the close friend whom she used to call her "wife." Two sisters and a cousin, three college friends, two former lovers, New Zealanders acquainted with her early background and some others who knew her well at various periods had all helped the book in various ways. But with one exception, all of them lived to read it. For a young and inexperienced writer that was not an easy situation. In conversations with people in their sixties to whom Katherine Mansfield was still a vivid presence in the room, I had often been told things which I didn't understand or didn't believe, at least with sufficient confidence to print them. Many personal impressions had been formed which could not freely play their part; many half-truths were at work. Besides, I wrote the whole book not knowing that when the time arrived, John Middleton Murry, Katherine Mansfield's husband and literary executor, would leave me entirely free to publish whatever I had discovered that was true.

Behind this last fact lay a situation that needs recalling briefly. In 1947, when I went to London with the book in progress, Middleton Murry was one of the most unpopular men to be found in the world of English letters. Very quickly I learned that another book on Katherine Mansfield which appeared to be sponsored by him would sink at its launching, if it got so far. For that reason I did not ask him for access to the notebooks and letters which he owned, and of which in any case he was then preparing new editions. We briefly met; he was friendly and helpful, he gave me the addresses of persons bound to be hostile to himself, and later he answered many questions by letter. When eventually I wrote from New Zealand asking his permission to use much copyrighted material (including letters of his former wife not known to him), and offered to arrange for him to see my text, he replied very simply: "Dear Mr Alpers, As a matter of fact I have already seen your book. It was submitted to me for my opinion by Mr Jonathan Cape. I recommended publication." But he refrained from sending me any comments at that stage; he only did so after the book was published—with some emotion, since it had told him much that he had not known.

Today, the personal situation has entirely changed. But the greatest difference now is in regard to documents, the biographer's surest sources for a truthful picture. Thirty years ago these were not freely available, copious though they were. Several friends of Katherine Mansfield had been willing to talk to me but not to produce the letters which they owned, nor was I able then to see the letters she had written to the father of her unborn child. Her sisters, mistakenly thinking I had discovered something embarrassing which in fact I didn't know, had been kind with their help but very cautious. Murry's new edition of the letters came out when I had finished all my text— too late for me to make substantial changes—and the fuller *Journal* only appeared in 1954. For all of these reasons, but especially because Murry was still alive, much that might have illumined Katherine Mansfield's relations with Murry himself, with D. H. and Frieda Lawrence, Virginia Woolf and the Bloomsbury circle, with S. S. Koteliansky, Bertrand Russell, Lytton Strachey, Aldous Huxley, Lady Ottoline Morrell, Dorothy Brett, A. R. Orage, and Francis Carco, eluded the previous book.

Since then, of course, the papers of that literary generation have acquired gilt edges. While some remain in England, great quantities have crossed the Atlantic—some to be hoarded away as sound investments, some to be stolen and recovered by the FBI, many more to be enshrined with care and made available to scholars. Deaths have lessened the need for privacy and reticence; our very notions of what is desirable in biography have changed; and I, this time, have been enabled by Queen's University and the Canada Council to visit all the open collections, including that which has now come into being in New Zealand. Under these conditions it has also been possible to discover much more about the catastrophic hidden years between Kathleen Beauchamp's arrival in London at the age of nineteen and her meeting Murry three years later—her extraordinary one-day marriage in 1909 to a man she didn't love; her months in Bavaria, where she lost the baby she had conceived by a young man whom she did; and her association after that with Orage's *New Age* and its team of desperate contributors.

But the book is now as much a picture of the period as a life of Katherine Mansfield, and in regard to both literature and the roles of women the period has come to hold exceptional interest. In the second decade of this century, as we've often been reminded, "human character changed." If that wasn't true of men, it was of women, and the "Mss. Bowden" of 1910 was a modern woman well before her time. More than that, she was an authentic early member of the "Modern Movement"—one of its shrewdest and wittiest observers, and unique in the range of her acquaintance with its principal members.

It would be hard to think of anyone who saw so vividly at the time so much of what was happening, with an eye for both the human and the literary fact. There is no other writer who knew Orage's *New Age* in 1910, the Lawrence who wrote *Women in Love* in 1916, *and* the emerging moth Virginia Woolf, along with Lady Ottoline Morrell's hectic Garsington, Middleton Murry's hectic *Rhythm,* and his distinguished *Athenaeum;* which is not to mention a short-lived intimacy with Bertrand Russell, a clash with Henri Gaudier-Brzeska, or the surprising walk-on parts that are played in her tragedy this time by T. S. Eliot, James Joyce, and Wyndham Lewis. Even Rainer Maria Rilke, like a terrible angel, makes a curious unseen visitation at one of the greatest moments of his own poetic career, and a strange affinity with his nature is observed. To accommodate this wider background, the book is some four-fifths longer than its predecessor.

Of the *New Age*, much more is now told, and while the chapters on *Rhythm* and the *Blue Review* are also treated as contributions to the history of the little magazine, I don't think these are the dullest parts of the story. Fresh darkness is thrown on Lawrence in his relation to the Murrys and his own most widely read novel; a literary debt of Virginia Woolf is brought to light; and the supposed indebtedness of Katherine Mansfield to Anton Chekhov is shown, I believe, to be mostly an illusion. The influence of Theocritus, because it was formative, is of much more interest now.

I strongly believe that a life of Katherine Mansfield must be a literary biography, so this is a book about the writer and her work. To depict the one without the other would be a betrayal of the only cause that justifies the biography of a creative artist; to describe what she did without describing what she did would be absurd. However, the passages that discuss the writing at any length are set off in such a way that readers who insist may skip or skim them—soon discovering, I would hope, that this was a mistake.

Antony Alpers

Queen's University
September 1979

Acknowledgments

As anyone who has helped a biographer must know, and as any biographer knows even better, printed acknowledgments can never express what needs to be expressed. In this case, moreover, since there are now two books, my helpers stand in ranks of the living and the dead, some thirty years apart and on three sides of the globe.

I would first thank the present book's Canadian friends: Dr. Geoffrey Andrew, the University of British Columbia, and the Canada Council; and Dr. George Whalley, Dr. J. A. Corry, and Queen's University. It was the former who fetched me to Canada on a visit from New Zealand in 1962, and the latter who in consequence invited me to join Queen's University in 1966, although I hold no degree of any sort. After Dr. Whalley had suggested in 1970 that the old book might usefully be "revised" (as we both mistakenly thought), a sabbatical year from Queen's, accompanied by a Canada Council Leave Fellowship and followed by further research grants from both of those sources, made possible what is now presented to the reader. My warmest gratitude goes to all those named.

Moving back some thirty years, and speaking as though all were still alive, I would again thank those who so generously sponsored or assisted the original, youthful venture in New Zealand: Joe Heenan, who as Secretary for Internal Affairs was a most enlightened official patron; Ormond Wilson and G. H. Scholefield, and with them the New Zealand State Literary Fund; G. N. Morris, who gave me the freedom of his Mansfield collection in Auckland; Miss Nola Millar; Mrs. G. G. S. Robison; Miss Maud England; Miss Ruth Herrick; Miss

Rose Ridler, Mrs. Harold Miller, and Miss Eva Butts. Those beginnings also drew, as this book does to a lesser extent, on the pioneer work of a young American librarian who went all the way to New Zealand in 1931 to attempt the first biography of Katherine Mansfield. Ruth Mantz was able then to gather information which but for her would not be available now, and every subsequent biographer is in her debt.

There followed all the practical help and many kindnesses of Miss Ida Baker and Mrs. Marjorie Clark, in Hampshire; Mr. G. C. Bowden; Mr. C. E. Bechhofer-Roberts; M. Francis Carco; Mr. D'Arcy Cresswell; Mrs. O. Raymond Drey; Mr. J. D. Fergusson; Lord and Lady Glenavy, in Ireland; Mme. Olga de Hartmann and Mme. Adèle Kafian, in Paris; Mr. S. S. Koteliansky, at No. 5 Acacia Road; Mrs. Sylvia Lynd; Miss Alice Marks; Mrs. M. J. Murphy; Mr. William Orton; the Rev. E. A. Payne, of the Baptist Historical Society; Mrs. C. M. Pickthall and Mrs. Charles Renshaw (Katherine Mansfield's sisters Chaddie and Jeanne); Mr. Edward Shanks; Mrs. J. W. N. Sullivan (Vere Bartrick-Baker); Mr. Frank Swinnerton; Mrs. Margaret Woodhouse; and of course John Middleton Murry, whose help is described in the Preface.

The task being taken up again under totally different conditions in the 1970s, outstanding assistance was given by Professor A. W. Riley, Department of German, Queen's University, and by Mrs. Riley, who comes from Schwäbisch-Gmund. It is thanks to their energies, by letter and in Bavaria, and also to the help of Herr Josef Wolf, Kneipp-Archivar, Bad-Wörishofen, and of Fräulein Maria Brechenmacher, that this book now can approximately plot what happened in 1909. Mrs. Jean E. Stone, of Sydney, with a kindness only matched by her persistence, has uncovered the background of the original "pretty Miss Mansfield"; Professor J. M. Stedmond, of Queen's University, searched through old dusty newspaper files in London when I could not do so myself; Dr. Whalley attended to my need to know more about Coleridge, and many other matters.

Without the access I have been given to papers in private hands (and permission to make use of copyright material) the book would obviously be much poorer, and I would acknowledge the generous help, not to mention the encouragements, of Mrs. Mary Murry, Mr. Richard Murry, Mr. Colin Middleton Murry, and the late Frank Lea, along with the late Mr. G. C. Bowden, his widow, and his son George M. Bowden. Professor and Mrs. Quentin Bell helped me to see the diary of Virginia Woolf before it began to be published, and the following all assisted my access to needed sources: the late Mrs. Mackintosh Bell (Katherine Mansfield's sister Vera); Mr. M. T. Bizony; Mr. David Drey; Mrs. Stephanie Fierz, Principal of Queen's College, London; Mr. Sean Hignett; Mr. John Manchester; Mrs. Jessie Orage and Mrs. Ann Orage; Mrs. Igor Vinogradoff; and Professor John Waterlow.

How much is owed to Mr. T. O. Beachcroft will be obvious from the text, and for help of various kinds I would also thank Mrs. Rickard Donovan; Mrs. Marjorie Gertler; Mr. Michael Holroyd; Mr. Warren Howell; Mr. Paul Levy; Mr. H. Clifford Maggs; Professor Wallace Martin; Mrs. Dorothy Morland; Mr. Stanley Olsen; Mr. Sankaran Palat, in India; Mr. K. G. Pope, of London Transport; Mr. Douglas Trowell; and James and Judy Wieland. For their help and hospitality in my widespread travels I gratefully remember Professor and Mrs. Joseph Jones, of Austin, Texas; Mr. Paul Gabites; Mme. Rosette Simon, of Montana-sur-Sierre; Mme. Jeanne de Sépibus de Preux, of Sierre; George and Carmen Bowden; John and Ruth Murry; Frank Lea; Mrs. Igor Anrep and Mrs. Arthur Waley; and, as always throughout thirty years, Mrs. Marjorie Clark, whose necessary role was so often to shout at Ida Baker, "Shut up, Lesley, and tell him the truth."

The following libraries or institutions have kindly allowed me to use materials in their possession: the Humanities Research Center, University of Texas at Austin; the Trustees of the British Museum; the Alexander Turnbull Library, Wellington; the Henry W. and Albert A. Berg Collection of English and American Literature in the New York Public Library, Astor, Lenox and Tilden Foundations; the Bertrand Russell Archives, McMaster University, Hamilton, Ontario; the Henry E. Huntington Library, San Marino, California; Stanford University Library, California; the Department of Rare Books, Cornell University Library; the Special Collections Department, University of Cincinnati Libraries; Windsor University Library, Windsor, Ontario; the Library of King's College, Cambridge; the Library of Sussex University; the Research Library, University of California, Los Angeles; the Archives of Smith College, Northampton, Massachusetts; and the Strachey Trust, London. Valuable help has been given by the General Assembly Library, Wellington, and the Douglas Library at Queen's University. As the bibliography records, much is also owed to the labours of Mrs. Margaret Scott in transcribing early Mansfield manuscripts at the Turnbull Library. To staff members who have helped me at all these institutions I would express my thanks for their patient attention to my inquiries, but for exceptional kindness that went beyond the call of duty I would specially thank Dr. Lola M. Szladits, of the Berg Collection in New York; Mr. Ken Blackwell, of the Bertrand Russell Archives; and Dr. Philip Larkin, who so kindly dug out unpoetic information in the Library of the University of Hull concerning something which didn't happen in Hull on the night of Guy Fawkes' Day, 1908.

To all of those whose permission to make use of copyright material is formally acknowledged I would express my personal thanks. In a few cases where all efforts to trace representatives have failed, I ask to be forgiven for any inadvertent trespass, and hope to be informed so that correction might be made at some time in the future.

Colleagues, staff and students at Queen's University, by their presence and their patience throughout nine years, have helped the work on occasions too numerous to acknowledge, but I would specially mention Anne-Marie Epp, Barbara Dunn, Anne Morton, and Noel King for their lively attention to certain critical and historical problems; Stella Wynne-Edwards; Lynda Lemaire and Kathy Abrams, for their patient and flawless typings and retypings; my colleague Catherine Harland, for a valuable reading of the typescript at a difficult time; and at home my wife, Margaret, for all the help that goes unseen.

The use of photographs is acknowledged in the List of Illustrations, but nothing there reveals what was contributed to the Picture Album by the photographic skills and the amused cooperation, over many months, of George Innes, of the Department of Geography at Queen's. When the album had been assembled with Mr. Innes' mischievous help, it passed to the obviously gifted hands of the book's designer, Ann Gold, to whom as well I am deeply grateful.

Lastly, and with exceptional pleasure, I have Amanda Vaill to thank for all that she contributed at The Viking Press by so brilliantly perceiving what in the text might be better said, or better not said, or said six pages later or round the other way, or by some exasperating change made far more helpful to the reader—whose thanks as well as mine are owed to her.

Contents

Contents

List of Illustrations

The photographs following page 246 are credited below. Pictures showing no acknowledgments are from the author's collection or were taken by the author. Abbreviations are as in the Reference Notes.

Childhood years: Thorndon and Karori

Queen's College, and New Zealand Again

out of the picture to the right; the Hôtel Beau Rivage faces the boats at the far end of the bay.

By Brett   A representation of "The Ark" (No. 3 Gower Street) from one of Dorothy Brett's letters to Lady Ottoline Morrell. TEXAS.

Uncaptioned   Lady Ottoline Morrell. By courtesy of Colin Middleton Murry.

Villa Pauline   The Villa Pauline in Bandol. TEXAS.

K.M.B. and L.H.B.   Chummie and Kathleen on a hilltop in Wellington, about 1907.

Leslie Beauchamp, 1915   Leslie Heron Beauchamp in his officer's kit, spring 1915.

Higher Tregerthen   The cottages at Higher Tregerthen, Cornwall, with "Katherine's Tower" in its original, castellated form. Photograph by courtesy of Colin Middleton Murry, with extract from a letter by K.M. to Lady Ottoline Morrell (TEXAS): "We are making a house—but everything seems to be made of boulders. We shall have to eat off stones as well as have them for our pillows. Money is dreadful: we've none."

Uncaptioned   Frederick Goodyear, four years before his death. British Library.

The cottage at Mylor   Sunnyside Cottage, Mylor, in 1972.

With Kot, 1915   K.M. with S.S. Koteliansky in the Gordon Campbells' garden, St. John's Wood, 1915. By courtesy of Colin Middleton Murry.

1917   K.M. in 1917, a studio portrait by courtesy of Colin Middleton Murry.

141a Church St., Chelsea   "The Studio" in Chelsea, taken in 1974.

Paris; Ospedaletti; the *Athenaeum*; Isola Bella

Katherine's mother, 1918   A late photograph of Mrs. Beauchamp, who died in August 1918.

J.M.M., Brett, and K.M., Hampstead   Jack, Brett, and Katherine (in deck chair), on the heath outside No. 2 Portland Villas. Photo by Ida Baker.

Ospedaletti, 1919   The Casetta at Ospedaletti *(see the waves below, at left).* A snap by Miss Fullerton, by courtesy of Colin Middleton Murry.

Villa Flora, 1920   On the steps of the Villa Flora: Miss Connie Beau-

Chalet des Sapins; Sierre; Fontainebleau

like an infant bishop"—"Elizabeth" at Montana. By courtesy of Colin Middleton Murry.

J.M.M., c. 1921   By courtesy of Colin Middleton Murry.

With Brett, Sierre, 1922   K.M. and Dorothy Brett at the Hôtel Château Belle Vue, Sierre, July 1922. Photo by Ida Baker.

Gurdjieff   George Ivanovich Gurdjieff, the father-figure of Katherine's last few months. The University Library, Cambridge.

Gurdjieff's throne   The Master's seat or alcove in the "study house" at Fontainebleau. From the *Graphic,* 1923. British Library.

Uncaptioned   Katherine Mansfield's passport photograph for the journey to San Remo in September 1919. By courtesy of Mrs. Mary Middleton Murry.

A Note on the Text

In her scribbled notebooks and her letters Katherine Mansfield wrote by ear much more than by eye, and very rapidly. In consequence the originals contain many slips of the pen, including spelling mistakes, which it would only be absurd to reproduce in type. But she also played the mimic on paper and made much use of deliberate misspellings, renderings of wrong pronunciations, and so on.

Modern scholarly practice might require an editor of her letters or notebooks to reproduce both kinds, with painfully frequent use of the voucher *"sic"* for all the inadvertent slips. But this book is a biography, and so, in the main, only her deliberate misspellings have been reproduced in quoted passages, the rest being silently corrected. For example, it is hardly necessary to insist on the reader's knowing, on page 49, that K.M. actually wrote, "which, being interpredeth, meaneth that I adore her"—a characteristic aural slip; or that lower down she ungratefully said of E.K.B., "also she will not achieve a great deal of gratefness"—even though the slip in that case might be "Freudian." For similar reasons, needed punctuation has often been supplied, though what to do with the innumerable short dashes in K.M.'s early writing (they are often no more than commas) is an unsolved problem.

One other kind of silent correction will only be noticed by readers familiar with the published *Journal,* where Murry sometimes could not read the original, or mistranscribed it. In 1909, for instance, the *Journal* has K.M. recalling for Garnet Trowell their times of sweetness and anguish in "Glasgow—Liverpool—Carlton Hill—*Our House.*" In the original notebook the last two words, *"but Home,"* are clearly legible, and that is how they are given on page 92 in this book. The reader's attention has not been drawn to all corrections of this sort. The misspelling of personal names, including Katherine's own, was such a common practice among her friends that it has been liberally reproduced, without recourse to *"sic."* Foreign words and phrases are normally italicised throughout the book, but in quoted passages the form of the original has usually been followed.

In order not to have too spotty a carpet, the titles of short stories by Katherine Mansfield are given in italics, but those of other authors are given in quotation marks, in the usual way.

THE LIFE OF
KATHERINE MANSFIELD

CHAPTER I

Places of Origin

We are born, so to speak, provisionally, it doesn't matter where; it is only gradually that we compose, within ourselves, our true place of origin, so that we may be born there retrospectively, and each day more definitely. For some people their spiritual birthplace coincides with that which one finds mentioned in their passports, and it must confer an unheard of happiness to be identical to such a point with external circumstances.
—Rainer Maria Rilke to Duchess Aurelia Gallarati Scotti, January 1923 (trans. E. C. Mason)

To say that Katherine Mansfield was born in Wellington, New Zealand, on 14 October 1888 would seem a simple statement of fact, beyond all contradiction, and in every way a sound beginning for an account of her life and her art and the time she lived in. Yet it wouldn't describe what actually happened that Sunday morning to Mr. and Mrs. Harold Beauchamp, and their child. Since the name is a pseudonym, which she adopted only nineteen years later, "Katherine Mansfield" can hardly be said to have been born that day. Or can she? There is no avoiding the fact that her story begins in complexity—and with a name problem.

Her father poses no such difficulty. An ambitious and vigorous young man with ginger hair, a neat red beard and rather prominent blue eyes, Hal Beauchamp worked for an old importing firm which had its office and warehouse down by the Wellington wharves. When he joined it as a boy of eighteen it had been quietly falling asleep, even though the colony was growing by shiploads every month. But eleven years of *his* energy had brought it back to life; in fact he had so increased its business that a partnership was promised him. On the morning when his third daughter was born, Beauchamp's thirtieth birthday was a month away.

Annie, his pretty little brown-haired, brown-eyed wife, less robust than he and even somewhat delicate since her bout of rheumatic fever, was six years younger, a woman who undoubtedly loved her husband, but who dreaded the monthly sessions when she had to sit beside him at the dining-room table and go through all the household bills, accounting for every threepence. Her own ambitions were social, in that town of thirty thousand people.

The Beauchamps had lately built themselves a square wooden house down in the suburb of Thorndon near the harbour, and had moved there (it was their fourth address), together with Annie's mother, Mrs. Dyer, and her two sisters, Kitty and Belle. They had two children so far, both girls. The house was full of women. It was time for a son.

The man of the house, it is true, wasn't yet the owner of W. M. Bannatyne & Co. He had not even begun to "make money" (the words are his). But old Mr. Bannatyne's death in England meant that a partnership was open, and another death soon was to leave him in control. Even better: by then Hal Beauchamp, born on an Australian goldfield to a rolling stone of a father whose example he did *not* intend to follow, would be a director of several companies in the capital, and a member of the Harbour Board as well—a man with the future at his feet. Perhaps Wellington society would never forget those goldfield origins, or Mrs. Beauchamp's rather noticeable hopes; but there would eventually be much grander residences than the box-like structure at 11 Tinakori Road, considerable wealth, financial power in the land, a knighthood and a crest, and in Beauchamp's seventies the *Reminiscences and Recollections,* bound in red cloth with a coat of arms in gold—our principal source for this Colonial story.[1]* If all that was ahead, and strictly speaking unforeseeable, it can almost be discerned in certain photographs of the young Hal Beauchamp. On this Sunday in the spring of 1888, it was high time for a son.

Apart from the *Reminiscences,* so proudly stamped with the motto *Vérité sans peur* (how his daughter would have loved that, and how it

---

*Reference notes, as distinct from footnotes, which have an asterisk or dagger, are gathered at the back of the book, beginning on page 426.

licences biography!), another account exists of the way things may
have gone at Tinakori Road that morning. A fiction, this time—a short
story, to be exact, entitled *A Birthday,* and written twenty-one years
later, with a certain licence as to facts but with the keenest possible ear
for *vérité*.

The setting is undoubtedly that house, with its back fence on the rim
of a deep ferny gully, a stone's throw from the iron suspension-bridge
which the man of the house must cross as he goes to fetch the doctor
—on edge, and without even breakfast to sustain him. It is the third
birth in the family, and the kindly grandmother is preparing to act as
midwife. In print, all the characters had German names, a disguise that
can be dispensed with here, where truth without fear is the aim. The
man of the house has arrived at the doctor's:

> "Well, Beauchamp," said the doctor jovially, brushing some crumbs
> from a pearl coloured waistcoat, "son and heir becoming importunate?"
> Up went Beauchamp's spirits with a bound. Son and heir, by Jove! He
> was glad to have to deal with a man again. And a sane fellow this, who
> came across this sort of thing every day of the week.
> "That's about the measure of it, Doctor," he answered, smiling, and
> picking up his hat. "Mother dragged me out of bed this morning with
> imperative orders to bring you along."
> "Gig will be round in a minute. Drive back with me, won't you?
> Extraordinary, sultry day; you're as red as a beetroot already."

In the story, it's a boy, but the baby that Dr. Kemp held up was a
girl: strong and healthy like her father, but with her mother's brown
hair and brown eyes. Boys' names could not be used. She was baptised
Kathleen Mansfield, the "Mansfield" being Mrs. Dyer's maiden name,
and a mark of the one love which the child later felt she had known
in her early years.

According to one who knew her well, Annie Beauchamp "didn't
handle babies," so the child was cared for from the start by Mrs. Dyer,
and became her Granny's Kass. The fact that her mother went off to
England with Hal on a business trip when she was one year old may
have hardly affected her. But Annie, returning pregnant, presented
Hal on 11 October 1890 with his fourth child not a boy, and this one,
by contracting infantile cholera, demanded all Mrs. Dyer's attention.
Gwen died, on 9 January 1891, but Kass by then had started having

nightmares. Beneath the chubby exterior there developed a nature that was insecure, and subject to terrors in the night not only when asleep.

The Beauchamps lived at 11 Tinakori Road for the next five years, with Granny Dyer and the young Aunt Belle (her sister Kitty having left). The house directly faced "Mount Wakefield"—a high, bare hill, once forested, but sprinkled now with gorse and sheep, whence photographers of the nineties took their panoramic views of leafy Thorndon, with the wharves and the ships beyond, and the birthplace visible in some. The road actually runs down a great crack in the land, a geological fault of vast extent,* which explains the gully behind the house and the towering hill before it. Katherine Mansfield was born on a fault line.

Thorndon's houses showed experience of earthquakes, and of cultural disturbance too. Invariably built of timber, they stood at fireproof distances among their trees—trying their best, however, to look as if they were made of stone, with imitation cornices and pillars gouged from native wood. The Beauchamps' home, more modest than most, was a bald, two-storeyed cube whose only decoration was a glassed-in entrance porch at the side, with strips of coloured glass surrounding its larger panes. The neighbouring houses, and the red-painted iron suspension-bridge beyond the Nathans' house next door, had far more frills.

From there, at any rate, Hal Beauchamp took a bracing daily walk in Wellington's wind to his office off Customhouse Quay, where he gave his profitable attention to supplying the colony with Nobel's dynamite, Eureka axes, and Light-of-the-Age kerosene, along with Teacher's Highland Cream, Dr. Townsend's sarsaparilla, Dresden pianos, Egyptian cigarettes, and Pain's Fireworks[2]—everything, in short, that was needed for the breaking in of a rude colony, and the comfort in the process of its uprooted middle class; which, however, was also being broken in, by a process that his daughter would observe more subtly than he.

The wharves and the ships, so close, were a constant invitation to departure, and by the age of six months Kass had made acquaintance with their sights and smells. *"Premier voyage âge de six mois,"* says a biographical note set down in her own sort of French in one of her

*Much farther north, it is the Tonga Trench.

letters;[3] which must mean that in 1889, probably at Easter, she was taken across Cook Strait to the little town of Picton, in Queen Charlotte Sound, on a visit to her father's parents. It is Grandpa Beauchamp, lying in bed "like a very old, wide-awake bird," who briefly appears in her story *The Voyage*.

He is a very important forebear, a sort of key piece in our story. Somehow, certain aspects of Arthur Beauchamp's character came down unchanged to his famous grandchild, who referred to them ruefully in the very last letter she ever wrote. It will help us, then, to know a little of *his* story—and of how it is told, also ruefully, by his son.

An incorrigible rolling stone who sought out every kind of Colonial bad luck and laughed at most of it in facetious frontier doggerel—or in lines of Byron if appropriate—Arthur Beauchamp as a young man was seldom to be found at one address for more than a few months at a time. He was forever pulling up stakes to move on, with such painful regularity that the family used to say that as soon as his hens heard the sound of packing, they lay on their backs with their legs up, ready to be tied; and if his human associates knew the limits of despair on such occasions, the Pa man, as likely as not, would respond with some stanzas of *Don Juan* making light of the human predicament.

He was one of the embarrassingly numerous sons of a certain John Beauchamp (born 1781), the last proprietor of a family silversmithing business in London which had once known better days. *That* ancestor's doggerel verses had earned him the name of "The Poet of Hornsey Lane"—he lived in Highgate, the business being in Holborn—but he seems to have had scant knack for either Poetry or Business. Although he invented a new kind of imitation silverware, he didn't patent it. He reeled off Byron by the hour (passing on this gift to Arthur); or he went out riding to hounds. By the decade that came to be known as the Hungry Forties, there was nothing for Arthur and his brothers to inherit.

Their mother provides a somewhat firmer connexion with the arts. She was a sister-in-law and sometime sitter to the painter C. R. Leslie, the friend and biographer of John Constable, which meant that Constable himself, as a letter records, once took his sons to "Mr. Beecham's" (his spelling records the correct pronunciation of the name) to see the "forges, smelting potts—metals—turning lathes—straps and bellows—coals, ashes, dust, dirt & cinders—and everything else that is agreeable to boys."[4]

The sons of the silversmith remained at school in Highgate until they were thirteen or so, but the cinders and dirt held no allure for them, and in any case the business was collapsing. With superb understatement, Hal Beauchamp sums up this painful situation: "My grandfather, in the circumstances, interposed no obstacles to the boys striking out for themselves." And of the Poet of Hornsey Lane no more is heard.

The first to get away was Henry Herron Beauchamp, future father of the Edwardian best-selling author "Elizabeth" (who became world-famous with *Elizabeth and Her German Garden*), and grandfather to a member of Bloomsbury who once proposed to Virginia Woolf. By the age of fifteen Henry was in Sydney, Australia, where he married, and made his pile in sixteen years. He then took his family back to Europe, living for some years in Lausanne. One day in 1889 his daughter May, aged twenty-two, was playing the organ in the American church in Rome when a recently widowed German count* came in, and a conquest was made. He proposed to May in Florence ("The Count looks such a dear," her mother wrote), and swept her off to his estate in Pomerania; whence some years later, without disclosing her identity, she began to publish her immensely popular books in a prattling prose that has an undeniable if egotistic charm.[5]

Arthur was the sixth son of the silversmith, the favourite of aunts with his twinkling eye and his constant spout of poetry. Seven years of apprenticeship to a stingy relative in the City resulted in some doggerel verses which had the refrain, "He kept his gold, and I my liberty," and so, in 1848, at the age of twenty-one, Arthur sailed for Sydney. A brief employment with his unpoetic brother having evoked the same refrain, he joined the gold-rush in Victoria with a similar result, and there followed almost sixty years of Antipodean wanderings as storekeeper, prospector, bushwhacker, sawmiller, "general merchant and auctioneer," popular tenor at concerts, and local politician. He did make one wise move. In 1854 he married Mary Elizabeth Stanley, the orphaned daughter of a Lancashire silversmith, who knew

*Count Henning von Arnim, "son of the ambassador disgraced by Bismarck and grandson of the Hohenzollern prince loved by Mme. Récamier. Alarmed by his passion but impressed by his grandeur and intoxicated by the music of Wagner, little Miss Beauchamp quickly married this widower sixteen years older than herself, and went to live among the Germans, whom she found absurd or nasty."—Raymond Mortimer, reviewing her biography in the London *Sunday Times*, 9 November 1958.

her duty as surely as the fowls. When her husband announced another move she meekly bowed her head—"Yes, Arthur"—and began to pack. "I can truthfully say I never saw her in a temper," writes her son in his style of slightly pompous charity. "I can only describe her as an earthly saint."

After two babies had died in the goldfields, the more vigorous Harold—Childe Harold, no doubt—was born in 1858, at Ararat, amid the diggings: probably not in a tent, since his father at that time seems to have been a "general merchant." His first bath, all the same, was probably a sluicing-pan. Perhaps the spoon was silver. Two years later, a wealthy aunt of Arthur's having left him a parcel of land in New Zealand (of which he was soon defrauded), the family crossed the Tasman Sea.

Arthur Beauchamp was what the family called a "Pa man"—an expression which his grandchild often uses in her letters, sometimes with reference to herself. It seems to mean a cheerfully feckless character who is always the first to make a joke of his own deficiencies. When Arthur spoke in the Marlborough Provincial Council for over ten hours, and at the end of five hours said, "Mr. Speaker, having made these few preliminary remarks, I will now proceed to address myself to the main subject," that was, as she would call it, "very Pa." His leaving town to take up a bush section in Pelorus Sound, where they lived on fish and mutton and native birds, and where, as Harold puts it, "my father continued our education," was purest Pa man conduct; and when, having moved to Wanganui, he sent his boys to school with a note to the teacher saying, "Dear Sir, Please receive, in good order and condition, my sons Harold and Arthur," that, too, was "true original Pa man" stuff.

By the age of seventeen Harold, having received the completest possible education in Pa-manship, had evidently resolved to find some better way. When his father moved once more he got his job with Bannatyne's, and so began an urban career devoted to uninterrupted gain.

Devoted in part, however, to Poetry as well; for he learned to play the piano, and once hoped to play the cornet. In Wellington he "met a lot of very fine young fellows," and he joined the rowing club, the football club, and also the Bijou Minstrels, who made him their accompanist: "The only pieces I can remember that I used to play would be considered quite obsolete today, for instance, 'The Maiden's Prayer,'

'The Golden Wave,' 'Les Hirondelles,' 'Le Poet Mourant,' 'The Joyful Peasant,' and so on."

There was one other clerk at Bannatyne's, a youth named Dyer, whose pretty sister Annie was thirteen years of age. Since their mother, the former Margaret Isabella Mansfield, is a figure of perhaps even more significance in Katherine Mansfield's life than Arthur Beauchamp, we need to know of her background as well.

Beauchamp's *Reminiscences*—which are openly concerned with what he calls "good lineage"—record no more of Granny Dyer than the claim that she was known in Sydney as "the pretty Miss Mansfield"; and his daughters, when asked, would never vouchsafe more except to add that they understood that she was "Irish," although in Australia's early days that could imply an ancestry not quite respectable.

In fact she was the daughter of a Sydney publican who had gone out to Australia from England—not as a convict but as a saloon passenger —and there seems to have been no "Irish" anywhere at all.

Samuel Worthington Mansfield, whose father was Ralph Mansfield, a potter, of Liverpool, reached Sydney at the age of twenty-two in 1825 ("came free," the records show) and within five years was the licensee of a pub called The Hope, in nearby Parramatta. Nine years more and he had married a girl just newly arrived from Somerset—Margaret Barns, who was born in Bath and whose father was a sailor; and in the year of their marriage he acquired or established two pubs in Sydney itself: The Rising Sun, and a sailors' pub called The Golden Anchor, which was down by the wharves where the Sydney Harbour Bridge now is. And that is where Kathleen's grandmother grew up. Born in Princes Street in 1839, Margaret Isabella Mansfield was baptised an Anglican, as her father nominally was; but at the age of sixteen, being then a Wesleyan by choice, she married an insurance clerk aged thirty-six named Joseph Dyer, the son of a well-known Baptist minister of Battersea, London, who had drowned himself in a cistern. Their fourth child, Annie, was born in Upper Fort Street, not far from The Golden Anchor, in 1864. Joseph was later sent to Wellington to open the first New Zealand branch of the Australian Mutual Provident Society, and by the time he died, in 1877, deeply in debt (like a brother who had worried his father to death), and beyond the help of his own insurance, there were nine children.[6]

From the outset, there was no doubt at all about Miss Annie Burnell Dyer. Hal of the ginger whiskers—who had clearly no thought of *marrying* money—began to court her when she was fourteen, and he gave her no peace until she was old enough to be his wife. He was then twenty-six, and able to put a roof over her mother and two of her sisters as well.

[2]

Such a relief it was for the man of the house to reach the doctor's residence that Sunday morning and "deal with a man again." It was an equal relief to the women (if we may trust his daughter's portrayals) to hear the door slam behind him as he left for his office on weekdays —as in *At the Bay*, in which "their very voices changed as they called to one another," and the young Aunt Beryl makes the New Zealander's gesture of companionship: "Have another cup of tea, Mother. It's still hot."

In Katherine Mansfield's stories of childhood the mother and the grandmother are always contrasted: the grandmother patient, tactful and affectionate, the mother languid rather than gentle, resigned rather than patient, warm to her husband's needs, but remote and even chilly to her children, as if she, too, had had rheumatic fever. Like Linda Burnell in *At the Bay*, Annie was the delicate wife of a hearty husband; her whole time was spent in "rescuing him, and restoring him, and calming him down, and listening to his story." One reads there, too, of Linda's dread of having children: "Yes, that was her real grudge against life. . . . .* She was broken, made weak, her courage was gone, through childbearing. And what made it doubly hard to bear was, she did not love her children."

Mrs. Dyer—"Mrs. Fairfield" in the Burnell stories—was the woman of self-effacing tact and practical good sense who, having borne nine children of her own, now cared for five of Annie Beauchamp's. With the help of servants and unmarried daughters she made the household run smoothly for thirteen years or so, and when there was a baby in the house her daughter did not have to touch it. That such a ménage survived so long while a succession of daughters arrived says something for Harold Beauchamp, if it says even more for the grandmother. The loss to the art of Katherine Mansfield if she had not known the

---

*In all quoted passages in this book five unspaced dots denote an elision by the present author. Three dots are Katherine Mansfield's own punctuation, and do not represent omitted words.

extended family of her Burnell stories is incalculable; one can hardly imagine it.

When Kathleen was four, and yet another girl had been born, Beauchamp decided to give his daughters a country childhood. Finding a large house vacant at Karori, a little settlement in an upland valley four miles from town by a winding road, he leased it for the next five years. Though exalted in the 1850's by the name of "Chesney Wold," the house was neither Bleak nor in any way Dickensian. After the cube in Thorndon it gave a pleasing welcome with its forty-year-old trees, its orchard equally "old," its conservatory, its sweeping drive, and its ample space for servants—who now could be added to. Beside the drive there grew a tall, solitary aloe.

In Dickens's time, when the house was built, the Karori valley had been filled with totara forest. Matches and Eureka axes had soon cleared that away, but the hillsides were still littered with the bones of unwanted trees, amongst which sheep now grazed. In the gullies, some folds of native bush remained, and in them native birds, so that at night one heard the little owl whose name is morepork. On the valley-floor lay the village—a scattering of bungalows with picket fences, a General Store, a wooden church, a blacksmith's and, some little distance off, the Big House with the literary name, later to be the setting for *Prelude*. "Quite a farmlet," as the *Reminiscences* inform us: "—cows, a couple of horses, pigs and poultry. It was here that Kathleen spent some of the formative years of her childhood, which she reconstructed so vividly in many of her stories that I often feel that the five years meant as much to her as they did to my wife and myself." To Linda Burnell, that is, and her husband Stanley (who seems in *Prelude* to have bought the place, not leased it):

> "The thing that pleases me," said Stanley, leaning against the side of the bed and giving himself a good scratch on his shoulders and back before turning in, "is that I've got the place dirt cheap, Linda. . . . ."

For Kathleen, the most important innovation may have been Patrick Sheehan, the Irish cowman-gardener whom she first described in a schoolgirl piece, *About Pat*. His duties included fetching his master by buggy at the end of the office day (he wore a brown bowler for this), spit-polishing all the family's shoes, proposing to each new cook, and amusing the children. While doing the shoes he would lift Kass on to

the table and recount "long tales of the Dukes of Ireland whom he had
seen and even conversed with," and at tea in the kitchen he would
put some salt on his knife and tap it off with his fork, "the little finger
of his right hand well curled." That was how the Dukes did it.
Along with the "Irish" granny—of course, her mother may have been
Irish but there is no evidence of that—he probably helped to germinate
the imagination of Katherine Mansfield. Certainly one thing he did
made a very deep impression, since it appears in three of her stories,
most vividly in *Prelude*. In the presence of their cousins Pip and Rags,
Pat invites the Burnell children to come and see "how the Kings of
Ireland chop off the head of a duck." On a stump, the tomahawk
descends, the head flies off, and the blood spurts over the feathers and
on to his hand:

> "Watch it!" shouted Pat. He put down the body and it began to waddle
> —with only a long spurt of blood where the head had been; it began to
> pad away without a sound towards the steep bank that led to the stream
> . . . That was the crowning wonder.
> "Do you see that? Do you see that?" yelled Pip. He ran among the little
> girls tugging at their pinafores.
> "It's like a little engine. It's like a funny little railway engine,"
> squealed Isabel.
> But Kezia suddenly rushed at Pat and flung her arms round his legs
> and butted her head as hard as she could against his knees.
> "Put head back! Put head back!" she screamed.

There were cousins present because the Beauchamps did not make
the move to Karori unaccompanied.[7] They had been followed there by
Annie's brother-in-law Valentine Waters, a Post Office official and
church organist with two small sons named Barrie and Eric—the
originals of Pip and Rags. Uncle Val and Aunt Agnes took a smaller
house nearby, and the two families moved in the same week, just after
Easter 1893.

Uncle Val was certainly no Beauchamp, but there was something in
him of the Pa man, which earned the lifelong affection of his niece. For
his garden, at the weekends, he used to clear the main road of its horse
manure, and to the children he was everything an uncle ought to be.
If shot with a popgun he could be relied on to fall to the ground,
moaning, "You've killed me, you brute." From Monday to Saturday

he accepted his dreary existence at the Wellington Post Office, finding solace in music. A popular singer in the town, in demand for opera and oratorio, he was the original of Jonathan Trout, in *At the Bay*, who habitually addresses the ladies in stage absurdities, as in this greeting in the garden:

> "Hallo, Jonathan!" called Linda. And Jonathan whipped off his shabby panama, pressed it against his breast, dropped on one knee, and kissed Linda's hand.
> "Greeting, my Fair one! Greeting, my Celestial Peach Blossom!" boomed the bass voice gently. "Where are the other noble dames?"

Beauchamp, like Stanley Burnell in that story, found Val's absurdities embarrassing. In Karori he still wore city clothes, and he drew the line at rolling on the ground or tidying the roads.

On 21 February 1894 came the longed-for blessing of a son, who was baptised Leslie Heron. The first name recalled the remote but illustrious connection who gave the family its lien on the arts, and the second was wrongly entered in the Karori register for Herron, after the great-uncle who had done so much to retrieve its honour in commerce. (The literary fame within that family still lay in the future.) But Leslie's name was put away, like fine china, and seldom used. As a child he was known as "Boy," which is hardly surprising, and later he was "Chummie," though his sisters also often called him "Bogie," or "Bogey" (which perhaps was velarised from "Boy").

Beauchamp now forged ahead in town. He walked there in the mornings—four miles, downhill—in just under an hour. He liked to race his neighbours, who went by the ninepenny horse-bus, with all its stops. In the evening he was fetched uphill by Patrick Sheehan. Only rain made Beauchamp use that bus.

He was thirty-six. He had become, as promised, the sole partner in Bannatyne's; he was a director of the Gear Meat Company (from which he always bought his mutton); he was chairman of the New Zealand Candle Company, a Justice of the Peace, and in line for some other directorships. He therefore took into the firm a partner of his own choosing, his Jewish friend and former neighbour from Tinakori Road, the ironmonger Walter Nathan, whose children appear in *Prelude* as "the Samuel Josephs."

At the beginning of 1895, when she was six, Kathleen went to school for the first time. She joined her sisters Vera and Chaddie, and all the children of the valley—farm children, the milkman's children, the bus-driver's, the storekeeper's, the washerwoman's, the children of a dentist—at the Karori Public School, to receive the "free, secular and compulsory" education which had been prescribed for all of the colony's children, white and brown, by its Education Act of 1877. She was good at arithmetic and bad at spelling. She learned to say "like I do," and "like he does," a habit that was never corrected, as one notices in her letters. Charles Darwin, however, did the same.

Few children in the colony began their education in private schools. For the Beauchamps to send their daughters to the local school was nothing unusual, and the move to Karori must have envisaged it. But a change later on was certainly in view, and at Karori certain traces of a social barrier did set apart these children from the "big house," with their starched pinafores and special voices, as in the well-known story in which Kezia would like to ask the washerwoman's children to come and see the doll's house:

> "Mother," said Kezia, "can't I ask the Kelveys just once?"
> "Certainly not, Kezia."
> "But why not?"
> "Run away, Kezia; you know quite well why not."

Kass was now the odd-one-out at home, being not of an age with Vera and Chaddie, nor with the babies. She felt herself less loved, save by her granny (in whose room she slept), and grew to be fat and moody and resentful. According to the Waters's "lady-help," Rose Ridler,* she had a penetrating gaze which disconcerted grown-ups. She would stare at them with those keen brown eyes, take them in, and go to someone else with a too-revealing comment. (An almost identical observation was made much later by Bertrand Russell.) Her mother had no affection for her, or so it appeared to Rose. She preferred her other daughters.

Kass took to reading far more than was good for her eyes. She would read by candlelight until her granny came to bed. Steel-rimmed glasses

---

*Val Waters would never have called his wife's domestic help a "servant-girl" (as the term was in the Beauchamp household). Rose Ridler, an informally adopted orphan, was treated as a member of the family, and was provided by Waters with an annuity which took care of her old age.

only made the gaze more disconcerting still. There were noticeable attempts to gain attention; and when she was eight or nine, she won the English composition prize at school, with her description of *A Sea Voyage*. An account of Kathleen by one of her teachers at Karori recalls a "plump, self-possessed little girl with bright alert brown eyes, always very amiable and well behaved," who wrote as if under compulsion: "When she first began to put her thoughts into words, her pencil literally ran away with her and she had to be restrained and taught to put her facts into shorter sentences so as to conform to the stereotyped lower-school essay."[8]

The inherited impulse to Poetry—or whatever it was—had found its way from Highgate to Karori.

[3]

In 1898 the lease of Chesney Wold was running out and it was time for town again. First, however, Beauchamp and his wife took another business trip to England, leaving Mrs. Dyer and Aunt Belle in charge of the children. They sailed in March, as the *Reminiscences* so helpfully record, by the S.S. *Ruahine* (6,127 tons), returning by way of Canada and the *Warrimoo*. "You will notice I gave the tonnage of these vessels," Beauchamp writes, "so that you can if you care note their gradual growth." In their absence the three elder girls, Vera, Chaddie and Kathleen, began attending the Wellington Girls' High School in Thorndon, awaiting the move to another Thorndon home.

The new school had a magazine, the *High School Reporter*, to which Kathleen lost no time in contributing. At the end of her first term it printed a little composition entitled *Enna Blake*, "by Kathleen Beauchamp, aged nine years," with the following delicious footnote by a sixth-former—the first printed criticism of any work by the Colonial writer who was to make her modest contribution to the literature of the older world: "This story, written by one of the girls who have lately entered the school, shows promise of great merit. We shall always be pleased to receive contributions from members of the lower forms.—Ed."

The story—no more than any child's account of "the happiest holiday she had ever had"—is set in middle-class England (where its author's parents were) and plunges confidently into those indications of indoor and outdoor weather that are so characteristic later on. The stance at the window, too, is something to be noticed here:

> "Oh, mother, it is still raining, and you say I can't go out." It was a girl who spoke; she looked about ten. She was standing in a well-furnished room, and was looking out of a large bay window. "No, Enna dear," said her mother, "you have a little cold and I don't want it made worse." Just then the gong rang for luncheon and they went into the dining-room. In the midst of this meal the maid came in with the letters. . . . .[9]

In November 1898 the family were reunited at No. 75 Tinakori Road, a house on high ground overlooking the harbour—"a big, white-painted square house with a slender-pillared verandah and balcony running all round it," as Katherine Mansfield's *Journal* tells us. The description speaks of "terraces and flights of concrete steps," of a visitors' gate, a Tradesmen's gate, and a "huge pair of old iron gates that were never used," which all makes it sound like a suitable home for a Colonial Forsyte in a suitable neighbourhood; but in fact, that part of Tinakori Road was "very mixed," as the *Journal* says. The Beauchamps' own washerwoman, most embarrassingly, lived in a "hovel" just over the fence, and farther along there lived "an endless family of halfcastes who appeared to have planted their garden with empty jam tins and old saucepans and black iron kettles without lids."[10] It was *not* where the capital's old-established families lived; and the Beauchamps were not of them.

What set No. 75 apart was its size and its raised position, owed to the geological fault. Eastward, its pillared balconies looked over the harbour, but in the other direction, down below the road, were the rusty tin roofs of mean little workmen's shacks, in a damp and sunless hollow. The lower orders were not merely in full view, but within earshot, night and day. The house was to be the setting, eventually, of Katherine Mansfield's story *The Garden Party*, in which the gulf of the social fault is bridged by pity and guilt; and the theme, in fact, of Kathleen's next story for the High School magazine, *A Happy Christmas Eve*, was the debt of the rich to the poor. The "Courteney" children are seen preparing for a party at which there will be "a tree for the poor children," and the scene that follows is a childish precursor of *The Doll's House:*

Such a funny crowd it was that came that night, ragged and dirty, but having a look of curiosity on their faces. When they had all come, the study door was thrown open and the Christmas tree was seen in all its splendour. I wish I could have let you see the delight on the faces of the children. . . . .[11]

One naturally wonders whether these little essays in correctness were really the burgeonings of a creative gift. Was it already determined that writing would be Kathleen's means of self-expression? It is hard to say, since by an odd chance her first appearance in print had coincided precisely with the bursting on the world of that other literary descendant of the Poet of Hornsey Lane, her father's first cousin May Beauchamp, now the Countess von Arnim.

Elizabeth and Her German Garden was also published that September, just before Harold and Annie sailed for New Zealand, and was soon giving widespread pleasure with its irreverent picture of the good life in Germany. They possibly brought a copy from London with them. Having no doubt stayed with its author's parents in Kent before they left, they knew about the romantic marriage, the sumptuous home in Pomerania; and now the book was well on its way to world-wide fame. By May of 1899, Macmillan's were announcing a "twenty-second edition." What effect all this may have had upon Kass Beauchamp's future, one can only guess. But the germ of *The Doll's House* existed.

For the present, she passed for an unremarkable child, and the family snapshots show a solemn little podge, dressed identically with two sisters who look much more at ease. She was reserved, she got the sulks, and she told fibs. She seldom unburdened herself to grown-ups (unless to her granny), and it is recorded by her first biographer, Miss Mantz, that when, to a visitor's customary question, she replied, "I'm going to be a writer," everybody laughed. With one exception she had no close friends at school.

The exception was Marion Ruddick, a Canadian, and an only child, who had crossed the Pacific with Kathleen's parents and thus had no friends when they met. Miss Ruddick once wrote up her recollections of the brief acquaintance. She remembered Hal Beauchamp striding ashore at cloudless Honolulu in a bowler and carrying a rolled umbrella, and his wife as a "languid woman" who greeted her third child on the Wellington wharf with "Well, Kathleen, I see you're as fat as ever."

At the end of 1898 Marion joined the Beauchamps in a holiday cottage at Island Bay, on the shore of Cook Strait, for a real New Zealand Christmas: buckets and spades, sunburn and citronella, shepherd's pie and bread pudding; a silver thimble in a green plush case With Love from Marion to Kathleen.[12] One hot day there turned up Santa Claus himself, in the hefty shape of Hal's good friend the Rt. Hon. R. J. Seddon, New Zealand's Premier, to offer *him* the biggest Christmas present of his life. The Seddon Government had lately rescued the Bank of New Zealand from collapse, and needed to put sound men in charge. "In December 1898," the *Reminiscences* record with all due modesty, "they did me the honour of making me one of the Government directors."

This appointment was eventually to make Beauchamp, as Chairman of the Bank, the strongest force, outside the Government itself, in the colony's financial affairs. It was not a *social* rise: he was still "in trade," a fact of which the gentlemen members of the Wellington Club were never unaware. But he now was made, for life. He had just passed his fortieth birthday. Perhaps Annie could even forget about that pub down by the Sydney wharves.

Kathleen and Marion Ruddick became "sworn chums," shared schoolgirl secrets, wrote poems ("Ode to a Snowdrop"), and found a dragon in a garden in Thorndon which they had decided was enchanted. But alien myths were soon to be forgotten in the sun and the sea and the bush of a true New Zealand childhood. By the following Christmas the Beauchamps had a new summer place of their own. To compensate for the return to town, their father had rented a cottage at Muritai, just south of Day's Bay, on the eastern side of the harbour.

Over there, the bush was still unspoiled; no road had yet been formed around the harbour, so one crossed from town by the *Duco* or the *Duchess,* which steamed sedately into the Day's Bay wharf, calling passengers for town with friendly hoots that echoed up empty gullies into the bush. The ferries, and still more, the bush, made Day's Bay seem a world away from Wellington.*

In the gullies the bush is dark and damp, and the birds stay high in

---

*The name "Day's Bay" (charmingly rendered by French translators as *La Baie du Jour*), was then loosely applied to an area including the bay itself, not yet subdivided by Mr. Day, and the modern Rona Bay and Muritai, which had been thinly settled. Katherine Mansfield's "Crescent Bay" is now called Muritai.

the tops. Climb higher, on a fine morning, and the bush thins out to become the more open beech forest, with sunlight streaming through. From there can be seen, beyond the harbour entrance, the ice-blue peak of Tapuaenuku, nine thousand feet high and ninety miles distant, on the other island. A thousand feet above the beach is the ridge, and beyond that another ridge, and then another, and clothing each ridge and each valley is nothing but the sombre bush, a "presence" of which one becomes more conscious as the darkness again creeps through it towards evening.

The sun goes down among the hills behind Karori; across the Strait the western face of Tapuaenuku glows with chilled fire; and very quickly, since there is not much twilight in New Zealand, Wellington is a darkening bank of lights twinkling over the water.

It was there that the children spent their next few summers, there that Christmas was celebrated, in a setting "full of sand and seaweed, bathing dresses hanging over verandahs, and sandshoes on window-sills, and little pink 'sea' convolvulus, and rather gritty sandwiches and the tide coming in."[13] It was probably at the bay, more than anywhere else, that Kathleen, in Rilke's fashion, began to compose, *within herself,* her true place of origin.

The sentimental story of *A Happy Christmas Eve* appeared in the *High School Reporter* at the end of 1899, just as the mistresses were getting the prizes ready for the break-up ceremony. Three of those prizes—for English, Arithmetic, and French—were for Kass Beauchamp, and it was from the distinguished hands of Sir Robert Stout, the Chief Justice and a former Liberal Premier, that she went up the aisle to receive them. Sir Robert, a member of the university Senate, then spoke on "Higher Education for Women," and he must have had the Chairman of the Bank in mind when he described that innovation as "better dowry than money." As everyone in the audience well knew, he was in fact recruiting students for Victoria University College, which had just been founded in Wellington at his instigation, without any build-ings yet, but with R. C. Maclaurin, the future president of the Massa-chusetts Institute of Technology, as one of its first professors.[14]

There was never any question, though, of the Beauchamps' daugh-ters becoming founding students of V.U.C. "Higher Education" in little Wellington did not compare with going "Home." After one more term at Wellington Girls' High School, Vera, Chaddie and Kathleen were sent to Miss Swainson's private school* in Fitzherbert Terrace, a stepping-stone to something in London yet to be chosen.

The big wooden house that was known as "Miss Swainson's" had its back to the same wild gully as Kathleen's birthplace. Miss Swainson employed Mrs. Henry Smith (a cousin of Charles Kingsley, author of *The Water Babies*) as head of the day school, and the whole atmosphere prepared its pupils for a life which looked on England as "Home," and New Zealand as "out here." It was seldom that a girl left it for anything but a finishing school in England or Europe.[15]

Two of the teachers there have told what they remembered of Kass Beauchamp. Mrs. Smith said she was "plain," "a surly sort of girl," and "imaginative to the point of untruth." Her compositions were too prolific, poorly written and poorly spelled, and "she put *herself* in too much."[16]

Miss Eva Butts, who was what Edwardians used to call a "well turned-out woman" (she would arrive magnificently mounted on a horse, in purple tweed), said that Kass was "shabby and inky" and her compositions were "never on the subject given." At the age of thirteen she approached Miss Butts after school for her views on "free love"— in those days a scandalously daring topic even for adults. She was dumpy and unattractive, "not even cleverly naughty," and "unambitious in the school."[17]

All the same, it was Kathleen M. Beauchamp who gave Miss Swainson's its first "magazine"—a foolscap effort in manuscript, containing stories and jokes. And when Miss Butts got up a charity performance of *Mrs. Jarley's Waxworks*, it was discovered that Kass possessed a wicked gift for impersonation, which perhaps was dangerous at home. Certain of her sketches drawn from the family life suggest an ability to prick her father's *amour propre* (in one, the child Kezia has called him "Bottlenose!"), and a subtler tension with the mother.[18]

Her performance in the part of Mrs. Jarley won Kathleen an admirer in an English clergyman, the Rev. Charles Prodgers, who seems to have taken some slight interest in her. The Church of England played scarcely more part in her life than it had in her father's, but

---

*Founded as a boarding school with Anglican affiliations, it offered some religious instruction (forsworn by the public schools under the Act of 1877). In Kathleen's time there were several Jewish pupils and one Maori girl, Maata Mahupuku, or Martha Grace, who was a wealthy heiress to Maori lands.

there was one rapturous moment of illumination which she recorded on a flyleaf of her prayerbook:

> Nov. 3rd 1901 went with E and D Bendall and Vera to St. Mark's Church to hear the Rev. Fred Bennet preach a sermon on Mauries. The most heavenly thing possible. He also read the Second lesson. The Betrayal of Jesus. I never enjoyed myself so much.* I am going to be a Mauri missionary.[19]

She was rebellious, she had a dangerous wit, she was capable of religious fervour (at any rate on Sunday evenings), and she was lonely: when Marion Ruddick went away, she seems to have had no close friend. It was at this time, aged thirteen, that she asked Miss Butts about "free love"; that her periods began; and that she met Tom Trowell.

"Caesar," as for some reason Kathleen called him, was the son of a Wellington music teacher, a boy who already played the cello so well (the famous Gerardy had heard him when in Wellington) that a fund was being raised to send him with his twin brother Garnet, a violinist, to study in Europe. The boys had the same red hair as Kathleen's father, if hardly his temperament; and Kass soon believed herself in love with Tom. His feeling for her was slight.

The beginnings of teen-age love usually pass into oblivion without delay, but in this case the meeting was later put into the opening pages of a turgid, untitled story of love and death now known as "Juliet." Scribbled in a fat black reporter's notebook, it is third-rate romantic fiction, but it does convey a sense of the hopes and fears of these two young casualties of Colonial life.

Juliet, calling for her parents after something which her unfeeling mother has referred to as "only a musical party," finds herself alone in the hall with the young cellist for whom a fund is being raised. He leads her to an open window for some dialogue like this:

> "Will you tell me your name?"
> "Juliet—and yours?"
> "David. I am a musician, and have been playing tonight—a 'cellist, you know. I am going to Europe next year."

*Bishop Bennett, as he later became, was a splendid orator and a valued leader of the Maori people.

· "I too, but not for music—to complete my education, you know."

"Do you want to go away?"

"Yes—and no. I long for fresh experiences, new places—but I shall miss the things that I love here."

"Do you like nights Juliet?" His face was transfigured. . . . .[20]

Now she had to have a cello, with lessons from Caesar's father. Her own father, delighted to see this healthy interest in music, bought an instrument without delay. She was soon transformed. In a family photograph taken during the voyage to England, Kathleen, beside her crushing parents, is a comely, well-poised young woman, her face finer, her eyes softened, the glasses gone. Whatever the reasons, Kathleen at fourteen looks more mature and composed than her Aunt Belle Dyer, who in her late twenties was still unattached and was about to be left in London to chaperon her nieces for three years—admittedly no prospect to produce a tranquil and fulfilled expression. The voyage was accomplished with the sort of flourish that was so endearing in him who paid the fares.

> What we did [he writes], was to take the whole passenger accommodation in the Tyser liner, *Niwaru* (10,000 tons),* for my wife and myself, our whole family of four daughters and one son, and the two in-laws [Belle and Sydney Dyer]. It was really a glorified yachting cruise, beginning with calls at Gisborne and Auckland and then via Cape Horn and Las Palmas, the whole voyage occupying forty-seven days. My wife was very fond of sea-travelling and always accompanied me on my trips, which added very much to their enjoyment.

They sailed from Wellington (Mrs. Beauchamp having just made her will) on 29 January 1903. To Tom Trowell, who had not yet left, Kathleen wrote from Montevideo, beginning an ardent correspondence—ardent on her side—that was to last for six full years.

The Trowell twins left for Germany seven months later, after the sum of £885 had been raised to support them. The subscribers in this charac-

---

*"You will notice," Beauchamp adds—the second time he did so in the *Reminiscences*—"my inveterate habit of putting in the tonnage of the steamers I travel in. It is not only because as a business man I have been accustomed to such detail, but because it is interesting to observe the growth in size of the ocean greyhounds." (In fact the *Niwaru* was a ship of only 4,061 tons.)

teristic New Zealand enterprise included Harold Beauchamp (£25), his partner Walter Nathan (£25), and various other businessmen, with Professor R. C. Maclaurin, one hotelkeeper, one typiste, one stevedore, one sheepfarmer, one poultry-farmer, and several "gentlemen."[21] The fares for the boys from Lyttelton to London cost £26 each, so that Bannatyne's all but covered that expense. After a year at the Hoch Conservatorium in Frankfurt they went to the Brussels Conservatorium, which Arnold—to give Tom his professional name—was obliged to leave, under the rules, when he had won the cello prize at the *concours*. Within a few years they were both in London, and had been joined there by their parents.

CHAPTER II

Queen's College, London

For the generation to which Katherine belonged, the decadents were the gateway to the imaginative life.

—John Middleton Murry, 1933

Queen's College, in Harley Street, was the first institution to be created in England for the higher education of women, and although it was quickly followed by other colleges it has an important place in the history of women's education. Even more important here is the role it played in the life of a girl who was to write a story called *The Little Governess* and a whole succession of pieces about young women who have to travel alone. So we need a little history, and while the S.S. *Niwaru* steams round the Horn with its precious cargo of young Colonials, their spinet, their sewing-machine, and their canary, there is time to pause for that.

A young lady of the Victorian middle class who was neither handsome, clever, and rich, nor married, faced that genteel form of slavery which led her to be called a "governess." There was nothing else that she could be: the only acceptable profession for women then was marriage. But women in England far outnumbered men, small children were to be seen and not heard while their parents enjoyed themselves, and so the governess was "a special victim of Victorian society,"[1] almost totally unqualified for her task, and exploited because she was "unwanted." What was done to rescue her—by men, since they alone had the power—is described in Elaine Kaye's excellent history of Queen's College.

One evening in 1844, with the intention of setting things right, a group of "noblemen and gentlemen" presided over by the Duke of Cambridge held a dinner in the London Tavern. As a guest speaker to urge them on they had engaged a famous young novelist, then thirty-two years old—Charles Dickens. It was Dickens who told the gathering that "Knowledge" had not its right place in society; that the governess was worse paid than the cook, the butler, the lady's maid, and the liveried footman; and that it was high time to "blot out a national reproach." Those present were subscribers to something called the Governesses' Benevolent Institution, which had its spacious premises in Harley Street; and four years later, as one of several charitable projects of the G.B.I., Queen's College was opened there, where it still is very much alive, in the self-same elegant houses that were once "the Home" for many an impoverished governess. The year of its founding was 1848—Europe's "year of revolutions," and the year in which Arthur Beauchamp left Hornsey Lane for the colonies.

Queen's College, then, was never a "finishing school" in any sense, but stood for a great reform: the idea that young women could be given a university education, in fact if not in name, and hence a status hitherto denied them. When its first two pupils met nervously in the Waiting Room they wondered if they ought to take their bonnets off. But the Lady Resident—she was never called "headmistress"—assured them that they should; and soon they were listening enthralled (it is apparently not too strong a word) as two of the founding professors began their instruction—the Christian Socialist F. D. Maurice, and the clergyman-novelist Charles Kingsley, the author of *The Water Babies*, already mentioned in another connection. Maurice rather daringly announced that the object of such a college should be to introduce its students to "the apprehension of principles"; and Kingsley began at once by urging them to read all kinds of English literature, including modern works. In fact both men were deeply involved just then in the Chartist movement—the college had opened its doors only three weeks after the "Chartist rebellion"—and Kingsley, rather soon, was obliged to withdraw under a political cloud. But the flourishing college could eventually lay claim to having taught not only those famous headmistresses Miss Buss and Miss Beale (who "Cupid's darts do not feel" as an old male-chauvinist jingle has it), but Gertrude Bell, the Lawrence of Arabia of her sex, and Sophia Jex-Blake, who helped to open the medical profession to women. These four, with "Katherine Mansfield," are the school's most famous pupils.

Of necessity, Queen's College long had men professors, and in 1903 there were several interesting persons on its staff who did *not* regard their pupils as future little governesses. Nor had they been picked for social reasons. J. A. Cramb, whose *Germany and England* later foretold the war (and who had a love affair with Lady Ottoline Morrell while teaching there), was a flamboyant lecturer in modern history; Hall Griffin, who had been a friend of Browning, taught English Literature; H. G. Wells's young friend "Rags" Gregory, the future Astronomer Royal (and son of the bootmaker at Clifton College), lectured on the heavens in an accent considered to be "common"; and Walter Rippmann, making his name as an innovator in language teaching, taught German with seductive charm. He also, on the side, introduced his pupils to the works of Ibsen, Oscar Wilde, Paul Verlaine, and Richard Dehmel. Kathleen Beauchamp learned from him, I believe, to think of literature as having "form."

How had Hal and Annie Beauchamp come to choose the college for their daughters? This is soon explained: Annie's first cousin on the Dyer side, Frank Payne, a Wimpole Street physician, was the son of England's first professor of education, Joseph Payne, of the College of Preceptors, and himself a man of modern attitudes. Having brought up his own two daughters on Froebel methods, he had placed them, after careful enquiries, at Queen's College. The three Colonials would therefore be joining their English cousins, Evelyn and Sylvia Payne, at a school not lightly chosen. Besides, their last headmistress was a cousin of Charles Kingsley.

Upon arrival they were taken to see Miss Camilla Croudace, the Lady Resident, a handsome little woman full of tact and good humour, who had once been chased by a wolf in the Crimea. Herself a former student and a pupil of F. D. Maurice—which meant that she had no time for "cleverness"—Miss Croudace wore a fine lace cap on her head, like Granny Dyer, but to Evelyn Payne she never seemed old-fashioned. When Miss Croudace noticed a case of *Schwärmerei* in the college she dealt with it lightly (a girl with a crush on another was said to be "D.V.," from the initials of a crush-prone niece of her own), and she was *never* sarcastic, unless in private. She used to invite girls down to her cottage at Haslemere, and a gushing entry in the visitors' book shows that Kathleen was invited there once, at least.[2]

Pupils of what we would now call school age usually took a four-year compounded course, but the lectures could also be taken à la carte by older women, known as "non-compounders," which made it all seem more like university than school. No uniform was worn. A hostel for girls from out of town was conducted in the house next door by Miss Clara Finetta Wood, a tall, thin stick of a woman with a topknot—and a twitch, which made the topknot wag—who dressed in shades of purple, or lavender for the opera. Miss Wood favoured violet ink, and the address from which she had applied for the post in 1873 was "Violet Cottage, Felixstowe."

The day-girls—West End daughters like the Paynes—set the tone of the place, and "Woodie" was an apparition who appeared at the end of the college day to lead her charges off to their unenvied regime next door. But the regime wasn't unkind. While they sewed after doing their homework in the evenings she read them Charlotte M. Yonge; on Saturdays she sent them in a crocodile* to uplifting places, and on Sundays she made them write their letters home, thus giving Sundays a poignancy for Katherine Mansfield which they never lost; Sunday remained her letter-writing day throughout her life. "Woodie" certainly understood Kass Beauchamp: as a parting memento in 1906 she gave her a thick black notebook, one of the sources of the *Journal.* Had she seen what went into it, her topknot would have flown off.

Kathleen's response to Queen's College was entirely personal, and would certainly have appalled the Founder, F. D. Maurice, whose portrait looked down upon her when she worked in the college library. History bored her—though Cramb as a man did not—and in English literature, Hall Griffin found her performance "disappointing" (but this was mutual). She enjoyed her German, and worked at that, but for a highly personal reason: she was charmed, or rather more than charmed, by Walter Rippmann, a most insinuating man.

By merest chance, her most important encounter at Queen's College occurred on the day she arrived, in April 1903. After the interview with Miss Croudace someone was needed to show the Beauchamps up to the room they were to share at Miss Wood's, and the choice fell on a tall, pale, fair-haired girl from Burma who was always ready to perform this sort of service—to do what was necessary, then disappear.

---

*For American readers: "*Brit. colloq.,* a double file of persons, usually schoolgirls, out for a walk."

English by birth but Anglo-Indian by upbringing, Ida Constance Baker was somehow vaguely out of contact with the rest. Her personality was a sort of *tabula rasa*, which awaited imprinting. It was only because her mother had lately died, and no one knew quite what to do, that she was staying at Miss Wood's that month. Her father, a former Indian Army doctor now practising in Welbeck Street, nearby, was a moody, unsociable, lonely man who had "ruined his digestion on curries." His terrifying presence can still be felt in the Mansfield story *The Daughters of the Late Colonel,* a story originally entitled *Non-Compounders.*

Since Ida's childhood had been spent in Burma the family home in Welbeck Street was full of Oriental carvings, but it was empty of a mother, and the role foreseen for her was that essentially Victorian role that awaits the Colonel's daughters in the story, Con and Jug. Though she wouldn't be a governess of course (there were investments to provide for her), she would be a "giver" all her days—but get her own back, too. Colonel Baker's withdrawal and melancholy were to end, eventually, in his suicide in Rhodesia. For the present, Ida was at Miss Wood's; she showed the girls from New Zealand to their room, then disappeared. However, she at once had a crush on Vera. "You know how it is with girls at that age," the latter once told the author. "I used to find her lying on the floor outside my room, waiting to ask if she could help me undress"—a remark that could easily be misunderstood, in the age of the zip-fastener, if one didn't hasten to explain that it was a matter of innumerable hooks and eyes, and quite the normal thing.

Ida was always giving food to animals, and always bending over prams. She played the violin, and even spoke in the Debating Society; but no one knew her well. The other girls felt "sorry for her," not knowing upon what firm self-confidence their sympathy was spent. She had a mighty appetite for puddings, and in one so sturdily made her soft, exquisite voice was always a slight surprise. Like Emily Dickinson's, her eyes were the colour of "the Sherry in the Glass, that the Guest leaves." The impression has somehow got abroad that Ida was a meek little thing, a "doormat," or, in her own dismissive phrase, "a little dog on a string." As the reader will discover, she was anything but that. She was an English type, long ago described by Geoffrey Chaucer in Madame Eglantine: "For hardily, she was nat undergrowe." She had a gift, indeed, for self-effacement in certain circumstances; but she took size nine in brogues. Beside her, Kathleen was short and slight.

It would seem from the accounts of two contemporaries* that Kathleen took to life in Harley Street with cool composure. No one felt sorry for her. The Beauchamps, after all, had had a whole ship to themselves for the journey from New Zealand; they stayed in expensive hotels, they always had the best seats at the pantomime, and Kathleen, when it suited her, was one of them (she was always a Beauchamp, a fact that should never be forgotten). She had her cello —a new one now, from Hill's, in Bond Street. She was writing to Tom Trowell, who with his brother came to Frankfurt in the summer; and in October she evidently went there to see them. Belle's chaperonage was hardly severe.

It was in the autumn, in Regent's Park as Ida recalled, that Kathleen startled her with the extraordinary proposal, "Let's be friends." To Ida, the Beauchamps at that stage were simply the Paynes' New Zealand cousins who had hired a ship, and whom she had happened to meet on the day of their arrival. She explained that you didn't start a friendship, a friend was something you became. But Kathleen got her way, since Ida in fact had lifelong need of a certain kind of friendship —one that would let her share vicariously the ambitions and achievements of another. If Miss Croudace ever remarked that Ida was "D.V. on Vera Beauchamp," it was soon on the sister instead. In this case, though, something more enduring than mere *Schwärmerei* was involved. A form of imprinting had occurred.

Ida's love for Kathleen is expressed in the book which she produced in her own old age, using as pseudonym Kathleen's name for her, "L.M."†The first thing it describes about Kathleen is her hair, which

---

*Mrs. M. J. Murphy (Evelyn Payne) and Miss Ruth Herrick, a New Zealander. Evelyn was Kathleen's monitor, which meant that she had to read her cousin's dreadful writing and endeavour to correct it. The relationship never recovered from this. At the end of her life Evelyn recalled Kathleen, with cousinly good humour, as impossibly conceited and perfectly detestable.

†Entitled *Katherine Mansfield, the Memories of L.M.*, this book was published in 1971, when L.M. was eighty-three. Its most noticeable characteristic is its loving and gentle tone, its angel-of-mercy sweetness. Most readers, however, would not notice—as even Elizabeth Bowen did not when she reviewed it for the London *Sunday Times* on 4 July 1971—the needle hidden in the cotton wool ("I hate to say it, but men are such beasts" could be the title of L.M.'s biography), still less the lethal fluid in the needle. An expert user of symbol and of that literary antimony known as innuendo, L.M. as author

she used to brush by the hour at Harley Street. They would talk for hours in Kathleen's room, and Ida, not always managing to aim her camera correctly, took snap after snap there of Kathleen with her cello.

These sessions were watched over by the silent photograph of Tom Trowell on Kathleen's chest of drawers, "her friend from New Zealand and great romantic idol," as Ida helpfully describes him (he was not a strongly masculine figure). Both girls were going to be great musicians, or writers, or something, and they would need professional names—like Tom (whose professional name was Arnold), and like Kathleen's famous cousin "Elizabeth," of the charming books on life in Germany. Ida, when she became a violinist, would have liked to use her mother's name, which was Katherine Moore, instead of the pair of trudging trochees she was known by. But Kathleen wanted "Katherine" herself, so another name was found for Ida: she could have Katie's brother's name, and be "Lesley Moore." This is how Ida eventually became "L.M."—which emphatically does not stand, as one American writer thought, for "Little Mouse."

In that same winter, at a meeting of the college poetry-reading circle, Kathleen took a crush on her own rather virginal cousin, Sylvia Payne, or "Jug." Here too the initiative was hers, and it remained so, since Jug, according to her sister, was "shy and reserved, modest and diffident." She was also "small and piquant, rather Dyer-like in appearance." Her hair, like Tom's, was red.

The only sign of any requital of Kathleen's feelings is the fact that Sylvia kept, in their envelopes until her death, the hectic effusions which her shyness drew forth. Kathleen's first two letters were girlish cousinly notes, but then, from the home in Kent of "Dee-pa"—Great-Uncle Henry Herron Beauchamp—just before Christmas 1903, came this sudden declaration:

> Dearest Sylvia,
>   I want to write to you this afternoon, so here I am. . . . . I like you much more than any other girl I have met in England and I seem to see

---

contrives minute assassinations of all the men in Katherine Mansfield's life save three, all her relatives save one, and many of her women friends. The few who survive this loving process are the true and the good, the pure and the faultless. But the book provides, almost for the first time, a satisfactory context for some of K.M.'s poems. Their highly personal character ceases to be a defect when they are come upon as private or secret messages within this nitric friendship.

less of you. We just stand upon the threshold of each other's heart and never get right in. What I mean by "heart" is just this. My heart is a place where everything I love (whether it be in imagination or in truth) has a free entrance. It is where I store my memories, all my happiness and my sorrow and there is a large compartment in it labelled *"Dreams."* There are many many people that I like very much but they generally view my public rooms, and they call me false, and mad, and changeable. I would not show them what I was really like for worlds. They would think me madder, I suppose.[3]

Announced there is the notion of "compartments" which was to characterise her later friendships. Revealed, as well, is a little duplicity in regard to Ida.

A story about children by "Kathleen M. Beauchamp" had appeared in the college magazine that month, and had earned some praise. Entitled *The Pine Tree, the Sparrows, and You and I,* it came from one of her "public rooms." In a private room as yet (it has never been published from the notebook that contains it) was something quite different and of darker significance: a story or fantasy entitled *His Ideal,* in which a death-wish theme makes its first appearance in her writing. The title refers to a nameless hero who, during a childhood illness, dreams of a beautiful woman appearing to him in a vision; he longs for her in manhood, and eventually is about to drown himself when she appears again to grant his wish—"and her name was Death."[4] That was written in August 1903, when Kathleen was still fifteen.

New Year's Eve, during holidays spent with relatives near Sheffield, found her addressing a poem to Sylvia Payne, a rather churchy prayer for knowledge and light, and later—after attending a midnight service —a message to Tom Trowell, set down in a notebook which she had begun to use as a sort of journal: "Now, at the entrance of this New Year, my dearest, I propose to begin my book. It will not be at all grand or dramatic, but just all that I have done. . . . . ."[5]

In her first year away from New Zealand, then, a pattern of some sort can be seen: she had secured one friend-for-life of a kind that New Zealand could never have supplied; she had written some stories about small children and had been praised for them, but she had also written a fantasy in which the hero longs for Death; she had composed some inferior verse; and she had formed the habit of talking to a notebook. Having found, in fact, a medium that competed with her music and her cello, she had begun to regard a day as misused if she hadn't *written* something.

There is one thing else: her "let's be friends" approach struck Ida as rather odd in Regent's Park, and it must have startled Sylvia Payne as well. It probably struck them as "Colonial." It is more than that. It is the essential, the shaping gesture of a good deal of her writing. One story after another seems to say to the reader, "Let's be friends." Many people do not like it. Literary criticism seems to have overlooked it, but a simple touchstone for distinguishing her best work is its absence.

[2]

41 Harley Street, W.

24 i 04

Dearest Sylvia—

It was ripping of you to write me such a long letter! I was very pleased to receive it. . . . .

O, how thankful I am to be back at College, but, Sylvia, I am *ashamed* at the way in which I long for German. I simply can't help it. It is dreadful. And when I go into class I feel I must just stare at him the whole time. I never liked anyone so much. Every day I like him more. Yet on Thursday he was like *ice!*. . . . .[6]

"Him" was Professor Rippmann, the idol of the German class—an exceptional teacher in fact, with the gift of stimulating youthful minds, and soon a most important influence in Kathleen's life. Not always like ice, Rippy was remembered by Kathleen's contemporary, Ruth Herrick, as "rather young for a girls' school" (he married a former pupil in 1905), and by Evelyn Payne as "rather fat and flabby, with very well oiled hair, and his voice had a rather thick lisp."

In Kathleen's eyes he stood for everything that was modern, daring, and exciting. Before his marriage he used to invite the keener and more attractive girls to literary evenings at the house in Ladbroke Grove which he shared with an artist and a journalist. Her devotion sensed, Kathleen was soon among the chosen, and her eyes were opened wide by all the *art nouveau.* The house had an "atmosphere," recalled a few years later when she saw herself as a novelist:

Walter opened the door. "Ha! you've come at last," he said, his voice full of intense hospitality. "Come along into the smoking room—second

31

door to the right." She pushed aside the heavy purple portière. The room was full of gloom but vivid yellow curtains hung straight and fine before the three windows. Tall wrought-iron candlesticks stood in the corners. . . . . There were prints of beautiful women on the walls and the graceful figure of a girl holding a shell in her exquisite arms stood on a table. There was a long low couch upholstered in dull purple, and quaint low chairs in the same colour. The room was full of the odour of chrysanthemums. . . . .[7]

"I am sure he helped many girls to find themselves," writes Ida Baker of Walter Rippmann, suppressing an *arrière pensée* which only emerges later in her book. "I think that young creatures reaching out into maturity were all the better for some masculine attention in that large hive of women." John Middleton Murry also credits Rippmann with bringing about Kathleen's imaginative liberation.[8]

A sharp little allegory Kathleen herself published in 1910 looks back to the encounter with an eyebrow, by then, ironically raised. Entitled *A Fairy Story*, it has a "woodcutter's daughter" being introduced by a Rippmann-figure to the works of Shaw and Ibsen, and to Arthur Symons, Oscar Wilde and Paul Verlaine—the "Decadents." From him, the little woodcutter's daughter learns that "unselfishness signifies lack of Progress," and that she must at all costs avoid the Seven Deadly Virtues.[9]

Of her reading *before* she came under Rippmann's influence, almost nothing is known—a significant fact in itself. Her sisters could not name for the present author *any* writers whom she read when young. Their home in fact was not a house of books; in this respect her background differed vastly from that of the English writers with whom she later consorted.

But there was now her famous cousin, the Countess von Arnim, with all *her* famous books. Did Kathleen, eager to learn, do more than glance at *Elizabeth and Her German Garden*?

May 7.—I love my garden. I am writing in it now in the late afternoon loveliness, much interrupted by the mosquitoes and the temptation to look at all the glories of the new green leaves washed half an hour ago in a cold shower. Two owls are perched near me, and are carrying on a long conversation that I enjoy as much as any warbling of nightingales. The gentleman owl says and she answers from her tree a little way off, beautifully assenting to and completing her lord's remark, as becomes a properly constructed German she-owl. They say the same thing over and over again so emphatically that I think it must be something nasty about me; but I shall not let myself be frightened away by the sarcasm of owls.[10]

This has a tinkling brightness (it is the opening paragraph of the book) and it seemed entrancing in its day, if one belonged to the appropriate classes, and the fortunate life was thought to be secure. But "Elizabeth's" style is thin; no shadows deepen, the inward life is never touched. The prattling pace lacks the thinking pauses, the intimations of compassion for victims of circumstance that one finds in the best work of the younger cousin.

Early in 1904 the *Queen's College Magazine* published a piece of Kathleen's which had got its title, rather promptly, from Elizabeth's latest amusing book, *The Adventures of Elizabeth in Rügen*, published one month earlier. There is nothing amusing about the story, though—at least, not intentionally. "Die Einsame," in the hands of the younger cousin, is a distracted virgin longing for romantic Death. She lives alone on the top of a solitary hill ("Her house was small and bare, and alone, too"), and she walks in the forest by day or beside the sea by night, until a figure in a white wonderful boat fashioned of moonshine beckons her, his lips smiling. "Take me," she cries; but then a great wave comes, and there is Silence.[11]

The piece marks the second occurrence in Kathleen's writing of the death-wish theme—no more than a literary "influence" at this stage perhaps, but alarmingly frequent later on. In the other book, "Die Einsame" denotes a watering-place on Rügen which has a pine forest, a pure sea air with ozone in it, "and works wonders on people who have anything the matter with their chests." The conjunction here of tuberculosis and the death-wish theme is obviously mere coincidence —though it also, of course, reflects the pervasive role of TB in the period consciousness. It was then the chief taker of lives.

The Beauchamp sisters did briefly meet the Gräfin von Arnim at some time during their years in London. It was not a success. Accustomed at Nassenheide to informing her visiting neighbours, most graciously, that they might sit down, she brought the habit to London, to the astonishment of English people who visited this Aussie at 32 Westminster Square. When acquaintance was attempted she brushed aside the daughters of her embarrassing commercial cousin from

New Zealand. In Vera's words, "We were little colonial frumps."

At this time—1904—the Countess had as tutor to her own three girls a Mr. Morgan Forster, a young Cambridge friend of her nephew Sydney Waterlow. He, too, had written a book—it was called *Where Angels Fear to Tread*—and he corrected the proofs at Nassenheide while his employer sat typing her play *The Princess Priscilla's Fortnight* in the summerhouse: "She read my proofs and hated the book because it spoke of underdone meat and spittle. 'Pfui, Mr. Forster!' "[12] Though their worlds seem remote at this point, Kathleen's acquaintance with these two writers was really no great distance off. In her own haphazard way, she was reaching toward an art that would lead her to meet them as equals in the next undecadent decade.

Suddenly there is a rush of information about her reading, if reading it can be called. A notebook she used that summer lists "All books which I have enjoyed," and some others which she hadn't. During one July weekend she polished off two volumes of Thomas Moore's life of Byron, and Anthony Hope's *Dolly Dialogues*. She enjoyed a life of Romney, but not Charlotte Brontë's *Villette*. Poe's poems have the asterisk of enjoyment, but there is no hint that she read short stories. The names of Kipling and Stevenson, Henry James and H. G. Wells are absent. She had written more poems of her own, and at the cello she had made a start on Boellman's *Variations Symphoniques*.[13]

Her accompanist for cello practice was her compatriot Ruth Herrick, who is mentioned and disposed of in Ida's book. Ruth and Kathleen went off to concerts, Ida writes, "in big floppy black ties and wide velour hats, and assumed a rather slouching walk, which made them seem young Bohemian musicians." Between writing and music as a ground for ambition, some choice had yet to be made; but as to the cello, Ruth Herrick simply says, "her fingers were too short."

For the present, with Tom sending his compositions from Frankfurt, it was time to reply in kind; and in fact the Misses Vera and Kathleen Beauchamp appeared in print in 1904 as song-writers. Two songs of theirs, "Night," and "Love's Entreaty," were handsomely printed by a Berlin music publisher, presumably at the behest of the chairman of directors of the New Zealand Piano Company, in whose presence they were sung by Val Waters at a Harbour Board dinner in Wellington a few months later. They are ghastly drawing-room ballads in the style of the songs of yearning that are sung by ardent young girls in the later stories of Katherine Mansfield. The third line here is correctly copied:

> *If thou wouldst take my heart, my life,*
> *If I thy slave might be,*
> *I'd reek not for the world's hard strife;*
> *Oh my love, I would live for thee—for thee.* [14]

Two more stories in the college magazine drew on childhood memories, in a style that is about as close to *Prelude* as *Blackie's Annual* is to Karori. But there followed, in December 1905, as her last contribution, the sketch, *About Pat,* already quoted in Chapter I. Like Pat himself it was much more vivid and alive, and it is the first piece of writing that can be said to have come from the pen of Katherine Mansfield. The pattern is clearer now. She was best at writing about New Zealand.

In 1906 a new friend, a sharp, cool young lady two years older than she, lent Kathleen a book that was to alter everything. Walter Rippmann had prudently refrained from introducing his admiring student to *The Portrait of Dorian Gray*, but Vere Bartrick-Baker, known to Kathleen as "Mimi," secretly lent her the old *Lippincott's Magazine* in which it first appeared (it is most significant that Kathleen first read this book in its original, unexpurgated form). Kathleen responded with *The Ballad of Reading Gaol,* and the two girls used to sit in alcoves of the Lower Corridor, having intense conversations about Wilde, and Tolstoy, and Maeterlinck. [15]

By *Dorian Gray* she was swept off her feet into a world whose enticements seem no outrage now. She was dazzled by the epigrams, which bespatter some "Reading Notes" she set down later. When she read, "Being natural is simply a pose—and the most irritating pose I know," she was all agreement. When she came upon, "To realise one's nature perfectly—that is what each of us is here for," she copied that out too. It was thus equipped, by Wilde and by the Decadents, that she awaited the arrival of her parents from Wellington. And a "European" episode now intervened, with undertones of Puccini and Murger, and of heaven knows who else.

[3]

The Trowell twins had moved from Frankfurt to the Brussels Conservatorium, and at Easter 1906 Aunt Belle (who had lately combined her task of chaperonage with assisting Miss Wood in Harley Street) took her nieces across to Paris and then to Brussels, so that Kathleen met the twins again, and met a student-friend of theirs, whose name apparently was Rudolf.

Tom (or Arnold) was composing trios in daring idiom and talking darkly about inversions of the chord of the Neapolitan sixth; as coming geniuses, he and Garnet were wearing huge black hats, and smoking the longest cigarettes ever seen.[16] It was a glimpse of the *vie de Bohème,* and a brief one, and in spring. But the cup was soon to be rudely snatched away, since Harold and Annie Beauchamp had just arrived by the *Athenic* to reclaim their educated daughters. The girls, returning to London, joined them for a time in their expensive hotel in Manchester Street, W. In spite of the news it contains, there is nothing rebellious in the letter which Kathleen wrote from there to Sylvia Payne (24 April 1906). For the moment, she was emphatically a Beauchamp:

> We have been staying here since last Friday with Father and Mother, and have had a very good time. I don't think I have ever laughed more. They are both just the same *and* we leave for New Zealand in October. . . . .
>
> A great change has come into my life since I saw you last. Father is greatly opposed to my wish to be a professional 'cellist or to take up the 'cello to any great extent—so my hope for a musical career is absolutely gone. . . . . But I suppose it is no earthly use warring with the Inevitable —so in the future I shall give *all* my time to writing.

She looks forward, she *says,* to the peace and quiet of that ideal little "cottage by the sea" which her father has had built for them at Day's Bay. Farther down, though, our chameleon declares herself. It is "impersonation" that attracts her now:

> I am enjoying this Hotel life. There is a kind of feeling of irresponsibility about it that is fascinating. Would you not like to try *all* sorts of lives —one is so very small—but that is the satisfaction of writing—one can impersonate so many people.

Back at Miss Wood's, Kathleen as a result of some bust-up with her sisters moved out of their room and arranged to share one with Eileen Palliser, another New Zealander; and about that time came news from

Brussels of the suicide of Rudolf. He had shot himself, with a pistol. The circumstances, which belonged to the world of Oscar Wilde and the love that dares not speak its name, were very disturbing to Kathleen. Did that sort of thing lead to *suicide?* The Trowell twins then left Brussels and came to London, to launch their careers with the obligatory West End recital. Perhaps there was too much excitement all at once, for Eileen witnessed at close quarters the effects of some upset in the supposed romance with Tom. After meetings with him, Kathleen came back to Miss Wood's in a terrible state: she threw herself weeping on her bed, and moaned in her sleep; she started visiting fortune-tellers, and she went to séances, "to try to discover the future."[17]

It sounds as if the love affair was more a symptom than a cause. The mental disturbance had possibly more to do with going "home"—with leaving all the enticements of London and Paris and Brussels for Thorndon's intolerable security. The providers of that security were very much in evidence now, and as parental talk of Wellington invaded her private world Kathleen began berating her father to Vere, speaking irresponsibly of taking a flat in London and "managing somehow." For a respectable young lady of 1906 that would have been impossible, but Vere's sister jokingly took it up, suggesting that *they* could share a flat together; and Kass in turn took her seriously.[18]

This trivial episode figures in the fragmentary "novel" on which Kathleen had just embarked. In May, only three weeks after writing the letter from the hotel about impersonation, she had opened a thick black reporter's notebook and begun the effusion now known as "Juliet," of which we saw an opening scene in the previous chapter, and which is packed with current information. Since its episodes were not put down in the narrative order, the shape of the story has to be deduced. It apparently would have gone somehow like this:

Juliet, aged fourteen, but no Capulet, meets the cellist David Méjin, in a town that is obviously Wellington. She falls in love with him, then goes to London for three years, sharing her room there with a girl called Pearl (or sometimes "Vere" in the manuscript, as David is nearly "Caesar" at one point). As the time approaches to return to Wellington and its "Suitable Appropriate Existence"—its perpetual society functions, its hours filled up with talk about clothes—she rebels against her father, decides to stay behind, and accepts Pearl's offer to share a flat in London. There are doubts about David then ("Think of a man always with you," says Juliet in a significant scene with Pearl. "A woman cannot be wholly natural with a man"), and all is ready for Rudolf.

In a purple episode entitled "The Triumph of Rudolf" Juliet calls at the studio which he and David share in London, to find that Rudolf is there alone. His opportunity has come! They chat away while he casually runs through *Tannhäuser* at the piano, but soon it is this, with Wagner and Puccini, "Shakespeare," Murger, and cheap romances all mixed up together:

> "Leave me alone" said Juliet. She raised her eyes to his face, and his expression caused her to suddenly cease struggling and look up at him dumbly, her lips parted, terror in her eyes,
> "You adorable creature" whispered Rudolf, his face close to hers. "You adorable creature—you shall not go out now . . ." She felt the room sway and heave. She felt that she was going to faint. "Rudolf, Rudolf," she said, and Rudolf's answer was "At last."

It has happened, it is over, when David returns from a Prom. with the convenient news that he is "madly in love with Pearl." And Juliet duly finds herself pregnant ("Terror took possession of her. 'O no—not that' she said, 'never, never that. That would be diabolical. . . . .' "), but expires, apparently following an abortion, in the presence of David and Pearl:

> She opened her eyes and saw the two beside her. "Ought I to join your hands and say bless you?" she whispered. Suddenly she raised herself. "O—o—I want to live," she screamed. But Death put his hand over her mouth.[19]

Something evidently suggested to the author that after such a wallow in the death-wish theme (such a strangely *prophetic* wallow in the death-wish theme) only irony could dismiss the actors from the stage; the manner in which the survivors go their various suburban ways has a bitter triviality.

Melodramatic and cheaply derivative though it is, "Juliet" is full of naïve disclosures about its author and her adolescence: her vulnerability to men who are "artists"; her relations with Vere and with Walter Rippmann; her unconscious attitudes toward childbirth and abortion;

and her ambitious drive, which shows clear signs of being as powerful as her father's. Many of its jumbled details illuminate events both past and to come.

The London scenes are the best, but the solidest figure in the manuscript, apart from Juliet herself, is of course her father, "wrapping up his throat in a great silk handkerchief, with all that care and precision so common to perfectly healthy men who imagine they wrestle with weak constitutions." Described as "thoroughly commonplace and commercial," he exudes, as he fetches his daughters from a college in London, "an undeniable *trade* atmosphere."

Thus with the uncharitable pen of seventeen, while its victim, unaware as any Forsyte of what he had let loose upon the world, was in London attending the sixth congress of the Chambers of Commerce of the British Empire, "and incidentally was one of the thirty members of the congress who were chosen to be received by King Edward VII at Buckingham Palace," as his book records. *Trade,* indeed!

The summer seems to have been passed in seeing the sights and visiting relations, but there was some sort of family scene as the sailing date drew near. Kathleen said she wanted to stay in London, and was naturally told she couldn't, but she knew what to do about that. "I'll make myself so objectionable," she told Eileen Palliser, "that they'll *have* to send me away."[20]

Aunt Belle was being left behind. But then Aunt Belle had become engaged to a wealthy stockbroker, who, as the *Reminiscences* add, "owned two fine properties, one at Lyndhurst in the New Forest, the other at Totland Bay, Isle of Wight." Kathleen might have begun her novel to prove to herself that she was a writer, but it was the last thing she could have shown to her parents to prove it to them. She would have to continue it at sea.

They left in October, a few days after her eighteenth birthday. This time, they had to share a ship with other persons. "We returned to New Zealand," Harold Beauchamp writes, "by the *Athenic*'s sister ship, the *Corinthic*, by way of Capetown, the sensation of the voyage being the discovery of a case of smallpox, which was landed at Capetown."

CHAPTER III

Wellington After London

There was an extraordinary mixture of comedy and tragedy in the situation which is here described, and those who are affected by the pathos of it will not need to have it explained to them that the comedy was superficial and the tragedy was essential.
—Edmund Gosse, Preface to *Father and Son*, September 1907

For Kathleen, the sensation of the voyage was a handsome member of the English cricket team that was going out to tour New Zealand and Australia. Nicknamed "Adonis" on the ship because of his wondrous beauty, he was flirting with her by the time they reached the tropics, causing certain scribbles in a notebook—of which perhaps we should specially note the first four words:

> So, smiling at myself, I sit down to analyse this new influence: this complex emotion. I am never anywhere for long without a like experience. It is not one man or woman that a musician desires—it is the whole octave of the sex, and R. is my latest. The first time I saw him I was lying back in my chair, and he walked past. I watched the complete rhythmic movement, the absolute self-confidence, the beauty of his body, and that quelque which is the everlasting and eternal in youth and creation stirred in me. . . . . When I am with him a preposterous desire seizes me, I want to be badly hurt by him. I should like to be strangled by his firm hands. . . . .

When the cricketers erect a practice net she watches the glorious bowling of Adonis; and that same evening he and she sit side by side in the tropical heat. They converse in the dangerous language of the French ("He has spent years in Paris"), and Adonis is "curiously excitable, almost a little violent at times." The more hearts you have the better, he tells her, and she feels his coat sleeve against her bare arm. "I want to upset him, stir in him strange depths. He has seen so much, it would be such a conquest."

—All perfectly normal and healthy, especially the strangling part. The notebook then turns to Kathleen's parents. They are worse than she had even expected, and her father's appearance fills her with disgust: "His hands, covered with long sandy hair, are absolutely cruel hands. A physically revolted feeling seizes me." He has spoken of her returning to England as "Damned rot," saying, "look here, he wouldn't have me fooling round in dark corners with fellows." But it isn't only fellows: there is something about Kathleen that attracts women as well as men, and her parents are aware of it. Her mother is always watching her, "constantly suspicious, constantly overbearingly tyrannous"; and as for her father: "I cannot be alone or in the company of women for half a minute—he is there, eyes fearful, attempting to appear unconcerned, pulling at his long drooping red-grey moustache with his hairy hands. Ugh!"[1]

This was the low point of Kathleen's comments on her parents. Although the torrent of egotism continued for some time in various notebooks, she was never again quite so nasty about her father as she was during this hateful, confined, symbolic journey out, this journey to "home" from the other place called "Home" that was now her spiritual home.

After Capetown and Australian ports, the chilly Tasman Sea, cold even in December. Last visits to the baggage room—those West End clothes and huge Edwardian hats all packed for shore. The windy strait; bleak rocky hills; the shacks of Island Bay. Then into the harbour, that curls round like a question mark.

"About nine o'clock," said the *Evening Post* of 6 December 1906, "the *Corinthic* glided imperially into the bay, in sunshine strong enough to thrill the pilgrims from the far north"; and on another page Mr. Harold Beauchamp was good for a loquacious interview on "Matters Imperial and Colonial." For him, the mood was confident. Why not? He had lately met the King. But what of those

> *Three little maids who, all unwary,*
> *Come from a ladies' seminary*

—what was their mood, and how would they now occupy themselves? Would they, like Father at seventeen, "meet a lot of very fine young fellows," and provide him with sons-in-law who would join young Leslie in the firm?

Colonial-Edwardian Wellington is nearly all gone today, since most of it was wood—"business Wellington of wood," as J. C. Beaglehole has piquantly observed, "where on Lambton Quay an occasional building soared three stories skyward, and at the corners the German Band cast its strains to the enraptured air."[2] The young Henry James might have sympathised with our returning resident, for on every gust of wind great clouds of dust and chaff were swept along the colonial streets. And London—where was London? But the booming capital of sixty thousand people held everything to delight her father, and her mother, too. On Customhouse Quay the telephone-poles had eight-score insulators each, for eight-score copper wires that hummed with trade. In Tinakori Road the big house on the rise awaited the return of the garden-party family; very soon they would all sign the visitors' book at Government House, and be invited there.

Master Leslie was still at Waitaki Boys' High School, in the South Island, so the sisters were on their own. Within weeks it was Chaddie —not Kathleen, but cheerful, bubbling Chaddie—who was posting Sylvia Payne a description of "what New Zealand is really like to live in":

> Well dear it is absolutely devoid of art and so naturally the people are most uninteresting. Take my advice dear & never come to the Colonies to live in, remain in England, how I wish I was there too. I would give the worlds to be back I can't tell you how miserable it is as we have absolutely no friends. All the girls we used to know have grown up & got married and don't seem the least bit interested in us, so it is rather a sad state of affairs n'est pas?[3]

The girls had returned with "accents," and were seen wearing veils to the nose. And their *dresses!* This was the Wellington of "girls' teas," of which all details would be reported by "Iolanthe" in the *Weekly Press:* "On Tuesday afternoon the Misses Beauchamp gave a girls' tea. After tea, which was served in the dining room, songs were sung by Misses Beauchamp, Fulton, McTavish and Seddon. Miss Beauchamp was wearing a dark red cloth dress, her sister [Kathleen] mauve taffeta."[4]

There were greater occasions, of course: "The English cricket team are all perfectly charming and it is just lovely when they are in Wellington," wrote Chaddie to Sylvia, describing a dance that was given for them. But they sailed away, being insufficiently replaced. "We have been to two very jolly dances lately," says another letter, "only I do wish the men had been English, the Colonial men are so different my dear." Meanwhile Kathleen was in this mood for Sylvia:

> The New Year has come—I cannot really allow myself to think of it yet. . . . . Life here's impossible—I can't see how it can drag on—I have not one friend—and no prospect of one— My dear—I know nobody—and nobody cares to know me— There is nothing on earth to do—nothing to see—and my heart keeps flying off to Oxford Circus—Westminster Bridge at the Whistler hour. . . . . It haunts me all so much—and I feel it must come back soon— How people ever wish to live here I cannot think—[5]

Visible here are the two destructive conflicts of Katherine Mansfield's life: the love-hate feeling for her father, and the love-hate feeling for her country. They tore her apart in two directions—quartered her, as it were—leaving psychic wounds that never would be healed.

The Victorian parent left his marks on many of those who shaped this century's literature—at every level, and not only on sons. From the creator of Peter Rabbit to the author of *The Waves* one can see the signs, and there was often another potent figure in the conflict. For Butler and Gosse it was the Father in Heaven of Puritanism; for Colonials and Irishmen, it was one's own dear native land. Katherine Mansfield, a nominal Anglican, had at least not to cope with Puritanism, but she did know its descendant the love of wealth. A full two generations back she loathed her father's money-making drive (she could hardly have seen it as the reaction it was to his own father's fecklessness), but unlike more recent counterparts she had no one to loathe it with. Later, she was able to write of him and of her country with deep affection; at present, she could only see the worst in both.

The creative temperament obviously had a difficult time in New Zealand before a cultural humus had begun to form, and it never has been easy to describe the causes, since paradox pervades them. Smallness, newness and rawness, remoteness from Europe, all must have played their part. In social and political terms these had positive effects, since they favoured experiment, but in the arts they became enemies of promise. The *writer* who would in Pound's phrase "make it new" needs tradition to join him to past and future, and the act of emigration broke that precious chain. Those who left England in the 1840's were either, like Arthur Beauchamp, cheerfully ready to sacrifice their cultural roots, or mistaken in supposing that they would transplant easily in a land that had not known man or even mammals in the time of Christ. They unloaded their pianos from the sailing ships and had them tuned again in wooden houses filled with comforting things from home, but the old songs never did sound the same again.

Coleridge, in *Table Talk,* says it is not the sod under their feet that makes men of one country, but identity in "language, religion, laws, government, blood." By 1920, when she read this in France as a sort of double exile, Katherine Mansfield could retort in the margin, "The sod under my feet makes *mine.* "[6] For she knew it by then: new mythologies must needs evolve. Identity in the things which Coleridge mentions cannot help the creative artist until several generations have shaped them again in one place—in organic relation to that place. When Christmas falls at summer's height and the Feast of the Resurrection occurs in the fall religion's roots are upside-down, and the human spirit must start again. (In a story called *At the Bay,* it does just that.)

All the same, Wellington in 1907 wasn't quite as barren as Kathleen Beauchamp's account would make it seem. Visiting theatrical companies and visiting musicians were plentiful—even Wagner, after a fashion, could be heard in Courtenay Place—and Kathleen met the exciting visitors in her home, since her parents captured them as house-guests. It was not that such things were not, but that they came and went, and made the sight of departing ships more painful. There was even, in 1907, a lively monthly called *The Triad,* devoted entirely to the arts, to which Kathleen contributed a decadent prose-fragment called "The Death of a Rose."

But all such imported cosmopolitanism was withering in the Colonial sun, and in any case was no part of the life her parents wanted her to join. She was expected to lead the "Suitable Appropriate Existence," as Juliet calls it, the very security of which she loathed. She might go to a lecture on "Girls' Responsibilities" at Government House, but not to the raw new university on its gashed-clay hillsite just above the town. Instead, the "Social Notes" report her presence (or rather, that of her clothes) at the Wellington College Sports: "Miss C. Beauchamp, plum-coloured shot silk, with purple hat; Miss K. Beauchamp, green shantung with green hat."[7]

The *Corinthic* had deposited its three unwary maids on the wharf three weeks before Christmas. The third one, in those weeks, was far too self-absorbed to visit her beloved Granny Dyer—now ageing, and living with another of her daughters in Thorndon. Mrs. Dyer remarked on it to a friend, without resentment. On New Year's Eve she suddenly died, and the letter to Sylvia Payne just quoted reports the event like this: "I have been living, too, in the atmosphere of Death. My Grandmother died on New Year's Eve—my first experience of a personal loss—it horrified me—the whole thing— Death never seemed revolting before."

Her moods were certainly noticed. Some relations shortly invited Vera and Chaddie to stay on their sheep station *without* their sister. "I wish dear old Kass was here too but sad to relate she was not asked," Chaddie wrote to Sylvia from there. "I always hate going away without her somehow."

Somewhere in the notebooks one finds four glum stanzas in imitation of Poe, and a creepy imitation of his story "Ligeia," with dull purple curtains that move, drops of blood, etc.[8] Now she began to fill them with "monotonous terrible rain," "narrow, sodden, mean, draggled houses" and so on. Even in glorious weather at Island Bay the sea was only blue with "the blueness of Rossetti; green—with the greenness of William Morris." There is not a trace of wit or joy or humour in those pages. On the other hand, there is this: "When New Zealand is more artificial, she will give birth to an artist who can treat her natural beauties adequately. This sounds paradoxical, but is true." Which isn't bad, for eighteen years.

It must have been about this time that Mrs. Beauchamp gave a certain garden party which figures in one of her daughter's best-known stories. In the fictional version, when the marquee has been put up on the lawn, the flowers and the cream puffs ordered and awaited, the hired band soon to arrive, word comes to the kitchen door that a poor young carter from one of those sordid hovels below the road has been thrown by his horse and killed. A grieving widow, five children fatherless, all within earshot of the party! And it is Laura, the "different" one, the more sensitive member of the family, who would call the party off. She is of course talked out of her extravagant compassion. The widow must simply endure the band; but after the guests have gone Mrs. Sheridan has one of her marvellous ideas: her daughter shall be humoured, and the stricken household comforted with party leftovers. So, in lace frock and enormous hat, Laura takes down a basket laden with sandwiches and cream puffs. Obliged to go inside, she sees the young man serene in death. Embarrassment and pity, love and condescension overwhelm her all at once, and to the dead man she blurts, "Forgive my hat." As she goes back up to the house, only her brother understands her feelings.

Kathleen's sister Vera, when asked by the author if there had ever been a garden party like the one in the story, and was there an accident that day, replied, "Indeed there was," and added, faintly bridling, "And *I* was the one who went down with the things!" She then described how absurd she had felt in "one of those enormous hats we used to wear in those days," and how she had had to tilt it sideways to get through the cottage door. At a distance of sixty years her comment had an edge to it; she and Kathleen never did get on.

The only time when the original garden party could have been given at No. 75 Tinakori Road, with the weather safe and the girls in such hats, is the early part of 1907; for the Beauchamps left that house in April. It was probably a farewell to the house, and given in February or March—not long, that is, after Kathleen's "first experience of personal loss," and her loveless account of her Granny's death. One suspects there was a good deal less grace in Kathleen's feelings on the day of the party than there is in Laura Sheridan's. All the evidence from the time suggests an unremitting self-absorption, of a most unpleasing sort. Some of her best-known stories were, it would seem, a form of atonement for the sins of her youth.

Obviously, some new kind of friendship was an urgent need: such self-inflicted isolation could hardly go on and on. The remedy came in two short love-affairs with girls. By her own testimony (in a document which belongs to a later moment) it was the first time Kathleen had experienced anything of the kind. By the same testimony, it occurred now under the direct influence of her reading Oscar Wilde.

Soon after returning she met again Maata Mahupuku, the Maori girl who had been at Miss Swainson's with her and whom she had also been seeing in London, after Maata had been to Paris. A passionate affair developed, of which there are records in the notebooks and in a dated fragment of Maata's diary.

"Dearest K. writes 'ducky' letters," says the fragment. "I like this bit: 'What did you mean by being so superlatively beautiful as you went away? You witch: you are beauty incarnate.'" Upon which Maata comments, "It's conceited of me to like it, but I do."[9]

Since that was in April, the affair must have coincided with another —the affair with "E.K.B." to which the *Journal* refers in June. Edie Bendall, a pretty girl with a sweet and simple nature and none of Kathleen's egotism, had lately returned from an art school in Sydney, where she had learned how to be a sort of Colonial Kate Greenaway. Kathleen thought her drawings the right match for her own child verses (it is exactly what they were) and proposed their doing a book together, so they used to meet on Saturday afternoons, when Kassie poured her heart out on the subject of "Caesar," or her dreadful family, and Edie did her best to be a "good influence."[10]

This friendship also developed into a passionate affair, reawakening the shipboard fears of Kathleen's parents—but they, meanwhile, had other things to occupy their thoughts. For in the middle of April the weekly paper called the *Free Lance* put this item at the head of its local news:

> Mr. Harold Beauchamp, the popular head of the go-ahead firm of W. M. Bannatyne & Co., has been cheerfully elected chairman of the Board of the Bank of New Zealand. . . . . He is the beau ideal of a dapper, suave, acute commercial man who has always known what to do at the right time and has done it. . . . .[11]

Henceforward Beauchamp was a powerful man in the commercial world of the growing colony. He must have known the vote was coming, and may have planned the move to a better address in anticipation of it. The new house was in Fitzherbert Terrace—a "good area," this time, with no more "hovels" close at hand—and it had a croquet lawn and a big garden. Like all its neighbours it was built of timber made to look like stonework at the front, with an imposing pillared porch. In Katherine Mansfield's letters and *Journal* it is referred to as "No. 47."

As soon as the move was completed Mrs. Beauchamp sent out invitations to an "At Home," not forgetting to ask the *Free Lance* to send its lady reporter. Lovely chrysanthemums in autumn tints were in profusion, her column duly reported, and bowls of palms and cosmeas were also used. Mrs. Beauchamp received in a black silk poplin gown trimmed with ivory lace and a smart black feather hat, while Miss Kathleen wore a dress of *ecru* lace with narrow pipings of flame-coloured silk. . . . .[12]

Sylvia Payne heard all the news from Chaddie: "We have a lovely ballroom, which we of course use for music, and it is splendid for sound. Kass has been playing her 'cello so well tonight. I do wish you could have heard her the dear old thing I hate to feel she is so unhappy here isn't it a horrid state to be in so early in life?"

Kass had a room of her own upstairs in which she now arranged her Watts prints, her postcards from the Louvre, and her photographs of "Caesar" and her college friends. She retired there after breakfast, her bed having been made for her by other hands (we can see the maid poking out her tongue at "Caesar"), and opened a notebook to describe how much she loathed herself. She wrote letters to "Caesar" signed "Kathie Schönfeld," and tried out different names: "K—Kathleen, Kathie, Kass, K, Kath." She was quite determined to be someone else.

When she went downstairs again she was a darling, the dear old thing. She was deliberately rude to the ships' captains whom her father was always inviting to dinner, and to the up-country parsons who were billetted with the Beauchamps when they came to town for the Anglican Synod. "Although there were no God," says a notebook entry, "God would remain the greatest notion man had ever had— Evolution—eventually God—nicht?" Was that tried out on the vicar of Johnsonville? Some of this must have been rather fun, but there is still not a glint of humour in her writing. Her father's secretary at the office, Mattie Putnam, who used to do some typing for Kathleen, "never saw her laugh." She only knew her to speak in a low monotone, "without inflection or vivacity."[13]

Early in June Kathleen was over at Day's Bay, with Edie, in the little holiday cottage which Beauchamp, with a pleasing absence of pretension, had caused to be built while his daughters were in London. This is not the inland cottage described in *At the Bay*, but a "bach," in the local tongue, which stood out on the rocks at Downes Point, and consisted merely of a kitchen–living room, a bunk room, and an outhouse with bath and woodshed. You cooked with rainwater, and a wood-stove and primuses. In a southerly buster, the waves crashed on the rocks outside.

A long *Journal* entry of 1 June (it is actually in the notebook Miss Wood had given her) describes what had just occurred between Kathleen and Edie: "Last night I spent in her arms—and tonight I hate her —which, being interpreted, meaneth that I adore her: that I cannot lie in my bed and not feel the magic of her body. . . . . I feel more powerfully all those so-termed sexual impulses with her than I have with any man." She now repudiates the handsome cricketer, and this time it is the last four words that demand our special notice: "Adonis was—dare I seek into the heart of me—nothing but a pose. And now she comes—and pillowed against her, clinging to her hands, her face against mine, I am a child, a woman, and more than half man."[14]

A nightmare follows, and is described with all its Baudelairean images of guilt and evil; it ends with Kassie's being comforted on Edie's breasts, "wishing that this darkness might last forever." There is beauty in the description of the loving; the feelings, at the time, were genuine enough, no doubt. But it is clear as well that some part of Kathleen's mind was capable of standing off and seeing them as "copy," even in the midst of loving—as though her account of them was a way of emulating her favourite writers. Edie once said (speaking generally) that Kass had no compunction at all about "using" people —she knew that she had been used herself—and she added: "That was a Beauchamp characteristic."

Just three weeks later the generous Edie was indeed being repudiated. "It was, I consider, a frantically maudlin relationship and one better ended," says Kathleen's notebook. "Also she will not achieve a great deal of greatness."

Kathleen then asked herself whether other girls of her age experienced desire as she did (her thoughts were turning now to Maata, not E.K.B.). Did they feel, like her, "so absolutely powerfully licentious, so almost physically ill"? The dashes in what follows are her own:

I alone in this silent clockfilled room have become powerfully—— I want Maata—I want her as I have had her—terribly. This is unclean I know but true. What an extraordinary thing—I feel savagely crude— and almost powerfully enamoured of the child. I had thought that a thing of the Past— Heigh Ho!!!!!!!!!!! My mind is like a Russian novel.[15]

[2]

Except for a fleeting reference to Tolstoy at Queen's College which suggests that her knowledge of him came from "Mimi," that passage is the earliest thing in Kathleen's notebooks or letters which might be interpreted as showing that she was acquainted with Russian authors. Dostoevsky was not yet generally available in English; Chekhov did not write novels (nor was she careless with such terms); Turgenev seems an unlikely model in the context. The point is of some importance, but will have to be left aside for the moment. There is no evidence that her knowledge of "Russian novels" was anything but secondhand as yet.

What she did read in Wellington is known in some detail, thanks to the fact that she had borrowing privileges at the General Assembly Library when Parliament was not in session, and many years later the librarian, Dr. G. H. Scholefield, went through the old cards for her name. She took out the lives of "innumerable artists and poets," and much poetry, including Browning and Yeats; some Ibsen, Maeterlinck, and Shaw; Nietzsche's *Dawn of Day*, Heine's *Ideas*, and Laura Marholm's *Psychology of Women*. [16] No Russians—although the library had a copy in 1907 of R. E. C. Long's translation of Chekhov, *The Black Monk, and Other Stories*, which Kathleen might have read without borrowing, since she often used the MPs' club-like reading-room.

One book that did affect her writing, and her behaviour too, is the *Journal* of Marie Bashkirtseff, that other young artist of passionate ambition who died of consumption before she could fulfil the gifts she possessed. Born to parents from the Russian nobility who separated while she was a child, Marie Bashkirtseff lived with her mother in a round of European health resorts, where her first ambition was to be a singer. When her voice failed at the age of eighteen she took to painting instead, and before her death at twenty-five she achieved some paintings of acknowledged genius, once very well known in France. She also poured out her inner life in an enormous journal of 103 notebooks, from which a two-volume selection, idealised and falsified at her mother's instigation, was published three years after her death and was very widely read in France and England, giving rise to a cult in both countries. Mr. Gladstone was much affected; and Stephen Leacock satirised the journal in his *Memoirs of Mme. Mushenough.*

Anyone who compares the lives of the two young egotists will be driven to conclude that Kathleen saw her own nature and her own features in those of the Russian girl, and embarked on the risky course of "identifying" with her, even to the extent of assuming the hairstyle seen in the frontispiece to an edition of Marie's letters which she probably knew.

Marie's entries were written mainly in French, but also in Russian and Italian. While daydreams abound, there are also many narrations of her actual dreams. When she describes herself, one New Year's Eve, "burning with impatience to tell my fortune before a mirror," the face we see is almost Kathleen's; while a passage like this (24 August 1874) is typical of either writer:

> The noise of Paris, this hotel as large as a city, with its people always walking, talking, reading, smoking, looking, makes me dizzy. I wish to live faster, still faster, faster. . . . . It is true, I fear, that this desire to live by steam is a forewarning of a short existence.[17]

The urge to self-expression now drove Kathleen to attempt short stories, of a sort—not the magazine kind, with a plot, which was then so widely approved, but in form more personal; and Mattie Putnam had been typing them for her at Beauchamp's office. She had evidently found them "morbid," since she was promised in a letter that there would soon be some poems full of cheerfulness—"though to tell you a secret I prefer the others—the tragic pessimism of youth—you see —is as inevitable as the measles!"[18] (Something made Miss Putnam keep the letters she received from Kathleen.)

Whatever had happened in London when the Trowell twins returned from Brussels, she was still inclined to believe herself in love with Arnold. In "Woodie's" notebook, at any rate, there is a draft of a letter to him (included in the *Journal*) which begins like this: *"Sunday. Beloved, though I do not see you, know that I am yours—every thought, every feeling in me belongs to you. . . . . To me you are man, lover, artist, husband, friend. . . . . etc."*

At this time Arnold's parents were still in Wellington. Kathleen was playing chamber music with Mr. Trowell, and one *Journal* entry refers to him emphatically as *"my* Father." So long as they were there, she could bear it. But they were leaving in September, to make a home for their sons in London.

Late in August, after a trio practice in the music room, Kathleen found herself having a discussion with Mr. Trowell about "marriage and music," and what a musician's wife must do for him (Mr. Trowell having doubts, apparently). By chance the next day's Frisco mail brought a letter from Ida with some gossip about Arnold's allegedly bohemian life in Brussels, which Kathleen seems to have believed, for she reared up primly, as the *Journal* shows.* One notes the incident mainly for the helpful role in it that Ida played. For some time Arnold vanishes from the notebooks; and Kathleen soon wrote a story that suggests a turning away from him.

The typing of the stories was part of a plan to make Beauchamp let her go back to London. But she needed advice on where to send them, and he knew where to turn for that. When the English cricketers were playing at the Basin Reserve in the previous summer he had sat down beside the *Evening Post* reporter, Tom L. Mills, who was covering the game. (Kathleen was probably in the pavilion too, admiring the bowling of "Adonis.") "I have a daughter, Mills, who thinks she can write" —so Mills eventually recalled the conversation in a magazine article.[19] "What does Father think?" said Mills. "Oh, I don't know anything about poetry and stories." Would Mills consent to read some of her efforts and give a candid opinion? He would—"so long as she doesn't fire the ms. of a novel at me."

After preparing a batch of short prose pieces which she called *Vignettes*, and some child-verses, Kathleen met Mills in a tea-room on Lambton Quay. He advised her to send the verses to *Harper's Magazine* (which declined them) and the *Vignettes* to a new monthly just started in Melbourne, called the *Native Companion*—in Mills's words, "a magazine that takes the sex story." It was apparently a prickly interview.

E. J. Brady was delighted with the *Vignettes* and accepted three at once. But he wondered whether this unknown writer on sex who wanted to use a pseudonym mightn't be his New Zealand contributor Frank Morton, trying to get more space. Inquiring, as delicately as possible, if she wasn't Frank Morton pulling his leg, he was assured in reply that nothing of hers was cribbed, as she hated plagiarism; and as to herself, she was "poor—obscure—just eighteen years of age—

---

*Arnold Trowell's sister Mrs. Dorothy Richards told the author in 1954 that she couldn't understand this incident at all. She said her brother was "never that sort of man, in fact his character is utterly conventional."

with a rapacious appetite for everything and principles as light as my purse." This must only have increased Ned Brady's doubts, but he replied with an astonishing cheque (he sent her £2, the best pay she received for years), and assuring the young lady that it was a compliment to be mistaken for Frank Morton, he kept the correspondence. She, of course, at once showed the cheque to her father, who reacted as a decent father should.

On 10 October, unknown to Kathleen, he dictated a letter from the office to this fellow in Melbourne. His daughter had shown him the correspondence, he said, and he desired to thank Brady for the "practical encouragement" he had given her; at the same time he would like to assure him that he need never have "any hesitation in accepting anything from her upon the assumption that it may not be original matter." She herself was a "very original character," and writing, whether it be good or bad, came to her quite naturally. As to her age, she had "spoken quite correctly"; she had been a student at a college in London, but had "left that institution to return to New Zealand." She had always been an omnivorous reader, and possessed a most retentive memory. Ah, yes—and would he be good enough "not to mention that I have written you concerning her."

Kass wrote again next day, reminding Brady that she wished to be known only as "K. Mansfield" or "K.M." He was on no account to use the name "K. M. Beauchamp."[20] It was in this manner that she assumed her pseudonym, and spurned her father's name, just before her nineteenth birthday. Stendhal, too, made parricidal use of masks and pseudonyms.

The three *Vignettes* that appeared in the *Native Companion* for October were, to use a phrase from one of them, "heavy with morbid charm." A shadowy nocturne depicts Kathleen mooning at her window-sill while London "stretches out her eager hands." A second window-sill piece* contains a day-dream in which Monsieur le

---

*Six separate sketches of this time all begin near windows or doors. "Marina stood at the scullery door and called "Pat, Pat,' " is the opening of one. Another begins: "On waking next morning Kathie slipped out of bed, ran over to the window, shook her hair back from her face, and leaned out." All six can be seen in the Mansfield anniversary number of *ADAM*, published in 1973. If one adds to them Kathleen's first story at the age of nine, the window scene in "Juliet," and other instances, a trick of her mind is evident: she is constantly inhabiting one space while observing another, and has her characters doing the same.

Musicien strolls by with lantern and fiddle-case from the café in the village, "softly whistling the opening bars of Max Bruch's D minor concerto." The third, a scene of girlish intimacies in London with "Mimi," affords a glimpse of its author's passionate hopes of fame, but ends in a sardonic gesture of dismissal—as yet, her only form of humour: "We talked of fame, how we both longed for it, how hard the struggle was, what we both meant to do. . . . . Today, at the other end of the world, I have suffered, and she, doubtless, has bought herself a new hat at the February sales. Sic transit gloria mundi."[21]

Those pieces were all signed "K. Mansfield," and so was a little tale called *In a Café*, which followed in the next issue. But this one wasn't a piece of decadent mood-painting, it was a Mansfield short story in embryo, written in bright self-mockery, its point well made within a thousand words.

Its unnamed girl is described as having an expression "at once of intense eagerness and anticipated disillusion"—all Katherine Mansfield, in a phrase. When she meets her musician-friend for luncheon in Bond Street, he wearily runs his white hands through his hair, declaring that "Life in its widest, fullest sense is granted to artists only"—once more the purest creed of a later Mansfield. But this must needs be mocked, and mocked it is—with a little joke about a portion of red-currant jelly. They talk of marriage, and he asks if he may have her violets to keep. "They are yours," she replies with emotion (the balance of emotion and mockery resembles that in *Bliss*, or in *A Dill Pickle*, which also mocks love with incongruous food). Just then his Fellow Student arrives to fetch him for rehearsal. The two go out into the cold: her lover's hands go into his pockets, her violets on to the footpath, where she, still musing on the proposal that was very nearly made, observes them a few minutes later. She kicks them into the gutter and goes laughing down the street.[22]

Bliss ends in a pear tree, *In a Café* in the gutter; and the emotion of its final gesture is unproductive, the irony no saving irony. But its author had found out how to use her gift for impersonation, extended to self-caricature, in something more skilfully made than anything she had done before. Moreover, she had given the result some form; and the fact that her mentor Walter Rippmann had made her aware of the need for that is revealed by a hectic letter she had written to Vera in Sydney at some time in this hectic year, which is quoted in Sylvia Berkman's critical study of her work. After fulminating against her fellow citizens and all the "firm fat framework of their brains," Kass assured her sister (who was not at all the sort of person to whom such things could be usefully directed), that what these Colonials needed was "a mad wave of pre-Raphaelitism, of super-aestheticism," in order to help them find some "balance and proportion."

"We want two or three persons gathered together to discuss line and form and atmosphere and sit at the street corners, in the shops, in the houses, at the Teas," she more than recklessly declared. And hectic and inappropriate though the context is those three words, line, and form, and atmosphere are there, to hint at the emergence of a new aesthetic, somehow linked to *art nouveau*. Then the letter threw off a heterogeneous list of necessary authors which must have dazzled Vera in the midst of her social gaieties in Sydney: Mendès, Meredith and Maeterlinck, Ruskin and Rodenbach, D'Annunzio and Shaw, "Whitman, Tolstoi, Carpenter, Lamb, Hazlitt, Hawthorne and the Brontës," all of whom the New Zealanders had better read, even if they have not yet been read by Kass.

The event of Kathleen's becoming a profitably published author had preceded, by only a week or two, her nineteenth birthday; and *that* was the occasion for one of Chaddie's headlong letters to Sylvia Payne, which broke a further piece of news. After describing all of Kass's birthday presents (greenstone earrings, Liberty brooches, and so on), Chaddie wrote, on 14 October 1907:

> More about Kathleen I am sending you an Australian magazine called *The Native Companion* which has accepted a lot of her work and the editor has written her several delightful letters. . . . . Isn't it splendid, I can't tell you how happy and proud I am. . . . . Fancy Kathleen going back to London after Christmas I can't bear to think of it, but I know she must go, it is the only thing for her and I feel her going will bring us all over the sooner. Oh! dear what absolute joy and bliss that would be.

That was the family, and that was Chaddie, as Kathleen turned nineteen. In the age of chaperons they were going to let her go, alone to London! Upstairs in her room just one week later, this was Kathleen, writing in the notebook supplied by "Woodie":

> 21 x 07 Damn my family! O heavens, what bores they are! I detest them all heartily. I shall certainly not be here much longer. Thank Heaven for

that! Even when I am alone in a room, they come outside and call to each other, discuss the butcher's orders or the soiled linen and I feel—wreck my life.[23]

It is hardly surprising that shortly after this Harold Beauchamp arranged to get his troublesome daughter out of the house for a few weeks. He arranged for her to join a party of friends (not actually known to him) who were about to make a caravan expedition through the volcanic central region of the North Island: through all that tortured, upthrown country that lies between Napier and the Urewera, and then to Rotorua. One of the party was a musical friend of Kathleen's in Wellington, Millie Parker, presumably a daughter of her piano-teacher (and her father's), Mr. Robert Parker.

It is tempting to wonder whether Beauchamp looked inside her copy of *The Importance of Being Earnest* and learned that "Anyone can be good in the country." More likely, no doubt, he was simply hoping that she would "settle down" if she went out and saw a little of the New Zealand that he had known in his boyhood. But the daughter of Harold Beauchamp was now a thoroughly urban product, who shortly had to ask one of her travel companions, in a Queen's College accent, how one peels potatoes.

With her Wellington companion she went by train to Napier to join the others. "There is something inexpressibly charming to me in railway travelling," says the *Journal*, introducing a personal trait that will often be noticed again. "I lean out of the window, the breeze blows, buffeting and friendly, against my face, and the child spirit, hidden away under a hundred and one grey city wrappings, bursts its bonds, and exults within me."[24] Trains—and windows, anywhere—made Kathleen want to write.

From Napier the party set off inland in a covered wagon, with a dray as luggage van, a large partitioned tent, and five horses—"such dear old things," wrote Kathleen to her mother. "They nearly ate my head through the tent last night."[25]

Beyond Tarawera they camped in a valley since identified as the setting for *The Woman at the Store* (they met a woman there who served as her original), and Kathleen's letter to her mother said that she was "quite fond of all the people." They were "ultra Colonial," but thoroughly kind and good-hearted, and "always more than good to me." Her companion Mrs. Webber, forgiving the condescension she must have sensed, described Kathleen kindly in later years as "a pleasant, plump-faced girl, bright, vivacious, and good company." But when Kass asked how you peel potatoes she had told her, "The same way as apples."[26] A New Zealander can almost hear the Kiwi accent.

The notebook extracts printed in the *Journal* are a little over-written, but they vividly portray the burned-off landscape, and they show us Kathleen forming a bond with her country (if not with its white inhabitants) which was later of much importance to her art:

> Everywhere on the hills, great masses of charred logs, looking for all the world like strange fantastic beasts: a yawning crocodile, a headless horse, a gigantic gosling, a watch-dog—to be smiled at and scorned in the daylight, but a veritable nightmare in the darkness. And now and again the silver tree-trunks, like a skeleton army, invade the hills.[27]

She loved the native bush, and the New Zealand species of pampas-grass prompts a pleasing image: "Below us lay a shivering mass of white native blossom—a little tree touched with scarlet—a clump of *toi-toi* waving in the wind, and looking for all the world like a family of little girls drying their hair."

She wrote a long, chatty, uncontrived description for her mother of the day when they reached Te Pohue; but then, for the notebook, compressed it into this:

> *Monday.* The *manuka* and sheep country—very steep and bare, yet relieved here and there by the rivers and willows, and little bush ravines. It was intensely hot— We were tired, and in the evening arrived at Pohue, where Bodley has the Accommodation House, and his fourteen daughters grow peas. We camped on the top of a hill, mountains all round, and in the evening walked in the bush, to a beautiful daisy-pied creek—fern, *tuis,* and we saw the sheep sheds. Smell and sound, 12 Maoris—their hoarse crying—dinner cooking in the homestead, the roses, the Maori cook. Post letters there—see Maoris.[28]

In the Urewera country they stopped at the Maori village of Te Whaiti, where, Mrs. Webber has recorded, some Maoris who had never seen such an outfit asked if it was a circus. They were told (by guess whom) that it was, whereon the rest of the district turned up to await the show. This *could* be the origin of an otherwise inexplicable assertion made some years later by Virginia Woolf about Katherine's adventures with "a circus on the Scottish moors."*

When they met white people Kathleen usually didn't like them—unless they happened to be English visitors with nice voices, and a little culture about them. "I am so tired and sick of the third-rate article," says a notebook entry. "Give me the Maori *and* the tourist, but nothing in between."[29]

In fact, unknown to her, Kathleen had some blood-relations in the Urewera who were Maoris, and whose name was Beauchamp†—some of whom could even have been present at Te Whaiti as disappointed patrons of the circus.

After leaving the Urewera the party made for Rotorua, pausing on the way at the Waiotapu thermal area, with its "Rainbow mountain" of varied colours, and its little daunting glimpses of emergent hell:

> We pass one oily bright green lake—round the sides the *manuka* clambered in fantastic blossoming. The air is heavy with sulphur and steam . . . By and by we go to see mud volcanoes—mount the steps all slimy and green, and peer in. It bulges out of the bowl in great dollops of loathsome colour, like a festering, filthy sore upon the earth. In a little whirling pool below, a thin coating of petroleum, black-ridged. Rain began to fall. She is disgusted and outraged.[31]

In her notebooks Kathleen was often uncertain as to whether she was "I" or "she." And when travelling in her native country, she wasn't sure whether she belonged there or not.

What Beauchamp seems to have hoped for didn't happen. The untamed beauty of her country made Miss Kathleen no fonder of its white inhabitants. The Maoris had something which she recognized, and was drawn to: they reminded her of Europe, where people had

---

*See page 249 below.

†This fact was only brought to light in 1974 when a gathering was held at Picton of descendants of the Poet of Hornsey Lane. Commander R. R. Beauchamp, RN (a grandson of Henry Herron Beauchamp), was delighted with the discovery and reported afterwards that an unrespectable brother of Arthur Beauchamp's who had also emigrated to Sydney had been "swept under the carpet" in Harold's *Reminiscences,* while his only son Fred, who had come to New Zealand, "was allowed to vanish into the mists of the Urewera country." (Harold had written, "What became of Fred I do not know.") Fred's Maori wife bore him five sons, who were all named after the uncles from Hornsey Lane, and this branch of the family was represented at the Picton gathering by Allan Tipene Beauchamp, Royal New Zealand Navy.[30]

roots. In her white compatriots she sensed no nutrient for her ambition, no humus of tradition.

As she was later to complain in a poem (composed in the manner of Walt Whitman, and therefore difficult to quote) there were impediments to creativity in a little island with no history—

> *Making its own history, slowly and clumsily*
> *Piecing together this and that, finding the pattern, solving the*
> * problem,*
> *Like a child with a box of bricks.*

My people, says the woman of the poem, "have had nought to contend with":

> *What would they know of ghosts and unseen presences,*
> *Of shadows that blot out reality, of darkness that stultifies morn?* [32]

[3]

"We spent a very quiet Xmas as most of the family were away as it was so awfully hot," wrote Chaddie to Sylvia on 10 January 1908. "Kathleen has just returned from her month away caravanning in the backblocks. She had the most interesting and delightful time, and came home looking so well and awfully brown. Don't be surprised to see her about April, it is quite likely she will be in London by then."

"I shall end—of course—by killing myself," says a *Journal* entry of 10 February. Another, of uncertain date but written at night, seems to have been scribbled in the Day's Bay cottage (since sheep would be a little unusual in Fitzherbert Terrace) while awaiting an assignation. If taken at face value, with its ominous lamb-to-the-slaughter image, it would seem to refer to her first sexual experience with a man—"the crisis of my life":

Night. J'attends pour la première fois dans ma vie le crise de ma vie. As I wait a flock of sheep pass down the street in the moonlight. I hear them cracking the whip—and behind, the dark heavy cart—like a death cart il me semble—and all in this sacrificial light I look lovely. I do not fear —I only feel. I pray the dear Lord I have not waited too long for my soul hungers as my body all day has hungered and cried for him—Ah come now—soon. Each moment il me semble is a moment of supreme danger

—but this man I love with all my heart—the other I do not even care about— It comes—I go to bed—[33]

"I purchase my brilliance with my life," says the *Journal* on 18 March. "It were better that I were dead—really." And then: "I am unlike others because I have experienced all there is to experience." What *was* she referring to? What was the "all"? There is then a cryptic allusion to Wilde, and his effect on her: "Of course Oscar— Dorian Gray has brought this S.S. to pass." And in May: "I am now much worse than ever. Madness must lie this way," etc. "O, Kathleen, do not weave any more of these fearful meshes—for you have been so loathsomely unwise. . . . . Be good—for the love of God—be good— and brave, and do tell the truth more. . . . ."

These are sparse notes for the months they cover, and they are rather less stagey than the others. There is later evidence that the allusion to Wilde holds the essential clue, and that Kathleen was wrestling with guilt over her desire for Maata, which she believed to be "unclean." Further reference is made to Maata in a notebook; and on 4 March, in the cottage at the bay, Kathleen began a love-letter to Sylvia Payne ("I must tell you—here tonight Sylvia—that I love you —far more than I loved you in England") which said she would be leaving soon for England: "I cannot live with Father, and I must get back because I know I shall be successful—look at the splendid tragic optimism of Youth."[34] Even the newspapers knew what was afoot: "Miss Kathleen Beauchamp is leaving for England this month, where she will study literary work for some time," wrote "Iolanthe" in the Ladies' Magazine section of the *Weekly Press* on 1 April 1908.

But she didn't leave in April. Something had happened which gave her parents second thoughts. Of this event, the only record is Ida Baker's recollection for the author of a letter she once received from Kathleen. It said she had been to a ball and had sat out one of the dances "with a sailor." An adventure followed, of which she afterwards wrote a description on some loose sheets of paper which she left in her room. The wind swung round; her mother went in to close the open window; she gathered up the scattered pages, and couldn't put them down. It isn't hard to imagine Mrs. Beauchamp's mounting horror as she read —and her husband's, when he came home. A terrible enquiry followed.[35]

Was the "sailor" an invention for Ida's benefit? Did the sheets de-

scribe an adventure with a man, or with Maata? Were the parents
concerned for their daughter's chastity, or was the ugly word "per-
vert" in their anxious minds? No wonder Kathleen was still in Wellington in May, when an earlier departure date had been publicly
announced.

Just then she read a feminist book by Elizabeth Robins, called *Come
and Find Me,* which prompted a rare burst of feeling in her notebook
on the subject of the role of women in a man-made world:

> Really, a clever, splendid book; it creates in me such a sense of power.
> I feel that I do now realise, dimly, what women in the future will be
> capable of. They truly as yet have never had their chance. Talk of our
> enlightened days and our emancipated country*—pure nonsense! We
> are firmly held with the self-fashioned chains of slavery. Yes, now I see
> that they *are* self-fashioned, and must be self-removed.

The note went on to say that Oscar Wilde had lost some of his hold
on her: she had been reading Tolstoi and Ibsen, Shaw and D'Annunzio, with this result:

> Here then is a little summary of what I need—power, wealth and
> freedom. It is the hopelessly insipid doctrine that love is the only thing
> in the world, taught, hammered into women, from generation to genera-
> tion, which hampers us so cruelly. We must get rid of that bogey—and
> then, then comes the opportunity of happiness and freedom.[36]

As things were, though, in the little world which her father ruled,
such freedom could only come as a gift from him, and that it did so
in the end is something which needs to be placed quite squarely to his
credit. Kathleen could hardly have recognised, nor could he have explained, how much she already owed to her father. He it was who had
given her Karori and Day's Bay in her childhood (another Day's Bay
more recently), and all those benefits of the extended family which
sustained her later work. He had given her an education in London
that was more bent to her purposes than his, and if he thwarted her
"musical career," he must be acknowledged to have prevented some

*New Zealand took pride in the fact that it had given voting rights to women in 1893,
and had established old-age pensions in 1898.

waste in that direction. It was he who took the first step toward finding an editor for her stories, and sprang to her defence when their originality was questioned; he who at a crucial moment sent her into the backblocks and the bush, on a journey but for which her knowledge of New Zealand would have been very limited indeed. However, Jeanne and Leslie weren't going to schools in England!

He now decided—albeit in a manner which left her filled with bitterness against him—to let Kathleen return to London, with an allowance of £100 a year. He tried, by cable, to arrange for her to stay with his cousin Henry Beauchamp, who taught at the London Academy of Music and had been guardian to the girls when they were at college. But Henry prudently referred him to a hostel for music students in Paddington, which happened to be known as Beauchamp Lodge. No escape yet from the name.

Late in June there began a round of farewell parties. In Aurora Terrace Mrs. Rankine-Brown, wife of the Professor of Classics, gave a "violet tea," at which, according to the morning paper,[37] "violets were introduced in every way that an artistic and ingenious fancy could devise." The lamp on the tea table had a violet shade from which were hung festoons of violets out of season. Crystallised violets were placed about the table in silver dishes, and dainty violet sandwiches were served. There was then a little competition. All round the room girls were seen busy with little violet pencils, trying to compose "a poem on a violet." The winner was Miss Kathleen Beauchamp, whose entry was entitled, "Why Love Is Blind":

> *The Cupid child tired of the winter day*
> *Wept and lamented for the skies of blue*
> *Till, foolish child! he cried his eyes away—*
> *And violets grew.*[38]

Second place went to Kathleen's former teacher, Miss Eva Butts, of the purple tweed. And then, one final party.

"My dear Kezia," wrote "Priscilla" on the Ladies' Page of the *Evening Post* of 4 July (Priscilla's column always opened in this striking manner), "..... Among the various farewell parties in honour of Miss Kathleen Beauchamp, who left today for England. . . . . was a most delightful afternoon tea at Awarua House."

A vast wooden mansion on Tinakori Road, Awarua House was the residence of the Rt. Hon. the Prime Minister, Sir Joseph Ward, and it was Lady Ward who gave the party. The beautiful drawing-room, said Priscilla, was gay and bright with softly shaded lights and cheery fire, masses of flowers and graceful foliage plants, while the brilliant tea table, beyond the folding doors, was lit with a low-set crimson-shaded light. Lady Ward wore a most effective frock of black silk voile, the bodice opening over a fine underblouse of white lace; the guest of honour wore a "dark tweed tailor-made, furs, and a picturesque hat wreathed with large purple asters."

A fortune-teller was "much in request" for a time. Great amusement then resulted from the compilation of a series of "blindfold drawings of pigs, sketched in a book presented to Miss Kathleen Beauchamp as a memento of the occasion." All the drawings were signed with the artist's name, which made the volume doubly valuable, and a prize was given for the Best Pig.[39]

As it happens, a little parting present which Beauchamp gave Kathleen to take to England was also a pig: it was a pen-wiper in the form of a little brass pig with bristles in its back, which had stood on his desk and which she was fond of. She kept it until the end of her life, and returned it to him in her will.

Kathleen's ship, the *Papanui*, was to sail from Lyttelton, the port of Christchurch in the South Island, on the following Monday, 6 July. She could hardly go down there alone. That Saturday evening, therefore, Harold and Annie Beauchamp took their daughter—clutching, we must hope, her book of pigs—on board the S.S. *Maori*, for Lyttelton. They must have spent a dreary Sunday in Christchurch. Sailing time was four-thirty on Monday afternoon. It poured hard all that day. Lunch in town, then through the tunnel in the gaslit train.

Time for a spot with Captain T. S. Weston in his cabin: "Well, Beauchamp, letting this one leave the family nest, are you? Mostly men on board this trip, I think—two other women though. *We'll* look after her! *Won't* we? Another whiskey there? More tea, Mrs. Beauchamp."

Captain Weston recalled his famous passenger ruefully in later years, with Weston terseness: "Couldn't abide the woman."[40]

The rain beat down on lifeboats, ventilators, wharf-sheds, while the Lyttelton seagulls swooped for scraps. Two dismal figures on the wharf receded, at last, into the rain and the gloom, and turned, and walked away together.

"After living in New Zealand for eighteen months," the *Reminis-*

cences say of this wretched parting (which for Beauchamp was merely the first one out of five), "she begged to be allowed to go to London, confident that she could make good in the real world of letters. Work she had already done showed undoubted promise. There could be no question of standing in her light. Accordingly, in July 1908, she sailed from Lyttelton by the *Papanui* (6582 tons) for London."

CHAPTER IV

Beauchamp Lodge,
1908

*A traveller! By my faith, you have great reason to be sad: I fear you have
sold your own lands to see other men's; then, to have seen much and to have
nothing, is to have rich eyes and poor hands. . . . .*

*Farewell, Monsieur Traveller: look you lisp and wear strange suits,
disable all the benefits of your own country, be out of love with your
nativity, and almost chide God for making you that countenance you are;
or I will scarce think you have swam in a gondola.*
—Rosalind to Jaques in the Forest of Arden

If you sailed from Lyttelton to London by way of the Horn in 1908,
the voyage took exactly seven weeks. The *Papanui* carried twenty-four
other passengers, only two of whom were women. In the dead of
winter they headed south toward the icebergs, for three weeks seeing
no land except Cape Horn, and made their first call at Montevideo.
Some thick black notebooks must have been filled, but they haven't
survived.

At Montevideo, Kathleen went ashore with one of the male passengers. She later told two separate friends in London, of whom Ida was
not one, that she thought she had been drugged for a time, and "didn't
know what had happened," but was afraid she might be pregnant.[1]
Two months were to pass before the fear was put to rest. Crossing the
Equator, so they say, can sometimes lead to this embarrassing mistake.

Meanwhile there had been news of another alleged pregnancy. The
Trowells were now all in London, living in St. John's Wood, and when
the ship berthed at Gravesend Kathleen evidently received a letter

from Ida which said that her college friend Gwen Rouse was pregnant by Arnold.[2] This was quite untrue. We are dealing, all through this part of the story, with hearsay and error and deliberate false trail, not to speak of misconception.

It was Ida the faithful, and Ida alone ("I cannot remember any of her relations being there"), who waited on the platform as Kathleen's train drew in on 24 August 1908. She took her straight to Montagu Mansions, and after spending a few days with Colonel Baker and his daughters Kathleen moved into the student residence in Paddington to which her father had been referred by his apprehensive cousin.

Beauchamp Lodge, which is part of the Warwick Estates and takes its name from that Warwickshire family, is a tall Regency house standing alone by the ungondola'd waters of "Little Venice," the Paddington basin of the Grand Canal. It once enjoyed a prospect of artists' studios and plane trees across the water. Today it is used for social work, but in 1908 it was run as a hostel for music students by two professional musicians, Miss Ann Mukle and Miss Rosabel Watson. A sensible pair, who well knew that music was a road to freedom for their charges, they imposed the minimum of rules. Every girl had her own latch-key, and she could have her meal kept late. She could practise on cello or drums, or even the trombone, in her room; but no one could live there who was married. If you did that, you had to leave. Most of the students *were* studying music, but there were also one or two actresses, and even a former Isolde, Quetita Crichton.

When Kathleen arrived with her cello at Beauchamp Lodge she took a nice big room upstairs, with its own little curved wrought-iron balcony overlooking the canal. It wasn't cheap: with board it cost her twenty-five shillings a week, which meant that once again she was regarded as the extravagant daughter of a rich Colonial.

Downstairs in the dining-room she met another new arrival. Margaret Wishart, who found herself sitting beside Kathleen at her first meal in Beauchamp Lodge, was also in flight from Father—in her case, a Rear Admiral—so confidences flowed at once. A violin student, of a warmer and softer temperament than Kathleen and a more straightforward person, Margaret was less driven by ambition and much more likely to make a contented marriage; but she had been expected to spend her days trailing round naval stations as a musical ornament to her parents' life, in Malta or wherever they might be posted. Rebelling, she had lately won the right to stay in London and manage on her dress allowance (£60 a year, compared to Kathleen's £100), plus anything she might earn, however demeaningly, by her fiddle. Before long, in fact, she met her future husband, the pianist George Wood-house, later a well known teacher in Wigmore Street; she became secretly engaged to him, and within a year, backed up by Miss Watson and Miss Mukle, was married from Beauchamp Lodge, her parents having "cut her off." All this made for a bond in 1908 between the two young fugitives—for Kathleen, too, very soon was "secretly en-gaged,"[3] although not to Tom Trowell.

The imagined romance with Tom had never been more than that. The idea of "love" between them had been mostly in her own mind. In his, she was a friend—"My very good friend Kathleen M. Beau-champ," to cite the dedication of his *Six Morceaux* for cello and piano —with whom he had, indeed, been exchanging letters for the last six years, but whom he hardly ever touched. With his twin brother Gar-net, a much more responsive young man, it was soon a different thing entirely.

At No. 52 Carlton Hill Kass was treated as one of the family, and the family atmosphere, in a house more full of music than of money, was warmer and easier than anything she had known. A few years later she tried to depict it in a "novel." Being hardly fiction the novel was soon abandoned, but some fragments exist. One of them has a girl, who is obviously Kass, arriving for an evening meal to find the mother, down in the kitchen, about to prick her name with a fork in the pastry of an apple pie, while one twin tries out chords at the drawing-room piano for his new quintet and the other practises the fiddle upstairs. After dinner comes this (the semifictional names being here replaced by the real ones):

Kass knelt by the dining room fire helping Dolly roast chestnuts. They had a packet of the little hard nuts beside them and a hatpin to prick them with, an old Daily Mirror leaf to hold the charred peelings. In the rosy glow of the fire the two children, leaning against each other laughed and whispered, very absorbed, very intent. By the table sat Mrs. Trowell darning whole new feet into a pair of Tom's socks. Her skirt was turned back over her lap, her little, slippered feet curled round the chair legs. Now and again she leant forward and opened her mouth for Dolly to pop in a "beautifully soft one," but she was, for the most part, pale and tired.

With a drawing board propped against the table, sheets of manuscript surrounding the big untidy inkstand, some pink blotting paper, the old man busied himself copying out Tom's latest score. . . . . The room was warm and all pleasantly scented with the roasting nuts. The window curtains in the flickering light looked heavier, and quite profound their ugly red colour—as though they wished for a little space to hold these four together . . . Now and again, in the hush, they heard Tom's piano. He was busy with something—a theme that had seized him at dinner and made him refuse pudding but carry an apple with him to the drawing-room. . . . .

"Mum," said Dolly suddenly, "where's our Garnet?" "Don't know, dearie—ask Kass," Mrs. Trowell doubling a strand of wool and laboriously threading the needle.

"Do you know where he is—he'd love some of these chestnuts."[4]

The longing for a home is obvious. And Kathleen's letters establish the fact that she very quickly (within a fortnight of arriving, to be exact) fell passionately in love with Garnet, and hoped to marry him. No hurt was done to Tom, for whom her feelings now became those of a rather indulgent elder sister.

Margaret Wishart remembered Garnet as "very tall and slender, dreamy, cultured, and loving books almost as well as his violin." He did not have a markedly masculine temperament, but was much more the sort of man that Kathleen was likely to marry (she was never attracted to the bull-male form; she positively disliked robust, "successful" men).

Here is another scene from the abortive novel. Upstairs in one of the bedrooms, Garnet and Kathleen have been confiding to each other how unhappy life makes them feel. Even his open violin-case on the white bed is like "a little coffin," as they talk of the darkness of the future and her feeling of being a "lonely prisoner":

In the pause that followed she felt that their speech had sunk into a deep unknown gulf that had been separating her from him—that the confused words had filled up the gulf. The door burst open. Tom came in, flicking his table napkin in his hand.

"Dinner bell's rung three times. Jenny has called you. Mother is in a wax. Meat's cold. What are you two birds doing? Out with it, Garnie, you sly dog."

"Oh I must fly down," said Kass.

"No—no." Tom spread out his arms to catch her. "Not until I know what you two have been up to."

"Don't be absurd, Tom. Let me go. Garnie, your hair's wild even in this light—they'll be so angry."

"Not so fast, my sweet sister."

"Don't be a fool, Tom," said Garnet, laughing. "We've been looking at the trees on the house wall opposite—that's all."

"What!" laughed Tom. "The ones that Kass said yesterday were holding each other's hands in the dark? Shame on you. Go down to your betters, miss."

"Oh you baby," she scorned, running down the stairs.

Tom went up and nudged Garnet in the ribs. "Lucky fellow," he said, and shouted after them all the way to the dining room, "I *knew* it, I *knew* it."

The real-life fact is that within one month of Kathleen's stepping off the ship—by which time Garnet had gone off on tour with the Moody-Manners Opera Company—she was addressing him as "husband" in her letters. Yet the letters contained strange hints of fear, from some unacknowledged cause. Even the very first letter which he kept showed this. While staying in the house at Carlton Hill she had left a note for him to read on coming home late:

My Dearest—

I feel I must just write you a little note—Fate has been so unkind to you both today. Dearest—I've wanted you ever since I saw you yesterday. I have been wretched—I don't know *why* exactly—but I feel we have so much to say and so little time to say it in before you go away.

Dearest, I love you so intensely that I feel I could tell you so now until we both are old. . . . . I feel as though your kisses had absorbed my very soul into yours.[5]

Those opening lines suggest precisely the expression of the girl in *In a Café*: an expression "at once of intense eagerness and anticipated disillusion." Was this built in? Or what was wrong?

On Sunday 13 September Kathleen saw Garnet off to Birmingham, for a winter season in provincial theatres and theatrical boarding-houses: playing six nights a week, and travelling every Sunday. He was in the Moody-Manners "A" company, one of its "one hundred and forty artistes," with Charles Manners and Fanny Moody in the leading roles, and Signor Romualdo Sapio conducting. It was not an easy life: in Hull that November they gave *Aida* on Monday evening, *Butterfly* on Tuesday, a Wednesday *Meistersinger* followed by "Cav. & Pag.," and after a brisk *Tannhäuser* matinee came Saturday night's big draw, *Maritana.* Then by train to Bolton, then Blackburn, and so on.

Kathleen's letters to Garnet gush over with the volatile, transitory happiness that marked her later years. With him she felt "secure and rested and content," and marriage was clearly in both their minds; yet always she was asking, "Do you understand?" or *"Du verstehst?"* or *"Tu comprends?"* On a windy day in London she spoke of "that frightful sensation of grief that used to come over me in Wellington," and added, "It is like suddenly finding myself face to face with this ghost which terrifies me."[6]

The letters give no hint of how they thought they would support themselves if they got married. Kathleen spells the Future always with a capital, and the house they talk of is a dream house. Margaret Wishart recalled long conversations with Kassie about how both of them would have to live on nothing, "since our families would be outraged at the idea of our marrying penniless musicians," and she remembered Kassie saying once that if she only had sixpence to buy food, it would be *very* important to buy a bunch of violets for the table, and less food. What of that when the gain was all to Art, and Thorndon far behind? "I seem to see all with *double force,* " one letter to Garnet exclaims. "You have transformed me utterly," says another. "I am a different person —or rather—pour la première fois—I feel so much myself."

Even so, she went to spend a weekend with Aunt Belle and her stockbroker husband in Surrey. From there she wrote to Garnet: "I feel as tho' Nature said to me—"Now that you have found your true self—now that you are at peace with the world accepting instead of doubting—now that you love—you can see."[7]

But the conflict left—or something left—this troubling sense of an unknown fear. As the Kass-figure tells her lover in the novel: "You know sometimes I feel I'm possessed by a sort of Fate—you know— by an impending disaster that spreads its wings over my heart, or maybe only the shadow of its wings—but it is so black and terrible . . . I can't describe it."

[2]

When Kathleen left Wellington she must have packed some of those expensive fashionable clothes she used to wear: her mauve taffeta, her green shantung, her dark tweed tailor-made. One and all they seem to have vanished, being doubtless sold, in some discreet little West End establishment, as representing an affront to her real ambitions; for accounts of what she wore at Beauchamp Lodge don't tally at all with what she wore in Thorndon. She was indeed, like Jaques, "out of love with her nativity." There is no trace, in Paddington, of the picturesque hat wreathed with purple asters, no sign of the dress of blue *chiné* silk patterned with pink rosebuds that had been worn, so recently, to a ball in the Star Boating Club's sheds on the Wellington wharves. If she had to replace all that high fashion, keep an expensive room, and make ends meet, how did she do it?

Once a month she was entitled to visit Mr. Kay, at the Bank of New Zealand in Queen Victoria Street, to collect her £8 6s 8d (plus a wink or two, for he was a man of the world). After paying for her board she therefore had 15s a week to pay for clothes, Parma violets, Abdullas (which Garnet smoked—they would smoke them on their honeymoon), frequent visits to Queen's Hall, and afternoon teas in Bond Street. Later, this was Ida's opportunity, and her cheque-book took it; but Ida at this time, not yet twenty-one, and living with her father, had only £12 a year of her own. Fortunately, she writes, in a bitter passage that casts aspersion on Harold Beauchamp, "Kathleen was able to use her great gift for recitation, mimicry, and music."

In those days a certain sort of West End hostess used to arrange paid entertainment for her guests, and Beauchamp Lodge was an obvious agency for talent, of a socially acceptable sort. The word was passed that Miss Kathleen Beauchamp could do the most amusing recitations, using skits that she wrote herself, and could also sing. (Her cello had no role in this; like the dresses perhaps, it was sold before long.) Here was a chance for the little chameleon of 1906 to try out her impersonations. She could easily pass as one of the guests, until, at a suitable moment, she would allow herself to be persuaded, and do a Salvation Army song or a coon song—"Ah'm a sinner, Ah'm an unlucky man"—and be slipped a tactful envelope as she left. Ida says that Kathleen accepted a number of such commissions at a guinea a time, and that at least one new long dress was paid for in this way.

The dress was made with the help of Amy Birch, another escapee from parental tyranny at Beauchamp Lodge, who was a great friend of Margaret's and Kathleen's. These three used to sit up late at night in Kassie's room drinking cocoa, and "talking of all things in heaven and earth," as Margaret recalled. Curled up on a rug in front of the fire, Kassie looked for all the world as if she must have "some Maori blood." She spoke of the episode at Montevideo, and wept a little as she told the tale. The two girls shared many secrets, one of them being a dear little Swiss hairdresser whom Kathleen had discovered in George Street, just off Baker Street, who was a perfect treasure—the sort of friend you would go to in time of trouble. In her sixties, Margaret said that she had never, at any period of her life, known such intimacy as she had known with Kassie at Beauchamp Lodge.

But what did "intimacy" mean? What of Ida's, for example, viewed as it were from these cocoa sessions? To Margaret, Ida was "a person who visited Kassie frequently and was a great bore," but was tolerated because of her loyalty, "although it was almost suffocating at times." She "worshipped Kassie in an abnormal fashion" and was "frantically jealous of her having any other associates," so Margaret kept out of her way, and made a point of disappearing when she came: "At the same time I couldn't help hearing a good deal about her, and what an incubus she was."

Ida, in her own book, speaks of Kathleen wanting to write but being distracted by a social life in the hostel that was irksome to her: "She made many acquaintances among the students, and one or two became constant companions in her small room. They were too constant, their attentions suffocating her and preventing her from working."[8]

Two suffocations, and an "incubus"? A little duplicity on Kathleen's part? She had indeed embarked, as we shall see, upon a risky histrionic adventure into made-up roles, putting her friends into different "compartments" and indulging to the full that whim to try "*all* sorts of lives."

Had she thought about her own? As a matter of fact she had, for one of her Wellington notebooks contains some snippets from an unnamed play she had been reading—among them this, from "Act II, Scene ii": "By dint of hiding from others the self that is within us—we may end by being unable to find it ourselves."[9] One cannot say she didn't *know* what dangers she invited in her life. Yet always one finds her *observing* the experiment. Margaret Wishart often saw Kassie talking to "herself" in front of a mirror at Beauchamp Lodge.

So the whole of her story at this point is a story done with mirrors, a thing of quick costume-changes, switches of voice and hemisphere and country, of allegiances of every kind; and I think the only way to tell it is with mirrors, admitting the view of each witness in turn with a sort of *Rashomon* effect, since only in the multiplex confusion can veracity be found.

The need to earn money led Kathleen soon to a brief encounter with one form of the Edwardian "New Woman." She was sending some kind of newsletter to a paper at home, and Garnet, in some provincial theatre, read of her going one evening to report on a women's suffrage meeting in Baker Street. Large upholstered women argued themselves hoarse and thumped the floor and applauded, and one of them even tried to rope her in for the cause; but Kass, no feminist at any time (save briefly, after reading Elizabeth Robins), felt that she could "remedy the ills of the world so much more easily."[10] By her writing, that is.

She was happier at the Palace music hall in Shaftesbury Avenue. There, somewhere between Juliette's Sealions and the Urbanora Bioscope, she could see the daring new danseuse Maud Allen, in her wisp of chiffon, who summed up "everything that is passing, and coloured, and to be enjoyed." While this was being described for Garnet, however, a girl in the room above her own was practising a drum part for "The Policeman's Chorus," and in the next room, someone had started trombone scales.[11]

Then the Venezuelan pianist Teresa Carreño came to town, to give a concert in the Bechstein Hall: Carreño of the many husbands and the famous "masculine" performances of Beethoven's great sonatas. Kathleen took Garnet's young sister Dolly to the concert, on a Saturday afternoon, and the letter she wrote for Garnet that evening is packed with information about Carreño, about Ida, about the depressing effect of letters from home ("the shadow of the old life creeps over me. . . . . They hurt me bitterly"). They went backstage to see Carreño (Kathleen must have met her in Wellington) and Carreño kissed her hands: "My dear child, I must see *much* of you. I am your friend, remember, and I hope you know I played the Erlkönig quite for you."[12] It wasn't all gush. Kass was invited to her flat the following

Sunday. But the day on which she described that visit was also the date of a notebook entry—one of the very few made at this time—which in the *Journal* appears in puzzling isolation. It may refer to the missing of a period: "*October 12.* This is my unfortunate month. I dislike exceedingly to have to pass through it; each day fills me with terror." Since the Wednesday was her birthday, she next wrote Garnet a rather special letter (13 October 1908), which began:

> Beloved—though I do not see you, *know* that I am yours. Every thought, every feeling in me belongs to you—I wake in the morning and have been dreaming of you—and all through the day, while my outer life goes on steadily, my inner life I live with you, in leaps and bounds. I go through with you every phase of emotion that is possible—*loving* you— etc.

—and there is of course something familiar about those lines. They are a repetition, almost word for word at first, as if they were a recitation that had long been in her head before the mirror, of the unposted Wellington letter of 11 August 1907 (page 51 above), which at that time was addressed to Garnet's twin. Whether Tom had received the same letter in London, or only Garnet ever read it, no one can say.

There are more divided selves (or cells) to be reckoned with than we thought. There is "Kathie Schönfeld," who signed the first draft in the notebook; there is "Caesar," who is Arnold (or is Tom); and there is nice uncomplicated Garnet—for whom, however, the envelope didn't bear his name either. It was addressed to "Mr. Carrington Garnet, Moody-Manners Company, Theatre Royal, Glasgow." They were *all* using other names.

On the birthday itself, Kathleen evidently received a ring from Garnet in the mail, and wearing it, she went to Carlton Hill to show it to his mother, and to Tom and little Doll. Then she caught the four-fifty from Victoria for Warlingham to stay with Aunt Belle— with the ring, presumably, on some noncommittal finger. Waking next morning with Garnet's name on her lips, she kissed "*our* ring," jumped out of bed and heard the gardener digging just below, and soon was describing it all for her intended husband, but asking, "Garnet— what is ahead of us both?—oh, we shall seek out the heart of the world."[13]

Kathleen's New Zealand friend Ruth Herrick was still in London at this time, and one day, to her astonishment, she was approached as a confidant in trouble. Knowing that Ruth had access to a certain woman doctor, Kathleen told her of the episode at Montevideo, explained that she had missed a period, and asked for an introduction. This doubtless explains a notebook entry made while staying with Aunt Belle: "Feel frightful and can't think why . . . . . feel awful, shocking terrible—what is to be done I wonder." And another note, written in a bus outside Victoria Station on returning to London: "I wonder if I will ever be happy again—that's the question. . . . . It seems my brain is dead. My soul numbed with horrid grief."[14]

There is no way of proving what produced these thoughts, but the fear of pregnancy would certainly explain them. Could she really sustain all her roles—and marry Garnet—if a child had indeed been fathered in Montevideo?

Next evening, however, she was gaily on her way to Paris, for a wedding. A naval friend of the Wisharts was to be married at the British Embassy Church on Trafalgar Day (21 October), and Kass had so charmed Margaret's father that he had asked her to join them as his guest—the result being a spate of travel descriptions in the notebook which of course accompanied her. A long piece addressed to Garnet as if it were a letter tells him of dozing in the train and dreaming that *they* were going abroad together.[15] Her letters skipped the wedding, but she told him all about Versailles, the Luxembourg, and Notre Dame; and soon was back at Beauchamp Lodge and seeing his family again. Then one more *Journal* entry, again in puzzling isolation. It seems to dispose of one cause of her fears: "October 29—Went to Mrs. Charley Boyd and at last put my mind at rest."[16]

Only two later letters to Garnet are at present known. A scribble in pencil is "just a note to say goodnight" after supping with Margaret on boiled onions cooked over her fire; the last one, written in someone's house at H.M. Dockyard, Devonport, on 8 November, describes the launching by Mrs. Asquith on the previous day of the Navy's latest Dreadnought battleship, the *Collingwood*—a most moving Imperial occasion, and prompting another of those little effusions that predict the character of future writing:

Oh, Garnet, why is it we so love the strong emotions? I think because they give us such a keen sense of *Life*—a violent belief in our Existence.

One thing I cannot bear and that is the mediocre— I like always to have a great grip of Life—so that I intensify the so called small things —so that truly everything is significant. . . . .

On the last page was this: "I dreamed last night that we were at a Tschaikovsky concert together last night—and in a violin passage, swift and terrible—I saw to my horror, a great flock of black, wide winged birds—fly screaming over the orchestra. . . . ."[17] In other words, whatever fears were removed on 29 October, still other dark fears remained. And the fears, and the love of "truth," were in some way connected; which means we should turn to the writing that Kathleen did at Beauchamp Lodge. It concerns us as much as her actions: at this stage especially, the life and the creativity are one.

[3]

There was first her Whitman phase, strong just now because Margaret Wishart was another enthusiast, and often made Kassie extemporise for her in Whitman's manner. One surviving product, metrically a sort of hybrid of Whitman and Swinburne, is a poem of Paddington in autumn called "October," which was dated "22 x 08"* and sent to Vera as a birthday present.[18] Since it didn't get into the collected *Poems*, here it is:

OCTOBER
(To V.M.B.)

Dim mist of a fog-bound day . . .
From the lilac trees, that droop in St. Mary's Square
The dead leaves fall, a silent, shivering cloud.
Through the gray haze the carts loom heavy, gigantic
Down the dull street . . . Children play in the gutter,
Quarrel and cry; their voices are flat and toneless.
With a sound like the shuffling tread of some giant monster
I hear the trains escape from the station near and tear
their way into the country.
Everything looks fantastic, repellent . . . I see from my window

---

*Vera's twenty-third birthday. With the title amended to "November," the poem appeared in the *Daily News* of 3 November 1909.

An old man pass, dull, formless, like the stump of a dead tree
  moving.
The virginia creeper, like blood, streams down the face
  of the houses . . .
Even the railings, blackened and sharply defined, look evil
  and strangely malignant.
Dim mist of a fog-bound day.
From the lilac trees that droop in St. Mary's Square
The dead leaves fall, a silent, fluttering crowd.
Dead thoughts, that, shivering, fall on the barren earth . . .
Over and under it all the muttering murmur of London.

So recently so longed for, London now was filled with symbols of
barrenness and death. But not because of reading Whitman, surely?
Whitman loved cities: he found them positive, vital, and attractive.
The poem reflects a change. The "blab of the pave" had lost its glamour. Yet the rhythms are neither her own nor his, and it is odd to find
Katherine Mansfield, of all writers, declaiming in Walt Swinburne's
manner.

At the same time she was filling notebooks with ideas for stories,
epigrams in imitation of Wilde ("Never relight a dead cigarette or an
old passion"), new words to be used, and names for characters seen on
shop-fronts from the tops of buses. "She wrote masses of short stories
most of which I imagine she destroyed later," Margaret Wishart said,
"and which had to be read aloud to me for criticism."

The stories revelled in sordid detail—"the cult of the foul," it was
called in those days. There was one about a little dressmaker who had
been seduced: she was dying of consumption in a slum tenement in hot
weather, and outside the window lay a pile of rotting bananas upset
from a barrow. "That fairly made me wilt," Margaret Wishart recalled, "but she insisted on retaining the bananas, with chuckles of
delight."

Margaret may also have seen a story called *The Education of Audrey,*
which was probably published in London about this time. (It appeared
in the Wellington *Evening Post* in January, but that doesn't mean it was
sent to them; it is much more likely to have been "lifted" from a
London source.) It is one of Kathleen's self-realising fantasies, a story
in which she endows herself, as "Audrey," with glamour and confidence and pretty clothes, a lovely singing voice, intoxicating freedom,

and an insolent admirer—an artist—whom she last saw sailing away
from some remote Philistia and who, on hearing that she is in London,
writes demanding that she come to his room this afternoon ("I'm
hungry for you, here, this minute with me. Are you coming?—Max.")
Her answering telegram reads simply, "I come," and after consulting
the mirror-face above her dressing-table she decides what she will
wear: "a Liberty dress of mauve face-cloth trimmed with dull violet
buttons, and a beaver hat of the same colour, with a long curled
feather."

She takes a hansom to No. 8 East Square at a quarter to four,
thoughtlessly ordering the driver to come back at five-thirty.* What
follows is like a scene from Elinor Glyn, though in fact it was rewrit-
ten from that section of "Juliet," already quoted in the previous chapter, which describes a *risqué* visit to Walter Rippmann, or "the Man."
He takes her to his smoking-room, pushing aside the heavy purple
portière. "Tall wrought-iron candlesticks" stand in the corners, and
there is a "long low couch upholstered in dull purple."

She is offered a cigarette. His sketches are produced from a green
suède case; they sit and talk of what Life means, and little erotic thrusts
are made—and parried—until the story ends in a gesture suspiciously
like the ending of that earlier piece of schoolgirl decadence, *Die Einsame:*

> "Ah, there are heights and depths in Art and Life that you have never
> dreamed of, Audrey. If you could only realise what might belong to you!
> You are playing on the outskirts of a forest filled with beautiful scarlet
> flowers. One day, sooner or later, if you want to fulfil your destiny, some
> one will take you by the hand and lead you there, and you will learn."
>
> Silence again in the dark room . . . the silver rain beat against the
> window.

---

*Taking a hansom in 1908 was cheaper than taking a taxi. Arnold Bennett, portraying
the middle class for socialist readers a month or two later, gave the following description: "I go to the [Army and Navy] Stores, to Harrod's Stores, to Barker's, to Rumpel-
meyer's, to the Royal Academy, and to a dozen clubs in Albemarle Street and Dover
Street, and I see again just the same crowd, well-fed, well-dressed, completely free from
the cares which beset at least five-sixths of the English race. They have worries: they
take taxis because they must not indulge in motor-cars, hansoms because taxis are an
extravagance, and omnibuses because they really must economise. . . . ."—"Jacob Tonson" in the *New Age*, 4 February 1909.

She suddenly turned towards him and stretched out her hands— "Teach me, Max," said Audrey.

The hansom presumably has to go away again, leaving us to wonder just what Kathleen's parents made of the piece when they read it, over the name "K. Mansfield," in their very own evening paper. A long low purple couch!

She soon moved on. What all this led to was a story, remarkably deft for a girl of nineteen, and called, this time, *The Tiredness of Rosabel.* The contrast is amazing. Her undeceiving masks discarded, a fresh young talent is revealed, and it is not satirical. In the opening sentences, with a few quick strokes, a reality is produced:

> At the corner of Oxford Circus Rosabel bought a bunch of violets, and that was practically the reason why she had so little tea—for a scone and a boiled egg and a cup of cocoa at Lyons are not ample sufficiency after a hard day's work in a millinery establishment. As she swung on to the step of the Atlas 'bus, grabbed her skirt with one hand and clung to the railing with the other, Rosabel thought she would have sacrificed her soul for a good dinner—roast duck and green peas, chestnut stuffing, pudding with brandy sauce—something hot and strong and filling. She sat down next to a girl very much her own age who was reading *Anna Lombard* in a cheap, paper-covered edition, and the rain had tear-spattered the pages. Rosabel looked out of the window; the street was blurred and misty, but light striking on the panes turned their dullness to opal and silver, and the jewellers' shops, seen through this, were fairy palaces.[19]

The plan of the story is simple enough. Through streets that make her think of Venice ("even the hansoms were like gondolas dodging up and down") Rosabel goes to her dingy, gaslit room in Paddington, unlaces her boots, and, kneeling by the window, falls into a daydream about the rich young couple—handsome insolent young man and haughty miss—whom she had served in the shop that day. (The man is called Harry, and the haughty miss could be Aunt Belle, or Mrs. Harry Trinder.) The dialogue in the day-dream is handled with a skill beyond her years. Gesture and movement, though barely described, are vividly apparent; they are felt in the prose.

The shopgirl's dream continues into marriage with the rich young man: a home with fires in every room and roses everywhere, a French maid who would fasten *her* hats for her, and so on; while into the dream reminders are slipped of Rosabel's actual surroundings, so that the story runs on three time-levels at once: in the shop, in the bed-sitter, and in the dream-home of the fancied marriage. On the fourth level, too, of literary criticism, since Rosabel's daydream is suddenly seen to resemble that of the girl in the bus who, licking a finger as she turned each page, and mouthing the words, had been reading about "hot voluptuous nights" in *Anna Lombard.* *

The tone is sustained until a final, give-away paragraph in which the author steps forward with an awkward little observation about "that tragic optimism, which is all too often the only inheritance of youth"—an echo of recent letters to Mattie Putnam and Sylvia Payne.

This and other details—the bunch of violets, the placing of Rosabel by the window, the setting in Venetian Paddington, the topical allusion to *Anna Lombard,* and the use of Miss Rosabel Watson's Christian name—all seem to confirm that the story was written in 1908. Kathleen's early writing often shows signs of following quickly upon direct experience, whatever it might contain of fantasy.[20]

Meanwhile, what did she *do* with all these pieces? If a London paper did print the story of *Audrey,* it appears to have been a solitary instance. Margaret Wishart, who knew of the attempted "newsletter" to a Wellington paper, recalled no rejections in London. It would seem that Kathleen was even more isolated in Paddington than she had been in Thorndon. She was a girl in a hostel writing things, struggling quite alone to discover a form, with no idea where to turn for the critical guidance that every young writer needs.

Her difficulty was not only that of being an out-of-touch Colonial and an out-of-touch musician: it was that of the form she was inventing. She was not by nature a novelist—she had nothing to offer to

*It is always worth looking up the allusions in Katherine Mansfield's stories. *Anna Lombard* was one of the salacious and very lucrative productions of "Victoria Cross," authoress of *The Woman Who Didn't* (1895), *The Night of Temptation, Electric Love,* and *A Husband's Holiday.* First published in 1901, it had lately been reissued as a paperback (received by the British Museum in April 1908), and the hot voluptuous nights occur on page 17. Gerald Ethridge is at a ball somewhere in "India," that fascinating Oriental country where the full moon *sinks* after sunset:

"I took her out on the terrace, found her a chair and then dutifully brought her the

publishers of books. And while it is true that London never had more magazines than it had during Edward's reign, the book was the thing. The magazine story, or the story of Wells and Kipling, was not the art-form towards which Kathleen Beauchamp was so urgently driving her unshaped imagination. It was expected to have what playwrights called a "curtain"—and she liked windows. The editors wanted "plot," and a happy ending, too. Her aim was something else—to "intensify the so-called small things," as she expressed it for Garnet, "so that truly everything is significant." The short story in that sense did not exist in England yet. There was no place for what Kass Beauchamp wished to do. No place, either, for what young Joyce had been up to, over in Dublin.

Edwardian periodicals of any standing were gentlemen's magazines —the *Cornhill, Blackwood's,* perhaps the *Strand*—exuding an atmosphere of port and leather armchairs which Kathleen would have sensed at once as belonging to her father's club in Wellington: to a world of received attitudes, received views of life. But Arnold Bennett can best convey for us what they were like.

Writing in April 1908, in a little upstart socialist weekly called the *New Age,* Bennett described England's periodicals as "the most stupid and infantile of any 'World Power,' the United States not excepted." The *Strand* and the *Pall Mall Magazine* were "hopeless," *Blackwood's* published "some of the feeblest fiction that can be found anywhere," and the *Cornhill,* he said, stood for "all that is worst in the British temperament. It has the smoothness and vacuity of a minor official retired from the Foreign Office. Look through a number; in the whole there is not a split infinitive nor an idea." When noting, two years later, the projected launching of a "purely literary paper" to be devoted chiefly to creative work, Bennett declared: "This will be something of a novelty in England."[21]

The respectable weeklies, the *Athenaeum,* the *Spectator,* the *Nation,* would hardly have seemed worth trying, had a girl in Beauchamp

---

ice and sat beside her. . . . . the purple sky above was throbbing, beating, palpitating with the light of stars and planets, and a low, large, mellow moon was sinking towards the horizon, reddening as it sank. What a night for the registration or the consummation of vows! One of those true voluptuous tropic nights when the soft, hot air itself seems to breathe of the passions. It was a night which, as the Frenchman said, all women wish to be loved. . . . . She sat sipping her ice cheerfully and diligently, for ice, like virtue, does not last long in the tropics. . . . ."

Lodge been conscious of them. They all belonged to the world that Kass Beauchamp wished to escape; and Ford Madox Hueffer had not yet launched the *English Review:* he did that in December 1908, "with the definite design of giving imaginative literature a chance in England."²²

With all her egotism, and all her falsities, there is something courageous and admirable about this lonely and persistent quest of Kathleen's. She needed, above all, to find and meet the fellow-worker. But how? And where? Among the English middle classes?

[4]

At some time during the winter it seems that Garnet's parents, or at any rate his father, developed a strong objection to his match with Kathleen. According to Ida Baker, the question of money was involved —for the family were now hard up. Mr. Trowell, having left his Wellington connections for the sake of his sons' careers, was trying to start again from nothing, and the boys were *not* embarked on the great careers that might have brought him pupils. He and his wife knew Beauchamp—they were sufficiently indebted to him already. To let their son marry Kass would have implied that they hoped for more from him. Besides, Kathleen's recent "sophistication" must have shown a little, and they must surely have viewed with some concern the sudden transference from one twin to the other. What they did accept was her own idea for easing their distress. For a while, she formally booked out of Beauchamp Lodge and paid her board to Mrs. Trowell. Since Garnet was away, she probably had his room.

In Margaret Wishart's memory the winter passed much as the autumn had, with Kassie and herself both "secretly engaged," and happily so. It was probably in November, after Garnet had been home for a week's leave, that Kass went to stay with his parents; certainly Kathleen was in London throughout the month.* But at some point later in the winter "something happened" at Carlton Hill: there was a stand-up row between Garnet and his father, who, whatever his wife may have felt, was not a man to let the young work out their destinies

---

*A mistaken note by Middleton Murry in the *Journal* says that Kathleen stayed with Garnet in Hull on 4 and 5 November 1908, but she did not do so. See Reference Note No. 8 to the following chapter, and its text, pages 91–92. Kathleen was not pregnant by Garnet in the autumn of 1908, as asserted by Jeffrey Meyers (1978).

themselves. He had a streak of hardness in him, a tendency to stamp on impulse, finally. Upon the instant, all the warmth and affection of the household were withdrawn from a Kass who clearly had urgent need of them. The longing for a home, which pervades her letters to Garnet and was depicted later in the "novel," was suddenly crushed. She returned to Beauchamp Lodge, and to a cheaper room. This was probably in January.

In February, events began to move rather quickly. Through friends of Margaret's, Kathleen met a tenor singer who was "pink and white, spick and span, with a little moustache, hair neatly parted, etc." The son of a Baptist minister, and eleven years older than she, he was a teacher, more of speech than of singing, at some colleges of divinity in London, and he lived not far from Beauchamp Lodge. He fell for her at once, according to Margaret, and "bombarded her with long passionate love-letters the very next day and every day, and she, gurgling with laughter, read these aloud to Amy Birch and myself interspersed with caustic comments, despite our protests that it was hardly fair to him."[23]

This was actually the first hint, unrecognised by Margaret at the time, of where the game of playing roles was leading Kathleen. (It was also the germ of two later "penitent" stories, both of which harshly satirise a young woman who reads out love-letters to be ridiculed.) Not until 1948 did Margaret realise that Kathleen had been "Kass" to her family and the Trowells, "Kassie" to herself, "Katie" to Ida Baker, and "Katherine" to all her later friends. "And with each name," she told the author then, "I'll warrant she assumed another personality. . . . . To me, she was always loving, *sincere,* and utterly *un*selfish, and so full of consideration in a thousand little ways, and utterly fascinating (without conscious effort). I don't know how to express it, but she was 'stripped' of all these meannesses, and worse, which were obvious to others. We never had an inharmonious moment until *suddenly snap!*— she cut off like a clam in the last two days before disappearing, to my utter hurt and bewilderment."[24]

"Suddenly snap!" refers to Kathleen's lightning decision to marry the writer of the letters, and her guilty desertion of the friends who had known of her love for Garnet. It was the end of February; she abruptly changed, became aloof and apart, and within a few days disappeared from Beauchamp Lodge, to a buzz of gossip. One of the girls recalled for Margaret long afterwards that Kathleen had appeared one morning

at nine o'clock breakfast, "as cool as a cucumber in a pink-and-white striped blouse and a brown tweed skirt, and announced that she had just been married." Then she left, without a word of explanation to the loving friend who had been so close. From the buzz it emerged that she had "done it just to know what it felt like," for a book she was writing. Two weeks later the same girl saw a marriage notice in one of the papers (it was in the *Morning Post* for 17 March). Kathleen had become Mrs. George Bowden.

Let it be Miss Rosabel Watson who shows us to the door of Beauchamp Lodge. In 1949, when Miss Watson, aged eighty-three, was in Cardiff as Musical Director to Donald Wolfit's Shakespeare Company, she described the departure of Monsieur Traveller in these words:[25]

> She was very young, and when I heard from the other girls that she was engaged and contemplating an immediate marriage I had a conversation with her, and begged that she would write to her parents and ask their advice and consent before taking such a serious step as marriage. She promised to do so, and seemed quite in earnest. A few days after, she left for a short visit to friends, as she said, and then came news that she was already married. When tongues began going, it was learned that she had told half a dozen different tales to different girls. I suppose her gifts as a Novelist led her to imagine herself as the heroine of several Romances. Soon after, she sent for her belongings and passed out of my knowledge or interest, leaving me the impression that she was untruthful and insincere. I can't even remember her appearance.

CHAPTER V

"Mss. Bowden,"
1909

I say, Vee. Half a minute, Vee. It's like this: You want freedom. Look here.
You know—if you want freedom. Just an idea of mine. You know how those
Russian students do? In Russia. Just a formal marriage. Mere formality.
Liberates the girl from parental control. See? You marry me. Simply. No
further responsibility whatever. Without hindrance—present occupation.
Why not? Get a licence. Just an idea of mine. . . . . No offence, I hope. All
right! I'm off. Due to play hockey. Jackson's. Horrid snorters! So long, Vee!
Just suggested it. See? Nothing really. Passing thought.
> —H. G. Wells's Ann Veronica being proposed
> to by Teddy, 1909

On the second of March, 1909, Kathleen went with Ida Baker to the
Paddington Register Office to be married. In signing the register she
falsified her age, giving it as twenty-two; she described herself, in the
appropriate space, as a spinster of "no occupation," and the chairman
of the Bank of New Zealand, in his, as a "General Merchant." Even
the bridegroom joined in the levity, describing himself with modest
understatement as a "vocalist."[1] Henry J. Wood, who once asked him
at short notice to take over a part in Debussy's *Le Martyre de Saint-
Sébastien,* knew he was more than that. All the same, it will not be
incorrect to think of him in this context as a man with a lifelong
interest in Voice, or what used to be known as Elocution, a subject
which Kathleen had taken as an extra when at Queen's.

What had really led to this event? What did it mean, and what did
it lead to, in its turn? It is still a tale that must be told with mirrors,

a tale of costume-changes too: more *Rashomon*. At least four separate narratives require to be unravelled and rejoined, and the first is that of the only friend to attend the ceremony—the only friend of either party.

Ida says in her book that Kathleen was dressed entirely in black, with a "dreadful shiny black straw hat on her head," which she declared she was wearing because it "gave her courage." They met Mr. Bowden in a "horrible little place," a dirty bare room with uncleaned windows and a low counter. A "small fussy man" came in, and since another witness was required, and Mr. Bowden hadn't thought of that, the fussy man fetched a clerk: "And there my beloved friend was married."[2]

Of the bridegroom's neglect to bring a witness, his wife a few years ago remarked, "That's exactly like George!"

The married pair then went their way—eventually, to an hotel—and Ida went home to Montagu Mansions. But as Kathleen possessed nothing but her heavy luggage from New Zealand, Ida had lent her for the occasion a brand-new dressing-case, a recent twenty-first-birthday present. While packing it for her she had popped a little note into one of its pockets, saying "Bear up," or something to that effect. And it seems that when this was read the whole affair collapsed. Kathleen changed her mind—it was evening—and left Mr. Bowden at once. Ida learned next day that Katie had left the hostel, for an address that she was not to give to anyone.

All Margaret Wishart knew at the time was that Kassie had suddenly become strange and aloof and had vanished from Beauchamp Lodge, to a buzz of rumours she couldn't believe. After some days she went round to the little Swiss hairdresser in George Street; she learned that Kathleen had gone there in tears on the third of March (the day of the announcement at breakfast), in great distress and begging to be taken in. The hairdresser and her husband had a spare room upstairs. There Kathleen had locked herself in, and "wept for a week." A Mr. Bowden had called to see her, but she had refused to leave with him, simply saying, "I can't come, I can't come." Then she had vanished, leaving no address.

She was not at Warlingham, with Aunt Belle. Someone had fetched her belongings from Beauchamp Lodge, since she couldn't live there any more. She had apparently seen Miss Watson, who had asked about Mr. Bowden, but Kathleen had simply said that she "couldn't be bothered with him." Eventually one girl produced the marriage notice in the *Morning Post* ("I think he put that in to force her hand"). Margaret was worried, and totally mystified.[3] No message at all had been left for her.

And now Mr. Bowden's account. For many years an unnamed figure of ridicule in the life of Katherine Mansfield, a distant sufferer in silence of all that followed some remarks made in print by Kathleen's second husband,* he consented to describe the episode for the author's previous biography, but at that time, out of a sense of decency, he held a good deal in reserve, to his family's cost. What follows is based on his original account, with crucial details newly added.[4]

"In an episode not without its dignity and good fellowship," Mr. Bowden wrote in 1949, "I do not care to be thought the villain in the piece. Its keynote was struck at the first moment of our meeting, and our capital error was in carrying it to the illogical conclusion of marriage."

They first met at the home in St. John's Wood of the well-known popular-science writer, Dr. Caleb Saleeby, whose wife was a daughter of Alice Meynell. It was a dinner party followed by music (the young Australian pianist William Murdoch was there), and after dinner Mr. Bowden noticed an "inconspicuous and somewhat demure figure" sitting in a low chair near the piano. His impression changed when he introduced himself. He found her witty, and they had "some rapid exchanges."

When they met again at another musical party he was astonished to find her appearance quite different. This time she was dressed "more or less Maori fashion," with some sort of scarf or kerchief over her shoulders, and there was "something almost eerie about it, as though of a psychic transformation rather than a mere impersonation." So much Mr. Bowden said in 1949, declining to elaborate. He has done so since: "She looked like Oscar Wilde."

Then Mr. Bowden gave a party. In St. Mary's Terrace, not far from Beauchamp Lodge, he shared a studio-flat with his engineer-friend

---

*In Miss Mantz's book in 1933 Murry spoke slightingly of Mr. Bowden from very little knowledge of his own. He described him as a musician who had advanced into the profession "by the flowery path of a choral scholarship at Cambridge" (it was King's), and as "the gentleman-artist with the bedside manner, of the type afterwards depicted with subtle understanding in *Mr. Reginald Peacock's Day.*"

Lamont Shand, a musical amateur who went in for Elizabethan love-songs. They had an elderly manservant, and when, on the day of the party, Charles opened the door and announced "Miss Kathleen Beauchamp" there was a hush in the room—"for here was another transformation." The hair was high this time, the dress almost girlish, and the deportment "something like regal simplicity." After that she became a regular visitor (Mr. Bowden's memory somewhat lengthened the time-span of these events), giving signs that she enjoyed "being a bachelor along with us."

Then Mr. Bowden went into hospital to have his tonsils out. Kathleen wrote to him there, offering to call for him in a taxi when he came home, and at that point they "became engaged." The news was announced at the next Saleeby dinner party, and conveyed to Henry Beauchamp, of the London Academy of Music, who was supposed to be Kathleen's guardian in England. Cousin Henry wrote off to New Zealand, but Kathleen was all for haste. Await *consent?* Besides, Mr. Bowden was in sympathy with the women's movement. In his view the marriage should "further her emancipation, rather than in any way cripple it." After all, it was 1909.

So they made the arrangements to be married. Kathleen would enter the bachelor life of the flat. She sat down and wrote her fiancé a long letter about it: they would meet at the "casual roadside campfire" rather than share the life of the Open Road together (she had been reading George Borrow), but he put that aside as "one of her frequent figures of speech." Her constant talk of Petulengro and gypsy life seemed merely symbolic; in any case the whole thing did have a bachelor character. Shand wasn't leaving the flat.

Though Kathleen talked freely of her writing, Mr. Bowden had little idea of her passionate ambition. He saw her mostly in her "lighter moods"; but there were also "dark humours" when she appeared unapproachable, and seemed to him to dramatise herself, to "enjoy the ill-health of the soul." He never saw her weep.

Then they met at the Register Office. As to her funereal appearance: "I don't want to be dogmatic about this, and it was a long time ago, but I'm sure I would have commented on it at the time—probably jocularly—had it been noticeable. My memory is that K.M. had *one* costume for street wear about town. It was black and well became her."

After the ceremony they didn't go back to the flat, but to a hotel suite. They dined together and "did a show" on their usual good terms, but after that it was *"suddenly snap"* for Mr. Bowden, as for Margaret a few days earlier. He knew nothing, at the time, of the note in the dressing-case. He only knew that in the hotel suite, *"she lay on the bed like a log."* Though ignorant of the note he said, "I think you'd better go and ring up Ida Baker." Which she did—or so he understood—and went away.* But not in tears. According to Margaret Wishart, not more than three weeks had elapsed between their first meeting and the wedding day. Kathleen told Ida that she couldn't bear the pink satin bedspread at the hotel, or the lampshade with pink tassels. She hated pink tassels.

So much for how the episode appeared at the time to Ida, to Margaret, and to Mr. Bowden himself. But now that various papers have come to light there are three documents, all in different countries and all emanating from Kathleen herself, which seem to throw some further light on her behaviour.

The first document is a rather odd typescript[5] giving extracts from something called "A Little Episode" which was evidently written by Kathleen in 1909, and which begins like this:

"Oh," she said, impulsively, childishly, "I have been so miserable." She felt she must tell him everything—confide in him—ask his advice —win his sympathy— She felt she must hear again that curious, caressing tone of his voice.

Then it seems to go into summary of words originally in direct speech:

Wishing to appear pleasing to them, she not only thru herself into the situation, whole-heart, absorbing all of it—but she seemed (to herself, as well as to them) to lean completely for a moment, though she always really stood alone.

Presumably the opening paragraph refers to Mr. Bowden and his voice, but who does "them" refer to in the second? To the Trowells? Resuming direct speech, the typescript goes on:

*It is clear now that she left that evening, and not next day. Presumably she spent the night at Beauchamp Lodge, to make her startling announcement at the breakfast table. But having said that she was married she couldn't stay there any longer; nor, without awkward explanations, could she go to Dr. Baker's. Hence the hairdresser's.

> When I came from Paris here, O, I really felt I should have died. I cried every night—they tortured me with everything. It went on for weeks —until at last I made up my mind that whatever happened—I should leave them.

That seems to refer to the house in Carlton Hill and to Garnet's parents, and all the trouble in the winter. The change from "she" to "I" is characteristic: as in New Zealand, Kathleen often did make that switch in her notebooks, as if uncertain which she was. Was the piece actually written in the Trowells' house? It continues by describing herself as penniless, "friendless, hopeless, loveless alone," and then adds cryptically that "——— came and engaged himself to me— Yes, that's the way to put it." She had thought that once married she would be freer: "but—I'm caged."

The typescript, after some further cryptic lines, ends like this:

> Never before had she needed so much love in her life. Primitive woman she felt. All scruples were thrown to the 4 winds——
> "Where have you been?"
> "I walked, and the wind has blown me about."
> She saw a bottle of eucalyptus, and the two clean handkerchiefs at his pillow. She was filled with disgust.

In some way those fragments all seem related to the marriage and the events that preceded it, though exactly how, it would be rash to say. Perhaps a tenuous clue is to be found in one of the letters Kathleen had written Garnet in the autumn. After seeing Maud Allen's dancing she had told him of a "strange ambition" of hers: she wanted to write things that she could recite on a darkened stage in a very fine way: "to study *tone* effects in the voice—never rely on gesture—though gesture is another art and should be linked irrevocably to it." She would like to be "the Maud Allen of this Art," she said.[6] It may be that when she met George Bowden—who spent a lifetime teaching Voice, and whose own voice she found "caressing"—she thought she had found the man who could help her. If that explains why she trifled with him in the first place, however, it hardly explains what she did on the second of March.

The third document is again in Kathleen's hand. When found, it was folded within another piece of paper, a torn-off sheet serving as an improvised envelope, on both sides of which Kathleen had written: "Never to be read, on your honour as my friend, while I am still alive. K. Mansfield." The letter asks the unnamed friend: "Did you ever read the life of Oscar Wilde—not only read it but think of Wilde—picture his exact decadence? And wherein lay his extraordinary weakness and failure?" It then goes on (a name being here suppressed):[7]

> In New Zealand Wilde acted so strongly and terribly upon me that I was constantly subject to exactly the same fits of madness as those which caused his ruin and his mental decay. When I am miserable now —these recur. Sometimes I forget all about it—then with awful recurrence it bursts upon me again and I am quite powerless to prevent it— This is my secret from the world and from you— Another shares it with me—and that other is ——— ———— for she, too is afflicted with the same terror— We used to talk of it knowing that it wd eventually kill us, render us insane or paralytic—all to no purpose—
>
> It's funny that you and I have never shared this—and I know you will understand why. Nobody can help—it has been going on now since I was 18 and it was the reason for Rudolf's death.
>
> I read it in his face today.
>
> I think my mind is morally unhinged and that is the reason—I know it is a degradation so unspeakable that——one perceives the dignity in pistols.
>
> > Your
> > Katie Mansfield '09

It is hard to be sure whom that was meant for. Was it meant for Ida ("on your honour as my friend")? But the name omitted is that of a Wellington girl whom Ida didn't know. Was it meant for Garnet, and written in his parents' house, where a photograph of Rudolf stood ("I saw it in his face today")? Whoever it was meant for knew of Rudolf's suicide and the reasons, and would read it (after the event) as a suicide note. Although it wasn't one *in fact,* it was obviously a part of some tense drama, of which the marriage on 2 March was another part: perhaps a desperate attempt by Kathleen, racked by guilt since her affairs in Wellington, to prove herself a normal woman—a man's woman. But these are all guesses, and only a man's guesses, and what follows by no means clears them up.

After leaving the hairdresser's Kathleen is said to have "vanished" for a time—that is, from the knowledge of everyone at Beauchamp

Lodge. But Ida once told the author (a fact forgotten when she wrote her book) that Kathleen went from there to Liverpool, joined the opera company as a member of the chorus and as Garnet's wife, and was "happy" for a time. Certainly, some years later Kathleen used to give her second husband amusing accounts of her life on the road with Garnet: how they used to cook themselves kippers over a fishtail gas flame in their boarding-house, and how she sang in the chorus, and learned all the absurd gestures that an opera chorus had to make in the provinces in those days.[8]

Well—the Moody-Manners Opera Company was in Liverpool at the end of March, and before that it was in Glasgow, playing all the week, and travelling on Sunday. And (to turn from guesswork to Kathleen's notebooks) there is a "Sunday morning" entry in the *Journal* a few months later, which is addressed to Garnet of poignant memory:

> Yet another Sunday. What has this day not brought us both? for me it is full of sweetness and anguish. Glasgow—Liverpool—Carlton Hill—*but Home.* It is raining again today—just a steady persistent rain that seems to drift one from one memory to the other. . . . . [9]

In other words, Kathleen went to Garnet in Glasgow about a week after the marriage, and then went on to Liverpool. Whether she told him what she had done in Paddington is impossible to say, and how long they were together is unknown. His parents may have seen the marriage notice on the seventeenth and sent it to him. His feelings then, if she hadn't told him and that's what happened, hardly bear thinking about. But the idyll of the kippers and the chorus line could not have lasted very long, and must have ended in wretchedness for both. One barely decipherable notebook entry, written in a train, speaks of some passengers getting on at Hereford,[10] which seems an odd way back to London.

Once there, the only place to stay at was Dr. Baker's. By early April Kathleen must have known that her mother, alarmed by cabled news of the marriage from Mr. Kay at the bank, was coming to England to see her; she sailed from Wellington by the *Paparoa* on the eighth. That was Good Friday—the date of a painful *Journal* entry composed of Crucifixion sentiments that make one want to look the other way.

Kathleen also learned, soon afterwards, that she was pregnant. A nurse-friend of Ida's had been summoned to examine a puzzling skin-rash, and her sharp eyes had noticed something. Also a period had been missed. Two poems in the *Journal* appear to belong to the moment of Kathleen's realising her predicament. It was real, this time.

With Mrs. Beauchamp on her way by another of those seven-week journeys, it was necessary to find a flat, and Ida describes one which they found in Maida Vale, "a part of London then of questionable reputation." Longing for Garnet's support, Kathleen wrote to him repeatedly, begging him to get in touch with her. Understandably, he didn't reply. She was Mrs. Bowden now. She went to the chemist, and bought some Veronal to help her sleep. In preparation for Mrs. Beauchamp's arrival she also went with Ida to the West End shops and bought a large, expensive hat—a garden-party sort of hat—to please her mother. It cost the enormous sum of twenty-seven shillings, as Ida never forgot, and was black, like the cheap hat of the wedding day.

Suddenly there was a trip to Brussels, a jaunt on the spur of the moment, referred to in a *Journal* entry written on the way to Harwich (trains *always* made her write): "The carriage is full but Garnie I feel that I am going *home*. To escape England—it is my great desire. I loathe England." Her thoughts were of Garnet all the time, since his child was with her. She travelled as "Mrs. K. Bendall," borrowing Edie's name to match the initials on her luggage.

It isn't clear how long she stayed in Brussels, nor even why she went there, but she was painfully conscious of her Pa-man rootlessness: "Almost before this is written I shall read it from another room, and such is life. Packed again, I leave for London. Shall I ever be a happy woman again? Je ne pense pas, je ne veux pas." Then back to Antwerp, wondering, in the train, "when I shall sit and read aloud to my little son."[11] And so to the flat in Maida Vale.

On 27 May, as Ida relates, Mrs. Beauchamp's boat-train drew in to a platform crowded with relations—Kathleen being somewhere on the fringe in her big black hat, "quite unacknowledged by any of the family." Annie was surrounded and embraced. Then, as if suddenly remembering her, she turned to look for her daughter. She didn't like the hat.

"Why, child! What are you wearing? You look like an old woman in that. As if you were going to a funeral."[12] Declining Maida Vale, she whisked her off to the private hotel in Manchester Street where they always stayed—the one in which Kathleen had written that letter about wanting to try *"all* sorts of lives." Mrs. Beauchamp told her daughter to give the hat to the chambermaid.

Kathleen once told John Middleton Murry that her mother could be as cold as steel. This, as he says, must have been one of those times, since Mrs. Beauchamp sailed for home again only two weeks later. Though it's hard to believe, she left without knowing of the baby.[13] What, then, did she know of?

She knew of her daughter's relationships with women. While in London she met Mr. Bowden (by appointment at the Bank of New Zealand), and she had a talk with Dr. Baker. It isn't necessary any longer to speculate about the nature of these conversations, for ten years later, when he wanted to marry in California, Mr. Bowden wrote to his prospective father-in-law as follows:

> The lady I married, though of excellent and well-to-do people, and herself of some literary reputation, was sexually unbalanced and at times was irresponsible, although at others perfectly normal. While her people in New Zealand were aware of this, her guardian in London was not, and as we married after a short acquaintance, it was only then conditions became known to me.

The letter went on to say that Mr. Bowden had "taken no steps towards divorce on the grounds of this perversion."[14]

It was decided that Kathleen ought to be sent Abroad, to be away from Ida, and previous accounts have said that Mrs. Beauchamp took her to "a convent in the mountains" and left her there. Ida, who says that she had no idea what was in the grown-ups' minds ("I did not know then what a 'lesbian friend' meant") was sent with her sister for a holiday in the Canary Islands. A sea trip in those days was supposed to cure such cases. They tried the same with Charles Baudelaire (who took to loving black women instead, and biting their wiry hair with his teeth).

Mrs. Beauchamp returned to New Zealand, as recorded in the *Reminiscences,* "by the *Tongariro* (10,192 tons)," sailing on 10 June and being met by her husband at Hobart, across the Tasman. A passenger who became ill on the journey touched her heart, and he actually died in her arms, as Beauchamp learned with dismay when the ship tied up. This led, eventually, to one of Katherine Mansfield's best-known stories.*

Immediately on reaching Wellington Mrs. Beauchamp saw her lawyer, to have Kathleen cut out of her will. She had yet to hear of the baby, but some version of the scandal had reached Wellington, for Vera's respectable Canadian fiancé, to Vera's deep embarrassment, found himself being taken aside and warned against marrying the sister of such a girl.

The will had been made in January 1903, just before the family left for Queen's College. Mrs. Beauchamp's personal estate at that time seems to have been worth about £250 a year, its main source being her husband. If he was not living on her death the estate was at that time to go in equal shares to all her children over twenty-one, but by a codicil of 13 August 1909 she revoked the trust in favour of Kathleen, the will to operate "as if Kathleen Mansfield Bowden had been excluded." An earlier declaration of trust relating to some Dyer property was also amended to exclude Kathleen.[15]

Mrs. Beauchamp then turned with relief to her preparations for Vera's marriage, in St. Paul's Pro-Cathedral on 23 September, to James Mackintosh Bell, a Canadian geologist with an extremely prosperous future awaiting him in his homeland.

[2]

The "convent" to which Annie Beauchamp supposedly took Kathleen turns out to have been the most expensive hotel in the little Bavarian spa of Bad Wörishofen. Not a mineral spa, and not a fashionable resort for the rich or the wicked, Wörishofen had become well known in the 1880's for the *Wasserkur* of Pfarrer Sebastian Kneipp, a Roman Catholic priest who propounded there a sys-

---

*In *The Stranger*, Mr. Hammond goes up to Auckland to meet his wife ("Yes, my wife's been in Europe for the last ten months. On a visit to our eldest girl, who was married last year"), and learns in a hotel room, at the height of his desire to be alone with her, that a man on the ship had died in her arms ("Yes, it did happen," his eldest daughter told the author. "Cut him to the quick, poor dear").

"Just as the voyage was drawing to a close a saloon passenger, Mr. D. M. Niven, breathed his last, and his body was committed to the deep."—the Hobart *Mercury*, 23 July 1909.

tem of nature therapy, consisting mainly of hosings with icy water, which still has many followers today. He had begun it with a watering can (still cherished in the town), when Wörishofen was not much more than a country village set in the pine forests, with oxen ambling down the street. The full regime eventually included arm baths, thigh baths, leg baths, paddling sessions, barefoot walks in the morning dew, a vegetarian diet for the good of the stomach, and so on. As the *Wasserkur* grew in fame, so did the town, and by 1909 it had acquired a *Kasino* set in pleasure grounds, a tennis club beside a lake, an International Club, and accommodations ranging from the modest family *pension* to the Hotel Kreuzer, all with their steep Bavarian roofs to shed the snows of winter. Kneipp died in 1897, but his books, *Meine Wasserkur* and *So sollt ihr leben*, are well known to the faithful, whose doctors still send them there in hundreds every year.

How does one discover what Kathleen did in Wörishofen? In Germany, the movements of travellers have to be registered with the police, and the records are kept. Those of Bad Wörishofen show that on 4 June 1909—eight days after the *Paparoa* had berthed at Gravesend—Mrs. Beauchamp and Kathleen were staying at the Hotel Kreuzer. No longer a spinster of "no occupation," Kathleen had decided that she really was an authoress: she registered as "Käthe Beauchamp-Bowden, Schriftstellerin, London."[16] Within a day or two Mrs. Beauchamp returned to London, to catch the *Tongariro*'s sailing on the tenth. To deal with her erring daughter had not engaged a great deal of her time, save fourteen weeks at sea.

One wonders what she said to Kathleen as she left her. What did she tell her to *do?* And why in Wörishofen? No doubt we mustn't push the facts too far, but there was one fact well known to every Edwardian mother: the most widely recommended cure for girls with Kathleen's difficult complaint was a course of cold baths and wholesome exercise. She was sent there to be hosed.

The Hotel Kreuzer was expensive. By 12 June Kathleen was registered, this time as Käthe Bowden, at the Villa Pension Müller, Türkheimer Strasse 2—the original, since it is mentioned there by name, of the *German Pension* which was soon to provide both setting and title for her first book of stories. It was run by the Stigelauer family (whose misspelled name also turns up in the book), and with them she stayed until the end of July.

At the height of the season as many as two thousand *Kurgäste* at a time would fill the little town. You were always welcomed into the fold when you arrived, and asked innumerable questions about your complaint and everything else. Newcomers were sized up by the regulars, such as Frau Fischer. That persistent lady came from Falkenau, Eger, where she owned a transport company, and not the "candle company" she is given in the story that bears her name.[17] The clientele consisted mainly of overfed bourgeois, but the social spectrum ran all the way from princes and archdukes to girls from New Zealand whose fathers were directors of candle companies.

To judge from her *Pension Sketches*, Kathleen seems to have let it be known that she would be staying until September; and she seems to have had (at any rate after her mother had left) a pattern for a baby's bonnet which someone asked to borrow. If you were serious about your cure you bought a pair of the open sandals that Pfarrer Kneipp had designed, from a shoemaker called Binzer; and you lived on fruit and vegetables and nuts, exchanging detailed news of your gastric progress with the rest. Not far away—a few miles' healthy walk— there was an inn at a little place called Schlingen (the German for gobbling, or wolfing it down) where recidivists went for secret eating.

Before breakfast one morning in June Kathleen went out walking barefoot in the dewy woods. *Barfussgehen* was a part of the *Kur*, but in this case it led to a chill, the subject of a piece in the *Journal* addressed to Garnet and making reference to their child:

> Some day when I am asked: "Mother, where was I born?" and I answer: "in Bavaria, dear," I shall feel again, this coldness,—physical, mental—heart coldness, hand coldness, soul coldness. Beloved, I am not so sad tonight. . . . .[18]

This was when she recalled their Sundays, "full of sweetness and anguish," in Liverpool and Glasgow. She was apparently still writing to Garnet (whose ring she still had). But the relationship with him now drops from sight, and precisely how it ended is not known, save that bitterness and guilt remained.

One day in the summer Kathleen lifted her trunk to the top of a cupboard in the *pension*. It was too heavy; she hurt herself, and had a miscarriage soon after.* This news was conveyed to Ida in a mystifying letter which she didn't understand, but she showed it to her friend Miss Good, who had nursing experience and had already guessed what was happening. (The letters of this period are only known from Ida's memory. Kathleen made her burn them all, with many others, ten years later.)

About the same time she wrote down something in an odd sort of German which is printed in the *Journal*, beginning: *"Ich muss streiten um vergessen zu können; ich muss bekämpfen, um mich selbst wieder achten zu können. . . . ."* The German is stilted and incorrect, and doesn't seem to be a quotation. It may be her attempt to state, in terms of which Pfarrer Kneipp would have approved, what she felt she must now try to do: "I must fight, to be able to forget; I must fight so that I can respect myself again. I must make myself useful so as to be able to believe in life again," and so on.[19]

At some time after writing that, she found that the loss of her baby was more than she could bear alone: she craved a child to care for. She wrote to Ida, who spoke to her friend Miss Good, and Miss Good knew what to do.

In a mews off Welbeck Street there was a little shopkeeper's son called Charlie Walter, who was recovering from pleurisy and needed a change and some sunshine. He was suffering from malnutrition, and he responded to affection. Arrangements were easier in those days, Ida writes (these are her actual words): "We got him a ticket, tied a label on him, and sent him across to her." By this time, perhaps in preparation for his coming, Kathleen had left the *pension* and was lodging with Fräulein Rosa Nitsch, the owner of a lending library above the Post Office, along the street from the *Kasino* and its gardens. He stayed for

---

*Middleton Murry, in the chapter which he contributed to Miss Mantz's biography in 1933, treated the occurrence as a stillbirth. He said there that the baby was "born prematurely, and born dead; and her own life was in jeopardy." But Murry believed (so he wrote to the author) that the child was conceived in Hull in the first week of November 1908. That would make Kathleen four months pregnant when she married, and seven months pregnant when her mother was in London, unaware of it; in any case she wasn't in Hull then. A stillbirth, under German law, had to be registered, and there is no record at Wörishofen of such a birth to Kathleen. It would seem the child was conceived in the spring and lost in the summer.

some weeks with her there, and Kathleen made him call her "Sally."

He was the only child she ever had. Some ten years afterwards he was transmuted into Lennie, the child who dies in her story, *The Life of Ma Parker*.

There exist some fragments of a strange, symbol-haunted story, also written some years later, which seem to comment on this episode. "Elena Bendall," a self-indulgent, exhibitionist young singer with a delicate child called Peter, takes him to somewhere in Germany where there are pansies in the *Kasino* grounds, and that winter, as Peter lies ill in a *pension*, she is overcome by a desire to sing to him. His terrified eyes implore her not to, and she knows it; but she must, for in her bosom there are "urgent wings":

> But she would only sing gently, only softly Peter. Listen. Snow is falling. Out of the sky falls the snow, like green and white roses and nobody sees but the moon. . . . . As she sang she stood up and singing still she went to the window and put her arms along the frame. Peter shut his eyes. He floated into his mother's singing bosom and rose and fell to her breath. His wonderful mother had wings. Yes, yes she could fly. She flew with him out of the window to show him the snow and to give him some of the roses. He felt the snow on his chest and creeping up to his throat it formed a little necklace round his neck. It crept up—but not to my mouth Mother. Mother, not over my eyes.

In the middle of her singing the doctor comes, and examines the child and finds him dead.[20]

The piece was written in 1914 by a Katherine Mansfield looking back upon an "Elena" who was always acting, always inclined to "play exquisitely" for strangers, even in railway carriages. It depicts, with a sort of unacknowledged guilt, a selfish young woman whose child exists for her satisfaction only, and who symbolically causes his death by her need to "sing." Apart from the *German Pension* sketches, it is the only piece of her writing to be set in Wörishofen, though not the only one that deals with the being disburdened of a child.

In mid-September Kathleen moved once more. With the boy, she took lodgings with Johann Brechenmacher, at Kaufbeurer Strasse 9. All this shows that *In a German Pension* is full of actual names, though doubtless they were moved around a little. In the mischievous *Frau Brechenmacher Attends a Wedding*, family circumstances are freely used.

The surviving daughter Maria, then only four, doesn't remember the young lady from New Zealand (and had never heard of her book until 1977), but she remembers well the precious brooch her mother used to wear on special occasions, and the big black crocheted shawl, which are mentioned in the story.[21]

Wörishofen, in its own small way, had a literary life. It seems to have attracted Continental *littérateurs* of one sort or another (even Rainer Maria Rilke dallied with the *Wasserkur*, though he never actually went there), and doubtless Fräulein Nitsch's library was a likely place to meet them. One shiftless and impecunious member of the tribe was a Pole named Floryan Sobieniowski, whom Middleton Murry is able to describe, since he got to know him too. Educated in Cracow, Sobieniowski lived by his wits on the fringes of literature, as a critic and translator. (He later put most of Shaw's plays into Polish, and much of Galsworthy, until Galsworthy tired of his attentions.) According to Murry, he was "charming, distinguished, and completely untrustworthy," he had a splendid singing voice, and he "might have served as the original of one of Dostoevsky's Poles."[22]

Through him, and through his friends the Yelskis, who were safer to deal with, Kathleen found herself being admitted to a brotherhood who were going to found important magazines and publish one another's work. Sobieniowski had a passion for the Polish dramatist Stanislaw Wyspiański, which he tried to pass on to her. He was also a fervent admirer of Walt Whitman, which explains how the poem quoted in Chapter III came to be addressed to Wyspiański, in Whitman's style; and Floryan translated it into Polish, and had it published in a Warsaw paper in 1910. So the lost Colonial had found the Fellow Worker—among a group of expatriate Slavs.

To accompany her Wyspiański poem Sobieniowski wrote a piece of flagrant puffery inflating Kathleen into "the young English poetess," who had displayed her sensitive soul in one poem entitled "The Wonder of Maoriland," and her knowledge of European literature in another called "The Old Mother" (both untraced, if they were ever published). She had given him to understand she was of "Irish" origin, and had talked of her adventures among the Maori savages. Of her *German Pension* sketches the article says nothing at all, which rather suggests they had not been written yet.[23]

It was perhaps through Sobieniowski and the Yelskis that Kathleen also made the acquaintance at this time of *Jugend*, the Munich illustrated magazine *"für Kunst und Leben,"* which gave the name of *Jugend-stil* to the German form of *art nouveau.* There is reason to believe that it had an influence, more by its illustrations than by its text, upon her writing, or on the way in which she "saw" her fellow *Kurgäste.*

At some time in the autumn of 1909, Margaret Wishart received a long, penitent letter, apologising for the way she had been treated at Beauchamp Lodge and telling her that Kassie was trying to straighten out "the tangled web she had made of her life." Her health came into it, too. A fragment written in Wörishofen tells of her conviction that she would die because of her heart—a conviction that persisted throughout the thirteen years that remained to her. It says she doesn't think she will live a long time: "Heaven knows I *look* well enough— like a Wienerin people say here and they could not say more—but I am not at all well—my heart is all wrong—and I have the most horrible attacks of *too* much heart—or far too little." That is why she wants to get so much into a short time: "when I am alone the böse or gute Geist jogs my elbow and says—'You'll have so much of this sort of thing later on—Make use of a short daylight.' "[24]

Then why did she stay in Wörishofen until the very end of 1909? Though facts are few, there is not much doubt about the reason: she had a love-affair, of sorts, with Sobieniowski. When they met, how it began, what Kathleen saw in him, and why she trusted him at all— all lost. No doubt she liked his voice. Ida Baker, recalling old burnt letters with the help of a shaky memory, gives a brief account of the little she knew. Katie, she says, "made plans with the Pole" to go with him to his homeland, and then to go perhaps to Russia. They were to meet in Munich (Kathleen did at some time go there), where he was to look for "two bed-sitting rooms in which they could study and read and work"; but Kathleen arrived there to find only one room and "a very different plan for living." So she ran away.

In fact it wasn't Munich, it was Paris; and Kathleen knew in advance of the single room, and she didn't go to it. On Sunday 12 December 1909 Sobieniowski was in Warsaw, longing for Kathleen and writing to her in German about their rendezvous in Paris after Christmas.

Warszawa. Niedzila (Sonntag.) 12/XII 1909

Kathleen, love! Will you not speak to me today—three times already the postman has been and brought nothing—but I hope it'll come in the evening.*Dear my†—you can't know how I long for you, how my thoughts are full of you all the time—where are you? What are you doing now? I see all of Wörishofen, and no matter where I look, no matter what I think of, you are instantly with me. . . . .

He talked to her of Whitman, and of Whitman's incompetent Polish translator, and said he would be going to friends that evening, but only because the publisher Przesmycki would be there, and he wanted to talk to him about their plan to translate Cyprjan Norwid's poems into English together.

On Monday, at last, her letter came, so he added a page or two. What happiness to read her words! When she wrote, "We are in Paris—I am going to make the tea—we will smoke, talk and read," then he really was with her in Paris! And when she said that she loved him—oh, why couldn't he express it! But she knew how he felt. A miracle had happened: "We are one."

He'd had a word at the party with Przesmycki. *He* was off to Paris too—they might run into him. But the party wasn't interesting. They had a singer there who sang "as Katziany plays her fiddle," and for his part he fell so silent that someone actually said, "I think we can take it that Sobieniowski is about to write a tragedy." Well—she must write to him next in Cracow:

> Goodnight, Kathleen, goodnight, and how will it be with that dream? The white forest, that I see in your room now, tells me, calls me to come to it. O Kathleen, perhaps in 18 days. Goodnight. Give me your hands. Your Floryan.[25]

This letter is not the only evidence of what Katherine had in mind. She had written of her intention to a friend in London named Vera French, an actress evidently, or a singer, presumably one of the women from Beauchamp Lodge, who had "nearly collapsed" when she read the news, and who now responded with nine affectionate pages of warnings and pleadings: pleadings which vividly suggest the view that was taken of "men" by single women of this time, a view that is also to be found in the stories Kathleen soon produced.

**Sic.* Four Sunday deliveries in Warsaw in 1909.

†In English in the original.

Vera wrote from an address in Kensington on 12 December, the Sunday of Floryan's letter. She had not been able to answer Kathleen's letter at once because she was overwrought when she read it, having just come back from the theatre, and might have said foolish things: "Childie, why should it have been difficult to make things clear to me, have I no intuition or knowledge of Life, did you think I wouldn't understand or sympathise? Dear little woman, it was bound to come, and I saw it racing along the road of Life, carrying you away with the unexpectedness and sweetness of it all."

She was going to be absolutely frank, and Kathleen mustn't mind. She would cast no imputation whatsoever on her lover, but when a man, *whatever* his nationality, met a woman with Kathleen's physical attractions and brilliant brains, half heartbroken, and learned the reason why, then it was in the nature of a man to want to possess her: "But the woman being a gentlewoman he cannot say 'I want you for my mistress.' No! he says, by coming away to Paris with me you force your brute husband's hand to such an extent that he *must* divorce you"— or suffer the derision of his friends. (All this is Vera's comment, and the only source of the facts implied.)

Had her Pole promised her that in the meantime she would be sacred to him—"as though you were guarded by your own brother"? Had he promised that they would only appear to be living together, in order to get the divorce? If so, no man could do it! And women were of course "so constituted that if they love they *can't* bear to refuse the beloved his heart's desire."

She was saying all this, not because she thought that what Kathleen was doing was wrong—she didn't think *that*—but because there might be a bitter cup for her to swallow afterwards; and the afterwards might be so desperate that "you will not care what you do or what becomes of you."

She therefore wanted Kathleen to give her a sacred holy promise: if, when her divorce from Bowden was pronounced, her Pole did not take immediate steps to marry her, "you will promise me by all you hold most dear and holy, *that you will come to me,* we will together patch up your cloth of Life somehow."

But she must keep this up her sleeve: "If your man fails, *I am your trump card,* but don't tell him about me." Naturally, if Kathleen could keep straight with him ("you know what I mean") then Vera's admiration would increase a thousandfold: but if she was overcome by her love and the thought of his pleasure, that would make *no difference* at all. She didn't wish to *judge*. Kathleen could come to her as confidently as to her work. ("I can think of no simile than your work, I know it means so much to you.") The promise she asked for was "the only thing to do, darling, unless you go to some other woman, and somehow most women have a knack of judging other women's moves through distorted glasses."[26]

Well, there was, of course, another woman, who could be equally relied on not to judge; and Katie turned to her for backing, and for money too. Just before Christmas, "Aida" wrote about the arrangements for her arrival.[27] She had telegraphed £6 to cover the fare; and would Katie arrive in the morning, "the time the child did," since otherwise it might be impossible to meet her? (There was an undertone of secrecy; Dr. Baker would disapprove.)

Arriving in London a few days after Christmas, 1909, Kathleen stayed for a time in the newly opened Strand Palace Hotel. In that mill pool of the lost she apparently met a fortune-teller, a bizarre acquaintance with whom she briefly considered going into partnership.* But then she received another letter—carefully addressed, years ahead of its time, to "Mss. Bowden":

Paris. Dimanche. 9/1 1910

Kathleen Dearest—I arrived at 1 P.M. today. I'm living as I told you, 4 Rue de Beaux Arts (Paris VI) and that's my address. I'm terribly tired, but happy that I'm in Paris at last. If only you were here already—this week will be an eternity. But I will be very patient—but this uneasiness always. How are you? Are you well again, or still sick? Oh, write me immediately, dear, write to me, Kathleen, so I can be at ease. . . . .

Floryan had found a hotel where one room, fairly large, in which they could live together, would cost 60–70 francs a month without board. Probably for that money they could get two rooms somewhere else. But wouldn't she write? Had she got his two letters? He had addressed them both to Mss. Bowden at the hotel—not *Poste Restante* —because he thought she must be ill. In the morning he would see a friend who had promised to help them find a flat.[28]

---

*It seems a pity she didn't run into Arnold Bennett instead, who was also staying there at the time, delighted with the place, and about to start work on *Clayhanger*.

She didn't go. It seems the fortune-teller may have saved her. For, when speaking of that lady's business scheme, Ida says that Kathleen "played with the idea for a little"; but then, abruptly, she told Ida that "partly for the sake of the family" she was going to live with Mr. Bowden and "try to make it work." The little monkey.

This move certainly was sudden. Mr. Bowden, who was at a house party at Easton Hall in Lincolnshire, was embarrassed to receive from the butler, "in quick succession on his salver, two or three open telegrams, delivered over the telephone, phrased with a crescendo of urgency, and signed 'Your Wife.'" They insisted on his coming to London at once. With "apprehensive reluctance"—since he concluded that Kathleen was acting under some sort of pressure from her relatives and not on her own judgement—he went, and Kathleen joined him in the flat where he now lived, at 62 Gloucester Place. This seems to have been in late January or early February 1910.

Why the crescendo of urgency? Had Sobieniowski come to London to look for her? Was he booked in at the Strand Palace? Was Katherine using her legal husband as a nominal protector? Was she simply short of money?

She lived in the flat for several weeks, but it was "only on the surface a success"—Mr. Bowden's words. She went to his studio in Bond Street once or twice, and "sang a little." She collaborated with him in a concert he gave at one of the institutions where he lectured, "delighting a large audience by her recital of some of her sketches."

During this interlude she had one of what Mr. Bowden calls her "dark humours"—a black mood, lasting a day or two—and out of it she wrote her sonnet, "Loneliness." She showed it to him, and he found it so pessimistic that he ventured to "alter a word or two, and substitute the title *Solitude,*" remarking helpfully that that lifted it out of darkness into light. "This was outrageous, of course, for it quite changed its tone," says his account of the matter. He had also inserted a comma, and what she said about that comma came as near to indignation as anything he ever saw in her.

Though he knew she had been abroad, Mr. Bowden knew nothing of what had happened to Kathleen since he last saw her—he didn't know about the baby—and she never referred to Wörishofen or her Polish friends. He could not have known—at least not in any detail— of the disarray her mind and body were in at this moment. But when she showed him some Bavarian sketches she had written, he suggested she take them in person to A. R. Orage, the editor of the *New Age*.[29] This meeting in February was a great success, and a turning point in Kathleen's life.

She had been ill in Wörishofen, as we know, and a month after meeting Orage she was ill again, this time seriously. Ten years later she became convinced that the health of the body is inseparable from the health of the spirit or moral nature, and it was, of course, while actually seeking spiritual repair that she died, in the Institute for the Harmonious Development of Man, at Fontainebleau. It may be that the road to Fontainebleau really began in Wörishofen, where she first encountered such a teaching. In the light of all that had happened to her lately, and was to happen in a few weeks' time, it would be surprising if there were not some connection in her anxious mind between her physical health and her moral worth. And now she had met, in Orage, a critic who proposed to show her the connection between her *writing* and her moral worth.

CHAPTER VI

The New Age

I want to tell you how sensible I am of your wonderful unfailing kindness to me in the "old days." And to thank you for all you let me learn from you. . . . . you taught me to write, you taught me to think; you showed me what there was to be done and what not to do.

—Katherine Mansfield to A. R. Orage,
9 February 1921

The *New Age* came out every Thursday from a printing works in Cursitor Street, off Chancery Lane, and in 1910 it was undoubtedly, with all its faults, the *liveliest* weekly that London possessed. Orage, stealing from Wilde, liked to say that it hadn't a friend in the world, but its enemies loved it. Nobody could accuse such an impudent rag of making anyone feel comfortable. So long as the writing was good it welcomed radical departures from established Edwardian ways of thought in regard to politics, literature, art, or anything else, and in consequence it had the reputation among young writers of being *the* paper to get into. Not for the sake of money: its payments to contributors were either nominal, or nothing. It was run at a loss of more than £1,000 a year, and Orage himself drew only £4 a week in salary from the funds which his backers provided, while his best-known contributors—Shaw, Wells, Bennett, Chesterton, and Belloc—had all been writing for no payment since his editorship began in 1907.

In Shaw's eyes at that time he was "a mystery man named Orage,"[1] and it seems the family name had once been Horrage. In the village of Fenstanton, twelve miles from Cambridge, he had once been Mrs.

'orrage's little boy Dickie—fatherless, but very bright. Helped by the local squire to go to a teacher's college, he became an elementary schoolteacher in Leeds, and from there he came up by the bootstrap methods of the day—reading Nietzsche on his own, and the *Mahabharata*, joining the Theosophical Society, and founding something called the Leeds Art Club, which he once got Shaw to speak to. He then became Orage, pronounced like the French for "storm." When Shaw wanted to annoy him, he called him Orrage.

In 1910 Orage was thirty-seven—tall, slim, and dark-haired, with lively, challenging eyes. He wore a soft felt hat (then a slight expression of revolt; hats in Edwardian England had immense importance as a badge), and his feline face and catlike movements, according to his Leeds friend Holbrook Jackson, made him look as though he were about to pounce on something.[2]

Many who had known him employed the word "charm" when describing Orage, and they praised the openness of his mind, which had a touch of mischief in it too. (It was because he would let them say things no one else would permit that they wrote for no pay.) He had a turn for epigram, and a taste for the balanced phrase: "Genius embraces the infinite; talent excludes it." Of the paper he used to say (to distinguish it from the *Spectator*) that it wasn't representative, but presentative. In some of his Edwardian wordplay there was a slightly phoney touch, and for all his solid intellect he had a sort of hole in him. It caused a mystical hungering for Ultimate Answers, so that from time to time he would drop everything to become the follower of some seer or shaman who possessed a key that was going to unlock the universe. Between those times he was a brilliant editor, though some of his gifts were self-destructive.

The paper called itself a "Weekly Review of Politics, Literature and Art." Orage and Holbrook Jackson had begun it in 1907 under the wing of the Fabian Society,* but after Jackson left in 1908 the emphasis

---

*Or rather, with backing from Shaw and from Dr. Lewis Wallace (a Theosophist merchant-banker from Leeds, said to have made his money sheep-farming in New Zealand), they acquired it from a previous owner in whose hands it had come to grief. Many facts in this section are owed to Wallace Martin's *"The New Age" Under Orage* (1967), to Philip Mairet's *Memoir* (1966), Paul Selver's *Orage and the "New Age" Circle* (1959), and some to John Carswell's *Lives and Letters* (1978). Others are drawn from the paper itself, in ways impossible to show without undue disfigurement. Only cautious use has been made of Beatrice Hastings's vindictive Blue Moon Press pamphlet of 1936. For Orage's

became more cultural than political—if "cultural" (a *New Age* word) is a fit term to use for all the arts, philosophy, economic theory and women's rights, plus the later heresy of Freudian psychology. Orage was especially proud of the paper's front page, which Eric Gill designed for him.

In the *New Age* you would hear what the European dramatists were up to, or you might encounter some little-known Russian writer— "Anton Tchehkoff," for example, some of whose stories it had printed, and whose plays were now being described for its readers by Ashley Dukes. In poetry, it helped the emergence of the Imagists in 1908–1909. It was discussing the Post-Impressionists several months before Roger Fry's first exhibition of their work in 1910, and when that occurred, and the rest of London scoffed, the *New Age* showed its open mind.

The "Notes of the Week" at the front were written mainly by Orage, and much admired, but the first thing many readers turned to was the "Books and Persons" column which Arnold Bennett contributed over the pseudonym "Jacob Tonson." A causerie packed with information and ideas, it reflected the best side of Bennett's then questing mind, before success had vulgarised him. Through it, he successfully urged William Heinemann to make the novels of Dostoevsky available in English. In March 1909 he had also written of "Tchehkoff" with great enthusiasm; but it is most unlikely that Kathleen saw that article. She was on her way to Liverpool just then.

Those whom we now call "Bloomsbury" probably never read the rag. Miss Virginia Stephen would have connected it with what she later called "the underworld," though she must have heard how it responded to the Post-Impressionist exhibition. Leonard Woolf never wrote for it; Lytton Strachey, according to his biographer, *nearly* sent an article to it once, but was prevented by the fact that he "did not have its address readily to hand." The *Daily Mail* never mentioned it (Orage was convinced there was a boycott), and in *Punch* not even jokes were made. It was left to Orage himself, who had one old suit, and wore boots that were patched on the uppers, to call it the *"No Wage."*

In the 1930's Ezra Pound declared that he hadn't the faintest idea who *read* that paper. He was exaggerating, of course; his friend T. S.

---

salary, etc., see the prospectus of the New Age Press, Ltd. (*N.A.*, 26 November 1908, p. 100). For Eric Gill's contribution, *N.A.*, 24 July 1913, p. 362. In November 1908 the *New Age* claimed a circulation of 21,205.

Eliot certainly read him there, and later admitted to a high regard for Orage. But it never was respectable, and although it caused alarm to the establishment (the boys at Haileybury* in 1912 were forbidden to read it[3]), that is hardly the same as influence.

Partly to blame was Orage's mischievous conception of his job as editor. He saw himself as the waspish chairman of a continuing and very open discussion, with no commitment even to the Fabian view. If he disagreed with an article from a good contributor he would simply print it, and then attack it himself next week or get another contributor to do so. This presented no difficulty, since the crew of homeless malcontents who were known as the "staff" were always ready to invent new pseudonyms. They, in fact, formed a sort of Verdian stage army of enormous size, marching grandly when in view but racing behind the backdrop to appear in other tunics before a gap appeared. Their exertions certainly made Thursday a lively day for the reader, but the opera could never meet its costs. Orage eventually quarrelled with nearly all his best performers, and in the end he even lost his Fabian backers. It was out of their dissatisfaction that the *New Statesman* was founded in 1913, to become the paper's chief rival.

Not one scrap of this information, of course, is needed to explain why Mrs. Kathleen Bowden should have been excited by Orage's acceptance of her first contribution in 1910. In the *New Age*'s policies she hadn't the slightest interest, and it is possible that she had not even heard its name until Mr. Bowden made his inspired suggestion. But she called on Orage herself. It was a personal encounter, and on both sides there was probably some "charm."

To visit him one went to the back of the printing works by an alley off Chancery Lane. Two flights of stone stairs smelling pleasantly of printer's ink led to the door of a tiny office in which there was room for two desks and a coat-hook, a set of pigeonholes, some files of the paper, and one chair for a visitor. The arrival we are thinking of was a vivid memory to Orage. "I am quite sure that K.M. brought the first ms. herself," he wrote long afterwards, "and within a few days of my publishing it. I well remember reading it while she sat in my office and offering to publish it *in the next issue.*"[4] But it seems that he never realised what that story actually was.

*For American readers: a distinguished public school, Haileybury was a training ground for the establishment and for future army officers.

The New Age

*   *   *

As Elisabeth Schneider first pointed out in 1935, the year after Orage's death, *The Child-Who-Was-Tired* is a free rendering into English, with many interesting changes, of Chekhov's story "Spat Khochetsia," of which a translation had in fact already been published in England.[5] Under the title "Sleepyhead," Chekhov's tale of an ill-used nursemaid who smothers the shoemaker's baby so that she can get some sleep was included in R. E. C. Long's collection, *The Black Monk, and Other Stories,* published by Duckworth in 1903. The edition was a small one, however, soon out of print, and little known,* so that the source of Kathleen's story escaped the notice of the *New Age*'s readers in 1910. These certainly included Arnold Bennett, who had mentioned Long's book there in 1909, and whose own column for 24 February began just under *The Child-Who-Was-Tired.* An overheading, "Bavarian Babies," had probably helped to put everyone off the scent.

Since it has long been standard practice for anthologists and writers of reference books to state without inquiry that Katherine Mansfield was "influenced by Chekhov," and even for respected critics to assume that the statement is true, the symbolic value of this early use of him is high—and heightened, too, when it is seen to have occurred in the context of deceit and pain that surrounded her return from Wörishofen. Yet "plagiarism" is not the term for what occurred—it is too simplistic. And even "influence" would be misleading.

In both tales a child enslaved by a brutal couple is cruelly overworked all day, but also forced to rock the baby to keep it quiet. Visitors in the evening prolong her drudgery, until suddenly she sees the baby as her enemy, she smothers it, and sleeps. Many resemblances in detail can be found, but more significant are the differences in method. Chekhov begins his story the night before, and brings in details of Varka's earlier life; Katherine Mansfield confines the action to a single day, and focuses sharply on the present. To heighten the sense of drudgery and mess, she adds more children, but she makes the time scale more compact.

She draws on Karori memories. A coal cellar containing a "mass of twisted dahlia roots" is bestowed on her impoverished peasants; the very ducks of Chesney Wold, with their lavish bucket of kitchen scraps, find a way into this "Bavarian" tale, along with the black bread

---

*Frank Swinnerton could not buy a copy in 1911. See his *Background with Chorus,* p. 143.

and sauerkraut, while the image of "a duck with its head off, wriggling," later made horribly vivid in *Prelude,* occurs at the moment of murderous climax. An excellent critical study of the two versions, conducted within the context of the whole Mansfield-Chekhov question, has been made by Ronald Sutherland,[6] who shows that *The Child-Who-Was-Tired* actually demonstrates its young author's ability to re-create the story in an independent way. (In her version, for example, the closing dream has a symbolic function which is her own idea. Chekhov's Varka has no dream.)

How did Kathleen come to know the story, and what was she up to when she offered it to Orage? She had probably read it in German in Wörishofen (there was a collected Chekhov in print in German at the time), and it is possible that the author's name meant little to her—though one of her added children has the name of Anton. Miss Schneider argues plausibly for something which she calls "unconscious memory," observing that a certain type of imaginative mind has the power of "taking in that which appeals to it with so much activity of its own, so little of mere passive appreciation, that the memory afterward will seem to bear the stamp of its own imagination." At all events, Kathleen would hardly have taken it to Orage as a first offering had she known of the English version. My own opinion is that *The Child-Who-Was-Tired,* while proving that its author had now made contact with her supposed "master," at the same time proved her imaginative freedom from his influence. It is far from being the proper starting point for an enquiry into how she evolved her method; that point is further back, and much more personal.

There followed in successive issues, and just in front of Bennett's column, *Germans at Meat* (their coarseness satirised), *The Baron* (their snobberies as well), and that brilliant little piece of mockery-self-mockery called *The Luft Bad:* all of them sketches rather than stories, a fastidious feminine recoil from crudity their theme, and satire their mode, but written with a gaiety and sparkle—insight, too—that was matched by nothing in the paper at the time. It is possible that some of them were written very quickly, in excitement after the meeting with Orage, with the prompting of her favourite *Jugend* artists and some good advice from her editor and mentor.

It is known that she had the habit of taking *Jugend* illustrations as a starting point for things she meant to write, and certainly one can find in it any number of paintings and cartoons which might illustrate her early work. All her Bavarian characters are there—the Baron, the Modern Soul, the Advanced Lady, young women dreaming by windows or smoking alone at café tables. There too, one can catch the ethos of pre-war Europe through its artifacts. The Thermos flask, the Auto-strop, the Vest-Pocket Kodak, the Zeppelin—these were the modern portents floating in the peaceful sky of 1910. (A *New Age* cartoon, however, turned the Kaiser's moustaches into cannons.)

The *pension* sketches, with their unannounced beginnings ("Bread soup was placed upon the table"), often suggest pictorial origins more than "influence of Chekhov." Their endings, on the other hand, are conspicuously pointed ("Tableau grandissimo!" one story ends) in a manner that was equally not his, and which was later dropped.

No sentimentality marred these pieces, but the same cannot be said of *"Mary,* a pathetic little story by Katharine Mansfield," which the popular magazine the *Idler* thus announced for March in its February issue. An expanded anecdote from Karori, in which Pat's beheading of a bird for the table is seen again, it is extremely sentimental, suggesting a case of touch-and-go. If the *Idler* had encouraged her to write more stories like that, and Orage had declined a borrowed plot, her career might have taken a different course entirely.

The *New Age* team of literary desperadoes rallied round its new recruit, writing "Letters to the Editor" about *The Child-Who-Was-Tired* immediately after its appearance. "With reference to the article in your issue of last week entitled 'Bavarian Babies,' " wrote "Vidi" (who was probably Beatrice Hastings), "I beg to state that, in my lowly opinion, I consider Miss Katharine Mansfield has given quite a wrong impression of the home life of these people." What was a *birch* rod, she asked, doing in a Bavarian home?

Retorting a fortnight later, one "He Visto" (who was probably J. M. Kennedy posing as a woman*) said that it was with great pleasure that she had read the little article. She and her sister had once stayed in a *Schloss* near Munich with a German school friend and, "while studying the people in their homes," had noted "the prevalence of the birch-rod,

---

*J. M. Kennedy (c. 1880–1918), a foreign editor on the *Daily Telegraph*, translator of Nietzsche, and author of *Tory Democracy* (1912), was one of Orage's main contributors. He used the pseudonym S. Verdad (= *es verdad*, Spanish for "it's true") when writing on foreign affairs. "He Visto" ("I have seen") is a Spanish retort to "Vidi."

how it seemed to occupy a place of honour at every hearth, and fell alike on boy or girl." All this nonsense immensely helped the correspondence page; and Kathleen, of course, soon made the acquaintance of these gifted writers.

It was Orage's custom to meet his contributors on Tuesday afternoons at the ABC tearooms in Chancery Lane—in the basement, where smoking was permitted even by women. The regulars in 1910 would have included Kennedy—"a fat squeaky man who lived with his mother," according to another of them,[7] and A. E. Randall, a lean, hungry-looking consumptive with staring eyes, who had not many years to live.

One woman only was a member of the team: Beatrice Hastings, or Beatrice Tina; or "T.K.L.," "Ninon de Longclothes," "Cynicus," "G. Whiz," or "Robert à Field." Born Emily Alice Haigh, she used some seventeen pseudonyms altogether, and as "S. Robert West" she once conducted a long debate against both Kennedy and Randall. Believed to be from South Africa (she did grow up there), she had married a pugilist, and borne him a daughter, but now was living with Orage in a flat in Kensington, with the gloves off. It seems that both were undivorced. She was nine years older than Kathleen, and like her she could always, in the last resort, fall back on her father's money. Mr. Haigh was a prosperous merchant in Port Elizabeth.

Beatrice Hastings contributed to the paper a vast amount of vituperative commentary, some flabby fiction, and some pretty-pretty verse. At one time a suffragist, she finished just as hotly in the opposite camp, and her writings on the agony of childbirth ("the ugliest fact of human life") were some of the paper's most vigorous polemics. Since her stories and verse were bound to attract no critical attention whatever, except for some dutiful pronouncements by Orage, her eventual fate was a fanatical jealousy of those who had eclipsed her, Katherine Mansfield especially being the object of her rage toward the end. She committed suicide in 1943.

Kathleen once told another friend after visiting "Biggy B.": 'It's terrible when two female women get together—I don't know which of the two of us was the more disgusting."[8] "Biggy B.," for her part, alleged much later (see Appendix B) that Katherine Mansfield never knew the worth of her satirical pieces, and thought her sentimental efforts "balls better."

*   *   *

During the first weeks of her association with the *New Age* Kathleen was living with her legal husband in the flat to which he had moved in Gloucester Place, near Baker Street. Ida, for obvious reasons, had been lying rather low, and when leaving messages there she always used the name of Lesley Moore, which Mr. Bowden didn't know about. In fact from now on it almost became her name, in the secret language of the friendship. Here too, then, she will mostly appear henceforward as "L.M."

Late in March L.M. received a sudden SOS. Asked to go to a strange address, she found Kathleen in a "second-rate nursing home" and was told there that she had just had an operation, for "peritonitis." Katie insisted on being removed at once—she said the surgeon was molesting her in bed. So L.M. called a "growler" (a horse-drawn four-wheeler), and because of the wound she told the driver to take it slowly, which only prolonged the agony. She took Katie to the flat which she and her sister at that time shared in Marylebone (their father having gone to Rhodesia), and Miss Good came to dress the wound each day. Then she found some rooms over a grocer's shop in Rottingdean, and later a cottage beside a meadow full of daisies, and so took Kathleen to the seaside to recuperate. Kathleen hadn't paddled in the waves since Island Bay. Her sad little sea poems are the product, in which the sea has become a reproving mother to "The Sea Child," and New Zealand has begun to be idealised as a "faraway home."

The spring had come; the countryside was beautiful; but Kathleen, though over her operation, was far from well; and now she was laid low by a new infection, or so she thought. At the time—it was just when Edward VII died—she understood that she had "rheumatic fever," as her mother once did, and for several years she suffered from rheumatic pains attributed to that: the pains which she always called her "rheumatiz." In fact the infection was gonorrhea, and the pains were caused by the arthritis that occurs when that disease goes untreated.*

---

*L.M., in her book, describes the pains and says that their true cause was "not correctly diagnosed nor was she fully cured until 1918 when Dr. Victor Sorapure took charge of her." She adds that Dr. Sorapure told K.M. that the pains were "the result of a disease which she had contracted before she was taken to the nursing home." This statement reflects an allegation which L.M. once made to the author in strict confidence. On the understanding that it was not otherwise known, nor going to be, no reference was made to it in the author's previous book, but it is evident now that the information was given to others as well. What L.M. hints in print, and elsewhere has asserted, must

* * *

Soon it was time to return to town—and, apparently, to send back Garnet's ring. For among the letters he kept was one from Ida, written in July at Kathleen's request to return some unnamed enclosure; it gave him her address (she was staying with Orage and Beatrice) and said: "She will never join G. Bowden again. . . . . Now she is Katherine Mansfield, 39 Abingdon Mansions, Pater Street, Kensington. That is her writing name and she is taking it almost entirely now."[9] Henceforward, then, she is "Katherine" in this narrative, as Ida is mainly "L.M."

While staying with Orage she was offered the use of a flat belonging to his friend the painter Henry Bishop, who was off to Morocco for the winter. She took it, of course—it was at 131 Cheyne Walk, Chelsea —and by the time she had moved, three more "Pension Sketches" had appeared in the paper. These were in the same vein as before, but with a new note added. Two of them, *At Lehmann's,* and *Frau Brechenmacher Attends a Wedding,* have an undertone of revulsion from childbirth and male sexuality. Since Katherine herself was unaware of the actual nature of her recent illness, their tone was probably the consequence of "female" sessions with Beatrice Hastings, who had lately been raging in print on the horrors of childbirth. Along with two sarcastic letters to the editor, they can be taken to reflect the baneful influence of "Biggy B."

One evening that summer Orage and Beatrice took Katherine to dine with Edmund B. d'Auvergne, another *New Age* contributor, who recalled her as a cool young lady with a cynical view of love.[10] In *their* presence she was like an actress trapped in comic roles—she had to sustain the part she had created in her sketches. But Bishop's agreeable flat, looking over the river through tops of plane trees, soon served as a retreat from this, and a new friend there became a quietist influence. For several months, in fact, she vanished altogether from the columns of the paper. There had been a rift of some sort.

---

be considered in the light of all her other loving denigrations of the men in K.M.'s life; and in a context which is far from making her marriage the only possible source of the infection. Its location in the upper genital tract explains why she had it for so long without knowing.

[2]

William Orton met Katherine at a tennis party in Hampstead in the late summer of 1910. An introspective young schoolmaster of her own age, he was eagerly exploring literature along paths already known to her. He had read his Pater, his Ibsen, and his Whitman, but he abhorred Swinburne—all this being from his autobiographical novel *The Last Romantic*, which has a chapter devoted to his relationship with Katherine, quoting entries she made in a notebook which they shared for the next year, on and off.*

This was not a love-affair in any usual sense, but something which a later Katherine would probably have described as "child love." It is clear that while it lasted they knew each other very well, being free to discuss without hurt their other, more fleshly affairs. Orton says that they did once talk of marriage, but it was doubtful whether "either seriously desired it." The mood can be caught from Katherine's published poem "There Was a Child Once" (a commentary on the friendship, according to L.M.), which ends:

> *There was a child once.*
> *He came—quite alone—to play in my garden;*
> *He was pale and silent.*
> *When we met we kissed each other,*
> *But when he went away, we did not even wave.*

In his book, Orton uses the name "Michael" for himself, and "Catherine" for her (which *is* how she signed herself when writing to him). He himself was then entangled in a difficult love-affair with another egotistical young writer, Edna Nixon (or "Lais" in the book), who had been "toying with decadence," and was embarrassingly fond of Swinburne. Here is the meeting:

> Catherine—Katharina she called herself (she was being very Russian just then)—had published several pieces in the *New Age*, which were shortly afterwards collected as her first book; and Orage had also taken

---

*Orton told the author in 1948 that "nothing in that book is faked, although the temptation to alter was often very strong. It was meant to be as authentic a document as I could leave."

a small essay of Michael's. But it was at the Berlings' they met in Hampstead, playing tennis. A sort of instant recognition passed between them, and going home, in the momentary silence of a tube station, Catherine suddenly said, "Do you believe in Pan?" So they got out of the noise and walked about, finding themselves at midnight somewhere near Euston. . . . .[11]

He was soon at Cheyne Walk:

She had made the place look quite beautiful—a couple of candles stuck in a skull, another between the high windows, a lamp on the floor shining through yellow chrysanthemums, and herself accurately in the centre, in a patterned pink kimono and white flowered frock, the one cluster of primary brightness in the room. . . . .

—all of which is clearly many thousand miles from Thorndon and Edwardian hats.

Throughout that summer, in fact, there had been at Shepherd's Bush an enormous exhibition from Japan: Japanese shrines and a village, miniature gardens, jugglers and wrestlers, prints and porcelain, the tea ceremony, the haiku. The kimono that Orton saw at Cheyne Walk is not the only hint of its effect on Katherine. She gave him the poems of Yone Noguchi, and she began to hanker after the spiritual repose of those beautiful houses from Japan. "Very Russian just then," she may have been, but Japan had beckoned as well. She was writing a good deal of poetry at the time, says Orton, but "all her writing was a kind of poetry," and she only felt secure when her life was subject to "art's pitiless demands."

One thing about her rather shocked him. Between Cheyne Walk and the King's Road in those days one had to pick one's way to the bus through swarms of children, and Katherine would observe them with an "amused but rather conscious detachment—I would almost say a cultivated detachment—which reflected her determination never again (N.B. again) to be taken in by her sentiments. . . . . But there was another element in her attitude. She was often bitterly lonely, and she wasn't going to expose her heart to any of those pulls that led, she thought, nowhere. This is very strong in the motivation of those years. The undertow was all in the other direction: you may take my word for that."

Reminded that the question, "Do you believe in Pan?" was later made fun of in Katherine's story, *Violet*, Orton answered: "I don't think at that time K. knew very much about Pan, and am pretty sure she hadn't read Nietzsche's *Birth of Tragedy*. But her later satirizing of the gambit is frightfully significant."

He saw her last in 1912, by when she had "decided to be businesslike about the literary career. . . . . She destroyed a lot of earlier mss. at this time, and so did I. I knew it was all wrong, and I think she knew but refused to know. It was like an abortion."

Ida, too, recalls those days at Cheyne Walk. She often slept in the little back bedroom, and says that one night after she had gone to bed Katherine called out that she was "thinking of going to Japan"; but she gave up the lovely thought at once when Ida said how lonely *she* would be. It fell to Ida to fend off one or two undesirable people (she describes an awkward encounter at the door with an unnamed man) and she says that Walter Rippmann came there and was attentive, but Katherine "would not start with him the relationship he seemed to want."[12] In this it would seem that L.M. may have been mistaken, or misled.

Among the attentive callers an exception was made of a young man named Francis Heinemann, a good-looking youth, hardly more than a boy in appearance, whom Katherine liked because he used to lie on the floor and wave his legs while the conversation went its airy way. He worked in the City somewhere, and had to go out selling something. He was attractive, though, and they talked of going away to Russia; in fact he gave her a Russian toy village, of painted wood. They were young and happy, writes L.M., they intended to marry, and "soon became lovers." But his family disapproved of his knowing a married woman who lived alone, so his visits came to an end. According to L.M., he was the father of a child that Katherine conceived while living at Cheyne Walk.

Such was Katherine's personal situation, more or less, in that historic December when, in a famous remark of Virginia Woolf's, "human character changed." Since July, she had been using the name of Katherine Mansfield "almost entirely." To Will Orton she was "Catherine," but he also knew that she was "Katharina." In a periodical invitingly called the *Open Window* she now appeared as "Katherina Mansfield," the author of an odd little fable called *A Fairy Story*, a Wildean fantasy (referred to on page 32) which makes ironic fun of the teachings she once imbibed from Walter Rippmann. She did wish to make a change, and it may well be that she wanted to shake herself free of the persona she had assumed to please Orage and Beatrice Hastings. There was nothing by her in the *New Age* between August 1910 and May 1911.

And as to "human character" at large? It is often assumed, not necessarily correctly, that when Virginia Woolf made the statement which is now almost done to death by repetition, she was referring to a specific event, namely, Roger Fry's first exhibition of the Post-Impressionists, which opened on 8 November 1910 and ran until early December, at the Grafton Gallery, just off Bond Street: an event granted far more importance now than the great forgotten visitation from Japan. In fact there were many other things which Mrs. Woolf may have been thinking of when she made her statement in 1924—for present purposes, it doesn't matter. What does matter is that for numerous young people at the time—and Katherine by her own account was one of them—the experience of stepping from London's November gloom into that luminous exhibition was like a sudden liberation, a shaking free from Victorian and Edwardian attitudes into wholly new ways of seeing.

Along with eight Manets (its title was "Manet and the Post-Impressionists") there were twenty-one Cézannes, twenty-two Van Goghs, thirty-six paintings and drawings by Gauguin, and smaller showings by Picasso, Matisse, Dérain and others. It was London's first real experience of "modern art," the whole at once being termed "degenerate," the work of madmen, an insult to the intelligence, and so on. But not in the *New Age,* where Huntly Carter did his best to see it through clear eyes, and George Calderon described amusingly the reactions of affronted Forsytes ("They are like dogs to music; it makes them howl, but they can't keep away"); while Arnold Bennett wrote, in a paragraph presumably never seen by Virginia Woolf:

> I have permitted myself to suspect that supposing some young writer were to come along and do in words what these young men have done in paint, I might conceivably be disgusted with nearly the whole of modern fiction, and I might have to begin again. This awkward experience will in all probability not happen to me, but it might happen to a writer younger than me. At any rate it is a fine thought.[13]

Katherine saw the exhibition, and eleven years later wrote to her painter-friend Dorothy Brett of the effect upon her of Van Gogh's "Sunflowers": "That picture seemed to reveal something that I hadn't realised before I saw it. It lived with me afterwards. It still does. That and another of a sea-captain in a flat cap. They taught me something about writing which was queer, a kind of freedom—or rather, a shaking free."[14]

[3]

Henry Bishop's return from Morocco early in 1911 meant that a new home had to be found. In Gray's Inn Road, at the top of a high pile of red brick called Clovelly Mansions, there was a three-roomed flat that seemed to have possibilities. From its kitchen, a timber yard, a multitude of chimney pots, and City of London spires; toward the setting sun, the roofs of Bloomsbury; from below, the rumble of traffic and the clash of trams.

L.M. and Katherine inspected it, and, since Katherine had no furniture, they of course went Japanese. They got some cheap plain bamboo matting for the floor and scattered cushions on it; in the sitting-room they put a roll-top desk, one arm-chair, and a basket chair of Mrs. Baker's. In the other front room they put more matting and a stone Buddha brought from Burma, before which Katherine placed a bowl of water with bronze lizards in it. There was a hookah on the mantelpiece, a pair of skull-like witches' heads, and somewhere, a guitar; but also a grand piano, for a certain Madame Alexander, who had heard Katherine singing at Cheyne Walk, had somehow persuaded her to take that over, together with liability for the outstanding payments. Such was No. 69 Clovelly Mansions, for which address some printed note-paper was next obtained. There also went with the flat a daily woman, Mrs. Bates, who was later the original for *Ma Parker*.

Orton saw the move to this flat as a great mistake. It symbolised Katherine's decision that her career as a writer was now definitely started, but it was "much too soon." For her, he says, the problem of achieving spiritual peace, in the midst of a life that insisted on being vivid and restless, was becoming urgent.

Besides, it would seem that another life had just begun, or Katherine thought it had. According to L.M.—who is the only source of this story —Katherine had reason to believe, soon after moving in, that she was pregnant again. Once more she wrote repeatedly to the young man begging him to come and see her, but received no answer. L.M. went to see Francis Heinemann at his office, but he never came—"So he never knew of his child." And six years passed before they accidentally met again, in Shearn's restaurant, when Katherine put it in a story.*

In April, when L.M. received an urgent summons to join her father and brother in Rhodesia, she was concerned about leaving Katie on her own. She was "expecting the child and happy at the thought," L.M. writes, and she was also "more capable of managing things now," but she had no money. L.M. therefore opened a bank account in Katherine's name, deposited £60 in it to cover the cost of having a baby, and left for Rhodesia. There is no other source whatever for this information.

When Middleton Murry read the author's previous biography in 1953 he said he did not believe that Katherine could have been pregnant at all, and he cited medical reasons which cannot easily be set aside. He said that he had lately found, by a strange chance, in the cover of one of Katherine's notebooks, a confidential medical report written for her in 1921 by Dr. A. Bouchage, of Menton, "the facts of which must have been given to Bouchage by K. herself." These facts made it clear, he told the author without revealing details, that after the operation of 1910 it was "highly improbable, if not absolutely impossible, that Katherine should ever be pregnant again."[15] He briefly said this in the *Journal* in 1954, again without disclosing the medical details, and then, apparently, destroyed Dr. Bouchage's report because of the private information it contained.†

This leaves us wondering whether Katherine *was* pregnant by Fran-

---

*A Dill Pickle, which begins: "And then, after six years, she saw him again." ("That 'Pickle' comes in my book! I wrote it in 1917. But there's a much longer story to be written about those two—the man and woman. When they *were* together."—K.M. to Violet Schiff, 31 August 1920.)

†But a copy of Dr. Bouchage's report, made by Miss Mantz in 1932 (a fact forgotten by Murry in 1953, if he ever knew it), is in Texas. It contains this paragraph: *"Previous History.* Age 32. Excellent health till 20. Married for the first time at 18. Had two years after an attack of peritonitis (very likely from gonococcal origin) white discharge for four months. Left salpinx was removed then. Since that time she has never been quite well. A short time after began to suffer from rheumatism, in various muscles of the body, hip joints and small joints in feet, and has been more or less troubled with it since." The rest is concerned with tuberculosis, and no pregnancies are mentioned. It is important to note that it was not Murry who placed this document in the public record.

cis Heinemann, as she gave L.M. to understand. And it now becomes necessary, though it is undoubtedly confusing, to mention the affair which she also had about this time with J. M. Kennedy of the *New Age* —whom L.M. unkindly depicts as nearly breaking by his weight her mother's basket chair, when telling Katherine at Clovelly Mansions that he would probably shoot himself for love of her (with Katherine's reply, "Oh, but do have a piece of this melon first").

In this regard L.M. is not the sole authority. The *New Age* contributor Edmund B. d'Auvergne was a friend of Kennedy's, and upon reading the author's previous biography he told the following story: after meeting Katherine Mansfield in 1910 he used to run into her in the British Museum Reading Room, "then a fashionable meeting place." They were not much interested in each other, but Kennedy fell for Katherine Mansfield. A few months later, "with a rather jubilant air," Kennedy told d'Auvergne that he feared he had "put a girl in the family way." Somewhat later again he appeared brokenhearted "and informed me that K.M. had thrown him over. . . . . Seemingly he was the father of the unborn child mentioned on your page 139."

"Many years after," wrote d'Auvergne, "I met a man named Norman, noted as a pacifist.* He told me that one day Kennedy burst in upon him and threatened him with a revolver, because as he alleged he had taken Katherine away from him. Norman represented himself of course as behaving with coolness and told Kennedy he had never seen K.M. in his life which was probably true."[16] The subject of Kennedy's relationship with Katherine will return in the next chapter.

L.M. left for Rhodesia in April. By that time Katherine's mother was on her way to England again—with Chaddie, Jeanne, and their brother "Chummie," who had now left school—for the Coronation of King George V. The expected baby, says L.M., was never born. When she came back in the autumn there was "no baby and no bank account." Katherine never once spoke of the matter again. Obviously it had all been horrible, and L.M. was "sure that Beatrice Hastings had been in some way responsible."[17]

It is not likely now that the true facts will ever be known. So far as the reputed baby and its fate are concerned the whole thing rests on

*C. H. Norman, who wrote on foreign affairs for the *New Age* under the pseudonym, Stanhope of Chester. Kennedy had muddled Norman with someone else, who will appear in due course.

the word of L.M., who left the country and with whom it was never afterwards discussed. There was probably no pregnancy at all: removal of one salpinx for the reason given virtually rules out the possibility of conception. D'Auvergne's assumption that Katherine was the girl of whom Kennedy spoke is nothing more than that. Was Katherine simply mistaken in thinking she was pregnant by Francis Heinemann? Did she unknowingly mislead L.M.? Or was she—against all medical probability—in fact with child? She was "happy at the thought" when L.M. left. Was her action—if there was one—connected with her family's decision to attend the Coronation? When was *that* made known to her? All mysteries.

Of facts not in doubt we have the following: In May 1911, just as her mother reached London (her father was detained in Wellington on bank business), Katherine returned to the *New Age* with a story about a birth; it appeared on 18 May. And two days later she was at the seaside with Beatrice Hastings. Whatever conjectures they may justify, these at least are facts.

The story represented a new departure for Katherine. The birth this time was, in a manner of speaking, her own, for the story was *A Birthday*—the first one quoted in this book—and it is the first piece of anything like mature quality to depict her own family: her father and grandmother, and the birthplace in Tinakori Road. But in order to admit it to the former series of *Bavarian Sketches,* its Harold Beauchamp was saddled with the Wörishofen name of Andreas Binzer—producing an odd effect in a story that belongs so vividly to Thorndon. She didn't even bother to remove the harbour. ("The dining-room looked over the breakwater of the harbour, and the sea swung heavily in rolling waves.") But she gave her parents in the story a son, instead of the decidedly disappointing daughter who had been born that day.

As to the other baby: whether Katherine *had* conceived, *had* turned to Beatrice Hastings, *had* found it necessary to take up the old relationship, stories and all—biography with some misgiving can only ask, then stay its hand.

There seems to have been some praise for *A Birthday,* or flattery at any rate: "She is exuberant, Idie, her work is conquering London," wrote Leslie Beauchamp to Ida Baker in Rhodesia (10 June 1911). "One Bavarian sketch made the New Age *the* most notable number, so said the editor."

Chummie was now seventeen, and he adored his sister. She had taken him to meet Orage, and his excitement in coming straight from Waitaki Boys' High School to find her "famous" in London is understandable. He had met "Aida" also, had been admitted, and now was keeping her posted in Rhodesia with Katie's news, and his. He had been taking lessons in shorthand with a view to a commercial course and joining the firm at home, but now he was thinking of becoming a surgeon: "and don't you agree that surgery has more shekels in it than trying to get the agency for van Houten's cocoa and Skipper sardines? . . . . . of course I shall be at either Oxford or Cambridge and that insight into varsity life I am greatly looking forward to."

Katie had provided him "with a latch-key which is awfully sweet of her"; but she *was* out rather often. In June, he said, she was attending "concerts and theatres nightly owing to her appointment as dramatic critic to the New Age.* But don't you see the triumph in sight?"[18]

What happened next was hardly the "triumph" Leslie had in mind, but it led to a crucial change in Katherine's writing. On 22 June King George V, whose ducal hand had shaken Harold Beauchamp's in Wellington ten years earlier, was crowned in the Abbey. Beauchamp, after all, missed the great occasion he would have enjoyed so much; but his daughter Kathleen made fun of it for the *New Age* in a satirical piece based on an ancient model that was eventually to influence her whole development.

Someone on the *New Age,* probably Orage, must have handed her a volume of Theocritus and suggested that she might make an amusing pastiche of the XVth Idyll by applying it to the Coronation. The result, a mere skit dashed off at speed, led to her learning, from Theocritus and not from Chekhov, the method which she later made her own.

The *Adoniazusae* is a brilliant little mime which takes its reader, within a hundred and fifty lines, into the engaging company of two prattling Syracusan wives in Alexandria as they head for the Adonis festival, about 250 B.C. Katherine's travesty of it begins like this:

---

*A little bit of nonsense thought up presumably by Katherine to explain her absences, though not *entirely* without a basis in events. It is evident from the files that Orage was having some difficulty just then in replacing Ashley Dukes, but no reviews of plays appeared that could have been by her.

THE FESTIVAL OF THE CORONATION
(With apologies to Theocritus)

Gwennie: Hallo, old dear!

Tilly: I'd given you up. Come into the kitchen and have some tea. We'll never be able to get a cup out.

Gwennie: Even the A.B.C.'s are closed.

Tilly: Squatty-vous.

Gwennie: Heavens, this rushing! I couldn't find a solitary 'bus or even a taxi—nothing in the streets but old scraps of newspaper and stray policemen. It's quite uncanny—a sort of Sunday without church bells.

Tilly: I know. The arrival of the postman seemed almost indecent. I got up this morning with a feeling of "early Communion" in the air. I'd never be able to live in London if it wasn't for the noise.

Gwennie: Pop on your things and let's start. I read in the "Daily Mail" the procession will be wonderful.

Tilly: In the "Daily Mail" everything is wonderful. Do you think I dare risk my best hat?

Gwennie: Doubtful. I've come out in rags. Trimmed this hat before I got into bed last night. The red velvet's off a cushion-cover, my dear, and I picked up the cornflowers for 2 3/4 d a bunch years and years ago.

Tilly: You're one of those people who never need good clothes. O, you know what I mean. And the hat's sweet—awfully ducky and appropriate . . . Where *is* my key? I lose the key of this flat simply through trying to find it.

Gwennie: Tilly, that skirt suits you down to the ground. Tell me, how much material is there in it? . . . . .[19]

That is actually a transposition into "modern suburban" of the Idyll's first forty lines or so, and it came as a pleasant surprise, a few years ago, to T. O. Beachcroft, to hear of its existence; for, in his survey of the English short story, *The Modest Art,* which was published in 1968, he had spoken of the XVth Idyll as a neglected model and example for the modern method. "In evolving over centuries out of spoken apologues and personal narration," he said at that time, "the written short story had a long way to come. Yet curiously enough, if it had developed from Theocritus it would have had a very short way to come."[20] Unknown to him at the time, Katherine Mansfield had taken exactly that shortcut in 1911. As we'll see, she later returned to the mime form with more awareness of the possibilities it held for her.

[4]

The summer of 1911 was one long heat wave. Everyone who had as much freedom as Katherine had spent it mainly out of doors. Yet in July she was ill. In Orton's words, "she had her first serious illness of the lungs," and her parents wanted her to go south to the sun. She dashed off to Bruges instead.

When L.M. returned from Rhodesia she heard peculiar descriptions of how Katherine had reacted to a very high fever, and the name then given to what she had had was "pleurisy." It has always been referred to by that name; but it is necessary now to call it tuberculosis. In 1955 Dr. Brice Clarke, in a paper published by the Royal Society of Medicine, reviewed all the facts then known and came to the conclusion that the disease was already present in 1911. It was well understood at the time, he said, that pleurisy was a precursor of phthisis.[21] Yet Katherine did not learn that she had tuberculosis until the end of 1917. Her only known recent contact was A. E. Randall; but little Charlie Walter, who went to Wörishofen, was almost certainly another, and a closer one.

This first indication of her illness coincided with an extremely subtle yet decided change in the quality of Katherine's vision. "Coincided" is the important word—too much must not be made of this, and perhaps it would have happened anyway—but the fact remains that just as phthisis gained admission to her lungs, Katherine began to see things in a subtly different way. The recuperative trip to Belgium had yielded two slight travel pieces, *The Journey to Bruges* and *A Truthful Adventure.* Insubstantial as they are, they show the beginnings of a new concern, to achieve that intricate delineation of the spaces between people which Katherine Mansfield later captured as the Impressionists had captured light.

In English fiction generally, the nuances of class had always performed this function, as they do in Jane Austen. For a Colonial writer, unattached to class, the viewpoint had to be somewhere else, and somewhere insecure: it had to float; and it is evident that Katherine assumed it most readily in a context of travel and movement, among other *deracinées.* Even Gorgo and Praxinoa (Syracusans in Alexandria) fall into this category, and perhaps that was true as well of Theocritus himself, in Alexandria. In Katherine's case, the factor of uprootedness is not in doubt. That of health is nothing but a question mark.

From Bruges, she went to stay with her Wörishofen friends the Yelskis, in Geneva—where a worried L.M., just back from Rhodesia, ran her to earth on hearing from Chummie Beauchamp of the illness.

On her return to London, she saw Orton again ("the world sprang to rights at her touch," says *The Last Romantic*); but then she committed to their common notebook a lurid piece of verbal sexuality, now in the *Journal* (6 September 1911), which seems to refer to a visit by Walter Rippmann, whom she had elsewhere called "the Man":

> When the bells were striking five the Man came to see me. He gathered me up in his arms and carried me to the Black Bed. Very brown and strong was he. . . . It grew dark. I crouched against him like a wild cat. Quite impersonally I admired my silver stockings bound beneath the knee with spiked ribbons, my yellow suède shoes fringed with white fur. How vicious I looked! We made love to each other like two wild beasts.

That recalls the sort of thing she used to write in Wellington, and it is followed by a piece declaring that "Michael [Orton] and myself alone are truthful . . . I want to begin another life: this one is worn to tearing point."

Shortly after that she wrote a fragment headed "Midnight" (it is also in the *Journal*) which read, in part:

> Après tout I live merely from day to day—taking, in everything apart from my work, the line of least resistance for the sake of my work. Do other artists feel as I do—the driving necessity—the crying need—the hounding desire that [will] never be satisfied—that knows no peace? . . . . . Then Catherine what is your ultimate desire—to what do you so passionately aspire? To write books and stories and sketches and poems.

The record of the friendship with Orton closes with a stagey and cryptic farewell (the *Journal,* 29 October) which declares, "I am become a little child again"; and in *The Last Romantic* Orton adds, very simply, "so they went their ways."

That autumn, the publishing house known as Stephen Swift and Co. announced a "six-shilling novel" by Katherine Mansfield to be known as *In a German Pension.* Charles Granville, or "Stephen Swift," was an adventurer with a flair for spotting authors of promise, and his "Books that Compel" had won him a reputation sufficient to ensure his authors the attention of reviewers, whatever else might be in store. He was a friend of Orage, and an occasional contributor to the *New Age*. He contributed poems, he could write a presentable book review, and many of the books he published had their origins in the paper. For this man Katherine had collected and very slightly edited her *Pension Sketches*, adding a pair of coarse unpublished pieces which Orage had probably declined. She received a £15 advance, and the book came out in time for Christmas, in full view of her parents and her admiring brother—for whose sakes, presumably, she had removed the name Kathleen from the stories that mention herself, and replaced it by "she" or "the Englishwoman."

The *Daily Telegraph*'s reviewer found the stories distinguished by "that peculiar touch of impishness—there is no better word—which has been foreign to English literature since the days of Sterne, although there are traces of it in a few modern Russian and French writers." The *Morning Post* said that Miss Mansfield wrote extremely well about the Germans, but she "dwelt a little too insistently on the grossness or coarseness, which is undeniable." A publisher's advertisement later quoted the *Times* ("these sketches are cleverly observant"), the *Pall Mall Gazette* ("a close and caustic description") and so on. The *New Age* reviewer (probably Beatrice Hastings, now with reason to be jealous) said with malicious accuracy that "when Miss Mansfield gets quite clear of the lachrymose sentimentality that so often goes with the satirical gift, she will be a very amusing and refreshing writer."[22]

It was a modest success—a *succès d'estime*—hardly to be compared with that of the book's cousinly precursor, *Elizabeth and Her German Garden*. But it rounded out a sort of pattern in the Beauchamp history.

Sixty years earlier, five sons of The Poet of Hornsey Lane had sailed for the Antipodes. The eldest, becoming a prosperous merchant in Sydney, begat a writing daughter who, restored to Europe and marrying a Count, made her name with a book about life in Germany and followed that profitable vein thereafter, well able to maintain herself in style when widowed. A younger one took the Pa-man character one stage further in himself, but his eldest son became a prosperous merchant in New Zealand and begat a writing daughter who, returning to Europe, made her start with a book about life in Germany—which she later called "a lie," "positively juvenile," and "not what I mean."

CHAPTER VII

Rhythm, *1912*

The chronology was rather mixed; her sister at least had once told him that there was one winter when she didn't know herself who was Nancy's husband. She had gone in mainly for editors—she esteemed the journalistic profession. They must all have been dreadful ruffians, for her own amiability was manifest. It was well known that whatever she had done she had done in self-defence. In fine, she had done things; that was the main point now! She was very pretty, good-natured and clever, and quite the best company in those parts. She was a genuine product of the far West—a flower of the Pacific slope; ignorant, audacious, crude, but full of pluck and spirit, of natural intelligence, and of a certain intermittent, haphazard good taste. She used to say that she only wanted a chance—apparently she had found it now.

—Henry James on Mrs. Headway, in
The Siege of London (1883)

Little magazines, those wayward pyrotechnics of the young, have provided countless brief illuminations of English literature since the days of the *Yellow Book*. It would be hard to say how, without them, Joyce and Eliot and Pound would have changed things as they did. Yet on which has their effect been the greater—on letters, or on lives? Rockets, Roman candles, Bengal lights, Jumping Jacks and Catherine wheels, sparklers and squibs: everyone knows what most of them have done in the literary sky; but what to the backyard lives of those who set them off? Burnt fingers, lost careers, broken friendships, printers' bills and bankruptcies—this is perhaps a neglected field of study which might be looked at in behavioural terms: The Little Magazine as Plumage; The Little Magazine as Threatening Behaviour; Territory and the Little Magazine.

In December 1911, having reason to be annoyed with the *New Age*, Katherine Mansfield sent a story to a new magazine with a most outlandish name. A hotch-potch of letters and art which had been launched by two young Oxford undergraduates, the quarterly called *Rhythm* was one of the jumping-jack variety, but, thanks to an expensive printer, did not look it. The young man who ran its literary side was awed by *The Woman at the Store*, and after looking up the book called *In a German Pension,* he took steps to meet its author.

John Middleton Murry, of Brasenose College, whom Katherine thought of as "that brilliant man from Oxford," came from a background she could not possibly have suspected when they met, since "Oxford men," in those days, were automatically assumed to be well-off. Born in a dreary South London street just off the Old Kent Road, he was in fact the child of parents who existed at the very bottom of the lower middle class, only one step up from the proletariat. His father, like something out of Gogol, toiled as a clerk in Somerset House: a narrow-minded civil servant, tyrannical at home, and utterly determined to see his son rise up—to the higher Civil Service. To make ends meet, the mother took in lodgers in their early years; and little Jack, at the age of two years and a half, was sent off to the Rolles Road Board School—*not* to learn to read, for his father had already seen to that; his biographer records that by the age of two he was encouraged to read newspapers aloud to the clients of his grandfather's pub, the Ordell Arms. From that lowly background, which by his own account was mean and even sordid, Jack Murry had been fished up by charitable scholarships, which themselves were the first of their kind.[1]

In the first month of this century he put on the yellow stockings and dark blue gown of the Bluecoat School, Christ's Hospital (then still in Newgate Street, in the City), soon learning what it was to be ashamed of his parents' home—and ashamed of being ashamed. He was *déclassé*, and was marked for life by the experience. By the premature reading, too.

A feeling for literature emerged. Like Coleridge before him he became a "Grecian" (one of the select band of sixth-formers destined for university scholarships), and in 1908 he earned his exhibition to Brasenose. At £170 a year, it was probably more than his father earned. But, like his father, Jack Murry always thought of himself as poor. His parents by then had moved, socially upwards an inch or two, to a house in Wandsworth Common.

When Murry first went up to Oxford there were perhaps a dozen Board School boys at Oxford and Cambridge together, and certain young men there soon let him know that he was what they called a "cad." If he now had prospects in his father's eyes, he needed acceptance more; which is why, in December 1910, when "human character changed," he was to be found not in Oxford but in Paris, frequenting a café society which readily accepted him, with book in hand, as what he felt himself to be—a "literary critic."

He had crossed the Channel to begin a new life, but his way of beginning it was to sit alone in a room on the rue Gay-Lussac, reading Bergson. Bergson was just then filling Sorbonne lecture halls with adherents to his new philosophy of the intuition (T. S. Eliot was present); yet Murry didn't join them—he sat and read. Timidly emerging from books to the Café d'Harcourt, he met a little bundle of intuitive responses named Marguéritte, who had brown eyes, and cherries on her hat, and was not like all the rest. A simple country girl from the Corrèze, she had no real inclination for the prostitute's life; but the story of how she loved him and made him sleep with her must be read in his autobiography, *Between Two Worlds*, where he tells it with a tenderness surpassing anything in his deadly novels. A nature's child, she *nearly* released him from his books. In later years he was haunted by poignant memories of her love.

Through her he met Francis Carco—another eye-opener, with his cynical views on women, and his elegant card announcing him as the *Secrétaire de Rédaction* of the literary review, *La Flamme*. Not yet famous for his seedy novels of Montmartre, Carco at once saw in Murry a man who might be of use to him.

Through his Oxford friend Joyce Cary, Murry also met a Scottish painter with a mordant wit who called herself George Banks. A big heavy woman with a flabby face like Oscar Wilde's, she wore men's clothes and was always weeping. In her chaotic flat he got square meals, and he picked up her enthusiasm for a wild young Spanish painter named Picasso. Looking at a picture of his Dot Banks once said, "I don't know what it is—I feel as though my brain had been sandpapered"—a remark that Murry quoted in an article, "The Art of Pablo Picasso," which he sent to the daring *New Age*.[2]

But his most important find in Paris was the Scottish painter J. D.

Fergusson. Clean-shaven and wholesome in a rakish bowler hat, blue collar, and fresh blue tie, with a studio which he kept like the deck of a racing yacht, Fergusson was one of the earliest British painters to be deeply influenced by the Post-Impressionists, and there was in everything he did, says Murry, "a clean strong reality of being." When Fergusson said, "But look now, Murry lad," all Murry's shyness went back to Oxford. He was a curious mixture of dependence and mild revolt.

Of what happened next the two men have left conflicting accounts, and this is because Murry seems to have had that unusual thing, a *genuine* bad memory. According to him, Fergusson was constantly using the word "rhythm" in connection with painting; and when Murry let slip that he and Michael Sadleir were thinking of starting a magazine at Oxford, Fergusson at once suggested that "Rhythm" must be its name; it would be the *Yellow Book* of the modern movement, and he would look after the art side for them.

According to Fergusson, Murry brought Sadleir to his studio one day while he was taking a shower (the shower was just inside the door), and asked him, while he was drying himself, if they could use his painting, "Rhythm," which they had seen in the Autumn Salon, as a cover design, and its name as the title of the magazine; and Fergusson objected that a queer word like that would seem affected, but they insisted.[3] None of this would matter, except that Murry's "memory" is going to play an intermittent role in this book from here to its end, and the sooner that is understood the better. There can hardly be many professional writers, especially critics, who have relied more recklessly than Murry did on such an undependable piece of equipment for information retrieval.

As to *Rhythm*, at any rate, it seems we can take his word for it that he had got himself into "a truly preposterous position" and become an editor and art critic by a sort of mistake. And that mistake had more to do with painters than with writers. For him, as for others in fact, it was the brush that was to liberate the pen. Returning for his third year at Oxford, he abandoned Marguéritte and her simple hopes (for she was much too like his mother) and with the help of Sadleir* and

---

*M. T. H. Sadler (1888–1957) later changed the spelling of his name to avoid confusion with his father, Professor Michael Sadler, then Chancellor of Leeds University and a well-known art patron.

his father, who contributed £50, *Rhythm* was launched in the summer of 1911.

There was nothing amateurish about its appearance. Splendidly produced by the St. Catherine Press on stout laid paper with deckle edges, it came in a cover of elephant-grey, with a design based on the formalised nude of Fergusson's painting. Its large type gave it a comfortable, Georgian look. Inside, though, was the first reproduction of a Picasso in England. Sadleir contributed an article on the Fauvist paintings of Anne Estelle Rice, an American friend of Fergusson's, and Murry an essay, very "intuitive," on Bergson's philosophy. On the back cover, a statement of Aims and Ideals proclaimed a slogan adapted from Synge: "Before art can be human again it must learn to be brutal."

The influence of Bergson on Murry's thinking was profound. Bergson's ideas had struck in his intellect the same chord that Marguéritte had struck in the rest of him, and the new philosophy (he declared in *Rhythm*) was "the open avowal of the supremacy of the intuition and the spiritual vision of the artist in form, in words, and meaning"; intuition was "the triumph of personality, the culmination and not the negation of reason." This he announced in the first number of *Rhythm;* and as critic he lived by that throughout his life.

That December, "Katherine Mansfield" was living alone at 69 Clovelly Mansions. Her family were in London, she was legally Mrs. Bowden, and flattering reviews were appearing of *In a German Pension.* She had therefore been taken up by W. L. George, a syphilitic Anglo-French Jew whose novel of a harlot's life in London, *A Bed of Roses,* had also just come out. Willy George was a collector of bright young people, and to him Miss Mansfield was a formidable cynic, an acquisition as a dinner-table wit.

Among the *New Age* set, on the other hand, there had been signs of coolness lately. Orage and Beatrice Hastings, having visited the flat, had begun to note with disapproval Katherine's promiscuity, both personal and intellectual. They once discussed it, Katherine stating that she believed absolutely in monogamy, but there was no man perfect enough for her. Of one of her affairs (probably that with Kennedy) she once asked Beatrice, "What does it matter? I don't love him."[4]

In the paper, too, there were indications of estrangement. One story had been printed which appears to be a parody of her manner,[5] a very clever one, while a little *symboliste* prose-poem of hers called "Along the Gray's Inn Road" had been made to look absurd by appearing among the Letters to the Editor with a "Sir" in front of it (the *New Age* had no time for French symbolism); and the hostile review of her book, with its reference to "sentimentality," had drawn on knowledge of rejected stories and not the book itself.

It was Willy George who arranged for the editor of *Rhythm* ("Art must learn to be brutal") to meet Miss Mansfield. She had first sent him a kind of "fairy tale" which only puzzled him (it probably came out of her "sentimental" drawer); but when she replaced it with *The Woman at the Store*, a stark murder story set in the backblocks of New Zealand, he was deeply impressed. Even Joyce Cary, who had no time for *Rhythm*, admitted that he had made a discovery; and Murry formed a strong desire to meet the exciting author.

George depicted her to him as some sort of fearsome mystery-woman. She was terribly clever, and difficult to meet, but a confrontation could be arranged: he invited them both to dinner; his pipe-smoking wife produced German red-plum soup in honour of her book, the conversation turned to a Russian writer called Artzybashev—and Murry had met his ideal. Two different accounts of that evening which he published in the thirties relied upon his unchecked "memory," and contain some giveaway discrepancies. As he recalled it then she had "subtly turned the tables on W. L. George," and had not been at all formidable. She wore a simple dove-grey evening frock, with a single red flower and a grey gauze scarf; she "cupped her hands unconsciously as if to hold some liquid in her palm," and when George spoke up for "starkness" in writing, she was for simplicity instead.

This doesn't fit with either what went before or what followed soon after. It was some years yet before Katherine spoke up for "simplicity." The accounts show Murry's memory idealising Katherine Mansfield and forgetting how tough and formidable she really had been. Before they met again he asked her, in fact, if she would like to do some criticism of Wells and Bennett and Shaw for *Rhythm*, "preferably appreciation with a sting in it."[6]

In February she told him from Geneva that she was ill and had been sent away, but soon she was back and staying with Beatrice Hastings in Sussex, having dashed off a clattering piece of satire called *A Marriage of Passion*, which appeared in the next *New Age*—a gibe at bourgeois marriage, portrayed in terms of velvet bedspreads, pink-shaded lights, and boredom when the party guests have gone.[7] It was probably never seen by her parents, who sailed for New Zealand on 8 March 1912, having not met Murry, who only met her brother at this time. Katherine, after this departure, never again saw her mother.

Then *Rhythm*'s fourth number appeared, the spring issue of 1912, with Katherine's story, and two of her poems, alleged to be translations from the Russian of "Boris Petrovsky." A prospectus said that the journal would henceforth be a monthly, with a short story in each issue, its "probable contributors" including Rupert Brooke, W. L. George, Holbrook Jackson, H. G. Wells and Arnold Bennett.

This of course was waving a red rag at Orage, who assumed that *Rhythm,* sumptuously produced as it was by a costly printer, must have money behind it. Orage could not have known that Professor Sadler's £50 was all it had, nor that Murry's home address just then was No. 13 Nicosia Road, Wandsworth Common. On the contrary, if he was up at Oxford, and had been writing from Paris on Picasso, he obviously had money. C. E. Bechhofer-Roberts, who was close to Orage at the time, asserted to the author that Murry *"must* have had money—there was always money about somewhere."

And so, on 28 March, the *New Age* began its extended onslaught on "the magazine called *Rhythm,* " with a full-page unsigned article written by Beatrice Hastings. Almost everything in the current number was either "stupid, crazed, or vulgar"; Laurence Binyon was apoplectic, the French contributor had "a little filthy mind," and the story by Miss K. Mansfield was, presumably, "also wilfully defiant of the rules of art, for it ploughs the realistic sand, with no single relief of wisdom or of wit." Her poems were even worse: "Miss Mansfield abandons her salt furrow and in two stanzas lies flapping and wappering."

Few could have guessed that the "J. M. Murry" who replied so effectively in the next issue was only twenty-two. It seems that Orage took a hand in the next engagement to prevent any further loss of ground, for this is his style, not that of Mrs. Hastings:

> Anyone who chooses rather to make an art of life than to exist as in an idiot's dream, must be set on making firm his basis. There is no finding a new basis. . . . . In advising young writers to value virtue as they value health, we spoke a very old truth, but one almost forgotten in our time. The word virtue, like some others that belong to men, has

been vulgarised by women's misappropriation: but its true meaning is still preserved from all botchers and sensation-seekers. The young artist who is virtuous will live for his art so that it may rank with the excellent. He will practice the duties of artists, cutting himself off from distracting influences, building up his power by practising in large and severe forms, fortifying his resolution by familiarity with the lives and works of great men. He will thus ensure the permanent health of his own work by cultivating his own character.[8]

That has a fine air of critical detachment, but in fact it was highly personal. Orage was addressing Katherine herself in terms she would know were meant for her.

The article ended, very obviously, in the hand that wrote the opening. *Rhythm*, it said, was the work of persons who were running after sensationalism, "dreaming of murderous hags and degenerate children. . . . . pampering pretty feelings until the very rivers seemed to lie in a sexual ecstacy" (allusions to *The Woman at the Store* and K.M.'s poem, "The Awakening River"). These were things for effeminates, they were things that ruined the mind! Germany for twenty years had been paddling in these dirty waters and now was bathing in them, and the editors of *Rhythm* were "sousing us with Continental wash."

All this was public use of personal knowledge: Katherine's fondness for *Jugend* was very well known in Cursitor Street, of course. ("She could take a picture out of *Jugend*," Bechhofer-Roberts once told the author, "and have a story round it in no time. I've seen her do it.") And there may indeed be more of *Jugend* in her early work than we have known. The theme of the brush that liberates the pen is persistent throughout this period, changing human character all the time. The really liberating things were happening in other media and other lands; the "dialect of the tribe" stood in need of renewal.

Murry and Katherine certainly noticed what the *New Age* was saying about them*—but what were words in print, compared with what was happening on the floor at Clovelly Mansions? There, while Katherine squatted on the bamboo mat and poured out tea in bowls—teacups and

---

*"Your reminder of the fierce warfare waged against *Rhythm* by the *New Age* was interesting to me. I had verily forgotten all about it. But at the time we both felt it bitterly."—J. M. Murry to the author, 18 September 1953.

chairs being equally marks of Thorndon—Jack Murry confided his problems. Oxford had become "unendurable"; he didn't belong there at all, among the "bloods." He wouldn't even write his Schools—his final exams—in June. He thought instead of going down, and staking all on *Rhythm:* it was sure to succeed. And Katherine, inclining an ear with a fine disregard for all that Brasenose had done for Jack Murry of Wandsworth Common, assured him it would be "wrong" to go on. Returning there, he broke the news to his classical tutor, H. F. Fox, a generous befriender; and Fox, forgiving what must have seemed rank ingratitude to his college, agreed to introduce him to J. A. Spender of the *Westminster Gazette,* for which Fox set the Greek and Latin competitions.

In the first week of April (just after the first *New Age* attack) Fox took Murry into Spender's office, and Spender promised him some part-time work—say £5 a week—on condition that he sat for his Schools. He went at once to tell Katherine he had "got a job," and on 6 April, or "Easter Eve," Katherine wrote one last farewell to William Orton in their notebook:

> Dear: the evening is slipping away and away like the river. Dark it is and warm.
>
> My life has been sad lately—unreal and turbulent. You know the absurd unreality of reality and the sense of chaotic grief that overpowers us when we attempt to fuse ourselves . . . So—blind I have been lately and deaf and frightened. But now I am utterly happy. I am at home again here—my rooms yield me their secrets and their uttermost shadows. I wander alone in them smiling, a silk shawl wrapped round my body, sandals on my feet. I lie on the floor smoking and *listening.* . . . .

A few days later Murry and Katherine dined near Piccadilly with Murry's Oxford friend, and *Rhythm* contributor, Frederick Goodyear, who was anxious to meet the brilliant satirist whose pieces in the *New Age* he had been admiring for the past two years. A handsome young man with curly brown hair, Goodyear was as much a trial to his Oxford tutors as Jack Murry—he insisted on reading everything except the books he was supposed to read—but he was thought to possess great gifts,[9] and Katherine immensely enjoyed him. He came from a bourgeois background (his father was a prosperous coal merchant), and he disguised a keen intelligence—to be encountered later on—

with a special line of nonsense, a gift of parody, and an odd sort of snorting laugh, which all reminded Katherine of the Pa man from Hornsey Lane. The fact is, Goodyear was envious now of his friend's good luck in meeting the bright young woman whom he would have liked for himself. He had nearly written to her once to say how much he admired her stuff, but felt too shy.

As the time came to part, in Piccadilly Circus on a warm spring night, Murry remarked that he was going to look for a room at 10s a week (he couldn't face Wandsworth Common any more). Upon which Katherine said that she had a suggestion to make: Would 7s 6d be too much to pay for her other front room? Poor Goodyear!

So it was that shortly after Easter 1912, Murry became Katherine Mansfield's lodger. The piano had been moved, with Ida's help, and a vase of catkins placed on a table by the window, with a £5 note wedged under it which Ida had supplied. Katherine, who was dressed to go out when he arrived, gave him keys and left him to work at his paragraphs for the *Westminster*—each one of which earned him one week's rent.

Ida, rather suddenly excluded as the masculine element in Katie took up its permanent role, went away forlorn, slightly resenting the £5, but with a special private poem for her comfort called "The Secret." Two months later she and her friend Miss Good went into business as The Parma Rooms ("Specialists, Scientific Hair-brushing and Face Treatment, Hours 10–7") at 59 South Molton Street, and that was her occupation for the next two years.

For a few weeks Jack and Katherine went about their separate affairs, meeting only when work was done. At midnight they partook of tea in bowls on the floor, and earnest talk, and always shook hands before going to bed: "Good night, Murry"—"Good night, Mansfield."

Michael Sadleir, finding himself despised by the Mansfield woman as an incorrigible bourgeois, was pushed to one side. J. M. Kennedy no longer called.* Katherine henceforward was designated the "Assistant Editor" of *Rhythm;* Murry was earning his £5 a week from the *Westminster,* and all looked well. But this was the moment for the

---

*Orage's secretary Alice Marks, who was fond of Kennedy, always resented on his behalf the fact that Katherine had accepted his gift of an expensive fur coat before she jilted him. The coat was eventually stolen by the *femme de ménage* of a flat which the Murrys took in Paris.

owners of the St. Catherine Press to acquaint him with the fact that *Rhythm* was heavily in debt—to them. He had innocently accepted their advice on how many copies to print (3,000 of every issue, so he says) and the returns showed that fewer than a sixth were ever sold. It was Murry who had ordered them, and Murry who must pay; and the change to monthly publication had already been announced.

Their pride now trapped them. Orage, out of loyalty to Kennedy, had demanded that Katherine make her choice: *Rhythm*, or the *New Age*. She had made it, and with Sadleir ousted there could be no more help from Leeds; but to let the magazine fold up at such a moment was unthinkable. They had Murry's £5 a week, as long as he earned it, and Katherine's £2. The magazine was losing £5 a week, but they carried on.

Murry once described all this as if he and Katherine were two poor babes-in-the-wood without enough to eat: he said they lived on penny meat pies, with bread and potato for a penny more, but to take the taste away they had to go to The Duke of York in Theobald's Road (ale was a penny a pint in 1912), where the landlady thought they were a music-hall couple down on their luck, and stood them free drinks. It is evident now that Murry had a Thing about money all his life, and went around convinced that he was hard up when he wasn't. On £7 a week in 1912 they were rather well-off, with a flat that cost £1. Only *Rhythm* made them "poor." They had no business accepting charity in a pub.

During the shaking-hands-at-bedtime stage, Murry unfolded his life-story. He told Katherine the story of Marguéritte, and told how he and Joyce Cary had gone to a brothel outside Oxford, the result for himself being gonorrhea. Apparently neither of them knew that she had it. He now thought that "falling in love was a complete mistake": when Marguéritte had made herself his mistress it had somehow "spoiled everything." One evening Katherine said, "Why don't you make me your mistress?" But Murry, who was lying on his back on the floor, waved his legs (which made him resemble Francis Heinemann) and said "I feel it would spoil—everything." As to how they eventually overcame the problem, Murry's account in *Between Two Worlds* is tragic, and Katherine's, given later to an acquaintance who preserved it in her diary, was comic.

Murry's version says that one evening in the pub they both, by coincidence, caught a glimpse in the mirror of a prostitute called Lil, who was gazing at herself in terrible self-knowledge. Against that vision, he said, they knew they must hold together—forever. And they "slept in each other's arms" that night. It is a most uncomfortable way to sleep. Katherine's less romantic version ended: "And then we got into this bed and we laughed and we laughed and we laughed without stopping, and since that time we have always slept together."[10] Tragic or comic, it probably happened at some time in May.

On the third of that month of spring, in Nottingham, Mrs. Frieda Weekley ran off with her husband's student, D. H. Lawrence. On the second of June, in Bloomsbury (which stops at Gray's Inn Road), Miss Virginia Stephen announced her "engagement" to Mr. Leonard Woolf.

In the *New Age* in May, behind a thin veil of fiction, and using his pseudonym "R. H. Congreve," Orage launched a personal attack on Katherine in a moral fable which ran for six full weeks, and which charged her at the last with "promiscuity of reflection, taste, judgement, character and intelligence." The story was actually one of a series entitled "Tales for Men Only," appearing in different years, by which Orage intended to expose the disastrous effects of female influence on the masculine mind. It exhibits his own male attitudes at their most illiberal, but it contains the first and for a long time the best attempt in print to describe what it was that made her work unique; and it is the only full-length portrayal of Katherine Mansfield in her *New Age* phase—her masks and her vanishing tricks, her flat with its bohemian décor, her literary small talk, and her tricky little ways with men, whom she keeps in separate compartments. It is full of hostile glimpses of the Katherine we know, or think we know. It is also, with its grating and dangerous tone, a reminder of what risks awaited any vulnerable young woman who chose to reveal her nature and her ambitions to the mainly masculine literary world of 1912.

Cast in Orage's favourite dialogue form, which he always used for eristic purposes, the story has three characters: Congreve himself (for Orage), a political scientist called Tremayne (for J. M. Kennedy), and Mrs. Marcia Foisacre, a "widow" whom Tremayne is trying to educate. It ends with Tremayne's being jilted for "that spark Stornell, the minor playwright."

Tremayne, as the serial opens, is explaining to Congreve that Marcia's late husband had been a brute and she is now indifferent to sex—"she is not fanatical on the subject, but as coldly logical as you could be"—and no longer has any desires; her thoughts have all turned to intellectual matters. But she needs some help, and so Tremayne is directing her reading, "and sending her long letters daily, to which she replies at length."*

Her taste? "I confess that her taste is very uncertain and rather promiscuous," says Tremayne. "For instance, she likes Whitman and at the same time loves Milton. Swinburne she thinks the greatest poet since Shelley."

And her intelligence? "Her genius," Tremayne replies, "is difficult to define; it is so very elusive, evanescent. She has an extraordinary gift of satire. Her letters are full of wonderful thumbnail sketches of people and places. She seems able to absorb an atmosphere and reproduce it in a sentence."

After hearing this out with friendly impatience, Congreve tells Tremayne that he has encountered, in Mrs. Foisacre, "the insoluble problem of promiscuity." Her early marriage is a sign of precocity and not of indifference to sex. She is "a bungler in the art of life."* But worse than that, she is a chameleon, capable of assuming very rapidly a variety of protective resemblances. With Tremayne, she assumes the mask of satire—"but I dare guess that in other circles she forswears satire with as much conviction." Undaunted, Tremayne still takes his friend to meet the lady, and we find ourselves in No. 69 Clovelly Mansions:

> Her room was quaintly furnished, for all the world as if relays of
> minor poets had each been given a cubic yard to decorate. On this wall

---

*K.M.'s letters to J. M. Kennedy were probably destroyed by Orage himself some six years later, when Kennedy died, and his mother asked Orage to go through his papers. Orage was almost violently opposed to the keeping and publication of private letters. In the *New Age* of 14 August 1913 he denounced the welcome then being given by London reviewers to an edition of Charlotte Brontë's letters to Professor Heger. Of Katherine's letters to himself, he destroyed a number that must have been written in the last year of her life, keeping only the one that is cited at the head of Chapter VI and given in full on page 325.

*Pot Orage and kettle Mansfield: Orage had first been married to "a lesbian" (so he told his friends) and now lived with a person who was legally Mrs. Lachlan Thomson, from whom he separated in 1913. Some years later, in America, he made a lasting marriage.

were the deposits of the French symbolist school—drawings of spooks and of male and female figures shaped like vegetables. . . . . The floor was covered with matting, and an earthenware fountain in the midst played by means of a pump. There was a piano and a host of divans. Oh, divans, I thought. Divans! What a lollipop life we are in for!

They sit there talking of Swinburne and Whitman, even of Lucian— "Isn't he a bit like Wells in places?" Marcia asks—and Tremayne would have Congreve appreciate her talents: "I've always thought [says Tremayne] that Marcia could write a play. Her dialogue is rapid and her characterisation is most effective. But her sketches are mere vignettes on which she spends too little time to do her justice. She needs a larger canvas."

Congreve suggests that a manuscript be produced, for an exercise in practical criticism, but Marcia dodges that. In any case, a young man has unexpectedly knocked at the door. There are whispers in the hall, but Marcia returns with a perfectly calm expression ("a Mrs. Buddha attitude was her masterpiece"), and doesn't mention him. With devious devices concerning a parcel at the door, and a sister to be visited in Vevers Square, Marcia gets rid of her visitors (this occurs in the sixth instalment, published in June). Congreve, however, sitting by the window, has already noticed "that spark Stornell" emerge on the street below. It is time for Tremayne to be informed of what he hasn't noticed—"And why in thunder didn't you tell me?"

"Look here, Tremayne," says Congreve as they leave the place, "if the whole afternoon, Stornell apart, has not convinced you that Mrs. Foisacre is an empty husk, as promiscuous as a rabbit, as responsible as a bubble, and as deceitful as a cat, find her out for yourself."

Orage recalled much later that Katherine had been "really hurt" by what he had said about her in this tale.[12] That may have been true of 1912; but in 1921, just after *Bliss* had appeared and had been rapturously praised, she was moved to write him the letter that is already quoted at the head of Chapter VI. "You taught me to write, you taught me to think," she said. And when she added, "But let me thank you, Orage—*Thank you for everything*," she underlined the last four words. By then, they applied even to his attack on her youthful character.

*   *   *

Murry obviously idealised Katherine from the moment he met her. "She was a woman simple and lovely in all her ways," we read in *Between Two Worlds*. "From the first to the last Katherine appeared to me a totally exquisite being. I do not think it ever entered my head, at any time, to criticise her in any way."* If that was what she had found, after three years in London packed with mischief, she was lucky indeed. She had the chance, with Murry, of becoming her "real self."

A fresh beginning, then. But what about Murry's exams, his parents, the financing of *Rhythm* as a monthly, and the fact that respectable tenants of Clovelly Mansions were now looking sideways at them? His exams, they took in holiday spirit, spending a week on Boar's Hill with their new friend Gordon Campbell, the result being "a tolerable second."

Taking Mrs. G. C. Bowden to 13 Nicosia Road was far more difficult. So much had been hoped of young Jack—and now this. There was a "curtain of ice" in the front parlour, and Murry's only brother, nine years old, stood there frightened by the tension. A fortnight later Murry's mother and aunt came to the flat, hysterical. Only force pushed them back from the door. "Go away, you women, go away!" cried Murry; and he did not see his family for the next three years. Both of them, now, were cut off from their families; both had younger brothers of whom they were very fond.

As to *Rhythm*, Katherine had a brilliant idea. She went to "Stephen Swift" (or Charles Granville), and proposed that he should take it over: it would bring him in more geniuses, more authors of "Books that Compel." He agreed at once. Nothing in writing of course, but he suggested that they should have a salary of £10 a month as editors, and gave them a check for four months in advance, which was duly honoured.

About the ambiguousness of their relationship there seemed little

---

*In 1953, after reading the author's previous biography, Murry thought about this again. "Looking back," he wrote in his journal, "it seems to me now that at first she was enchanted by my innocence, and wanted to preserve it, and (to be in harmony) to put away her own 'experience,' which was considerable and much of it an unhappy memory. She wanted to annihilate her past. Of that I am *sure*. . . . . I was deeply conscious that she wanted to start afresh, and that she was in some way afraid of my making any contact with her past."—quoted in Frank Lea's biography, p. 31.

that they could do. If marriage wasn't possible, at least they could take a honeymoon: a few days in Paris, enabling Fergusson to pronounce his blessing, and Francis Carco to notice Katherine and her apologetic *"je ne parle pas français"* to him when they were introduced. After that, they would find a cottage in the country.

Murry said in *Between Two Worlds* that if Katherine had been free they would have been married at once, but that "Katherine's husband refused to take proceedings against her. They were begun and dropped." He was relying, when he wrote that, on what she had told him or had given him to understand, and the word "refused" was not true. The six years' delay resulted, in fact, from Katherine's mischievous contempt for middle-class taboos.

Hearing that they were living together, Mr. Bowden called at the flat unannounced, to ask Katherine her intentions. "She did not seem to be concerned," he wrote, "about any proceedings that would make remarriage possible for her, at any rate for the moment. For on leaving I asked her in Murry's presence—half jokingly—if they wanted to marry, and she looked quizzically at him and said something like 'Do we, J.M?' "

Then Katherine had the idea of getting an American divorce—Mr. Bowden to go to America for the purpose. She wrote to him about it ("I think it is in every way the wisest plan for us both") and went alone to see him at Gloucester Place, displaying, this time, "another of those changes in appearance I have noted, which revealed an aspect of her personality I had never seen before." But it was found that the decree would not be valid in England.

Once it was clear that an undefended case on the ground of adultery would have to be heard in London, with attendant publicity, Mr. Bowden got the impression that if there must be a divorce it was up to him. He gathered that she was "less averse to her way of life with Murry—with its suggestion of the romantic literary tradition of George Eliot and George Sand—than to the stigma of being the guilty party in an undefended suit in London as it was then."[13]

With her scheme for sending him to America, however, Katherine had inadvertently done Mr. Bowden one good turn. He did go in the following year, and began a successful career, teaching "Voice in Public Speaking" at the Divinity College of the Pacific in the University of California, where the subject was new. But his work so preoccupied him that he did not follow up the preliminary formalities he began before leaving London. There was a verbal understanding that he would hear from her, but he never did. From 1912 onwards he knew nothing of the details of her life until they became public knowledge. "So far from ever feeling any 'pique,' " he once wrote, "I still feel that of the many facets of her multiple personality, K.M. presented to me what was fascinating and attractive."[14] His wife once remarked to the author: "I sometimes think George was the only gentleman in the whole darned bunch."

By the summer of 1912 Jack and Katherine were known as the Two Tigers. The novelist Gilbert Cannan, delighted by a woodcut in *Rhythm*'s first number of a tiger stalking a monkey, had bestowed the name, and they had taken it up themselves, Katherine later being "Tig" to Jack, and eventually "Wig."

One of the first to hear the name being used in the flat was the young Irish barrister Gordon Campbell, who had met Katherine at Willy George's house. On his third or fourth visit he was alone with her for a time, until, to her summons, "You can come out now, Tiger," there emerged from the other room a slight figure in a navy blue fisherman's jersey. He gathered that certain tests had been passed, and an introduction could now be safely made; in fact he was soon much more Jack's friend than hers.

"Mansfield," he told the author once, "was always acting a part, or going off on the tops of buses to Poplar to see what "the people" looked like, and presumably putting her real self down on paper somewhere. But Murry, like himself, was exploring *literature*, and a friendship developed from which she felt shut out. It was his opinion that she could never really love a man because there would always be some part of her mind a foot or two above her head, observing what was happening.[15]

The Diaghilev ballet burst upon London in June, and the cult of things Russian became the rage. Bloomsbury was present; Lady Ottoline Morrell entertained Nijinsky at Bedford Square; perhaps the Tigers were able to afford the gallery. Dostoevsky's novels were at last coming out in English—apparently at the instigation of Arnold Bennett, who had urged this in his *New Age* column;[16] and other periodicals were now translating Russian stories. A witty parody by Katherine of the Russian manner, entitled *Green Goggles,* * which must have been sent in earlier and held, appeared in the *New Age* on 4 July; but then there was another lurid attack, and nothing more of Katherine's appeared in the *New Age*—at least, not until the autumn of 1915, when she surprisingly sent in one more satirical contribution.

Four years away from Thorndon, from girls' teas, charity bazaars and green shantung; four years away from dainty violet sandwiches, from Lady Ward and blindfold pigs, from that parting in the rain at Lyttel- ton. What Kass Beauchamp needed more than anything else at this moment was something like a home. One purpose of *Rhythm* for the Tigers of course was to bear them away from their origins toward recognition and security—not the bourgeois sort, which is intolerable, but the sort that one earns for oneself. Such ventures, however, confus- ingly attract both friends who already have those things, and others who do not. Danger and help come knocking at the door impartially.

In the spring of 1912, on holiday in Germany, Rupert Brooke had received a letter from the editor of *Rhythm,* inviting him to contribute. He had lately written his most famous poem, and was soon to become a Fellow of King's College, Cambridge. On returning to London in August he stayed with Edward Marsh, who was Winston Churchill's private secretary at the Admiralty and, since he had some money to

---

*A hint of something which seems to have escaped all notice these six decades: that Nikolai Gogol, rather than Chekhov, might be the Russian writer to examine for signs of an influence on Katherine Mansfield. What emerges, instead, is a remarkable affinity between their creative natures, of which apparently Katherine remained entirely un- aware.

Gogol, when young, possessed an impish and brilliant gift for mimicry and caricature, which he transferred into writing. He also could plunge ill-advisedly from satire into sentiment (and he began by writing sentimental verse). Both were compulsive liars, compulsive letter-writers, and compulsive travellers, who found in travel a sense of well-being and a cure for all ills. Both were outsiders in the capitals to which they took their talents (but Gogol took, from his Ukraine, a powerful folk tradition which carried him sooner to success), and were in similar ways misunderstood for what they did with vernacular speech. Both, lacking either the inclination or the gift for inventing "plot," were at their best in episodic narrative in which absurdity disguises an underlying melancholy. Both destroyed much work in self-disgust, and the end of K.M.'s creative life astonishingly resembled that of Gogol.

The author of *Green Goggles,* of course, would no more have known how "Gogol" is pronounced than her associates in 1912. For the piece itself, see Appendix A.

spare, a patron of poets and painters. Clovelly Mansions being not far away, Brooke called—"I suppose to spy out the land," says Murry.[17] Having inspected the Tigers in their fearful symmetry he invited them to lunch in Soho so that Marsh could meet them too. They were shy of him at first—he was so evidently from another sphere—but he took a liking to them both (which wasn't quite shared by Brooke), and in this way Eddie Marsh became *Rhythm*'s best friend and most generous helper.

They still were longing for their cottage in the country, when another young artist came to see them. This time it was Henri Gaudier-Brzeska, who had sent them some of his animal drawings, which greatly impressed them. He soon came again, bringing his "sister." Thus danger came through the door in the persons of Pik and Sophie, who were respectively twenty years old and approaching forty, and were neither siblings nor yet lovers in any usual sense.

Gaudier, undoubtedly a genius, and very prickly, was a Frenchman —small and feline, with eyes like a leopard's; according to both Richard Aldington and Ezra Pound, he stank. The unstable Sophie Brzeska came from Cracow; it was she who made Gaudier put their names together, connecting hers with all his work.

On his first visit to the Tigers Pik was enchanted, and wanted to model Murry's godlike head, which he fondled warmly. On the next occasion confidences were swapped, and the comic tale was told of how the Tigers had got into bed and laughed and laughed. It was learned that the Murrys were looking for a cottage. Marvellous! Pik and Sophie would be able to go down for weekends!

A pretty little house was found at Runcton, near Chichester, costing only £40 a year. "It's lovely, it's our place," said Katherine with her head on Jack's shoulder as they stood in the dining-room; and a three-year lease was signed. Perhaps it was rather far away for the Gaudiers? The fare might be beyond them? Heavens, no. "All the *better!*" said Pik; Sophie would come and live with them—it would be good for her health—and he would get down when he could.

"But it's our house," Katherine moaned to Jack, "our wedding house!" Hateful Thorndon and its tried conventions were twelve thousand miles away. More confidences flowed. Sophie, feeling recklessly safe with Katherine, poured out the story of her wretched life. (This part is from H. S. Ede's account in *Savage Messiah*, which draws on Sophie's diary.) As she "opened the abysses of her soul," she took hold of Katherine's hand and pressed it warmly. Soon it was, "Tiger darling, we must go." Sophie knew she was disliked.

Some days later a note from Jack asked Pik if he would come to the flat without Sophie. Since he "still loved Middleton Murry," he did so, but he found that Katherine had suspected him of being homosexual. She asked him point-blank if he didn't have "peculiar longings" (the fondling of the head). He reported to Sophie that he now felt sorry for Murry, who was being "squeezed dry" by too much love-making.[18] In any case it was August, and in hot weather Gaudier "stank." But the ever-scrupulous Murry makes no allusion of any sort to that difficulty.

The Tigers moved into Runcton Cottage on 4 September 1912.* With Murry's £250 a year from the *Westminster*, Katherine's £100 from her father, and £10 a month from Stephen Swift for editing *Rhythm*, they reckoned to have £450 a year between them—a very good income then, with only £40 to pay in rent. They were well inside the professional class. Down in the working class, whole families were managing on 25s a week; a telephone girl began at 11s a week. J. B. Priestley's father, as headmaster of a large elementary school in Bradford, earned £350. This was the England in which Orage (£208 per annum) was able to run the *New Age* as he did on very low printer's wages. There was, then, nothing *financially* absurd in the Tigers' going to Runcton. That they furnished the house on hire-purchase at Maples, had the grand piano, their books and the Buddha all sent down; that Katherine engaged a soldier-servant, and had some notepaper printed for "Runcton Cottage"— these things in themselves were not absurd. But as to *Rhythm*, and Stephen Swift, they were living in a dream.

Soon a painful incident removed at least the threat of Sophie. Gaudier came down to see the cottage, walking miles at the last for lack of the train fare. Arriving worn out, he had the bad luck to hear Katherine (who was fixing curtains at an open window), telling Jack why she didn't want Sophie there. Gaudier withdrew unseen, and was thenceforward a most malignant enemy of theirs. The whole thing had been a sort of model in advance—the resemblances are really very odd

---

*"All through August we painted and stained and polished"—*Between Two Worlds*, p. 227. But a letter from Murry in Sir Edward Marsh's papers establishes the date given here. It would seem that the Runcton sojourn was a whole month shorter than Murry thought when he wrote his book.

—of the friendship that was soon to follow with D. H. Lawrence and *his* overpowering wife.

Eddie Marsh went down for a weekend. Frederick Goodyear, "boisterous and blushing and brilliant," was joined there by Rupert Brooke, and all four tramped the marshes singing the choruses of Goodyear's many songs. The *English Review* paid its respects in person, since Ford Madox Ford and Violet Hunt (also living together out of wedlock) lived nearby. Ida went down, and saw her Buddha sitting in the garden. The sales of *Rhythm* were improving. Golden days!

But a strange feeling of precariousness, says Murry, began to invade their lovely house, as though it were merely a stage-set that could all be snatched away. They were longing to have a child, yet there was an "agonising premonition" that he would never be: "In the half-dusk, by the window, at such a moment, I could see Katherine's eyes brimming with tears."*

At that point a figure from the past turned up. "Suddenly," says Murry's account in *Between Two Worlds*, "a Slavonic friend of Katherine's came to England, and being penniless, came to us, with two big black trunks full of books and manuscripts, for he was a writer." It was therefore Sobieniowski, not Sophie Brzeska, who invaded their wedding-house, becoming a burden to their economy as well as their souls. He was always touching them for a "loan," and in the autumn evenings the house used to echo to his forlorn Slav songs. Once again they were spellbound by a sense of "the precariousness of all things human and lovely."

Even more suddenly, Murry was called by urgent telegram to London, and Katherine went up with him, to hear that her publisher "Stephen Swift" had absconded, leaving behind him a trail of devastation, bigamy, and fraud. At the printers', no formal notice had ever been given of a change in the printing order. It had actually been

---

*Katherine did not know in 1912 what had been done to her reproductive system in 1910. As yet, she knew of nothing but "peritonitis," and in fact she asked Murry to have a fertility test. As late as 1918 she still believed that she was able to conceive; two letters to Murry of that year (23 March and 2 June) in which "Aunt Martha" refers to her menstrual period, make this quite clear. She first learned the full facts when Dr. Sorapure explained them in 1919. No doubt she told Murry then, but Murry forgot even that, for he once remarked to Frank Lea (speaking of 1912, and the inability to conceive), "I do think she might have told me." That her infection was not in the lower tract explains their continued ignorance of its presence.

increased, since subscriptions were improving; but Granville (whose real name, it emerged, was Hosken), had done that in Murry's name, and had now run off with Louise Hadgers and the assets, leaving Murry all the debts. He owed the St. Catherine Press £150.* The story of this catastrophe, which seriously affected the Murrys' financial freedom for the next six years, has not been told before.

Charles Hosken, alias Charles Granville, referred to in certain publisher's announcements as "the English Tolstoy,"[19] was already married when, in November 1905, as "Henry Charos James," he married Emily Esther Parker. On the day of the ceremony, however, having had "something to drink" at her house, and his mind a blank, he left in the afternoon, and she never saw him again. Three years later, as "Charles Granville," he married Mrs. Caroline Fawcett, his first wife being still alive (and the second one, too).

By 1912, as "Stephen Swift," he had a fairly extensive list of "Books That Compel," with Hilaire Belloc, Max Beerbohm, Ezra Pound and Arthur Ransome among his authors. But the strain of being both James *and* Swift, and Tolstoy as well, was evidently too much for him. On 29 September 1912 he went to his doctor in a highly nervous condition and "much overworked," as the doctor later told the court. Being advised by the doctor to give up his business and "go abroad," he naturally did so at once, taking the name of Godwin this time, and "accompanied by a young lady." He was arrested in Tangier on 28 October and charged with bigamy and fraud.

At the Old Bailey, on 2 July 1913, he was convicted of fraud to the tune of £2,000. When he later came up for sentence a witness for him was Orage, who told the court that he had a high reputation and was "always known as the English Tolstoy." He was sent to prison for fifteen months.[20] After his release, Ezra Pound gave him a fiver.

When the Tigers got back to Runcton, having learned as much of this as was known in October 1912, it was "almost a comic relief" to find their soldier-servant drunk on the proceeds of some valuables he confessed to having stolen. "Oh, go away," they said, "and don't come near us again." That left Floryan Sobieniowski striding up and down the living room, "as though in travail of some impossible solu-

---

*According to Murry's "memory," in *Between Two Worlds*, £400; but the figure given here is correct, being established by a letter of his, and other evidence.

tion for our disaster," singing his melancholy songs. They gave him some money to fend for himself (thinking that would be the last of him), and prepared to leave their cottage in the country, for which all the rent had not been paid. Murry told the printers he did not regard the debt as his; and he wrote asking Maples to take away the furniture. A man in a bowler hat and yellow gloves arrived with a writ from the printers, and leaned on "Katherine's grand piano" with a familiarity that made it "indescribably his own." Somehow the Buddha came safely through all this. He was not, in fact, left sitting in the garden of that cottage, but accompanied the Tigers to their next.

CHAPTER VIII

The Blue Review

It's a daft paper, but the folk seem rather nice.
—D. H. Lawrence to Ernest Collings,
24 February 1913

She can *write, damn her.*
—Rupert Brooke to Edward Marsh,
29 June 1913

The *Pall Mall Gazette* used to carry a daily item by Filson Young entitled "The Things That Matter." To make it stand apart from the hurly-burly of the news it was set in italics, and on 23 October 1912 the Thing That Mattered was a pretty little fairy-tale which began: *"Once upon a time a young man and a young woman loved each other and poetry so much that they decided to devote their lives together to the furtherance and encouragement of English poetry—especially the poetry of young and unknown writers like themselves. . . . ."*

It described how they founded a magazine, devoted all their days and strength to it, and were content to find their joys in "the sublime and ideal region of the things that are eternal art." But then, "their rainbow bridge (in this case the publisher) gave way beneath them." They owed the printer £150, and they had no money except "the transmutable currency of youth." It would help them keep their cockleshell afloat, said Filson Young, if the reader would order a year's subscription to *Rhythm*.

This little plug for the Tigers had been inspired by Eddie Marsh,

who posted it to Runcton and hoped they "wouldn't mind." Not at all
—"You're a darling," wrote "Jack Tiger," adopting Eddie's language
in reply: "We think it awfully sweet of him."[1] It was probably the least
effective of a series of moves by *Rhythm*'s supporters to keep the cockleshell afloat. Amazingly, it was kept afloat for five more issues under the
name of *Rhythm,* and then for three more as the *Blue Review*—in effect
a separate chapter.

Mere pride on the Tigers' part could not have accomplished that.
There was another publisher willing to help—for the accounts had
been showing a small profit when Granville ran off—and the contributors, as Frank Swinnerton explains,[2] felt that *Rhythm* was youth's
alternative to the far too opulent and well-established *English Review*
of Ford Madox Ford, which had Hardy, James, Conrad and Wells all
writing for it. They were willing to contribute for nothing in the hope
of being rewarded later. In other words the "profit" was literally
fictitious—it consisted of their work.

Murry's first impulse after the crash had been to temporise with
the printers. Convinced that he must have money, they thought
that if they only pressed hard enough they would get everything. J.
A. Spender urged him to file a petition to bankruptcy, since the
debt was really Granville's and the Court would see that.[3] It was
the right advice, but perhaps the daughter of the chairman of the
Bank of New Zealand could also see danger in it. Instead, it was
arranged that the whole of her allowance would be pledged to pay
the printers off. The next move was also hers: she went to call on
Gilbert Cannan's publisher. "Secker has been charming about
Rhythm to Tiger," Jack wrote to Marsh from the Strand Palace
Hotel in late October, "and I think he will take over the publishing and work hard for it."[4]

A scheme of Willy George's to float a company with £500 capital
came to nothing; and by mid-November the Tigers were working and
sleeping in a gloomy flat at 57 Chancery Lane (Orage was at No. 59),
six friends having put up £10 each to carry them through November.[5]

Katherine did manage to write one new story at this troubled time
—for Frank Harris, who had lately acquired *Hearth and Home,* a glossy
magazine devoted to fashions and the Royal Family. Called *The House,*
it resembles the minor stories that she later wrote with London set-
tings, but has an odd sort of biographical interest, being somehow

connected with Sobieniowski's appearance on the scene at the time when a baby had been hoped for.

Its worn-out office-girl (another Rosabel, but her name is Marion) takes shelter from rain in the porch of an empty house for sale which she and her lover have lately inspected. Falling asleep there she dreams of a perfect marriage in that house—a cheerful manly husband, a baby boy and a nanny, log fires and toasted buns—but the dream turns to nightmare when she hears a voice downstairs, the voice of a former lover: "What, what was he doing there—yes, it was he. Something within her seemed to crash and give way—she went white to the lips. . . . ."

"White to the lips," she rushes down to prevent him from being let in, and the front door bangs behind her. She is then found dead in the porch by people who drop their aitches: "I remember 'er face as pline as yestidy. She comes with a young feller to look over this 'ouse. . . . . And when 'e'd gone, she comes back, laughin', and says, 'We ain't got enough money to furnish a cottage,' she says, 'we're just dreamin' true,' she says."[6]

Literally antipodal to that were the three down-under murder stories published in *Rhythm*, *The Woman at the Store*, *Ole Underwood*, and *Millie*. Less than murder stories, they were really insights into the social isolation that used to be common in New Zealand, especially in the backblocks; and they were written in a cultural isolation that was total for their author: no one who read them in London could have known what in fact they achieved.

The woman at the store, a yellow-haired backblocks hag who keeps a loaded rifle ready for strangers, is as much a part of the landscape as its rocks and hills and glaring light. Ole Underwood, the wild-eyed outcast of Colonial bars, is likewise dominated by his environment to the point of madness. And Millie, a childless backblocks female whose compassion for an exhausted fugitive turns to bloodlust when the hunt is on, belongs there as surely as the hideous details of her house.

Far from representing any "Continental" perversion of aesthetic principles, as the *New Age* thought, the stories were something that only a New Zealander could have written at that time. They succeeded (and only seventy-five years after settlement) in relating character to environment in a land of "no tradition." This is especially true of Millie, sweaty in her tin-roofed bedroom with its packing-case dressing table, its fly-specked mirror and its coloured print of "A Garden Party at Windsor Castle," all in a burning landscape where men have dogs with names like "Gumboil."

In the same issue of *Hearth and Home* that contained *The House* were articles on Murry and Katherine written by Hugh Kingsmill and Enid Bagnold, the former making Murry sound like a young critic of substance, and relating (though the matter was now *sub judice*) how *Rhythm*'s publisher had run off and the Tigers were "encumbered with this man's debts." Those words, appearing only a month after Granville's arrest, were too much for his loyal friends, Orage and Beatrice Hastings; and the *New Age*'s response to them was a paragraph by "T.K.L." which will show what she was capable of writing when aroused, and what Orage was willing to print. It was headed, "To *Rhythm*," and was probably written next door, in Chancery Lane:

> What a nest of crickets you've become! Crickets on the "Hearth and Home." Or is it rats? I think it must be rats. The captain has gone down, and the ship— Watchman, what of the ship? To be sure, it was a horrid captain to go and jump overboard like that, but really, was he so bad while he was alive? Was there not any amount of food for little rats? And all of his providing?

It went on to ask who had been gulled by the *Pall Mall Gazette* exploit. Nobody cared, of course—"only, considering the legal disability, from the Hanover Square view,* of the lady in love, perhaps the joke was not quite the ticket. I should not have mentioned it in public, however, except that I actively dislike rats."[7]

No wonder the *New Age* wanted friends. Under a different pseudonym the same issue contained an even fiercer piece on Katherine called "The Changeling" (see Appendix B). Something was wrong, and Orage knew it was. A few months later he deposed Mrs. Hastings as the paper's literary critic, and began his own column, "Readers and Writers." In the following year they parted, and she went to live in Paris.

The piece about rats could scarcely have done much harm to the

---

*St. George's, Hanover Square, was then a fashionable place, for the respectable, in which to get married.

Tigers, and the next few months brought a generous rallying of support as plans were laid to put *Rhythm* on a firmer basis—the change of name being part of this. (According to Marsh, it was changed because the word "rhythm" was too much for the bookstall staffs of W. H. Smith.[8])

Marsh had just successfully launched the first volume of *Georgian Poetry*—it was selling rather well—and when Murry needed a guarantor for a three-year loan of £100 intended to give *Rhythm* the capital it required, Marsh agreed within the week. "Your surety means that you guarantee that we *will* repay the £3. 16. 0 per month for 3 years," Murry told him, "and you know we will."[9]

Rupert Brooke stood up for *Rhythm* when the artist Gwen Raverat told him how much she hated it: "Of course, it's modern. It's all by people who do good work and are under thirty-five."[10] And the new man, D. H. Lawrence, even though he had run off to Italy with his professor's wife and needed anything he could earn, wrote from there agreeing to *Rhythm*'s having a story of his for nothing—for though the paper was daft, the folk seemed rather nice.

Murry next tried Hugh Walpole, and soon a letter to him described a meeting of contributors at which some grand new plans had been outlined. In an atmosphere which had been "extraordinarily enthusiastic and sane," about sixteen of the younger artists had "sworn adhesion." They would give their work unpaid, with Murry meeting the loss of £10 a month in the meantime. When that became a profit of £15 to £20 by the end of the year, it would be shared in proportion to work done.

The artists who had sworn adhesion were Albert Rothenstein, Ambrose McEvoy, Eric Gill, Norman Wilkinson, Duncan Grant, R. Ihlee, Derwent Lees, Mark Gertler, Maresco Pearce, Gerard Chowne and Lucien Pisarro. (In the event, only the first three and Lees ever had work printed in the *Blue Review*.) About half of the sixty-four pages were to consist of poetry, short stories, critical articles and so on; the other pages, in smaller type, would have Gilbert Cannan on theatre, Walpole on novels, Swinnerton on general books, D. H. Lawrence on German books, Murry on French books, and Katherine Mansfield on, of all things, "dress." (This must have been decided in her absence by an all-male-chauvinist meeting. There is no further mention of it anywhere.)

These were the so-called "staff members" (so Murry explained it to

Walpole), but Rupert Brooke, Walter de la Mare, J. D. Beresford, John Drinkwater and W. H. Davies would contribute two or three times a year. All these were "keen on the scheme," and there were two more to be approached—Oliver Onions and "M. E. Forster." Walpole agreed to come in, and was asked to do the approaching of "M. E. Forster" ("he's one of the men we really want").[11] And so it was that the *Blue Review* came out in May 1913 under Martin Secker's imprint, with Max Beerbohm's "A Study in Dubiety" as its frontispiece,* and with Lawrence's "The Soiled Rose" and Katherine's *Pension Seguin.*

Meanwhile, having experienced the gloom of their office-flat in Chancery Lane—where the electric light was on all day, a canary of Katherine's died, and her "novel" about the Trowells would not break through—Gilbert Cannan suggested their taking a cottage near his windmill in Cholesbury, Bucks. They moved there in the spring—or rather Katherine moved, with some furniture that once belonged to Ida Baker's mother, and Murry went down for the weekends. A consequence is that Katherine's letters now contribute glimpses of their life, which are far more amusing and vivid than Murry's could ever be.

The whole *Blue Review* episode, short and unfruitful as it was, marked a kind of watershed in the Murrys' joint career. It led to their first encounter with Bloomsbury; and it marked the end of two stormy Slavonic relationships that belonged to their early days.

One day Murry went to the home of Katherine's distant relative Sydney Waterlow, "to meet these Woolff people." "I don't think much of them," he wrote to Katherine at Cholesbury (12 May 1913), "they belong to a perfectly impotent Cambridge set."[12]

The same letter told of a visit to Chancery Lane by Gaudier-Brzeska and George Banks, who had now joined forces in a passionate hatred of the Tigers, fuelled mainly by Sophie. Arriving unexpectedly, they got inside the door and turned violent—Gaudier demanding payment for the drawings used in *Rhythm,* and Banks some actual drawings, which Katherine had at Cholesbury. Murry's face was slapped, pictures were torn from the walls, and the pair departed, vowing, "We've only begun." They then went about the town saying they were going

---

*"Mr. Edward Marsh wondering whether he dare ask his Chief's leave to include in his anthology of 'Georgian Poetry' Mr. George Wyndham's famous and lovely poem: 'We want eight and we won't wait.' " (A caricature of Marsh and Churchill in Churchill's office.)

to "knock Murry's block off," but in fact this was done in effigy only: Gaudier and his friend Horace Brodzky (whose book on Gaudier describes this) put the godlike head of Middleton Murry against a wall and—to our loss—smashed it to bits in a highly satisfying orgy of brick-throwing.

In the same week came Sobieniowski, who owed *them* money, and whom Katherine now called "a rather dangerous fraud."[13] He seems to have been fended off, at least for the next few years, thus closing the hazardous Polish side of their lives—in which one can see now that the parricidal Katherine had a tendency to fall for frauds of the opposite sex, a fate that befalls many women in her stories.

By midsummer Murry was despondently admitting to Marsh and Walpole that sales were below £800 and the loss was £15 a month. The "epoch-making story" had not turned up,[14] and the "rubbish sent in by geniuses of modern English art"* was too awful. He was also "bursting to write a novel," and had been for a year. A man called "Wolff" had sent in a good story, but what was the use, unless the team as a whole were keen to *make* a paper?[15]

Rejecting bankruptcy (his letter told Marsh), he was going to compound with his creditors, raise £100 on a life policy, and pay them about 7s in the pound. He would then be free to earn his living and write his novel, and Marsh's surety would not be touched in any way, as he had just made arrangements with the bank for repayment of the loan; they were going to give up Chancery Lane and take a cheap flat at Baron's Court. A closing paragraph left the door ajar for Marsh to save the venture even yet, but Marsh let slip that opportunity.

A form letter then went out to inform contributors that there would be no August number to contain their work. One copy went to "Mr. Wolff," whose story, said a handwritten postscript, Murry would have liked to print; it was "undoubtedly the best we have yet received from outside sources" (Katherine's work was better!—the first move in a long and subtle game between the Murrys and the Woolfs). But he didn't think England was ready yet for "an honest literary magazine." Would he and Mrs. Wolff care to visit them in their "remote address" at Baron's Court? "My wife, who could not meet you at Waterlow's,

*McEvoy? Mark Gertler? Duncan Grant?

also wishes to meet you both."[16] But three years passed before this happened.

That summer, D. H. Lawrence and Frieda Weekley came back to England after their elopement. They came from Irschenhausen, where Lawrence had just written his story "The Prussian Officer." A call at the office of *Rhythm* led to meetings, and the two unmarried couples took to each other at once. "I was quite unprepared for such immediacy of contact," says Murry, in his book. And Frieda, in hers, called it "the only spontaneous and jolly friendship that we had." She fell for them when she saw them on top of a bus making faces at each other and poking their tongues out.

So began the famous alliance filled with danger that was to alter, and at times almost govern, Jack Murry's life for the next twenty years, and Katherine's for three; and in which an important factor, not to be forgotten, is the very strong attraction which the good-looking, dark-haired Murry held for Lawrence from the outset[17]—an attraction fully borne out now by the long-suppressed Prologue to *Women in Love*, which speaks of the "trembling nearness" of Gerald Crich and Rupert Birkin when they met.[18] The blond Gerald Crich probably has much more in him of the fair-haired David Garnett than he has of Jack Murry; and Murry—who never forgot a nasty experience that had befallen him at the Bluecoat School—had no leaning whatever toward homosexual feelings. But one does read in the Prologue of the desires that Rupert Birkin felt for his *dark-haired* friends; and it follows, from other facts now known, that there was danger from the outset of some dark jealousy being aroused in Lawrence, as it is in the Prussian Officer, by the younger man's feelings for his girl, and his writing poems for her. For the present, though, the friendship was cheerful and "jolly," in the 1913 prewar way—making faces on bus tops, poking out tongues, and so on.

The Lawrences, staying at Broadstairs with the Herbert Asquiths, invited their new little friends to visit them there, and they did so, and read the opening pages of *Sons and Lovers* in the train going home. Such richness made Murry envious of Lawrence's gifts; and he confessed in his journal much later that he had been "a fool, a jealous fool,"[19] in these early days, when each man saw himself as the Novelist of the Age.

In August, Lawrence and Frieda went back to Bavaria, and by October they were living cheaply and delightfully at Lerici, in Italy, from where it seems that Lawrence must have written urging Jack and Katherine to join them. But Murry had become tied to his London journalism and his debts, which Lawrence despised, and he also did not feel that he could "live on Katherine's money." Lawrence of course despised that too, the result being one of those splendid postal lectures in his cheerful pre-war style, informing Murry that his refusal to take Katherine's money only meant that he didn't trust her love for him: "When you say she needs little luxuries, and you couldn't bear to deprive her of them, it means you don't respect either yourself or her sufficiently to do it."

At this stage it is clear that Lawrence contentedly accepted Katherine's role as Murry's wife, and wanted to help them both, though perhaps he didn't quite understand what being a Beauchamp meant: "You insult her," he said. "A woman unsatisfied must have luxuries. A woman who loves a man would sleep on a board." They should come to Lerici, live very well on £7 10s a month all told, and be greeted as "Signoria" when they went out together—"that would be luxury enough for Katherine."

As for writing: Murry must "stick to criticism," writing essays like Walter Pater, or somebody of that style; he must get the *Westminster* to give him two columns a week to fill from abroad; he must take Katherine's money to the last penny and let her do her own housework (Frieda had a servant, however, at £1 a month); he mustn't be silly and floppy, he must get up and be a man for himself—"I think Oxford did you harm."[20]

The catch was this: if Jack were man enough to live on Katherine's allowance instead of paying it to the adamant St. Catherine Press, they would have the bankruptcy officials after them, even if they skipped the country. In that case, would the chairman of the Bank of New Zealand continue to pay it?

So the Murrys didn't go to Lerici. But according to his journal Jack *had* set his heart on "getting abroad at Christmas for some years." Bursting to get to that novel, and determined to have written something before his twenty-fifth birthday (because Stendhal said that was essential), he had decided that Paris was the place. If he couldn't earn money from Lerici, perhaps he could from Paris? And if the *Westminster* couldn't help him, perhaps some other paper would—the *Times Literary Supplement*, for example.

CHAPTER IX

Indiscreet Journeys

*There is really, my friends, no salvation in Geography. Paris, it is true,
is the arbiter of European taste; but arbiters do not create! . . . . The best
advice that can be given to young English writers is to shun Paris and cease
reading French. The best preparation for writing great English is living
in England and reading, writing and, above all, talking, English.*
— A. R. Orage in "Readers and Writers,"
the *New Age*, 28 August 1913

"It's curious," Murry wrote in his journal in October 1913, "how I
have a childish and implicit faith that, once across the English Channel, inspiration will run free, thought be profound, and word come
back to the speechless."[1] Still looking for a fresh start, Katherine was
ready to turn her back on London too, and so, one night in December,
they disappeared from Baron's Court and flitted to Paris, with the
slenderest prospect of Jack's being able to earn a living there by sending articles to London. He had scratched an interview with the editor
of the *Times Literary Supplement*, who had said he would "do his best."

The move is called a flitting by Ida Baker. From a personal interest
in various pieces of her mother's furniture that crossed the Channel
with them, she remembered it well. And Murry himself told Marsh
that he had left "in order to prevent my life becoming intolerable by
the interference of creditors." From an Oxford man, they wouldn't
accept seven shillings in the pound.

But Marsh was one of the creditors too. Being suddenly asked by the bank to honour his guarantee, he had written to ask Jack what was up, and the answer he received from Paris was so embarrassed and involved that it had to be followed by another, making things plain. What he had been trying to say, Murry wrote this time, was that when they came to Paris he had left £19 in the bank for Barclays to draw on. Probably two of his quarterly instalments had been paid, but as he was earning only £3 a week and was now the subject of bankruptcy proceedings (some papers had arrived from the bankruptcy court in Carey Street), he couldn't answer for the next two. Would Eddie pay them?[2]

At Baron's Court he had been earning £12 a week by his journalism, but after paying £25 to ship their belongings over, taking a flat next to Foyot's in the rue de Tournon, and starting a huge Stendhalian novel, he had found that his articles for the *T.L.S.* were not appearing (Lord Northcliffe had ordered economies). So they were using all of Katherine's allowance for themselves, which explains the bankruptcy proceedings.

Murry doesn't mention it in *Between Two Worlds*, but it seems that Frederick Goodyear went to Paris with them. He, too, was labouring at a long autobiographical novel, and a letter of Katherine's records that he gave her the *Oxford Book of English Verse* while they were there.[3] The flitting and the dodging of creditors were thus no secret from him.

In February, J. A. Spender wrote offering Murry the post of art critic to the *Westminster*. He therefore returned to London to discuss it, and stayed with Gordon Campbell. It was just as well: a lawyer-friend of Campbell's said that if Murry went to Carey Street at once, the officials would see that it wasn't his fault and would be nice to him; if he didn't, they would put out a warrant for his arrest. He went at once, and was treated as the injured party, being made to feel that bankruptcy was a gentlemanly accident.[4] It was an advantage, after all, to have been at Oxford.

There was not much choice. In London, a job worth several pounds a week. In Paris, next to nothing. But they had leased their flat for a year, and named *Le Times* as a reference! No flitting this time, then. Needing £30 to break their lease, however, they had to sell up everything they had, and *Between Two Worlds* gives a comic account, which Ida in due course read, of Murry's being taken by Francis Carco on a bizarre expedition through the brothels of Paris in search of buyers for "all our precious belongings." Ida's mother's carved oak writing table, a writing desk, a carved screen, and various other things of hers, remained in Paris, at addresses of ill repute.

The only thing Murry brought back from Paris was the knowledge that his right place was in England. But Katherine brought back *Something Childish but Very Natural*—her longest story yet. Named after a poem of Coleridge,* which it quotes, it tells of two shy young things who have met in a suburban train. Both longing to touch and kiss, they are afraid of "spoiling it," but they dream of being married in a cottage in the country, a dream that ends when Edna (who is all of seventeen) simply fails to arrive. Illusion is shattered for Henry by a telegram, though not sardonically. The tone is neither destructive, nor is it exactly sentimental; no trace of Chekhov can be seen, and the day-dream, here directly sanctioned by Coleridge, is central to the method.

There are hints of its author's relations both with Orton and with Murry: Henry works in an architect's office, and Edna was the name of Orton's girl-friend in 1910; but Henry, at the end of the story, while waiting for Edna to arrive, is day-dreaming in Murry-Mansfield terms: "And then we shall light our candles and she will go up first with her shadow on the wall beside her, and she will call out, Goodnight, Henry —and I shall answer,—Goodnight, Edna."

The story's queer, half-lit sense of unreality also pervades the *Journal* entries that belong to Paris and the first weeks back in London. Some actual dreams are described, but in the daylight entries, too, the firmly concrete and the faintly mysterious are mixed with an effect peculiar to Katherine's mind. In a rather expensive borrowed flat in Beaufort Mansions, where they stayed for a time on returning to London, she writes:

> Today the world is cracking. I am waiting for Jack and Ida. I have been sewing as Mother used to—with one's heart pushing in the needle. Horrible! But is there really something far more horrible than ever could resolve itself into reality, and is it that something which terrifies me so?[5]

---

*Coleridge's lines were written in Germany in 1799 and sent in a letter to his wife, being given by him the title, "Something Childish but Very Natural," when published later. They are an imitation of the German folk-song, *"Wenn ich ein Vöglein wär."*

And then, on 27 March: "I am waiting for Ida to come. She's very late. Everything is in a state of suspense—even birds and chimneys. Frightened *in private.*"

These and neighbouring entries from a *Straker's Diary for 1914* and a *Straker's Monster Exercise Book* mark the beginning of her *Journal* as it is generally thought of. Most of what goes before lacks the characteristic slant of her imagination, but it is evident in these notes belonging to a year when not only Katherine, but all of Europe, even birds and chimneys, had good reason to be "frightened *in private.*" It would be tempting to find some cosmic awareness of doom in their strangely dislodged vision, across which birds in various guises pass with an almost Yeatsian symbolism, but the strangeness is more readily explained by immediate circumstances: she was ill, without knowing it; she was beginning to be discontented with Murry; and at the same time her feelings were turning toward L.M., for L.M. was going away. She had received a summons to Rhodesia to care for her father—no knowing *when* she might return. It was the prospect of an indefinite parting that brought to the surface those disturbing emotions expressed in a *Journal* piece called "Toothache Sunday,"* in which Katherine wonders, "Have I ruined her happy life? Am I to blame? . . . . . She gave me the gift of herself. . . . . I ought to have made a happy being of her." This is the first surfacing in the *Journal* of the mystery of that extraordinary relationship, filled with both love and its opposite; as when Katherine is comforting an exhausted L.M.: ". . . . . not as I usually do, one little half-kiss, but quick loving kisses such as one delights to give to a tired child. 'Oh!' she sighed, 'I have dreamed of this.' (All the while I was faintly revolted.)" Nearby is the admission, "Nobody knows, or could, what a weight L. is upon me. . . . . The strongest reason for my happiness in Paris was that I was safe from her."

Both needed and dreaded, L.M. was going away, and the "birds and chimneys" note of 27 March belongs, in fact, to the day of their parting. But that was also the day of Murry's public examination in bankruptcy court: no wonder everything was in a state of suspense. Katherine's poem, "The Meeting" (actually about the parting), belongs to that day too.[6] Highly personal, as her poems mostly are, it conveys some notion

---

*"Toothache emotional not physical"—Miss Baker's note of 1951, explaining a term in their private language.

of the iron ring within which she and L.M. had somehow sealed their lives:

> *You said, "I cannot go: all that is living of me*
> *Is here for ever and ever."*
> *Then you went.*
> > *The world changed. The sound of the clock grew fainter,*
> *Dwindled away, became a minute thing.*
> *I whispered in the darkness, "If it stops, I shall die."*

From that date onward Murry was an undischarged bankrupt, and Katherine bore a burden of indebtedness to Ida which biography cannot weigh. She seems to have produced no work for many months.

As to the role which should be accorded to her illness when considering the shift in Katherine's imagination, one speculates at risk, of course. According to Dr. Clarke's pathography she had now had tuberculosis for nearly three years, and another bout of "pleurisy" was at hand. Though still entirely unsuspected, the bacillus was at work. What, indeed, was that "something which terrifies me so," of the *Journal* entry when the world was cracking? What did she "know" when writing that?

From the expensive flat in Beaufort Mansions they moved for economy into two dingy top-floor rooms in Edith Grove, off the Fulham Road, with two tables, two chairs, and a mattress on the floor: a smelly hall, a common WC, and scraps in open buckets on the landing. Almost at once (while trying to educate himself as an art critic), Murry came down with pleurisy, and Katherine followed one week later: "She dropped into a chair, white and unable to speak, her heart was galloping so."[7] Dr. Croft-Hill cared for them kindly, but the real risk escaped his notice. She *looked* so well.

Soon Murry had to answer Eddie Marsh: "I was rather dreading your letter. Somehow I couldn't write. I haven't any money at all. I haven't had any since I came back." He was trying to get a job in a museum or an art gallery; his earnings were down to £4 a week from the *Westminster,* but Bruce Richmond of the *T.L.S.* was to take some articles in August, so he could faithfully promise £10 when they were paid for in September. Katherine, he astonishingly said, was "trying to get on the stage, but it's a damnable and sordid business without influence."[8]

The real reason for the drop in Murry's earnings was probably that novel of his. It is very long, very laboured, and painfully revealing. Its hero, Maurice Temple—"Morry" to his friends—is a young writer who has run off with his editor's wife, thus cutting off his earnings (a touch of Lawrence, perhaps). She is older than he and has some money of her own (a touch of Katherine), and the good life in the country is a central theme. There are kindly rustics down in Sussex who will warm the cottage beforehand if sent a telegram, and fetch one from the station without so much as noticing impropriety. ("The missus put a light there, sir, and lit a fire. . . . . It's not kindly to come to a cold house. She'd have done more, though, if she'd known that you were coming, ma'am.")

Morry and Mrs. Cradock sleep in separate rooms at first, but later all is childish but natural, and he "snuggles up," with his head on her breast. "We'll have to go and find someone to look after us," says Anne; and nice Mrs. Fletcher from across the fields offers the services of her daughter Alice, who, with a blush and a curtsey, agrees to start work *tomorrow.* [9]

There are glimpses in *Still Life* of Francis Carco (as "Dupont") with his cynical views on love; of the Scottish painter "Ramsay," and of George Banks and of Frederick Goodyear too, who as "Dennis Beauchamp" falls in love with Anne because Morry has done so, and later chucks his job to join them in Paris. There is a great deal of talk (Dennis Beauchamp is also Gordon Campbell), but it is always speeches, never lifelike dialogue. Katherine's comment was this laconic *Journal* entry: " 'I am afraid you are too psychological, Mr. Temple.' Then I went off and bought the bacon." And she still wrote nothing herself.

The Lawrences came back from Italy in June, free to marry, as the Murrys were not, and gay and confident because Methuen had offered a £300 advance on Lawrence's next novel. Those two were happy, and seemed to have all the world before them. When they came for a meal at Edith Grove, Katherine, understandably, let go her feelings about the sordidness in which she and Jack were living, which caused a quarrel afterwards—and another move. They found a pretty little house in Chelsea, and had signed the agreement before they discovered that it was crawling with bugs; they were waging war on those with kerosene and sulphur when, on 13 July 1914, at the Kensington Register

Office, Lawrence and Frieda were married—with Jack and Katherine and Gordon Campbell present as their witnesses.

The Murrys must have been filled with envy. But then Frieda, on the spur of the moment, thought of giving Katherine her former wedding ring; and Katherine, Murry says, was "really moved." She put it on and kept it on—"nor would she change it even when we married. She was buried with it on her finger at Fontainebleau."[10] So the symbol on Katherine's left hand thenceforward was the symbol of a broken union.

They all went back to the Campbells' house in Selwood Terrace, and in the backyard, beside a towel on the clothesline, they lined up for a wedding photograph which made the four of them look thoroughly bourgeois. Not a thought could have been in their minds of what had happened two weeks earlier, when at Sarajevo, the schoolboy Gavrilo Princip had fired the shot that was to burst the planet into flames and utterly change their lives.

The declaration of war, and the unreal events of August that surrounded it, found Murry at one moment enlisting in a bicycle battalion with Hugh Kingsmill simply because he liked bicycles, and the next day being examined by Dr. Croft-Hill, who told him he was overworked and needed a holiday. He gave Murry a chit for the military which mentioned his pleurisy, and added, "Query T.B."

Like everyone else that fatal summer, Jack and Katherine had already arranged a holiday: the novelist J. D. Beresford had found them a cottage in Cornwall for part of September. "We go to Cornwall tomorrow, I suppose," says Katherine's diary on 30 August. ". . . . . Tell me, is there a God? I do not trust Jack. I'm old tonight. Ah, I wish I had a lover to nurse me, love me, hold me, comfort me, to stop me thinking."

She had no one specially in mind; but she was just on the point of getting to know a certain Russian friend of Lawrence's, a mystery man who soon became a most important figure in her life—not as a lover, but in an oddly paternal way as a sort of father-figure, admirer-from-afar, and frowning disapprover. His name, which for some time Katherine could not spell correctly, was Koteliansky. It was simpler to call him Kot.

So began the war, for Murry and Katherine—with Murry in need of some mothering, and Katherine hankering after something different from Jack, although she didn't know quite what. From St. Merryn in

Cornwall, Eddie Marsh received a gloomy letter informing him that Jack had been rejected for the army because of his eyesight, he had not been able to get a job, and they had decided to live cheaply in the country, "writing as hard as we know how in the hope of a peace in three years' time." Meanwhile, as he only had £4, he wouldn't be able to send the £10 he had hoped to. Marsh's response was typical. He sent them a cheque for £5; but it missed them in Cornwall, and was forwarded in a towel they had left behind. Only after they had spent some time at Rye, vainly hunting for a cottage at 5s a week,[11] did Murry go to use the towel in Chelsea, when the cheque fell out: "I don't know why you do these things, Eddie. Is it to heap coals of fire? I'm sure it isn't—but it struck me all of a heap."[12] By then the Lawrences had taken a cottage at Chesham, not far from Cholesbury and the Cannans' windmill, and the result of a weekend visit was that the Murrys found themselves a cottage nearby.

Rose Tree Cottage, at The Lee, was *exactly* suited to their situation: it was small, and gloomy, and damp, and had the usual outside privy. But with Lawrence's help it was soon redecorated and ready to be the scene of those tremendous intellectual disputations which Gordon Campbell once described as "the great Dostoevsky nights, when Mansfield was always at her worst." Since his wife was away in Ireland he often went down for weekends, and in one cottage or the other the three men would spend a weekend locked in metaphysical discussions. (There are twenty clotted pages of them in *Between Two Worlds.*) This perhaps was when Katherine observed to Anne Estelle Rice that "Murry couldn't fry a sausage without thinking about God."[13] The men were altogether too intense for her; "I want lights, music, people," she cried one night to Beatrice Campbell. And here she was making jam, or chasing a neighbour's fowls from the garden with a tea-towel.

Lawrence, they soon discovered, had somehow changed. His Oedipal struggle with Frieda, and his despair over the war, were eating into him, and he appeared distinctly ill. His face looked green, for he had grown his new red beard, and violent quarrels with Frieda were occurring. If she began keening for the "childeren" she had left in Nottingham, Lawrence flew into a rage. The fact is, he had TB.

The Lawrences' marriage, which they now began to observe at close quarters, completely puzzled Jack and Katherine—as witness this unpublished passage from Murry's journal:

The more I think about it—and K. and G[ordon] have the same ideas—the less I can understand the why of it. There is no high degree of physical satisfaction for him. That is all wrong between them. F. accuses him of taking her "as a dog does a bitch," and last night he explained his belief that even now we have to undergo a dual "mortification" by saying that very often when he wants F. she does not want him at all, and that he has to recognise and fully allow for that. Sincerely I do not believe she loves *him* at all. She is in love with the idea of him as a famous and brilliant novelist—and that's all. And the idea that she should have been allowed to tyrannize over him with her damnably false "love" for her children is utterly repulsive to me. I have all my work cut out to prevent myself from being actively insolent to her. She is stupid in any case, and stupid assertiveness is hard enough to bear. I do not understand why L. goes on with it; not *really, intimately* understand. K. and G[ordon] both hate her. Tig also is certain that F. loathes her. I think she is terribly jealous of her too.[14]

The "K" near the end of that may in fact refer, not to Katherine, but to their new friend, Kot.* He had come to spend a weekend with the Lawrences, only to find that there was tension at lunch because his hostess was lamenting for her abandoned children. Never known for any reluctance to speak his mind, Koteliansky possessed the useful gift (for a short man) of being able to make his friends feel unworthy and small, and humbly conscious of their *souls,* simply by drawing himself up and pronouncing, in his firmest Russian tones, monolithic utterances of enormous moral weight. On this occasion he rounded on his hostess (he had met her only once before) with the information that she had left her children to marry Lawrence, and that if she chose Lawrence she must stop complaining about the children.[15]

In his friendships with married couples, Koteliansky had a lifelong habit of siding with either one spouse or the other. Being Lawrence's friend-for-life made him Frieda's enemy, and for a long time it was made to appear that he was also Katherine's friend-for-life—her refuge in time of trouble, and the one person she could always trust. It was a maxim with him, wrote Murry in *Between Two Worlds,* "that Katherine could do no wrong." This is quite untrue; it was rather Murry who held that view. There came a time, of which Murry gives no hint,

---

*A later pencilled note of Murry's beside the text reads " ? Kot—or Katherine." The reason for this extract's remaining unpublished until now will emerge in Chapter XI.

when Kot was by no means Katherine's friend. But he was for the present, and in the approaching estrangement from Jack she leant on him a good deal, though rejecting a show of sexual interest which seems to have been prompted by some misunderstanding on his part.[16]

It was not because of Kot, but rather with his conspiratorial approval, that Katherine began to turn from Murry at Rose Tree Cottage. She had come to feel that Francis Carco—in whose instructive company she had spent some time in Paris the previous winter because of her *"je ne parle pas français"* when they met—in some way represented what she wanted in place of Jack. Carco was writing to Murry at this time, and when Katherine read his letters she liked his "warm sensational life." She found herself wishing, as the *Journal* shows, that he were her friend.

By Christmas 1914, says Murry, it was understood between them that he and Katherine were about to part. For she, breaking an unwritten law, had looked inside his little red notebook, and had read there of his confessing to Gordon Campbell that he didn't know whether she was "more to him than a gratification."[17] Whereupon she had written in her own *Journal* (18 December): "That decides me, that frees me. I'll play this game no longer. . . . ."

By then, she was conducting her own correspondence with Carco. She had told Jack about it, says the *Journal,* but he was "not really interested." (Quite so, says Murry in *Between Two Worlds.* Knowing Carco rather well, he was "curiously certain" that if Katherine went to him she would come back disillusioned.) In a different notebook, a little later, Katherine wrote this:

> One night when Jack was with Goodyear and I had gone to bed and he said that what he really wanted was a woman who would keep him— yes, that's what he really wanted. And then again, so much later, with Campbell, he said I was the one who submitted. Yes I gave way to him and still do—but then I did it because I did not feel the urgency of my own desires. Now I do and though I submit from habit now it is always under a sort of protest which I call an *adieu* submission. It always *may* be the last time.[18]

That was how things stood at Rose Tree Cottage as the season approached for hilarious parties, of which three were originally planned, though only two eventuated. Altogether, in four buildings ceded to art by agriculture, three novelists and one short-story writer were at work.

In the cottage at Bellingdon Lane—as Murry heard from Frieda when he went over there on his bike—Lawrence was writing a big novel about marriages in three generations which had "Marlowe and Fielding in an account of a genuine English wedding" and would be called *The Rainbow;* he would soon have a good top room to work in which Frieda was preparing—to the envy of Murry, who had to be creative in a shed. In the windmill at Cholesbury, Gilbert Cannan had as houseguest the young Jewish painter, Mark Gertler, and was busily pumping him for a novel to be entitled *Mendel.** Inside the Murrys' cottage, Katherine was probably writing her story called *Brave Love,* and the unfinished Wörishofen piece about Elena and Peter. She was constantly tearing up what she produced.

The first party was at the Lawrences', on the twenty-third: a gay feast with holly and mistletoe, at which Koteliansky chanted Hebrew songs in a voice like a wind from the Urals, and a "murder entertainment" (the phrase is Murry's) nearly resulted when Lawrence maintained that the novel is "not creation of character." At those words Jack, with a tumbler of rum inside him, flung out his arms and declared that when Lawrence had created a character he would take off his hat to him "several times a day." (This was written down by Murry in a sodden haze before he went to bed that night.)

On the evening of Christmas Day, approximately the same company gathered at the Cannans', for a party that had to be split between their "long room" and the round room in the windmill. While Cannan worked the pianola, Murry (according to his journal) became "very distinctly conscious of a hostility" between himself and Gertler. Everyone got drunk, and no one could carve the suckling pig, yet somehow two short plays were performed after the meal. In the first play, no one had thought of a part for Murry, and Koteliansky kept urging him to devise "a play within the play," which led to the second one.

It would take a map of the premises to convey all the ins and outs

---

*The son of very poor East End Jews of Polish origin, Gertler had come into this circle by way of the Slade School of Fine Art, and his passion there for Dora Carrington, who eventually spurned him for Lytton Strachey. At this time he was being supported by Eddie Marsh, having succeeded Murry in that patronage.

of what then happened in the house and windmill; but Murry set the idea in action (his and Katherine's actual situation), while "Lawrence, Frieda and Tig all began to have a curious idea of the meaning of my sincerity."

Jack was supposed to be a cynical husband whose wife (acted by Katherine) had a sentimental desire to comfort a sentimental foreigner (Kot), but was seduced from this by a strong strenuous lover (Gertler), and then was to be reconciled to her husband. Drunk as he was, this last point was all-important to the author. The play proceeded, and the rejected Kot lay dead on the floor, a suicide. As the love-scene between Gertler and Katherine became too realistic for others' tastes, first Lawrence pulled Murry aside and told him, with intense severity and genuine concern, not to go on and expose himself like this. Taking him outside on to the road, he said, "It's not as though we didn't love you."

Then Frieda intervened. Katherine had started kissing Gertler (in the play) and when the Lawrences said, "You don't love him," she answered, "Yes I do, I *do,*" and refused to enact the return to Murry. So Frieda took Gertler out onto the road, and told him that Kath was a bad woman and she tempted him. Gertler then burst into tears. "Discussing it we went to bed together," says Murry's journal (they slept at the Cannans'). "But it was an extraordinary atmosphere—and very like a Dostoevsky novel."[19]

It also gave Lawrence a plot for his next book. Mark Gertler, describing the occasion for Carrington, said that "all the writers of Cholesbury" were going to use it in their work. But Lawrence was the only one who did. Gilbert Cannan, describing it for Lady Ottoline Morrell as "like a chapter out of a Dostoievsky novel," connected its immense emotional relief with the horror of "the months we have been through."[20] Like everyone else, he thought the war would soon be over.

The Murrys' party was never held. It was first postponed, and then thought better of, perhaps by Dostoevsky. In any case, Katherine's thoughts were now taken up with the soldier in France who had written to her, "*Ah, Madame, vous devrez être au soleil.*"[21]

[2]

Francis Carco was stationed at Gray, in the Zone of the Armies, where his duties were those of a military postman. With a little Colonial audacity, it would be possible to go there and see him. The years with Jack which Katherine now called their "three-year idyll" seemed over, and she wanted a life that was to be "more natural to that which I suppose I am." So the opening pages of her 1915 diary are full of references to the Frenchman whom Jack knew better than she, but whose birthplace, like hers, was in the sunny South Pacific.*

She had her photograph taken for him, and sent him a lock of her hair. When she and Jack made love in front of the fire she tried, "Quite vainly, to forget." When they did so in Jack's room she shut her eyes, leant her cheek against his and dreamt, and found it horrible ("I felt I betrayed F. and slept hardly at all"). All this in the *Journal,* published eventually by Murry in 1954.

Katherine wasn't the only one indulging in fantasies. Lawrence was seriously talking of gathering up some friends and sailing away from this world of war and squalor to found a little colony—Rananim—on an island where there would be "some real decency."[22] The name of Rananim for this bright vision came from one of Koteliansky's gloomy Hebrew songs; and Katherine it was, according to Koteliansky—Katherine, the fantasist in regard to men but not in regard to living on small islands in real decency—who went out and obtained a lot of detailed information about real islands. After which Lawrence fell sadly silent.[23]

Her attempts to write reflected the tension in which they were living. The abandoned piece about Elena and Peter in Wörishofen has already been quoted in Chapter V, and the long story called *Brave Love,* which was finished on 12 January, was the prototype of a sterile formula Katherine later used again: a young woman has a sudden romantic passion for someone more exotic and imaginative than her mate, but runs back home when sense returns.[24] This theme of the "Prudent Wife" will be noticed again. Unpublished until 1972, *Brave Love* is almost a parody of her manner (it might have been done by Beatrice Hastings at her most malicious), but like *The House* it has some interest as a personal disclosure. The sordid rendezvous with Mitya takes place in Marseilles, a sordid place. If Marseilles is not exactly Gray, the story remains an oddly prophetic enactment of her own approaching rendezvous in France.

---

*François Carcopino-Tusoli, to give him his full name, was born of Corsican parents in Nouméa, New Caledonia, in 1886.

The next weeks brought a series of blows for Murry, each one worse than the last. First, the Lawrences went away, because they had been offered the use of a cottage in Sussex. He was feeling that loss when Gordon Campbell, by not arriving for an expected visit nor explaining why, suddenly appeared to end *his* friendship; and this coincided, says Murry, with Katherine's definite decision to leave him. Moreover, her brother just then arrived from New Zealand to join a British regiment, met her in London, gave her the £10 she needed to "go to Paris for a week,"²⁵ and generally assisted the whole collapse.

That is how Murry saw it in his journal at the time. An entirely different story emerges from the letter Leslie Beauchamp sent his parents on 11 February—his first after reaching England, and one which reveals that Kathleen's skill at keeping her life in separate "compartments" had not diminished in the least since 1909. Leslie was twenty-one; his letters glow with the bloom of youth, and with much affection for his parents. Perhaps, as well, they were slightly protective of his sister, though this is hard to tell.

Writing from Aunt Belle's luxurious home in Tadworth, Surrey, he told his father and mother how he had gone into the bank to see Mr. Kay, and on leaving his room, "who should I run into but Kathleen who had come to draw her money." She looked "wonderfully fit" and was thrilled to see him, "not having the faintest idea that I was coming over." Then lunch, and a session of flagrant fibbing:

> She is more than ever in love with J. M. Murray which is a thing to be thankful for and with a new contract with one of the monthlies for a series of war sketches, they have prospects of a little money coming in, though these times are exceptionally trying for their itinerant sort of writings. They are going over to Paris at the end of this week to collect materials for the new job. I do not expect to see K. again for some time.²⁶

Murry saw Katherine off at Victoria on 15 February. He then went down with flu and took himself to Greatham, where he collapsed and was fondly nursed by Lawrence. This undoubtedly means that Lawrence, unconsciously seizing an opportunity, gave Murry an oil massage like the one that Rawdon Lilly administers in remarkably similar circumstances in *Aaron's Rod*. ("He rubbed every speck of the man's lower body—the abdomen, the buttocks, the thighs and knees," and so on.) But Murry was as yet so naïve about all this that he did not perceive the nature of Lawrence's attachment to himself.

Meanwhile Katherine, armed with a fetching muff—and a notebook, as always—brought off that jaunty escapade filled with wartime ironies which figures in the *Journal*, and later in the story called *An Indiscreet Journey:*

> Are all these laughing voices really going to the war? These dark woods lighted so mysteriously by the white stems of the birch and the ash—these watery fields with the big birds flying over—these rivers green and blue in the light—have battles been fought in places like these?
>
> What beautiful cemeteries we are passing! They flash gay in the sun. They seem to be full of corn-flowers and poppies and daisies. How can there be so many flowers at this time of the year? But they are not flowers at all. They are bunches of ribbons tied on to the soldiers' graves.

Four days later, having charmed some imposing colonels into letting her enter the "Zone of the Armies," she was in lodgings with Corporal Carco at Gray—all very secret and exciting: "The room. The little lamp. The wooden ceiling . . . . . And F. quite naked making up the fire with a brass poker. . . . . and brushing his hair with my ivory hair-brush." The "act of love seemed somehow quite incidental," they talked so much.[27]

Carco himself, not knowing what lurked in the notebooks, gave his account of the episode in 1938, in *Montmartre à vingt ans:* "I for my part was utterly sincere . . . . . and in a place like that, where everyone knew everyone, I would never have suggested that the young Australian should come and join me if my intentions had not been absolutely correct and disinterested." He was on duty all day; only in the evening was it possible to have a leisurely chat.

In Murry's *Still Life* the character Dupont, who is Carco's fictional equivalent, tells "Morry" that he must never love a woman more than three or four days, but that during those three or four days he must "never think of anything else, never leave her for a moment, and thus, knowing her to the last hiding-places of her mind, break with her once for all, leaving no thread of the unknown or the unexplored to bind you to her." Since this is on page ten of the novel, it had probably been written before the escapade at Gray; it would not be like Murry to put it in afterwards.

When Katherine had been at Gray for *four days,* a telegram told Murry that she would be arriving at Victoria next morning (25 February) and the Prudent Wife returned: "She was strange, her hair was cut short, and she was aggressively defensive. I was not to imagine she had returned to *me.*"[28] At Rose Tree Cottage a sort of weary truce between them "deepened into peace," and they decided to look for rooms in London.

In the meantime, somehow she had written *The Little Governess,* which is everything *Brave Love* is not, as well as *Spring Pictures.* Her "Dame seule" theme was turning into art. Fairly soon, after a happy visit to the Lawrences at Greatham, she knew she needed to return to Paris, this time in order to write. She had the use of Carco's flat on the quai aux Fleurs. He was still at Gray.

Orage, no doubt, would have told her that—as he once wrote in the *New Age*—there is "no salvation in Geography," and that the best preparation for writing good English is "living in England and reading, writing and, above all, talking English." She was, after all, though not an English writer, a writer in English. A epiphyte of the language, drawing sustenance from the atmosphere rather than the soil, she had all the more need to breathe the air that he prescribed. The fact remains that her trips to France in 1915 were fruitful for her writing, and the second one germinated the story now known as *Prelude.*

Her letters this time were gay and sparkling: in love with Jack now, she wanted to share it all with him. It is therefore surprising to find her hobnobbing at 13 rue Norvins with Beatrice Hastings, who, after leaving Orage and becoming desperate over Wyndham Lewis for a time,[29] had since grown thick with Max Jacob, Modigliani, and Picasso. "Beatrice's flat is really very jolly," says a letter to Jack. "The faithful Max Jacob conducts her shopping . . . . . She has dismissed Dado [Modigliani] and transferred her virgin heart to Picasso, who lives close by. Strangely and really beautiful though she is, still with the fairy air about her and her pretty little head still so fine, she is ruined."[30]

This doesn't sound at all like the author of "I actively dislike rats" and of "The Changeling"—which Katherine can hardly have seen if they were friends again so soon. The reason for the ruin: "I go to the cupboard and nip cognacs till it's all over for me, my dear." Katherine got drunk with her there, and vowed never to drink like that again. On 21 March, after a fearful row, they parted for life. (But a brief, unavoidable encounter seems to have occurred in 1918, in a moment of difficulty.)

It was three days later that Katherine fell, as Murry read, "into the open arms of my first novel." This, almost certainly, means that she had begun work on her story set in Karori, entitled *The Aloe*, from which *Prelude* was eventually to be refined.

Had she anywhere to publish such work, now that she had broken the spell of sterility? "No, you won't find anything of mine in *The New Age*, because I won't send them a line," she told Murry on the twenty-seventh. "I think Orage is too ugly." She had at last found her "real self" in her writing, but had nowhere to present it.

During this absence, Murry had been happily doing up some rooms at Elgin Crescent, in Notting Hill Gate, for a fresh start, and it was to that address that Katherine returned with as much as she had written of *The Aloe*. She spent the whole of April there, but found that she couldn't get on with it in those two rooms; and so back in May to the quai aux Fleurs, and all that visual pleasure which fills her letters. One morning near the end of this visit she heard the concierge refer to her on the stairs as "la maîtresse de Francis Carco," and she also heard that he was coming to Paris; so she fled in haste, assuring Jack that he now meant nothing to her at all. By 19 May she was back in London, with the story completed, as she thought. In the following year, by which time a catastrophe had altered her life and her attitudes, she started afresh, and, even then, it had not the qualities she wanted. Only in 1917 was it reshaped into *Prelude*, under the influence of Theocritus and the stimulus of talking at last to a fellow writer.

Carco was delighted to find that his guest had left behind a pretty bowl of English china. He then became an aviator rather than be sent to Turkey, and within a year or so he had written his novel, *Les Innocents*, in which Katherine is depicted as "Winnie," a predatory huntress out for "copy." There is a "Beatrice" as well, who murders Winnie. But Carco had only heard of her, and physically, seems to have based her on George Banks. Carco himself is "Milord" (more or less), who with his young friend Reggie here meets Winnie in a certain café on the boulevard St.-Michel:

> C'était une petite femme menue, gracieuse avec froideur, dont les immenses yeux noirs se posaient partout à la fois. . . . . Elle n'avait guère

de tournure au goût de Milord et n'était ni poudrée convenablement ni chaussée comme les filles de Paris.

When Katherine Mansfield had become famous, Carco wrote up his recollections in *Montmartre à vingt ans,* portraying a friendship, *"folle d'ailleurs, mais absolument pure."* It confirms that he really did think she was an Australian:

> To anyone who would not have understood it, I can honestly state that what counted in this friendship was the deep and natural taste that Katherine Mansfield shared with me for the poetry of night, of rain, of absurd and dangerous existences—in a word, for a kind of plaintive romanticism where the exotic mingles with the marvellous, not without a touch of humour, of disillusion. Having both been born in a distant country, scarcely separated by an arm of the sea and some islands, we involuntarily felt an affinity, thanks to the subtle schemes of an ironic destiny.
>
> Life, which makes light of everything, had no wish that this meeting should last. Yet it is to Katherine Mansfield that I owe having written my best book; for she, to a certain extent, furnished the elements of it for me. If it is she whom one recognizes in many a detail of Winnie in *Les Innocents,* she has prompted only the pure and innocent part of the character . . . . . and I myself am depicted, in the traits of Milord, only in the bizarre exchange of double personality which he makes with Winnie.[31]

In May 1950 the present author, whose limited French would not have served the occasion, went with Monique Furth as interpreter to visit Carco in his flat on the quai de Béthune. By coincidence he had just found a copy of *Katherine Mansfield et moi* (the French edition of *Between Two Worlds*), in a book bin beside the Seine, and had marked the page where Murry described the episode at Gray. The initials R.D. had been used there for Carco—the original of Raoul Duquette in *Je ne parle pas français,* as he well knew. To help along the awkward South Seas interview (the interpreter being distractingly pretty and most of the conversation meant for her), the page was produced and shown to Carco. His comment, relayed in English afterwards, was "That's annoying. I didn't know Jack knew."

CHAPTER X

Acacia Road and the Villa Pauline

Well dears most people think that by the time my training etc. is over there will be no more men off to the front. If there are it will be summer time and more of a picnic than anything else, so DON'T WORRY!
—Leslie Beauchamp to his parents, 11 February 1915

For the families of Britain, 1915 was the year in which the fatal telegrams began arriving at the door with more alarming frequency. And yet it was a year of strange anomalies in civilian life, and grotesque ironies. For a spectacle, one still went to Charing Cross to see "the wounded" being carried from the trains, an indulgence which Katherine had allowed herself in the previous autumn. Now, while she could still move back and forth across the Channel as it suited her, England was beginning to experience what France and Belgium already knew. In February, the Lawrences' maid at Greatham came bursting into the room: "Oh, Mam, my poor brother's killed at the war!" William Orton survived the Dardanelles, but in May it was Rupert Brooke, and in June, Henri Gaudier-Brzeska, killed in battle. The Germans had sunk the *Lusitania* and begun to use poison gas. French losses were in the tens of thousands. Young men came home on leave unable to speak of what they had been seeing.

Leslie Beauchamp, on an officers' training course with two hundred others—"all varsity men except myself, it seems"—had spent the month of March in rooms of unaccustomed luxury at Balliol College, Oxford, by no means unaware of the absurdities of his new existence. At home, there had always been flowers in the house; in an English

180

April, billeted near Bournemouth, he had loathed the route-march sacrilege of "trampling underfoot masses of primroses, violets and snowdrops." In camp near Aldershot in June (provided with a batman who brought him shaving water at 5:45 A.M., helped him into his uniform, and waited upon him at breakfast) he had been given instruction in the handling, and the throwing by primitive catapult, of the delicate hand-grenade.

The Lawrences were returning to London, and Lawrence, now in the midst of his short-lived philosophical encounter with Bertrand Russell, had decided to make his Rananim in Hampstead. He and Russell would give lectures, and with Murry he would start a magazine. It was the autumn of the world, and those who really cared would take the magazine and come to the lectures. To be near him therefore, but not too near, the Murrys took a house (and the servant who went with it) at No. 5 Acacia Road, St. John's Wood. This was possible because Katherine's allowance had been increased, and Murry was now established as the *Times Literary Supplement*'s reviewer of French books. The Gordon Campbells lived nearby. (The Trowells, as well, in Springfield Road.)

They were installed there when Leslie Beauchamp came to London for a six-day course on Clapham Common ("These bombs are frightfully deadly and very tricky to handle," he told his parents. "Now I have to instruct the whole Battalion, officers and men"). And so it came about that Chummie was able to visit his sister and the odd fish she was living with, of whom he sent home as charitable a picture as he could:

> I had a most comfortable roost at Kathleen's dear little house in Acacia Road St. John's Wood—Jack Murray is a very kind quiet soul and he and Kass are perfectly sweet to each other—in fact I was awfully glad to see how smoothly things were running—they pay £52 per year for the house and it is the acme of comfort *and* cleanliness—marvellously cheap, don't you think?[1]

That was late in August. And shortly after, all was ready to launch the *Signature*, as a fortnightly costing 2s 6d for six issues. Lawrence told a friend that he was going to "do the preaching." Murry would do "his ideas on freedom for the individual soul," and Katherine would do "her little satirical sketches."[2]

That is by no means what they were, though it may have been all that Lawrence could see in them. While Chummie was at Acacia Road, he and Kathleen, sitting under the pear tree in the back garden, in a sort of ecstasy of fear and nostalgia, had been playing the game of "Do you remember?"—as reflected in the *Journal:* "Do you remember sitting on the pink garden seat?" "I shall never forget that pink garden seat. . . . . Where is it now? Do you think we shall be allowed to sit on it in heaven?"

Out of this mood she had written a piece called *The Wind Blows,* the first of her haunting evocations of adolescence in a Wellington setting. With its curious time-shift or dream-shift toward the end, it is touched by the numinous, as her best work later was, and along with *The Little Governess* it was noticed in the *Signature* by Bertrand Russell, and by Lytton Strachey and some others. It appeared on 4 October, after Leslie had left for France.

Except from his boyish letters, it is hard to discover what sort of young man Leslie Beauchamp was. He had a strong resemblance to his sister—at a fancy-dress ball in Wellington he was once mistaken for her—and he was evidently something of a dandy. In 1912 he returned to Wellington wearing spats and carrying a cane, seeming oddly unaware that they were inappropriate on Lambton Quay, and one of the original "Samuel Josephs" children recalled him long afterwards (without any animus whatsoever) as "what would nowadays be called a pansy."[3] Murry is noticeably silent about him. In the *Reminiscences* his father says: "I think he would have liked to follow a literary career, but in deference to my wishes he adopted business and came into the firm to learn."

It happens that at Bournemouth Leslie shared a billet with Edward Shanks, the Georgian poet. Shanks remembered him, long after, as a pleasantly intelligent young man of no pronounced interests, whom he had liked. Leslie had talked a great deal to Shanks about his family in New Zealand, but had never mentioned Kathleen, though it came out that he knew Orage. After the war, when Shanks was surprised to learn that his friend had been Katherine Mansfield's brother, he concluded that Leslie had not wanted to run the risk of discussing her way of life with a comparative stranger.[4]

In proud high spirits as a bombing officer in the South Lancashire Regiment, and taking with him a scribble from Katie which was "not a letter" but "only my arms round you for a quick minute," Leslie left for France at 6:00 A.M. on 22 September, and for two weeks was not allowed to write. On 4 October—by when the "summer picnic" had deteriorated—he asked Aunt Belle to send him some Norwegian trench boots, some preserved fruits, and some salmon waders. He also wrote to Kathleen on that day.

Three days later, at Ploegsteert Wood, near Armentières, he was showing his men how to lob the hand-grenade. The one he used was faulty; it blew up in his hand, and killed his sergeant also. Before he died he said, over and over, "God forgive me for all that I have done," and then, "Lift my head, Katie, I can't breathe." On 11 October Murry made this note:

> Three minutes ago Tig had a telegram to say her brother is dead . . . I cannot believe it yet; and she cannot. That is the most terrible of all. She did not cry. She was white and said: "I don't believe it; he was not the kind to die." And now she has gone off to Kay for news. . . . . She wanted to know what day was the 7th. It was the day before she got his letter saying that he felt like a child of seven—the day she bought the badge of his regiment to wear. I don't know what will come to be now. I feel terrified of the future: he was so much to her; and that last letter—[5]

That evening, it seems, there was a dinner party at Acacia Road (which Anne Estelle Rice described to the author). Koteliansky was present, and Katherine was wearing the bright Russian peasant dress that he had given her. The Campbells joined the party later, but were told nothing. Katherine seemed to Beatrice unusually talkative and gay, but when a few days later she inquired about Chummie, Katherine looked at her "in a queer, wild, hard way," and then said, "Blown to bits!" His cap was later sent to her.

This bereavement altered Katherine's life. Her grief completely changed the balance between her cynical side and the other, and so released her main creative stream. The process began in private, with *Journal* entries addressed to Chummie in this vein: "You know I can never be Jack's lover again. You have me. You're in my flesh as well as my soul." She spoke of having "things to do for both of us," and by that time (29 October) Murry knew that she felt she could no longer live at Acacia Road. Within another fortnight they were heading for the South of France—such was that war—in order that Katherine could write, about New Zealand.

*   *   *

By mere coincidence, Lawrence in the same month suffered a blow which likewise changed his life. On 28 September he had given the Murrys a copy of his new novel, *The Rainbow*.[6] Two days before Leslie's death he came round to show them the hostile review that Robert Lynd had written for the *Daily News*. Scenting the danger, he sat there very silent while the Murrys read it; and it was indeed the start of his being hounded for that book, which was suppressed soon afterwards, and its publisher prosecuted. But Murry and Katherine had found it hard to comfort him; they didn't like *The Rainbow*, and Katherine "quite definitely hated" certain parts of it; she hated the "female" parts for which she felt that Frieda was to blame.[7]

The *Rainbow* prosecution in November drove Lawrence, as well, to seek salvation in geography. Suddenly, he was all for escaping to a Rananim in Florida, and was gathering up a phantom band of followers, mostly very new acquaintances (they included Philip Heseltine and an Indian law student named H. S. Suhrawardy). Influential friends helped him to get passports for himself and Frieda, but a visa for America required a medical rejection from the army; and at that, while actually standing in the queue, his pride rebelled. He stomped out, wasting his friends' exertions.[8] So it was that feelings between the two couples were a tangle of loyalties and dislikes as the Murrys got ready to leave for France, abandoning Lawrence to his misery over *The Rainbow* and the failure of the *Signature*, which only ran to three issues.

Just before they went, their new friend Dorothy Brett threw a noisy party at her studio near the Earl's Court Road. Correctly, as a daughter of Viscount Esher, she was the Honorable Dorothy Brett; as a former student of the Slade School of Art, however, she was always addressed as "Brett," and she treated her "position" as befitted a Slade girl in a smock. Upon writing her first letter to Lady Ottoline Morrell, using her father's ennobled stationery, she put a disrespectful chinless drawing of herself beneath the coronet as she stuck the envelope down. Being rather deaf, she carried a kind of ear-trumpet which she called her "Toby."

Brett's party on 5 November seems to have been meant for the Lawrences—at that stage off to Florida. And that fireworks day, as it happens, was the day on which Guy Fawkes Lawrence heard that his novel had been seized. There is a comic account of the party in Brett's own book on Lawrence. "Everyone" was there, including Mark Gertler, Clive Bell, and Lytton Strachey, and it was probably Katherine's first encounter with Bloomsbury and with Lady Ottoline's Garsington friends—any of whom, had they been *New Age* readers, might have seen in that week's issue her experiment in mime called *Stay-Laces,*[9] a satire on suburban women's attitudes to the war. ("I *love* the wounded, don't you? Oh, I simply love them. And their sweet blue and red uniforms are so cheerful and awfully effective, aren't they?") Its tone is hard and bitter, and the fact that she sent it to Orage, so recently "too ugly" to be trusted with her work, is obviously significant. Yet it marked the first appearance in her writing of a theme that was later of immense importance; it was also one further step in the use that she was making of her 1911 encounter with Theocritus and the mime form. Her really important advances often had trivial beginnings.

Although Lawrence had been too proud to seek rejection from the army, Murry was not, and early in November he received a fresh bill of ill health. No. 5 Acacia Road was made over to some friends of Koteliansky's, who also took in Kot himself,* and by 19 November Murry and Katherine were in Marseilles, preparing to find a cheap place along the coast where both could write. It was in Katherine's mind to retrieve the past from grief in a way that would make her brother live again, and Murry was to write a book on Dostoevsky for Martin Secker, to clear off the debt still owing on the *Blue Review.* He could do his reviewing for the *T.L.S.* from there, and he had lost his compunction about living on part of Katherine's allowance, which was now £120 a year. This feeling wasn't shared, however, by Katherine's father, who felt that the man she was living with was dodging his duties in every sense.

At Cassis the mistral blew, and they shivered in their hotel room, wondering why they had come. One day when they walked round the point and sat on the rocks, Katherine, overcome by her grief, began to weep as though she would never stop, and Murry, discovering that he "knew what jealousy was," burst out in a rage against her, then felt

---

*The house then remained Koteliansky's home until his death in 1955.

ashamed. In describing this in *Between Two Worlds* he takes the reproach upon himself for having been jealous of a dead brother. But pure grief in a family bereavement does not usually make a spouse feel jealousy or rage.

There is no need to doubt Katherine's love for Chummie or the strong affinity between them—there is evidence for that from 1907, and his last words were addressed to her. But their adult acquaintance was really *not* extensive. She had obviously deceived him about the purpose of her "week in Paris" in the previous spring, and what is known of her reactions to his death (strangely traversed by a streak of her satiric hardness a few weeks later) would suggest that there may have been guilt as well as grief in her weeping on the rocks at Cassis: that all the guilt, in fact, which she must have felt toward her family, and the Trowells, since 1908, now made a virtue of itself. These are hard words, but it does seem possible that her tears at Cassis were as much for her past offences as for Chummie's death, and that it was by this that Murry felt shut out.

He found himself arranging to return to London, to plod on with the *Signature* perhaps, and have a printing press, and stand by Lawrence. Before he left they found the village of Bandol, a few miles farther along the coast, where Katherine was happily installed at the Hôtel Beau Rivage when Murry, already regretting his decision, returned to London.

It was agreed that as soon as she had broken the silence with her writing she would come back too, and her letters from Bandol, her first from the warm south, are almost too bright-eyed with Keatsian responsiveness. Murry, for his part, took a furnished room in Hampstead at 9s a week and settled in to solitude, having meals when he could with the Lawrences and the Campbells.

But Katherine now fell ill, first with the "Marseilles fever" they had both had in that place, and then with her so-called "rheumatism." Confined to bed in a strange hotel, she longed for his letters, and there was a gap, of two whole days, to which her reaction (in a country engaged in a war on its own territory) was out of all proportion—"Do not leave me like this without news," she wrote, "It is so cruel—cruel." Murry, whose own letters from a lonely room disclose an almost abject dependence on her love, was reduced to saying that he wasn't worthy of her and was "only a *little* man," but he had given her all his love.[10] It is clear from what follows that this abnormal outburst should be attributed in part to her third illness, her phthisis, still totally unsuspected.

While in the depths she had written to Lawrence—a "wild kind of letter," as she later confessed to Murry, "and not fair to 'us.' You understand?" It happened to arrive at Byron Villas while Murry was there. Lawrence didn't show it to him, but after reading it he went for Murry; it was all his fault, he was a coward, he had never offered Katherine a new life, her illness was due to misery, and that was due to Murry's always whining and never making a decision, and so on.[11]

The upheaval led to a decision. Since Lawrence had now been offered a cottage in Cornwall and was going to it after Christmas, Murry was free to return to Bandol, so he suggested that Katherine should find a villa for them. Meanwhile, at Lawrence's instigation, he had been invited by Lady Ottoline Morrell to spend Christmas at Garsington Manor, along with Lytton Strachey and Clive Bell. He described his new friends to Katherine as "a fairly decent lot," but said that he felt like a babe-in-the-woods among them, and when he returned to his little top room in the cottage where he slept he could imagine that he and Wig were snuggled up together, "and the birds cover us with leaves."[12]

It was on Boxing Day that Katherine received his telegram from Garsington to say that he was definitely coming back. Next morning, wishing to "have a small fête," she went to the Post Office and put *"new Relief nibs* in all the awful old crusty pens." In a state of high excitement she then found the Villa Pauline and the friendly couple who owned it, and was ordering the wine and the wood. On the thirtieth she stood among the buyers at the flower market and bought, "wholesale, you know, at the auction in a state of lively terrified joy 3 dozen rosebuds and 6 bunches of violets."

Katherine's letters to Murry from Bandol that December—at least one every day for three weeks—are all marked by that "lively terrified joy." Even her letters from Paris of the previous spring do not approach their vividness, and hindsight finds in them, and in the *Journal*, the tell-tale signs of phthisis.

On 27 December: "I knew I would not sleep. What drowsy bliss slept in my breast! Oh Jack, I hardly dared to breathe." Three days later: "I am still so frightened that my breast hurts me to breathe." Or in the *Journal*, earlier: "Even my heart doesn't beat any longer. I only keep alive by a kind of buzz of blood in my veins."

As the year was closing she wrote: "I have loved you before for 3 years with my heart and my mind, but it seems to me I have never loved you *avec mon âme* as I do now. . . . . I have never felt anything like it before. . . . . I seem to have only played on the fringe of love and, lived a kind of reflected life that was not really my own. . . . ."

"This Katherine," Murry writes in *Between Two Worlds* without connecting it to her illness, "I had never known." As at Runcton, they still were bound to hurt themselves, and yet the Villa Pauline was for them an interlude of safety, while not very far to the north there lay Verdun, awaiting what was soon to happen there. Throughout this time one seems to be watching not only the private lives of Katherine and Murry and Lawrence and their friends, but the dolorous path of hope and cynicism along which creative artists stumbled during the First World War, of which the ironies alone can convey its unrealities.

"We get up at seven and go to bed at half past nine," Murry wrote to Lady Ottoline on 21 January 1916. He and Katherine were sitting, as they did most evenings, at opposite sides of the kitchen table, in the warmth of the stove, and she also was writing a letter to Garsington; for ever since Murry had told her that there was "a perfectly wonderful woman in England," she had been wanting to send her things, "like this hour of bright moonlight, when the flowering almond tree hangs over our white stone verandah a blue shadow with long tassels."[13] Sometimes they both sat at that table writing poems about their happiness.

"We pay 22.50 for rent—and live on the rest of 75 francs,"* Murry went on. "The amount of honey we absorb is beyond belief. A Spanish girl does for us in the morning. Part of the rest of the day we roam about."

Or they got down to work. While Murry read for his study of Dostoevsky, Katherine, as the *Journal* records, was preparing herself for something unlike anything she had so far written. Her desire had

---

*About 17s and £2 16s respectively, the second sum being Katherine's allowance, more or less. They also had whatever belonged to them of the rent which their tenants were paying for No. 5 Acacia Road—£7 10s a week, according to John Carswell's *Lives and Letters*, but that must be an error for £1 10s (see page 181 and "£52 per year").

never been more ardent: "Only, the form that I would choose has changed utterly."

What she wanted to write *now* was "recollections of my own country"—as a "sacred debt," a "debt of love." She wanted for one moment "to make our undiscovered country leap into the eyes of the Old World. It must be mysterious, as though floating. It must take the breath." All must be told with "a sense of mystery, a radiance, an afterglow."

Having re-read her Karori tale, *The Aloe*, and found that it was "right," she made some notes for a fresh beginning, with a new idea that would not have been there in the previous spring: the story was now to end with Leslie's birth (in fact it doesn't). The name of *Prelude* had not been thought of yet.

The Aloe is one third longer than *Prelude*, and it does not "take the breath," nor have an afterglow: there was first much dross to be removed. No doubt because it represented such a departure from her usual manner and usual material, it gave more trouble than anything else that Katherine wrote—nothing else was worked on in three different years—being at first digressive and diffuse in form. She more than once spoke of it as her "book," and in the *Journal* she describes its structure as "really thirteen chapters." But it never was really a book, nor are the parts into which it eventually fell really chapters. They are episodes, and of atmosphere rather than action.

In either of its versions, it is a picture of movement. It shows a New Zealand family moving from a house in town and settling into another in the country, the whole being seen through the eyes of its characters rather than those of its narrator. The "narrator," in fact, is hardly perceptible, merely inhabiting all the characters in turn. No "plot" is discernible, in the sense of a prearranged scheme of causes and effects requiring to be brought to just conclusion, the expectations awakened in the reader being rather those of life itself than those of a "story." The piece simply sets out to show what all the members of the household think and feel, and how they behave, during their adjustment to the new home—their whole Colonial life, of course, being exactly that —so that the movement is of two sorts, acknowledged and unacknowledged. It shows them realising, in their different ways, how their lives are going to be altered by the new surroundings. When it has done that, it stops.

The child Kezia is central, as we'd expect. She is Kass, of course,* but she is not the only representative of Katherine's "self." The character of Beryl owes more to introspection than it does to recollections of Belle Dyer. Thus Kathleen is depicted at two stages: there is an idealised picture of the child she never was and another of her "divided self," and at the end, these meet.

In its final form, *Prelude*'s peculiar magic probably derives, in part, from the effect of shifting focus as the viewpoint moves from the inner thoughts of one character to those of another. The narrator seems able to be everywhere and nowhere all at once, without confusion. That the method is Katherine Mansfield's own can be seen by comparing the story's opening with that of a story by her supposed "master," Chekhov: *The Steppe,* which also describes a child's journey to a new home. Chekhov, admitting his presence from the outset, begins with an exterior description, giving the reader certain information that is going to be needed, if only for convenience, later on. In Constance Garnett's translation of 1919 *The Steppe* begins like this:

> Early one morning in July a shabby covered chaise, one of those antediluvian chaises without springs in which no one travels in Russia nowadays, except merchants' clerks, dealers and the less well-to-do among priests, drove out of N., the principal town of the province of Z., and rumbled noisily along the posting track. It rattled and creaked at every movement, the pail, hanging on behind, chimed in gruffly, and from these sounds alone and from the wretched rags of leather hanging loose about its peeling body one could judge of its decrepit age and readiness to drop to pieces.
>
> Two of the inhabitants of N. were sitting in the chaise; they were a merchant of N. called Ivan Ivanitch Kuzmitchov, a man with a shaven face, wearing glasses and a straw hat, more like a government clerk than a merchant, and Father Christopher Sireysky, the priest of the Church of St. Nikolay at N., a little old man with long hair, in a grey canvas cassock, a wide brimmed top hat and a coloured embroidered girdle.

---

*Kezia—whose name means cassia—was the second daughter of Job. There is a pencilled note to this effect, in K.M.'s mature handwriting, on an endpaper of her Bible, now in the Turnbull Library. She must also have been familiar with its use in the Wellington "Social Notes" (see page 62 above). The name is often mispronounced. K.M. herself gave it the Biblical pronunciation, that is, rhyming with "desire" and not with "easier."

That is an external description: the writer is outside the event and is hardly felt to be participating in it—at any rate, not yet. By contrast Katherine Mansfield, seeming very much a participant (although she isn't), drops us without warning or explanation into the midst of a scene and situation which we have to interpret for ourselves, the mother's pregnancy and all, as though we had happened on it by accident in real life:

> There was not an inch of room for Lottie and Kezia in the buggy. When Pat swung them on top of the luggage they wobbled, the grand-mother's lap was full and Linda Burnell could not possibly have held a lump of a child on hers for any distance. Isabel, very superior, was perched beside the new handy-man on the driver's seat. Holdalls, bags and boxes were piled upon the floor. "These are absolute necessities that I will not let out of my sight for one instant," said Linda Burnell, her voice trembling with fatigue and excitement.
>
> Lottie and Kezia stood on the patch of lawn just inside the gate all ready for the fray in their coats with brass anchor buttons and little round caps with battleship ribbons. Hand in hand, they stared with round solemn eyes, first at the absolute necessities and then at their mother.
>
> "We shall simply have to leave them. That is all. We shall simply have to cast them off," said Linda Burnell.

That is the method of oblique impersonation, first used in *The Tired-ness of Rosabel*, but now extended to a group. Katherine Mansfield is outside the event and yet she isn't. What is more—and this is the real difference—she is making a presentation of her own sensibility in every line, and this is of equal interest with the event, as in a lyric poem. Swiftly and unpredictably, she flits from the inside of one character's mind to another one, and the reader, treated as someone who already knows them all, is tricked into familiarity before having time to feel lost.

Not that Chekhov always wrote as leisurely as in *The Steppe* (which for him, too, was a new departure), but he did consistently use the external method of description and rely, as a Russian author could, on reference to known types. Katherine Mansfield could not have called her buggy "one of those buggies with buttoned-leather cush-ions in which no one travelled in New Zealand in those days except certain merchants' families." Swiftness apart, it would have had no meaning, anywhere. She could never have described Stanley Burnell, on his appearance later, by saying whether he was or was not a typical New Zealand merchant, since no such animal had yet evolved. She could not assure her reader's familiarity with any containing society or class. Chekhov virtually had to, since he wrote for the readers of Russian magazines; but Katherine Mansfield hardly knew whether her story would be published at all. She had somehow to pretend her reader's familiarity with her "undiscovered country," then hasten to establish it before the sleight of hand was noticed. If there is an ancestral method, it is that of the XVth Idyll of Theocritus.

A device which probably helped the private process was her use of family names, whereby she gave her characters, as it were, a drop of family blood from the outset. The Harold Beauchamp of real life becomes Stanley Burnell in the story, a compound of two family names. (His mother was a Miss Stanley, his wife's paternal grandmother a Miss Burnell.) Granny Dyer becomes Mrs. Fairfield, or Beauchamp Anglicised, and Aunt Belle (whose name was Isabel) becomes Beryl; Vera then turns into Isabel, and Chaddie (short for Charlotte) into Lottie. And the comic uncle, Jonathan Trout—a jocular derivation from Waters? Not quite. A great-aunt of the Dyer sisters, another Miss Burnell, of Plymouth, was married in 1814 to a Baptist missionary, Bro. Thomas Trowt.[14]

The system went beyond the family. The original of Mrs. Samuel Josephs was Mrs. Walter Nathan, but her father was Mr. Joseph Joseph. The lower orders, such as Pat and Alice, and Thorndon's Chinese fruiterer, Chung Wah, kept their names unchanged.

The transformation which the story later underwent has been well described in Miss Sylvia Berkman's critical study of Katherine Mansfield. Countless minute changes were made to sharpen an image, compress an episode or clarify a situation, and one whole episode was dropped. One difficulty, with the character of Beryl, was never quite resolved, for personal reasons noted by Katherine herself on the manuscript. Beside the passage in which Beryl, after writing a very false letter to a friend, is sitting in her room thinking about her true self and her false self, this note occurs:

> What is it that I'm getting at? It is really Beryl's *Sosie*. The fact that for a long time now, she hasn't been even able to control her second self:

it's her second self who now controls her . . . There was a kind of radiant being who wasn't either spiteful or malicious, of whom she'd had a glimpse—whose very voice was different to hers. . . . . I want to get at all this *through* her, just as I got at Linda *through* Linda. To suddenly merge her into herself.[15]

It seems that *The Aloe,* with all else that it was, was an attempt by Katherine "to suddenly merge her into herself"—as if, for Katherine, learning to write was learning to be. It is one more instance of the close relationship, in her case, between the personal life and the creative work.

"You will be glad our darling Leslie was the means of bringing poor old Kass *right* into the fold again," Annie Beauchamp wrote to a friend while Katherine was at Bandol, "and she writes to us all most loving letters, she *adored* Leslie."[16] Already, in December, Katherine had committed to her *Journal* a significant remark about wishing to embrace her father; and two months later he again increased her allowance. The Turnbull Library, in Wellington, has some typed copies of letters from Katherine to her father which he deposited there toward the end of his life (he died in 1938). Among them is one that she wrote on 6 March 1916:

My dearest Father,
This morning I received from you a letter telling me that you had instructed the Manager of the Bank to pay me £13 a month instead of £10 as formerly. I scarcely know how to thank you for yet another proof of your unexampled generosity to me, darling. It puts my finance on such a secure and easy footing at a time when so many are in want and it gives me a very real feeling of security and added comfort. Thank you a thousand times, my darling Father, I am deeply grateful. . . . .
Our dear one, when he was here seemed to bring me so near to you, and talking of you with him I realised afresh each time how much I love and admire, and how very much you mean to me. Forgive my childish faults my generous darling Daddy, and keep me in your heart. . . . .
Well dearest and best of fathers, I must end this letter. Again from my heart I thank you. I think of you every day, and I long for the time when we shall meet again. God bless you darling.

Always your own child
Kass

On first seeing longer passages from that letter in 1953, Murry regarded them as faked.* It is true that they do not sound like Katherine's letters as he knew them, but I think that apart from one phrase she wrote them just as they are, using phrases that Beauchamp would understand—"secure and easy footing," "when so many are in want," "our dear one," etc. The phrase to be excepted is "the Manager of the Bank." To her father she would have written "Mr. Kay" (as she does farther down), but this would have seemed to Beauchamp to need explaining. Anxious to be helpful, he probably inserted it as naïvely as he withheld the originals of the letters. One original letter to him does exist, and is given in full on pages 348–50. In its light, Murry's charge against Beauchamp can hardly stand.

The Lawrences, almost as soon as they got to Cornwall, had decided to stay on there, and Lawrence had started urging Murry to come and join him. They would all find "a nice place where one can be happy," he said, and live there in peace, "having nothing to do with the world, no connection." But he wanted a relationship (with Murry at any rate) that was based on *purpose* and not on the personal. As he wrote to Katherine: "I am tired of this insistence on the *personal* element: personal truth, personal reality. . . . . I don't want a purely personal relation with him; he is a man, therefore our relation should be based on *purpose:* not upon that which we *are,* but upon that which we wish to bring to pass." They mustn't be forever fingering over their own souls, or the souls of their acquaintances, but trying to create a new life, a new common life, "in unanimity."[17]

It was very confusing, to say the least: "no connection with the world," yet based on *purpose,* underlined. Based on *purpose,* underlined, yet not in the consciousness—only in the unconsciousness. Since Murry was a man, *therefore* it should be impersonal. No fingering of souls, and yet "unanimous"—and so on round and round, without a centre, without respect for the roots and meanings of the words involved; and very insistent, though "tired of this insistence."

---

*"The only letters of K. which make me *thoroughly* uncomfortable are those to her father. They are so obviously faked. But you are quite right. It was his lack of generosity of heart which upset her, not his closeness about money; and his utter lack of appreciation of her work."—J.M.M. to the author, 18 September 1953.

Katherine didn't want to go. She was very fond of Lawrence, but afraid of the disturbance of his mind, and afraid of Frieda, too, whom she saw as the cause of it; even more afraid of Lawrence's latest pair of disciples, Philip Heseltine and the Armenian writer Dikran Kouyoumdjian (later well known as the composer Peter Warlock and the novelist Michael Arlen). They, at this stage, were both included in the scheme, though both were soon to fall out with Lawrence, or he with them. Nothing more was heard, for the time being, of the Indian law student, Suhrawardy.

By the end of February—just as Katherine was starting on *The Aloe* —the Murrys had capitulated, though not because of Lawrence. Conscription for single men had been introduced, making Murry, a single man with short sight, liable for non-combatant service. For that reason alone he had to return to England. On the twenty-sixth Katherine was writing to Lady Ottoline: "I am thankful that the Armenian has gone but I wish he had taken Heseltine with him. . . . . What a pity it is that dear Lorenzo sees rainbows around so many dull people and pots of gold in so many mean hearts."[18] And Murry added, in a postscript: "We are going to stay with the Lawrences for ever and ever as perhaps you know; I daresay eternity will last the whole of the summer." Soon Heseltine also left.

The Lawrences then found the group of stone cottages known as Higher Tregerthen, near Zennor, on Cornwall's northern coast, which form the scene of the next chapter. For themselves they had taken a small cottage facing the sea, for £5 a year, and there was a longer one, standing at right angles to it, which the Murrys could have for £16. There was a tower at one end of it which at that time had a castellated top. "I call it already Katherine's house, Katherine's tower," wrote Lawrence eagerly.

It was only twelve strides from one house to the other—they would be able to talk from the windows! They could have a maid, and later on perhaps Heseltine could have a room in the Murrys' house. There would be lambs skipping about like little explosions, and seagulls fighting with the ravens, and sometimes a fox, and a ship on the sea. "We count on you as our only two *tried* friends, real and permanent and truly blood kin," wrote Lawrence on 11 March. "I know we shall be happy this summer." Frieda told Katherine that all she wanted now was "to *live* without any more soul-harassing. . . . . just let's live like lilies in the field."[19]

Toward the end of March, Murry was informing Lady Ottoline that they hoped to see her soon. The little iron gate of the Villa Pauline clanged for the last time, and soon they were back in England, with Murry's book on Dostoevsky finished, and *Prelude* existing in the rough.

Sporadically, from Bandol, Katherine had been exchanging jokey letters with Corporal Frederick Goodyear, who was now in the meteorological office, GHQ, BEF, suffering from ineffable boredom and, like many another soldier, tragically in need of converse with a woman. (In fact he had probably been in love with Katherine for some time past.) "You wrote some good stuff in the *Signature*," said Goodyear in a letter to her of 14 February—a letter written in an Armstrong hut with the aid of a little champagne and stout. "I understand that Lady Ottoline was so impressed that she invited you to her bed." Was it so? And was it true that Lawrence had sent her a certificate of consummation? Was she consummated? Or Jack only? He had come to mock—could she make him remain to pray? "You of the vivid pen, have you ever saved a soul? What's the good of writing if you don't? Save mine then."

As a matter of fact he had only one regret—that she had never been "brought to bed of tennis" by him. He could imagine no higher bliss than to be "discussing art and life with you and our kidneys in bed. May your breasts blossom and your navel never grow less." STEADY! He wasn't as tight as all that. But he greatly missed her talent for *double entendre*, which made conversation with her one of the consolations of life. Anyway, she was a genuine old darling, for all her mendacity, and he would like to get something more like a letter than the postcard, wrongly addressed, which he had just received from her.

He got one later in the month, which hasn't survived. He answered it on 28 February. "Our intellectual sympathy is, I think, near enough perfect," he wrote this time, but insufficient intimacy had prevented its appearing properly: "All the time I have known you you have been fixt up with Murry, and that's been final so far as I was concerned, though it has made things very awkward between us." Now, in the army, he had deteriorated, and lost his taste for everything: "My ordinary vice of masturbation is greatly accentuated by this life; and I am very doubtful whether anything worth having will survive." He was always surprised that he continued to exist at all: "The rest of my sexual life has been 5 whores, 1 engagement, several interminable sentimental friendships. Like the hedgehog, I've never been buggered at all." In fact he was in a chronic surly temper with life, and "Personally, I think everything everywhere is bunkum."

The unposted letter from Katherine to Goodyear which is printed with excisions in the *Journal* was perhaps a draft of the reply he got: "Yes, you're bad tempered, suspicious and surly," she wrote (4 March 1916). "And if you think I flung my bonnet over you as a possible mill, my lad, you're mistook. So shut up about your Five Whores *and* a Hedgehog and send me no more inventories of those marbil halls wherein of aforetime they did delight to wander." And she went off into an amusing passage on how she loathed French furniture—so uncomfortable that bed was the only place: "I quite understand the reason for what is called French moral laxity. You're simply forced into bed—no matter with whom."

This wasn't posted, and what she did send cannot be known; but on 9 April—by which time the Murrys were with the Lawrences in Cornwall—Goodyear in all sobriety sent Katherine a criticism of her character and attitudes that went much deeper than Orage's of four years earlier, and sprang from a wish to put her right, because he was fond of her. "I shall proceed to lecture you a little," he wrote after a jocular preamble, "along obvious lines." He then recalls their rue de Tournon days, and the flitting from Baron's Court:

> The demand you used to make on life was prodigious. You were like Froissart's knight who found that to rob and pill was a good life. You boasted of nothing more wholeheartedly than your successful lies and cheats. You openly and avowedly despised human beings in their social compacts and considered them fair game. Now you say humanity is on the whole detestable, which is your old attitude in a more humble phase. You still cut yourself off, but admit (by experience, I take it) a force, where previously you recognized none. Therefore you have two courses open to you, so far as I can see: (1) reunion (2) back to the old superior contempt.

The first was a religious sort of gesture on quasi-Christian lines; the second was more philosophic and stoical. If she was right before, she could be right now by simply wrapping herself up in herself:

But you hanker after and greatly feel union with external things. You seem to live happily and egalitarianly enough in a republic of sounds and scents and grasses and dews and café-mirrors and odd things and appearances generally. I don't see why you should draw the line at man, only another phase of nature, unless you remain *plus sentimentale qu'artiste*, like Mme. Bovary, about these sunsets and things.

Was it the brutal competitive W. L. Georgishness of man that repelled her? Every blade of grass, every delicious bud was just the same; in fact, the more delicious it appeared, the better presumably it was succeeding: "It seems to me that the literary significance of people and things is too thin a thing to live on. It reduces life to a single process of criticism. Sell your criticism and there is something added—a potentially growing process."

He didn't think an absorbing sense of the literary significance of things helped anyone to write, not when it was self-conscious. An active life of some description (she had expressed a wish for an active life) would therefore likely enough repose her "overtwanged inelastic literary nerve."

By an active life he did not necessarily mean a life of physical activity, but one in which there was an external aim, "apart from spectating or enjoying or detesting."

The game of "Do you remember," he added in a closing exhortation, should certainly be sidetracked somehow:

You will always do plenty of it. It is a case of burning your boats, mentally, every morning, when you get up. It is there that an active life comes in useful. But of course it should be used entirely for your own purposes—it needn't attract you for its own sake. Send a further sample of water (spiritually speaking) for analysis.

No one who knew her—neither Lawrence, who saw much more of her, nor Orage, nor Murry of course—ever described more acutely the defects of Katherine's attitudes to life and nature and art than Goodyear in this letter. "Your overtwanged inelastic literary nerve"—in four words, there she is.

Goodyear had actually known Katherine as a writer longer than Murry had, since Orage had printed a piece of his in the same issue as her own first contribution. "When I first read the German Pension in the *New Age*," he told her, "I said to myself, 'If this woman were young, she could be absolutely the Thing. But I have no doubt that she is married, 45, climacteric.' So I never wrote then. Probably I shouldn't anyhow, as it wasn't the sort of thing I could do."

They met only once, and briefly, after this, while Goodyear was on leave in England. But Katherine kept these letters (and so did Murry) and they are now in Wellington.[20] Later in 1916, evidently with a feeling that he had missed the marriage he would have liked, Goodyear decided to obtain a commission in order to get to the Front and put an end to boredom. It was his turn to feel cynical.

CHAPTER XI

Cornwall, 1916

Cari Miêi Ragazzi: I am very glad you are happy. That is the right way to be happy—a nucleus of love between a man and a woman, and let the world look after itself. It is the last folly, to bother about the world. One should be in love, and be happy—no more. Except that if there are friends who will help the happiness on, tant mieux. Let us be happy together.
—Lawrence to the Murrys at the Villa Pauline,
17 January 1916

In response to Lawrence's affectionate urgings the Murrys went down to Zennor early in April 1916, and for more than a year then Katherine wrote nothing which she thought worth keeping. No stories exist which belong to her five months spent in Cornwall, nor any journal entries, and there followed seven months in London almost totally barren of writing. Did Goodyear's home-truths destroy her faith in her pen through all that time? But there are other factors, too: Celtic Cornwall, "so full of huge stones," and something equally alien and disturbing in the Lawrences; and then, this business of always moving, though always with some good *reason* for the move.

"Like an emigrant, Katherine looked." The words are Frieda's, in her book, *Not I, but the Wind . . .*, where she describes how the Murrys arrived, "sitting on a cart, high up on all the goods and chattels, coming down the lane to Tregerthen"—and *we* are reminded of that other emigrant Arthur Beauchamp, whose hens used to offer their legs for tying when the sounds of packing were heard.

By a conservative count Murry and Katherine had now moved sixteen times since they came together in 1912; but Katherine, for her part, had amassed a total of twenty-nine postal addresses since coming to London in 1908 (this is not counting her jaunts to Belgium or her escapades with Garnet Trowell), and since the meeting with Lawrence there had been six moves somehow influenced by him. A seventh was not far off. Perhaps heredity is irrelevant, given four such products of the age as the Murrys and the Lawrences. And yet those ancestral hens keep turning on their backs.

The goods and chattels were a few belongings fetched from Acacia Road. Taking a room at the Tinner's Arms in Zennor ("I shall never like this place," said Katherine), they bought some cheap old furniture in St. Ives, told the postman to bring their mail to the Lawrences', and set to work on the other cottage with distemper and paint and Lawrence's enthusiastic help.

The two slate-roofed structures that constituted Higher Tregerthen had once contained five small worker's dwellings ("cottages"). In the Long House, facing eastwards along the coast, three had been knocked into one, and this was what the Murrys took for £16 a year. Of two cottages in the other building, looking down to the sea, one stood empty, but the Lawrences had taken the other—one room up, one down, with a long scullery—for £5 a year. They shared an outside privy, and you went up the hill to a spring for water. "Higher Tregerthen" distinguished the cottages from the farm, Tregerthen itself, which was down toward the sea.

Much told as the story is of what went on at Higher Tregerthen, certain elements of it have been long suppressed, because of Murry's loyalty to Lawrence. Principally, there were letters of Katherine's which he never felt free to publish as long as Frieda was alive; but other suppressions have also been at work. We have seen already how Murry viewed the relationship between Lawrence and Frieda at Chesham, when she spoke of his "taking her as a dog does a bitch." Those words could simply be general in meaning, but in the light of the "Excurse" chapter in *Women in Love,* and other evidence, they are probably more specific. They almost certainly do mean "from behind." Whatever was wrong, the Murrys believed that the blame lay with Frieda entirely. ("What a great fat *sod* she is," Katherine had written once to Jack. "Lawrence has got queer blind places, hasn't he?"[1])

At present, Frieda was raging against Lady Ottoline, to whom in the week of the Murrys' arrival she posted a violent outburst[2] accusing her of "arrogance and insolence" and of wanting "some sort of unwholesome relation" with Lawrence.* A few days later the postman gave the Lawrences, as usual, some mail for the Murrys. There was a letter from Garsington, and Frieda, apparently, either steamed it open while the Murrys were busy painting, or simply by clairvoyance knew that her outburst was enclosed; for an hour or so later Lawrence said point-blank to the Murrys, "O. sent you Frieda's letter."

Lawrence was completely on Frieda's side in the matter (Murry wrote), and had spent a long time trying to convince him and Katherine that their remaining friends with Ottoline was black treachery to him. So they might be going to drift into a "final rumpus" with her, though for Lawrence's sake they would do their best not to.

Then Murry tried to "diagnose their condition" for Ottoline. He said that Lawrence now seemed in many ways much younger and happier, but he had bought this happiness at a price, and had quite definitely lost something: "I feel that he will not create anything very much in the future." (Lawrence in fact had begun rewriting *Women in Love* in the other cottage, with its symbolic treatment of two couples who do bear some resemblance to these four.)

As for Frieda: "Really we are frightened of her." She was sure to break out against the Murrys sooner or later, because she felt they imperilled her present triumph over Lawrence. They had been trying to like her for three years, but her "ultimate vulgarity" appalled them both, and was probably the reason for her turning against Ottoline: being no longer married to a man who could keep three servants she was *déclassée*, and despised herself. They would write again soon when they got into their cottage; at present they were "suspended over the abyss," living at the inn.[3]

It remains to add that this was the moment at which the postman brought Katherine her "spiritual analysis" from Goodyear, which was followed by the longest period of sterility (or of self-discipline) in her writing life.

Frieda's rage apart, there was at first contentment in the "community." Only in January Lawrence had been calling Murry "one of the

---

*"Frieda wrote to you. I am glad she said what she feels. That is always best. Then if anything remains, it can begin to grow, free from the weeds."—Lawrence to Lady Ottoline, 7 April 1916.

very few people I count on," and now the two would march off happily to St. Ives with rucksacks on their backs, Lawrence, like a friendly gardener, making Murry feel that there was something in him which could grow. But that which Lawrence really wanted from Jack was something he didn't understand, and shrank from when it came to his notice. This is when Lawrence started talking about *Blutbrüderschaft* and hinting at the need for some inviolable blood-sacrament between them, as in the novel; and Murry drew back, having not the slightest idea—though "The Prussian Officer" might have given it to him—of what that rejection might do to Lawrence.

Today, when the subject can be discussed more easily than it could in Murry's lifetime, the facts fall into place. Some of them, however, derive from a source unknown to Murry all his life—the suppressed Prologue to *Women in Love*, which Lawrence had possibly written in the other cottage while waiting for his orderly to arrive.

In a critical context it would of course be wrong to speak as though Rupert Birkin "is" Lawrence, or Gerald Crich "is" Murry, in *Women in Love*. But this is biography; and Lawrence in fact was sitting in the other cottage writing a novel in which there is a man, like him, who longs to be able to love women but cannot (because with women he feels there is either too much spiritual sisterly love, or else only a "brutal, callous sort of lust"); and that this same character feels attracted to two kinds of men—the white-skinned, keen-limbed men with eyes like blue ice, and the other kind "with dark eyes that one can enter and plunge into," the "dark-skinned, supple, night-smelling men," at one with the "viscous universal heavy darkness." The words come from the Prologue,[4] first published in 1968.

Later, in the novel itself, when Rupert longs for a "further conjunction," the *Blutbrüderschaft* scene occurs, with Gerald withdrawing his wrist from the threat of Cornish flints, or the viscous universal heavy darkness or whatever it was. It is a fact that something like this scene took place at Higher Tregerthen.

Meanwhile Katherine, depressed because "everything seems to be made of boulders,"* felt that her Villa Pauline Jack was being drawn away from her, and drawn, moreover, toward a way of looking at life which she found absurd. "I *shall never* see sex in trees, sex in running

---

*From a letter to Lady Ottoline. The cottages had that appearance, especially the end wall of the Lawrences', which Katherine's tower overlooked.

brooks, sex in stones and sex in everything," she wrote to Beatrice Campbell;[5] but there is nothing whatever in her letters that could be read as hinting at *homo*sexuality, which seems to have been as far from her mind as it was from Murry's. Moreover, she held Frieda responsible for all the "symbols."

Finding that if he turned toward Lawrence, Katherine became engulfed by a sense of "belonging to no one here," and that with Katherine miserable he was only half a man, Murry withdrew toward her. The effect on Lawrence was disastrous. He had for some time been subject to rages that were in some way connected with his illness, and these now became more frequent.

The worst explosion—its uglier details always suppressed by Murry —took place in the first week of May, prompting two descriptions by Katherine, one for Koteliansky and the other for Lady Ottoline, neither of which Murry ever published.

As Katherine told Koteliansky, she and Frieda were not speaking at present, and Lawrence was a million miles away, all because she couldn't stand the situation between them. She didn't know which disgusted her most—when they were loving and playing with each other, or when they were roaring and Lawrence was pulling out Frieda's hair and saying, "I'll cut your bloody throat, you bitch." He wasn't really healthy any more. If he was contradicted about *anything* he got into a frenzy, which went on until he was so exhausted that he couldn't stand, and had to go to bed. Whatever the disagreement, he said it was because you had gone wrong in your sex and belonged to an obscene spirit. She thought he was suffering from "quite genuine monomania at the moment," through having endured so much from Frieda.[6]

On Friday 5 May Katherine went across to them for tea, and most unfortunately mentioned Shelley. "I think that his Skylark thing is awful footle," said Frieda. "You only say that to show off," said Lawrence. "It's the only thing of Shelley's that you know." Then Frieda: "*Now* I have had enough. Out of my house, you little God Almighty you. I've had enough of you. Are you going to keep your mouth shut or aren't you?" And Lawrence: "I'll give you a dab on the cheek to quiet you, you dirty hussy," etc. Katherine fled—the whole twelve strides to home.

That evening Lawrence came over to dinner with Katherine and Jack, but Frieda wouldn't come (in the version sent to Ottoline[7]). "I'll cut her throat if she comes near this table," said Lawrence. After dinner, Frieda appeared; in the dusk, she walked up and down outside. Suddenly Lawrence made "a kind of horrible blind rush at her," and they began to scream and scuffle. He "kept his eyes on her and *beat* her," he beat her head and face and breast and pulled out her hair, while she screamed for Jack, "Protect me! Save me!" Then they dashed into the Murrys' kitchen and raced around the table—Lawrence quite green with fury. He stood back on his heels and swung his arm forward, and "thumped the big soft woman." "And though I was dreadfully sorry for L. I didn't feel an atom of sympathy for Frieda. . . . . Murry told me afterwards he felt just the same—he just didn't feel that a woman was being beaten."

Then Lawrence fell into one chair, Frieda into another. No one said a word. "A silence fell except for Frieda's sobs and sniffs." Lawrence could scarcely breathe. He sat staring at the floor, biting his nails. After a long time Lawrence looked up and asked Murry a question about French literature. Murry replied to it. Little by little the three drew up to the table. Frieda poured herself some coffee. In half an hour they had almost *recovered,* and were remembering, "*mutually* remembering a certain very rich, very good, but very extravagant macaroni cheese they had once eaten."

Next day Frieda stayed in bed. Lawrence took her meals up the little stairs and started trimming a hat for her, and by afternoon she was singing (*intentionally,* says Katherine), with Lawrence joining in. She seemed to thrive on a beating, and to take some Awful Relish in it; for she began to make herself dresses, and put flowers in her hair, and sustain a girlish prattle with Lawrence "which left Murry and me speechless with amazement and disgust—disgust especially!"

So their relationship was over. The "dear man" in him whom they all had loved (so Katherine wrote to Ottoline) was hidden away, absorbed, completely lost—"like a little gold ring in that immense German Christmas pudding which is Frieda. And with all the appetite in the world one cannot eat one's way through Frieda to find him. One simply looks and waits for someone to come with a knife and cut her up into the smallest pieces that L. may see the light and shine again. But he does not want that to happen at all."

In all of Murry's and Katherine's letters there is hardly a word against Lawrence himself. For him, all is sympathy and sorrow. The Murrys then began looking for somewhere else to live, and the two couples withdrew somewhat to their respective cottages, each pair thankful that its way of loving was not like the other's, and each employing the word "disgust." As in the novel: "The hot narrow intimacy between man and wife was abhorrent. The way they shut their doors, these married people, and shut themselves into their own exclusive alliance with each other, even in love, disgusted him."

And so Gudrun and Gerald were portrayed as headed for damnation. As to their "originals," the letters of one, at least, now make it all seem much simpler and more human. Jack and Wig at that time simply loved each other, as human beings sometimes do, and wanted to be on their own. But that, to the man who was writing *Women in Love* just then (with Frieda in the room) was abhorrent and revolting.

Although it has been widely accepted that Gudrun and Gerald were portrayals of Murry and Katherine, they didn't see that for themselves when the book came out; which perhaps is not surprising when the outline of the story (Gudrun leaves Gerald for Loerke) derives from the Cholesbury play (Katherine leaves Murry for Gertler) and not from their own real lives. There are only a few passages, mostly near the beginning, which seem to have been written by Lawrence with a picture of Katherine in his mind. Gudrun is a sculptress with a liking for small things, and she likes to watch people with objective curiosity, to place them in their true light and settle them forever until they are "finished, sealed and stamped and finished with, for her." Lawrence on Katherine, perhaps—though it hardly compares with Goodyear on Katherine.

As for her "overtwanged inelastic literary nerve," it was reposed by this active life, and lay quite slack. A letter to Beatrice Campbell, written in a black mood when the roof was leaking and the floor was studded with Cornish pitchers to catch the drops, said that she had just re-read *The Aloe*, "and now I can't believe I wrote it."[8]

Using the dampness as an excuse, the Murrys went house-hunting on the softer, leafier south coast, and thirty miles away at Mylor, on the shore of the inlet known as the Carrick Roads, they found a charming cottage for rent at £18 a year. Leaving Lawrence and Frieda to watch the seagulls fighting the ravens, they moved in the middle of June. In *Between Two Worlds* Murry says that he parted from Lawrence with the feeling that he had said good-bye to him forever. They were meeting again, for a reason not foreseen, within three weeks.

* * *

Sunnyside Cottage, which stood among trees on a tidal creek not far from the village of Mylor Bridge, was one of the prettiest places of abode the Murrys ever knew. It had a kitchen garden sloping gently to the water's edge, and beyond the water, peaceful farmlands. You could keep a boat there and go sailing, as Murry was longing to do. His only source of income, however, being his reviewing for the *T.L.S.*, he contented himself with a hired dinghy. He rowed back from Falmouth with a boat full of second-hand French books, and read and read; but Katherine, finding him now withdrawn from her, didn't write and write. Once more there was something wrong between them; she wanted to escape again, and within ten days she was informing Koteliansky, in a sort of coded private language, that she was coming up to London, and when she saw him she would tell him of her "plans."⁹

Then Frederick Goodyear, home on leave from France, came down to stay. He had leave because he had accepted a commission in order to get to the Front. Ostensibly, he had come to see both Murry and Katherine; more probably, in fact, he had come for one last indulgence of his gallantly hidden (or perhaps not hidden) love for Katherine; and finding her discontented, it seems that he planted in her mind the idea of going to Denmark, a country which he knew.

While there he expressed a wish to see Lawrence, which meant that Murry had to take him across to Zennor for a night (they slept on the floor in "Katherine's tower"). In this way Lawrence heard what was afoot, and told Koteliansky that the Murrys had made "some sort of contract whereby each of them is free." Katherine also used that word in writing of her "plans" to Kot: she told him now that she was coming up to stay with the Campbells and find some rooms, and she thought of going to Denmark for September; life now felt wonderful and different, she said, "for at last I am free again."¹⁰ Exactly how much this had to do with Goodyear can't be known; and Murry's own account of the time at Mylor, though it hints at the domestic strain, gives no hint of an outside cause.

Lawrence's interpretation, offered to Koteliansky on 10 July, was that Katherine wanted to run away from herself—"but also from Murry, which complicates matters." Perhaps a sojourn in Denmark might be useful, he remarked. "After that, I do wish she could learn to be still—and alone." It was all very well for Lawrence: he had a book under way.

To mention what was *really* in the background of these personal events means seeming to renounce all notion of proportion. Goodyear went to Mylor about the first week of July. It was, of course, on 1 July 1916 that the British army launched its calamitous offensive on the Somme, perhaps the most destructive act of war the world had ever known; and to get over there as soon as possible had now become Goodyear's foremost thought. On the visit to Zennor he shocked Lawrence deeply with his cheerful nihilism. He was bored, simply bored, with his job in the meteorological office of the Royal Engineers, and *wanted* to get to the Front. At Lawrence's incredulity he merely laughed, with his cheerful snorting laugh. The only way was to get a commission; he wouldn't come back, but what did it matter? Life, he told Katherine's *husband* when at Mylor, was a boring business anyhow.

Murry was very fond of Goodyear, and had, like others, expected much of him in the future. That he felt depressed to hear him talk like that, with the carnage on the Somme just started, is not surprising. A letter of Katherine's written some weeks later looks back on the visit with misery.[11] No doubt the cottage had been filled with lacerated feelings for all three of them.

Meanwhile Katherine had arranged, as part of her escape plans, to pay her first visit to that wartime refuge of the arts and the peaceable conscience, Lady Ottoline Morrell's Garsington. She went up to London on 8 July, being met at Paddington by Koteliansky, and after spending a few nights with the Campbells in St. John's Wood she went to Garsington. A letter which Murry received at Mylor shows in what annoyance she had gone off from him. Koteliansky, her secret friend, understood that she was "leaving" Jack, and discussed the fact with Gertler, who predicted her prompt return.[12]

Since the Garsington visit opened a whole new chapter in Katherine's life we had better pause a moment, notwithstanding all the descriptions and the travesties that now are so well known, to consider what Garsington was. Some loosely think of it today as a part of "Bloomsbury," which it emphatically was not.[13]

The Morrells—that is, Lady Ottoline and her Liberal MP husband Philip Morrell—had formerly lived in Bedford Square, which is geographically in Bloomsbury of course; but they had never been —nor had they wished to be—a part of the "Bloomsbury group." Both, in spite of some individual friendships, were as much observers of the Bloomsbury phenomenon as were Katherine and Murry.

The Elizabethan manor house of Garsington, with its 1,500 acres of land, was a bike-ride from Oxford, not merely for students of those days, but for Lady Ottoline herself. The Morrells had actually bought it before the war, but had only been able to take possession in 1915, and they had done so then in the hope of making it a wartime refuge for artists and pacifists, including Lady Ottoline's former lover, Bertrand Russell.

By now, in 1916, a number of conscientious objectors had been installed in various cottages in the grounds, nominally as agricultural labourers, in the terms of their exemption. Virginia Woolf's brother-in-law Clive Bell was one of these—*echt* Bloomsbury indeed, like Lytton Strachey, who was a frequent visitor; but Dorothy Brett, decidedly one of Bloomsbury's outsiders, was also much in the house—so much in fact that she almost seemed to live there. Mark Gertler and Carrington, pursuer and pursued, were also in and out. Lawrence, overruled by Frieda because she hated Lady Ottoline, had earlier declined the offer of a cottage; the young Aldous Huxley, exempt from military service because of his eyesight, was soon to move in as a resident; Bertrand Russell was a constant visitor; and hordes of others came down for weekends—being joined now in July by "Katherine Mansfield," whose exact relationship to the wispy figure of Middleton Murry was something one had to establish by tactful inquiry.

The guests on that particular weekend had included (according to Lady Ottoline's little green silk visitors' book), Lytton Strachey and Carrington, David Garnett, Fredegond Shove, G. F. Short, and J. T. Sheppard (later Provost of King's College, Cambridge; at present working in "MI7d," a department of the War Office). Those are the ones who signed the book; but Strachey wrote to Virginia Woolf that he, for his part, had lost count of the arrivals and had gone into a trance from which he was only awakened by the stamping of thirty feet and the frenzied strains of the pianola playing desperate ragtime. The paragraph that follows, the first known "Bloomsbury" account of Katherine, shows how she could expect to be regarded in that circle:

Among the rout was "Katherine Mansfield"—if that's her real name— I could never quite make sure. Have you ever heard of her? Or read any of her productions? She wrote some rather—in fact distinctly—bright storyettes in a wretched little thing called the *Signature*, which you may have seen, under the name of Matilda Berry. She was decidedly an interesting creature, I thought—very amusing and sufficiently mysterious.

She had said some flattering things about *The Voyage Out*, and wanted to meet its author, so Strachey had said he "thought it might be managed," for he did think that Virginia might find her entertaining: "I may add that she has an ugly impassive mask of a face—cut in wood, with brown hair and brown eyes very far apart; and a sharp and slightly vulgarly-fanciful intellect sitting behind it." To which Mrs. Woolf replied that Katherine Mansfield had been "dogging her footsteps for three years," but she had never met her or read her stories.[14]

Lady Ottoline herself has also described those weekends, in her memoirs. "They all used to rush in on a Friday or a Saturday, some by motor bikes, some by train," she writes, in an account which characteristically shows far more generosity than those that some of her guests have left—and far more recognition, too, of the role that was played by her devoted household staff (her middle-class guests describe their visits as though the servants never existed).

The farm supplied the ample food, but even the manor house had not enough rooms and beds for *all* the guests, nor modern plumbing either. One fact that seems to have escaped research is that Garsington had only one bathroom and one water-closet, both upstairs, for which the water was manually raised each day by one of the gardeners, who spent an hour or so at a semi-rotary pump attached to an outside wall. It fell to the servants every morning to empty all those "overflowing jordans" which Carrington somewhere mentions in a letter.

On a summer weekend, after crowding round the table for a meal, the guests would clamour for bathing suits, says Lady Ottoline (these apparently were provided, rather than brought along), and then would splash about in the ornamental pond that served as a swimming pool—a somewhat slimy swimming pool, but it was better than the trenches; after which they would sit or lie about, "endlessly talking, talking."[15]

Can we hear a sample of that endless talk? Thanks to Katherine, I think we can. An uncollected *New Age* piece of hers, published ten months later, is probably the sharpest recollection of it that exists.

A group of five young men, clever young Clives and Davids and Aldouses, are having no end of an argument in a big shadowy drawing-room. Two are hugging their knees on the floor while one sprawls on a sofa, cutting a French book with a jade paper-knife. All are tremendously at their ease, while "Marigold," their aureate hostess (Lady Ottoline used henna on her hair), murmurs from time to time, "How true that is," or "Do you really think so?" Their talk is of France, though hardly of what was happening on the Somme:

> *4th Gentleman:* But look here, all I wanted to say is that the lack of prudery in France merely seems to me to prove that the French do believe that man is *au fond* a rational animal. You don't dispute that, do you? I mean—well—damn it all! their literature's based on it. Isn't it?
>
> *2nd Gent:* And that, according to you, explains why they seek their inspiration, their very inspiration, in realism. Does it?
>
> *4th Gent:* (superbly): Of course it does. Absolutely. How else are you going to explain it?
>
> *1st Gent:* Then a nation that's "got prudery," as the Americans would say, is a nation that believes man is not a rational animal?
>
> *5th Gent:* (very bitterly): There are things, say the English, which are not to be talked about. *Fermez la porte, s'il vous plait.*
>
> *3rd Gent:* (greatly excited): But look here—half a minute—don't go too fast; this is damned interesting. Now we really are getting at something. If what you say is true, then prudery is a step towards real art —what? For what do we mean by prudery? Prudery is false shame, the negative to real shame, which again is, as it were, the negative to reverence. Reverence being the positive quality, the thing that great art's got to have—what?[16]

Did Katherine flee from that? She had arrived on Thursday, 13 July, evidently meaning to stay for some days, but even before the weekend she had written to both Lawrence and Beatrice Campbell, pointedly informing them that she would be back in Mylor on the Monday. Whatever was behind this sudden change, she evidently did become the Prudent Wife of some of her minor stories, *Brave Love* included; and Gertler, in reporting to Koteliansky that she had already left when he arrived at Garsington, recalled foreseeing as much, to which Koteliansky replied, "Well, your maxim about couples came once more true."[17] They were probably all remembering the Carco escapade.

The offensive on the Somme—"ninety miles of uproar," as the *Times* described it—was in its third disastrous week as Katherine left the lawns and ponds of Garsington and returned to Jack at Mylor. On 1 July, 20,000 British soldiers had been killed between dawn and night; over the next three months, 400,000 more fell to the machine guns or the shells, or died of stinking gangrene in the sweltering tin-roofed sheds in which that summer's wounded lay. In quick succession came news of the deaths of two friends of Murry's youth.[18] If truthful descriptions had been printed in the papers of what was going on, people in England, enjoying that beautiful August, perhaps could hardly have believed them. Goodyear was still in training at Newmarket, among his papers being a piece of verse entitled "Confessions of a Meteorologist," written at some time in this appalling year. Here are its closing lines, from the British Museum copy of his *Letters and Remains*, the pages of which remained uncut until the present author sadly opened them a year or two ago:

> *Yet a little time for sorrow—*
> *I'll be more decayed tomorrow.*
> *Slow and sweet Decomposition,*
> *Sloth and softest Inanition*
> *Stealthily I feel you grow;*
> *And the still diminished glow*
> *Welcome, as I watch my verse*
> *Retrogressively grow worse;*
> *Till at last my senses balked*
> *Tell me that enough I've talked,—*
> *Sink me to my settled term,—*
> *Time for silence and the Worm!*

As an officer in the Essex Regiment, Goodyear crossed to France in March 1917. On 17 May he wrote to his parents from a Canadian casualty clearing station near Arras, telling them that an high explosive shell had buried him in a dugout a few days earlier, his left leg had been smashed, and the foot taken off; the copy of Joyce's *Dubliners* which he had asked for had arrived, and he was "feeling better this morning."[19] But the other leg had soon to be taken off as well. On 23 May he died, having just, apparently, missed reading the beautiful closing lines of Joyce's story about those who have loved and are dead.

The war was closing in on Murry and Katherine. New call-up papers had been served on Murry in Cornwall, and while at Mylor he had gone to the Bodmin recruiting centre to be medically examined, being classified B.2. Although his eyesight ruled him out for active service, he was fit for a labour battalion, and might find himself building breakwaters at Aden. A friendly colonel said that was silly, for an Oxford man: he ought to be an interpreter, or something of that sort. Had he not some friend who could help him? So Murry wrote, as a voice out of the past, to Eddie Marsh. He was not a CO, he said, but he didn't want to be employed in tidying the Viceroy's garden at Simla. He had until 1 October to find some nationally useful job. Could Eddie arrange some introduction for him?[20]

In August, the way prepared by Marsh, Murry went up to London to see about a job in the Home Office (which he didn't get), leaving Katherine, at Mylor, wondering what would become of them. He popped down to Garsington as well, where J. M. Keynes and J. T. Sheppard also were, and a letter of Clive Bell's to his wife Vanessa provides a Bloomsbury glimpse of how things were done then in matters of this sort. Keynes was not being as helpful as he should be, said Bell, and "might have done more" for certain friends by dropping a word to a high official here and there. For example: "Murry was condemned to a labour battalion at Aden. We have all taken a great liking to Murry. Maynard was asked if he could do anything and refused. Sheppard, who came here for last weekend, immediately got him a good job at 5£ a week in the War Office."[21]

Murry's novel, *Still Life*, after many rejections, was published by Constable soon after this, to be greeted with a silence you could cut with a knife. There is not a word about it in all the Garsington correspondence, nor anything in Katherine's letters, but Lawrence did mention it to Koteliansky: "merely words, words. It is the kind of wriggling self-abuse which I can't make head or tail of."[22]

Lawrence and Frieda had in fact returned the Zennor visit by going, a little reluctantly, to Mylor for a summer's day, and something evidently went wrong—something more than the gale that nearly drowned them after their picnic upriver in the dinghy.

"He wrote me a most comminatory letter when he got home," Murry reported to Lady Ottoline, "the most violent I have ever had from him, saying that I have the same soul as Sir William Robertson. But I don't feel any the wiser, nor any the less fond of him."[23] General Robertson was Chief of the Imperial General Staff, and the drift of Lawrence's remark is no clearer now than it was to Murry, though doubtless it reflected on his willingness to serve. The letter must have been self-destructing, since Murry took care to keep all that Lawrence sent him, and this one no longer exists.

Jack's book on Dostoevsky also came out in August. Naturally, he sent a copy down to Zennor. For anyone but Murry, the acknowledgement he got would probably have ended the friendship there and then. Lawrence had "just looked in it here and there," and Murry (he implied) was digging his head in the sand to find the revelation, like the disgusting ostrich, and squirming his behind, most disgustingly. Dostoevsky, too, could nicely stick his head between the feet of Christ and waggle *his* behind in the air.

"You want to be left alone," he said. "So do I—by everybody, by the whole world, which is despicable and contemptible to me, and sickening." As for her: "I don't know what Katharine is going to do," he told Koteliansky two days later, "—and don't care. They weary me, truly."[24]

What Katherine *did* was to follow Jack to London, since his job as a translator in the War Office, at Watergate House, was to start at the beginning of September. Having nowhere to live, they split up temporarily: Katherine slept in Brett's studio, near Earl's Court, which only had one bed; and Murry went to a cheap hotel in Bedford Place. For the present, they left their bits of furniture in the cottage at Mylor, and even Katherine's box of manuscripts, including that of *The Aloe*. If she ever began to write anything in Cornwall, it hasn't survived. All the evidence would suggest that she wrote nothing there at all.

CHAPTER XII

Gower Street and Garsington

I sent the precious book back to Garsington. It made sumptuous reading.
As usual, it struck me that letters were the only satisfactory form of
literature. They give the facts so amazingly, don't they? I felt when I got
to the end as if I'd lived for years in that set. But oh dearie me I am *glad*
that I'm not *in it.*
—Lytton Strachey to Lady Ottoline Morrell,
31 October 1916[1]

Nothing that had happened in Cornwall could alter Katherine's loyalty to the Lawrence she believed in—as she proved, a few days after her return to London, in a scene which he himself promptly used in *Women in Love,* and of which the facts have always been wrongly given.

One evening she went with Koteliansky and Gertler to the Café Royal, near Piccadilly Circus—the sort of place that Lawrence contemptuously referred to as "the World." In those days it was a favourite resort of bohemians and writers, with a florid atmosphere that William Orpen's painting has preserved: narrow marble tables, turquoise columns topped by caryatids, and the faces of George Moore, Augustus John and Nina Hamnet among the patrons. Some people sitting at the same small table as our party had with them a copy of Lawrence's latest book, *Amores,* and were jeering at the poems. Katherine couldn't stand that, so she politely asked for the book, stood up, and strode with it out of the café, followed by Kot and Gertler.

Reported to Lawrence by Kot, this became the "Gudrun in the Pompadour" scene in *Women in Love,* and thanks to Murry, who allowed his "memory" to conflate that version with what he remembered of Katherine's account, it was long supposed that Philip Heseltine and Michael Arlen were the mockers that evening—they being the known "originals" of the characters in the novel. But neither was even present.

What did happen was recounted for Lady Ottoline next day by *two* of her correspondents—Mark Gertler, who was there, and Aldous Huxley, who was not. Both accounts expose the racist attitudes of Liberal England. Gertler's letter described how he and Kot and Katherine (a Polish Jew, a Ukrainian Jew, and a Colonial), finding the café packed, were obliged to sit at a table already occupied by a coloured man, "an Indian perhaps—but a weak type," whom they hardly noticed. After a time a "Long Thin White Herring of a Woman with a Terrific High Bunch of Crimson Hair" came to join him, and then another coloured man made a third:

> We immediately hated all three of them. Soon to our astonishment they began to talk "Intellectually,"—they were University Blacks—using "perfect" English very long words carefully chosen. They talked about Dostoevsky, Russia, the New Age, all in a very advanced manner. All this irritated us enough, But imagine our Hatred and Horror when the red headed peice of dried Dung produced a Volume of Lawrence's poems and commenced to discuss Lawrence with the other, in this perfect English and carefully picked, long words! We had been ragging them all the time, but now we knew something drastic must be done. We sat and thought. Suddenly Katharine leant towards them and with a sweet smile said *"Will* you let me have that Book a moment?" "Certainly" they all beamed back—even more sweetly. Imagine their horror and utter amazement when Katharine without a word more, Rose from the table, Book and all, we following most calmly—most calmly we walked out of the Café!!![2]

Katherine never did like prostitutes, or women whom she thought were prostitutes.

Lady Ottoline probably received Huxley's letter by the same mail, and read them both at breakfast. Huxley was twenty-one, and was soon to join the "manual labourers" at Garsington. By sheer coincidence he had run into one of the "University Blacks" on the morning after the episode, heard his account of it and, aware that Lady Ottoline knew him—it was the Indian law student, H. S. Suhrawardy—hastened to pass on the tale.

"London is entirely filled with the Indian population of Oxford," wrote Huxley. "These strange children with devils' faces are omnipresent. They come up on padded feet and pluck one familiarly by the sleeve in omnibuses, in railway stations, in public lavatories, in restaurants. You cannot escape them. . . . ." After some polysyllabic humour about curries, Huxley went on to relate that Suhrawardy had recognised Gertler (having met him at Garsington), but could not name the "other man and a woman." No sooner was the book in her hands, Suhrawardy said, than all three swept out and vanished in a taxi.

Lady Ottoline, understandably intrigued, told Huxley what she had heard from Gertler, so that Huxley wrote again, fishing for more information; and *this* letter was evidently sent to Katherine, who was not amused. "I am a little hazy about Suhrawadi," she replied. "Was he one of Lawrence's Bing Boys last winter?*At any rate, Huxley's languid letter doesn't tempt me dreadfully to tell him. . . . ."[3]

Meanwhile Koteliansky's account had gone to Higher Tregerthen. "Your 'Dostoevsky evening' gives me a queer contraction of the heart," wrote Lawrence (4 September 1916). "It frightens me, when I think of London, the Café Royal—you actually there, and Katharine, terror comes over me. . . . . It is a real feeling of horror." Not a word of gratitude for "Gudrun in the Pompadour"—no message of thanks for her. Still, it made good copy for the book.

It is time to leave the Lawrences to their isolation in Cornwall, but there was one more burst of animosity, with a consequence that Murry never disclosed. Shortly after the Café Royal episode Frieda came up

---

*This shows Katherine correctly remembering Suhrawardy as one of Lawrence's chosen team for Florida, but happily muddling his name perhaps with "Kouyoumdjian," and so helping to launch the episode on its sixty years of misbestowal.[4]

The musical comedy *The Bing Boys* (with George Robey and Violet Lorraine) was all the rage in 1916; and Huseyn Shaheed Suhrawardy, a Bengali Muslim hailing from what is now called Bangladesh, was a noncollegiate law student at Oxford who gained his B.C.L. with third-class honours in 1917 and later practised in Calcutta. He was the leader of the Muslim League in undivided Bengal, and one of M. A. Jinnah's main supporters. Before the partition, he was Chief Minister of Bengal, and after August 1947 he became Chief Minister of East Bengal in Pakistan.

to London for a few days. She did *not* wish to see Katherine, but she saw both Kot and Gertler, and she told them something about the Murrys (it involved "duplicity" and "meanness" on Jack's part, and was presumably connected with Katherine's deserting him at Mylor to place her confidence in Kot). "I know she will not face anything," Frieda wrote to Kot next day from Hampstead. "Yet there is so much that is good in them, must one not *fight* their dishonesty?"[5] Whatever was said, and whatever was true, the incident caused Koteliansky to break off all relations with the Murrys for the next two years.

The Murrys, too, being evidently told what Frieda had said, withdrew into silence and wouldn't write, and Lawrence told Kot (7 November 1916), "I have done with the Murries, both, for ever—so help me god." In Frieda's words: "in fact it is over, but if she comes this minute I would have to be nice with her. She has the terrible gift of nearness, she can come so close, but it's really no good in the long run!"[6] This time, it was two years before they met again.

Katherine was down at Garsington within a week of the book-snatching and sharing a room with Carrington, who wrote excitedly to Gertler: "I now possess the pink-haired whore's book for she Katherine gave it to me! What a Dostoeffsky subject!" The same letter broke the news that she and the Murrys had joined in a scheme with Brett to share J. M. Keynes's house in Gower Street, thus moving all of them to Bloomsbury, in the geographical sense at least.* Technically speaking, Brett became Keynes's tenant for the next nine months, taking the others as her lodgers, the rent being £27 10s per quarter, shared among the four. The Murrys were to live on the ground floor, close to the front door and the telephone, with Brett on the next, and Carrington in the attics.[7] Keynes's housekeeper, Miss Chapman ("Chappers"), went with the house, and lived in the basement.

Until Gower Street was vacated the Murrys stayed in Brett's studio in Logan Place, with Murry trying to adjust himself, for the first time in his life, to a regular routine, his job in MI 7d (Military Intelligence, room 7d). This meant, since Sheppard had sponsored him as a person competent in German, that he had to spend every spare minute mug-

---

*Since Clive Bell was at Garsington for the duration, and his wife, Vanessa, was now living with Duncan Grant, Keynes had decided to occupy the Bells' house in Gordon Square, with J. T. Sheppard, and to let his own house, No. 3 Gower Street.

ging up the language to conceal his deficiency from the colonel in charge, and he found himself turning into a machine, something to which his father was accustomed, but he was not. "I became an automaton," he writes in *Between Two Worlds*. "I worked desperately hard in a kind of mental stupor. Life, or what I regarded as life, had simply ceased."

In fact he had forgotten, when he wrote those words, what relief he had found in knowing Lady Ottoline—to whom, in a tortuous letter of 22 September,[8] he recklessly declared himself:

> I have at times a queer suspicion that I must be in love with you. I don't know. It's very hard to get at what I feel: so rarely do I feel towards persons any emotion more intimate than amusement or blank terror. But when I try to find a name for my feeling towards you,—then it is that I begin to suspect that I am in love with you.

So began, for Jack Murry of Wandsworth Common, a self-doubting affair of the heart that was riddled with his uncertainties as a former member of the proletariat, and entangled with his and Lady Ottoline's attitudes toward the war and toward the arts. With her, he now saw the war as part of a process that was turning human beings into machines—it hadn't taken him long to forget how the mass of men, including his own pen-pushing father, had been living for most of a century—and the two now wrote back and forth about the "other life," that shut out art, and was "nothing but a great machine." On the other hand, so Ottoline read, Bertie Russell had been coming to Gower Street, and had been admirable: "We enjoy him immensely," Murry wrote on 2 November, "and to talk with him is one, I believe, the only one of our delights, in the inspissated gloom of this abominable life." If Murry was indeed "in love" with Ottoline, that didn't mean shutting out Katherine.

By December the harmless little *amour* had become a piece of Bloomsbury gossip. "Ottoline is trying to get up an affair with Murry," wrote Clive Bell to his wife Vanessa from Garsington.[9] "She writes to him and he leaves her letters about." Whether this happened at Gower Street itself or at Watergate House, where Murry worked, is not recorded. The espionage element in Bloomsbury is one of its neglected moral aspects.

*   *   *

Number 3 Gower Street came to be known as The Ark. Its animals went in two by two, more or less, as soon as Keynes and Sheppard had moved out; and Brett, picking up all she could with her hearing-aid, kept Lady Ottoline informed of what went on. Once again, as at Beauchamp Lodge, it is a tale that needs to be told with mirrors, or perhaps with hearing-aids. No doubt the simplest telling might be simplest reading, but in this place "truth" is the aim, and the dire complexity of what follows derives from Katherine's own. More *Rashomon*, therefore.

Katherine was installed very *comfortably*, Brett wrote from The Ark to Ottoline on 2 October, and so was Carrington. But Carrington didn't like Katherine now: she suspected her of being double-faced. Besides, she had feathered her nest in The Ark too quickly and too snugly. So Brett was going to watch events with relish.[10]

Brett at the time was writing to Ottoline every day, and should probably be described as being in love with her. Ottoline for her part felt sorry for Brett—her upbringing as the daughter of Viscount Esher had been so cruel. Certainly Brett was trusted by her friend: so much so, that Ottoline shortly posted her a letter of Murry's which disclosed that he was not happy in The Ark, and because of that was "only the more sure that I am in love with you."

Well, said Brett in her reply (for Ottoline was puzzled, and hoped for elucidation), this interested her enormously, and it threw a *great* deal of light on a curious feeling *she* had had. But "for Heaven's sake gang warily with Murry!! do be careful, Murry will make love to you and I don't entirely trust either of them. . . . ." Brett could dimly see, she said, the utter darkness of Murry's present life, but why, oh why, were people dragged away from their own lives to lead the lives of others, especially such shrinking dreaming souls as Murry?

Brett then reported that Carrington was "coming round about Katherine," and for her own part she didn't think she *was* a fraud:

> She is *not* double faced I'm certain, only inclined to be witty about one —and why not? and perhaps not that when one is once a friend. You *must* come up to London for a little after Christmas Katherine and I want you so badly to come and lead a cheap low life with us, and cast your Ducalness—such lots of things to do—and oh such Wonderful things to say.

If Ottoline did come up to London she would try to get hold of Bertie Russell. He had called to see Katherine, but they were out. Toward the end of October Brett told Ottoline that there were some little queer things going on which she didn't like to *write,* and which Ottoline must on no account let out. "Old Lytton," she said, "calls at The Ark, and to our chagrin no one gets further than Katherine!! Bertie, Lytton, etc. all disappear like magic—and I have my little instrument trained to the cracks in the floor."[11]

Just then Ottoline received from Katherine a constrained, self-conscious letter, her first for some weeks, which spoke of wanting to explain why she had been so silent for so long. It was *only* because she had been so wretched and distracted, and not herself at all. The diabolical thing was that she couldn't break through and explain. How incomprehensible that must be!

Lady Ottoline found this *very* puzzling, and must have wondered what connection it had with the letters she had been getting from Murry. So this one too was posted back, to the house from which it had come. "Most interesting," said Brett's reply, "and I think I can give you the key." Poor Katherine was in a veritable hell:

> *I* think she is in *Love,* some man has risen like the dawn on her horizon like they all will all her life—the Call of the Wild is in her and she can no more resist the call when it comes than any other wild animal. Poor Katherine she is torn in two I believe— Pity for the shy gentle clinging man she lives with and the passionate desire for freedom—new life, new faces, a minute here, a minute there, the great and wonderful world— and behind her if she goes a knife left buried in Murry's heart, the loss (possibly) of valued friends—that I believe to be her particular Hell— I long, as I told you, to tell her that I understand, but I can't yet—may never.[12]

It is evident that Brett had not yet learned the identity of the man. If she had known, she would hardly have written thus to Ottoline, for it was Bertrand Russell. Nor did Ottoline guess, or at least not yet, that the man was her former lover. She did know that Russell's feelings were drifting away from her, but she did not know to whom until he explained himself some months later.[13] The fact is, he had lately met Lady Constance Malleson—the actress Colette O'Neill, married to

Miles Malleson—and the two were already deep in a passionate affair,*
unknown to Katherine of course.

Everyone knows how important was Truth to Bertrand Russell, and
to Bloomsbury, and to those who lived the good life at Garsington,
including Katherine herself, whose one aim as a writer was to get at
truth.

Ten days later Russell dined with the Murrys, telling Ottoline that
he "liked her [Katherine] again very much," and that Murry seemed
unhappy because he was "working for the war," so he had tried to
induce him to change. Then he must have asked Katherine to dine
with him, for a letter of hers is preserved among his papers, accepting
his invitation to dine on the twenty-third. It is the first of a sequence
of twelve letters of hers which he kept—all of them devoid of saluta-
tion, most of them undated, and growing by degrees more intimate in
tone, though never intimate in fact. On some of them Russell put dates
at the time, and in 1949 he wrote a note to accompany them which
states that there was no "affair," nor going to be. After they had dined
together she wrote to him:

> Yes, it was a wonderful evening. The thrill of it stayed with me all night.
> Even after I had fallen asleep I dreamed that we were sitting at the same
> table, talking and smoking, that all the mirrors of the café were windows
> and through them I could see long waves of green water gleaming and
> lifting without sound or break as though we were far out at sea.[14]

Russell was just then telling Ottoline that a terrible longing for *her*
had been growing in him: it wasn't passion because the war had all but
killed that, but a longing for companionship. He had been in the
"absolute abyss" over the war. He had been seeing "Katharine" Mansfield, and liked her—she talked of her brother who was killed. In a gay
boyish mood, he continued, he had become intimate with Constance
Malleson; but she didn't suit serious moods. What held him to Ottoline
for ever and ever was religion—everyone else hurt him by lack of
reverence.[15]

Three women and a war, religion and a doxology, with reverence
as well ("reverence" was a Garsington word), all in one paragraph. A

---

*His autobiography does not say this, but his letters to Colette, now in the Russell
archive, leave no doubt of it at all.

day or two later Russell was telling Ottoline that he wanted to get to know Katherine really well, because she interested him mentally. She had a very good mind. But he didn't think she had much heart.

Then, having described her in identical terms to Constance Malleson, he wrote to Katherine herself, who could hardly have known how many would be listening-in when she replied:

> I have just re-read your letter and now my head aches with a kind of sweet excitement. Do you know what I mean? . . . . . It is such infinite delight to know that we still have the best things to do and that we shall be comrades in the doing of them. . . . .
>
> You have already, in this little time, given me so much—more than I have given you, and that does not satisfy me. But at present my work simply springs from the wonderful fact that you *do* stand for Life.
>
> Adieu until Tuesday. I shall not read your letter again. It troubles me too greatly. But thank you— Thank you for it.[16]

Her next letter ended, "Ah, but it is not for nothing that we know each other. We shall do great things—great things." And just then Brett told Ottoline: "Bertie is a skunk. He rushed in this morning to see Katherine and never dreampt of looking in on me—you can tell him I have got the Booming Ump!!"[17]

One more letter shows that Katherine had trusted Russell—trusted him with intimate confessions about her creative vision and her hopes of what she might achieve with it; about her fits of despair, when all was ashes; but then life *could* be sweet again, and she could go among the flowers and leaves and fruit and grass—"to air oneself among these things, to seek them, to explore them and then go apart and detach oneself from them—and to write after the ferment has quite subsided."[18]

The relationship was, perhaps, more important to her than anything else that happened in that hectic autumn of 1916. But, in the attempt to describe it, two quotidian events which we need to know of have been passed over.

Shortly after the peopling of The Ark, Ida Baker had returned to England by troopship, bringing her lonely father with her. Finding that Katherine was staying in Gower Street with her new friend Dorothy Brett and "a woman called Carrington," and that the atmosphere in the house was somehow uncomfortable, she realised that it would not be possible for her to live there too. So she went to stay—after parking her father at the Strand Palace Hotel—with an old friend of Burma days who lived in Chiswick; and this led to her becoming, before Christmas, one of the thousands of educated Englishwomen who worked with their hands at machines, in overalls, with cotton caps on their heads. After a training course she started work as a machinist at an aeroplane factory in Putney, and Katherine got her some lodgings in Hampstead, vacated by a man who had gone to the war.[19]

The other event belongs to literature. In the first week of November it seems that Lytton Strachey took Katherine to Hogarth House, to meet the author of *The Voyage Out*. "I have had some nice visions of Virginia at Richmond," he wrote to Ottoline, "and hope this week to bring her and Katherine together—though what the result of that will be, Heaven knows!"[20] Albeit conjectural, this is the first recorded meeting; and Strachey's misgivings were justified.

[2]

And now the question was, who should be invited to Garsington for Christmas? Russell and Strachey were going, and the Murrys and Brett, while Aldous Huxley was already in residence (Clive Bell, as well). But Lady Ottoline was in a quandary about her Belgian refugee, Maria Nys, whom Aldous had fallen in love with, and also about Carrington, who was behaving rather oddly over Mark Gertler—or over Lytton Strachey.

Maria, who was eighteen, had been a source of motherly concern to Ottoline for some time past, because of her coltish liberties since escaping from her respectable Belgian parents.[21] She had been put at Newnham, but had removed herself from there and briefly joined the human fauna at The Ark. ("Maria started her first morning's work today," Brett told Ottoline on 18 October. "She is attached to a Russian general. I have her here in the Ark because then *we* shall know what she does with her evenings and how often she does it.") Philip Morrell didn't want her back in the house for Christmas because she flirted with *him*, but Brett said that was cruel and he must be made to give in, since "otherwise it means a dreary Christmas for both in London —or else Aldous gloomily spoiling everything for you and Maria crying her eyes out in London—alone. Tell him he mustn't be *cruel* because a silly girl is silly."[22]

Nor had Ottoline meant to ask Carrington. She had lately turned against her, deciding she was a fraud because she wouldn't sleep with Gertler, even after being lectured by Philip in a walk around the pond.[23] By a week before Christmas, however, Brett had got her way:

> Please don't think I don't *like* Philip. I *do* very much. . . . . I feel he makes it difficult for you sometimes, but I do so feel you are really top dog and get the best of Philip in the *end* which is right and as it should be—because Philip with too much of his own way would have us all combing the pigs and adding up the milk bills and finally sitting on eggs, our lives would be a perfect Hell!!! Carrington has received your invite I hope she will be able to come.

In this way did Brett help to compose the assemblage that gathered at Garsington for the middle Christmas of the war—a gathering held in a sort of hyperventilated tension, a mixture of amorous frenzy and despair, that was doubtless a product of the war, and which actually touched at several points the emerging literature of the time. She also, inadvertently, helped to assemble the cast for yet another play-within-the-play.

Christmas Day was a Monday, that year. Brett in her excitement arrived with her presents on the previous Wednesday, in time to help festoon the house with garlands and Chinese lanterns, but the Murrys' arrival was governed by Jack's overwhelming duties at the office. He arrived on Saturday without any presents, and the "Bumblepup" (as Brett and Ottoline called Carrington) arrived then too, in time to spend all Sunday walking and talking over fields and ditches with "Grandfather Lytton"; and to go at evensong to the village church since the Bishop of Oxford was to preach and come to dinner afterwards. So it was that Carrington was able to write to her soldier-brother in France on Boxing Day, listing the company for him as follows:

> Hon. Bert Russell, Maria Nys, a Belgium lass of little repute and worth, the lady of Gower Street Katherine Mansfield and her melancholy spouse, Lytton, Brett, Aldous Huxley of Balliol (attached to Maria Nys and she to him) a lanky youth with one eye gamey who writes poetry, and is well versed in the literary accomplishments which the lads

of Balliol do acquire. Madmoiselle who perhaps you remember, the little
girl Julian, her parents (our host and hostess) and that is all.[24]

"Madmoiselle" was Julian Morrell's Swiss governess, Juliette Baillot
—the future wife of Julian Huxley, as Maria Nys was the future wife
of Aldous.

Bishop Gore was a good friend of Lady Ottoline's. With Russell,
Strachey and Clive Bell all present on Sunday evening, the dinner
conversation turned to President Wilson's offer of the previous week
to mediate in a compromise peace, and the Bishop was set upon by "the
C.O. dogs" for wanting victory. But he stood his ground and refused
to budge, says the Bumblepup's engaging burble, being "very intelligent and unpompous for a Bishop."

In the drawing-room afterwards—the Bishop having left—Clive
Bell declared that the Germans as a nation were better educated and
"more receptive" than the English—a greater appreciation of art pre-
vailed over there. This brought all the voices down on Bell save that
of Strachey. The one person in the room who had written a book about
the Germans probably kept rather quiet about it.* Discussion on the
Germans raged, and Middleton Murry, says the Bumblepup, "stood
for democracy on every occasion whether it bore on the subject or
not."

Meanwhile Katherine began to think out a play for the company to
act; and Murry took some manor-house note-paper and wrote two
letters, in lieu of the presents he hadn't brought.

The first told Ottoline: "Tomorrow I shall be the only wedding
guest without a wedding garment: I who so deeply admire and so truly
love you shall have no gift for you. . . . ." He had thought of fibbing
about a book that was ordered and had not come, but no, he wouldn't
practise that small deceit. He did not think that their friendship—"our
love, I will not call it by another name"—would ever die. A year had
proved it. No gift would have said this for him; nor could his words
—but they were the best, as yet, that he had to give.[25]

The other note was to Brett: "This is my Christmas present—only
what I am writing now—nothing more. And this is only to say that
you are a darling, and that I hope we shall always be in the same house

---

*Three weeks later she offered to lend Ottoline a copy of her "wretched old book."
It was "young and bad," Katherine said, but it might amuse Ottoline a little.

for Christmas until—forever—if every Christmas Eve you will either kiss me or let yourself be kissed by me."[26]

Katherine, of course, never saw such letters of Murry's, but she knew all about the side of him from which they came. She called it his "sham personality," and she saw it once in an essay of his, and wrote him a note about it: "I feel that you are going to uncover yourself and quiver. . . . . What is it? Is it your desire to torture yourself or to pity yourself or something far subtler? I only know that it's tremendously important because it's your way of damnation."[27]

On Christmas Day, while the rest went out for walks and talks across the fields to have an appetite for dinner, she worked at her dramatic piece. After that (Noel Carrington learned from his sister), Grandfather Lytton read the company "an essay he has written on Dr. Arnold." A section of the book that was later to make him wake up famous, the essay was full of in-jokes for the present company. What a titter in the drawing-room, when one well-cadenced paragraph closed with this: " 'The public schools,' said the Rev. Mr. Bowdler, 'are the very seats and nurseries of vice.' "

At last, on the evening of Boxing Day, came the play that Katherine had devised, a "kind of Ibsen-Russian play," as Carrington told her brother, "marvellously witty, and good." Or as Aldous Huxley told his brother Julian: "We performed a superb play invented by Katherine, improvising as we went along. It was a huge success, with Murry as a Dostoevsky character and Lytton as an incredibly wicked old grandfather."[28]

The play was an ephemeral thing, and those two references might have been all we ever knew of it. But somehow seven grubby little sheets of pencil scribble, torn from a notebook and very difficult to decipher, have survived to provide a partial text of what the distinguished company acted or watched that evening. Katherine must have kept them herself, since they eventually went to Wellington with the rest of her papers, and they may be all that was actually written down, the rest being supplied in plot form. They preserve "Act I, Scene I," no more—slight enough, but apparently the first thing she had written since *The Aloe,* and the cause of a change of direction in her work.

She had chosen to amuse herself as much as the others. In the list of characters the long-lost Florence Kaziany is a private joke, a reference to her Wörishofen days and near maternity. (The allusions to Floryan and the female fiddler Kaziany—who is mentioned in one of

Sobieniowski's letters in Chapter V—would have gone completely over Murry's head.) To Ivan Tchek and his cloak of gloom no introduction is needed, and The Laurels may be taken for the cottage in the country for which Carrington was hunting at the time to share with Strachey. If the name Dr. Keit contains some joke it escaped even Strachey himself, since he signed the visitors' book that Christmas as "Dr. Kite." In the text that follows,[29] illegible words are represented by dots, and a few conjectured words are supplied within square brackets.

THE LAURELS

Lytton:	Dr. Keit
Carrington:	his grandchild, Muriel Dash
Mansfield:	Florence Kaziany
Aldous:	Balliol Dodd
Maria:	Jane
Murry:	Ivan Tchek

Act I, Scene I. Breakfast Room

Ivan enters, pours out a cup of coffee, lights a cigarette, stubs out the cigarette, [sighs].

    Ivan: And so it goes on. *(Walks out, wrapped in gloom. Enter Jane* [. . . . .] *brushes away cigarette ash.)*

    Jane: Why clear away?*(Resets the table, goes to the door and calls)* Miss Muriel!

    Muriel Dash *(in the distance):* Just coming. *(She comes in, with a bird in a cage; takes off cover and hangs the bird in the window.)* Now you can look out and sing and see the sun *(sighs enviously)* shining on the land.

    Jane: Mr. Tchek has had his breakfast, Miss. It's all ready for the Master.

    Muriel: Oh, very well, Jane—I'll call him. *(Looks at Jane)* What's the matter, Jane? You've been crying.

    Jane *(resetting table):* Oh, don't notice me, Miss Muriel. I'm nobody, I'm *nothing*.

    Muriel: [. . . . .] Whatever do you mean, Jane? *(Jane puts her hand over her eyes and sobs.)*

Muriel (taking her hand away): Poor Jane, you do look so dreadful.
(*Brightly*) [. . . . .]

Jane: Oh Miss, if you knew what I feel. [It do] seem funny, don't
it Miss? But things happen like that. When I saw 'is boots in
the passage this morning—those black button ones with the
brown tops—I felt I couldn't bear it no longer. I felt quite
wild, Miss, in the kitchen jest now. Oh, Mother what 'ave you
been and gone and done? And it isn't as though it's my fault,
Miss. That's what makes it so 'ard to bear.

Muriel (bewildered): What on earth *are* you talking about, Jane?

Jane: Oh, Miss—it's Mr. Tchek. The Russian gentleman.

Muriel: Are you in love with him, Jane?

Jane: Oh, Miss!

Muriel: But whatever is there to cry about in that, Jane? Oh, Jane
—You lucky girl! Just to be in love—isn't that enough? Oh,
how I envy you—how I envy you! I've nothing—nothing to be
in love with except (*she points*) my canary. There comes a time,
Jane (*taking the cage*), when even a canary isn't half enough.
One seems somehow to want more. Oh, Jane!

Jane: But you don't understand, Miss. If I was like you, with me
Pa and me Ma in a lovely double frame on the dressing table,
it'd be all right. But there—I've got to tell somebody. (*Beats her
breast*) I'm a love-child, I am!

Muriel (clasps her hands): A love-child, Jane? How too divine!
What is it? How pretty it sounds! (*Dreamily*) A *love* child!

Jane (leaning towards her): [. . . . .] Do you mean to say you *don't*
know, Miss? It means I 'aven't got no Father—

Muriel: But oh, Jane, how perfect! Just like the Virgin Mary!

Jane (furious): You ought to be ashamed of yourself, Miss Muriel.
That you ought. Don't you know it's the most horrible thing
that can happen to anyone, not to have a Father? Don't you
know Miss that's the reason what young girls like me jump off
bridges in front of trains and eat rat poison and swoller acids
and. . . . .

Just then "Grandfather" totters in (Lytton Strachey in a beard of red
wool, which Lady Ottoline's daughter still has somewhere in a box
upstairs), and after a comic scene in which Muriel/Carrington pleads
to go out and know the world beyond The Laurels, he decides that the

time has come to tell her the Awful Truth about her father, and the mother whom she has never seen. "Mr. Tchek is not our first lodger, Muriel. Once upon a time another lived in Mr. Tchek's room. . . . ."

Grandfather: Time passed . . . One fine day Florence and the first lodger—went away. And after a long time, while Grandfather was all alone, he found *(groans)*—How shall I tell her?—a basket under the laurel hedge—with a baby and a bottle and a bonnet in it.

Muriel (radiant, flings her arms around him): The baby was *me*, Grandfather!

Grandfather (clasping her to his breast): My treasure is a love-child.

Muriel (awed): Just like Jane! *(Leaves his arms.)* But did Mother never come back, Grandfather?

Grandfather: Never—when grass was green and water flowed— Never came back. *(They swing to and fro, clasped in each other's arms. Suddenly the door opens and Florence bursts in, in a travelling cape, carrying a bag, followed by Jane. To Jane):* Pay my taxi. *(Rushing forward):* Father!

Grandfather (horrified): Florence!

Florence: Now don't get up—my old, feeble, [. . . . .], white-bearded old Father.

Muriel (very embarrassed): Good afternoon, Mother. I am your daughter, Muriel.

Florence (as to a child): Well, my little darling. *(Turns to Grandfather.)* How old you have become, my poor Father. I should have warned you before I came. I had no right—I didn't realise how old you were—how feeble—how almost—*(shakes her head at him)* It was high time.

Grandfather (trying to "carry it off "): I have never been better in my life, Florence.

Florence [. . . . .]: There, there. *(She unbuttons her cape, Muriel takes it from her and stands holding the cape in her hands.)* How hot and stuffy it is in here—*(walks over to the window)* Hemmed in by laurels!

The rest is lost, leaving Florence—or Katherine—standing once more at a window.

Next day, after trouble with trains, most of the guests dispersed into a London fog, but meanwhile the mail brought a Dostoevskian parcel containing a horrible surprise for Lady Ottoline, which would have totally changed that Christmas had it arrived a few days earlier. This is when Lawrence (at her request—she had heard some rumours) sent her the manuscript of the novel he had been writing in Cornwall. When she read it, she felt herself go pale with horror.

So far as she recalled it when writing her *Memoirs* some years later, she found herself called by every name from an "old hag," obsessed by sex mania, to a "corrupt Sapphist" whose dresses were dirty, and in one scene she was depicted as making love to a "glorified Frieda." The house and garden and its inmates were accurately described. The whole thing seemed to have been written expressly to humiliate her, the only assuagement of the shock being that "all the worst parts were in Frieda's handwriting."[30]

She evidently took this to mean that Frieda had actually written those parts, and it may be so (there was not much work for Frieda in that tiny cottage); or the manuscript may simply have been a spare one that she had helped to assemble, doing some copying in the process.

Ottoline wrote at once to Russell and Katherine, describing the book. Unable to reply at length just then, Katherine said she hoped that Lawrence could be persuaded not to publish it, adding: "I think that living alone engenders in him a kind of madness." Later, when she had heard more about it from Brett but had still not read it, she said:

> There is no doubt about it: left to himself Lawrence goes mad. When he is with people he expands to the warmth and the light in them—he is a darling and often very wonderful, but left to himself he is cold and dark and desolate. Of course Frieda is at the bottom of it. He has chosen Frieda and when he is with real people he knows how fatal that choice is. But his cursed obstinacy eggs him on in his loneliness with her to justify his choice, by any means—by even the lowest methods. [She urged Ottoline to laugh at Lawrence and not let him see how hurt she was.][31]

Both her husband and Clive Bell gave similar advice, in vain. As Bell told his wife: "Ottoline returned Lawrence his MS. with an incredibly foolish reply, in spite of excellent counsel from me, and some desperate admonitions from Philip against falling into the depths of folly. Every line of her letter that I was allowed to hear revealed a wound: Lawrence must have rejoiced."[32]

All this happened little more than a year after Philip Morrell, at risk to his own political career, had asked a question in the Commons about the suppression of *The Rainbow*, and Ottoline had exerted herself to raise money to help Lawrence go to Florida. Morrell shortly wrote to Lawrence's agent, J. B. Pinker, warning him that there would be libel proceedings if the book were published in its present form, and according to Ottoline's memory (but her emotions are involved), it was not. It was her impression that the "worst parts" had been toned down, but a manuscript that would establish this does not seem to have survived.

Evidently no one yet realised that Gerald and Gudrun were supposed to be Murry and Katherine. That the "learned dry baronet of fifty" bears the name Sir Joshua Malleson (or Matheson) suggests a vindictive change made by Lawrence after hearing of Russell's affair with Constance Malleson (that is, in 1917 or later).

On returning to town from Garsington, Murry and Katherine decided to leave The Ark. No bust-up had occurred (Brett's letters continue friendly), but Katherine, having produced no new work except the burlesque *Laurels* since leaving France, now felt urgently the need of a place where she could write, and Keynes's house was not that place. As we'll see, what she wanted to write now took dramatic form.

She began the year with fruitless visits to land agents, only to find that the war had begun to affect civilian life. Rents had gone up, flats were harder to get, and land agents were requiring three-year tenancies. She found she couldn't any longer face the old ordeal (so Murry read), of "ALL those houses, ALL those flats, ALL those rooms which we have taken and withdrawn from."[33] This was why she started looking for a studio in January, and Murry for some rooms in which he, too, would write. "The rumour went around," says his commentary in the 1951 *Letters*, "that Mansfield and Murry had separated. It was nothing of the kind." The letter just quoted, and an entry in his journal describing a night they spent together, would seem to bear him out. All the same, she still was engaged in her little venture of the heart and mind with Russell.

Her letters to him do not resemble any others that she wrote. They are like wisps of cloud across the moon—they exist, but cannot be touched and felt and compared with other substances. That emotion is in them one would not deny; there is awe, and there is fascination. Brett's "Call of the Wild" seems hardly the term, but in order to correct it one would need to have sat near them in a Soho restaurant while they talked at their table by the window—somewhat at cross purposes, one suspects. Did Russell know that the ring on Katherine's finger was the symbol of Frieda's broken union? They talked, a good deal, of "truth."

In the first week of the new year Katherine told Russell how much a letter of his had meant: "To feel that we are going to be truthful with each other, quite without reservations—that promises so great an adventure that it is difficult to remain calm."[34] A few days later she told him she was acting for the movies in something called "exterior scene in walking dress"; later again, in a big bare studio, she had to walk about in what the producer called "slap up evening dress," and so many *absurd* things had been happening to her. She had just been gypped of a flat by a most perfidious Pole, and the whole thing had been like a "perfect little Dostoievsky novel."[35]

It was in the midst of all this that she and Murry went one evening to dine with the Woolfs at Hogarth House, with her relative Sydney Waterlow to act as buffer. She must have talked too much about the movies, or about the perfidious Pole, for one month later Virginia told her sister: "I have had a slight rapprochement with Katherine Mansfield, who seems to me an unpleasant but forcible and utterly unscrupulous character."[36] Mrs. Woolf had probably been hearing the Bloomsbury gossip, fostered with relish by Keynes and Clive Bell, connecting Katherine with Russell. Ottoline, too, was aware by now that Russell's affections were being drawn away from her. But she did not know to whom, any more than Katherine did.

Late in January Katherine wrote this letter to Russell, who did not keep it as he kept her others:[37]

You wrote me such a lovely letter, mon cher ami— Yes, let us dine together on Friday evening. I shall be well enough if you will please come for me here. Then *we shall talk*. I feel there is so much to be said that I'm quite silent until then; that it is an age since we have seen each other—and yet while I haven't seen you my "friendship" for you has gone on and grown ever so much deeper and profounder.

Let us be very happy on Friday night. I give you my two hands.

Katherine

Now Russell gave that letter to Constance Malleson (or "Colette"), and its phrasing left her convinced that Katherine *was* having an affair with him. Here, from the Russell archive, is the note he attached in 1949 to those letters of hers that he did keep, when sorting out his papers for posterity:

The following batch of letters from Katharine Mansfield has surprised me as I have come upon them (1949). They read as if we were having an affair, or about to have one,* but it was not so. She withdrew, possibly on account of Colette, though I never knew. My feelings for her were ambivalent: I admired her passionately, but was repelled by her dark hatreds.

Russell's autobiography says that in the autumn of 1916 he "half supposed that he was having a light affair" with Colette—a statement wholly belied by the passionate letters which she received from him —and of Katherine he says:

. . . . . it was at this time that I got to know her well. I do not know whether my impression of her was just . . . . . but when she spoke about people she was envious, dark, and full of alarming penetration in discovering what they least wished known and whatever was bad in their characteristics. She hated Ottoline because Murry did not. It had become clear to me that I must get over the feeling that I had had for Ottoline, as she no longer returned it sufficiently to give me any happiness. I listened to all that Katherine Mansfield had to say against her; in the end I believed very little of it.[38]

It is hard to know whom to believe. The only person whom Katherine is known to have called perfidious at this time was the Pole who had

---

*"I don't agree. The letter from K.M. to B.R. which I own does read like that, though." —Lady Constance Malleson, commenting on the note for the author in 1971. The placing of the asterisk is hers.

gypped her of a flat. It is true that Brett wrote, "Bertie is a skunk."

In February, Katherine left The Ark for a studio flat at 141a Church Street, Chelsea, which had the largest window she had ever lived with —"my Thou-God-seest-Me window," as she called it—and Murry took rooms half a mile away at 47 Redcliffe Road. (J. D. Fergusson now had a studio in that street.) From her "nunnery," Katherine wrote Ottoline a letter which reveals that there had been some embarrassment and she had been afraid of meeting her, but all had been forgiven.[39] Her last extant letter to Russell, dated 24 February, shows that the affair between them foundered upon an intellectual difficulty. He had sent her an article of his on "The World After the War," which ended by saying that unless the truth about the war could be brought home to ordinary men and women, and especially to children in the schools, civilised man would perish off the earth. "Whether that would be regrettable," he concluded, "I do not venture to determine." Katherine was shocked. She had climbed so high with him in reading the article, only to learn that the journey had been more or less cynical: "I am not yet recovered."[40]

Five months later, after Russell had insisted that it was he, as the author, who should have been imprisoned for a certain No Conscription leaflet, and not the men who distributed it, he was brought before the court and fined.

"I am so sorry about B.R.," wrote Katherine to Ottoline a few days earlier,[41] "as I saw him once; he was awfully kind about my work, and I enjoyed talking to him. He was 'in the mood.' We didn't talk about present people and present affairs but of all kinds of 'odd' things—like flattery and Praise and what it is one really wishes to convey in writing you know."

The letters of Russell and Lady Constance record that Katherine saw him again in August to talk about her work, and seemed very anxious to be friends with him. But then she must have heard about Colette.

CHAPTER XIII

A Studio in Chelsea

I am a recluse at present and do nothing but write and read and read and write—seeing nobody and going nowhere.
—K.M. to Bertrand Russell, 24 February 1917

As "European history" was totally transformed by events of the year 1917, so was the minuscule life of Katherine Mansfield. The scale of the comparison is extreme, but what invites it is the presence in each case of a fertile paradox of destruction and renewal.

From a masculine viewpoint the nature of Europe's transformation in 1917 is vividly expressed in A. J. P. Taylor's history of the war. If Napoleon could have come back to life in January, says Taylor, he would have found "European history" still in existence: czars, kings, emperors and Liberal politicians, the Great Powers fighting much the sort of war that he had known. All that, Napoleon would have recognized and understood; but in the following December he would have been bewildered. At one end of Europe by then was Bolshevism, a wholly new system of thought and government; at the other end, the United States, beginning to intervene on a scale that would eclipse all the "Great Powers" put together. Within a single year, the modern political world was born.

Another immense overturning had also occurred, however—a social one, concerning women, hence not the concern of Taylor's book. For England's young men and young women, the war brought contrary effects. Along the Front, the machine-guns and the shells slew half the seed of Europe, one by one. But for women at home—and because of machines, not suffragettes—a whole new life was springing up. One of these was Miss Ida Baker, the Colonel's daughter, working in a cotton cap at lathes in her aeroplane factory in Putney.

"I enjoyed my work there very much," she writes, not meaning at all to describe this change. "Mr. Gwynne was extremely kind to us, and I met there Stella Drummond (later Lady Eustace Percy) who became a great friend, and Lady Mary Hamilton." If lathes were hardly liberation for those two, they were for L.M. In Hampstead she had a landlady, "good old Mrs Butterworth," who made it her war-work to provide a good solid breakfast at 5:30 A.M., and a "nice fire and supper when I came back, in the little sitting-room where I could rest and read."[1] This is a perfect unconscious portrayal of the new rights, once a masculine privilege, which thousands of English women tasted for the first time in the middle years of the war. The bus conductress discovered a role—bossing all her passengers around. The "business girl," a new phenomenon, finished her lunch in public with a cigarette. The American dance called ragtime had completely changed accepted notions of how a young woman might move her limbs. Short skirts and short hair, the brassiere—all these things had put both women and the young on the way to the 1960's.

For Katherine Mansfield also, 1917 was a year of creative growth and fatal news. In January, she was that ragtime intellectual whose vitality had attracted Bertrand Russell and disturbed Virginia Woolf. The spring and summer saw her germinate, under glass, as it were, and from classical seed, the gift of mime that was to yield her strongest work. Its autumn, after fruitful days, brought first a chill, then phthisis, diagnosed at last. Her whole existence changed, and so did the character of her work. Turning its back upon Goodyear's "café mirrors, dews and grasses, and outward appearances generally," her work became, instead, an inward quest. Her art, henceforward, was the bright-burning flame of her consumption.

The compensating movement, of creative renewal, probably had its start in the frivolity of her Christmas play at Garsington; but then, in the spring, it would seem that Orage took a hand once more.

The *New Age* had fallen on difficult times—or on more difficult times than those it normally survived. With his best men away at the war, and Beatrice Hastings no longer at his side, Orage was running the paper single-handed, writing much of it himself, and appealing to old friends for support. He seems to have got financial help from Shaw (who also contributed again), and new names appeared. T. E. Hulme was sending contributions from the Front, and Ezra Pound was wildly prolific. One cry for help must have gone to Katherine, who relented. In April she contributed some "Fragments"—short pieces of the kind that one finds in her *Journal*—and she followed them with eight pieces in the dialogue form that Orage himself was so fond of. She had also begun a play. When Lady Ottoline invited her to Garsington for Easter she replied that she *dared* not interrupt what she was doing: "I've a play half written and God knows how many short stories and notes and sketches for portraits."[2]

The play amounts to very little: but the dialogues, slight as they are in subject matter, all drew on what she had learned from Theocritus, and, like her Coronation piece, had probably been written at Orage's prompting. They included *The Common Round* (later set out as narrative and renamed *Pictures*), *Two Tuppeny Ones Please*, *The Black Cap*, and the Garsington sketch already quoted, called *In Confidence*. All six were light-weight stuff, but it is not for their substance that they matter here, but for the part which they played in changing the modern short story in English—in particular, for what they contributed to the development known as "getting rid of the narrator."

It was T. O. Beachcroft who first pointed this out, though only *after* he had written his book, *The Modest Art*, already cited in Chapter VI. Until the twentieth century the English short story, from Chaucer to Stevenson, Kipling and Maugham, had in general retained the well-proven services of the audible narrator, a figure of implied authority whose function was to establish values, scene and tone, and who could offer explanations—and also moralise, of course. The art had not yet learned from Theocritus the shortcut which Katherine Mansfield now was taking to a form that suited the age by dispensing with authority, a form that is dramatic in character, revealed rather than told. This, very briefly, was how Beachcroft saw it after he had learned in 1974 of Katherine Mansfield's 1911 encounter with Theocritus.

Less a narration than a "small picture" (the root of *eidyllion* almost permits this reading), the fifteenth idyll of Theocritus was, he wrote, a mime in verse in which, although it was intended to be read, the action was presented to the reader as a "happening," without any palpable narrator to stand between the reader and the truths which he perceives with his inward eye. By dispensing with the narrator it got rid of moralising and explaining; it lent itself to the portrayal of everyday life rather than great events, and it forswore long periods of time. Its brevity was "that of the flash, not of a condensed narrative." Equally, the modern short story was not just a story told in a different way, but a different *kind* of story, dealing in a different kind of truth.[3]

In other words, while Katherine's Coronation piece of 1911 does not displace *The Tiredness of Rosabel* from its key position in the development of her art, it does, with its successors, replace Chekhov by Theocritus, making him an ancestor rather than a neglected model. For the *New Age* mimes soon led to *Mr. Reginald Peacock's Day* and *A Dill Pickle* (the method carried into narrative), and, concurrently, to her refashioning of *The Aloe* into *Prelude* for Virginia Woolf to print; thence to her own best work, and in turn to the influence of that upon the modern short story—Beachcroft's completion of the puzzle.

Meanwhile, something similar had been happening in English poetry, with the two outsiders, Pound and Eliot, learning from Browning's dramatic monologues his way of "getting rid of the narrator"; and in June of 1917 there appeared in London a slim volume entitled *Prufrock and Other Observations,* which went at once to Garsington. Clive Bell came back from town with several copies, which he handed round (he mistakenly says it was at Easter) "like so many Good Friday buns." "Prufrock" itself caused a stir, he says, and much discussion, and of one thing he was sure: "It was Katherine Mansfield who read the poem aloud."[4]

She admired it then, and its cadences certainly lingered in her mind.* To Virginia Woolf she later made the interesting remark that she didn't think of Eliot as a poet, because "Prufrock is, after all a short story."[5]

In considering what had led to all this, the success of her Garsington playlet is obviously significant, and so is Orage's liking for the dialogue form; but she had also, as we've seen, been "acting for the movies" in the winter. Since the films were silent it would be rash to assert that her experiences in that "big bare studio" had anything to do with her *New Age* pieces, but they are a sort of "visualising for the voice." They also take a cinematic liberty with shifts of scene—as does the *Adonia* itself.

The 1915 piece called *Stay-Laces* follows its monologuing lady from

---

*"Is that all? Can that be all? That is not what I meant at all."—the *Journal,* 1917 (page 124).

a footpath onto a bus and then into Selfridges. *The Black Cap* begins with wife and husband at their breakfast, cuts suddenly to a taxi (she has left him), to the station to meet her lover, into the train, into a hotel, and to a taxi once again (she has now left *him*), all with the speed of film—old film. Yet another prudent-wife piece called *A Pic-nic* takes a party of Wellington ladies and gentlemen across the harbour by ferry to Day's Bay, into the sandhills, into the water, up the hill for a walk, and home again by ferry, all in dialogue, with Katherine Mansfield's shortest daydream (two lines) worked in as well.

All were pictures of people in movement— εἰδύλλια κινητικά. As acted mimes they would present some difficulty on a stage, but none at all in film, or on sound radio, which media they anticipate as the *Adonia* did.

The "play" that Katherine mentioned to Lady Ottoline is of little account when compared, for potential, with the mimes. It was called *A Ship in the Harbour,* and was an attempt to put the Beauchamp family on a more or less Chekhovian stage at the time of Vera's marriage in 1909, to which it makes detailed allusions.[6] But the living room which is its static opening scene was all too real—no stage at all, in fact—and some of the dialogue is facile. There was more vitality in *The Laurels.* The Brandon family of the play are two-dimensional figures who could never have been illumined from within by the process that Beachcroft has so happily termed "interior mime."

Writing apart, the spring and summer were for Katherine an uneventful time. She was hard at work now, discovering something; and Goodyear had died. If it is true that his dead-sure criticism had stilled her pen for the past twelve months, then perhaps that effect was past.

She was not quite living alone in her "nunnery." L.M. was a constant visitor, though it meant much travelling for her: up at five to get to the works in Putney, then to Chelsea, and home at last to her bed in Hampstead. This is one of the *New Age* "Fragments"[7]—yes, it was published in full view of L.M., but she would not have minded in the least, and Katherine knew that:

L.M. came to see me the other evening; she brought me some oysters. Oh! I said, the smell of them reminded me so of a little café in Marseilles. And how well I remembered one particular evening! Just then I looked up. L.M.'s face had changed—became curiously blank and then serious and distressed. "One moment, dear," said she; "I must fly away and pay a little visit." She flew, and came back all smiles and readiness. "Yes, dear, one evening in the little café," said she, composing herself. But while she was away it occurred to me that something of this kind invariably happened whenever I wished to describe anything to her . . . "Would you just wait, dear, while I get a hanky?" Or, "Shall I put on a lump of coal before you begin?" Or, "Shall I just dash up to the kitchen and put the kettle on?" . . . Then, "About the little café, dear. Do go on!" "No, I've forgotten." Very distressed: "Oh, you haven't! Not really." "Yes, absolutely. Have you washed your hair lately? It's such a pretty colour—like lager beer." "No, I haven't washed it for ages. I must, though. It's coming out in handfuls, simply." Which is the correct reply according to the Book of Female Conversations?

One notes a female friendship (there were many hours of hair-brushing) that would *always* be on the verge of bickering. Fairly soon, since the long daily journeys were too much for L.M., and Katherine had need of her useful services, it was decided that she had better move in.

The studio had no bedroom, however. There was only a curtained space beneath a sort of balcony, and behind that a bathroom. Beyond the gallery above, a kitchenette. L.M. gave up her Hampstead digs and slept up there, behind another curtain; and Murry's unpublished journal gives this glimpse of life at the studio *à trois*, perhaps his record of an incident described by Katherine:

> L.M. was bathing in K.'s bathroom. K. had her back turned to the door. Suddenly she heard the door open and she *knew* that L.M. was standing naked there, knew that she desired that K. should turn and look at her and say "You're not so bad-looking after all." And K. would not turn. She felt the humiliation and the bitter disappointment of L.M.— and, of course, was glad.[8]

If visitors came when L.M. was in bed she had to lie still so as not to embarrass them. One of the visitors to Katherine's "curious little kennel" was Aldous Huxley, who told his brother Julian of a Sunday evening's conversation being interrupted when Katherine suddenly gave a shout and was answered by "the sleepy voice of somebody who was in bed behind a curtain and whose presence I had never realised."[9] On a Sunday there was no avoiding it, perhaps; but as to weekdays, it was arranged that L.M. would not come in before nine o'clock. She declares in her book that Katherine and Murry were "parted" at this time, but Murry's journal makes that seem unlikely; and in any case there may have been a quite different and overriding reason for Murry and Katherine to have different addresses in 1917. In April 1918 Katherine was finally divorced by Mr. Bowden. Just when the proceedings were begun isn't known, but as soon as they were begun it would be true, as John Carswell points out in his *Lives and Letters,* that "all could have been ruined, as the law then stood, if the King's Proctor had been able to show that she was living with Murry." Mr. Carswell has particular authority for making the remark: his barrister-father, Donald Carswell, was an acquaintance of Katherine's at this time (it was with his help that she had found lodgings for L.M. in Hampstead). L.M. herself was always mysterious about the "separation," asserting that it was one, but evasive when asked for the reason.

However all that may be, it can be said of both Murry and Katherine at this time that the creative drive was stronger in them than anything else. Both were burning to make their names, and for Katherine, certainly, this was a time for her being "a writer first and a woman after" (in her own words of a later time). Her *Journal* for 1917 testifies to that; and this further *New Age* "Fragment"[10] conveys the atmosphere of her studious retreat:

> Late in the evening, after you have cleared away your supper, blown the crumbs out of the book that you were reading, lighted the lamp, and curled up in front of the fire—that is the moment to beware of the rain. You are conscious of a sudden hush. You open your eyes wide. What's that? Hullo, it's raining! Reluctant at first, and then faster and faster, tapping against the window, beating on the door, comes the rain. The air seems to change; you are so aware of the dark flowing water that your hands and cheeks grow cold. You begin to walk up and down. How loud the rain sounds! You catch sight of yourself in the mirror, and you think that you look very plain. You say to that plain creature in the wavy glass: "I am twenty-eight, and I have chosen, but absolutely deliberately chosen, to live quite alone for ever." The creature in the glass gives a short laugh and says: "C'est pour rire, ça." But you reply severely: "Don't speak French if you're English; it's a vulgar habit." Now there are quick steps coming up the garden path, stopping at the door. Someone is coming. But nobody knocks. Again there are steps and again that pause as though someone felt for the wet door-knocker in the dark. You are

sure that somebody is there. Nobody. You remember that the kitchen window is wide open. Run up and shut it. Is the rain coming in? No, not really. You lean out a moment. Two little roof gutters flow into the garden. In the dark they sound like two women sobbing and laughing, talking together and complaining and laughing, out in the wet garden. One says: "Life is not gay, Katherine. No, life is not gay." But now the rain is over. The lamp-post outside, yellow in the light, with a spray of shining tree across it, looks like a very bad illustration out of a Dickens novel. Yes, it is quite over. You make up the fire and squat before it, spreading out your hands, as though you had been rescued from a shipwreck, and just to be alive and safe were bliss enough.

First impressions being somehow overcome, Katherine's friendship with Virginia Woolf began at the studio—but it calls for a chapter to itself. Out of the past again came Floryan Sobieniowski. Sought out, apparently, by him, Katherine briefly collaborated in translating one of Wyspiański's plays.[11] Called on by Huxley, and by Strachey too, she also met the new young poet T. S. Eliot more than once, and in fact was at a dinner party with him only a few days after her reading of "Prufrock" at Garsington. A letter describes for Ottoline an evening at the St. John Hutchinsons' at which the other guests included Eliot, Robert Graves, and Roger Fry. In this excerpt "Mary" is the hostess, and "Jack" the host. As it ends, the recently published *Rhapsody on a Winter Night* would seem to be in Katherine's mind:

Oh, God! those parties. They are all very well in retrospect but while they are going on they are too infernally boring. Mary, of course, went all out for Roger Fry and Robbie Ross, with an *eye* on Greaves, and an *eyebrow* for Elliot. From Mary's end of the table whiffs of George Moore and Max Beerbohm and Lord Curzon floated. While Jack tied a white apron round himself and cut up, trimmed and smacked into shape the whole of America and the Americans.* *So* nice for poor Elliot who grew paler and paler and more silent. In the middle sat Greaves chatting incessantly of what I told my sergeant and what my men said to me and how I brought them back at the point of my revolver etc. etc. I did not like that young man at *all*. In fact I longed to snub him and tell him that one does not talk unless one has something to say. He seemed to me, too, to be so stupidly callous about the war and he was so frightfully boring

*St. John Hutchinson was a big man with a red face like a butcher.

about how the beer was diluted at La Bassée..... I came away with Elliot and we walked past rows of little ugly houses hiding behind bitter-smelling privet hedges; a great number of amorous black cats loped across the road and high up in the sky there was a battered old moon. I liked him very much and did not feel he was an enemy.

In another letter, at the speed of electronic flash, she captured Eliot's manners on her high-speed film: "I want to talk to you about Sassoon. .... I want to make you laugh about my times with Rasputin & Aldous & his khaki brother & French polish Elliot—and I want to ask if I may come to Garsington at the end of next week perhaps."[12] ("Rasputin" was probably Sobieniowski. The real Rasputin had been murdered a few months earlier.)

Some years after Katherine's death, prompted by the frequent question, "What was she really like?" Lady Ottoline tried to put the answer down on paper. She said she had often been made to feel inferior by Katherine's insistence on the apartness of artists, and that looking back she couldn't recall an hour when Katherine had seemed entirely "off duty" as a writer. She was as much aware of that "as Queen Victoria was of being a Queen." Yet a want of insight made her pitiless and scornful, and great sincerity in people baffled her—"she did not know how to respond." She once told Ottoline that she sometimes did not know when she was acting, and when she was living her own life, adding, "Have I any real self left?" Yet somewhere behind all this there seemed to have been, in her magical New Zealand childhood, a secret refuge which had known a "real self," a truly simple child which had existed once.[13]

It was in April, soon after a printing press had been unpacked on the dining-room table at Hogarth House, that Virginia Woolf had told her sister she was going to see Katherine Mansfield, "to get a story from her perhaps." The only manuscript suitable for that occasion was of course *The Aloe,* hitherto thought of as the opening chapters of a "novel." It now was treated for the first time as an independent story, and its new name, as it took new form over the summer, was Murry's contribution.*

---

*The Woolfs got it wrong to begin with. On the opening page, and in the running heads up to page 20, they printed Wordsworth's title of "The Prelude," and it was published like that. Even Katherine made the same mistake a few years later.

The whole work was sharpened and tightened, diffuseness noticed and removed, slack dialogue condensed or cut. Recent practice in the dialogue form no doubt played a useful part, and no doubt Virginia and Katherine talked of what was under way—but Virginia had not yet begun to keep the diary in which such conversations are described. That only began, properly speaking, in October. In Katherine's letters and notebooks no reference to the work of revision is made, although one letter to Ottoline does, in an odd way, seem to reflect on something in the final episode.

It speaks of letters to Ottoline which Katherine hadn't posted, they seemed so "hopelessly superficial and fatiguing. . . . . I heard my own little mocking, mechanical voice, *loathed* it, and chose silence."[14] If the Bandol manuscript did not exist to disprove it, that observation might seem to have found its way into the final episode, the one already quoted on pages 192–93, concerned with Beryl's *sosie*. But it wasn't that way round. The scene in which Beryl re-reads her letter to Nan Pym, finds it "flippant and silly," and detests the sound of her voice in the letter, was written at Bandol in 1916, and echoed in the letter.

As an example of the sort of attention that now was given to small points of rhythm and concreteness, here is Beryl before the mirror, in *The Aloe:*

> Lovely long hair. And such masses of it. It was the colour of fresh fallen leaves, brown and red, with a glint of yellow. Almost it seemed to have a life of its own, it was so warm and there was such a deep ripple in it. When she plaited it in one thick plait it hung on her back just like a long snake. She loved to feel the weight of it drag her head back; she loved to feel it loose, covering her bare arms.

The equivalent lines in *Prelude:*

> Lovely, lovely hair. And such a mass of it. It had the colour of fresh fallen leaves, brown and red with a glint of yellow. When she did it in a long plait she felt it on her backbone like a long snake. She loved to feel the weight of it dragging her head back, and she loved to feel it loose, covering her bare arms.

There followed at once in the longer version (where Nan Pym was a more culinary "Nan Fry") a description of how Nan used to brush

Beryl's hair when they were girls together at "Miss Birch's." It is a recollection of Kathleen and Ida at Miss Wood's:[15]

> But nearly always these brushings came to an unpleasant ending. Nannie did something silly. Quite suddenly she would snatch up Beryl's hair and bury her face in it, and kiss it, or clasp her hands round Beryl's head and press it back against her firm breast, sobbing: "You are so beautiful! You don't know how beautiful you are—beautiful, beautiful!"
>
> And at these moments Beryl had such a feeling of horror, such a violent thrill of physical dislike for Nan Fry. "That's enough. That's quite enough. Thank you. You've brushed it beautifully. Good-night, Nan." She didn't even try to suppress her contempt and her disgust . . . And the curious thing was that Nan Fry seemed to understand this, even to expect it, never protesting, but stumbling away out of the cubicle, and perhaps whispering "Forgive me" at the door. And the *more* curious thing was that Beryl let her brush her hair again, and let this happen again . . . and again there was this silly scene between them, always ending in the same way, more or less, and never, never referred to in the day time.

On reflection, out it went, since there are different kinds of truth, and that kind was not for *Prelude*. Then Beryl's session at the mirror is ended by a most significant interruption. It is Kezia, carrying her grubby little calico cat—Kezia, the true Kass of Karori, the child without complexity whom Ottoline believed to have existed once—who bursts in to tell Aunt Beryl that Father is home and lunch is ready. "Botheration!" And when Beryl has run out, Kezia unscrews a jar of face-cream, puts the calico cat before the mirror, and sticks the lid over its ear. "Now look at yourself." The cat topples over in surprise. The top of the cream jar flies through the air, it rolls like a penny in a round on the linoleum—and does not break. "Then she tiptoed away, far too quickly and airily . . ."

Three selves, then: of Innocence and Experience, and false experience. Thus *Prelude* ends, in a glimpse of what Wordsworth might have called tranquillity recollected with emotion.

Kass in infancy

Arthur Beauchamp, the Pa Man

Chaddie, Leslie, Vera, Jeanne, Kass

Granny Dyer
with Gwen

No. 11 Tinakori Road

Granny Dyer, 1855

No. 75 Tinakori Road

Uncle Val

On the garden seat

Karori, 1893

Kass

Pip and Rags

Chaddie, Vera, Kass

Las Palmas

Aunt Belle

At Queen's
College

Frankfurt, 1903

Rippmann

Arnold Trowell

At Miss Wood's

The Corinthic

No. 75 Tinakori Road

"Damn my family!"

Miss K. Beauchamp

Maata Mahupuku

Te Whaiti, 1907

Garnet

Beauchamp Lodge

Annie Beauchamp

Rottingdean, 1910

George Bowden

Sobieniowski

The German Pension

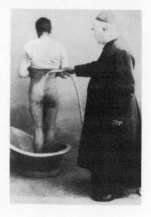

Pfarrer Kneipp,
hosing

1910

Orage

At Cheyne Walk

Beatrice Hastings

The editors of Rhythm

J. M. Kennedy

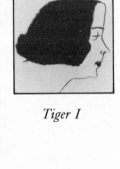

Tiger I

L.M.

"The Gables,"
Cholesbury

Baron's Court, 1913

At Chaucer Mansions,
Baron's Court

Anne Estelle Rice

Jack, Frieda, and
Lawrence

Lawrence

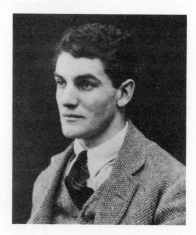

J.M.M.

Carco: Quai aux Fleurs

Villa Pauline

K.M.B. and L.H.B.

Leslie Beauchamp

The cottage at Mylor

With Kot, 1915

By Brett

Higher Tregerthen

FREDERICK GOODYEAR—1913.

1917

*141a Church St.,
Chelsea*

Katherine's mother, 1918

J.M.M., Brett, and K.M., Hampstead

Passport:
Paris 1918

K.M. and J.M.M. with
Richard, 1920

First day at sun.

Villa Isola Bella,
Menton, 1920

Ospedaletti, 1919

Villa Flora, 1920

Harold
Beauchamp

The detested 1913
photograph

Isola Bella

Wingley, Athenaeum, and
The Heron Press

The Chalet: L.M. entertains

Farewell, Isola Bella

Randogne, 1922

*L.M. and
Wingley*

J.M.M., c. 1921

With Brett, Sierre, 1922

The Chalet, 1922

From the Sphere

In her Swiss Garden

Gurdjieff

Gurdjieff's throne

Katherine Mansfield.

CHAPTER XIV

Katherine and Virginia, 1917-1923

Neither had "arrived" when they met and both were concerned to do so, in order that their gifts might flourish and something permanent be created. It was the elder one, *apparently* much more secure, but cursed with a rival-complex, who feared that the younger might surpass her.

Virginia Woolf was already thirty-four when she first met Katherine Mansfield. All that she had to her own name then was *The Voyage Out*, a novel in traditional form which had taken her seven years to write and had cost her two breakdowns. Denouncing it herself as "long and dull," she was afraid it deserved to be condemned. She was now at work on the tedious *Night and Day*, but had not yet produced the short story "Kew Gardens"—her first departure from conventional narrative—whereas Katherine, a confident, healthy young woman of twenty-eight, had long since disavowed one book as "young and bad" and had lately begun to find new forms, in stories which Lytton thought "distinctly bright."

Both hurt by early wounds, both women were obliged to live behind some sort of mask. There was so much that neither could avow: in Virginia's case, the threat of insanity, brought nearer by her creative bouts. Publication of *The Voyage Out* had been followed by a harrowing breakdown of which Katherine knew nothing—screaming fits and violence, four mental nurses in attendance, her devoted husband scarcely seeing her for weeks. All that, Woolf covered up from the outside world.[1]

What Katherine saw when she went to Hogarth House was a

woman secure in her husband and her home, with a room to write in, a background of relatives distinguished in the arts, and no need at all to repudiate her family or feel estranged by being creative. A Miss Beauchamp from Thorndon and a daughter of Sir Leslie Stephen did not begin as equals in the race, if race it had to be.

There was so much more unknown about the future. That Katherine would be dead before she reached the age of Virginia when they met, leaving only two more books that contained inferior work, Virginia could not know for her comfort; nor that she would then have eighteen good years in which to achieve what she hoped, with fame as well.

The social barrier was of a kind that couldn't be removed. Virginia's family tree included Thackeray, John Addington Symonds, and even Ralph Vaughan Williams; as a girl she knew Henry James, and she and her sister grew up knowing the Cambridge conversation of brother's friends from Trinity—from among whom came both their husbands.

When Middleton Murry, the Oxford scholarship youth from Peckham, told Hal Beauchamp's daughter in 1913 that these Woolf people belonged to "a perfectly impotent Cambridge set," he implanted prejudice, no doubt—as did Strachey for Virginia two years later: " 'Katherine Mansfield'—if that's her real name—I could never quite make sure. . . . . decidedly an interesting creature. . . . . wanted to make your acquaintance. . . . . ugly impassive mask of a face. . . . . sharp and slightly vulgarly fanciful intellect sitting behind it."

She has "dogged my footsteps for three years," Virginia had replied; and now the footsteps met. It is true that Virginia's one-time suitor Sydney Waterlow, who was fit to propose if not to be accepted, was Katherine's second cousin, and another intermediary. But *his* grandmother, the Australian one, as he once admitted to Virginia, was a ratcatcher's daughter ("which he profoundly regrets. And so do I"), and Virginia had since come to hold a low opinion of him,* which

---

*"By God! What a bore that man is! I don't know why exactly, but no one I've ever met seems to me more palpably second-rate and now the poor creature resigns himself to it, & proposes to live next door to us at Richmond, & there copulate day & night & produce six little Waterlows. His house for a long time stank to me of dried semen— And it's only a kind of mutton fat in his case."—V.W. to Lytton Strachey, 22 October 1915 (the Strachey Trust, London.) The remark about the ratcatcher is in the *Diary*, 22 August 1922.

went still lower when, a few years later, he actually joined, by sharing Murry's house in Katherine's absence, what Virginia by that time called "the pigsty." Dogs, rats, pigs, the lot.

One other impediment existed. Woolf never liked Murry. He bore his sufferings in his own wife's illness with selfless dignity, and Murry's "strong Pecksniffian vein," as he called it, left him "irritated and revolted." He did like Katherine—"I don't think anyone has ever made me laugh more than she did in those days"—and he thought her a "very serious writer," who was in some way perverted and destroyed by Murry.[2]

There is no telling now what caused the first brush when they met, but by midsummer the two women had got to know each other well enough for Virginia to tell her sister that Katherine seemed to have "gone every sort of hog since she was 17," but had "a much better idea of writing than most." She also told Violet Dickinson that Katherine had had "every sort of experience, wandering about with travelling circuses over the moors of Scotland."[3] It sounds as though Katherine's confidences were either gaily inventive or not followed very closely.

A letter of Katherine's to Ottoline in July suggests how things stood then. Katherine had gathered that Virginia was "still *very* delicate," and seldom well enough to leave her own home and surroundings; she had dined with her last week and found her charming: "I do like her tremendously—but I felt then for the first time the strange, trembling, glinting quality of her mind—and quite for the first time she seemed to me to be one of those Dostoievsky women whose 'innocence' has been hurt— Immediately I decided that I understood her completely——I wonder if you agree at all."[4]

In August, something happened which has not been brought to light before, and which now puts a different complexion on the relationship between the two women as writers.

When the Woolfs moved down to Asheham, their house in Sussex, Katherine was invited for a weekend. She was to take with her the typescript of *Prelude,* or as much as the typist had done of it, but neither she nor Virginia looked forward to the occasion with much eagerness, the reason being, on Virginia's side at least, that Clive Bell and Maynard Keynes had lately been spreading Bloomsbury gossip about Katherine, no doubt connecting her with Bertrand Russell. So it happened that on the Wednesday before the visit Virginia wrote to

Lady Ottoline, having just read a letter from Katherine that seems to have set her teeth on edge:

> Katherine Mansfield describes your garden,* the rose leaves dying in the sun, the pool and long conversation between people wandering up and down in the moonlight. It calls out her romantic side; which I think rather a relief after the actresses, A.B.C.'s and paintpots.[5]

The letter from Katherine which prompted that has not survived—which is unusual, when the Woolfs were such meticulous keepers of her letters, and seem to have lost no others. By the same day's post, however, Lady Ottoline received one from the studio which almost alludes to it and must have resembled it. This is Katherine writing to Ottoline that same Wednesday (15 August 1917):

> Your glimpse of the garden—all flying green and gold made me wonder again *who* is going to write about that flower garden. It might be so wonderful, do you see *how* I mean? There would be people walking in the garden—several *pairs* of people—their conversation their slow pacing—their glances as they pass one another—the pauses as the flowers "come in" as it were—as a bright dazzle, an exquisite haunting scent, a shape so formal and fine, so much a "flower of the mind" that he who looks at it really is tempted for one bewildering moment to stoop & touch and make *sure.* The "pairs" of people must be very different and there must be a light touch of enchantment—some of them seeming so extraordinarily "odd" and separate from the flowers, but others quite related and at ease. A kind of, musically speaking, conversation *set* to flowers. Do you like the idea?. . . . . Its full of possibilities. I must have a fling at it as soon as I have time.[6]

The emphasised *"who"* at the beginning shows Katherine thinking that someone else might write such a story, while the "again" suggests that she is somehow repeating herself.

On returning to London after the weekend with her *Prelude* typescript Katherine wrote Virginia a bread-and-butter letter containing a

---

*Although the Morrells had been at Garsington for more than two years, the Woolfs had not yet been there. Because of Leonard's reluctance they had been putting it off. "A. B. C.'s," a few lines lower, were the tea-rooms of the Aerated Bread Company, found all over London—tea-rooms of the common people, of *New Age* contributors and so on.

sentence that has often been cited as evidence in general terms of the literary relationship between the two: "We have got the same job, Virginia and it is really very curious and thrilling that we should both, quite apart from each other, be after so very nearly the same thing." But the letter also contained a much more specific piece of information. "Yes," it said, "your Flower Bed is *very* good. There's a still, quivering changing light over it all and a sense of those couples dissolving in the bright air which fascinates me."[7]

This means that Virginia had shown Katherine her story "Kew Gardens,"* in which four couples stroll among the flower beds in various states of enchantment, exactly as prescribed in the letter to Ottoline, and *possibly* as prescribed in the missing letter to Virginia. The pairs are symmetrically distributed: there are Eleanor and Simon; there is William, walking with another man; there are two elderly women "of the lower middle class," and a young man and young woman "in the prime of life." We do see their slow pacing, we see the "bright dazzle" of the tulips, and some insects; we hear snatches of conversation, and some of the people are indeed extraordinarily "odd." They are not at Garsington, since Virginia did not know that garden yet; but she did know Kew.

The resemblance of the story to the idea in the letter is so close that there must have been some connection. What was it? When was "Kew Gardens" written? Apart from the details given here there seems to be no evidence for dating it. Nothing on record suggests that it had been written previously. Mrs. Woolf's diary (which is full of Asheham insects in that week) says nothing anywhere about its writing, but does show that there was time for it to have been composed between the reading of the letter and Katherine's arrival late on Saturday. If it wasn't written then, and at Katherine's direct prompting, some extraordinary coincidence needs explaining.

Whatever *had* happened in that week, the question still remains why it was that Virginia, who had published one long novel when they met, but no short stories, soon afterwards wrote two important short pieces —"Kew Gardens" and "The Mark on the Wall"—of which one is an experiment in dialogue and is also her first departure from traditional ways of seeing. The evidence is very strong that Katherine Mansfield

---

*So identified by Murry in a footnote, in the *Letters* of 1928.

in some way helped Virginia Woolf to break out of the mould in which she had been working hitherto.

There followed some last revisions, no doubt, of *Prelude* in typescript, and then some more short stories. A *Journal* entry has Chekhov appearing in the role of a writer *confirming* Katherine's desire to write things of uneven length. It was a productive, fruitful autumn—the studio full of figs and quinces, and ideas. An invitation to Garsington was declined by Murry with the news that Katherine had disappeared into retreat in order to write some stories "which will be as good as the extraordinary achievement which she has handed over to the tender mercies of the Hogarth Press."[8]

"Tender mercies" meant something like this: faced with hand setting, from a newly acquired typecase, the seventeen thousand words of *Prelude* (their "Publication No. 2"), Woolf and Virginia made a start on returning to Richmond in October, and pulled a proof of one page which they invited Katherine to come and see. They then had the bright idea that Alix Sargant-Florence, aged twenty-two and just down from Newnham, might be the person to take on the tedious chore of setting. She accepted because she thought it would be "an introduction to literary work of some sort," and on going to Richmond, all ready to be literary with literary people, she was put on a stool in the top-floor room and shown how to pick up tiny pieces of metal, with forceps, and put them in "a metal frame," face up. Having shown her what to do (with forceps), Leonard and Virginia then went for a walk with their dog. They were surprised, on their return, to learn that Alix had decided she couldn't possibly do anything so boring. They were "very nice about it," so she packed up and left[9]—the first of a succession of intelligent young persons who were to discover, over the years, the extraordinary notions that Woolf and Virginia had of how to engage and treat employees. No doubt the Woolfs eventually learned, as they undertook corrections, what the forceps supplied with a typecase are meant for. After a while, a new apprentice was found in Barbara Hiles, a girl from the Slade with bobbed hair and a fringe, who for some weeks continued the setting of *Prelude*.

It happens that the week in which Katherine dined at Hogarth House and saw her page proof was also the week in which Virginia began a new volume of her diary—or rather, in its proper sense began the regular keeping of her diary as we know it. Thus the entry for 10

October 1917 records "the prospect of K. Mansfield to dinner, when many delicate things fall to be discussed." These were not in fact to do with *Prelude*, but with Clive Bell's gossip and its consequences.* Then on the following day:

> The dinner last night went off: the delicate things were discussed. We could both wish that ones first impression of K.M. was not that she stinks like a—well civet cat that had taken to street walking. In truth, I'm a little shocked by her commonness at first sight; lines so hard & cheap. However, when this diminishes, she is so intelligent & inscrutable that she repays friendship.

This interesting passage has been rather freely interpreted by Leonard Woolf. Falling into a masculine error which Virginia herself did not commit, he has written, a little symmetrically perhaps, of Virginia's disliking Katherine's "cheap scent and cheap sentimentality."[11] Katherine was fond of a rather expensive French perfume called Genêt Fleuri (it probably reminded her of Wellington's hills aflame with gorse). Whether this is what she was wearing on the night she went to Hogarth House, her biographer must not presume to say, but I think that anyone who has known her three sisters would declare with some vehemence that no Beauchamp, even the fallen Kathleen, could ever have worn "cheap scent." That it was a capital error to use scent at all when going to dine with Leonard and Virginia and look at page proofs is obvious, of course, and it may be that we have here discovered a whole new field for doctoral researches—Class and the Olfactory Symbol in Virginia Woolf. One simple fact remains, however:

> *That perfume chaste*
> *Was but good taste*
> *Misplaced!*

---

*"I think these rumours that are put into motion, whether by Clive or the other Bloomsburies, too preposterous to be taken seriously."—Murry to Lady Ottoline, 15 September 1917. "Clive, that plump marrow, hiding under the leaves, and every leaf an ear, can't be taken seriously—do you think?"—K.M. to Lady Ottoline, 23 September. "All very odd, isn't it? And quite unimportant. Such people are not to be taken seriously."—Clive Bell to Vanessa Bell from Garsington, at about the same time,[10] the background to all of which is suggested in Katherine's letter to Virginia of 22 August (after the visit): "But don't let THEM persuade you that I spend any of my precious time

To Virginia, that evening, Katherine stank. But cheaply so? Or expensively so? Did Virginia dislike perfume altogether? Is there any in her novels? The Bond Street scene in *Mrs. Dalloway* contains a passing reference to "Atkinson's scent shop" which sounds distinctly slighting —but then what references to shops do not, in Virginia Woolf? Perhaps the question really turns upon a deeper difference between the two women, a larger issue altogether. Katherine, with a touch of Lawrence's "good animal" in her, did go in for the life of the senses, and Virginia shied away from it, which is why she had such curiosity in this regard. Katherine did love food and scents and colour and music (above all verbal music), with a passionate delight that ruled out *curiosity* altogether. And Virginia, though drawn by curiosity toward that side of her, at the same time found it somehow vulgar ("she seems to have gone every sort of hog since she was seventeen"); and this very distaste is a defect in her writing.

If Leonard Woolf was stretching the terms a little when he wrote of "cheap scent," then I think, with all respect, that Professor Quentin Bell is guilty of something similar when he writes, as it were on his aunt's behalf, that Katherine "dressed like a tart."[12] Mrs. Woolf doesn't say so in her diary; in fact she scarcely refers to Katherine's outward appearance or her dress (those "lines so hard and cheap" must refer to something else, since they diminished during the evening), whereas in other cases she is as generous with such information as Chaucer himself. That Katherine may have "behaved like a bitch" is for the family to say, and not for a mere biographer to question; but neither photographs nor reliable witnesses known to the present author have ever put Katherine Mansfield into clothes that would be suitable for duty in Leicester Square. "Dainty in appearance. . . . . great charm in her femininity" (Anne Estelle Rice); "Exquisite in her person. . . . . always scrupulously groomed" (Frieda Lawrence), and many similar accounts by word of mouth. Admittedly Lady Ottoline has described Katherine's dress as "rather a cheap taste, slightly Swan & Edgar," and the wife of Frank Harris is on record as calling her "no beauty," about five foot four in height, "and square everywhere," while Francis Carco

---

swapping hats or committing adultery—I'm far too arrogant and proud." See also Virginia's diary for 27 October 1917. It should be recalled, perhaps, that Clive Bell's wife was living with Duncan Grant and he himself had an attachment to Mrs. St. John Hutchinson. Katherine's letter had therefore trodden rather heavily on family matters.

seems to have known a dowdy phase.[13] But the further one tries to pursue this matter by authorities, the further certainty recedes. How a woman's dress strikes other women is one of the greater mysteries.

And so back to a scented dinner. Since Virginia was writing an article on Henry James which had to be ready two days later there was some discussion of him, a subject on which Katherine was "illuminating," Virginia thought. But then the doorbell rang. A "munition worker called Leslie Moor. . . . . another of these females on the border land of propriety, & naturally inhabiting the underworld," had arrived to take Katherine back to Chelsea.

That is all the diary said of their talk next day. Although it often mentions the conversations Virginia had with Katherine, it seldom gives reports. However, Katherine too sat down at her desk, not with a notebook—for there is in all her notebooks not one word about her friendship with Virginia, at least avowedly—but to write to Brett. The long, informative letter which then went off to Scotland is almost certainly a record of that evening's talk, set off as it was by Henry James. For *Prelude,* she said, the Woolves had served her up "so much praise in such a golden bowl that I couldn't help feeling gratified," and the whole letter seems an overflow from that:

It seems to me so extraordinarily right that you should be painting Still Lives just now. What can one do, faced with this wonderful tumble of round bright fruits, but gather them and play with them—and *become them,* as it were. When I pass an apple stall I cannot help stopping and staring until I feel that I, myself, am changing into an apple, too, and that at any moment I can produce an apple, miraculously, out of my own being, like the conjuror produces the egg. . . . . When you paint apples do you feel that your breasts and your knees become apples, too? Or do you think this the greatest nonsense. I don't. I am sure it is not. When I write about ducks I swear that I am a white duck with a round eye, floating on a pond fringed with yellow-blobs and taking an occasional dart at the other duck with the round eye, which floats upside down beneath me. . . In fact the whole process of becoming the duck (what Lawrence would perhaps call this consummation with the duck or the apple!) is so thrilling that I can hardly breathe, only to think about it. For although that is as far as most people can get, it is really only the "prelude." There follows the moment when you are *more* duck, *more* apple, and *more* Natasha than any of these objects could ever possibly be, and so you *create* them anew.

Brett (switching off the instrument): "Katherine I *beg* of you to stop. You must tell us all about it at the Brotherhood Church one Sunday evening."[14]

There is not much doubt that the foregoing provides a sample of the sort of conversation with Katherine that Virginia valued.

How much it did mean to her is casually revealed by a mere three words slipped into the diary a few months later. One Saturday morning Virginia sat with her sister Vanessa and Duncan Grant in their studio, talking about art. Nessa and Duncan, unfavourably comparing a painter's life in England with that in France, said that there was no one worth considering as a painter in England, and no one like K.M., "or Forster even," with whom it was worth discussing one's business.[15] Forster by then had published all of his novels except *A Passage to India.*

There was still much delay in getting *Prelude* into type, and Katherine and Virginia seem not to have seen each other for some time—no doubt because of the Clive Bell episode. By January 1918, a sixth of the pages had been printed off and Virginia thought the rest would take five weeks, but it took five months. They were months, as it happened, in which Katherine's life was completely changed by illness. To that, the next chapter returns; but I think it will be easier for the reader if we follow the story of Katherine and Virginia to its end in this one.

By the end of June 1918, *Prelude* was ready to receive such publication as it got, Virginia's diary remarking that although it seemed "a little vapourish" and was freely watered with some of Katherine's "cheap realities," it had the living power of a work of art. Then her new story, *Bliss,* was published in the *English Review,* and Virginia threw it down with the exclamation, "She's done for!" Katherine's mind, after all, was very thin soil, and the story's whole conception was "poor, cheap, not the vision, however imperfect, of an interesting mind."

During the autumn, Virginia began visiting Katherine almost every week at the house which the Murrys by then had bought in Hampstead, and she found herself liking her more and more. Then, just after Christmas, she was puzzled, and as the *Diary* shows, very hurt, by the fact that Katherine seemed to have "dropped" her, and had not acknowledged some Christmas gifts which she had sent. She could never have known what agony on Katherine's side had caused this break—but it belongs in a later chapter.

Katherine's life then fell into the painful pattern of English summers and Mediterranean winters which disrupted her marriage, her friendships, and everything else, and Virginia watched the process with a sympathy which seems rather chilly at times.

It was in the spring and summer of 1919, after Murry had been appointed editor of the *Athenaeum,* that the two women had their best meetings and the longest diary passages were written, recording, for instance, on 22 March, Virginia's annoyance with "the inscrutable woman," but then, as well, "a sense of ease & interest, which is, I suppose, due to her caring so genuinely if so differently from the way I care, about our precious art." These passages are known by now; here is the other side, a letter of Katherine's to Lady Ottoline:

> I understand *exactly* what you say about Virginia—beautiful brilliant creature that she is and suddenly at the last moment, turning into a bird and flying up to a topmost bough and continuing the conversation from there . . . She delights in beauty as I imagine a bird does; she has a *bird's eye* for "that angular high stepping green insect" that she writes about*
> and she is not *of* her subject—she hovers over, dips, skims, makes exquisite flights—sees the lovely reflections in water that a bird must see—but *not humanly.* [16]

It was possible for them in that summer to spend an hour together very happily. Virginia found herself really liking Katherine, and felt they had reached some kind of durable foundation. But, alas, there were rocks ahead.

In the autumn, Katherine went south to the Italian Riviera, from where she was reviewing novels for the *Athenaeum,* and Murry sent her *Night and Day* to review. Virginia had conceived that book as an "exercise in the conventional style" (the words are her own), perhaps as a recuperative work, after the terrors of *The Voyage Out.* Well knowing that it had not come from the best part of her mind, she even called it "that interminable *Night and Day.* "

Katherine, knowing none of this, and assuming, as one does, that a serious writer's latest work puts her best foot forward, saw the novel

---

*In "Kew Gardens." V.W.'s phrase is actually "the singular high-stepping angular green insect."

as a pedestrian affair; but there were also elements in it which she hated, and she dreaded the task of reviewing it. She was under great stress at the time, from her fear of death and other causes, but in sixteen days nine letters refer to her anxiety over the review. Her private opinion was that "it is a lie in the soul. The war never has been: that is what its message is. . . . ." It reeked of intellectual snobbery, but she couldn't say so: "I tried my best to be friendly and erred on the side of kindness"—and so on.[17]

There is no doubt of the review's sincerity, or the serious thought that Katherine put into it.* As Quentin Bell says, it was perceptive and discreet, and by no means unfair to the novel. Unfortunately, in comparing the novel to a ship sailing serenely into port, the review had slipped into a hurtful phrase, occasioned by the fact that ships are feminine: "The strangeness lies in her aloofness, her air of quiet perfection, her lack of any sign that she has made a perilous voyage—the absence of any scars."

Virginia saw spite in the review, and so did Woolf, as the diary records. They had, after all, expected praise. They knew nothing of Katherine's dreadful state in Italy just then.

All questions of snobbery apart, there lay behind this episode a feeling of Katherine's which went beyond the personal: her conviction (of which she had spoken to Virginia in the week of the Armistice) that the novel must respond profoundly to the world's first total war. After telling Murry that *Night and Day* in effect denied the war, she went on:

> I don't want (G. forbid!) mobilisation and the violation of Belgium, but the novel can't just leave the war out. There *must* have been a change of heart. It is really fearful to see the "settling down" of human beings. I feel in the *profoundest* sense that nothing can ever be the same—that, as artists, we are traitors if we feel otherwise: we have to take it into account and find new expressions, new moulds for our new thoughts and feelings.[18]

Those closing words led, eventually, to her own little masterpiece, *The Fly*. A few days later she enlarged on what she meant about the postwar novel in general. The passage is important to an understanding of her own later work and cannot safely be condensed:

*It is printed in *Novels and Novelists*.

I can't imagine how after the war these men can pick up the old threads as though it had never been. Speaking to *you* I'd say we have died and live again. How can that be the same life? It doesn't mean that life is the less precious or that "the common things of light and day" are gone. They are not gone, they are intensified, they are illumined. Now we know ourselves for what we are. In a way it's a tragic knowledge: it's as though, even while we live again, we face death. But *through Life:* that's the point. We see death in life as we see death in a flower that is fresh unfolded. Our hymn is to the flower's beauty: we would make that beauty immortal because we *know*. Do you feel like this—or otherwise —or how?

But, of course, you don't imagine I mean by this knowledge let-us-eat-and-drink-ism. No, I mean "deserts of vast eternity." But the difference between you and me is (perhaps I'm wrong) I couldn't tell anybody *bang out* about those deserts: they are my secret. I might write about a boy eating strawberries or a woman combing her hair on a windy morning, and that is the only way I can ever mention them. But they *must* be there. Nothing less will do. They can advance and retreat, curtsey, caper to the most delicate airs they like,* but I am bored to Hell by it all. Virginia, *par exemple.* [19]

It seems a pity that neither Katherine nor Virginia could ever speak "bang out" about their deserts of vast eternity. One wants to show that letter to Virginia—even to show Virginia's later work to Katherine Perhaps artists would be better not to live their lives until their biographies have been written.

A winter passed with no correspondence between them, and when Katherine returned she seemed not anxious to meet again—but a fever was to blame. The *Diary* portrays her now as "of the cat kind: alien, composed, always solitary—observant." (Virginia never knew, of course, how much of Beauchamp or Dyer she was describing.) But then they fell into step, and Virginia found the other expressing *her* feelings as she never heard them expressed: to no one but Leonard could she speak in the same disembodied way about writing without altering her thought more than she altered it in the diary.[20]

More meetings occurred over the summer. Virginia went up to the

*"Curtsey and retreat" was a phrase she had lately used in a letter to Murry of an *Athenaeum* article by Clive Bell. It perfectly describes his prose style, which makes much use of elegant inversion.

house the Murrys had bought in Hampstead, to visit a Katherine who drew herself across the room "like some suffering animal." After a farewell visit, Virginia probed the strangeness of her emotions. Did she feel it as much as she ought to? Would Katherine mind their parting? She noted her own callousness, but then at once came "the blankness of not having her to talk to."

When *Bliss and Other Stories* was published in time for Christmas, and praised for a column in the *Times Literary Supplement,* Virginia saw the prospect of paeans to come, and felt a little nettle of jealousy growing in her, which she plucked by writing a little note to say how glad and proud she was. Katherine modestly said she didn't deserve the letter, and closed her reply with an odd note of finality: "I wonder if you know what your visits were to me—or how much I miss them. You are the only woman with whom I long to talk *work*. There will never be another. . . . . Farewell, dear friend (may I call you that?)"²¹

It sounds as though Katherine had heard something she didn't like. At any rate, that letter of Katherine's was the end of the friendship, on her side at least. For, some weeks later, after hearing how ill and lonely she was at Menton, Virginia wrote again, but received no answer, and was hurt, as she later told Brett. Some "odious gossip" had assured her that this was Katherine's game, and so on; but she wished she had tried again, for Katherine had given her "something no one else can."²²

In the meantime she had finished *Jacob's Room,* the novel in which new techniques, and experiments with the sense of time which probably owed something to her talks with Katherine, began to take her toward her future manner; the novel, as well, which repeatedly declares that human beings can never really know the truth about each other.

When Katherine died, Virginia confessed in her diary that Katherine's writing was "the only writing I have ever been jealous of," and she later told Ottoline that while Katherine was alive she could never, from jealousy, read her books. No doubt we must look upon this jealousy as part of her illness, and not regard it in a moral light. Yet Katherine only envied what Virginia had (her home, and her security in her husband), whereas Virginia was jealous of what Katherine might attain. Perhaps that caused the guilt she also felt.

A diary entry made by Virginia within three weeks of Katherine's death[23] describes the feeling of melancholy that had been brooding over her for the past fortnight. She was alone now, with no competitor: cock of her walk, but a lonely one. She would go on writing, of course —"but into emptiness."

CHAPTER XV

Bandol, 1918

Late in the summer of 1917, while *Prelude* was still being revised at the studio for the Hogarth Press, Wig and Bogey had been nursing their dream of a lovely farmhouse in which they would live at peace when the war was over and be successful authors—married at last (the divorce was coming through), released from all former stress, and devoting their lives to literature. It would be Runcton Cottage without all the things that had gone wrong there. Bloomsbury, except Virginia, would never cross the threshold, and would no longer be able to snigger about their problem in regard to Katherine's name. They would have a little son—someone else would care for him—they would read Wordsworth and Coleridge, the smoke would curl lazily from a fire of autumn leaves, and they would both do their finest work in their peaceful, separate rooms.

This was first heard of in a letter that Murry wrote to his schoolboy brother Arthur (later known as Richard), who was in fact already on a farm: by his brother's contriving he was working at Garsington, to help him recover from some operations for tuberculous glands; after which, with Jack's support, he was to take up printing at the Central School of Art and Design. On 9 September 1917 Murry wrote to him at Garsington about the "wonderful old farmhouse with walls six foot thick, an orchard, a meadow, and plenty of good farm buildings," which the three of them would find when the war was over. They would turn the "finest barn" into the printer's shop; Richard would have to look after the garden and the butter-making, and they would all (in strictest secrecy) "become very famous together."[1]

This dream-farm came to be known as The Heron, in memory of Katherine's brother. There is a little self-mockery in Murry's description, which was expressly shielded against Clive Bell, but the dream was serious too: they shared the general belief that after the war the old good life would still be possible. For the present, they both worked hard.

In Murry's case, too hard: in November he went to pieces. Dr. Croft-Hill once more told him he was in danger of tuberculosis (the disease was then taking 1,000 lives a week in Britain) and suggested sick leave and a rest. So Katherine wrote to Ottoline asking if they could have him in the cottage: "One of his lungs is slightly affected but the principal thing is fever, *complete* exhaustion—a collapse at last after this appalling depression and overwork."[2]

It is plain from her letters that she herself felt perfectly well at the time. Her only complaint this year was her accursed "rheumatiz," and there is no hint that she knew of any risk to her own lungs; which makes it all the more extraordinary that only a few weeks earlier she had done a translation, and published it in the *New Age,* of Alphonse Daudet's story "La Chèvre de M. Seguin."

A cautionary tale from Provence designed to make small children appreciate their homes, the story is addressed in the *Lettres de mon moulin* to a fifteenth-century French poet who had preferred his ill-clad poverty to security. Very well, says Daudet to Gringoire, M. Seguin's goat longed for freedom too; she broke her cord, went up on the mountain, met the wolf, and fought all night until the dawn:

> "At last!" said the poor creature, who was only waiting for the daylight that she might die, and she lay down on the ground in her lovely white fur, all spotted with blood . . . And the wolf jumped on to the little goat and ate her up. . . . .
>
> You understand me well, Gringoire.
>
> In the morning the wolf ate her up.[3]

In all the circumstances, it isn't possible that Katherine—who soon was heading for the South of France when ill, in time of war—could have fallen upon this Provençal tale, translated it, and published it, without seeing herself (as a letter to Murry did make explicit some time later) in M. Seguin's goat. It was not her habit to make translations: this was the only one she ever published, and it clearly belongs with some other strange "predictions" of the fate which she had almost seemed to court since her adolescence. She knew about the price. Her freedom on the mountain was her art.

Murry went to Garsington on 24 November,[4] and was housed in the manor, of course. They had meanwhile decided that they must live apart no more, King's Proctor or no King's Proctor,* and Katherine vowed while Jack was away to "house-hunt by day and write by night."

Then she went down for a weekend visit, in very cold weather. After the drive in the dog-cart from Wheatley station she was chilled. She took to bed, but returned to Chelsea, and soon was ill, with "pleurisy" again. A neighbor called in Dr. Ainger (a New Zealander in fact), who told her she must stay in bed; which she reported to Murry, adding: "I am still feeling *prestissimo*. In fact, I can't sleep for a nut. I lie in a kind of *furious bliss.*"

Murry came up to town. Christmas at Garsington was abandoned, and Dr. Ainger said that Katherine must escape the English winter, himself suggesting the South of France. (That would also remove any legal risk to her divorce.) It was decided that L.M. was to go as well, to help Katherine and get her settled in, so armed with medical certificates, Murry and L.M. went off to get passports. The news was conveyed to Ottoline as the greatest of jokes, but behind the jokes was fear. For Dr. Ainger shortly said that there was a "spot" on Katherine's right lung. To get to the sun was now imperative. At this stage, she could possibly still have been cured, were she willing to put that first.

The news brought family help to the door of the studio. Katherine's sister Chaddie, widowed in India and now in London working at War Graves Registration, called in a car with Aunt Belle, bearing lashings of food, which was hard to get. Aunt Belle (who had herself once had TB) would have liked to sweep Kathleen off to her place in the coun-

---

*The case of *Bowden* v. *Bowden* had been heard in London on 17 October 1917. The decree *nisi* was to become absolute at the end of April 1918.

try, *de luxe*—"furs and motor-cars from here to there"—but Dr. Ainger said no, she must stay where she was and be quiet. So Christmas saw no partying. As a present from Aunt Belle, so Wig told Jack, there arrived "an IMMENSE apple-green padded silk dressing-gown. . . . . big enough for at least three Wigs great with child," which had to be taken to Knightsbridge and changed.

By New Year's Day, Katherine felt well enough to join Murry at Garsington for a rest before her journey. Returning to London, they learned that L.M., after all, had been refused a permit to go with her. It was the moment when, as hindsight can so easily say, they should have cancelled the whole idea; but defying the war, they went ahead. On the Sunday afternoon at Jack's place they made love together (this is mentioned in letters), and on Monday 7 January 1918 Katherine set off alone from Waterloo, armed with a pretty new muff. She would come back in April to be married. What bliss! Meanwhile Jack must remember to address his letters and telegrams to "Mrs. Bowden"—the name on her hateful passport.[5]

She landed at Le Havre in a snowstorm, and wrote about the beauty of it. She had a hot place in her chest, which she called "the flat-iron." Although the train to Paris was unheated, with snow coming in through a broken window, her uppermost thought was to write of that. There followed the journey past Fontainebleau to the Midi, in a compartment with two ladies dressed in black who talked of what a fatal place it was for anyone with lung trouble; and then the alarming trip from Marseilles to Bandol in a train besieged by soldiers in a very ugly mood; of which Murry, Ottoline and J. D. Fergusson all received amusing descriptions some days later. Always, the danger or the misery was a stimulus to write, to burn with brightened flame.

Of course the journey took its toll. After reaching Bandol Katherine told Murry that she felt like "a fly who has been dropped into the milk-jug and fished out again, but is still too milky and drowned to start cleaning up yet."[6]

At the Hôtel Beau Rivage, new people had taken over. A strange woman greeted her, wiping her mouth with a serviette. Nothing was known of her reservation; the hotel was unheated—and it cost much more. In the town, familiar shops had changed: no one recognized her now. A destroyer and two submarines were anchored in the bay—"quantities of black soldiers everywhere." No cigarettes to be had—until the submarine captain gave her some roll-your-own. Under the palm trees there now was human excrement. Late as it comes, all this was Katherine's first real experience of what the war was doing to Europe. England was still only learning that.

The ninety-odd letters from this four-month separation amount to one-fifth of all that Katherine wrote to Murry. In them are found some of her most courageous words, and some of her cruellest and most despairing. Some are brimming with love, not only for Murry (the Corsican maid, Juliette, is unforgettable), while others freeze with hatred. They race from one extreme of fever to the other.

Her first response to France—from Paris, on the way through—was to recognize her love for it ("It is because I never feel *indifferent*"), but within three weeks she was scribbling in a notebook that she hated the French, and on the same page starting a story which served to sublimate that feeling. She herself noticed the resemblance to Lawrence's condition. She could not control her moods of exasperation, and she developed an irrational dislike for Ottoline, whose present of a costly shawl was keeping her warm in the evenings.

Her reckless resolve that Jack must not be worried with bad news went by the board; she had no one else to tell. And from Redcliffe Road he began to take what steps he could to help. They had a slightly embarrassing acquaintance in Carpentras, Mme. Régine Geoffroi, whose husband was a doctor and now the mayor (they must have met in Bandol three years before); and it seems that Jack wrote to her, since to Katherine's dismay she turned up unexpectedly, after an exhausting journey, for a one-night visit on 18 January. Her passion for Keats made her a tiring visitor. Murry had also told L.M., of course, how Katherine was, and she was trying once more to get a travel permit.

"My left lung aches and aches," wrote Katherine while Mme. Geoffroi was there. "It is like an appalling *burn.*" But "don't send Lesley," says the same letter. "I can stand it, and if I do get worse I will tell G[eoffroi]." Next day she was admitting, "It is quite true. I have been *bloody ill*"; and she went into the town to buy a rubber-tipped cane to help her walk.

The pain and anxiety, far from preventing "work," had just the opposite effect. She began one piece which came to nothing: "tame, diffuse, 'missed it,' " was her comment in a letter.* But then, at the end

---

*It was probably *Love-lies-bleeding*, a fragment printed in the *Scrapbook.*

of January, immediately following some remarks against French sexuality, she began to write her story *Je ne parle pas français,* which was to prove a turning point as important as *Prelude* had been, though in such a different way.

She began it in a state of feverish excitement—a state that from now on typified productive periods—and under conditions one would hardly wish upon one's own worst enemy. "My work excites me so tremendously that I almost feel *insane* at night," she wrote to Murry when halfway through. Half knowing that that was a danger sign, she added: "there is a great black bird flying over me, and I am so frightened he'll settle—so terrified. I don't know exactly what *kind* he is."

Night terrors and insomnia returned, night terrors from a long way back. Her only relief was in reading Dickens: "if I read him in bed he diverts my mind." And yet, if she were not working, "with war and anxiety I should go mad, I think. My night terrors here are rather complicated by packs and packs of growling, roaring, ravening, prowl-and-prowl-around dogs."[7] The howl in the night of Daudet's wolf, perhaps.

In London, while all of this was happening to Katherine, a dead-tired Murry had to return alone each night to Redcliffe Road after eating out, re-read her letters there, and try to be adequate in reply. His job was now much bigger (he was soon to become Chief Censor), and yet his own ambition in the evenings was to be—no less—the finest English poet of his day. While convalescing at Garsington in the previous autumn he had made his first acquaintance with Keats's letters, and that experience, as his biographer has shown, was to prove a turning point in *his* life. It had befallen him, moreover, at the very moment when fate seemed to have transferred Keats's illness from his own lungs into Katherine's, a fact that impressed him deeply. As he told her somewhat later, he felt he had it in him now to write "such love poetry as had never yet been written." And then he declared:

No, my darling, you and I are English, and because we are truly English we are set apart from our generation. That has gone whoring after strange gods, and only you and I and Wordsworth and Coleridge, Lamb Keats and Shelley abide. . . . . You are the perfect flower of England—the thing that Shakespeare dreamed. . . . . I know I become fantastic; but these fantastic ideas of mine are true somehow.[8]

Poor Murry! The fantasy had picked ironic words. It was the "strange gods," in fact, who were to alter English poetry. The two outsiders, Eliot and Pound, were already at their work of overthrow, and the joint retreat from cities and corruption was not to be, for Jack, a way to greatness. The poetry he was writing at this time, though drawn from live emotion, was written in dead language. In their household, at least, it was Katherine, and in a most un-English way, who was to "make it new" in English literature.

But alarming news had reached her room: She could soon expect L.M. With no encouragement from Jack, Ida had gone to the passport office on her own, burst into tears at the counter, and won her way. Hysterical letters began to arrive from her. *Much* worse than Mme. Geoffroi! Ida really was coming—coming to feed on Katie's need of her. Cannibalistic metaphors, of the sort that Brigid Brophy has noted in her Freudian study[9] of Katherine's life and consumption: "She *is* a ghoul in a way. . . . . As long as I am to be massaged she's an angel, for then *c'est elle qui mange.* . . . . That's why I used to get so furious at the studio, for there she ate me before my eyes, and I really *revolted.*"[10]

On February 10 (just in time, as it happened) Katherine finished copying out the last of *Je ne parle pas français,* and sent it off to Jack. "Take it. It's yours," she wrote. "But what I felt so curiously as I wrote it was—ah! I am in a way *grown up* as a writer—a sort of authority— just as I feel about your poetry. Pray God you like it now you've got it all."

She told him she had *dreamed* a story in the night, complete even down to its title, which was *Sun and Moon;* by the next day she had written and copied that, and was ready to start something new and big, except that L.M. might appear at any hour. What *could* be the reason for her coming? Was *he* ill? If that was so, she'd understand.

Bearing some squashed *babas au rhum* from Paris, L.M. arrived on 12 February—"completely hysterical about me," so Jack was told. Succeeding letters described her with a revulsion only paralleled at times of fever: "She's a revolting hysterical ghoul. She's never content except when she can eat me" (12 February). "You should have seen her face drop when she said, 'I thought you were very ill.' My blood turned ice with horror" (14 February). "Oh, I do *detest* her personality, and her powerful broody henniness—and her 'we' and 'our.' " One day L.M. asked: "Katie mine, who is Wordsworth? Must I like him? It's no good looking cross because I love you, my angel, from the little tip of that cross eyebrow to the *all* of you. When am I going to brush your hair again?"[11]

But this occasion was Lesley's greatest triumph.* For it was only seven days after her arrival, as the *Journal* records, that Katherine glimpsed the scarlet tongue of Daudet's wolf:

> February 19. I woke up early this morning and when I opened the shutters the full round sun was just risen. I began to repeat that verse of Shakespeare's: "Lo, here the gentle lark weary of rest," and bounded back into bed. The bound made me cough—I spat—it tasted strange— it was bright red blood. Since then I've gone on spitting each time I cough a little more. Oh, yes, of course I'm frightened. But for two reasons only. I don't want to be ill, I mean "seriously," away from Jack. Jack is the first thought. 2nd, I don't want to find this is real consumption, perhaps it's going to gallop—who knows?—and I shan't have my work written. *That's what matters.* How unbearable it would be to die— leave "scraps," "bits" . . . nothing real finished. . . . . L.M. has gone for the doctor.

The doctor was an Englishman, of sorts, and when writing to Murry after she had seen him Katherine played the whole thing down, or tried to. "Bogey," she wrote, using the pet name that had once been Chummie's and now was Jack's, "this is *not* serious, does *not* keep me in bed, is absolutely curable, but I have been spitting a bit of blood. See?" In fact, of course, she had "nearly had a fit" (as the letter went on to confess) when she saw that bright arterial blood. She had known it at once. Keats had known it; so had Lawrence; and so had her own Aunt Belle, at one time.

"Doctor Poached Eyes," as Katherine called him, was one of those shady characters whom she loved to hate encountering in foreign parts —"a maniac on *venereal* diseases and *passion*" and a "filthy little brute." She was "sure he is here because he has killed some poor girl with a dirty button-hook."[12] To endure his leer, and to write to Dr. Ainger, was the best that could be done, meanwhile, for M. Seguin's goat. Except that, of course, she could apply the balm of humour, and write

---

*"I had *no word* from Katherine telling me not to go out to France. Murry tried to dissuade me. *But I knew I had to go.* Later I think my feeling proved right?"—L.M.'s comment on the typescript, at this point, of the author's previous biography.

the comic lines which head this chapter; or she could get on with her "work." She would fight all night, until the dawn.

[2]

The original manuscript of *Je ne parle pas français* comprises forty pages of pencil-scribble in one of Katherine's notebooks, with a few later changes in ink, which she apparently began on 30 January 1918— exactly two weeks before L.M. arrived.

There were three main impulses behind its writing. One was the irrational loathing that she had developed for the French since coming away this time; another was her profound despair about the war and what it was doing to everything she loved ("it's never out of my mind, and everything is poisoned by it"); but the strongest impulse that she acknowledged was her love for Jack. She later told him that she had "fed on our love" as she wrote it, and she called it "a tribute to Love, you understand, and the best that I can do just now."[13]

It was her first major story to be written through a persona not her own. Its method is simply a total impersonation of its cynical narrator, and the fact that Katherine was reading so much Dickens at the time—"I am not reading Dickens *idly,*" Jack was told—is not without significance. Always impersonating, as she was, she had now found a way to use that faculty throughout a major piece. One other, more visible influence, is that of Dostoevsky: in the story's tone, and in the self-revelation of its seedy narrator, there is more than a trace of the *Notes from Underground,* which she probably had read at the Villa Pauline when Murry was writing his Dostoevsky book.

Je ne parle pas français is the story which Katherine called her "cry against corruption," and it prompted one of her most revealing general statements of artistic aim. The paragraphs that follow have been quoted rather often, but we need them here for an understanding of what she was about. They were written before she had completed half of the story:

> I've two "kick offs" in the writing game. *One* is joy—real joy—the thing that made me write when we lived at Pauline, and that sort of writing I could only do in just that state of being in some perfectly blissful way *at peace.* Then something delicate and lovely seems to open before my eyes, like a flower without thought of a frost or a cold breath

—knowing that all about it is warm and tender and "ready." And *that* I try, ever so humbly, to express.

The other "kick off" is my old original one, and (had I not known love) it would have been my all. Not hate or destruction (both are beneath contempt as real motives) but an *extremely* deep sense of hopelessness, of everything doomed to disaster, almost wilfully, stupidly, like the almond tree and "pas de nougat pour le noël."* There! as I took out a cigarette paper I got it exactly—*a cry against corruption*—that is *absolutely* the nail on the head. Not a protest—a *cry*, and I mean corruption in the widest sense of the word, of course.

I am at present fully launched, right out in the deep sea, with this second state. . . . .[14]

Since, after *Prelude, Je ne parle pas français* was the longest piece in *Bliss and Other Stories*, it must have contributed to the stir which that book caused in 1920. Yet criticism has largely overlooked it, perhaps because it has only been known, through all these years, in an expurgated version, with cuts that have blunted its meaning. The little private-press edition in which it first appeared is very rare. It has never since been reprinted, and few know the story in its intended form.

Its narrator, through whose mind the whole of it passes while he sits musing in a café, is a cynical young Parisian called Raoul Duquette, a "little perfumed fox-terrier of a Frenchman." He writes for two newspapers, but is going in for serious literature (he is the author so far of *False Coins, Wrong Doors,* and *Left Umbrellas*) and he has a taste for English things of quality: he wears an English overcoat, and has an English desk in his flat; he likes that ridiculous song about "One fishball"; and he has a homo-erotic liking for the young English writer, Dick Harmon, whom he met in Paris once and who was far too fond of his mother.

In the café Duquette picks up a writing-pad, to find that someone has written there "that stupid, stale little phrase, *je ne parle pas français,* " and it is this that suddenly brings back the whole tragic tale of Dick and the helpless pretty English girl whom he brought across to Paris and at once deserted there.

Her name is Mouse. Dick calls her that (an echo no doubt of Tig),

*An allusion to a poem in Provençal by Henri Fabre, the naturalist, telling of the withering of the almond blossom by the cold (Murry's note).

and she acquires no other name. Duquette has been asked to book two separate rooms for them, in a "discreet" hotel. He meets them at the station. Exquisite and fragile, Mouse wears a long dark cloak with cuffs and collar of grey fur, and her hands are in a minute muff—"Mouse II." Her first shy words to him are, *"Je ne parle pas français."* She knows no one else in Paris.

He takes them to their rooms, and stays awhile. Mouse asks for "Tea. Immediately!" He observes in a while—as a writer observes—that all is not well between them; then suddenly Dick darts out to "write a letter" in the other room: "It's to my mother." He never returns; and Mouse, after a long, embarrassing wait, goes across the passage and finds that the letter is for her:

MOUSE, MY LITTLE MOUSE,
It's no good. It's impossible. I can't see it through. Oh,
I do love you. I do love you, Mouse, but I can't hurt her. . . . .

Duquette (a pimp, in fact, as we learn in the café where he muses on this little tragedy), is not the man to comfort Mouse. She shrinks from his tendered hand, and is doubtful of his "Do feel that I'm your friend." But she accepts his offer to call tomorrow, because "it is all so difficult"—and because, *"Je ne parle pas français."*

So he departs; and he never goes near the place again.

The story was, obviously, in some measure a riposte to Carco's *Les Innocents,* which Murry had reviewed for the *T.L.S.* in the previous July. "The subject, I mean *lui qui parle,* is of course taken from Carco and Gertler, and God knows who," she told him now. "But I hope you'll see (of course, you will) that I'm not writing with a sting. I'm not, indeed!"

In fact the original pencil draft[15] starts immediately after a note, written with the same pencil, which begins: "But Lord! Lord! how I do hate the French. With them it is always rutting time. See them come dancing and sniffing round a woman's skirt. . . . ."*

In posting a copy of the first half to Murry, Katherine said she had just re-read it and couldn't think where the devil she had got it from —there was so much less taken from life than anyone would credit:

---

*The note is printed in the *Journal,* but with nothing to indicate its close connection with the story, and with the rutting-time sentences suppressed.

"The African laundress I had a bone of—but only a bone—Dick Harmon, of course is, partly is—"

She broke off just there. There is not much difficulty in seeing that Dick Harmon "partly is Murry" (though she may have been about to write Garnet's name); and that Mouse, with her muff, is partly the Katherine he took to Paris in 1912 and partly the one who had left Waterloo six weeks before; though also, surely, the Marguéritte whom he deserted in Paris in 1911 and allowed to think his mother was to blame. While Raoul Duquette, like Scott Fitzgerald's Nick Carraway, is Katherine seeing herself see herself. His part is full of implied self-condemnation for her clever self—for the copy-hunting Winnie of *Les Innocents*. Of course it is not on that plane that the story endures.

Two years later, when Constables were about to publish the collected volume that included *Je ne parle pas français*, Michael Sadleir insisted that certain passages be cut. They were all to do with sex misused, and their purpose was to make Duquette's self-portrayal explicit and evil. To examine them in detail here would be tiresome, but it is only in the light of their harsh ironies that the story's full intention can be seen. In a sense, it was really Katherine's *Waste Land*.

The ending, where Duquette is about to leave the café in which he has recalled the tale of Mouse and Dick, originally had the extra lines here given in italics:

> I must go. I must go. I reach down my coat and hat. Madame knows me. "You haven't dined yet?" she smiles.
> "No not yet, Madame."
> *I'd rather like to dine with her. Even to sleep with her afterwards. Would she be pale like that all over?*
> *But no. She'd have large moles. They go with that kind of skin. And I can't bear them. They remind me somehow, disgustingly, of mushrooms.*[16]

In 1920, when she heard from Murry of the excisions that Constables were demanding, Katherine replied that she was furious with Michael Sadleir and would never agree: "Shall I pick the eyes out of a story for £40? . . . . . The *outline* would be all blurred. It must have those sharp lines." She gave in next day, deciding that she had been "undisciplined," but she later changed her mind once more, and wished she hadn't cut one word: "I was wrong—very wrong."[17]

If the story has a weakening fault, it lies in the slightness of the character of Mouse. Not quite enough is known of her, and she can hardly bear the intended weight of "a tribute to Love." It is high time, all the same, that *Je ne parle pas français* should be known, after sixty years, in the form its author meant.

[3]

After the queer hallucinatory experience of *Sun and Moon*, Katherine embarked on something which she thought of as another *"big* story"; but it was only *Bliss.* This story has been much admired, and its fame persists. I find it ultimately heartless, for while its women are human beings, the men are mere types, and their relations thus fall apart. Bertha herself derives painful reality from an obvious source—

> . . . . . in her bosom there was still that bright glowing place—that shower of little sparks coming from it. It was almost unbearable. She hardly dared to breathe for fear of fanning it higher, and yet she breathed deeply, deeply.

—but her husband, Harry, is a sort of stock stockbroker, while the fatuous Eddie seems to have stepped out of a *Punch* tennis party of the twenties, and in the end we don't much care what happens to anyone, even Bertha. The satire of arty London drawing-rooms is as clever and thin as that of Aldous Huxley, himself the model for Eddie.[18]

T. S. Eliot, in his *After Strange Gods,* although commending the story's "perfect handling of the minimum material," also justly observed that "the moral implication is negligible." But *Je ne parle pas français,* in its intended form, escapes that stricture.

"Quick March" passed by with no more writing. All that Katherine wished for now was to be home with Murry and away from L.M.— who threatened to go in her taxi to Redcliffe Road and help her unpack, even if Jack was there: "You will be bound to want somebody to look after you *decently* after the journey," she said, to which Katherine added: "And if you saw her eyes rivetted on me while she says that 'decently' you'd know why I hate her."[19] But now came the crowning calamity of this war-defying trip to France.

The two women left Bandol on 21 March 1918, expecting to go straight through to London, though Katherine's permit was only good for Paris. They thus reached Paris—Paris in the spring—on the very same day that the Germans began to shell it with their huge new long-range gun. In the confusion which this caused, all hope was lost of crossing the Channel. They found a hotel next to the Sorbonne, and settled in.

Like history itself, the Kanon made a very loud ominous sound every eighteen minutes—or once a day; you never knew. To sit in the hotel cellar on a heap of coal, "listening to the bloody Poles and Russians," was all too vividly like something out of Dostoevsky; and Murry seemed rather to enjoy the symbolic conjunction.

"I am in that state of mind, not seldom with me now," he wrote to Katherine helpfully, "when I see symbols in everything. . . . . the weeks have been indescribable—as though my soul, and something far more precious than my soul, an ideal of beauty by which it lives, had been torn out of me and turned into thistledown or a glittering bubble."[20] L.M. resented all her days this self-absorption in the man her darling loved.

For a few mad hours both women worked in a services canteen beneath the Gare du Nord—Katherine's only recorded war work. Daily journeys had to be made to Cook's for mail, to the Military Permit Office, to Cook's again. According to L.M. they ran out of money, and Katherine had to visit "someone she would have given anything *not* to see," returning with some cash. Not daring to ask, L.M. suspected it was Carco, and says so in her book; more likely, it was Beatrice Hastings.

Three hideous weeks turned into what Katherine called "another Sodom and Gomorrah." When one shell fell nearby with a deafening roar, she went to look. The whole top of a house had been "as it were, bitten out," and the road all covered with ruin. The trees along the street, just come into their new green, had many branches broken, but on those that remained strange bits of clothes and paper hung—a nightdress, a chemise, a tie, all dangling in the sunny light. And then:

> Two workmen arrived to clear away the débris. One found, under the dust, a woman's silk petticoat. He put it on and danced a step or two for the laughing crowd . . .That filled me with such horror that I'll never never get out of my mind the fling of his feet and his grin and the broken trees and the broken house.[21]

Three hideous weeks of seeing humanity degrade itself: "This is *not* Paris, this is Hell," wrote Katherine, remarking that L.M. in that place assumed the role of fiend-guardian: "stopping in front of all the shops and murmuring 'I should like one day to see your little hands covered with *fine rings.*' "[22] Her conjugal gift for *le symbole juste* was unsurpassed.

Katherine's own dream was of being married to Jack as soon as possible after reaching London—no longer to be "Mrs. Bowden" in every telegram or document. In the midst of all the destruction and waste of life, that hope alone had been sustaining her. Then, they would look in the country for a "Heron." She even entertained this reckless feminine hope: "I want to see a medicine man and ask if there is any divine reason why I have never seen Aunt Marthe *since that Sunday afternoon.* I shan't hope a bit till I have asked him."[23]

But she had not conceived. Already seriously ill before they left Bandol, she was a frightened, haggard waif (as a ghastly passport snap reveals) before she and L.M. at last escaped and crossed the Channel, on 10 April 1918. The disease now had its hold.

"European history," as it had been known four years before, was at an end. For domestic service and its aid to art, the writing was on the kitchen wall; and Wordsworth's England, the England of the Man of Letters and his wife, with lovely old farmhouses to write in while the smoke curled lazily from a fire of autumn leaves—for Wig and Bogey that was over too.

CHAPTER XVI

Waiting for The Elephant

The man in the room next to mine has the same complaint as I. When I wake in the night I hear him turning. And then he coughs. And I cough. And after a silence I cough. And he coughs again. This goes on for a long time. Until I feel we are like two roosters calling to each other at false dawn. From far-away hidden farms.

—the *Journal*, Looe, June 1918

Within a few days of the Channel crossing Katherine saw Dr. Ainger, and learned that she had "definitely got consumption." But she had also got him to agree that a sanatorium would "kill me *much* faster than cure me," and so she was to try a "cure at home," in Hampstead, perhaps. In her mind, the plan was to find a house before the winter and meanwhile to stay in Jack's rooms in Redcliffe Road, in Fulham, which she liked because it was "not at all bourgeois," and the people who lived there went about "without their hats on."[1] Naturally, Murry had other ideas. His rooms were not sunny, and she had been recklessly talking of doing the shopping while he was at the office. She had no idea what the food queues were like in London now.

The divorce became absolute on 29 April, and on 3 May, with J. D. Fergusson and Dorothy Brett as witnesses, they went to the Kensington Register Office (where the Lawrences took them in 1914) and so at last were truly married—though Frieda's ring was not replaced. Having shed the name that must have smitten her with guilt every time she saw it written, Katherine soon proudly closed a letter to Virginia Woolf with her new initials, "K.M.M." Yet so divided was she about this bourgeois joy that she belittled it when they met—an anti-Blooms-bury defence, perhaps. A few days after the marriage she went to the Woolfs in Richmond for dinner, and Virginia shortly wrote to Otto-line of having found Katherine inscrutable and fascinating as usual, but making out that marriage was of no more importance than engag-ing a charwoman: "Part of her fascination is the obligation she is under to say absurd things."[2]

In fact her wedding day had been another day of misery:

> Our marriage. You cannot imagine what that was to have meant to me. It's fantastic—I suppose. It was to have shone—apart from all else in my life. And it really was only part of the nightmare, after all. You never once held me in your arms and called me your wife. In fact, the whole affair was like my silly birthday. I had to keep on making you remember it. . . . .[3]

But what is it like, after being emotionally dependent for six difficult years on a young woman of immense vitality, to marry her when she is looking frail and doomed, and has just been told that she has the disease which is taking 1,000 lives a week?

In Wellington the news that Kathleen and her Jack were soon to be properly married had been gladly and generously received (they had both had approving letters from her parents), but the other news had also been cabled by Mr. Kay, and Mrs. Beauchamp had written about it to a family friend. Her affectionate prattle *in extenso* will best convey the tone:

> Kathleen had to go to the South of France at the end of the winter, as she has had to do on previous occasions for her health sake, and when she last wrote from Bandol sur mer she was getting better from pleurisy and rheumatism but unfortunately since her return to London we had a cable last week to say she was very seriously ill with advanced lung trouble, and required Sanatorium or home treatment at once. This was a great grief and shock to us as you may imagine. I had to repeat the cable to poor Harold who is on a short visit to Sydney on business matters, but of course I wired them authority for any extra special expenditure for the dear child, and I know everything will be done for her that is possible, for she has been taken into Belle's and Dora's fold by Chad long ago and is quite a pet with them all. Chaddie has been marvellously good to her ever since she arrived in England, and Kass has so enjoyed the

attention of this loving and generous sister, but it seems that nothing much can be done for her now but make the remainder of her life as happy and comfy as possible. Of course if it was possible* I should go home to her by the next steamer, for I know she would love to see me again, for she has at last learnt to love her Mother and Father, and has written us adoring and adorable letters lately, and so sweetly and quaintly put, poor poor darling she has missed so much in life, but it was quite her own choosing, fortunately she was the last to see Leslie off to France, and she has never forgotten this privilege for she simply worshipped her only brother and he had such loving compassion for her always through all her misdeeds. Even when at school he used to write and ask forgiveness for her in the most learned and clever way.[4]

The Middleton Murrys were quite alone. They had no wish to go to Garsington to celebrate their marriage: a cloud had come over Katherine's feelings for Ottoline while in France because of something she had learned, and she never went there again. The Lawrences were now in Derbyshire, and not in communication. L.M., back at her lathes in Putney, was living in a munition workers' hostel, and rather enjoying it. Koteliansky wasn't speaking to the Murrys (he had been saying some nasty things to the Woolfs about Katherine's "soul"). Brett was off to Scotland for the summer; Anne Estelle Rice was down in Cornwall with her husband, painting; Bertrand Russell was off to Brixton Prison for sedition; Lytton Strachey, now living with Carrington at Tidmarsh, was about to be raised to dizzying heights by his *Eminent Victorians;* when it came out in May and Mr. Asquith praised it, all social London desired to meet its brilliant author.

Down in Richmond, the Woolfs had not quite finished setting the type of their "Publication No. 2." "My poor dear *Prelude* is still piping away in their little cage and not out yet," wrote Katherine to Brett in Scotland. She had been counting on that to make a difference, and certainly Murry was hoping for its success.

In the *Journal,* at this period, are some vivid short pieces of the kind she could do so well when her "real self" held the pen: sharp glimpses of urban life in the Redcliffe Road; a visit to Fergusson's studio; a fragment of film catching the poor underfed dog that haunts the street,

*Mrs. Beauchamp was herself seriously ill and died three months after writing this.

"nosing along the dry gutter." This last is like something from Rilke's letters. But one piece also records the old division of her nature between satire and sentiment. After recording some snatches of charwomen's gossip, Katherine asked herself whether she really liked that sort of thing: "What about the Poets and—flowers and trees?" Then she answered herself: "As I can't have the perfect other thing, I *do* like this. I feel, somehow, free in it. It has no abiding place, and neither have I. And—and—Oh well, I *do* feel so cynical." Frederick Goodyear, perhaps, could have told her where the trouble lay. She needed to abandon that Georgian pastoral and somehow unify her vision of modern life, finding poetry in city streets as she does in the *Journal* fragments. But under consumption's threat, the ability to do so kept coming and going.

Truly, everything was changed. Never again would Katherine be the life of the party. There could be no more escapades. One can live all sorts of *lives,* indeed, but death is different. There is only one, and it happens to oneself.

> Nearly every night at 11 o'clock I begin wishing it were 11 A.M. I walk up and down, look at the bed, look at the writing table, look in the glass and am frightened of that girl with burning eyes, think "Will my candle last until it's light?" and then sit for a long time *staring* at the carpet—so long that it's only a fluke that one ever looks up again. And, oh God, this terrifying thought that one must *die,* and may be *going* to die ...[5]

The suspicions of the phthisis sufferer among the healthy and the strong now afflicted her. She had lately seen Jack put a handkerchief to his lips and turn away when she was coughing; there had even been a moment when he asked her if she "still believed in the Heron." And now, within two weeks of her precious marriage, he was proposing that she should get out of London for the summer!

They had their eye on a house in Hampstead, a tall, grey-brick monster which they called The Elephant and could have in August; and while they waited, he wanted her to be cared for in more suitable surroundings. That meant he was "trying to get rid of her."

Anne Estelle Rice, from Looe, which had a good hotel, was proclaiming it "just the place for Mansfield," and there was money for such things now. Murry, as Chief Censor, got more than £500, and Beauchamp had stepped up Katherine's allowance; it was now £200 a year.* And so, on 17 May, she was installed by Anne Rice in the Headland Hotel at Looe, with a nice big expensive room looking out to sea, ample food in spite of wartime shortages, and all the motherly attentions ("There do be a handsome hot bath for ëe") of the delightful Mrs. Honey—a Grandma figure in the letters that came from Looe.

After the usual cheerful arrival, Murry learned that she was in bed again, with "pleurisy"—every cough a fiendish pain. Looe's nice young Irish doctor came to see her at midnight, and soon she was breathing more easily—and wanting, of course, to write, despite the usual trouble in breaking through. A *Journal* piece reports her as feeling, "in my hideous modern way, that I can't get into touch with my mind." She saw herself standing gasping in one of those disgusting telephone boxes, unable to "get through":

> "Sorry. There's no reply," tinkles out the little voice.
> "Will you ring them again—Exchange? A good long ring. There must be somebody there."
> "I can't get any answer."

Then the building must be empty—not even an old fool of a watchman; it was dark and empty and quiet, and the queer thing was that she kept seeing it, this empty building, as *her father's warehouse:* "I see the cage of the clumsy wooden goods lift and the tarred ropes hanging."

On that day or the next, impelled by bitterness, she did get through. She began a new piece, "another member of the *Je ne parle pas* family," as Murry learned, a "big story," and "a devastating idea." There is some difficulty about identifying this story, which was clearly an important one, to judge by several references in her letters which do not name it; but it does seem to have been at least an early version of the uncompleted *A Married Man's Story*—her only use, after *Je ne parle pas français*, of a male narrator on such a scale, unmistakeably a "cry against corruption," and the only thing of hers that could be described in the terms she used.

Once again it is a piece that critics, and even fellow writers such as Elizabeth Bowen, have overlooked when attempting what André Mau-

---

*"I can't possibly live here under £5 a week alors, and I've only just four."—K.M. to Murry from Looe, 17 May 1918.

rois once called "the difficult task of analysing Katherine Mansfield's talent."[6] Because it is incomplete? But its five thousand words of tensely compact writing make it longer and more substantial than most of her best-known stories, and for other reasons too it is an important one to examine for signs of what its author was moving toward.

Neither nostalgic nor satirical, it has the sharp concreteness found only in the best of her later work. Its self-centred narrator, the son of a chemist who has poisoned his wife, is a new invention. The child's recollections of the dying mother's visit to his bed, of a battered harlot lurching into the shop for his father's famous pick-me-up, and the domestic scene of frozen hatred in which the tale itself is written—all are signs of an intention to strike out in new directions.

Presumably someone has the manuscript of *A Married Man's Story*, since Murry seems to have parted with it. It is thus impossible at present to say how much of the whole represents the "first little chapter of my big story" which Katherine posted to him on 2 June, but since there is nothing to suggest that that was lost (there were in fact two holograph copies), and nothing else that could answer her description, it does seem to have been *A Married Man's Story* that she began at Looe, while the Woolfs, at Richmond, were printing the final pages of *Prelude*, now left so far back in the past.

[2]

Murry joined Katherine three weeks later, and after a week's holiday together they returned to Redcliffe Road—Katherine four pounds heavier, thanks to the hotel puddings she so despised. By then the Woolfs were glueing on the covers of *Prelude* and preparing for its publication, which for both the Murrys was to have been the main event of July. As things turned out, however, it was overshadowed by something else which caused a sensation among their literary friends.

A little before this Lady Ottoline, wishing to do a good turn to Siegfried Sassoon (whose act of protest against the war in 1917 was remembered with admiration, and who was now back at the Front), had asked Murry to review his book of war poems, thinking he would praise them highly. The result, which appeared in the *Nation* on 13 July, was one of those ill-starred demonstrations of his integrity which cost him so dearly at various moments of his life. For what he wrote,

one can only commend him,* but in all the circumstances he might
have been wiser not to publish it. His action had the following consequences:

Philip Morrell wrote a magisterial letter of protest to the *Nation,* and
Lady Ottoline, who had just heard of Sassoon's being wounded in the
head, wrote to Murry declaring melodramatically that the article "may
just send him to his death"; to which Murry, unaware of the wound,
retorted with a noble defence of his role as critic ("You seem to forget
that in my eyes poetry is of infinitely more importance than persons").
Lady Ottoline at the same time wrote for comfort to Bertrand Russell
in Brixton Prison, slipping her letter sheet by sheet between the uncut
pages of a book to get it past the guards. Russell in the same manner
smuggled out an indignant letter to the *Nation,* signed "Philalethes,"
and assured Ottoline that he admired the poems very *much.* Katherine
wrote to Ottoline, "Oh—these misunderstandings. . . . . I should hate
S.S. to think ill of Murry." Sassoon, from France, asked Ottoline who
had done the review, and when told replied: "I wish I could do something to make Murry happier." Russell, to whom Ottoline sent a copy
of *Prelude* to read in prison, told her he thought it trivial and worthless
—it was bad enough that such trivial things should happen, without
having to read descriptions of them; to which Ottoline replied that she
quite agreed, really. The Murrys backed out of a visit to Garsington
on 27 July, when the Woolfs were also to be there. The Woolfs went,
but were not at all ready to approve of Philip's letter, so that "little was
talked of save the Murry crisis," to the high amusement of Clive Bell
("Virginia seems to have stood uncompromisingly for critical integrity
and nevertheless to have been a roaring success"). And Russell told
Ottoline that Katherine hated her because Murry had liked her, and
that meant Katherine had to hate Sassoon because Ottoline didn't; so
Murry had to hate Sassoon as well. Those two were exactly like the
Lawrences, a little toned down, said Russell, and Katherine was
to blame entirely, out of jealousy. When he had been in that mood him-

---

*"It is the fact, not the poetry, of Mr. Sassoon that is important. When a man is in
torment and cries aloud, his cry is incoherent. It has neither weight nor meaning of its
own. . . . . We long to silence the cry, whether by succour or sympathy, or by hiding
ourselves from it. . . . . Mr. Sassoon's war verses—they are not poetry—are such a cry.
They touch not our imagination but our sense. . . . . Their effect is exhausted when the
immediate impression dies away."

self she suited him, but really she was a person to be avoided.

And Brett, about this time, told Ottoline that Bertie made her feel like an enraged fly in the window, she so hated his certainty and his human weakness: "The God in him is overwhelming—but the humanity of him is rather footling and below standard."[7]

For the little blue book called *Prelude* there was no general enthusiasm, no body of allies ready to promote it, and no demand in the bookshops. Few review copies were sent out, and the papers hardly noticed it, for its appearance was unprofessional. Then Virginia opened the *English Review* containing *Bliss,* and threw it down with the words of disgust already quoted in Chapter XIV. Such was *Prelude*'s almost soundless launching on the world, just at the moment when Katherine heard the news that in Wellington on 8 August, after long illness, her mother had died.

"Yes, it is an *immense* blow," says a letter to Brett a week later.

> She was the most precious, lovely little being, even so far away, you know, and writing me such long, long letters about the garden and the house and her conversations in bed with Father, and of how she loved sudden, unexpected cups of tea "out of the air, brought by faithful ravens in aprons"—and letters beginning "Darling child, it is the most exquisite day"— She *lived* every moment of life more fully and completely than anyone I've ever known—and her gaiety wasn't any less real for being *high courage*—courage to meet anything with.

The Murrys then moved into No. 2 Portland Villas, East Heath Road, overlooking the Vale of Health, and the "cure at home" began. From her summer garden Lady Ottoline placed her blessing on The Elephant by sending boxes of flowers to Katherine, and the two began to heal things over; for, as Ottoline told Russell: "I really do like her —you know—in spite of everything. She has just lost her mother and feels it very much."[8]

L.M. had been enjoying the freedom of her bondage to machines. The factory and the hostel took decisions for her, and she enjoyed them both. She had made new friends, and had "become integrated" into the routine life. If she left the factory she would lose all that. But the idea had been in Katherine's mind that when they moved to Hampstead L.M. would go there too, to manage the household. She would "cost £2 a week," and Katherine was afraid of taking her "for better and for worse," but when it came to thinking of the move there was simply no one else. Only she could be trusted to pack things at Redcliffe Road and know where they should go at the other end; only she could do the measuring for curtains, and so on. But they could hardly ask her to do all that and then depart: "If we took her like that it would have to be forever." Thus Katherine had written to Jack from Looe in May —and a letter from Lesley, offering herself, had crossed that in the mail.

At Redcliffe Road, one evening shortly before the move, Katherine asked her (L.M. writes) if she would like to go to Hampstead with them, "to look after things," and some sort of quarrel resulted: her heart sank at the thought of all she would be giving up. But she did it. She got herself released from war work, and for the rest of Katherine's life except the last three months they were together almost constantly, "for better and for worse." What Murry felt about this, and how he accepted the arrangement, will be heard of in due course.

The Elephant was the first house the Murrys had owned, and since Murry was still an undischarged bankrupt, there were difficulties in financing it. Richard Murry remembers furniture got from junk shops and government surplus, including Katherine's "government table," on which, when it had been painted bright yellow, she did all her work at Hampstead. In the living-room were cretonnes, and Ida made the curtains. Originals of *Rhythm* drawings were framed on the walls, while in the basement a large workroom became the press-room of the Heron Press, with the typecases in a greenhouse at the rear. For it was there that the Murrys, in a mood of some annoyance with the Hogarth Press, set up their own press with Richard's help. Its first production was Murry's *Poems, 1917–1918*, a more professional affair than *Prelude*, thanks to Richard's training; its second was *Je ne parle pas français*.

With the move came another innovation, of the greatest importance to Katherine's health. Anne Estelle Rice now introduced her to Dr. Victor Sorapure, the first doctor she had ever had whom she felt she could talk to freely, and he soon brought about one crucial change. Her "rheumatism," as she always thought of it, had been causing much pain in June. It was Dr. Sorapure who at last was to put the right questions, diagnose the gonococcal origin of her arthritis, and remove the infection,[9] thus earning the gratitude which is evident in the *Journal* and some of the letters. Exactly when he did this will emerge.

But now that there was a house with a door to open, there were rather few friends. At Acacia Road, one day soon after the move, Koteliansky was surprised to receive a telegram which simply said, "Come tonight, Katherine." The Gordon Campbells, at their house nearby, received a similar wire. Thinking she must be gravely ill, all went, and Katherine, certainly looking ill, received them brightly with, "It's such ages since we met I thought it would be fun if you all came here tonight." She behaved as though nothing had gone wrong in 1916, and nothing whatever was said about that quarrel.[10]

This opened a new phase of Katherine's relationship with Kot, a matter of days before Lawrence and Frieda turned up in Hampstead to stay with friends.

Another reunion: Lawrence called at The Elephant two or three times, and although Katherine noted in her *Journal* that he and Murry would never hit it off ("they are both too proud, and Murry is too jealous"), there was in her case a renewal of the old, warm friendship. "For me, at least, the dove brooded over him, too. I loved him," she wrote to Brett. They kept to things like nuts and cowslips and fires in woods, and his black self *was* not: "Oh, there is something so loveable about him and his eagerness, his passionate eagerness for life—that is what one loves so."[11] Lawrence even sent her a present from Derbyshire on returning there—a little golden bowl of fluorspar; but they never met again.

Just then Katherine agreed to be seen by two separate lung specialists. One was her father's cousin Sydney Beauchamp (the brother of "Elizabeth"), who saw her in a high fever on the night of her thirtieth birthday, 14 October, as a sort of birthday present from her father. He said a sanatorium offered the only hope. The other, recommended by a War Office colleague of Murry's, was a "big gun," who said the same, to Murry downstairs, as he left the house. Otherwise: "Four years, at the outside." The idea was evidently considered for a time, since Virginia Woolf shortly told her sister that Katherine was "going to Switzerland with Murry and will be cured."[12] But soon it was dropped, Dr. Sorapure dissenting from the specialists on the ground that they did not understand the importance of Katherine's work to her will to live. In a sanatorium, she would have been forbidden to work.

The eleventh of November came, and guns boomed out the peace at 11:00 A.M. Crowds in the streets went mad. "I thought of my brother and of you," wrote Katherine to Lady Ottoline on 17 November 1918, "and I longed to embrace you both. I shall always feel that you have understood all that this war has meant to the world in a way nobody else has—just because of your wonderful 'feeling' for life." The diary of Virginia Woolf shows that a few days earlier Katherine had been saying that in her opinion most people had grasped neither war nor peace. In Wellington, her father must have been thinking out the important speech he was about to give as Chairman of the Bank:

> Those responsible for the perpetration of the countless inhumanities, barbarisms and iniquities that have made this War a horror of horrors, should be arraigned at the bar of an international judicial tribunal and receive from that august Court the just punishment of their offences. . . . . The braggart and blaspheming "All Highest" if shown to be responsible, should receive the same treatment as the lowest common soldier.
>
> Thus we shall perfect the work which our gallant dead have had to leave unfinished, and fill up the measure of their sacrifices, so that the splendour of their completed achievements shall go down with un-dimmed lustre to a grateful posterity, and shine for ever with an imperishable glory. (Applause).[13]

Soon Lady Ottoline and Murry made it up, and were friends again. Virginia wrote down the last words of *Night and Day* on the twenty-first, and from 7 December the people of Britain were allowed once more to make cakes and pastries, and to cover them with sugar and chocolate. Pre-war flour returned, the street-lamps blazed, and preparations were being made for festivity throughout the land, filling Katherine's mind with nothing but "the wretched little picture I have of my brother's grave."

Still, they held a Christmas party at The Elephant—Kot, Gertler, and the Campbells—which must have made them think of Cholesbury: stockings and a tree, decorations, crackers, pudding and drink; and they played charades. Beatrice Campbell says that little bags of sweets for everyone had been tied to a tree and that Katherine cut them off and handed them round as though it were a Last Supper, which Kot disliked; and he would only play a dead man in the charades.[14] As a matter of fact it *was* Katherine's last English Christmas.

It was also, strictly in private, an agonising time for her, for reasons not visible until now. As noted already, Virginia Woolf had lately got into the habit of coming to see her every week, having found that she "liked her more and more." It has also been remarked that there is nothing at all about Virginia in Katherine's notebooks; but that may not be true. To whom does this 1918 *Journal* piece refer if not to Virginia, almost her only visitor at this time? Does it not portray a parting between them on the steps of 2 Portland Villas, with the willows bare in winter?

> And once again the door opened, and she passed as it were into another world—the world of night, cold, timeless, inscrutable.
>
> Again she saw the beautiful fall of the steps, the dark garden edged with fluttering ivy—on the other side of the road the huge bare willows —and above them the sky big and bright with stars.
>
> Again there came that silence that was like a question—but this time she did not hesitate. She moved forward, very softly and gently—as though fearful of making a ripple in that boundless pool of quiet. She put her arm round her friend. The friend is astonished—murmurs "It has been so nice." The other—"Goodnight, *dear friend.*" A long tender embrace. Yes, that was it—of course that was what was wanting.

Professor Quentin Bell, speaking from his much closer viewpoint, once told the author that he thought there was perhaps some element of "a little love affair" in Virginia's feelings for Katherine; nothing comparable, of course, with her later passion for Victoria Sackville-West, but a fascination, all the same, with Katherine's elusive personality and all her wide "experience." If ever that was true it would have been so in this autumn of 1918, the time of the weekly visits; and if ever Katherine did break the silence of her journal on the subject of Virginia, the passage just quoted would fit the case, with its echo in the letter already quoted that calls Virginia "dear friend." But the matter of Katherine's shocked unhappiness still waits to be explained.

Just after Christmas Virginia got the feeling that she had been "dropped"—because her presents had not been acknowledged—and by mid-February she doubted whether Katherine could any longer be classed "among my friends." Quite possibly they would never meet again says the *Diary,* and the question "very decidedly pained" Virginia. They had been intimate, "intense rather than open," but Virginia had felt fond as well as curious; and now: "she falls silent; I get no thanks, no answers, no enquiries."[15]

A few days later Katherine did invite Virginia to tea, explaining that "some new treatment gives her fever for two days & makes it impossible for her to see people." In fact a month went by before the visit could come off, and when it did (the *Diary,* 22 March 1919), Katherine, in a "momentary revelation" as Virginia was leaving, spoke briefly of something that had happened since they last saw each other—"something dark & catastrophic possibly to do with Murry." So much she had hinted, but she said that she wanted to forget it now—"something that had absorbed her, apparently."

Virginia, of course, never knew what the something was; but biography, with reasonable confidence, can volunteer the explanation. Almost certainly it was in late December that Katherine learned from Dr. Sorapure that the cause, through all the last eight years, of her wretched "rheumatiz," was gonorrhea, dating from 1910.

Her remorse and shame would amply explain the sudden silence which Virginia encountered. One can sense it in the *Journal* too, which has a long gap after New Year's Eve. I believe the closing entry for 1918 is a private comment on the news—conveyed as it was by Dr. Sorapure with a kindness and wisdom to which later entries bear grateful tribute:

> December 31. 4:45 P.M. Oh, the times when she had walked upside down on the ceiling, run up glittering panes, floated on a lake of light, flashed through a shining beam!
>
> And God looked upon the fly fallen into the jug of milk and saw that it was good. And the smallest Cherubim and Seraphim of all, who delight in misfortunate, struck their silver harps and shrilled: "How is the fly fallen, fallen!"

CHAPTER XVII

The Athenaeum
and the Casetta

I have discovered that I cannot burn the candle at one end and write a book with the other.

—the *Journal*, 10 June 1919

In January 1919, three months after being told that his wife was dying, Murry was offered the editorship of the languishing weekly the *Athenaeum*, which the philanthropist Arnold Rowntree proposed bringing back to life to serve the new, post-war society. It was Murry's first opportunity, at the age of thirty, in the direction that was right for him; for if he still saw himself as a poet, he had admitted himself no novelist. It wouldn't be easy: he would have to get on with the best available writers whether they liked him or not, and somehow form a team and hold their confidence. Katherine's help would be essential; ideally, she would need to be a hostess at Portland Villas. If the *Athenaeum*, abandoning its clubland readers to their leather armchairs, were to start afresh as a post-war "Journal of Literature, Science, the Fine Arts, Music and Drama," it would need her touch.

They could hardly begin by printing her stories (short stories were not an accepted ingredient of the serious weekly, they belonged in magazines), but she could review the weekly batch of novels. Virginia Woolf might contribute, and Forster, too. Lytton Strachey, now famous, would be a catch. Although Murry had lately spoken in print of his "patently cynical showmanship,"[1] he wrote to him at once. They might have to ask Clive Bell to join the team—and Bertrand Russell. Perhaps even Lawrence could be induced to write in a manner suited to the delicate enterprise. "Golly, what a paper!" exclaimed a character of R. L. Stevenson's in 1889, after he had had a little trouble with the pronunciation of its name. In 1919, he could say that again.

On hand for science there was Murry's admirer J. W. N. Sullivan; and there was Eliot, decorously toiling in his bank, whom Murry did try to get as his assistant editor; or the clever young Huxley, not yet working for *Vogue*. The Rowntrees offered Murry a salary of £800 a year—£300 more than he was getting at the War Office. To maintain L.M. would be no problem, and servants under her. That drain on Katherine's energy could end.

The news was not unwelcome at Garsington or in Bloomsbury, since it held the prospect of an alternative to the *New Statesman*, whose literary editor was the unspeakably coarse Jack Squire, marching with dog and tankard at the head of Georgians and Philistines alike. "It is rather exciting that he's got the *Athenaeum*, isn't it?" wrote Strachey to Lady Ottoline on hearing of Murry's appointment. "I really think it ought to give poor old English Kultur a leg up." Virginia privately hoped that Katherine wouldn't be reviewing *Night and Day*. In Derbyshire, it was rather Jack who was mistrusted.[2] "I like Murry as the benevolent patron of us all: tra-la-la!" jeered Lawrence in a letter to Kot.*

So it was that the Tigers, their tails a little limp now, their lives turned to sadness by the bacillus that was present even when they met, greeted an English spring for the seventh time since the days of *Rhythm* and Clovelly Mansions. The willows on the heath in front of the house were not yet green when Murry's first number came out on the fourth of April, to give its name next day to the Elephant's first kitten. (A little is heard of "Athy" at Portland Villas but much more, in due course, of his brother Wingley.)

So it was, also, that 1919 was a year almost barren of stories by Katherine. When William Heinemann declined a volume of her stories she wrote a wry little piece called *Perambulations* for the *Athenaeum*,[3] and silence followed. Even her notebooks have a four-month gap. Her energies went to the paper (frequent callers and discussion), to the

---

*Murry invited Lawrence to contribute, and printed "The Whistling of Birds," over the pseudonym, "Grantorto," but he returned a short story about a rabbit called "Adolf" which employs the French word *merde*, thus setting off once more all of Lawrence's hatred, which soon was transferred to Katherine as well.

running of the house (managing servants and L.M.), but above all to a steady flow of excellent reviews which soon were giving widespread pleasure with their sprightly wit.

"M. and I seem to work like niggers at the *Athenaeum,* " said a letter to Lady Ottoline. "I wonder if you really like it. *I* feel rather like the pink icing butterfly on the dark sumptuous tragic cake—very unworthy." The tone of the paper, apart from the articles signed "K.M.," was indeed lugubrious at first, causing Mrs. Woolf to remark of Murry to the same recipient, "It is at least a channel for some of his miseries." It had its triumphs, all the same. One of its first contributions, written at the editor's request, was Paul Valéry's "The Crisis of the Mind."

As juniors—Eliot having decided to stick to his bank—Murry took Sullivan and Huxley. Katherine was never happy about Huxley's appointment, finding him silly and "watery-headed."

All this led to the holding of a party at The Elephant to bring together those who might contribute or befriend—probably the first such party Katherine had ever given, and certainly the last. No Woolves, for they were at Asheham, and no Eliot, since Lloyd's had sent him into the provinces; an apology from Lytton, and in place of Lady Ottoline a gift of peonies, delphiniums and lilac. But Swinnerton was there (so a letter of Katherine's records), and E. J. Dent, the music man—another old hand from the *Blue Review;* and while Dent embarked on a too-long anecdote, and the kitten tried to tear off Bertie Russell's trousers, Clive out-Clived himself, Jack Hutchinson sat on a sofa like Humpty-Dumpty ("but alas! never falling"), Roger Fry leafed through Hopkins's poems, and L.M. went round "offering sweetness as though she had the head of John the Baptist on a charger."

That was one week after a coughing fit that brought up blood. How Katherine endured it without collapse is astonishing—an instance of her remarkable ability to live on her nerves for special occasions.

Her unaccustomed role as lady-of-the-house is amusingly depicted in a *Journal* entry written next day (30 May), but there is one art that Katherine practised which has never been described. Few writers of this century have conveyed more vividly than she the exquisite pleasures, the absorbing satisfaction, of really good food. It happens, by chance, that there survive a number of her excruciating recipes.* This

---

*She posted them to Murry from Italy in November 1919, unaware that meat had just been taken off the ration.

is Tinakori Road in Hampstead with a vengeance, the favourite adjective here being "thick":

Just a few ideas in case Violet might like to look at them.

Curried Vegetables
Have some mixed boiled vegetables (carrot, turnip, parsnip, artichoke, potato). Cut them into dice. Fry some onions. Add the vegetables. Make a thick white sauce, flavour it with curry powder and mix it with the fried vegetables. Serve with a border of rice. . . . .

Savoury Rice (risotto)
Fry some onions in a saucepan a pale brown. Shake the uncooked rice with them (about a cupful) and just let it absorb the fat. Then add liquid —either stock, or if you have none add some Oxo or any remains of gravy. . . . .

Rabbit en casserole (If Wing can catch one.)
Cut up some nice pieces. Fry them with an onion. Season. Put into the casserole with some mixed vegetables and a tomato or two if you can get them. Brown the gravy, thicken it with tapioca. Add a little mushroom Ketch up and let all cook very slowly. If people are very hungry it is nice to cook with this a few very small savoury dumplings.

Cornish Pasties
Meat turnovers with vegetable added, potato, onion or turnip or artichoke, make a nice change. They can be nearly all vegetable. Serve with a thick brown gravy.

Cinnamon Rice
To an ordinary baked rice pudding add a thick sprinkling of powdered cinnamon and some sultanas or raisins. Serve with hot vanilla custard.[4]

Those are quite a surprise. They come from the one who speaks with such distaste of L.M.'s appetite for puddings, and whose Looe notebook declares, "I despise terribly English cooking." Let us rinse our mouths with dry white wine, go upstairs to Katherine's yellow-painted table, and experience an altogether different cuisine:

Very often, after reading a modern novel, the question suggests itself: Why was it written? And the answer is not always immediate. Indeed, there is no answer; it is perhaps a little reflection on our present authors that there can be so many and of so diverse a kind. One of our famous young novelists half solves the problem for us by stating, in a foreword to his latest book, that he wrote it because he could not help himself, because he was "compelled" to—but half solves it only. For we cannot help wondering, when the book is finished and laid by, as to the nature of that mysterious compulsion. It is terrifying to think of the number of novels that are written and announced and published and to be had of all libraries, and reviewed and bought and borrowed and read, and left in hotel lounges and omnibuses and railway carriages and deck chairs. Is it possible to believe that each one of them was once the darling offspring of some proud author,—his cherished hope in whom he lives his second richer life?

That was her opening paragraph as the *Athenaeum*'s new reviewer of novels—deceptively discreet, pronouncing a manifesto without declaring war; still another part that she could play, complete to the obligatory "we," and no vernacular. The style was a sort of female mandarin, or mandarine, most delicately judged for the needs of the moment as its author's husband tried to win new readers without losing *all* of the paper's old ones. It established a tone which she was able to maintain through a sea of troubles for the next eighteen months, and which served for discussing anything from Virginia Woolf and E. M. Forster to H. de Vere Stacpoole (of *The Blue Lagoon*) or an even more watery author whose name was Horace W. C. Newte and who sold in millions.

After touching on Dorothy Richardson in her opening article (found wanting because "she has no Memory"), Katherine ranged perforce over numberless nonentities of the day, but she also managed to write on novels by Conrad, George Moore, V. Sackville-West, Gertrude Stein ("negro music with all its maddening monotony done into prose"), Gilbert Cannan, Hugh Walpole, Jack London, and John Galsworthy—whose *In Chancery* she discussed with keen insight in her final article. Her criticism was always tactful, courteous and fair, and was totally free from literary jargon or reviewers' clichés. When Forster's *The Story of the Siren* gave her the opportunity, she made amends for something clever which she had once said in the *New Age* about *Howards End* (a little gibe about Leonard Bast's umbrella, now in the *Journal* for 1917). The following does them both more justice:

There is in all his novels a very delicate sense of the value of atmosphere, a fine precision of expression, and his appreciation of the uniqueness of the characters he portrays awakens in him a kind of special humour, half whimsical, half sympathetic. . . . .but in *Howards End,* though less than elsewhere, we are teased by the feeling, difficult to define, that he has by no means exerted the whole of his imaginative power to create that world for his readers. This, indeed, it is which engages our curiosity. How is it that the writer is content to do less than explore his own delectable country?

One does not easily discover an aesthetic in Katherine's reviews— T. S. Eliot in any case is on record as saying she didn't have one, or not a pure one.[5] Always elusive on the subject, she avoided making any overt statement on the short-story form. As for the novelists, she found them, for the most part, simply not serious writers. The fact is, most of their output was concocted according to just those appetising principles which she posted to the kitchen at Portland Villas. The "pastime novel," as she called it, was produced, like its televised equivalents today, by hacks who knew very well that a narrative Cornish pasty can be nearly all vegetable—a want of meat being atoned for by "any remains of gravy"—and that in the last resort one can always produce a nice hot vanilla custard. Anyone seeking an explanation for the tremendous welcome that awaited Katherine Mansfield's own work will find it in *Novels and Novelists,* the volume that Murry put together of her reviews.[6] It depicts a barren land awaiting the rains of 1922; in which year, of course, *The Garden Party* was not the only flowering in the desert.

A single winter at Portland Villas was enough to change Katherine's mind about the "cure at home." By June of 1919 she was hoping that Ottoline might come to stay in her "little villa in San Remo," and a powerful drive to earn money is evident in the letters and the notebooks, reflecting her discovery that tuberculosis was a very expensive disease.

Murry's £800 a year, plus her allowance (now £300), and her £100 a year from reviewing, had now put hardship behind them. But Katherine's money relations with Murry were bedevilled by the same thing that troubled relations with her father. It was not so much the amounts concerned as the feelings involved in dealing with amounts. From the outset, there had always been an element in their marriage of Katherine's supporting Murry; he had never been the "husband" in that sense, and even now they kept entirely separate accounts.* But a part of her hated that. When she heard by accident one day that Murry was still working for the War Office and was paid £250 a year for it, but hadn't told her, she was much annoyed, as the *Journal* shows.

She was really very divided about it. Although one half of her longed to be an old-fashioned wife relying on a nice solid husband, the other half insisted on its *in*dependence, and expected her sisters' sympathy: "I cannot get five pence out of my sister," says a letter of 18 June to Ottoline, referring to Chaddie. "Somehow, at sight of me, her gold purse vanishes. She is far poorer than I am. I almost offer to pay her fares from Dover Street to Hampstead."

In August her father arrived from New Zealand, widowed and lonely, and bringing with him his youngest daughter Jeanne, to leave her in England as the last bird flown from the nest. Katherine at that time was feeling sufficiently ill to contemplate a sanatorium once more, and (as a letter told Anne Estelle Rice) she looked upon her father as "a kind of vast symbolic chapeau out of which I shall draw the little piece of paper that will decide my Fate." That is, she hoped he would offer to pay the costs of going to a sanatorium. Looking more like Edward VII than ever, he came to tea (it was the first time they had met since 1912) and she found him adorable—"just as I had imagined, but even fuller of life, enthusiasm, with his power of making all he says vivid, alive, and full of humour." She had hoped that he and Murry would get on. But Murry, that day, was in "one of his moods" (so Ottoline read). When Beauchamp laughed he looked the other way —"never spoke *once* to him, paid him not a moment's attention. It could not have been more fatal."[7]

This no doubt explains the tragic circumstance that while Katherine's £300 a year continued until her death it was never again raised or supplemented, although her needs increased enormously. No hand went into that vast symbolic chapeau, no relief from her "money complex" was ever drawn out of it. Indeed, she gathered from a relation that the allowance itself was grudged; and he forgot her birthday

---

*"Never think any money I send you deprives Jack of anything. As you know we keep our money affairs entirely separate. He doesn't give me a penny and he never has."— K.M. to Richard Murry, January 1921.

in October. The saddest consequence was a grave effect on her artistic output, to be noticed in its place.

It isn't hard to see what restrained the paternal hand. This fellow Murry had lately been Chief Censor, and now had got himself made editor of the paper called the *Athenaeum*. Wasn't he Kathleen's *husband* now—whatever had been going on before? And couldn't he pay his own wife's doctor's bills, or send her abroad for a while? There remained in the family some painful memories of earlier days—when Kathleen, for instance, taking advantage of Vera's presence in London, had "borrowed" some money from her for the rue de Tournon venture of 1914. As a member of the family once expressed it: "Yes, money for Aunt Kathleen, certainly—but *not for the clique.*"

At this moment, however, while Katherine did hope for some extra money, and felt that her sisters were unfairly better off,* it was not money only that she longed to receive from Beauchamp, it was his love. She longed for him to show affection, perhaps even forgiveness, to his erring and loving, but now dying, daughter Kass. Unhappily, it sounds as though Murry's demeanour on the fatal afternoon made that concession quite unthinkable. Years later, Beauchamp referred to Murry as "a perfect rotter."

On Dr. Sorapure's advice, it was decided that Katherine, after all, should spend her next winter on the Riviera (but in Italy, this time), and that L.M. would go with her. Tickets were bought for three, since Jack would go too and see them settled in. While Lesley attended to the packing, Katherine took a piece of paper and wrote this letter:

My darling Boy,
    I am leaving this letter with Mr. Kay just in case I should pop off suddenly and not have the opportunity or the chance of talking over these things.
    If I were you I'd sell off all the furniture and go off on a long sea voyage

---

*Vera's husband was now earning £11,000 a year in Canada, as the *Reminiscences* record with satisfaction, and Chaddie, a colonel's widow, was also well off. Mrs. Bell once assured the author that Kathleen received from her father exactly the same as they, and Bank correspondence now deposited at the Turnbull Library corroborates this. However, while the sisters' income derived mainly from capital held in their names which could be left to their husbands, Kathleen's was a cash allowance only, which would cease on her death. The arrangements were clearly intended to prevent any of Beauchamp's capital going to Murry in Kathleen's will.

on a cargo boat, say. Don't stay in London. Cut right away to some lovely place.

Any money I have is yours, of course. I expect there will be enough to bury me. I don't want to be cremated and I don't want a tombstone or anything like that. If it's possible to choose a quiet place, please do. You know how I hate noise.[8]

The rest of it asked that some personal mementoes be given to certain friends, including Lawrence—his little golden bowl to be returned. Then followed one important line, borne out by a later, formal will: "All my Mss. I simply leave to you." The letter ended: "That's all. But don't let anybody *mourn* me. It can't be helped. I think you ought to marry again and have children. If you do give your little girl the pearl ring." She sealed that up.

They set off two days later, calling at Menton on the way to see a rich relation—Harold's first cousin, Connie Beauchamp. She was seventy, and she and her friend Miss Fullerton, who was sixty-four, ran an expensive nursing home in London, but spent the winters at the Villa Flora, in Menton. Katherine thought of them jointly as her "Catholic cousins."

[2]

The trio spent some days at a hotel in San Remo—until the English manager, Mr. Vince, who looked like a gaol-bird and reminded Katherine of Charles Granville, had to come and explain that for the sake of the other guests, and *their* health, it was hoped that they would leave. He had a small villa for rent, he said, on a hillside above the sea three miles away, which the ladies could have. And so Katherine and L.M. were installed in the Casetta Deerholm at Ospedaletti (with a revolver, supplied by Mr. Vince), and were assured that running water would be laid on very soon. Murry left for London on 2 October, and Katherine was presented with a bill for the fumigation of her room. In Italy, tuberculosis was a notifiable disease and regarded with horror.

Lesley for some days had to bring up buckets of water from a spring, and she had to find out how to manage a charcoal stove.[9] Her muscular coordination suffered. Within two days—Jack was told—she had broken, "(1) the big fruit dish (2) our plate (3) a saucer, all at one go, from leaning on the sideboard." Two days more, and she had broken Katherine's thermometer. Never mind—they got another in San Remo for

six shillings, "which seems to play the same tune, though the notes are
not so plain." The first letters from Ospedaletti, as always after an
arrival, were witty and un-self-pitying, and filled with the beauty of
the scene, as thus on 1 October:

> I have taken this little villa for the winter, perhaps for longer. It is
> nice, Koteliansky; you would like it. It is on a wild hill slope, covered
> with olive and fig trees and long grasses and tall yellow flowers. Down
> below is the sea—the entire ocean—a huge expanse. It thunders all day
> against the rocks. At the back there are mountains. The villa is not very
> small. It has a big verandah on one side where one can work and an
> overgrown garden. No hideous Riviera palms (like Italian profiteers);
> everything very simple and clean. Many lizards lie on the garden wall;
> in the evening the cicada shakes his tiny tambourine.

With no previous experience of housekeeping, and very little of
cooking, Lesley had suddenly to produce regular meals for an exacting
patient with primitive equipment (she scrubbed the pots with sand),
and to do all the shopping without a word of Italian; in the village they
called her "the woman who doesn't count her change." She once came
back from San Remo (*"such* a funny little shop") with four ounces of
black-market coffee at 10s a pound (read 10 dollars, modern reader). Yes,
she said, the parcel did seem rather small for the money, "but the beans
felt very tightly packed." She smashed a glass jug: "It was very frail
from the beginning." She kept saying, "Give me time!" and "I'll learn
by degrees, Katie," which put her darling in a rage. They did have a
maid to start with, but she left, and no other would come (it was
learned from an English doctor later) because of Katherine's *disease.*

Insects plagued them, huge ones, and little deadly ones, and nothing
then known was effective against them. One day Lesley caught one
and, following the Way of the Buddha, gently put it out the window.
Beggars kept coming to the door (which had no lock, and the locksmith
couldn't fit one), so Katherine, against Lesley's absences, took the
revolver into the garden and practised shooting. The doorbell used to
ring alarmingly at night.

Her birthday came and went. From Chaddie and Jeanne in the New
Forest, where Beauchamp had settled them in a house, there came an
"ordinary small ld match-box, enamelled yellow and painted (very
badly) with an ugly little Chinaman. Oriental department, 1/11¾ ."

From her father there was only a communication not mentioning her birthday: "so all my fervour has gone to nothing so far. I thought my opinions on the Labour Crisis were good for a fiver—but *no*. He gave Marie* £10 on hers. Isn't it *awful minge?*"

Soon the letters began to show signs that her sense of humour wouldn't last the winter. The Casetta's lovely situation had made it seem a perfect place to get well in, and there are beautiful descriptions of the flowers, the clouds, and the home-reminding sea; that lift of white, seen far away, was the *very thing* she would like to express in writing. But then some wintry weather, the fantastic prices and the cheating Italians, the loneliness and the silence, broken only by the utterances of the Albatross (no longer Ottoline's "Rhodesian Mountain," she was someone whom Katherine had killed, and now was killing her)—all of these things, plus knowledge of a fact, brought on the melancholy fit once more (19 October): "Shall I send this letter? Or write another one—a gay one? No, you'll understand. There is a little boat, far out, moving along, *inevitable* it looks and *dead silent*—a little black spot, like the spot on a lung."

In London, Koteliansky inconsiderately passed her news on to Lawrence, whose mood he well knew. "Let us hope the insects will bite K. to death," Lawrence replied, and wasn't joking. And Murry now had reason to be worried about the future of the paper. J. C. Squire, resigning from the *New Statesman,* was about to found the *London Mercury.* With the *Literary Supplement* also mounting a campaign, that would mean stiff competition for both readers and contributors, and it drove him once more to overwork. It was against this background that Katherine took so seriously the reviewing of Virginia Woolf's *Night and Day.*

Then came a family invasion, so remote in tone that it seemed unreal. Katherine's father was visiting Miss Beauchamp and Miss Fullerton at Menton, so the whole party came purring over in a "motor," and took her for a drive, described for Murry: she felt corrupted by the luxury, the furs and the cushions, the chauffeur and the speaking-tube (down which her father talked Maori to the driver). Back at the Casetta the Albatross got lunch, but cut up the onions so coarsely that

*Chaddie had long been known in the family as Marie because of her resemblance to the actress Marie Tempest.

it was "like a workman's meal," and she felt absurd and clumsy. Miss Beauchamp picked up Katherine's *Oxford Book of English Verse:* "There are some quite pretty things here, dear. Who are they by?" Katherine pretended not to hear.

Preparing to leave, the widower Hal Beauchamp hugged his daughter (he was glad to see her without that husband of hers) and said: "Get better, you little wonder. You're your mother over again." He had picked her some daisies and an orchid, had tied them with grass, and handed them to her. He even left her five Three Castles cigarettes.

Beauchamp then sailed for New Zealand from Toulon, to marry, out of loneliness, on the day after landing, his late wife's closest friend, Mrs. Laura Bright, who was far from poor. There seems to have been no birthday present for Katherine, nor any cheque to help with expenses. "We shall not get another *sou* out of Father, darling, not on any account," says a letter that Murry received about this time. Something had been said, apparently; and Katherine soon found herself unable to write to her father, falling, as we'll see, into a long and painful silence.

How does someone who has no religious faith and is only thirty-one "accept" the imminence of death? How does anyone do that at thirty-one? How does a woman possessed of a talent which is just on the point of turning into something more—something very much more—accept the fact that this may never be? And if there was once, when young, a romantic wish to die, and a courting of death, what then? Will there be guilt, and a dark attempt to shift the blame?

From Hampstead, Lady Ottoline had received a comic portrayal of L.M. as the perfect undertaker. Katherine had been having fearful fits of depression and weeping, and she reported (February 1919): "This was roast meat and drink to the Mountain. It made me realise more than ever that she is the born *Layer Out.* " If ever a village flower show had a prize for the Most Beautiful Corpse, L.M. would win it: "It's very horrible. But I begin to feel that every man or woman has his murderer."

Something had also happened which made her think that Jack had moments of wishing it were over. Some poem of his had evidently given him away, and a letter from Ospedaletti speaks of "the fact that you have thought of me as dead and written as though I were and that L.M. is always preparing for that."[10] Other letters record in copious detail her alternations of exultation and despair.

Late in October her irritation with L.M. turned into violence. She cursed her, called her a murderer to her face, and threw things at her ("yes, even that") and when she wrote of it to Murry two days later they were not speaking. Peace followed as Lesley talked to the bread instead ("It lets her fill herself with it to her content and is made to be devoured"), but then she became "the albatross around my neck," and one letter gave expression to a physical loathing that Murry perforce suppressed while Lesley lived:[11]

> Christ! to *hate* like I do. It's upon me today. You don't know what hatred is because I know you have never hated anyone—not as you have loved —equally. That's what I do. My deadly deadly enemy has got me today and I'm simply a blind force of hatred . . . . . Her great fat arms, her tiny blind breasts, her baby mouth, the underlip always *wet* and a crumb or two or a chocolate stain at the corners—her eyes fixed on me—fixed— waiting for what I shall do so that [she] may copy it. Think what you would feel if you had consumption and lived with a deadly enemy!

That, said Katherine, was one thing she would grudge Virginia all her days: "that she and Leonard were together." The worst of it was that she couldn't write a book while living with Lesley. She had tried, and it wouldn't work.

Then Murry, as well, became a victim of this phthisical rage, and at a time already difficult for him. Overworked, and worried about the future of the paper, he was obliged to show his paces as a critic in November, when the fourth anthology of *Georgian Poetry* appeared with all its pre-war attitudes intact, and the Sitwells' *Wheels* collection was also published.

As with Sassoon, integrity meant a risk. The *Georgian* anthology was weak, and he would have to hurt dear, kindly Eddie Marsh, to whom he owed so much. Yet his article on both books, in the *Athenaeum* of 5 December 1919, was one of the high points in his career as a critic. Surefootedly exempting Wilfred Owen (and poems by de la Mare, D. H. Lawrence, and W. H. Davies) he found in both collections a corporate flavour that was "distinctly disagreeable": in the Georgians, "false simplicity"; from the *Wheels* group, "a strange blend of technical skill and an emotional void." He asked whether English poetry at this moment should be serious or not, and his article had the result which Christopher Hassall describes in his life of Marsh: the *Georgian* anthologies lost their acknowledged position, and Murry appeared as "the spokesman of the new trend in literature"[12]—a statement which may seem surprising now; but the rise of Eliot was still to come. Eddie Marsh was keenly hurt.

It was Murry's bad luck, however, just as his critical gift was gaining stature in this way, to have Katherine turn on him in a rage as cruel as any rage of Lawrence's. She had forgotten how overworked he was, she had even forgotten her own sympathetic warnings on that score when, just as his article appeared in London, she sent him those bitter verses called "The New Husband" which are included in the *Letters.* This is the first stanza only; it seems to refer to Harold Beauchamp's recent visit, and to make a most unfair comparison of Jack with him:

> *Someone came to me and said*
> *Forget, forget that you've been wed.*
> *Who's your man to leave you be*
> *Ill and cold in a far country?*
> *Who's the husband—who's the stone*
> *Could leave a child like you alone?*

There were in fact three poems,[13] but that was the one that hurt him most when they arrived, in a just-as-usual letter with a note requesting him to keep them for her because she would polish them up someday and "have them published." As it happens, there is a strong suggestion in the diary that this action—if not those that followed it—may have been connected with the hormonal disturbance of her menstrual period. Perhaps that was also the case when in 1918, at Looe, she had done something very similar: she had *casually* sent him something that was bound, indeed could only have been meant, to hurt him as deeply as she knew.* These facts, for what they are worth, may throw a personal

---

*A piece which Murry included in the *Journal* under the heading, "An Idea." It begins, "Are you really, only happy when I am not there?" and proceeds, in a notably vindictive tone, to accuse him of being glad to have got rid of her again by sending her to Looe. Her diary entry for 2 January 1920—twenty-eight days after she had sent the poems—bears the private symbol, A.M., for "Aunt Martha."

light on a passage in *Prelude* that was written in those halcyon days at the Villa Pauline, wherein Linda Burnell longs to send her husband a little packet of her secret thoughts, her hatred, just as real as her other thoughts: "She wished she *could* have done them up in little packets and given them to Stanley—especially the last one—she would like to watch him while he opened that."[14]

The rest of this unkindly episode can be followed in the *Letters*, if it must. And Frank Lea's biography of Murry gives the helplessly pained reply that came from London; it is far too long and tortured even to summarise here. Murry was notoriously bad at defending himself when he had a good case to make—*cet animal n'était pas méchant*. He muffed this occasion badly, using so many "I's" in his letter that Katherine went through it underlining them all, with some of his other self-absorption words. Ignoring telegraphed commands, he then set off to join her for Christmas; and she, on the day before he reached her, wrote the long piece in the *Journal* which asserts that the experience had caused her despair to disappear: "I am (December 15, 1919) a dead woman, and *I don't care.*"

This account has left out much that went on while she was ill: her fantastic notion, at the height of fever, that she might "adopt a child," and her secret turning to Koteliansky (who has suppressed one letter that he received). For a brief while Katherine was almost, in her own words, "*mad*—but really, medically mad," and was filled with envy for Virginia: "There is always in her writing a calm freedom of expression as though she were at peace—her roof over her, her possessions round her, and her man somewhere within call."[15]

Unwanted and wanted, Murry arrived, and although L.M. declares that *she* slept on the sofa in Katherine's room throughout the visit, they made it up: it was agreed they must part no more—they would live in England. Jack would find them a house in the country, and the Albatross must go—*forever*. Murry left for London, with some figs from the garden, on 2 January 1920.

The little black diary which Katherine then began to use, in a manner suggesting that its purpose was to help her through a personal ordeal, records a series of Black Days and *nuits blanches;* of palpitations, or "heart attacks"; dreams of being at sea, tossing forever; hearing of her father's marriage on stepping off the ship at Auckland; and then, a reconciliation with L.M., and the breaking through, to write in one day a crucial story called *The Exile,* now known as *The Man Without a Temperament.* *

In the end it was only writing that could save her, and what it had to save her *from* was an old remorse. After she had posted the story to Murry the sea below the Casetta "howled and boomed and roared away" and she could not sleep: "I lie *retracing* my steps—going over all the old life before . . . The baby of G.T."[16]

On the following day the Albatross fell from her neck, and Katherine sent Murry a tremendous recantation with regard to L.M. She saw her as her murderer no more; the hate was gone, "like a curse removed," and something positive was in its place that was "very like love for her."[17]

The nightmare over, she wanted L.M. to share the calm: "I think I would have died without Lesley these last terrible times"; and Lesley knew this: her self-respect had all come back. They must cancel the house in the country. She would go to Menton, to the welcoming arms of Connie Beauchamp and Jinnie Fullerton.

Miss Fullerton booked her into an expensive nursing home called L'Hermitage, and in the midst of a serious Italian strike—the start of post-war revolution there—they got away, at great expense, by taxi across the border. In the confusing disorder of their final days, Katherine's good overcoat was stolen by beggars who came and found the door open; but the news of her escape was written from "a superb place in every way"—doctors, maids, a masseuse, and "a sort of Swiss nurse in white!" A big writing table awaited her with a cut-glass inkstand on it, and a box of Abdullas. They had called in at the Villa Flora to announce their safe arrival: "Now Katherine, my dear. The garden is yours—and you must take tea with us every day and when you come here to work, *growl* when you see us and we'll disappear." After describing all this for Jack she said: "I'm here with people, with care. I feel a different creature *really*—different eyes, different hair."[18]

---

*Not a few have supposed—the present author being among them once—that this acute portrayal of a man whose wife is hopelessly ill on the Riviera was a picture of Murry himself (whether consciously so or not), and a hostile one. That is not at all what he thought. After reading the author's previous biography in 1953 he said that its comment struck him as "a quite fantastic misreading of the story," and he added: "If ever a character was drawn with loving admiration, Salesby was. I should be very well content to go down to posterity as his original."

It would cost five guineas a week. She would write to Mr. Kay and tell him she would have to overdraw for a bit. But people like Frank Rutter of *Art and Letters* were *asking* her for stories now—*The Man Without a Temperament* had gone to him—and the publisher Grant Richards was even talking of a book. She felt quite sure that she could earn the extra that was needed, and so reimburse her father's account. She must keep that straight, whatever happened.

CHAPTER XVIII

Conquest of the Personal

Everything in life that we really accept undergoes a change. So suffering must become Love. This is the mystery. This is what I must do. I must pass from personal love which has failed me to greater love. I must give to the whole of life what I gave to him.

—K.M.'s *Journal,* 19 December 1920

If going to Bandol in 1918 had been a mistake, going to post-war Italy had proved another, and it was Katherine's "Catholic cousins"—in effect Miss Fullerton, who was no relation—who plucked her out of that experience in the hope of getting her well again, and of converting her to their faith. They could hardly succeed in either, but their care and support gave her the strength to embark on a courageous and lonely endeavour of her own: an endeavour, by means which lay outside their understanding, to bring out wholly new resources in herself that would be both religious and creative. Her enemy was Despair—to use the dark word which she hated so much when Murry used it. And against despair her best resource, in the end, was her love for the beauty of the external world, and her summons to perfect small works of art that might compare with it. What Katherine now attempted, in a year spent mainly in Menton, thus embraced both her personal destiny, as a woman in love, and something very much larger, that concerned her on a scale beyond the personal, as an artist of the post-war period.

Her thinking about her own death had begun, perhaps, or at least was first recorded, down at Looe, alone in her hotel room. For a week or so there, while writing *A Married Man's Story*, she had briefly found it possible to "drown the melancholy fit in a flood of work." But then, in that letter to Murry which she sealed but never posted, and which he found only after her death, she described the agony of her nights alone, when she would sit for a long time *staring* at the carpet, alone with "this terrifying thought that one must *die*, and may be *going* to die."

The unfinished story had drained her best resource, and left her at the mercy of despair, or of distraction. She returned to London and the so-called cure at home. The publishing of *Prelude* gave none of the boost that had been hoped for, and the *Athenaeum* then fatigued her in a different way. Only at the Casetta, after her fearful crisis of loneliness and fever and mistrust, did she again "break through" by writing *The Man Without a Temperament*, and so regain some faith. Then she crossed the border into Menton, and her room in the nursing home; and on 27 January 1920 she scribbled an entry in her little pocket diary which reads, or appears to read, as follows:

> January 27. The woman who does the massage is not really any good. My life is queer here. I like my big airy room, but to *work* is so hard. At the back of my mind I am so wretched. But all the while I am thinking over my philosophy—the defeat of the personal.[1]

When given the authority of print, those closing words seem filled with significance, and some writers have understandably accepted them as a record of defeat accepted. It may be so. But they were almost not written at all. Scribbled with a hard pencil and only just squeezed in in the space available, they are all but illegible, so that Murry's transcription is almost a guess. What *did* she mean? That "the personal" had been defeated, or that it was something to defeat?

To ponder this question is to consider at once her religious dilemma, her artistic aims, and her separate relations with Murry, Lawrence, her father, and her "Catholic cousins." Lawrence comes into it because he was almost certainly in her mind when she wrote those words: it was he who in Cornwall had attacked Jack's and Katherine's reliance on "the personal"—which is a theme, as well, of *Women in Love*. The religious question comes in because it was toward their church that her "cousins" were hoping to direct her thoughts when they persuaded her to come to Menton. They rightly saw her problem as partly religious; what they did not realise was that her solution to it would have to be creative, not submissive.

In Murry she had, of course, a husband uniquely fitted to support her belief in her art as a form of salvation. To him alone could she speak of the "tragic knowledge" which the war had brought, and of what she felt must be demanded of "the novel after the war." To no one else, as she had told him when censuring Virginia Woolf in this regard, could she speak "bang out" about those deserts of vast eternity, than which nothing less would do. Yet Murry was far too fond of the word "despair," and she, who knew the experience so well, more than once told him he should not use the word: he must not be personal, *bang out*. Sometimes in his reviewing (she told him) he cried of things which had happened to *me* or to *us*, but she felt as a critic that *me* and *us* were superfluous. If they must be there, then he should write a poem or a story:

> If you speak for your generation, *speak*, but don't say, "I speak for my generation," for the force is then gone from your cry. When you know you are a voice crying in the wilderness, *cry*, but don't say, "I am a voice crying in the wilderness."[2]

There was her courage, stated as a principle of art. Yet we still do not quite know what the note in the diary meant. Defeat or conquest? Failure admitted, or challenge accepted?

On 29 January, two days after writing it, Katherine received from Murry what the diary calls "an abnormally selfish letter"; and on that day a hurricane blew up once more from the gulf of her despair. It is hard now to see how the letter could be blamed: the attack which it brought him seemed most unfair, to him and to his own biographer.*

Yet she, as a woman in love, can hardly be said to have deserved what happened next.

She had imagined, when she told Murry how expensive L'Hermi-

---

*It was not even normally selfish, but was one of Murry's affectionate letters, full of his pleasure in walking thirty miles on the South Downs in the hope of finding the ideal farmhouse they were looking for. It is quoted in full in Frank Lea's biography of Murry, where Lea suggests that what had cut her was "his inability really to enter into her feelings of loneliness and relief." That may be so; but in fact she received his letter, and began to experience her rage, just twenty-seven days after her visitation on 2 January by "Aunt Martha," who returned on 1 February.

tage was going to be, that he would wire £10 at once. He didn't, because in fact he had already sent her all he had, and was "cleaned out" until his next pay cheque. Unaware of that, she sent him an angry ultimatum asking that he contribute £10 a month toward her expenses at the nursing home; and in the little diary she wrote: "At night old *Casetta* feelings, like madness. Voices and words and half visions."[3]

It was just then (7 February 1920) that she received from Lawrence, on Capri, a vile attack which seemed to end forever the personal friendship which had meant so much. Two rages, it would seem, came into horrible collision by merest chance. Jack meanwhile had sent her £20, explaining why it hadn't been possible before, but "Damn the £ 20," she shouted, "I wanted love and understanding. Were you cleaned out of those until February 1st?" Ruled off on the same sheet was this:

> I want to mention something else. Lawrence sent me a letter today. He spat in my face and threw filth at me and said: "I loathe you. You revolt me stewing in your consumption. . . . The Italians were quite right to have nothing to do with you" and a great deal more. Now I do beseech you, if you are my man, to stop defending him after that and never to crack him up in the paper. *Be proud!* In the same letter he said his final opinion of you was that you were "a dirty little worm." Well, *be proud.* Don't forgive him for that please.

She didn't destroy the letter, since Lawrence's letters, like Jack's, were exempt from her ùsual throwings-out. But Murry eventually did destroy it, probably in 1932, after Lawrence's death, when an entry in his journal records a few more words. It had also said: "You are a loathsome reptile—I hope you will die."[4]

Exactly why Lawrence did this, and why at this moment, has never really been explained. No biographer of his has tried. Murry's rejection of "Adolf" for the *Athenaeum* seems hardly enough to explain all the hatred that ensued. Obviously Katherine must have written to Lawrence out of her recent misery (as she also had to Kot)—perhaps a trusting letter, like the one she sent him from Bandol in 1915. But even so, and even allowing for TB rage, why should he turn on *her* with words of such violence?

The only explanation that makes any sense demands that one recall "The Prussian Officer," the discarded Prologue to *Women in Love*, and Murry's naïvely innocent rejection of the personal Lawrence in Cornwall. We know what happens in the story: that "horrible breaking down" of something inside the officer and those bruises on the orderly's thighs, which it made him sick to touch. What would have happened if the officer had met the girl?—"You are a loathsome reptile —I hope you will die"?*

Next day Miss Fullerton called at the nursing home in a carriage with cushions and rugs. She knew that Katherine had grown to hate the place, with its noisy trays and banging doors, and she said to her over tea: 'Now, my dear, we want you to come here, and live here. It's *dead* quiet. You can be alone all day if you like. . . . . You're going to get well." Then she laughed and said: "The Lord has delivered you into our hands, and please God we'll cure you."

Reporting this to Jack, Katherine asked, "*Why* should they do that?" though she knew, of course, perfectly well. In her diary she wrote: "I for the first time think I should like to join the Roman Catholic Church. I must have *something.* "⁵

In the letters to Murry, the hurricane died down. He had sold a book of her stories to Constable for an advance of £40; he had bought her an overcoat to replace the stolen one; he had sworn that when he next saw Lawrence he would hit him, and that was *exactly* what she had hoped for when she read the beastly letter. Jack's vow struck an atavistic chord in a very feminine, instinctual Katherine, whose reply discloses that she liked her man to be a caveman with a club, just occasionally. And so, after all they had just been through together, she loved him *more:* "And loving I simply cannot face desolation—the desert *persists* in blossoming—the flower *persists* in turning to the light."⁶

Katherine shortly moved into the Villa Flora, with its cousinly affection and all its welcome corrupting luxury, and she stayed there until April. L.M. got work in another nursing home nearby (the town was full of English hypochondriacs), and used to see her in the evenings.

As Murry observes in his commentary, the letters he received from

---

*John Carswell, in his *Lives and Letters* (1978), noting that Lawrence's letter no longer exists, has questioned K.M.'s account and suggested that it may have been "impressionistic" because of her state of mind. That is certainly possible: but the present author first heard of the letter from Ida Baker in 1949, well before K.M.'s account of it first appeared (in the 1951 *Letters*). Miss Baker said that Katherine had shown it to her at L'Hermitage; that it said Lawrence loathed her and hoped she would die, and contained the words, " 'Stew in your sputum,' or something like that." Later, when reading the galley proofs

the Villa Flora are less spontaneous and more artificial than any others, and of course he is right about the reason: although Miss Fullerton and Miss Beauchamp did indeed want to see their little friend get well, they were also in hopes of her conversion. In accepting their lavish hospitality and their presents she accepted a false position, and the falsity shows. In one brief moment of infidelity to Wingley she even fell in love with their Peke.

One day, after coffee and liqueurs on the balcony, they took her driving on the hills near La Turbie, and in the evening Lesley received an extremely self-conscious note which told her that when lying on the hills that afternoon Katherine had "known there was a God" and one day she was going to "become a Roman Catholic."[7] Lesley was forbidden to mention the note or even acknowledge having received it.

On St. Joseph's Day, two weeks later, Miss Fullerton inscribed to Katherine a leather-bound copy of *The Imitation of Christ*, which proved a false move. A note in the margin shows that Katherine recoiled from the opening of Chapter 5: "It is a very great thing to be in a state of obedience, to live under a superior, and not to be one's own master."[8] Beside those words she scribbled, "Nonsense"; and Murry soon learned that she had no use for the "personal deity" of the Catholic Church.

With a nod toward Father Kneipp, of Wörishofen, we can probably date from that day on the hills at La Turbie the spiritual conflict which troubled the remainder of Katherine's life, and which led her precisely into a state of obedience under a Master. On the Casetta verandah she had written one day: "I don't want a God to praise or to entreat, but to *share* my vision with. This afternoon looking at the primula after the rain. I want no one to 'dance and wave their arms.' I only want to *feel* they see, too."[9] That sounds "personal," to a degree; and it exactly describes the rituals that were favoured by the Master in whose Institute she was to die. Her spiritual problem with "the personal" was profound.

---

of the *Letters* for Murry, the author saw K.M.'s text, and checked Miss Baker's memory again.

When Katherine *had* died, Lawrence referred to her in print as a "shabby little slut." His preface to Verga's *Mastro Don Gesualdo* (1925) contained, in a context clearly indicating her, the following sentence: "No matter how much of a shabby little slut you may be, you can learn from Dostoevsky and Tchehov that you have got the most tender, unique soul on earth, coruscating with sufferings and impossible sympathies."

In fact it was compounded by another, which was new, and on which her letters of the time are silent, so much shame it caused. Somehow, during her stay with them, Katherine was given to understand by Connie and Jinnie that her father felt she wasn't really entitled to the allowance she got from him: her husband was the one who should be supporting her, and it was an extreme concession on Hal's part to pay her so much every year. This was probably a misunderstanding of something else he may have said: he had indeed so arranged things that Murry would receive no capital on her death, and may well have let fall some remarks about his son-in-law that were capable of the interpretation conveyed to her; but he did intend the allowance to go on. She, however, believing what she had been told, was so deeply hurt that she couldn't write to him, and the silence lasted for nearly two years.

More hurt was piled on that. She had proudly sent him a copy of *Je ne parle pas français,* fresh from the Heron Press and Richard Murry's hands, only to learn from a relative, later, that he had said of it, "I chucked the thing behind the fireplace. It wasn't even clever."[10] A little imprudently she had also shown it to her hosts, with a result that was more amusing but only slightly less dispiriting.*

Young Richard Murry was an artist though, and Katherine started writing affectionately to him during this sojourn abroad. He was now eighteen, and there is a pleasing generosity in the letters which he received. "I think she looked on me as a sort of mascot," he once remarked, "because I was someone who had recovered from TB." In this way Richard became a sort of substitute for her brother Leslie, receiving affections that had formerly gone to him, and some kindnesses which he remembered all his life.

Yet even Menton could sometimes produce appreciative friends. In April, the publisher Grant Richards put Katherine in touch with Sydney and Violet Schiff, two wealthy patrons and collectors of creative persons, who were staying at Roquebrune. (Katherine had briefly

---

*Raoul Duquette, in the café, is pleased with his smart little joke about the Blessed Virgin, "riding upon an ass, her meek hands folded over her big belly." Miss Fullerton, confusing Duquette with K.M., reproached her: "But how could you say that about the Blessed Virgin! It must have hurt Our Lady so terribly." On which K.M. comments in the *Journal,* "And I saw the B.V. throwing away her copy of *Je ne parle pas français* and saying: 'Really, this K.M. is all that her friends say of her to me.' "

met Schiff in London once, and had since reviewed a novel by "Stephen Hudson," unaware that this was Sydney Schiff.)

"Schiffs are coming to tea," says the *Journal*. "Connie lies on the couch and reads. I feel I must live alone, alone, alone—with *artists* only to come to the door." And there follows the remark, which sounds more like Van Gogol than Katherine Mansfield: "Every artist cuts off his ear and nails it on the outside of the door for the others to shout into."

The Schiffs, like Connie and Jinnie with their coffee and liqueurs, lived a life of luxury that oscillated between the West End and the Riviera; but they invited artists into it, not book-burners, and Katherine took to them eagerly at this time of need. Schiff could pontificate on the art of the short story, and his wife, a sister of Ada Leverson ("The Sphinx," to Oscar Wilde), was a singer of *Lieder*. Their tastes ranged from Katherine to Wyndham Lewis, to Joyce, Picasso and Stravinsky, and to Marcel Proust (whose final volumes Schiff translated). They do not seem to have left their card in Bloomsbury.

Soon Katherine was back in London, having written to Murry since September some 110,000 words in letters, or twice as many words as are in her whole *Collected Stories*. Some passages in those letters are more worthy to endure than many of her stories, and the same might be said of the *Journal*.

[2]

In Hampstead, she rejoined her Wandering Tribe. Mark Gertler came to tea. "Well, Katherine, I hear you've got it. Do you spit blood and so on? Do all the things in the books? Do they think you'll get over it?" Then he laughed outright. There was also Brett, now playing much tennis with Jack, and offering jocular remarks about how many of her friends had "spotty lungs."[11]

By hired car she ventured into town, to the office of the *Athenaeum*, which shared a staircase in Adelphi Terrace with the *Nation*, the scene being described for Violet Schiff:

Unthinkable disorder and ugliness. Old Massingham like a cat dipped in dough slinking in the doorway. . . . . Huxley wavering like a candle who expected to go out with the next open door, poor silly old men with pins in their coat lapels, Tomlinson harking back to the mud in Flanders, Sullivan and E.M. Forster very vague, very frightened. . . . .[12]

As for Jack, *he* was a literary man who had now confessed he had little vitality to spare, and "doesn't ultimately care for people except as symbols."[13] At the instigation of the Schiffs, all the same, the Murrys invited the Coming Man to dinner, with his encumbrance:

> The Elliots have dined with us tonight. They are just gone—and the whole room is *quivering*. John has gone downstairs to see them off—Mrs. E.'s voice rises—"Oh don't commiserate Tom; he's *quite* happy" . . . . . She really repels me. She makes me shiver with apprehension . . . I don't dare to think of what she is "seeing"—from the moment that John dropped a spoon and she cried, "I say you *are* noisy tonight—what's wrong," to the moment when she came into my room and lay on the sofa offering idly: "This room's changed since the last time I was here." To think she had been here *before*. . . . .
>
> And Elliot, leaning towards her, admiring, listening making the most of her—really minding whether she disliked the country or not——
>
> I am so fond of Elliot and as he talked of you both tonight I felt a deep sympathy with him. . . . . But this teashop creature.[14]

A wary and hesitant Virginia, still conscious of that review of her novel, and wondering who would make the first move now that Katherine was back, sent a friendly postcard from Richmond, only to get in reply a "stiff formal note" inviting her to call. Her description of Katherine's "steady discomposing formality" on this occasion has been given in Chapter XIV. Yet it melted: they fell into step, and had their "2 hours priceless talk."

It is hardly surprising that Katherine, after these encounters with her Wandering Tribe, should withdraw to her yellow table for some reflections on the Flowering of the Self, which appear in the *Journal*. She must certainly have wondered often just to which tribe—blood relatives, or artist-nomads, her "real self" did belong. "True to oneself!" she exclaimed, after making some allusions to Polonius. "Which self?" Which of her many—well, hundreds of selves, since that's what it looked like coming to? Was it not possible that the rage for confession, autobiography, especially for memories of earliest childhood, was explained by "our persistent yet mysterious belief in a self which is continuous and permanent"?—a self which, untouched by all that we acquire and shed, thrust a green spear through the leaves and through the mould until at last, one day, it flowered for one moment on the earth—

"the moment which, after all, we live for—the moment of direct feeling when we are most ourselves and least personal."[15]

These observations had coincided, approximately, with a decision that must have followed some discussion between Murry and Katherine about the publication of her fiction. At the risk of offending old subscribers, they decided to open the pages of the *Athenaeum* to short stories; and Katherine, in June, made a weak start with the story *Revelations,* which served to set Virginia's teeth on edge, and gave no hint of what was to be done a few months later. The reason is plain enough.

"Last week here I hadn't time to write a word," says a letter to Violet Schiff. "This week is already covered, covered under manuscripts to read, poems, essays to choose 'finally'; novels to review, schemes to draft, an article to write on 'Why we intend to publish short stories,' and then there's a special smashing review to be written for the *Nation.* "[16]

So a London summer slid away in toiling for the paper. The *Rhythm* contributor Thomas Moult, briefly a houseguest, noticed that Mrs. Murry "sat down at her type-writing machine each Tuesday morning and refused to leave it until the task was complete in the afternoon," her lunch having been simply a cup of beaten eggs and wine.[17] Sylvia Lynd, an occasional visitor, noticed that her rings slid up and down her fingers as she poured out tea.

Her visitors were few. But "Elizabeth," now an admirer of her cousin's reviewing, came to call, and perhaps to repair any slight that Kass Beauchamp may once have felt. Having lately been divorced from Bertrand Russell's horrendous brother, she was received with some reserve, but seems to have dropped a remark or two on the mutually interesting subject of "men." Discussing her with Murry some months later, Katherine evidently recalled the meeting; and, incidentally, put on paper what seems to be her only explicit statement anywhere on the subject of sexual relations, generally considered:

> All that you said about Elizabeth is extremely interesting..... Forgive my frankness: she has no use for a physical lover. I mean to go to bed with. Anything but that. That she can't stand—she'd be frightened of. Her very life, her very being, her gift, her vitality, all that makes her depends upon her *not surrendering*. I sometimes wonder whether the act of surrender is not the greatest of all—the highest. It is one of the [most]

difficult of all. Can it be accomplished or even apprehended except by the aristocrats of this world? You see it's so immensely complicated. It "needs" real humility and at the same time an absolute belief in one's own essential freedom. It is an act of faith. At the last moments like all great acts it is *pure risk*. That is true for me as a human being and as a writer.[18]

But this first real meeting of the two writers was misleading. A valued friendship lay ahead.

Virginia called again, and was begged to write the *Athenaeum* review of *Bliss and Other Stories* when that came out. Much against her better judgement she agreed, and they parted for the last time in August with the understanding that she would.

At Hampstead in this year, Murry's self-absorption was astonishing to those who noticed it. Thomas Moult was in the house when he completely forgot his own birthday (6 August), and Katherine soon afterwards wrote a *Journal* note about his reaction to her constant coughing: "And J. is silent, hangs his head, hides his face with his fingers *as though* it were unendurable." Years later Richard Murry told the author (remembering of his own wife's death): "My brother simply didn't have what's needed there. He'd hang around with a bloody awful face, and only make her worse. He couldn't buck her up at all."

Unhappily Katherine now became aware of the feelings that had grown up in the previous winter between Murry and Brett—who now was living in Thurlow Road, not far from The Elephant. In March, while she was at the Villa Flora, Murry had written a letter to Brett which contained these words:

> You know I love you, just as I know you love me. And your tenderness during a time when I was going to pieces through strain and anxiety has done more than anything else to help me pull myself together. It sounds strange I know; but it's true that it's been chiefly the experience of your loving me that has made me realise how sacred is my marriage to Katherine. I was in danger of going to pieces over that. There was some excuse for me, but not very much.[19]

"That's rather obscure," he added, "but you'll understand." Perhaps even Katherine would have understood, could she have seen that letter with its ring of simple truth. Perhaps not. What she did somehow see was what Brett wrote to him.* About the third week of August Katherine wrote these bitter words:

> Brett in her letters to Murry is unbalanced. This morning when she wrote how she wanted to rush into the cornfield—*horrified* me. And then he must *smack* her hard and she threatens to cry over him until he's all wet. Poor wretch! She's 37, hysterical, unbalanced, with a ghastly family tradition—and he has "awakened" her. Her face is entirely changed: the mouth hangs open, the eyes are very wide: there is something silly and meaning in her smile which makes me cold. And then the bitten nails —the dirty neck—the film on the teeth! Whatever he may feel about it the truth is she flattered him and got him! She listened and didn't criticize and sat at his feet and worshipped and asked for the prophet's help and he told her the old old tragedy. . . . .[20]

A week or so later she was adding:

> August 19. J. let fall this morning the fact that he *had* considered taking rooms with Brett at Thurlow Road this winter. Good. Was their relationship friendship? Oh no! He kissed her and held her arm and they were certainly conscious of something far more dangerous than *l'amitié pure.* And then he considered taking rooms with her. . . . . The lack of sensitiveness as far as I am concerned—the selfishness of this staggers me. This is what I must remember when I am away. Murry thinks no more of me than of anybody else. . . . . I must remember he's one of my friends—no more. Who could count on such a man! To plan all this at such a time, and then on my return *the first words:* I must be nice to Brett. How disgustingly indecent! I am simply *disgusted* to my very soul.

One can only think with sadness of them all, for what they suffered in their various ways. Murry's own biographer, Frank Lea, who did not know of the letters to Brett just quoted, cited in this connection a passage from Murry's journal of thirty years later which spoke of the longing he had felt for some feminine warmth and tenderness, and of *"how* one is starved for it when one has spent years tending, and anxious for, a sick wife!"[21]

---

*On two occasions the *Journal* reveals that Katherine read Murry's private mail, no hint being given there as to whether he knew this at the time. If she did it secretly, it would be like him not to say so in a note. For her part, she told him on 15 September 1920 that he could open anything of hers.

[3]

Full of anticipation and hopes of health, Katherine left for Menton and the Villa Isola Bella about 11 September 1920, taking Chaucer, Spenser, Coleridge and Chekhov in her luggage, and accompanied by L.M. With *Bliss and Other Stories* due out in time for Christmas, she was planning a sort of "journal book" for Methuen to publish as well, and she began writing pieces for it even in the train. Ships and notebooks, trains and notebooks, always went together.

The house had been aired and the kettle put on by Miss Fullerton's maid, and in the morning Katherine wrote the first of those ecstatic letters from the Isola Bella that sparkle with all the enchantments of the Midi: its colours, its scents, its flowers and its fauna—including the wonderful Marie, her *bonne,* who was an artist in the kitchen. It was all delightful, all full of beauty and warmth and light. But just as she got there she was blackmailed. A voice had come out of the past and out of Wörishofen, as it does in that early story called *The House.*

Floryan Sobieniowski, now married and working for the Polish Embassy in London, must have seen the advance notices of *Bliss.* He had therefore, from the most considerate of motives, approached the now substantial Mr. Murry with the suggestion that a packet of Katherine's Wörishofen letters might be worth, say, £40 (or exactly what Constables had paid as her advance).

"It is imbecile and odious that you should be so troubled," she was forced to write to Murry only three days after arriving. "What F. refers to as the Chelsea period and good received beats me. But *it is true* that he does possess letters written during my acquaintance with him which I would give any money to recover."[22] L.M. supplied the needed £40, and after Murry had been to a lawyer's office the letters eventually reached Katherine and were destroyed, thus closing that chapter, more or less.*

---

*By the "Chelsea period," Sobieniowski presumably meant the time in 1917 when he caused Katherine to put into English part of a play by Wyspiański. But as he still had the manuscript, and later sold it in America, it was hardly "good received" by her. In 1946 he turned up in London again, still cadging, and Katherine must have turned in her grave when Murry supported his application for help from the Royal Literary Fund, vouching for his work as an expositor of English literature (translating Shaw into Polish) and for "his straitened circumstances in this country at the present time."[23] Sobieniowski died in Warsaw, aged seventy-three, in 1964.

She had come away resigned in some degree to the cruelties which her illness now inflicted. With Brett in mind, she could write to Jack, "I hope you have good tennis and that all goes well"; and when he forgot her birthday in October she took it calmly enough.

Then, on 18 October, something caused her to write one of those remarkable letters to Murry which really belong among her "works" —as in a similar way do many of Rilke's letters. She had been thinking, she said, of Walter de la Mare—she had been "haunted" by him as one who shared her joy in what she called "the silent world"; and the letter went on:

> You know, I have felt very often lately as though the silence had some meaning beyond these signs, these intimations. Isn't it possible that if one yielded there is a whole world into which one is received? It is so near and yet I am conscious that I hold back from giving myself up to it. What is this something mysterious that waits—that beckons?
>
> And then suffering, bodily suffering such as I've known for three years. It has changed for ever everything—even the *appearance* of the world is not the same—there is something added. *Everything has its shadow.* Is it right to resist such suffering? Do you know I feel it has been an immense privilege. . . . . It has taken me three years to understand this—to come to see this. We resist, we are terribly frightened. The little boat enters the dark fearful gulf and our only cry is to escape—"put me on land again." But it's useless. Nobody listens. The shadowy figure rows on. One ought to sit still and uncover one's eyes.

When Katherine wrote so directly out of suffering, yet with such hard objective courage, potent symbols simply materialised upon the page in front of her, without being sought. The affinity of her mind with that of Rilke is a strange phenomenon of the period: no other writer of her generation stood so close. Yet she never knew of him. The letter continued:

> I believe the greatest failing of all is *to be frightened.* Perfect Love casteth out Fear. When I look back on my life all my mistakes have been because I was afraid . . . Was that why I had to look on death? Would nothing less cure me? You know, one can't help wondering, sometimes. . . . No, not a personal God or any such nonsense. Much more likely— the soul's desperate choice . . .

That moral strength she had to find, and hold, by herself. But now her *physical* strength was low. She was thinner than she had ever been, and her weekly stint of reviewing was only preventing creative work. Well aware that much of *Bliss* was not good enough, she knew that better must soon be done, and within three weeks she had abandoned the "journal book" ("I should always be trying to tell the truth"). Yet she went on reviewing.

Then one of her queer hallucinations produced the story, *The Young Girl* (it came presented to her in a dream). It was quickly followed by *The Stranger,* which is based on what happened when her father met her mother at Hobart in 1909, and belongs with the best of her later work. Concurrently, she had been doing some hard reflecting on her earlier life (the packet of Wörishofen letters from Sobieniowski was still on its way). "It wasn't flattering or pleasant or easy," she wrote to Jack: "I expect your sins are of the subconscious; they are easier to forgive than mine. . . . . I've *acted* my sins, and then excused them or put them away with 'it doesn't do to think about these things' or (more often) 'it was all experience.' But it hasn't ALL been experience. There is waste—destruction, too."[24]

She knew, and said: "as I write I falsify slightly." But she believed she'd escaped from her enemies—emerged. And her inspiration had been Love: "It was the final realization that Life for me was intimacy with you." It was a danger sign, had Murry known it, when she talked like that. The barometer was low.

A spate of well-known stories followed: first *Miss Brill,* then *Poison,* and *The Lady's Maid,* and soon she had written about half of *The Daughters of the Late Colonel.* All those are on the level of the best work in *Bliss,* not of its minor pieces, and she asked Murry to act as her agent in placing them. Yet in the midst of this, the most productive period she had known since 1917, her despair swept up once more with hurricane force—the *apparent* provocation being a photograph of her which Murry had allowed to be published in the *Sphere.*

Asked for a picture to be used in publicity for *Bliss,* he had innocently given Michael Sadleir a certain studio portrait, taken about 1913, which he liked, and which shows her in good health, if a trifle sulky. When she saw it she was so outraged that she sent a telegram commanding him to burn it. "I know you know how I *detest* it," said the furious letter that followed; she didn't have such beastly eyes and long poodle hair and a streaky fringe. She was *not* an ox, she wrote, her hold on life was weak. She was thin and ill, but that was the real her—didn't he *know?* She continued in a rage for some days, even borrowing a typewriter to send him a "business" letter dismissing him as her agent;[25] and Murry, in London, simply crumpled and went to pieces. Since it was the sort of thing that married couples later put out of mind as insignificant, it might be truer to life if biography did the same. But that would be to overlook the conditions under which Katherine wrote two of her best-known stories, and the agony *she* went through. "I must tell you something else," she wrote when the storm was at its height and she was hurt by how little he had written to her about *The Stranger:*

> I have been ill for nearly four years—and I'm changed, changed—not the same. You gave twice to your work (which I couldn't see) what you gave to my story. I don't want dismissing as a masterpiece. Who is going to mention "the first snow"?* I haven't anything like as long to live as you have. *I've scarcely any time, I feel.* Arthur† will draw posters 100 years. Praise him when I'm dead. Talk to ME. I'm lonely. I haven't ONE single soul.[26]

What the episode did to Murry went somehow like this: on the Saturday following her onslaught he went to dinner with Anne Estelle Rice and her husband, Raymond Drey, feeling acutely miserable, as a confessional letter eventually told Katherine. On leaving the house with Mrs. Bonamy Dobrée he unexpectedly kissed his hostess; walking to the gate with Mrs. Dobrée he then kissed her on the cheek (and later began a letter explaining, but tore it up). On the Monday, walking to the Leicester Square tube in the same state of misery, he saw a tart near the Express Dairy and stopped to speak to her. After taking a few steps in the direction she wanted him to go, he said, "No, it's not my game, I want someone to talk to," and he stood her a dinner at Malzy's (she was a Lancashire girl, and kind to him). Next evening he rang up Brett, went down to her house at ten in the evening, and took *her* in his arms, but felt a great loathing of himself and her. On the Wednesday he had "almost recovered his senses," but then he was invited by Mary Hutch-

---

*In *The Stranger:* "But her words, so light, so soft, so chill, seemed to hover in the air, to rain into his breast like snow."—Murry's note

†Richard Murry.

inson to dinner on the next Monday with Princess Elizabeth Bibesco, the daughter of Margot Asquith whose *Memoirs* he had just reviewed; and coming away with her in a motor-car (she too had now invited him to dinner) he suddenly kissed *her* on the cheek. He returned to Portland Villas "in an agony of nerves."[27]

The Princess then sent Murry a story for the *Athenaeum,* which he told her by post was "clever" and said he might publish, with some changes. But Monday being so far off she called at his office on the Friday; he felt embarrassed about the kiss, but she was kind, and very flattering, and when she had left the office he wrote her a letter saying he had been terrified she might interpret the kiss as making love, and so on; all of this, surely, being the behaviour of a man almost ill with a longing for affection.

In fact he *had* found it in Elizabeth Bibesco (who seems to have fallen in love with him), but he spilled out his misery in letters to Katherine and, to make matters very much worse, posted the clever story for her opinion. No, no, she said—she wouldn't read it for £5, she was much too busy. Instead, she finished *The Lady's Maid* and sent him that for the paper, at the same time telling him that "K.M." would have to stop reviewing, forthwith.

The pouring out of his own wretched story provoked an angry telegram on 12 December: "Stop tormenting me with these false depressing letters be a man or don't write me, Tig."[28] And on the following day she completed that masterpiece of love and pity—and of technique—*The Daughters of the Late Colonel.* From the manuscript, and other references, it appears that she wrote the whole second half of it in one session, ending in exhaustion after midnight, when L.M. brought her tea and egg sandwiches.

The misery that both of them suffered in this episode goes back to 1912, and the root of the matter: in that brave year Jack Murry was a soft young man in need of support and mothering; but it was "Mansfield" whose timely offer of a room he then accepted. Since her illness, he had progressively lacked more and more of what he needed most, as also had she, of course. "I'm a writer first and a woman after," she had told him twice in recent letters—a fact she had admitted first in 1911. Since 1907 she had known that she was "more than half man." *He* now had little but the wrong half left; and that was ill, and far away.

For her part, she had come to terms with it more or less—at least to the extent that is acknowledged in the notebook piece on Suffering

("I should like this to be accepted as my confession") which she wrote on 19 December 1920. In the *Journal,* this part was abridged: "Life is a mystery. The fearful pain of these letters—of the knowledge that Jack wishes me dead—and of his killing me—will fade. I must turn to *work.* I must put my agony into something, change it. 'Sorrow shall be changed into joy.' "[29]

By the time she wrote that, he was on his way to Menton for Christmas (which they had planned in any case); and so this second hurricane died down. L.M. being present, and a witness to it all, they lived together quietly for the next few weeks. "Mysterious fitness of our relationship!" says the *Journal* shortly, when Jack's brush and comb had somehow altered the very room they shared. "It is all part of this feeling that he and I, different beyond the dream of difference, are yet an *organic whole.*"

On the day after arriving, Murry wrote to tell Brett that he wouldn't, after all, take rooms in her house when he returned. It would be wrong to let the good feeling he had had for her get corrupted and grow bad. He didn't have it in him, he said, to take a lover-mistress relationship simply. Perhaps he ought to, but it couldn't be so with her: "It seems as though I'm too fond of you in one way, ever to make anything of a physical relation with you." He had always been told that he had never faced the "female element," and perhaps that was true—"We must wait and see."[30] (These words left Brett hoping that Jack would marry her when Katherine died.)

There were no more stories for a time—merely life itself, in a somewhat calmer form. Upon seeing how ill she was, Murry decided that this was the moment to let the *Athenaeum* be absorbed by the *Nation,* and the business discussions were begun. The reviews of *Bliss* came in, their meaning being that Katherine, just as her illness took a turn for the worse, was "made," and some letters display her consciousness of that.

One was a nostalgic letter to Koteliansky, recalling the old days of their early friendship in a curiously wheedling tone. But Koteliansky was *very* annoyed with her just then, because she had somehow lost a whole notebook of his Chekhov translation work, and he seems to have retreated into another of his monolithic silences.

There was a more important letter to Orage—important because of its bearing on events to come. It was evidently prompted by her knowledge that he would be seeing the paeans of praise for her books, and the references to Chekhov as her "master." Although this letter has been quoted already, it needs to be seen in full at this point. Orage, on his death, was found to have kept very few personal papers, but this letter was among them, suggesting that for him, as well, it possessed a special significance:

9
ii
1921
Dear Orage,

This letter has been on the tip of my pen for many months.

I want to tell you how sensible I am of your wonderful unfailing kindness to me in the "old days." And to thank you for all you let me learn from you. I am still—more shame to me—very low down in the school. But you taught me to write, you taught me to think; you showed me what there was to be done and what not to do.

My dear Orage, I cannot tell you how often I call to mind your conversation or how often, in *writing*, I remember my master.* Does that sound impertinent? Forgive me if it does.

But let me thank you, Orage— *Thank you for everything.* If only one day I might write a book of stories good enough to "offer" you . . . If I *don't* succeed in keeping the coffin from the door you will know this was my ambition.

Yours in admiration and gratitude
Katherine Mansfield

I haven't said a bit of what I wanted to say. This letter sounds as if it was written by a screw driver, and I wanted it to sound like an admiring, respectful, but warm piping beneath your windows. I'd like to send my love, too, if I wasn't so frightened.   K.M.[31]

It was only now, when *Bliss* was out, that she could really see—for the first time—what her writing looked like when it was collected, and how it appeared to others.

The reviews evoked distaste, however, in Taormina. "Spit on her for

---

*"This week I read a new book *Bliss* by Katherine Mansfield which knocked *Books in General* out of my head. Miss Mansfield's master in the art of fiction is Tchehov. . . . . "—the opening of Desmond MacCarthy's weekly *Books in General* article in the *New Statesman*, 21 January 1921. Her remark to Orage would seem an express rebuttal of the second sentence, which she knew Orage would see.

me when you see her," wrote Lawrence to Mary Cannan (who went to Menton in February). "She's a liar out and out. As for him, I reserve my language. . . . . Vermin the pair of 'em." He wrote to Kot shortly after: "I hear the *Athenaeum* lost £5000 a year under our friend the mud-worm. . . . . I hear he is—or was—on the Riviera with K.—who is doing the last-gasp touch, in order to impose on people. . . . . Two mud-worms they are, playing into each other's long mud-bellies."[32] Plainly, Lawrence couldn't *bear* the fact that those two loved.

For English prose fiction 1920 was not a memorable year, in retrospect or at the time. Wells and Bennett had begun to lose the regard they had once enjoyed as novelists, being no longer voices of the age. Forster, Huxley and Dorothy Richardson had brought out minor works only, and *Women in Love,* though available in America,* was not yet published in England. The name of Virginia Woolf was known to few, of Joyce to fewer still, and "K.M." herself had spent the year reviewing undistinguished books, from which the only name that seems to stand out now is that of Galsworthy's *In Chancery.* This is why *Bliss,* in spite of being short stories, which the world is never waiting for, both seemed, and was, an important event: a fresh way of seeing, a new voice in English prose.

The critic who best knew how far that was undeserved was naturally Katherine herself. She knew that apart from *Prelude, Je ne parle pas français* and *The Man Without a Temperament* (though she also thought well of *Bliss* itself), its contents were mostly slight or even makeweight stuff. It was, in fact, a collection of the windfalls of her years of growth. Two of her less worthy 1917 *New Age* pieces were included, along with two light *Athenaeum* sketches at the end, and she knew that she must either do better very soon or die with her purpose unattained, leaving "scraps" and "bits."

As to *how* she must do better she was perfectly clear, and had been since the experience of reviewing *Night and Day* had caused her to think about the novel and the war. Not only were Bennett, Galsworthy and all the pastime novelists prepared to take up the old

---

*"Lawrence has brought out another dirty book, procurable at enormous expense from America. It is full of thighs and loins and Midland hecticness. It is probably good weight in the way of temperament, but a little silly."—Wyndham Lewis to Violet Schiff, 6 February 1921.

threads of Edwardian life, but Virginia too, it seemed. Katherine knew that for her, at least, as a result of the war and her illness, "new expressions, new moulds," must be found for new thoughts and feelings. That much she had already said; and from Menton in September, when telling Murry that much of *Bliss* was *"trivial*—not good enough," she returned to the theme:

> You see it's too late to beat about the bush any longer. They are cutting down the cherry trees; the orchard is sold—that is really the atmosphere I want. Yes, the dancing and the dawn and the Englishman in the train who said "jump!"—all these, with the background. . . . . I cannot conceive how writers who have lived through our times can *drop* these last ten years and revert to why Edward didn't understand, Vi's reluctance to be seduced or (see Bennett) why a dinner of twelve covers needs remodelling. If I did not review novels I'd never read them.[33]

It would be natural to examine her new spate of work for signs of her achieving what she had in mind. But the precepts implied in her letters were always more explicit than her practice, which worked obliquely, and by elusive means. Of the eight stories she wrote at the Villa Isola Bella, five, including *The Daughters of the Late Colonel,* were variations on her *dame seule* theme, and two (*Poison* and *The Stranger*) were portrayals of solitude in marriage, leaving only *The Young Girl* as a story where the focus falls elsewhere. In three of the eight, a death is mainspring to the whole. The stories of *Ma Parker, The Stranger,* and *The Daughters* are all concerned with the way in which a death affects the living. The last is of course concerned with much more besides, and its marvellous dexterity in handling shifts of time—a technique owing nothing to any other writer, and indeed without parallel in 1920 —implies that time itself is one of the characters.

There is a visible escaping from the self, a conquest of the personal, in the Isola Bella stories. Even in *The Young Girl,* one no longer thinks of the narrator as being Katherine herself. If it be true that there was a sort of "thinness" in these spinster stories, and if that thinness is a defect, then it was so also in the lives of all the world's Miss Brills and lady's maids and Cons and Jugs and little governesses—Edwardian victims of an age in which Queen's College itself had represented an attempt to do something humane for England's surplus women; that is what Queen's was founded for, and it was there that Kass Beauchamp was educated. Her *dame seule* stories have more of history in them than has been acknowledged.

They don't, of course, have an overt message for society with regard to the roles of women. Kass Beauchamp was never an incipient feminist—even if reading Elizabeth Robins briefly made her feel and talk like one in Wellington—and of all her numerous *dame seule* stories and fragments, not one would have bestirred an Edwardian reader to "sit down and write a cheque"; which is one reason why Virginia Woolf respected her work. From the outset (when was that?) she perceived her task as wholly creative, concerned with vision itself and not with circumstance. The central value which her work proclaims is the value of vision itself. "We are ARTISTS," she kept exclaiming to Murry, and if there was ever anything she wanted to reform it was a literary form, through which her vision could be given the force of truth. After fleeing that suffragette meeting in September 1908 she wrote to Garnet Trowell (who was to her an "ARTIST" too):

> The room grew hot and in the air some spirit of agitation of revolt stirred and grew. It was over at 10.30. I ran into the street—cool air and starlight. . . . . And decided I could not be a suffragette—the world was too full of laughter. Oh, I feel that I could remedy the evils of this world so much more easily—don't you?[34]

In the light of all that followed there is certainly something ironic in that "easily": when Katherine Mansfield tied herself to the railings of Art, no benevolent policeman came forward to set her free. And time and again, in fact, she returns to her *dame seule* theme, to her suffering feminine victims, to give them life through vision:

> Was it simply her own imagination, or could there be any truth in this feeling that waiters—waiters especially—and hotel servants adopted an impertinent, arrogant and slightly amused attitude towards a woman who travelled alone? Was it just her wretched female self-consciousness? No, she really did not think it was. For even when she was feeling her happiest, at her freest, she would become aware, quite suddenly, of the "tone" of the waiter or the hotel servant, and it was extraordinary how it wrecked her sense of security. It seemed to her that something malicious was being plotted against her, as though everybody and everything —yes, even to inanimate objects like chairs and tables—was secretly "in

the know"—waiting for that ominous, infallible thing to happen to her which always did happen, and which was bound to happen to every woman on earth who travelled alone.

And yet, a little like Jean Rhys (whom oddly enough she seems never to have run into in her numerous cafés, and who would at least have offered her a Pernod), she also gave them chains. A few moments later in the story just quoted, that same young woman—in fact she isn't Mouse, though she very well might be—is alone with the mirror in her hotel room:

> She said to herself, as she stroked her muff, "Keep calm!" But it was too late. She had no more power over herself. She stammered: "I must, you know . . . I must have love. . . . I can't live without love, you know . . . It's not . . ." At the words that block of ice which had become her bosom melted into warm tears, and she felt these tears in great warm ripples flowing over her whole body. Yes, she wept as it were from head to foot. She bowed herself over her darling familiar muff and felt that she would dissolve away in tears. It was all over—all over. What was all over? Everything. The battle was lost.[35]

By giving them life, and vision, and painful insight, perhaps she did, in a sense, speak out for those who travelled alone. But the *aim* always lay elsewhere. For her, the "purpose" of the art of literature, if it had such a thing, was rather as Murry expressed it some years later: "the power to awaken in the reader an intense and understanding contemplation of all that is."[36] Even so, the founders of Queen's College, and the ghosts of the first sad occupants of its gracious rooms, had left their mark upon her practice of the art.

What is lacking perhaps, especially if one places her story *The Stranger* alongside Joyce's cognate masterpiece "The Dead," is a sense of security in the culture to which it seemingly belonged. Kass Beauchamp, from her earliest letters onwards, is constantly heard to ask of even her most trusted friends, "Do you know what I mean?" *"Du verstehst?"* and *"Tu comprends?"* and except in a handful of stories where that sense of insecurity is overcome one hears the same question implied—it is one source of the extraordinary intimacy of her work. But it is never heard in Joyce or Chekhov, nor in Henry James (where one could sometimes wish it was), since their conception of the implied reader was complete. Outsiders all, they yet had "European" minds. As a "Colonial," she stood much more alone.

One notices the problem often in those letters that refer to stories lately written or published. ("Oh God! Is it good? I am frightened, for I stand or fall by it"—to Murry, of *Je ne parle pas français* in 1918; and many other examples). And although she had confidence in *The Stranger* and *Miss Brill*, all certainty left her when *The Daughters of the Late Colonel* came out in the *London Mercury* in 1921. Very few readers had understood it, she told William Gerhardi. They thought it was "cruel," or "drab," and at the end she was "poking fun at the poor old things." She later told Brett that "even dear old Hardy told me to write more about those sisters. As if there was any more to say!"[37]

And yet those last astonished words express in the end her total confidence in the *form* which she had made her own, but which in English was not yet sufficiently familiar. Joyce's *Dubliners,* though out six years, was a neglected book in 1920 (and no proof is known to the author that Katherine Mansfield ever read it). The problem, even yet, was the loneliness not merely of herself but of the form—indeed, of the very idea that form could have equal status with the content, in a "story." That idea, being essentially poetic, seemed foreign to what so visibly was "prose." In the hands of other practitioners it later became so familiar that the boldness and originality of her innovation began to be forgotten. That this could happen suggests, in turn, that David Daiches was right in calling her work "almost a unique species of writing." Its character has certainly been found extremely difficult to describe. Perhaps Daiches came nearest to solving that problem in this passage:

> It is not the most obvious way of telling a story, nor is it the easiest. To make the content so dependent on the form, as it were, by relying on the method of presenting the situation in order to make it a situation worth presenting, without distorting the facts to meet the idea and without any comment, is to risk complete failure. There can be no half measures with this method; the critic cannot say, "A thoroughly well-told story, though a little pointless," because the point is so bound up with the telling that if it cannot be brought home the telling has no purpose—indeed, no separate existence—at all.[38]

"At the last moments like all great acts it is *pure risk*. That is true for me as a human being and a writer"—Katherine Mansfield on the act of loving. Art and love for her were almost one.

Her illness showed no real signs of remission, but early in November, when she still had peace of mind, Katherine had arranged with Miss Fullerton to rent the Villa Isola Bella until 1922, her hope being to stay there and recover. Should the *Athenaeum* really fold, as now seemed likely, she would have Jack there as well. Both could write from the South of France once more.

At Christmas Murry resolved to speed this plan, and in February he returned to London to clear up his affairs. During that visit he met Virginia Woolf, and his news of Katherine prompted her to write the letter which Katherine never answered. His visit marked, in fact, a parting of the ways between the Murrys and Bloomsbury as a whole. No doubt it was only his being an important editor that had kept them in communication until now. The house in Hampstead, where Sydney Waterlow was Murry's lodger at this time, was already, in Virginia's eyes, a part of what she called "the underworld," and later it became "the pigsty." Virginia did glance at Katherine's stories later in 1921, but they made her want to rinse her mind. It was not until Katherine was safely dead that Virginia really thought about her further, as the diary reveals.

In March L.M. went to London, to clear out the house and arrange for Wingley to be boarded. The plan was now to move to Switzerland, the cat being included in that. Murry, who had been invited by Sir Walter Raleigh to give some lectures at the Oxford he had found unbearable eight years before, was busy at the Isola Bella, composing *The Problem of Style*.

Cousin Connie and Miss Fullerton, having sensed what a letter of Katherine's calls her "no Popery manner," were rather hoping they could have the villa for someone else. They needn't have worried: she had grown dissatisfied with Menton and with Dr. Bouchage, and had written to an old school friend in Geneva to ask about hotels. She also got Dr. Bouchage to provide her with the note on her medical condition, already cited on page 122.

Murry wrote asking Sydney Waterlow (who was in the Foreign Office) for help in finding out about the treatment being offered in Switzerland by a certain Dr. Spahlinger, and Katherine on the same day (20 March 1921) told Ida that she was leaving Menton for good. She said that Jack was going to England in May for his lectures and she had "arranged with him not to return abroad," at any rate until the winter: "It would be *impossible* to have him in Switzerland while one was 'looking round' and deciding. . . . . He is v. willing not to come."[39] But this was one of her anti-conjugal lies to Lesley, the result of her being in a very bad mood about Jack.*

Just then some letters had come for him which somehow Katherine read, though she evidently wasn't meant to, so that Ida was told in the same communication: "Elizabeth Bibesco has shown signs of life again. A letter yesterday begging him to resist Katherine. 'You have withstood her so gallantly so far how can you give way now.' And 'You swore nothing on earth should ever come between us'. . . . . I hope he will go on with the affair. He *wants to*. 'How can I exist without your literary advice,' she asks. That is a very fascinating question. I shall write to the silly little creature. . . . ." Which was done:

24
iii
1921

Dear Princess Bibesco,

I am afraid you must stop writing these little love letters to my husband while he and I live together. It is one of the things which is not done in our world.

You are very young. Won't you ask your husband to explain to you the impossibility of such a situation.

Please do not make me have to write to you again. I do not like scolding people and I simply hate having to teach them manners.

Yours sincerely
Katherine Mansfield[40]

There were no more stories from the Villa Isola Bella—only note-

---

*In September 1953 Murry wrote to the author: "This letter to Ida is very mysterious to me, because it contains a plain lie. 'I have arranged with him not to return abroad, at any rate till the winter' etc. This is totally untrue. It was clearly understood between us that I was coming to Switzerland with her as soon as my lectures at Oxford were over. Why on earth did she tell this tale to Ida? There is no trace of it in her letters to me. . . . The only reason I can suggest for this story to Ida is that it was to bring pressure on her to come out by representing that she would be alone."

book scraps, and some painful probings about Jack's evasions on the subject of Elizabeth Bibesco. "I thought, a few minutes ago, that I could have written a whole novel about a *Liar,*" says one jotting made in March (but placed in the *Journal* for December). "A man who was devoted to his wife, but who lied. But I couldn't. I couldn't write a whole novel about anything. I suppose I shall write stories about it."

She had in fact already written *Poison,* a bitter little story about a marriage being poisoned by mysterious letters; and Murry had declined it for the *Athenaeum,* finding it "not wholly successful." In the end, her Menton year left a nasty taste. After the Bibesco affair she felt as though she were *dirty* or *disgusted* or both—"Everything I think of seems false."[41] She had a longing for something pure, and there is in the *Journal* a short prose-poem which anticipates the purity of obliterating snow: "Forget! Forget! all is blotted out, all is hidden— long ago, said the snow. Nothing can ever bring it back, nothing can ever torture you again. There is no trace left."[42]

In April, having arranged for Wingley's temporary board in England, Ida went south again, and it was decided that she should spy out the land around Montreux, returning for Katherine while Murry gave his Oxford lectures, and fetching Wingley later. On 4 May 1921, accompanied by L.M., Katherine left Menton for a hotel at Baugy, behind Montreux, and saw the Mediterranean no more.

CHAPTER XIX

The Chalet des Sapins, Montana

Why is it so difficult to write simply—and not only simply but sotto voce,
if you know what I mean? That is how I long to write. No fine effects—
no bravura. But just the plain truth, as only a liar can tell it.
                    —the narrator of *A Married Man's Story* (1918/1921)

After Menton—and a villa which had no bath—the spotless Hôtel
Beau Site and its prospect of immaculate mountains were at once a
refreshment to the spirit. Murry in England received ecstatic accounts
of Switzerland's fresh clean laundered whiteness, though Anne Rice
heard how ugly all the people were—the women with their fat be-
hinds, the men in tight felt hats and check suits far too small. Soon
afterwards, joined by Murry, Katherine ascended to the higher altitude of Montana-sur-Sierre, where she had her last big spate of writing, and *nearly* achieved the book that would have put beyond argument the position she deserved. Her work at the Chalet des Sapins is
thus the summit of her creative life, and this chapter must try to
describe it. But not without first disposing of a hanging question; it
concerns her relation with her father, and began to be resolved while
she was still at Baugy, with L.M.

Katherine had left Menton believing that her book-burning father
begrudged her the allowance he was paying her, and still not knowing
that her richer sisters got the same. Now, with her account at the bank
in London showing a healthy balance thanks to *Bliss,* she was afraid
that "Stanley Burnell" might get to hear of it. At the same time she
was expecting a rather nasty bill from Dr. Bouchage of Menton, she

had still not paid Dr. Sorapure's bill for the previous autumn, and she had pinned her next hopes on the vaunted and expensive Dr. Spahlinger of Geneva. She thought that if Beauchamp heard what *Bliss* was bringing in he might suddenly end the allowance which alone made possible all this travelling in search of health. L.M. knew of her fear, and asserted years later that the allowance was cut off; but she only had the facts half right.

What happened was this: first, while Murry was in England Katherine rang up Dr. Stephani of Montana. She made an appointment to see him in Sierre, engaged a motor-car ("It is years since I have done such things"), and had herself driven there for a consultation at the Hôtel Château Belle Vue—altogether an expensive Beauchamp outing, but it showed her the beautiful Rhône Valley, in the canton of Valais. Then an envelope turned up from Wellington which she was afraid to open. In dread she sent it to Murry with a note (which he never published) saying she felt certain it contained "that Blow I am always expecting. Will you open it and read it and *wire* me the result?" In a postscript she asked him not to spare her any of it: "I can hear anything from you."[1]

Well, the envelope did contain a copy of her passbook, which Mr. Kay, the London manager, had seen fit to send to his Chairman of Directors. A note enclosed by Beauchamp, however, said that it had come to him "by mistake."

From London, Murry sent it straight back to Katherine. He had written to her father at once, he said, "because it's monstrous that you should be so worried by the thought that he may cut you off." He had described her condition as nearly as possible, explaining that she had been too ill to write and had not wanted to worry him; and he now enclosed the sole contents of the letter that had frightened her: "It's very nice of your Pa to return it as sent apparently in error—I mean that's a gentleman's behaviour—but by what earthly right does Alex. Kay send a copy of your private account to New Zealand? If I were you, Tiggy, I would bank all other moneys except the allowance with another bank."

This she arranged for at once, while Murry wrote again, saying, "Really, Wig, I think you're much too frightened of what your Father may do. I am perfectly certain he would never dream of cutting off your allowance for such a cause."[2] The incomes of £300 a year continued to all four daughters, in sickness or in health and regardless of their circumstances; and Katherine thenceforward banked her author's earnings at Barclays branch in Hampstead.* But she still couldn't write to her father.

Meanwhile *The Daughters of the Late Colonel* had come out in the *London Mercury* and had been much admired. In sending this news to Katherine J. C. Squire wrote: "Don't forget to send us whatever you do next. . . . . I wish you could do a long book into which you could pour your whole vision of the world. The novel seems to be temporarily dead."[3]

That seems to have set her thinking, since a few days later (on 23 May, 1921) she was asking Murry, "Don't I live *in glimpses* only? There is something wrong, there is something small in such a life. One must live more fully and one must have more *power* of loving and feeling. One must be true to one's vision of life—in every single particular— and I am not."

A day or two more, and she was telling the novelist Mrs. Belloc-Lowndes that she was dissatisfied with her work and longed above all to write about *family love*—"the love between growing children—and the love of a mother for her son, and the father's feeling—but warm, vivid, intimate—not 'made up'—not *self-conscious.* "[4]

The date of this comment—26 May 1921—and its connection with some later remarks, suggest that it may have been prompted by Katherine's hearing that *Women in Love* was about to appear in London.

As Montreux began to swarm with tourists, Katherine and L.M. went up the Rhône Valley to the peaceful little town of Sierre, lodging at the Pension du Lac, set in the rock face beside the Lac de Géronde. The Valais, with all its miniature mediaeval towers and terraced vineyards, had delighted her when she drove to see Dr. Stephani, just as it had delighted Rainer Maria Rilke in the previous October. It was all so beautiful that the only person she could think of meeting there was "Lawrence before the war." Sierre, however, was really a station for Montana, three thousand feet higher, to which she also went. Recoiling from the expensive Palace Hotel, full of Magic Mountain invalids and doctors, she soon had her eye on the Chalet des Sapins, nestling

---

*Murry eventually forgot this episode entirely. Commenting on the incorrect version given in the author's previous book he wrote (15 September 1953): "I didn't know her father stopped her allowance. I don't think she can have told me, if it was so. Kay would certainly have had no compunction at all in reporting K's earnings to her father."

among wild flowers and pine trees just below the village. On 10 June Murry arrived, and they moved into Sierre's main hotel, the Château Belle Vue, while deciding whether to take the chalet for at least a year.

They were still there on the twenty-third when a man booked in who was also looking for a house in the Valais in which to write—a rather military-looking man, courteous and modest, trimly dressed in waistcoat and spats, but almost visibly a poet. It was Rilke, in fact, whose *Duino Elegies,* frozen into silence by the war, were to come to him again that winter and be completed, along with the *Sonnets to Orpheus.* They must have noticed him in the dining-room, with his odd thin drooping moustaches, and the woman-friend who was with him, Baladine Klossowska. The house in Sierre which he had come to look at was unsuitable, but in a hairdresser's window next to the hotel he saw a photograph of an enchanting little castle not far away, which was for sale or rent.[5] Thus Rilke found his Château de Muzot just as the Murrys prepared to ascend by funicular to the Chalet des Sapins.

They settled in, with Ernestine Rey to do the cooking in her peasant costume,* and began to make the closer acquaintance of a neighbour whose presence they must have known of beforehand. The Chalet de Soleil, owned by Katherine's cousin the Countess Russell, was only half an hour's scramble down the mountainside at Randogne, so that Elizabeth and her Swiss Garden were soon offering hospitality and the use of a library, and sending the Chalet des Sapins armfuls of flowers and baskets of apricots. Elizabeth and Murry got on well at once and became good friends. On Katherine's side there were some prickly reservations to be overcome (her cousin had "a vulgar little mind"), but overcome they were, by Elizabeth's bright and generous nature, and the last of Katherine's friendships was in this way formed with some-one of her own blood. Later, L.M. brought Wingley over in a basket.

The chalet's rooms were small, and dark varnish made them gloomy, but it had a bathroom with hot water, which was more than the Isola Bella did, and central heating for the winter. (Rilke's Muzot had nei-ther electricity nor running water.) Katherine established herself on the top floor, with a balcony overlooking the valley, and in no time she

---

*Ernestine's niece, Mme. Rosette Simon, with her husband, today maintains the chalet as an annexe to their Pension Helvétia. Mme. Simon, whose childhood authors were "La Fontaine and Kat'rine Mansfield," now uses the desk on which Katherine wrote. Guests can book her room.

and Murry were living like "two small timetables."[6] Both worked all morning, and from tea until supper—Jack at articles for the *Nation* and the *Literary Supplement,* and Katherine at things to earn money to pay her doctors' bills.

There being no spare room for Ida, she took a little room in the village, and later got a job in a clinic. *Her* account of these events concludes: "In June Murry finished his Oxford lectures, and, as he had left the *Athenaeum* and had no home in England, he decided to join Katherine in Switzerland; he stayed with us in Montana all through that summer and winter until the following January."

Katherine's financial saviour at this moment was Clement Shorter, of the *Sphere,* a paper he conducted with more appetite than taste. He had commissioned six short stories at ten guineas each, the highest pay she had ever known.[7] She obviously couldn't refuse, but in fact this contract did lasting damage to her reputation. It caused her to return to the vein of *Bliss* for some more of those clever stories of "English" couples toying with love, which came out in the *Sphere* with hideous illustrations. Wyndham Lewis, some months later, referred to Katherine with disgust as "the famous New Zealand Mag.-story writer,"[8] and doubtless the taint stuck in other minds too. What no one knew, until the *Journal* came out, was that the sternest and most perceptive critic of these bill-paying pieces was Katherine herself.

She knew that *Mr. and Mrs. Dove,* the first piece she wrote for Shorter, was too made up, "not inevitable," and "not quite the kind of truth I'm after."[9] Declaring that "all must be *deeply felt,*" she turned from it to a Wellington story, thus establishing a pendulum pattern for all her work at the chalet. It alternated between stories set in Europe and others set far more concretely in New Zealand—with death, in most of these, a silent figure in the shining background.

Even as she began to discover this way, however, she worried that what she was doing had *"no form!"* Of the Thorndon story *An Ideal Family,* she averred that she "didn't get the deepest truth out of the idea, even once," and she decided that after two more stories for the *Sphere* she would tackle a long story, adding: *"At the Bay, with more difficult relationships. That's the whole problem."*[10]

But it wasn't the whole problem. "More difficult relationships" was only part of it. What she did in this story was to conceive a major piece of symbolic representation that would unite her feeling about her country, her childhood memories, and her sense of the nearness of death, all at the same time as it constituted, in a surprising connection, an utterance by her on the subject of love.

At the Bay was begun at the end of July, and finished on 10 September. It was interrupted, however, for the writing of *The Voyage*, the story of Fenella Crane's being taken to Picton on the death of her mother; and again interrupted in August, during an attack of fever, for the resumption of that horrific unfinished febrile work begun at Looe, *A Married Man's Story.* *

All this makes an extremely complex picture of Katherine's creative state in the month of August 1921—too complex to be considered in detail here; it would interrupt too much. What is needed is a fresh look at *At the Bay*. But first, there is no avoiding another of those awkward irruptions which the facts of biography impose from time to time— the cause being Lawrence once more.

Women in Love had been announced for London publication by Martin Secker in May or June, and the news most likely prompted those remarks of Katherine's concerning the kind of love *she* wished to write about. In due course a copy came to Murry for review. It was in the chalet by 24 July, when Katherine briefly mentioned it to Ottoline, exclaiming for her comfort, "Really! Really!! Really!!!"[11] It now put all their friendships to the test—and, at Montana, more than that.

Katherine had already told Murry (in a letter of December 1920) that in *The Lost Girl* Lawrence "denies his humanity." His hero and heroine were merely "animals on the prowl," who did not feel, who scarcely spoke—"This is the doctrine of mindlessness," she said. Of the passage where Alvina feels "a trill in her bowels" and discovers herself with child, she asked: "A TRILL—what does that mean? And why is it so peculiarly offensive from a man? Because it is *not on this plane* that the emotions of others are conveyed to our imagination. It's a kind of sinning against art." And now *Women in Love* was in the house, to be reviewed by Jack.

---

*Murry told Sydney Schiff on 23 August (in a letter now in the British Museum): "K. is in the middle of the longest and last of her stories for her new book which is to be called (I believe, though this is confidential) 'A Married Man' and other stories. It's the married man she's in the middle of now. I think it's an amazing piece of work." C. K. Stead (*New Review*, September 1977) has taken this to mean that the piece was not begun at Looe. But if it wasn't, what became of the work she did write there, and regarded as so important? Two copies existed: her own, and the one she posted to Murry (both are presumably now in private hands). My own opinion is that Katherine could hardly

Since no surviving letters mention them, we can only guess what confabulations must have gone on in the little *salon* of the chalet where Jack and Katherine were soon to be "Snowed Up." That Gerald and Gudrun were headed for damnation because their love was wrong was not exactly hidden, and it is hard to believe Murry's assertion that they did not recognise themselves at all, with both the Café Royal and the *Blutbrüderschaft* scenes to go by: that sounds more like his "memory."

At any rate, Murry must have had to compose his review for the *Nation* just as Katherine was beginning *At the Bay,* for it appeared on 13 August. Sadly recalling what Lawrence's gifts had been before the war when he "thrilled us with the expectation of genius," he lamented that those gifts were now dissolved in the acid of "a burning and vehement passion." The characters were impossible to tell apart, because the same adjectives were used for all of them, and all they did was "writhe continually, like the damned, in a frenzy of sexual awareness of one another."

On the question of the consciousness and the "unconsciousness," so confusingly put to Katherine at the Villa Pauline, Murry wrote: "We stand by the consciousness and the civilisation of which the literature we know is the finest flower; Mr. Lawrence is in rebellion against both. . . . . He is the outlaw of modern English literature; and he is the most interesting figure in it. But he must be shown no mercy."[12]

In all the circumstances, it was a judicious and just review. No one would have taken it for the work of a man to whose wife Lawrence had written, "You are a loathsome reptile—I hope you will die." No other critic of the time approached its justice.

Unlike the enemies who pursue him yet and never suffered anything at Lawrence's hands, Murry had known Lawrence intimately in 1914–15, and had a clear impression in his mind of what, but for the threefold rages caused by his illness, Frieda, and the war, he might have become: he might have been a better novelist than the one we know. "If onlys" have certainly no place in criticism, strictly considered, but in living friendship they are very real, and nothing could be more unjust to

---

have *begun* a story of this character while in the midst of *At the Bay*, let alone complete five thousand words. The interposing of *The Voyage* is more easily accepted and explained: begun on 11 August, it seems to have been prompted by the third anniversary of her mother's death.

Murry than to ignore, from this safe distance, what a task it must have been for him to review that novel at that time.

He alluded only briefly (and in such a way that probably no one guessed his meaning) to the revulsion he must have felt on reading the "Excurse" chapter, with its *penetratio per recta* theme ("She had thought there was no source deeper than the phallic source"): "Mr. Lawrence's consummation is a degradation, his passing beyond a passing beneath, his triumph a catastrophe." He knew what he knew, and he shut up about it—except to close by referring to something "sub-human and bestial" that our forefathers had rejected "when they began to rise from the slime." Which does sound prim today, of course; and Jack was prim, as his editing of Katherine's papers has disclosed.

Meanwhile Katherine had written, somewhat guardedly and cryptically, to young Richard Murry about some "modern work" she had been reading lately, in which it seemed to her that the blight upon it was a kind of fear: "Writers, at any rate, are self-conscious to such a pitch nowadays that their feeling for life seems to be absolutely stopped—arrested." Obviously alluding to the hurtling motor-car of the "Excurse" chapter, she continued: "They know they oughtn't to say 'driving fast, eh?' and yet they don't know what they ought to say. If I am dead sincere I'd say I think it is because people have so little love in their hearts for each other." The expression is awkward and oblique (for Richard), but the object of it is clear enough, and soon she was writing more openly to Brett: "What makes Lawrence a *real* writer is his passion. . . . . But L. has got it all wrong, I believe. . . . . It's my belief that nothing will save the world but love. But his tortured, satanic demon love I think is all wrong."[13]

What all this means, since she finished it twelve days after writing those words, is that *At the Bay,* among all the other things which it is, is a response by Gudrun to Gudrun's creator on the subject of *"family love. . . . . warm, vivid, intimate—not 'made up'—not self-conscious."* So it needs to be viewed with that in mind as well. I propose to look at it now in three ways: first, as a story planned with a skill deserving more attention than Katherine Mansfield's narrative structures have usually received; second, as an example of the vernacular prose style (in Cyril Connolly's sense) to be put beside an example of the mandarin style of Virginia Woolf; and above all as a symbolic representation (in this, a clear riposte to Lawrence) of matters too elusive to be here put lamely into non-symbolic terms.

[2]

At the Bay depicts the passage of a single summer's day, from sunrise to night, and from necessity to dream, in the lives of all the Burnell family at their summer cottage in "Crescent Bay." Aunt Beryl and the grandmother are with them, and Alice the maid, while Uncle Jonathan has taken a cottage there as well, so that we meet again the extended family which was Harold Beauchamp's richest gift to his daughter's art. The baby boy that Linda was expecting in the time of *Prelude* has been born; down at the beach we encounter the tribe of the Samuel Josephs, dragooned by the whistle of their "lady-help"; and the "fast" Mrs. Harry Kember, who smokes and is vulgar, and plays bridge on a summer afternoon. She and her equally hasty husband, whose crude advances will horrify Beryl after nightfall, stand for such evil as obtrudes upon the after-Christmas pastoral. To remind us of town and of necessity there is Stanley Burnell, blustering and practical and bossy, who must dash off to the office in a stiff collar, leaving the women and children—their relief is immense—to enjoy what he provides.

The story is given outward shape by the ancient universals, sun and moon and tide, and by the "sleepy sea," which is heard before sunrise and in the moonlit, Debussyan close. The cycle of the day affects the lives at first of sheep and sheepdog and the shepherd with his pipe (it is one that smokes), but in due course of every living thing that is present in the story, not least the flowers, nearly all of which are little insignificant invaders, like the human colonists—who, as in *Prelude*, are colonists come out from a Colonial town. Their sense of isolation in time and place is implied by numerous local details, wonderfully remembered, and made explicit by Alice's thoughts as she walks along the empty road.

Though outwardly shaped by the ancient rhythms, more profoundly the story is structured within by something else. As *Prelude* shows the family's move to a new home and their thoughts as they go to sleep, *At the Bay* contrives for most of them to reflect, in their different ways, on the mysteries of birth and love and death, and in the process we notice that some are capable of dream or of deep reflection, and some are not. The story opens in the freshness of a dewy sunrise, its prose all alert and free of symbol. It ends, with a little envoi of a mere five lines, in the poetry of night and sea and moon. By then the littoral is symbolic.

The events of the day provide contrasting glimpses of the characters' thoughts on love and death. For some, this is done through their daydreams. Some wear masks, which are removed for us; others, like Stanley Burnell, wear none. Death makes at first a comic entry to the story, when the lewd Mrs. Kember (whose husband will surely have to murder her someday) is imagined by the other women, "stretched as she lay on the beach: but cold, bloody, and still with a cigarette stuck in the corner of her mouth." It tinges with sadness the siesta taken by Kezia with her grandmother, who has been drowsily thinking of the past and of her son who died; it returns in comic mode with Alice's visit to the widow Stubbs; it is a passing shadow over Jonathan's little talk with Linda in the garden about his wasted life, and over Linda's thoughts of her romantic youth. For the children, at their card game in the wash-house, it is reduced to the fear of spiders or Uncle Jonathan's sudden appearance at the darkening window. For Beryl, nightfall means the transformation of her romantic daydream into Harry Kember's cat-like snatching by the garden gate; after all of which come these few lines to enclose the whole:

A cloud, small, serene, floated across the moon. In that moment of darkness the sea sounded deep, troubled. Then the cloud sailed away, and the sound of the sea was a vague murmur, as though it waked out of a dark dream. All was still.

The little envoi, impeccably shaped, with its three-word close, returns the story to the tonality of its lovely opening, and restores its dominant symbol, the sleepy sea.

Let us turn back to that opening, to its effects and purposes. This story with a three-word title and a three-word close has also a three-word beginning—in effect a stage direction:

Very early morning. The sun was not yet risen, and the whole of Crescent Bay was hidden under a white sea-mist. The big bush-covered hills at the back were smothered. You could not see where they ended and the paddocks and bungalows began. The sandy road was gone and the paddocks and bungalows the other side of it; there were no white dunes covered with reddish grass beyond them; there was nothing to mark which was beach and where was the sea. A heavy dew had fallen. The grass was blue. Big drops hung on the bushes and just did not fall; the silvery, fluffy toi-toi was limp on its long stalks, and all the marigolds and the pinks in the bungalow gardens were bowed to the earth with wetness. Drenched were the cold fuchsias, round pearls of dew lay on the flat nasturtium leaves. It looked as though the sea had beaten up softly in the darkness, as though one immense wave had come rippling, rippling—how far? Perhaps if you had waked up in the middle of the night you might have seen a big fish flicking in at the window and gone again . . .

Ah-Aah! sounded the sleepy sea. And from the bush there came the sound of little streams flowing, quickly, lightly, slipping between the smooth stones, gushing into ferny basins and out again; and there was the splashing of big drops on large leaves, and something else—what was it?—a faint stirring and shaking, the snapping of a twig and then such silence that it seemed some one was listening.

Round the corner of Crescent Bay, between the piled-up masses of broken rock, a flock of sheep came pattering. They were huddled together, a small, tossing, woolly mass, and their thin, stick-like legs trotted along quickly as if the cold and the quiet had frightened them. Behind them an old sheep-dog, his soaking paws covered with sand, ran along with his nose to the ground, but carelessly, as if thinking of something else. And then in the rocky gateway the shepherd himself appeared. . . . .

That is fresh and enticing for many reasons—perhaps chiefly because of its underlying assumption that the scene is already part of our experience. There is no narrator telling us of things we do not know. The sudden raising of the curtain has made us feel that we are the sole observer and it governs all that follows, making one bright wakeful instant of the whole first paragraph: an enchanting pop-up, sharp and specific, yet full of mystery to a child, in which adjectives are few and of the simplest sort. The Master, here, might be Theocritus.

There is at first no sound. The author, refined almost out of existence, only sees. But then when sounds take over, deep in the bush we only hear a clear cold stream, not a *writer*. When something disturbs the quiet, it is not the predictable bird that twenty other authors would produce, but the "snapping of a twig," and then, "such silence." Let us now put beside the opening of *At the Bay* this other sea-dawn opening:

The Chalet des Sapins, Montana

The sun had not yet risen. The sea was indistinguishable from the sky, except that the sea was slightly creased as if a cloth had wrinkles in it. Gradually as the sky whitened a dark line lay on the horizon dividing the sea from the sky and the grey cloth became barred with thick strokes moving, one after another, beneath the surface, following each other, pursuing each other, perpetually.

As they neared the shore each bar rose, heaped itself, broke and swept a thin veil of white water across the sand. The wave paused, and then drew out again, sighing like a sleeper whose breath comes and goes unconsciously. Gradually the dark bar on the horizon became clear as if the sediment in an old wine-bottle has sunk and left the glass green. Behind it, too, the sky cleared as if the white sediment there had sunk, or as if the arm of a woman couched beneath the horizon had raised a lamp and flat bars of white, green and yellow spread across the sky like the blades of a fan. Then she raised her lamp higher and the air seemed to become fibrous and to tear away from the green surface flickering and flaming in red and yellow fibres like the smoky fire that roars from a bonfire. Gradually the fibres of the burning bonfire were fused into one haze, one incandescence which lifted the weight of the woollen grey sky on top of it and turned it to a million atoms of soft blue. The surface of the sea slowly became transparent and lay rippling and sparkling until the dark stripes were almost rubbed out. Slowly the arm that held the lamp raised it higher and then higher until a broad flame became visible; an arc of fire burnt on the rim of the horizon, and all round it the sea blazed gold.

The light struck upon the trees in the garden, making one leaf transparent and then another. One bird chirped high up; there was a pause; another chirped lower down. The sun sharpened the walls of the house, and rested like the tip of a fan upon a white blind and made a blue finger-print of shadow under the leaf by the bedroom window. The blind stirred slightly, but all within was dim and unsubstantial. The birds sang their blank melody outside.[14]

Since the author of *The Waves* is looking out to sea and thinking much of time, the aim is not identical, but comparison can fairly be made, and the first thing we notice is that our own experience is not assumed. Not trusting us with "sea" or "sky," the writer first fetches a cloth, with wrinkles in it, then endows it with strokes, which turn to bars. The bars being found to be waves, each one gives a sigh, "like a sleeper whose breath comes and goes unconsciously"—laboured words and laboured breathing; no match for the natural poetry of its equivalent in the other place: "Ah-Aah! sounded the sleepy sea."

Rather confusingly, there is then a different bar, and alas, a wine-bottle too, in which dark sediment has sunk, to leave the wine "green." There is next white sediment, and on a couch, a Thurber-like woman with an arm which levitates a lamp. When the sun's rays have spread like the blades of a fan, hardware images have taken us far from sea and sky—though only "gradually," with all those nudging adverbs and over-numerous "as ifs." The ensuing description of the bonfire-dawn becomes at moments almost absurd, as the writer wrestles with the language and seems not to *like* the things of which she writes, or to know their names. At length the birds, one up, one down, leave us unsatisfied, and the passage closes flatly with "blank melody." On the showing of this comparison, Virginia's envy of Katherine Mansfield is understandable. True images came naturally to her.

At the Bay has indeed its weak moments, and it does not improve on *Prelude* at every point. The scene in the water between Stanley and Jonathan is flawed, the portrayal of Jonathan being worthy of the young James Joyce, but that of Stanley more like something out of Galsworthy. A more serious defect occurs in the portrayal of Alice: the dislike of her which Beryl feels becomes the author's too, and distracts attention from her important role.*

It is Alice who gives overt expression to the sense of isolation of the little summer colony, the sense of there being no "others" in the background—an element of which V. S. Pritchett once actually complained when discussing Katherine Mansfield's work. He declared that the sense of a country, the sense of the "unseen characters," was as weak in her writing as it was strong in Chekhov's, where we are conscious all the time of "Mother Russia." Of *At the Bay* he asked, "Who *are* these people, who are their neighbours, what is the world they belong to? We can scarcely guess. . . . . There is no silent character in the background."[15]

Of course there isn't, and that was the point, and it was Katherine Mansfield who made it. The "silent character" was the stillness of the

---

*"You scarcely say anything about the black holes in my book (like the servant's afternoon out)."—K.M. acknowledging a fan letter from the novelist Berta Ruck (Mrs. Oliver Onions), 24 March 1922.

bush, which had not known man or even mammals in the time of Christ. Even Beauchamp understood this, in his own rough way. He had known, as a boy, the emptiness which Alice feels, and wanted something different for his children. There being no Mother Russia, nor anything remotely like her, he gave them the extended family as their defence, and "Jonathan Trout" conjoined him in his wisdom. After their fashion, these two admitted history to the unhistoric scene. Thus, another of the things that Katherine Mansfield wished to do, and did do in *At the Bay*, with art that conceals if not with intellect that obtrudes, was to give expression in symbolic form to a Colonial experience, now passed and not to be known again, which might perplex an old-world mind, but which still holds good as material for literature. Yet this is one of the least of its aims. Much more than for that, I believe that she meant it for Lawrence.

At the Bay was finished in a burst of nine hours' solid writing on 10 September, and Katherine needed a week to recover from it. At that stage she thought it would give its title to the book she was assembling (the *Married Man* being put aside) but one month later she wrote *The Garden Party*, and gave it that name instead.

What she needed, after so much creative work, was simple rest; yet within two weeks of finishing *The Garden Party* she was planning her next book, and it is evident that this one would have had a conscious design, and would not have had to draw on make-weight stuff. Two lists of projected titles and briefly noted ideas exist, and are printed in the *Journal*. In both, the titles are alternately marked, "N.Z." and "L." (for London). The fuller list, made on 27 October, includes the note for *The Doll's House:* "N.Z. At Karori: 'The little lamp. I seen it.' And then they were silent. (*Finito:* October 30, 1921.)"—which shows how she worked for her shorter pieces—in "glimpses," certainly, but now with a plan as well, an expatriate's plan, to make the best of both hemispheres. Various other *Journal* entries testify that all this work represented not merely a creative endeavour but, no less urgently, a process of personal regeneration. It was in this autumn at the chalet that she prayed in her notebook, "Lord, make me crystal clear for thy light to shine through."

In almost her next act after planning the new book, and as one of a series of moves toward certain reconciliations—with her past as well as her present—which she knew to be imperative, Katherine wrote a letter to her father which is crucial to their tragic story. It evidently broke a silence going back almost to their meeting at Ospedaletti: she mustn't die with *that* between them.

Because of what the Pa man did to the letter, we need to see it whole, and so the whole text follows.

It is plain—most painfully plain—that when Katherine wrote it her heart was full of affection for the father she had spurned in her adolescence, and that *her* main concern was to regain whatever of love might be regained before her death; but in trying for that she was forced to speak of what she had been told about his begrudging her allowance.

It is equally plain—and as painfully too, from the strokes of his sharp steel businessman's nib—that when Beauchamp read the letter ten weeks later, it was the money question that touched him most deeply, at least in private. What he wrote to her on 7 January cannot be known (her acknowledgement will be seen in due course). What he wrote to himself—diagonally across the top of the letter, in his firm, businessman's hand—was this: "R[eceived]. 7/1/22. A[nswered]. Idem." And on reflection two days later: "I can emphatically state that in *thought, word, & deed* I have never begrudged any of my children the amounts I have paid them by way of allowances. On the contrary, I have always considered it a *pleasure* and a *privilege* to do everything possible for their comfort, happiness & worldly advancement. H.B. 9/1/22." In the vigorous strokes, and the stab of the nib in the inkwell—how she knew that inkwell in his office!—one sees as nowhere else what it was that Kass had been afraid of all these years. On the later pages of the letter Beauchamp also made the two marginal notes that accompany this printed text:[16]

Confidential	Chalet des Sapins
I	Montana-sur-Sierre
xi	(Valais)
1921	Switzerland

Father darling,

I must get over this fear of writing to you because I have not written for so long. I am ashamed to ask for your forgiveness and yet how can I approach you without it? Every single day I think and wonder how I can explain my silence. I cannot tell you how often I dream of you. Sometimes night after night I dream that I am back in New Zealand and sometimes you are angry with me and at other times this horrible behaviour of mine has not happened and all is well between us. It is simply agony *not* to write to you. My heart is full of you. But the past rises before me, when I have promised not to do this very thing that I have done and it's like a wall that I can't see over.

The whole reason for my silence has been that, in the first weeks I was ill and waited until I was better. And then events conspired to throw me into a horrible depression that I could not shake off. Connie and Jinnie made me understand how very much you considered you were doing for me. They made me realise that for you to give me £300 a year* was an extreme concession and that as a matter of fact, my husband was the one who ought to provide for me. Of course I appreciate your great generosity in allowing me so much money. And I know it is only because I am ill in the way that I am that you are doing so. But it is highly unlikely that I shall live very long and consumption is a terribly expensive illness. I thought that you did not mind looking after me to this extent. And to feel that you did—was like a blow to me. I couldn't get over it. I feel as though I didn't belong to you, really. If Chaddie or Jeanne had developed consumption husbands or no husbands they would surely have appealed to you. One does turn to one's father however bad one is. Have I forfeited the right to do so? Perhaps . . . There is no reason, Father dear, that you should go on loving me through thick and thin. I see that. And I have been an extraordinarily unsatisfactory and disappointing child.

But in spite of everything, one gets shot in the wing and one believes that "home" will receive one and cherish one.

When we were together in France [*sic*] I was happy with you as I had always longed to be but when I knew that you grudged me the money† it was simple torture.

I did not know what to say about it. I waited until I saw if I could earn more myself at that time. But it was not possible. Then I had waited so long that it seemed impossible to write. Then I was so seriously ill that I was not in a state to write to anybody. And by the time that crisis was over it seemed to me my sin of silence was too great to beg forgiveness, and so it has gone on.

But I cannot bear it any longer. I must come to you and at least acknowledge my fault. I must at least tell you, even though the time has passed when you wish to listen, that never for a moment, in my folly

---

*In the margin at this point: "Quite Untrue. H. B."

†In the margin at this point: "Quite untrue. Never made such a statement to anyone. H.B."

and my fear, have I ceased to love and to honour you. I have punished myself so cruelly that I couldn't suffer more.

Father don't turn away from me, darling. If you cannot take me back into your heart believe me when I say I am

Your devoted deeply sorrowing child

Kass

After that letter, three weeks passed with nothing completed. Tantalising openings were written for stories that would probably have ranked with her best—*Six Years After,** The Weak Heart* and *Daphne* were all to be New Zealand stories. The *Journal* reveals an almost puritanical Katherine chastising herself (even while haunted daily by the nearness of death) for being "idle," and having "failed," and for "wasting time." Since the only photograph of the period shows her pathetically emaciated, it is easy to agree with Murry that she had set her ideal too high, and "ought" to have been taking rest.

But it was, unfortunately, just at this moment that Koteliansky (whom Murry always cursed for it, though he says not a word in print) wrote to Katherine with news of Dr. Manoukhin, formerly Gorki's doctor and now a member of the Russian colony in Paris, who claimed to be able to cure pulmonary tuberculosis by a highly priced and nonsensical process of irradiating the spleen with X rays. At Kot's instigation she had written twice to Manoukhin without receiving any answer when, only half in jest, she wrote to Brett (19 December 1921): "I am disappointed. I had made him my 'miracle.' One must have a miracle."

The approach of Christmas moved her to write warmly to Kot (she wanted *him* back, too; she was gathering up her father figures) about a long-ago Christmas party—not the mad one at the Cannans', but the Lawrences' party that preceded it:

> Wasn't Lawrence awfully nice that night. Ah, one must always *love* Lawrence for his "being." I could love Frieda too, tonight, in her Bavarian dress, with her face flushed as though she had been crying about the "childeren." It is a pity that all things must pass. And how strange it is,

---

Six Years After, which is easily the best of these fragments, depicts the feelings of a man and his wife on board ship, six years after their son has been killed in the war. It is a loving portrayal. But at the end of the original manuscript (now in the Turnbull Library) are the three words, in Katherine's writing, "Oh, my *hatred!*"

how in spite of everything, there are certain people, like Lawrence, who remain in one's life for ever, and others who are forever shadowy.[17]

But Lawrence himself had lately written to Kot (and there is no sign that he was ever rebuked for such things): "I see Murry and the long-dying blossom Katharine have put forth new literary buds. Let 'em."[18]

This was the manner, in a mood of reconciliation sought and given, but also of inordinate hopes for some miracle of health, that Katherine awaited publication of *The Garden Party and Other Stories,* a book which, if you were living at the time, was one of the first bright events of that literary *annus mirabilis,* 1922—the year of *Ulysses* and *The Waste Land,* of Proust's last work and Brecht's first play, and of Rilke's *Duino Elegies.*

CHAPTER XX

In Search of a Miracle

I have a suspicion like a certainty that the real cause of my illness is not my lungs at all, but something else. And if this were found and cured, all the rest would heal.

—the *Journal*, 20 January 1922

In the autumn of 1921, on a mountainside above Sierre and in dread of her death, Katherine Mansfield was endeavouring to draw together all that was of value in her art—trying to master by symbolic means some utterance of greater value than her own unworthy "self." By then she knew, like Yeats, that all that is personal soon rots if it isn't packed in ice and salt. The war being three years past, she was soon to write *The Fly.* Around the corner, as it were, downstream at Lausanne, was T. S. Eliot, granted sick leave by his bank to recover from a breakdown caused by his marriage. He had brought with him the long poem that had been in his mind for some time, hoping to make it connect with itself and with the present and the past. A bundle of fragments as yet, it awaited the hand of a "better craftsman" to draw it together in Paris, and to agree that *The Waste Land* should be its title. A mile or so upstream from Sierre, at Muzot, was Rainer Maria Rilke, whose *Duino Elegies,* held in suspension throughout the war, would soon miraculously complete themselves within a space of eight days. In Paris, James Joyce awaited the publication of his Odyssey composed from the fragments of a single day in Dublin in 1904, while at 44 Rue Hamelin, racked by asthma and all the ills of a youth whose mother had unmanned him with her kisses, lay Marcel Proust, completing his own great work about time present and time past. At Hogarth House, Richmond, on 4 November, Virginia Woolf, who had been ill again during the summer, wrote the last page of *Jacob's Room,* an experimental novel which declared that for one human being to know another is not possible. Lawrence, down in Sicily, was about to spit on Europe for the last time and depart. Living next to Basil Blackwell's bookshop in Oxford, in the best of psychic health, was W. B. Yeats, whose latest volume contained some of the poems we now most value for their symbolic vision and their unity of being. Some rough beast slouched. The world that read in English was ready—and by no means ready— for *Ulysses* and *The Waste Land.*

The Garden Party was to appear at the end of February, bringing much praise, and money with which to pay bills. There was no real need for Katherine to continue subjecting herself to the strain of the autumn months; but stronger than all of her desires (says the *Journal* on 24 November) was the desire "to *make good* before I do anything else. The sooner the books are written, the sooner I shall be well, the sooner my wishes will be in sight of fulfilment."

They had taken the chalet on a twelve-months lease, intending to stay there for a year or two.[1] Had that been adhered to we should have had Katherine's best book, and her first intentional one: her first to consist of mature work only, and the first one designed to a plan. But through the agency of her friends Koteliansky and Orage, two mysterious persons had just unwittingly intervened in her destiny. Koteliansky had sent her the news of Dr. Manoukhin's treatment, and Orage—who could never have known where this would lead—had arranged for a review copy to come to Murry of a privately printed book called *Cosmic Anatomy, or the Structure of the Ego,* by "M. B. Oxon" —his Theosophist contributor, Dr. Wallace.

Murry intensely disliked this "book of occult doctrines," and would have none of it. But Katherine, as the *Journal* records, eagerly took it up for what it had to say about "mystic expansion of consciousness," "the evolution of reality," and so on, and she began to correspond with Orage about it. She was reading it in January, in the intervals of working on *The Doves' Nest:*

January 4 . . . . . I have read a good deal of *Cosmic Anatomy* and understand it far better. Yes, such a book does fascinate me. Why does Jack hate it so?

To get even a glimpse of the relations of things—to follow that relation and find it remains true through the ages enlarges my little mind as nothing else does. It's only a greater view of psychology. It helps me with my writing, for instance, to know that hot + bun may mean Taurus, Pradhana, substance. No, that's not really what absorbs me; it's that reactions to certain causes and effects have always been the same. It wasn't for nothing Constantia chose the moon and water, for instance!

There is a good deal hidden away in that. The allusion to the closing episode of *The Daughters of the Late Colonel* is her only admission anywhere, to the present author's knowledge, of her use of symbols, and it is typical of her to make Constantia responsible for them—with a double negative, at that. She had an almost Polynesian reluctance to refer directly to the penetralium of mystery.

If the book did seem to "help her with her writing," its main effect was of a different sort. Through the correspondence with Orage it was to lead her, in nine months' time, to Fontainebleau. For the moment, however, her mind was still set upon that other miracle, Dr. Manoukhin's costly wonder-working with his meaningless machine.

At this point Murry's words express the matter best. She had precipitately turned, he says, to "two alternative and in essence contradictory notions: one, that there was a physical or medical technique which would abolish her disease and annihilate her limitations; the other that there was a psychological or spiritual technique which would enable her to ignore them."[2]

For his part, he could put no faith in Manoukhin at all. Too many reputable doctors had told him what they wouldn't say to Katherine. Since, at the chalet, she had come nearer to following a regime than at any other place, he had come to look upon it as a symbol of salvation and sanity, and he wished she would simply stay there.* In his commentary to the letters he blames himself, regretting that when Katherine was enticed to visit Dr. Manoukhin in person he did not "reso-

---

*L.M.'s comment on the typescript of the author's previous book at this point reads: "Lesley, personal note, forgive her. His strong man, possessive, *I* arranged, *I* found a chalet, sickens and infuriates me. He was quite happy at the chalet, skating, being fed, kept warm, nothing to do but enjoy himself, work if he wished . . . 'symbol of salvation and sanity!' . . . She was making no progress, the height was trying her, the doctor had nothing to say . . . and as nothing stands still she was going slowly back and down." In fact Murry nowhere made the claims here ascribed to him by L.M.

lutely oppose her going," and perhaps prolong her life a little. When writing that, however, he had forgotten the role that was played at the time by Katherine's "wife." Against the conjugal alliance of Katherine and L.M., not all the resoluteness Murry could have summoned in a lifetime would have stopped them going to Paris.

The need for money again played its familiar part. On 9 January Katherine told Brett that she was thinking of Manoukhin "more than anyone can imagine," but that she had £100 saved up for "this *Last Chance,*" and as soon as she knew that he could help her she would make some more. Just then the *Sketch* wrote asking if she could supply something like *Marriage à la Mode* for its series of "Tales with a Sting";[3] although wretchedly unwell just then she meekly declared in a notebook, "I must obey." She then began making arrangements to go to Paris, giving Murry to understand that she would return after a few days' consultation, but telling Elizabeth that her treatments were to start in a fortnight.[4]

If all this sounds like desperate and tragic folly, it was also Arthur Beauchamp—and Annie Beauchamp, too. In her appetite for travel, Katherine was her mother over again. Steamer tickets and train bookings were a sort of adrenaline to her: when lured by the thought of hearing Manoukhin pronounce the magic word *"guéri,"* all she needed was someone to do the packing, and she would put a notebook in her bag and be off.

On 11 January she wrote *A Cup of Tea* in four or five hours. Next day she had a daydream about being cured and adopting a Russian baby to be known as Anton. Eight days later, she was sure that the real cause of her illness was not her lungs but something else. In one more week (having written *Taking the Veil* in a three-hour burst) she was sending Ida down to Sierre to book the seats. So it was that Katherine, abetted by Ida, left the chalet on 30 January 1922. Anne Rice had recommended the Victoria Palace Hôtel, avenue Blaise Desgoffe.

Murry promptly heard that Manoukhin had said, "I can promise to cure you." Then why not start at once? She would need at the outset fifteen treatments (the French word happens to be *séance*) at 300 francs apiece, followed by a rest in the mountains, and then ten more, "to prevent recurrence": £112 for the first round, and then another £75. She had in the bank £103, and editors with cheque-books waiting for her clever type of story.[5]

In the privacy of her notebook, after writing this news for Murry,

Katherine confessed something altogether different. Although she could feel that Manoukhin was a really good man she also had a sneaking feeling that he was a kind of unscrupulous impostor: "Another proof of my divided nature. All is disunited. Half boos, half cheers." But the die was cast that evening. The chalet saw Katherine no more.

Murry, who was embedded in another misguided novel and had not expected to be uprooted, now realised that Katherine expected him to join her. He wrote to her offering to come, being told very bitterly that that was "like Father's telling me that I could count on him up to £50 if the necessity arose. It is not the gesture of people who deeply understand each other." On the evening of the day when her reproaches reached him (9 February 1922) he left Sierre, in such a state of nerves that he tipped the railway guard a whole golden louis instead of a franc, and taking with him an abject letter declaring his love and admitting all fault.[6]

Rilke, that day, having completed a seventh "Duino Elegy," sent his friend Frau Wunderly an excited telegram from the Sierre post office at ten past five to tell her so; as he walked back to Muzot another one formed itself in his head and was written down that night. In Paris, *Ulysses* had just been published by Miss Sylvia Beach.

L.M. returned to Montana two days later to mind the chalet and care for Wingley, and if possible to find some way of taking in lodgers to recoup the rest of the lease.

Murry's arrival in Paris had interrupted the writing of *The Fly*, which Katherine began within a week of going there, and which now is widely regarded as one of her principal achievements. Aside from its connection with the war, it has been more discussed and interpreted than anything else she wrote. It has also been found to have an analogue in Chekhov, on which she may well have drawn unconsciously when writing it.* A little masterpiece of symbolic attention

---

*But surely less so than on her feelings toward her father, whose reply to her letter of 1 November she soon expected to receive. A letter to Brett of 26 February describes it as "a queer story called *The Fly*. About a fly that falls into an inkpot and a Bank Manager."

In America *The Fly* attracted, between 1945 and 1965, a long series of academic explications. More fruitfully, F. W. Bateson and B. Shahevitch submitted it in 1962 to "the kind of close analysis that has been so successful in our time with lyric poetry."[7] Chekhov's story "Small Fry" (translated by Constance Garnett in 1920) is about a helpless over-to what the war had meant, its genius eludes most explorations of the academic sort, and defies belittling, too. It was not dashed off, but took, it would seem, three weeks, from beginning to completion.[9] Nor was it destined for a magazine. It went, unlike her recent pieces, to the *Nation,* as did that brilliant little soufflé, *Honeymoon,* which she also wrote in Paris—a farewell to her sparkling Riviera manner. She knew quite well now which her best work was, and whether it was written for money or for perceptive readers.

Meanwhile her book had come out, had been greeted with rapture by reviewers, and had gone at once into further printings. The *Observer*'s critic, noticing the theme of death, said that her treatment of it had "a tenderness in its irony, a dignity in its tragicomedy," which reminded him of Hardy. The *Nation* found *The Garden Party* a happier book than *Bliss,* leaving the reader convinced that "it is a good thing to be alive on this shining planet." The *Times Literary Supplement* still found a wry taste in the cup, but said the result was wider in range: "You might say that pity has entered in." Rebecca West, in the *New Statesman,* was alone in dwelling on *At the Bay* and seeing it as a continuation of *Prelude*—"that section of a work of genius which was the best thing in *Bliss.* "[10]

Meanwhile also, Murry had written an article for the *Nation* on *Ulysses,* which prompted its author to seek a meeting, since both were in Paris. It was arranged by Sydney Schiff, for 29 March, and described by Katherine in a letter to Violet Schiff a few days later:

> I was so distressed that Sydney stayed such a short time on Wednesday. But Joyce was rather——difficile. I had no idea until then of his view of *Ulysses*—no idea how closely it was modelled on the Greek story, how absolutely necessary it was to know the one through and through to be

---

worked clerk who, when trying to write a sycophantic letter to his hated superior, sees a cockroach run across his desk; he slaps his hand on it, it wriggles and dies, and when he has tossed it into the flame of the lamp he feels better. When *The Fly* is considered on its own ground, any role in its conception that Chekhov's cockroach may have played seems merely trivial. In fact the helpless insect, or the "fly in the milk-jug," had been one of Katherine Mansfield's favourite images for years, and anyone familiar with her notebooks knows that it was her habit, when one of her fountain pens made a blot, to see the blot as an insect and give it legs. There is an early example in the "Juliet" notebook, and a sort of Rorschach moth in one of her letters to Murry.[8] All this is not to mention her father's familiar inkwell, or the little brass-pig pen-wiper that he had given her when she left home in 1908, and which she still had with her.

able to discuss the other. I've read the Odyssey and am more or less familiar with it but Murry and Joyce simply sailed away out of my depth. I felt almost stupefied. It's absolutely impossible that other people should understand *Ulysses* as Joyce understands it. It's almost revolting to hear him discuss its difficulties. It contains *code words* that must be picked up in each paragraph and so on. The Question and Answer part can be read astronomically or from the geological standpoint or—oh, I don't know! And in the midst of this he told us that his latest admirer was *Jack Dempsey.**

That letter owes its preservation to the fact that Violet Schiff sent it—in no kind mood, in fact, for she knew of his contempt for Katherine—to Wyndham Lewis, with this further information: "J. told us last night that Mrs. Murry seemed to understand his book better than her husband which would have surprised her."[11]

Most of the comments on *Ulysses* which are scattered through Katherine's letters are ill-considered expressions of revulsion (like those of Virginia Woolf), but an exception occurred when she wrote of it to Brett:

> Joyce certainly had not one grain of a desire that one should read it for the sake of the coarseness, though I confess I find many "a ripple of laughter" in it. But that's because (although I don't *approve* of what he's done) I do think Marian Bloom and Bloom are superbly seen at times. Marian is the complete complete female. There's no denying it. But one has to remember she's also Penelope, she is also the night and the day, she is also an image of the teeming earth, full of seed, rolling round and round.[12]

With so much praise for her own book coming in from every side —and indications, too, that money would be no problem now—Katherine understandably felt well. It was also spring. But she gave the credit to Dr. Manoukhin, who had shrewdly ordered a fattening diet. "I hardly ever cough," says a letter to Ida at the chalet. "I have gained 8 pounds. I have no rheumatism whatever. . . . . My voice has changed back. I take no medicines."[13]

---

*A quaint mistake on Katherine's part. Joyce must have mentioned George Stanislaus Dempsey, his English teacher at Belvedere College, Dublin, who had kept in touch with him and probably wrote to him at this time.

It was therefore decided, since "repose in the mountains" was prescribed, that they would return to the Valais—not to Montana's altitude this time, her heart being the sole remaining weakness, but to Randogne. Would Ida pop down and choose two rooms at the Hôtel d'Angleterre? She, of course, would not be needed any more.

Splendid, said Elizabeth when told: "But it seems so incredible that you will be able to be there without someone like the Faithful One to hover round you. . . . ."[14] After that, and the final treatments, they might go south, perhaps to Bandol again. Even Murry, when he wrote to Elizabeth, was almost ready to believe: "I begin to feel that the horror may move away," he said, "and that there is a big round spot of real daylight at the end of the tunnel. I feel I can tell you. I'm damned if I can tell anyone else. I'm terrified even at mentioning it."[15]

Ida had meanwhile completed the evacuation of the chalet and taken Wingley in a basket to England, where she found a home for him. Her services to Katherine being superfluous at last, she began to think of some occupation for herself. Perhaps she might start a little tearoom somewhere with a friend.

On 4 June Jack and Katherine went to catch the train—but they'd quite forgotten it was Whitsun. No porters to be had, crowds of people wheeling their own luggage, "fifteen thousand *Gymnastes de Provence* pouring through one," and so on. There were no couchettes, only an ordinary first-class carriage and no washing arrangements. Jack, who had Katherine's money, gave away a 500-franc note instead of a 50; luggage tickets lost at Lausanne; a rainstorm at Sierre; and then, those bare and poky rooms that Ida had booked ("whatever made you tell such bangers?"), in which it dawned on them that Jack had lost his only fountain pen, and also had left Katherine's little square clock in the train.[16]

All they could do about the hotel was pretend that it was "the sort of place R. L. Stevenson would stay at." Then they began to relax, and think of all the work ahead. What a pleasure, as one of those English reviewers had remarked, to think of all the years of writing Miss Mansfield had before her.

[2]

Hôtel d'Angleterre
[about 8 June 1922]

Ida,

If you are not finally fixed up for the summer—listen to me. It's no go. I am almost as ill as ever I was, in every way. I want you if you can come to me. But *like this.* We should have to deceive Jack. J. can *never* realise what I have to do. He helps me all he can but he can't help me really and the result is I spend all my energy—every bit—in keeping going. I have none left for work. . . . . It would have to come entirely from you. I'll draft a letter and send it on chance. If you agree, write it to me. It's not wrong to do this. It is right. I have been wanting to for a long time. I feel I cannot live without you. . . . .[17]

The Faithful One supplied the needed letter, was told that it had had "precisely the effect it was intended to have," and abandoning her plan to start a tearoom she prepared to return to Switzerland.

It was not until 1953, when he first read that letter to L.M. and some others like it, that Murry began to realise the extent of the deceptions with which he had lived throughout his years with Katherine. She, for her part, had long taken the view that his "self-absorption" and his "memory" left her free to practise the deceptions, with impunity.

To Elizabeth in London she now confessed that the Furies had returned in full force, adding: "My only trouble is John. He ought to divorce me, marry a really gay young healthy creature, have children and ask me to be Godmother. He needs a wife beyond everything. I shall never be a wife and I feel such a fraud when he still believes that one day I shall turn into one."[18] And Murry's difficulty was that she *demanded* that belief from him.

She had also to think of her father, who was on his way to England again. His reply to her letter of the previous November had reached her in Paris, breaking the news that all four sisters were receiving similar incomes from him, and she had answered him on 18 March, in one of those letters that Murry thought "so obviously faked":

My darling Father,

I can't express to you my feelings when I read your letter. How you can possibly find it in your heart to write like that to your undeserving little black sheep of a child only God knows. It wrings my heart to think of my ungrateful behaviour and I cannot understand how I have been the victim of my fearfulness and dread of misunderstanding. You have been—you are—the soul of generosity to us all. Then how, loving you as I do, feeling your sensitiveness and sympathy as I do, can I have made you suffer? It is a mystery. I sometimes wish that we could have been nearer to each other since I have been grown up and not the intolerant girl who returned to New Zealand with you years ago. But fate has willed otherwise. . . . . .

> God Bless you darling.
> I am, ever your loving and grateful child,
> Kass[19]

Conscious of his fears on his own behalf, she now told him she was "no longer actively consumptive, i.e., no longer infectious in any way," and talked of seeing him in London in August and handing him copies of those books which she had never felt were good enough to present to him.[20] No doubt she meant to give him an American edition of *The Garden Party*, in which (though rather too late) she had made some prudent changes in *The Stranger*, altering the place-names of Wellington and Auckland, which would have forced him to see who "Mr. Hammond" was, and to notice that the story was connected not only with the incident at Hobart but with his second marriage, on the day after his ship reached Auckland on 5 January 1920.

Having the hotel's glass verandah all to herself, she went to work on *The Doves' Nest*, supposedly as the "serial" which Clement Shorter had requested. It was meant to be delivered by 1 July. She worked every day, Sundays included, until lunchtime, and from tea until supper; but the labour of getting up (she told L.M.), of "tidying, brushing clothes, carrying cushions and so on," was so great that mentally she was exhausted. She further tired herself with typing. All of which amply explains why nothing remains of *The Doves' Nest* but the portion she had written at the chalet. What was written at Randogne under these conditions was probably torn up.

L.M. arrived on 24 June—"I don't deserve such a wife," says a letter to Brett—but, discreetly keeping her distance, she took a room in a remote wing of that bald hotel.

Then it was—just a few days after the arrival which made it possible —that the troubled question of Belief brought Jack and Katherine to the sorriest of their partings. She had evidently been writing to Orage since January ("Heard from China," "Wrote to China," says the January notebook in some obviously coded references), and had come to look on *him* as the friend who could help her in her purposes. She had withdrawn into a secret plan of which she obviously could not speak to Murry, but for once it seems she hardly spoke of it to L.M. either. And so, although it was potentially the most grievous parting of all— for as things turned out it was very nearly final—not much is known of what really took place in the Hôtel d'Angleterre.

In his commentary to the *Letters,* Murry is clearly at pains to avoid passing judgement:

> A deep restlessness had now taken hold of Katherine. She found it very difficult indeed to work. Her mind was now moving fast towards the expectation of the other miracle—the attainment of such psychic control as would enable her to ignore her bodily condition. Into this realm I could not enter at all. Disagreement on a matter so fundamental created a situation that was painful for us both. It was at this point that we agreed to separate for the time being.

It was quite beyond his power, he says, to pretend that he saw any hope for her in "occultism." And so it was decided (he uses the passive mood) that he should remain at Randogne while Katherine, with L.M. to care for her, descended to Sierre: "We agreed that we now had a depressing effect upon one another, and that we ought not to live together until one or other of us had found a faith to live by."[21]

L.M., the only other person who might have described the event in detail, never did so to the author, leaving the impression that she did not really know what had taken place. Her published account reads as if it were based on Murry's.

Elizabeth, who was keenly disappointed, and smelt a rat, was told that the reason for the move was Katherine's "heart."

"Walked round to say goodbye to Katherine after breakfast up by the back way, through wet grass and rain," says Elizabeth's journal entry for 29 June. "Talked a long while with her. Back to lunch. . . . . Intercepted Katherine's procession at 5.30 on way to station and got into her tumbril and went with her and saw her off. An idle day, like Sunday, and I felt seedy all day." So *she* knew nothing, either. Indeed, it may well be that Murry himself hardly knew, and had to reconstruct it afterwards. But a few days later this was written in

Katherine's notebook: "Today is Tuesday. Since Leaving M.* I have written about a page. The rest of the time I seem to have slept! This of course started all the Old Fears, that I would never write again, that I was getting sleeping sickness and so on."[22]

Then Brett arrived, to spend a month at the same hotel, which was tiring for Katherine because she always felt so sorry for Brett. According to L.M. (there was mutual jealousy between the two), Brett wore Katherine out by sitting up talking far too late, ear-trumpet and all. But the visit prompted the writing of Katherine's last completed story. It was one she had promised as a gift to Brett from Paris, where some canaries in a cage across the street had caught her imagination. The idea now took shape in her little requiem for a lonely woman's dead canary—it is terribly objective, never sentimental, and is actually set in New Zealand, not Paris—which marks the end of Katherine's creative life: from *The Tiredness of Rosabel* to *The Canary*, not quite fourteen years. At this time too she wrote her poem "The Wounded Bird." Like Rilke in the same hotel not very long after, she was ready to admit that she was winged.

Though she dragged on with the typing, there was no more question of finishing *The Doves' Nest*. Its delivery date had passed, and she knew she could not go on.

At such a moment a little money would have been some comfort— all the more so if it could have come as a loving gesture from her father, perhaps after a family conference with the sisters to consider the fact that Kass was unlikely to participate in Beauchamp's will. Was no such conference ever held, as in other families it often is? Had something of the sort been done in time, Katherine need not have written all those magazine stories by which the output of her final phase is tainted. There would have been no need for her to deal with men like Clement Shorter wanting serials. Awareness of the need must have reached Elizabeth, for soon these letters were exchanged:

Chalet Soleil
Sunday [30 July 1922]

Dear Katherine,
　　Do let me lend you £100! I'd love to. I'd send it with this but I'm so

---

*In editing the *Journal* Murry mistakenly read this reference to himself as a reference to Montana. But Katherine had not left Montana, she had left Randogne.

afraid you'd send it back. You can pay it back when your book is paid for if you like. I know if you had just finished a book as I have and got paid and I was temporarily hard up I'd *certainly* ask you to give me a hand for the moment. Men do these things so simply and never give it another thought. Is it *really* impossible for us to be brothers?

So much love
Elizabeth

Hôtel Château Belle Vue

Monday

My dear Elizabeth,

It would be too marvellous if we might be men and brothers for once, and I am more grateful than I can say. I will pay it back the moment my book is paid for. But that will not be before the late autumn ... May I keep it as long as that? Of course, if in the meantime my Papa shakes a money bag at me— But it is far more likely to be a broomstick.

Thank you from my heart, dearest cousin. . . . .

Lovingly yours,
Katherine

Chalet Soleil
Wednesday

Dear Katherine,

Here you are. What do you think—the cook I had engaged for this month, on whom all my hopes were fixed, has failed me and we are cookless! Also I have a sore on my lip and feel too revolting for words. . . . . John says you've written a wonderful story. . . . .

Ever yours
Elizabeth

Hôtel Château Belle Vue

Thursday

Dear Elizabeth

Many many thanks once more.

I am so sorry to hear of your misfortunes. . . . . My story isn't a bit wonderful; I wish to God it were. But I'm panting for new scenes, new blood—everything brand new! In fact, you've lent that £100 to a fearfully desperate character.

Ever, dearest Elizabeth,
Yours lovingly,
Katherine[23]

So the help came from a "brother" after all.

Throughout that month, Rilke was constantly in the Château Belle Vue—it had an atmosphere of old Europe which gave him pleasure. His publisher, Anton Kippenberg, had come there with his wife to hear the elegies, which were read to them at Muzot, and since the hotel had few guests the curious trio of Englishwomen—the one in the smock with an ear-trumpet, the big one with the large feet, and the thin and tragic dying one—must have been a familiar sight to Rilke and the Kippenbergs. Rilke feigned to loathe the English, but there must have been some little nods and small politenesses.

On 7 August, upon some kind of premonition, Katherine wrote a farewell letter for Jack—the "secret you"—to receive in due course from the bank:[24]

> Dearest Bogey,
>
> I have been on the point of writing this letter for days. My heart has been behaving in such a curious fashion that I can't imagine it means nothing. So, as I should hate to leave you unprepared, I'll just try and jot down what comes into my mind. All my manuscripts I leave entirely to you to do what you like with. Go through them one day, dear love, and destroy all you do not use. Please destroy all letters you do not wish to keep and all papers. You know my love of tidiness. Have a clean sweep, Bogey, and leave all fair—will you?
>
> Books are yours, of course. . . . . Monies, of course, are all yours. In fact, my dearest dear, I leave everything to you—to the secret you whose lips I kissed this morning. In spite of everything—how happy we have been! I feel no other lovers have walked the earth more joyfully—in spite of all.
>
> Farewell—my precious love,
I am for ever and ever
Your
WIG

On 14 August a telegram asked Brett in London if Katherine could stay with her. She wanted to see Dr. Sorapure, and no one must be told that she was coming—not even Kot. On that day too, she drew up a formal will, which was witnessed by two of the hotel staff.[25] It followed the terms of her letter to Murry. It left her gold watch and chain to L.M., her Spanish shawl to Anne Estelle Rice, her fur coat to her mother-in-law, her large pearl ring to Richard, and her Shakespeare to Elizabeth. It left all her books to Murry, but asked that he give one each to Walter de la Mare, H. M. Tomlinson, Dr. Sorapure, A. R. Orage, Sydney and Violet Schiff, J. D. Fergusson and D. H. Lawrence; her writing case to Chaddie, her piece of greenstone to Jeanne, the brass pig to her father and her Bible to Vera; her Italian toilet boxes and her carved walking-stick to Koteliansky. Of her writings it said: "All manuscripts note books papers letters I leave to John M. Murry likewise I should like him to publish as little as possible and to tear up and burn as much as possible. He will understand that I desire to leave as few traces of my camping ground as possible."

It happens that Lawrence, on the day on which that will was made, was in Katherine's birthplace, en route from Australia to New Mexico. There had been no communication of any sort from him since his letter to Katherine from Capri, in which he wished her dead. But in Wellington his thoughts were sufficiently gentle to permit him to buy a postcard, write on it the one word, "Ricordi" (approximately, "memories") and send it through Lady Ottoline. The two thus made their parting gestures, the one a little more generous than the other's, on the same date, at opposite sides of the earth.[26] But Lawrence in fact never got his book. Murry eventually chose a little volume of Milton —perhaps because one title in it referred to something lost—which had been given to Katherine by Ottoline, and which she treasured. But he entrusted to L.M. the task of posting it; and L.M. never did, because, as she told the author, she "couldn't find Lawrence's address." So Lawrence never knew of it.

Jack came down from the Hôtel d'Angleterre; no doubt Elizabeth also came, to see them off; and all three left for London on 16 August 1922. It had been arranged that Katherine would stay with Brett in her house at No. 6 Pond Street, Hampstead, and that Jack would have a room in Boris Anrep's house next door.

CHAPTER XXI

To Fontainebleau

It is all memories now—radiant, marvellous, faraway memories of happiness. Ah, how terrible life can be! I sometimes see an immense wall of black rock, shining, in a place—just after death perhaps—and smiling—*the* adamant of desire.

—K.M. to J.M.M., 7 November 1919

In Moscow, in 1910, a Caucasian Greek named George Ivanovich Gurdjieff founded what he called his Institute for the Harmonious Development of Man, an exercise in changing human character which at that stage was as much a ballet troupe as a school of higher thought. During the war one P. D. Ouspensky, a journalist who had studied both mathematics and the occult, became his follower and chief apostle, and by 1921—the Institute having meanwhile fled the Russian Revolution by way of Tiflis, Constantinople and Dresden—Ouspensky was in London giving lectures on Gurdjieff's teachings to a circle which included A. R. Orage, the novelist J. D. Beresford, the psychiatrist J. C. Young, and various others who were looking for some new way. Among them was Lady Rothermere, who had been converted by reading Ouspensky's *Tertium Organum* in America. With money provided by her and by other supporters it was hoped to bring Gurdjieff and his Institute to England, but the current fear of Bolsheviks prevented that. And so, in 1922 at last, it found a home in France, near Fontainebleau.

What sort of man was the "Mr. Gurdjieff" whom Katherine Mansfield speaks of in such respectful tones in the letters of her final months? When Ouspensky sought him out in St. Petersburg in 1915 he found himself meeting, in a small café, a man of Oriental appearance whose black moustache and piercing eyes, bowler hat and black over-coat with velvet collar all suggested someone amateurishly disguised —something between a carpet dealer and a spy. He spoke bad Russian with a thick Caucasian accent which sounded all wrong for the expres-sion of philosophical ideas, but he obviously knew a great deal about carpets (he made a profitable sideline of selling them, and had cun-ningly mastered the art of mending them), and Ouspensky gathered that he had spent his childhood among nomadic peoples of Asia Minor in almost biblical circumstances, amid mysterious persons and flocks of sheep, in an atmosphere of fairy tales, legends, and old traditions.

He used to tell of village life in certain parts of Asia where, on winter evenings, a whole community would gather in one large build-ing and work together, the young and the old, upon a single carpet, all to the accompaniment of songs and dances which shaped their movements as they spun and wove. About schools, and where he had acquired all the knowledge he undoubtedly possessed, he would say very little. He might say one thing today and something quite different tomorrow, and "one could be sure of nothing in regard to him." He mentioned Tibetan monasteries, Mount Athos, Sufi schools in Persia and Bokhara, and dervishes of various orders, but all of them "in a very indefinite way."[1]

One of his beliefs was that civilisation, in developing certain of man's faculties, has thrown the others out of balance, so that the task is to correct this and to balance what he called the "centres": the intellectual centre, which thinks and formulates, the emotional centre, which feels, and has likes and dislikes, and the physical centre, which acts and moves and creates. A man with his centres balanced would be a four-dimensional man, like Jesus of Nazareth, and possess extraor-dinary powers. One might say that D. H. Lawrence needed his centres balanced in one way, and Middleton Murry in another.

The means of attaining Harmonious Development included what were called the "exercises." Whether in Tiflis, Constantinople, or Dresden, Gurdjieff's pupils had to walk about for tiring periods with arms outstretched; to stop a dance at the moment the music stops and hold that pose, or to get up and work hard in the small hours of the night. A pupil fond of sugar would be surfeited with sweetness or, capriciously, a heavy smoker would be ordered not to smoke, and so on.² Nothing would be easier than to ridicule what went on; but a send-up would hardly help us to understand what happened to Katherine Mansfield in 1922.

Orage had been fond of saying that Freud was the great analyst of the age, and what was needed next was a great synthesist. From what he learned in 1921 through Ouspensky, it seemed that Gurdjieff was that man. The London group used to meet in a Theosophical lecture room at 28 Warwick Gardens, off Kensington High Street, and it was doing so at the time when *Cosmic Anatomy* was posted to the chalet. A few weeks later Gurdjieff himself reached England, only to learn that he could not stay, and Katherine must have heard of him then directly from Orage (who had decided to join the Institute) at about the time her book came out. Then followed Paris and Manoukhin, Randogne, and the parting from Murry in June, of which the real meaning was probably disguised from him so that he scarcely knew *what* was happening.

Katherine arrived in London, with Murry simply tagging along in misery, on 17 August 1922, and stayed with Brett in Hampstead, Murry being next door at first. On the very next morning she saw Dr. Sorapure and "went over the battlefield with him." He thought she looked amazingly better and said her heart was not diseased: its condition seemed connected with the state of her left lung. Anyway, "the more exercise I take in the way of walking and moving about the better."³ That is what she wrote to her father, who had just arrived from New Zealand, to be joined in London by Chaddie and Jeanne. She had soon seen him as well: "He will live for hundreds of years," she told Elizabeth, "growing redder and firmer and fatter for ever. As to his 'fund of humorous stories,' it doesn't bear thinking about."⁴

To the Schiffs, and to her "wandering tribe," she let it be known that she would be with Brett for the next three months, taking the Manoukhin treatment with a London radiologist who knew how to do it. She wrote affectionately to Ottoline—she simply longed to see her soon. In fact all this was smokescreen. Though both Elizabeth and Murry had understood that she was heading for Manoukhin in Paris, Murry says he was surprised by the speed with which, instead, she joined the Ouspensky circle to which Orage and Beresford belonged.⁵

Her letters disclose that she now made Koteliansky her secret friend. She told him soon that she had arranged a "splendid scheme" by which

Murry would share Vivian Locke-Ellis's country house in Sussex and "live there for ever and ever."[6] He shortly did go there; then she summoned Orage. He came to Pond Street on 30 August, and the conversation occurred which the *Journal* records a little later: "On that occasion I began by telling him how dissatisfied I was with the idea that Life must be a lesser thing than we were capable of 'imagining' it to be. . . . ." Nearly everyone she knew, when his youth was past, "stopped growing," and beneath presumed maturity there sounded "an undertone of deep regret." She *knew* this need not be. How did one know? "Let me take the case of K.M. She has led, ever since she can remember, a very typically false life. Yet, through it all, there have been moments, instants, gleams, when she had felt the possibility of something quite other." Thus (or something like it) to Orage, her personal critic of 1912. She met him twice again; and following the advice of Dr. Sorapure she undertook all those strenuous engagements that are recorded diary-fashion in the *Journal.* She had tea with her father and her sisters, an X-ray session with Dr. Webster, lunch with Edward Garnett, her sisters to tea with her; and then, all in one day: "*September 14.* Lunch with Papa. Saw Marion Ruddick. Lecture at 28 Warwick Gardens."

Thanks to a vivid description given by Dr. Kenneth Walker of *his* first visit to that house a few months later, it is almost possible to follow Katherine into an Ouspensky lecture. In the hallway, Dr. Walker first had his name ticked off a list by a Russian woman with a "reassuring sense of humour." Then he went into a room like thousands of other such rooms: rows of small uncomfortable chairs facing a blackboard and a table; a carafe of water, a duster, and some chalks; one small painting on the walls, and on the windowsill a vase of artificial cherry blossoms made from shells. People trickled in in twos and threes and whispered. Most were middle-aged. Very few were young.

A solid man with close-cropped hair and strong glasses came to the table and sat down; he looked like "a scientist or a lawyer." Pulling some notes from his pocket he said, "Well?" and began without further introduction.

He said that man misunderstood himself: he thought he had a permanent self, a master "I," which integrated and controlled his thoughts and actions. But this was an illusion. Instead of the single "I" there were innumerable "I's," many of which said contradictory things. Then Ouspensky got up and drew a circle on the blackboard, and divided it by crisscross lines until it looked like a fly's eye seen under the microscope. In each little space he put an "I," and then he said, "This is a picture of man."

Someone asked him how long an "I" lasted. He said it was impossible to answer that: every thought, every desire, every sensation said "I," then disappeared into the background; what made it worse was that these ephemeral "I's" did not know each other. Were none of them connected, someone asked. All of them, in some way—"but we usually don't know the connections."

Ouspensky then expounded Gurdjieff's method whereby a man might examine his nature and discover himself, eventually acquiring powers at present denied him. He was at present a machine. When asked by a "lady with a very sensitive face" whether artists like Leonardo and Michelangelo were not free spirits, he replied: "They also were machines; very fine machines, no doubt, but machines. . . . . All the art that we know is mechanical and subjective." The lecture lasted for about an hour, leaving Walker convinced that Ouspensky was "as honest as he was unpretentious."[7]

On the Sunday after hearing all her "I's" described like that, Katherine excused herself from meeting Ottoline at Oxford Square on the grounds of exhaustion. But she did go out that day—to have lunch with the Schiffs at their home in Cambridge Square, an occasion recorded by a single line in the *Journal:* "Lunch with Sydney and Violet. *Odious.*"

She had had, in fact, a horrible experience. From letters and conversation the Schiffs knew very well that Wyndham Lewis (who was painting Violet's portrait just then) had nothing but contempt for their little friend;* but she had been wanting to meet him because she greatly admired his paintings, so he was there too. Evidently no one had warned her about him. She must have talked too recklessly of what was uppermost in her thoughts, and he, in some way, attacked her for her credulity: or, as Murry expressed it in a letter to Violet Schiff years later, "He positively outraged her, and she felt that Sydney and you

*"Your neighbour Miss K.M. continues to reap a monotonous harvest of offensive notices (you see them I expect). I have not read her book [*Bliss*]. But the notices are not of the kind that inspire one to procure it."—Wyndham Lewis to Violet Schiff at Roquebrune, 6 February 1921 (British Library).

did not protect her, as she thought you should have done. She quivered for days afterwards."[8] (He must have heard that from Brett, or made it up; he wasn't in London at the time.)

From Pond Street Katherine evidently sent Violet Schiff a note about the meeting, which Violet passed on to Lewis with this result:

> Dear Violet:
>
> K.M.'s note arrived. I don't see how, short of possessing such powers of divination as the Paris Institute would provide you with, you could have foreseen this rather comic dénouement of my meeting with the famous New Zealand Mag.-story writer, in the grip of the Levantine psychic shark. I am rather glad not to be troubled with her, though I hope she won't be too venomous. I shall expect you tomorrow at 3 or a little after.
>
> Yours,
> Wyndham Lewis[9]

She must also have sent some sort of protest to Lewis himself, who told Sydney Schiff that in considering these semicomic events a little he felt that Miss K.M. had picked a quarrel with him, who had merely been too sincere:

> For me of course she is nothing but a writer of 2 books of short stories, as she puts it, which have been advertised and pushed cynically out of all proportion to their merit. I find them, as I have always said, vulgar, dull, and unpleasant. And when there are so many fairly amusing, pretty charming people in the world, on principle I find it as well to *avoid* those few who write stories or paint or whatnot stuff for which I have a contempt.[10]

The encounter marked the end of Kass Beauchamp's relations with eminent creative artists of her time, a side of her life in this age of violence that began with Gaudier-Brzeska, included Lawrence, and closed with Wyndham Lewis.

She remained in London only two weeks more, and the diary shows no further appointments. On 30 September she wrote to her father explaining why she had drawn her next month's allowance in advance, and on 2 October, accompanied by L.M., she crossed the Channel for the last time, having booked in at the Select Hôtel —the one where they sat out the bombardment in 1918. On arriving there she remembered to write an affectionate "Good-bye for just now" to Richard Murry:

> I hope all goes well with you, my dear no longer little brother. Even if dragons come along don't forget that ten to one (the best dragons at any rate) they are guardians of treasures.[11]

She also had to write explaining her sudden departure to Mrs. Schiff, who wrote to Lewis, "Did the mere sight of you so completely bowl her over as to make her leave this country for good?"[12]

Such was Katherine's farewell to London, and to her Wandering Tribe. It was given out that she was returning to Manoukhin for further treatments, and she did in fact have some more. But L.M. says that they made her feel much worse, and really frightened her.

In the *New Age* office the news that Orage was leaving to go to Gurdjieff came as a bombshell. To the faithful Alice Marks it seemed the end of the world, and all he could say to her by way of explanation was, "I am going to find God."[13] His last issue was that of 28 September. He arrived in Paris on 14 October, Katherine's thirty-fourth birthday.

One or two of the letters from the Select Hôtel have some of the wit and gaiety of the Katherine we used to know, but after 14 October everything was changed. On that day—surely aware that it was probably her last birthday, yet denying the knowledge in every line—she wrote a long *Journal* entry which she tore out of the notebook, intending to post it to Jack: her renunciation of the world for which she had lived since stepping ashore at Gravesend in 1908, and her account of her reasons for what she now had in mind.

Since coming to Paris (she told herself) she had been as ill as ever. She couldn't walk; she could only creep. She had become "an absolutely hopeless invalid." It made her calmer to be writing ("Thank God for writing!"), but all the same she felt "so terrified of what I am going to do": "Do I believe in medicine alone? No, never. In science alone? No, never. It seems to me childish and ridiculous to suppose one can be cured like a cow *if one is not a cow.*" Then her thoughts perhaps slipped back to Wörishofen and Father Kneipp, as she went straight on:

> And here, all these years, I have been looking for someone who agreed with me. I have heard of Gurdjieff who seems not only to agree but to

know infinitely more about it. Why hesitate? . . . Risk! Risk anything! Care no more for the opinions of others, for those voices. Do the hardest thing on earth for you. Act for yourself. Face the truth. . . . .

Farther down she asked herself what she meant by health, and what did she want it for. Now the principal word was the verb "to live":

> By health I mean the power to live a full, adult, living, breathing life in close contact with what I love—the earth and the wonders thereof—the sea—the sun. All that we mean when we speak of the external world. I want to enter into it, to be part of it, to live in it, to learn from it, to lose all that is superficial and acquired in me and to become a conscious, direct human being. . . . .

> Then I want to *work*. At what? I want so to live that I work with my hands and my feeling and my brain. I want a garden, a small house, grass, animals, books, pictures, music. And out of this, the expression of this, I want to be writing. (Though I may write about cabmen. That's no matter.)

> But warm, eager, living life—to be rooted in life—to learn, to desire to know, to feel, to think, to act. That is what I want. And nothing less. That is what I must try for.

She had written that for herself. Now she must "risk sending it to Bogey." He must see how much she loved him:

> And this all sounds very strenuous and serious. But now that I have wrestled with it, it's no longer so. I feel happy—deep down. May you be happy too.

> I'm going to Fontainebleau on Monday and I'll be *back here* Tuesday night or Wednesday morning. *All is well.*

> Doctor Young, the London man who has joined Gurdjieff, came to see me today and told me about the life there. It sounds wonderfully good and simple and what one needs.

She didn't, after all, "risk sending it to Bogey." She left it among her papers, to be discovered by him later. And after that date, everything was changed; her very writing changed its tone. In the notebook she had written (just after the injunction, "Face the truth"):

True, Tchehov didn't. Yes, but Tchehov died. And let us be honest. How much do we know of Tchehov from his letters? Was that all? Of course not. Don't you suppose he had a whole longing life of which there is hardly a word? Then read the final letters. He has given up hope. If you de-sentimentalize those final letters they are terrible. There is no more Tchehov. Illness has swallowed him.

—and the same words could describe the letters which she herself wrote after this. The wit and the gaiety are gone.

On 16 October Katherine went to Fontainebleau, ostensibly for the night, but with every intention of remaining.

[2]

The Prieuré des Basses Loges, at Avon, was an old Carmelite monastery (and former home of Mme. de Maintenon) set in beautiful neglected parkland on the edge of the Forest of Fontainebleau. Gurdjieff had acquired it from the widow of Dreyfus's defending lawyer, complete with all its paintings, including some by Rosa Bonheur; but the grounds had run wild, the paths were overgrown, and the fountain in the courtyard didn't work. An advance party consisting of Dr. Young and some Russians had come ahead, with Mrs. Ouspensky to cook for them, to begin the task of cleaning up. They had weeded the paths and washed innumerable windows by the time the main body arrived— among them Orage, who now shared a room with Dr. Young in the servants' quarters. The best rooms were reserved for visitors and for Gurdjieff himself, in a part of the château which soon was known as "the Ritz," to those who did not live there. (Lady Rothermere stayed briefly in the Ritz.) In a row of small houses in the grounds were Gurdjieff's mother and his married sister, his brother Dmitri and his family, Dr. and Mrs. Stjoernvall, and M. and Mme. de Salzmann.

About sixty people were in residence when Katherine went, but much had still to be done in the way of adapting and furnishing, stocking up with cows and goats, poultry and pigs, and then—the main job of all—erecting a meeting-house like those in the East which the Master had known. Gurdjieff himself was extremely capable with his hands. Out of an old stone ruin, under his direction, a Russian bathhouse was improvised, with Gurdjieff doing most of the brickwork, and while the men turned labourers for that, the women set to work on the costumes needed for the exercises and dances that would be given in public as well as at the Prieuré itself. In this case too, says Dr. Young, Gurdjieff "cut out the materials with great skill," and the women had merely to sew, cut stencils to his designs, and print the fabrics as he showed them.

For the "study-house" an odd symbolic tribute was exacted from the self-destroying West. The frame of a wartime aeroplane hangar was obtained, was miraculously erected without loss of life, and was lined inside and out with rough wooden laths. The space between being filled with the Prieuré's autumn leaves, the whole was then covered, says Dr. Young, "with the materials out of which the Hebrews made their bricks," a mixture of mud and straw. Its walls, above a certain height, were cleverly glazed with the help of old cucumber frames; the glass was then coloured with Caucasian designs, the hard earth floor, when dried with stoves, was covered with matting, and all was ready for the arrival in December of sixty-three carpets from Bokhara and Baluchistan, and a matching ritual number of fur rugs.[14]

When finished it resembled, according to a later observer, a Dervish tekke. There were Eastern instruments and drums therein; before a raised earth platform at the far end a perfumed and illuminated fountain played, and around the walls were numerous panels inscribed with wisdoms of the East in some Near Eastern script: "Work in this place is an end and not a means," and so on. Just inside the entrance, somewhat raised, was a richly ornamented alcove with crimson hangings—Mr. Gurdjieff's own seat: "The atmosphere was that of a holy place."[15]

"A new way of being is not an easy thing to *live*," said a letter that Murry had received just before Katherine's birthday. ". . . . . I have to die to so much." The only thing to do was get the dying over—court it, almost—"and then all hands to the business of being reborn again." Couldn't he, for his part, get "nearer the growing earth"? He ought to be gardening and have some animals. Playing chess with Sullivan could only feed his "overdeveloped intellectual centre." Yes, she did care for Lawrence, and thought of seeing him in the spring; but she didn't want any more *books* just now of any kind.[16]

Her next letter was written from the Prieuré on 18 October. She told Jack that she had asked "Mr. Gurdjieff" if he would let her stay, and he had agreed to her remaining for a fortnight, "under observation." If he did let her stay she would be really cured. She had written only

long or short scraps since *The Fly*, "for I was dying of the poverty of
life." Ida, for the time being, would remain at the Select Hôtel. She,
of course, had been "very tragic."[17]

Alone in Paris with her loss, Ida sat down in "a completely empty
world," and she wrote in her diary that Saturday: "Indeed I have said
goodbye to Katherine." Somehow knowing that they wouldn't meet
again, she looked about for some way of staying and working in
France, and heard of a job on a farm at Lisieux, near Deauville.

"It is too isolated," Katherine told her. "You will only get depressed
and *dull*. . . . . But you do see that our relationship was absolutely
wrong now? . . . . If you loved as you imagine you do how could you
make such a moan because I was no longer helpless. Try and look at
it like that."[18]

Katherine described her day for Jack: up at seven-thirty, wash in
ice-cold water, down for a lavish breakfast—"make my bed, do my
room." In the garden during the day. Then after dinner there was
music: "tambourine, drums and piano—dancing and perhaps a display
of all kinds of queer dance exercises." Dr. Young came at bedtime to
bank up her fire, and she was patching his trousers in return. Do send
Lit. Supps., she said: "They are so good for lighting fires."[19]

He mustn't feel they were moving apart! She was only trying to put
into practice ideas she had had for a long time, of another and *"far more
truthful"* existence. Her next letter had this in it:

> Mr. Gurdjieff likes me to go into the kitchen in the late afternoon and
> "watch." I have a chair in a corner. It's a large kitchen with 6 helpers.
> Madame Ostrovsky, the head, walks about like a queen exactly. She is
> extremely beautiful. She wears an old raincoat. Nina, a big girl in a black
> apron—lovely, too—pounds things in mortars. The second cook chops
> at the table, bangs the saucepans, sings; another runs in and out with
> plates and pots, a man in the scullery cleans pots—the dog barks and lies
> on the floor, worrying a hearthbrush. . . . . Mr. Gurdjieff strides in, takes
> up a handful of shredded cabbage and eats it. . . . . It's just the same all
> through—*ease* after *rigidity* expresses it more than anything I know.[20]

Another letter told Jack how she had spent the morning in the work-
shop: the forge was alight, Mr. Gurdjieff was planing, and Mr. Salzmann was making wheels. And Mr. Gurdjieff was going to build her
a high couch in the stable as soon as the cows were bought, where she

could sit and inhale their breath. Everyone called them already "Mrs. Murry's cows." So she *was* going to stay!

What we are seeing here can be explained quite simply, without any mystery at all. Kass Beauchamp, who was always a Beauchamp, whatever else she may have seemed at times, had been longing for years for the gregarious unthinking active life of her own extended family: Grandma Dyer in the kitchen with her shelves of bottled fruit, Aunt Belle discussing shoulder-straps, Pat Sheehan saddling up the horse or bringing in the cow's milk—or chopping off the heads of ducks. The other life, that arid life of "being a writer" along with Jack—who scarcely knew such things except through her—had simply gone too far, and the compulsion to regain some life more like her memories of Karori was made immensely urgent by the nearness of her death.

Forty years ago it was common to refer to Gurdjieff as "the man who killed Katherine Mansfield," because in those days one had read of how she suffered from the cold as the winter advanced, and worked in the kitchen scraping carrots, peeling onions and so on. It is easier now to see what those things meant to her. One of the best friends she made at the Prieuré, Olga Ivanovna (who later married Frank Lloyd Wright), gives it all in a single glimpse, when describing Mrs. Murry's arrival: "She stood in the doorway of our main dining-room and looked at all and at each with sharp, intense dark eyes. They burned with the desire and hunger for impressions. She wanted to sit down and eat with all the students, but someone called her to a different dining-room. . . . ."[21]

Close friendship followed, and in an article which is full of intimate knowledge of Katherine Mrs. Wright declared: "One of the most humane acts Gurdjieff ever did was to accept her into the Institute."

There is no reason to doubt this view. It was obvious from the start to everyone, not least to the doctors, that Mrs. Murry had not long to live; and the Institute was not even running yet. If Gurdjieff had considered his own interest he would hardly have taken the risk of a bad press—which he got—by having a famous writer die of tuberculosis at the Institute within the first year of its existence. She was not a potential source of funds, like Lady Rothermere (who rather soon abandoned her expectations, and went away).

As for Gurdjieff's teachings, they barely concern us here. They were either too naïve or too well worn, and were mainly suitable for persons not well read. Of moral content they had none. His "know thyself" was hardly modern Greek; his notion of "balancing the centres" came from the sort of man who could make a good firm milking stool, but would hardly depose the Trinity. Yet he comes out of all the literature as a kindly and decent friend to Katherine Mansfield in her last and most desperate endeavour to locate her "self." He told her she was "Not to think, not to write. . . . . Live in your body again."

He was not a fraud. A man who lays bricks and planes wood, cuts out dress materials and printing stencils, designs all the decorations of a "holy place," mends Oriental carpets, and picks up a little shredded cabbage in the kitchen, is something else.

He apparently supported a copious family by his work, but he never "made money" by it. As a father figure he was all that Kass Beauchamp had never known. "He spent comparatively little on himself and had no interest at all in money except as a means of carrying out his work," writes Kenneth Walker, who says that money poured out of Gurdjieff's pocket as quickly as it was poured in. He was "always very princely with his gifts," and sometimes covered the expenses of people who wanted to see him but could not afford it.[22]

About the middle of November Gurdjieff moved Katherine to a room in the workers' quarters that was "small and plain and very simple," and in which she felt the cold: "the kind of room that Gertie Small might have," as L.M. read. "Bare boards, a scrubbed table for the jug and basin etc." Yet a letter of New Year's Eve records the astonishing fact that throughout her stay she did not have to spend a single day in bed. And from that room she wrote to Jack: "I never think of Ida except when I get letters from her. Poor Ida! When I do, I am sorry for her."[23]

She also felt sorry for Jack, condemned now for good to "being a writer," simply emerging from his study and disappearing into it again. "Don't you *sicken* of shutting that door and sitting down to that table?" she asked him, wondering whether it even had flowers on it.

She did know of two men who could understand this place if they would—Lawrence, and E. M. Forster. But Lawrence's *pride* would hold him back, she said. For herself, she no longer was "a little European with a liking for Eastern carpets." The West now seemed "so poor, so scattered." But Jack had a horror of anything Eastern, hadn't he?[24] (By return of post he was able to tell her that he was just then immersed in *Rajah Yoga,* for he was living now at Ditchling, where he had taken up with an English mystic, named Dunning.[25])

Katherine told Jack early in December that she would rather they didn't meet again until the spring. Meanwhile Gurdjieff had had the hayloft furnished and decorated for her so that she could lie there in comfort and inhale the breath of the cows, which was good for the lungs. She used to climb up some steps, and there, awaiting her exclusive use, were divans covered with Persian carpets, while the ceiling and the walls had been decorated for her pleasure by Mr. Salzmann with flowers, birds, animals and butterflies, all with faces that everyone would recognise (Orage was an elephant). There she went for a few hours every day, and toward evening she heard the pingle-pangle of the milking, just below. By orders of the Master she even managed to swallow some fresh milk straight from the cow. He had restored her to her comfortable room.

All this was simple kindness to a young woman near death; and Katherine was grateful to Mr. Salzmann (a friend of Chekhov's widow) for the pleasure he had given her by his gentle arts. "He dresses like a very shabby forester and carries a large knife in his belt," said a letter to Jack. "I like him almost as much as I like his wife."[26]

As Christmas approached, Katherine altered her appearance. "I no longer have a fringe—very odd," she told Jack. On Boxing Day she wrote: "You see, my love, the question is always: *'Who am I?'* and until that is answered I don't see how one can really direct anything in oneself. *'Is there a Me?'*. . . . . I don't believe for one moment these questions can be settled by the head alone." Indeed: "If I were allowed one single cry to God that cry would be: *I want to be* REAL."[27]

It is natural to wonder what passed between Katherine and Orage during these weeks when they saw each other every day. The article which he published two years afterwards, "Talks with Katherine Mansfield," is disappointing. He was no reporter, and one hardly hears the sound of her voice, still less of any new ideas. It uses the style of Plato's dialogues, and the voice purporting to be hers sounds far more like his own.

The article has Katherine declaring that the greatest literature is "still only literature" if it does not have a purpose commensurate with its art, and that even if she could write like Shakespeare there would still be something missing, because "literature is not enough"—a clanger we must doubt she ever dropped. Then it describes how she sent for him one day because she had something very important to tell him, and when he entered her room "her face shone as if she had been on Sinai." She said she had found her idea: "Katya has felt something that she never felt in her life before, and Katya understands something she never understood before."

She said she had a whole new attitude toward life and literature, and she meant in future to "make the commonplace virtues as attractive as ordinarily the vices are made." She would present the good as the witty, the adventurous and the alluring; and the evil as the platitudinous, the dull, the solemn and the unattractive. In the past she had been a camera—a selective camera, but one without a creative principle, and so on. "I saw her a few hours before her death," says Orage, "and she was still radiant in her new attitude."[28] It all sounds more like Book III of *The Republic* than it sounds like Katherine,* and we are probably safer in the hands of "Olgivanna":

We both looked at the fire in pleasant repose.

"What do you do in life?"

"I am a writer."

"Do you write dramas?"

"No." It sounded as though she were sorry she did not.

"Do you write tragedies, novels, romances?" I persisted, because she looked as if she should write these.

"No," she said, and with still deeper distress; "only short stories; just short stories."

Later on she told me she felt so wretched at that moment she would have given anything if she could have answered at least one "yes" to the "big" things.[29]

There was another young person who had been detailed to look after Mrs. Murry, a Lithuanian girl named Adela (later Mme. Kafian), who spoke no English then; they could only converse in simple French.

---

*It also sounds like Gogol at a similar stage in his life. From 1840 Gogol wandered Europe, moving from spa to spa in quest of health and friends. In 1845, facing death, as he believed, and "standing before God," he burned all the manuscripts of the second part of his projected greatest work, *Dead Souls*. He became convinced that all the human failings he had depicted were his own, and his satirical fiction merely an attempt to put them outside himself; he vowed instead to create an art of moral regeneration. Returning to Russia, he turned for spiritual guidance to an ill-educated, fanatical priest with the manners of a peasant, who made him promise to give up his trivial scribbling. Complying, and submitting himself to an excessive Lenten fast, he died in 1852, aged forty-three, after destroying the work of his last seven years.

Adela has since described how Katherine would go to the cowshed "carrying a notebook," and she stated, surprisingly, that at the Christmas party which was held on 25 December for the English contingent Katherine recited "some character sketches in an English dialect."[30]

Christmas Eve and New Year's Eve were Sundays—letter-writing days for anyone who learned good habits at Miss Wood's. On the first of them Katherine described for Ida all the preparations being made for the Russian New Year on 13 January and the opening of the study-house. She enclosed 100 francs, saying she had lost her "money complex," and signed the letter, "With love from, KM."[31]

On New Year's Eve Olga Ivanovna had the feeling that "something had happened" to her friend: Katherine spoke of how hard it was to push away "old feelings, habits and desires," and needed reassuring that she was "still on the right way." She said she was going to ask Mr. Murry to come and see her.

Then she wrote, that day or that evening, some final letters, all with different signatures: a hasty note to Jack in pencil, inviting him to come for a week on the eighth or ninth as Gurdjieff's guest, for the opening of the study-house. It was signed, "Your ever loving, Wig." Then a letter to her cousin Elizabeth, enclosing a cheque for the £100 that Elizabeth had lent. Katherine said she hadn't written a word since October and didn't mean to until the spring ("I am tired of my little stories like birds bred in cages"). But then she dropped her guard, and said: "Goodbye, my dearest Cousin. I shall never know anyone like you; I shall remember every little thing about you for ever. Lovingly yours, Katherine."[32] She began a letter to Chaddie and Jeanne, but somehow couldn't finish it.[33] If she wrote to Kot, he put it with other intimate letters from Kissienka that cannot yet be seen.

Then she wrote, at leisure and with deep affection, to her father, back in New Zealand. She described her gallery above the cows ("I feel I must look a great Pa-woman, perched up aloft"), and said she was going to stay there for six months at least. Jack seemed happy, and she only wished that she could look forward to settling down in England: "But the idea of settling is to me what it seemed to be to Grandpa Beauchamp. Only I am driven there: he went willingly." This letter was probably her last, since it ended: "The New Year is already here. I must leave the fire and go to bed. God bless you darling Father. May we meet again at not too distant a date. Ever your devoted child, Kass."[34]

There was one more Sunday, but, apparently, a Sunday without any letter-writing. A silent week, of simpleness, perhaps, and of Epiphany. Jack was to arrive after lunch on the Tuesday, 9 January. After asking Olga Ivanovna if she thought it would be very foolish, Mrs. Murry combed her hair down again, to have a fringe for his arrival.

He, too, felt when he saw her that "something had happened." As they talked in her room she seemed "a being transfigured by love, absolutely secure in love." She didn't try to defend the Institute to him; she simply spoke quietly of her feeling that perhaps she had now gained all that it had to give her, and might be leaving very soon.[35]

Olga Ivanovna met them in the study-house, which was still not finished, feeling somehow uneasy. She sat with Katherine on the rugs while the women worked at the painting of the glass. To Katherine's delight, Jack took a brush and worked with the others: "It pleased her that he was nice and friendly to everyone."

After supper all were summoned as usual to the living-room for the exercises. Katherine was at her favourite place by the fire and Olga Ivanovna joined her, but she seemed impatient and remote. "I want music," she said. "Why don't they begin?" She was pale and strange and "dreadfully far away from me." When the dancing was over Olga Ivanovna said goodnight and returned to the study-house, in some way puzzled.[36]

Adela Kafian was nearer when it happened. She says that in going up with Murry to her room, Katherine forgot every caution and ran ahead as a healthy person might, and something loosed the flood. At the top she began to cough, she spun on her heels to Jack, and blood came spurting from her mouth. Poor Kass had not seen anything like that since Patrick Sheehan chopped off the duck's head at Karori. She managed to say to Jack, "I believe . . . I'm going to die." He led her to the bed and rushed down the stairs for Dr. Stjoernvall, meeting Adela at the bottom and pointing to their door.

Adela flew up the stairs, prepared by Murry's paleness for the worst, to find Katherine sitting on her bed, fully conscious of what was happening to her. The blood came in gushes from her mouth, and Adela grabbed a towel which Katherine pressed convulsively to her lips, her eyes on the door for Jack. Two doctors came with him. They pushed Murry out of the room before Katherine's eyes, and Adela went to hers and sobbed on her bed.[37]

When Orage fetched Olga Ivanovna from the study-house, the doctors were "going through hopeless motions with hot-water bags," but Kass was dead.

Lesley came next day from Lisieux, was given Katherine's room, and began to sort out her things, taking for herself the gold watch and chain which she knew was left to her in Katie's will. Next morning, in a small chapel, she relieved the bareness of Katherine's cheap white coffin by putting over it the brilliantly coloured black silk Spanish shawl that was to go to Anne Estelle Rice.

Chaddie and Jeanne, and Brett as well, arrived in time for the funeral on Friday afternoon. Some unidentified "young literary men," Lesley writes, also came from London. They sat talking in an intellectual way about why Katherine Mansfield should have come to this place, so Lesley stood up and told them off. There were not many flowers, but Brett put some lily of the valley at the head of the coffin.

From the Protestant church at Fontainebleau the hearse was drawn by two black horses wearing funeral plumes before a long, slow procession of cars, in which were Gurdjieff and some of his people, to the communal cemetery at Avon. Since a long devious route had been chosen, Lesley got out and walked. Still wearing Frieda's ring, Katherine was lowered into French soil, with her brother: unlike Chummie, to be later lidded from the sky by unsmiling stone.

There was a moment's confusion when Murry, not understanding what was expected of him, did not sprinkle something on Wig's coffin. Lesley touched his arm, "but he jerked away from me." Someone suggested the shawl, but that was Anne's, so Lesley dropped in some marigolds that she had brought. The company then returned to the Prieuré, the edge taken off its New Year celebrations on the morrow, and the visitors went their ways.

"Yes, it is something gone out of our lives," Lawrence wrote to Murry from New Mexico. "We thought of her, I can tell you, at Wellington. Did Ottoline ever send on the card to Katherine I posted from there for her? Yes, I always knew a bond in my heart. Feel a fear where the bond is broken now. . . . . We will unite up again when I come to England. It has been a savage enough pilgrimage these last four years."[38]

E. M. Forster wrote to Murry: "What you say has given me a curious feeling. I had never for an instant thought that she might be thinking of me. Death *interests* me for more than one reason. It is largely connected, for me, with the problem of remembering. Sorrow I find indirectly rather than directly painful: it obscures."[39]

The grave was blanked over by a large stone slab, bearing as epitaph a quotation from Hotspur of which Katherine was fond, in lettering designed by Richard Murry. The inscription reads: "Katherine Mansfield, Wife of John Middleton Murry, 1888–1923. *But I tell you, my Lord fool, Out of this nettle, danger, we pluck this flower, safety.*"

CHAPTER XXII

Afterwards

Forget! forget! all is blotted out, all is hidden—long ago, said the snow.
Nothing can ever bring it back, nothing can ever torture you again. There
is no trace left. All is as if it had never been. . . . . You have your wish,
your wish! whispered the snow. You are safe, hidden, at peace—free.
—the *Journal,* 1921

In the New Year honours of 1923 Harold Beauchamp was knighted for his services to the Dominion of New Zealand in finance. Then came the news that his famous daughter had died, and a few weeks later he publicly acknowledged a debt which he felt the businessman owed to the arts. "A handsome bequest," said the *Dominion* on 7 February, "of a valuable freehold property valued at between £5,000 and £6,000, was made yesterday by Sir Harold Beauchamp towards the establishment of a National Picture Gallery in Wellington." It was the house in Fitzherbert Terrace, Kathleen's last home in New Zealand, and the last true home she ever had. He had intended, Sir Harold said in his letter to the Minister of Internal Affairs, to leave it as a posthumous bequest: "Recently, however, I have decided to act in my lifetime." Kathleen does seem to have been at the back of his mind as he did this, since the letter also mentioned his desire to create in the minds of the rising generation a love for art "in its best and truest form." A few months later, his partner Walter Nathan having died, the firm of W. M. Bannatyne & Co. was sold for £150,000. As can be seen from the Chronology, the money cost to Beauchamp of "Katherine

Mansfield" (as her name is printed in his book) had been about £2,600. He later gave the Turnbull Library £200 so that it could purchase her first editions and preserve them in "suitable bindings." Her own estate, apart from personal possessions, came to £232.[1] The little brass pig was willed to him.

After the funeral, Murry and Ida travelled back to England with their loss, and Murry shortly invited Ida down to Sussex to help him sort out Katherine's papers and date her early manuscripts. "Now the only thing that matters to me," said his reply to Ottoline's letter of sympathy, "is that she should have her rightful place as the most wonderful writer and most beautiful spirit of our time."[2] It was Brett's resentment of Ida's part in this work (she went to Ditchling too) that drew from Murry a ringing defence of L.M., from which it is possible now to form some idea of how he had accepted her role in his life with Katherine.

Brett, in fact, had hoped to marry Jack when Katherine died; as early as 1 February he had to tell her that she must put the idea right out of her mind.[3] Herself in deep distress in every way, Brett found in Ditchling that she could not bear seeing "this great porpoise of a woman" handling Tig's belongings and putting clothes of hers on her own body. She let fly in a letter to Murry, which he answered as follows (4 April 1923):

My dear Brett,
 I have your letter, and I tell you frankly I don't like it. You make a great many insinuations about Ida which I don't like. You *ought* not do these things. They are unworthy. . . . . I feel your letter is *all wrong*. And some of the insinuations are intolerable. You have no right to say "Ida tortured Tig." Do you imagine you never tortured Tig? Or I, for that matter? "She is so very insensitive." Really? If you can't see that you *must not* say such things, then you have a long way to go. . . . . believe me, your attitude to Ida will have to change *absolutely*, be really changed, uprooted and planted again, before any good will come to you. What does Dunning matter or Virginia's sympathy or anything else in comparison with this one plain and simple duty of putting right your relations to a fellow-creature, who loved Tig just as much as you, was as loyal to her as you were? Why this pretence of superiority to her? "This solid school-girl type." Really! Do you imagine that Katherine would have relied on her for twenty years, had she been that?

Murry didn't often write with such heat, and the tone belies, in fact, the utter disarray of his own emotions; of which Frank Lea, as well as he could, has told the story in his biography. One sad result of Murry's devastation was that since he forgot to pay the bill for Katherine's funeral, her wanderings were not ended even yet. In 1929 a New Zealand admirer discovered that her grave was not in perpetual ground but had been moved to the *fosse commune,* the pauper's part that is re-used. She informed Sir Harold Beauchamp, who commissioned his English son-in-law, Charles Renshaw, to go to Avon and put things right.[4] The grave was moved again, and today an imposing plot a yard or two away holds Gurdjieff and his family, so friends are near.

Murry brought out *The Doves' Nest and Other Stories* in June 1923, followed by the *Poems,* then by *Something Childish,* and in 1927 by the original *Journal of Katherine Mansfield,* which sealed her in porcelain for twenty years—for the *Letters* of 1928 were of necessity somewhat sweetened in the editing, many harsh comments on friends and fellow writers being removed. The image of Katherine thus presented to the world had far more resemblance to Murry's "perfect" Katherine than to the Beauchamp actuality. In England, its adoration was followed in due course by embarrassment, and by a feeling that Murry had exploited his dead wife's work. In France, what arose was something like a cult.

Meanwhile Murry had founded the *Adelphi* with a huge following of fifteen thousand readers, but by shedding far too many tears for Katherine in it he squandered his account, being also brutally lampooned by Lawrence and Huxley in works of fiction that were very widely read. By the 1940's his own unpopularity in England had obscured the worth of her work as well as his, and the notion of an English Chekhov had taken hold. For a long time it was impossible for either criticism or biography to escape the effects of what had happened.

By now she has had her natural death: she has been through that phase of disregard which commonly follows the death of a writer much admired. It should be possible to start afresh—for our own sake of course, not hers. A satisfactory complete edition of her work has yet to be produced, its "sources" straightened out, its originality perceived.

Christopher Marlowe was stabbed in a tavern brawl at twenty-eight; had Shakespeare been stabbed at that age we should have known him as a minor Elizabethan dramatist with some lyric gift. Katherine Mansfield died at thirty-four; had Virginia Woolf gone under the waters at that age we should have known her by *The Voyage Out* and nothing else; she would never have read *The Garden Party* and written *Mrs. Dalloway*. It would seem that modern criticism has been ill-equipped to deal with potential and the *colonne brisée*. That is one part of the problem. One legitimate aim of biography, of course, is to make criticism more difficult.

"Our missing contemporary," as Elizabeth Bowen called her in a notable preface in 1960, already had tuberculosis when she first met Murry in 1911. Unknown to her it probably touched *The Aloe* at Bandol, and from 1917 onwards all her art, like that of Keats or Stephen Crane, was a function of her dying. This makes it wrong to ask what might have happened "had she lived." The question is philosophically absurd. But a certain wrong decision to leave Montana makes it feasible to contemplate what might have happened could she have gone on dying a little longer—long enough, say, for the book already conceived —by remaining quietly at the chalet. With the help of her own clear words, and the lists and beginnings that she made, it is not impossible to form an idea of the qualities which that book would have possessed.

Murry once said that the new subjectivist novelists, such as Joyce and Proust, appeared to be trying to express "the truth alone," whereas writers like Chekhov and Katherine Mansfield aimed at "an *art* which is compatible with the truth."[5] Of one impurity she certainly was free by 1921: she had no trace of a desire to be in the intellectual fashion of the day. Her missing book would probably have given her a place among the modern writers somewhat resembling that in modern music of Maurice Ravel. Impeccable ear, superb technique in the use of existing tonalities, intuitive classicism, along with texture, scale and sharp-edged clarity, all make the comparison seem apt. As it is, we have a Ravel without a *Daphnis:* no mean composer, and not a minor figure to be left aside because the form she employed lacks heavy weight.

The moral implications of the life, from which it is so hard to disengage the work, are rather more difficult to appraise. How should we esteem a pursuit of truth in art by one who used so many deceits in life? Compassionate biography must turn to life's evasive ironies in such a case. Let irony, at the last, choose Katherine's compassionate enemy Frieda Lawrence, whose ring she stills wears—"a bracelet of bright gold about the bone"—for closing words, written from Cornwall[6]: "She must become simple, as we all must learn to be. But I do love her, if she tells lies, she also knows more about truth than other people and don't let us see too much the *ugly* things."

APPENDICES, CHRONOLOGY
BIBLIOGRAPHY, NOTES, AND INDEX

APPENDIX A

Green Goggles

Katherine Mansfield's send-up of Russian novelists, which appeared in the *New Age*'s "Pastiche" column on 4 July 1912, was preceded by two lines alleged to be from a Russian folk song: "Green Goggles, green goggles, / The glass is so green." Here are the beginning and the end of the parody, showing that almost any Russian writer, from Gogol to Chekhov, could have been in her mind when she wrote it:

The servant girl, wearing a red, sleeveless blouse, brought in the samo-var. "But it is impossible to speak of a concrete ideal," thought Dimitri Tchernikofskoi. "In the first place, concrete is a composition. It is not a pure substance. Therefore it must be divided against itself."

"There is a gentleman in the passage," bawled the servant girl. Dimitri Tchernikofskoi disguised his nervousness by frowning deeply and plucking at the corners of his collar, as though the starch were permeat-ing his skin and stiffening the throat muscles. "Show him in," he mut-tered, "and"—he closed his eyes for a moment—"bring some cucum-bers."

"Even so, Little Father."

A young man, wearing a bear-skin coat and brown top boots, entered the room. His head was completely covered in an astrachan cap, having enormous ear-flaps, and his pale, kind eyes smiled timidly from behind a pair of green goggles.

"Please to sit down," said Dimitri Tchernikofskoi; and he thought: "How do I know those eyes? Are they green? Da, if they were green I should not know them. I feel that they are blue. Lord help me! I must try to keep calm, at all events."

The young man sat down and pulled his coat over his knees. Twice he opened his mouth and twice he closed it. A round spot of red, about the size of a five-rouble piece, shone on his cheek-bones.

Dimitri Tchernikofskoi fumbled in his waistcoat pocket for his watch, and then he remembered that he had pawned it three months before—or sold it, he could not remember which—to Ivan Dvorsniak. And he saw again the little evil-smelling shop and the grotesque, humped figure of the Jew, bending over a green-shaded lamp, weighing the watch on the index finger of his right hand. He fancied he heard it ticking quite sharply and distinctly. Then he realised it was the voice of the young man.

"My name is Olga Petrovska."

"Eh? What's that? What's that you're saying?"

Olga Petrovska raised her hand. "Please do not speak so loudly . . ."

—and so on for a page or so, until:

And suddenly all that he had imagined and thought and dreamed—the values and revalues and supervalues of good and evil, his hopes, his ambitions—faded away. He knew only one thing. He must go with this woman. That settled, action became easy. He drew his handkerchief from his pocket and spread it on the table. She watched him. He went over to the washstand and, taking a toothbrush and a half-used cake of some yellowish soap, he wrapped them neatly in the handkerchief. "What are you doing?" she asked, vaguely troubled. "Come," he said, "it is time."

APPENDIX B

The Changeling

After Katherine Mansfield had left the *New Age* for *Rhythm* and Middleton Murry in 1912, Orage more than once allowed Beatrice Hastings to make pseudonymous attacks on her in print. One was the piece about rats (page 156), which was published on 2 January 1913, just after the return from Runcton, and another was the following, which appeared on the same page over the pseudonym, "Alice Morning":

THE CHANGELING

Oh, surely, she was in love! Reflecting both in her mind and the mirror—she had nearly lived at the mirror since once He brought her, a willing Vashti, before all his friends and they proclaimed her Venus's double—she was quite sure she was in love. Yet, to convince herself, she took a look round the room, strewn with hats and a pink bed and little duckey boots and the best cigarettes and ever so many perfumes with the spray tops she had always coveted. With a weeny sigh of security, she smiled back to the mirror.

Yes, he was a coming genius, and a catch in every sense of the word. How vulgar the commercial traveller seemed now, how boorish the engineer, how most inexpensive the provincial actor! Yet for the engineer she had scrubbed floors, for the actor she had lived on oatmeal, for the bagmen she had endured what unholy tedium of quick-lunches, the longest things on earth sitting on those hard high stools! She was not critical in those days. N-no! But why had she even thought she was having such a Life?

"No use blinking facts, my dear," she said to her face. "You *did* enjoy yourself. You were a real child playing real games, and now you are only

Dinky's Baby. . . . . Good heavens, I look perfectly ugly. I look forty. Marie!. . . Marie!!. . . Oh, bring me a little thimbleful." Two tumblersful made all the difference. "I'll pin my hair up. . . . He'll be sure to pull it down when he comes in. Oh, Dinky, darling, come, come, *my* LOVER!"

She rattled on to the mirror: "Well, miss, I really hopes as how you'll be happy. Dearly beloved brethren, all we are lost and have strayed from our ways like false teeth. But, my good woman, it's all the difference between optimism and peptonism, and if I don't do this in Dinky's absence I shall fairly break one of these days. Mah, mah, mah!"

So for ten minutes, clattering about the room, punching the pink bed, whistling, singing, mimicking all sorts and conditions of people, and as suddenly she sat down on the chair before the mirror and was "only Dinky's baby."

"I think my white velvet will suit me to-night," said Baby; so she put it on, arching her throat and getting an amazing look like the advertisement mannequins, something tame-tigrish, very Scarlet, alluring—no, leery. The final grimace was of *hauteur*, real white velvet mannequin *hauteur*. Her very nails, as she cut them off, dropped with an air. Slowly she fitted on a ring or two. Slowly she turned from the mirror. Slowly and solemnly she leaned upon the post of the pink bed. Enravished she flung forth her arms. And just then he came in.

"My beautiful one!"

"Oh love!"

"Eons since I saw you."

Sotto voce: "Oe-er!" *Aloud:* "Silly darling. Oh, his little hair's quite wet. Naughty boy. I told you not to run up the hill. Now trot off and take a bath."

"One more—exquisite!" Mummumm.

"There, now di-rectly! And what boots! Oh, it is a bad boy. I'll beat him!" And she did fetch him a pretty hard slap, covering its weight with kisses all over his habitually mal-de-merish countenance. "Now—trot!"

For the first five minutes of his bath she sat on the edge of the pink bed and looked very like an interesting but bored suburban female. Then she snatched up a volume—the journal of Eugenie de Guérin, and, reading, decided almost, to enter a nunnery. Do not ask why, when the bath was over, the knock at the door turned her once more into Dinky's baby. She was a changeling, and you can't explain changelings. The "real child" threw a hair-brush at Dinky the very next evening, but Dinky's Baby lisped it "wuth tho thorry thweetheart!"

ALICE MORNING.

The Changeling

There are barbed allusions in that to Mr. Bowden (or rather his flat-mate, the engineer), to Garnet Trowell, to Francis Heinemann, and of course to Murry himself.

Identification of the Changeling as Katherine is established by another piece which Beatrice Hastings wrote some twenty years later for her own short-lived publication, the *Straight-Thinker Bulletin* (June 1932, page 7)—a reminiscence purportedly describing the arrival in the *New Age* office of the *German Pension* sketches in 1910 ("I told her that I only wanted MSS. of that level. She thought her sentimental efforts better, in her favourite oath, 'balls better.' ") Here is an extract:

> In the old days, A.R.O. scarcely threw her a serious word in three weeks. He nicknamed her the *marmozet,* thought her vulgar and enterprising and couldn't understand my putting up with her. She used to sit among us, silent and furtive, beady, obsequious, or suddenly pompous, picking up everything everyone said and did, grist for the sketch-mill, as A.R.O. called her memory. But it was the only way she could take, completely lacking intuition. . . . My estimate of Katherine as a critter was expressed in "The Changeling," also she served me for "Echo" [an earlier item]. In 1914 she came to see me in Paris, on her way to Francis Carco, on whom she had a shake. She meant to write him up, of course, but that was Carco's own game; and he had a head as well as a pen. The result was *Les Innocents,* a book rigidly boycotted by the K.M. publicity department. Carco regarded her as belonging to the "floating consciences" *(consciences flottantes)* around a rigid ego, and potentially dangerous; the which treatment corresponds with my "Changeling."

Four years later again, in her Blue Moon Press pamphlet, *The Old New Age—Orage and Others,* Beatrice Hastings closed the account with the following, which quotes Olive Moore's *The Apple Is Bitten Again:*

> I never knew until this month of January 1936 that Katherine Mansfield came back on the paper. The sketches published in 1917 look like the incredibly vulgar stuff I rejected. That this "fiendish" (Gaudier-Brzeska) pole-cat (me) was on the scene instructs me considerably; among other things I divine what a mess she and Orage made of poor J.M.K.[ennedy]. That she must have fancied she was triumphing over me, although I never knew that she was offered to the readers in the place of "Alice Morning," is not completely amusing; and it rather gladdens me to

reflect that when Francis Carco's terrible study, *Les Innocents,* showed her that she was detected and classified, *she* had to reflect that poor Sophie Brzeska, by lending her Carco's *Bubu de Montparnasse,* that led her to court this inexorable psychologist, had been fate's innocent instrument of revenge. After that book, Katherine began to play saint, prate about God and, as Olive Moore says, "twittered" her way out of a world she had fouled wherever she went.

Chronology

1825   Samuel Worthington Mansfield, aged twenty-one, emigrates from Liverpool to Sydney, New South Wales. In March 1838 he marries Margaret Barns (b. Bath, Somerset, in 1820).

1839   Margaret Isabella Mansfield born 21 January in Princes Street, Sydney. Her father becomes licensee of The Rising Sun and The Golden Anchor.

1848   Arthur Beauchamp, aged twenty, emigrates from Highgate to Sydney, where his brother Henry is already established in business.

1854   At Port Fairy, Victoria, Arthur Beauchamp marries Mary Elizabeth Stanley, aged eighteen, daughter of Timothy Stanley, silversmith, of Preston, Lancashire.

1855   In Sydney, Margaret Isabella Mansfield, aged eighteen, marries Joseph Dyer, aged thirty-six, son of the Rev. John Dyer, of Battersea, London.

1858   Harold Beauchamp born at Ararat, Victoria. The family moves to New Zealand in 1861.

1864   Annie Burnell Dyer born in Upper Fort Street, Sydney. Her family also moves to New Zealand.

1866   Henry Herron Beauchamp's daughter May (later Countess von Arnim) born in Sydney.

1884   In Wellington, Harold Beauchamp marries Annie Dyer. Her mother and two sisters, Kitty and Belle, join the household. Two daughters, Vera and Charlotte, are born in 1885 and 1887.

1888
14 October   Kathleen Mansfield Beauchamp born at 11 Tinakori Road.

1889
Easter   Kathleen's "first voyage"—to Picton.
November   Mr. and Mrs. Beauchamp go to England for several months.

1890
11 October   Gwendoline Burnell Beauchamp born at 11 Tinakori Road; dies there, 9 January 1891 (see also 9 January 1923).

1892
20 May   Jeanne Worthington Beauchamp born at 11 Tinakori Road.

1893
Easter   The Beauchamps move to "Chesney Wold," Karori, for five years. The Waters family move to Karori at the same time.

1894
21 February   Leslie Heron Beauchamp born in Wellington.
December   Kathleen visits Picton again.

1895   Kathleen begins attending the Karori village school.

1897   Kathleen wins school composition prize with *A Sea Voyage.*

1898   Mr. and Mrs. Beauchamp are away in England, March–November.
25 May   Kathleen is registered for the second term at Wellington Girls' High School—a bus trip from Karori.
September   *Enna Blake,* "by Kathleen Beauchamp, aged 9 years," published in the *High School Reporter.*
(In London, *Elizabeth and Her German Garden* is published by Macmillan.)

November	Harold and Annie Beauchamp return across Canada and the Pacific from England. The family is reunited at No. 75 TINAKORI ROAD.
December	Harold Beauchamp appointed (by his friend the Premier) a director of the Bank of New Zealand. The family spends Christmas at Island Bay.

1899

April	*A Happy Christmas Eve,* "by Kathleen M. Beauchamp, aged 10 1/2" published in the *High School Reporter.*
June	Vera, Chaddie and Kathleen leave Wellington Girls' High School for Miss Swainson's, in Fitzherbert Terrace. Kathleen there begins a magazine called *The School.* She is taking piano lessons from Mr. Robert Parker.

1900–1902	Kathleen and her sisters at Miss Swainson's. Maata Mahupuku, or Martha Grace, is also there.

1901

3 November	Kathleen's first journal entry, in her prayerbook: "I am going to be a Mauri missionary."

1902

	Kathleen, aged thirteen, meets Arnold Trowell, aged fifteen, who expects to go to Europe soon.

1903

29 January	The Beauchamp family, taking the entire passenger accommodation of S.S. *Niwaru,* sail for London via Cape Horn and Las Palmas.
After Easter	Kathleen and her sisters enter QUEEN'S COLLEGE, Harley Street, meeting Ida Baker on the day of their arrival. (Arnold Trowell and his twin brother Garnet leave Wellington to study music in Frankfurt.)
23 August	Kathleen's earliest surviving letter—to her cousin Sylvia Payne.
Autumn	Kathleen proposes to Ida Baker, "Let's be friends." She gives Ida the name of "Lesley Moore."
17 October	On the evidence of a torn-up, dated postcard, Kathleen is in Frankfurt (Eschersheimer Landstrasse).
10 November	Harold and Annie Beauchamp, with Jeanne and Leslie, sail for New Zealand. Aunt Belle remains in London, "to chaperon the girls."

December	*The Pine Tree, The Sparrows, and You and I,* published in *Queen's College Magazine*—the first of several contributions.
23 December	Kathleen and her sisters are with the Henry Herron Beauchamps (parents of "Elizabeth") at Bexley, Kent, for the Christmas holidays. They also spend some time with relations near Sheffield.

1904
March	*Die Einsame* published in *Queen's College Magazine*.
Summer	Kathleen visits Bollendorf, Germany.
	Two songs composed and written by Vera and Kathleen are printed in Berlin.
December	*Your Birthday* published in *Queen's College Magazine*.

1905
Summer	*One Day* published in *Queen's College Magazine*, of which Kathleen is now sub-editor (with Ida Baker as treasurer).
December	*About Pat* (a Karori reminiscence) published in *Queen's College Magazine*, Kathleen now being "head editor."

1906
16 March	Kathleen inscribes to Ida Baker a copy of Poe's *Tales of Mystery and Imagination*.
Easter	Aunt Belle Dyer takes Vera, Chaddie and Kathleen to Brussels. They meet the Trowell twins there, and also "Rudolf" (who later shoots himself). Kathleen is reading Oscar Wilde.
c.20 April	Mr. and Mrs. Beauchamp arrive in London to take their daughters home.
24 April	From a West End hotel at 3 MANCHESTER STREET, Kass writes to Sylvia Payne: "Would you not like to try *all* sorts of lives?"
June	Kathleen and her sisters leave Queen's College.
14 July	Miss Clara Wood gives Kass a thick notebook, "In very affectionate remembrance of No. 41 Harley Street."
	Arnold and Garnet Trowell come to London to give a joint recital in the West End.
October	The Beauchamps sail for Wellington by the S.S. *Corinthic,* arriving 6 December and resuming occupation shortly afterwards of No. 75 TINAKORI ROAD.
31 December	Granny Dyer (née Mansfield) dies suddenly, aged sixty-seven, having noticed that Kathleen has no time to visit her. The

girls now have the use of a summer cottage on the rocks at Day's Bay.

1907	
? March	Mrs. Beauchamp gives a garden party at "No. 75," the day being marred by a fatal street accident to a poor neighbour.
April	Harold Beauchamp becomes Chairman of Directors of the Bank of New Zealand.
	Kathleen has love affairs in Wellington with Maata Mahupuku (Martha Grace) and Edith Bendall. With the latter as illustrator, she produces a book of child verses.
May	The Beauchamps move to No. 47 FITZHERBERT TERRACE. Leslie is at school in the South Island.
1 June	Kathleen is in the cottage at Day's Bay with E.K.B.
	(In London, A. R. Orage and Holbrook Jackson purchase the *New Age.*)
July	Mattie Putnam is typing stories for Kathleen.
23 September	Kathleen learns that the *Native Companion* (Melbourne) has accepted her *Vignettes.*
26 September	New Zealand becomes a Dominion.
12 October	"Such a jolly dance" to celebrate Kathleen's eighteenth birthday (14 October).
	Vignettes by "K. Mansfield" published in the *Native Companion,* Melbourne; *Silhouettes,* in November.
15 November	Kathleen leaves to join a caravan party for an expedition into the "King Country," returning to Wellington 18 December.
December	*In a Café* published in the *Native Companion.* K.M. also contributes a Christmas story to Tom L. Mills's paper, the *Feilding Star,* of which no trace remains.
1908	
10 February	"I shall end, of course—by killing myself" (K.M.'s notebook).
4 March	Kathleen and Chaddie are in the cottage at Day's Bay.
6 July	After much unhappiness, and a farewell party given by the Prime Minister's wife (Lady Ward), Kathleen leaves per S.S. *Papanui* (via Montevideo and Tenerife) for London.
24 August	Mistakenly afraid that she may be pregnant, Kathleen reaches London and moves into BEAUCHAMP LODGE, Warwick Crescent, Paddington. The allowance from her father is £100 a year.
September	Three weeks after arriving, Kathleen is in love with and wishes to marry Garnet Trowell, twin brother of Arnold. She fre-

quently stays with his parents in St. John's Wood while he is away with the Moody-Manners Opera Company.

The Education of Audrey and *The Tiredness of Rosabel* written (?) at Beauchamp Lodge. The former is probably published in London.

(John Middleton Murry enters Brasenose College, Oxford.)

14–19 October   Kathleen stays with Mrs. W. H. Trinder (Aunt Belle) at Upper Warlingham, Surrey.

21–24 October   Kathleen is in PARIS for a naval wedding, with Margaret Wishart.

29 October   "Went to Mrs. Charley Boyd and at last put my mind at rest."

7 November   Kathleen is in Devonport with Margaret Wishart for the launching by Mrs. Asquith of the Dreadnought-class battleship, H.M.S. *Collingwood*.

December   Ford Madox Hueffer launches the *English Review* "with the definite design of giving imaginative literature a chance in England."

1909

2 March   After 2–3 weeks acquaintance, and falsifying her age, Kathleen suddenly marries G. C. Bowden, aged thirty-one, at Paddington Register Office, but leaves him the same evening. She also leaves Beauchamp Lodge, and shortly joins Garnet Trowell on tour in GLASGOW and LIVERPOOL (c. 10–28 March), becoming pregnant about this time.

17 March   Bowden-Beauchamp marriage notice published in the *Morning Post*.

April   Kathleen takes a flat in MAIDA VALE, knowing that her mother is coming to London.

29 April   Kathleen is in BRUSSELS, alone, for a few days. She has been taking Veronal to get to sleep.

27 May   Mrs. Beauchamp reaches London, has interviews with Mr. Bowden and Dr. Baker, and takes Kathleen to BAD WÖRISHOFEN.

4 June   Mrs. Beauchamp and Kathleen register at Hotel Kreuzer, Wörishofen. Mrs. Beauchamp returns to London a few days later.

12 June   Kathleen now at Villa Pension Müller, Türkheimer Strasse 2.

Late June?   Kathleen has a miscarriage. Shocked by the loss, she asks Ida Baker to send her a child to care for, and Ida arranges this.

Late July   When the *Tongariro* reaches Hobart, Tasmania, Harold Beauchamp meets his wife in circumstances which later form the basis of K.M.'s story *The Stranger* (1920).

31 July   As Mrs. Kathleen Beauchamp Bowden, Kathleen is now lodg-
                ing with Frl. Rosa Nitsch, owner of a lending library above the
                Wörishofen Post Office.

13 August   (In Wellington, Mrs. Beauchamp cuts Kathleen out of her
                will.)

23 September With the child, Charlie Walter, Kathleen is lodging now with
                the family of Johann Brechenmacher, a postman, at Kaufbeurer
                Str. 9, Bad Wörishofen. (In Wellington, on this date, Vera Beau-
                champ marries James Mackintosh Bell, of Ontario, Canada, at
                St. Paul's Pro-Cathedral.)

12 December   By letter, Vera French begs Kathleen not to live with Floryan
                Sobieniowski, but to come back to London.

21 December   Ida Baker sends Kathleen £6 and makes arrangements for her
                return.

1910

January   Kathleen returns to London, living first at the STRAND PALACE
                HOTEL. She then lives briefly with G. C. Bowden at 62 GLOUCES-
                TER PLACE. At this time Ida Baker becomes "L.M." so that she
                can keep in touch with Kathleen.

February   At Mr. Bowden's suggestion Kathleen takes *The Child-Who-Was-
                Tired* to A. R. Orage of the *New Age,* who prints it on 24 Febru-
                ary and asks for more. It is followed on 3 March by *Germans at
                Meat.*

March   After an operation for "peritonitis," Kathleen goes with Ida
                Baker to ROTTINGDEAN to recuperate.

May   At Rottingdean, Kathleen suffers a febrile illness referred to as
                "rheumatic fever." Unknown to her, it is in fact of gonococcal
                origin.
                Just after the death of King Edward VII, the Japanese-British
                exhibition opens at Shepherd's Bush.

7 July   After an interruption due to illness Kathleen resumes her *Ba-
                varian Sketches* in the *New Age.*

29 July   Now using "Katherine Mansfield" as her name (not only in
                print) Katherine is staying with Orage and Beatrice Hastings
                at 39 Abingdon Mansions, Kensington.

Autumn   K.M. moves to 131 CHEYNE WALK, CHELSEA. Friendship with Wil-
                liam Orton; affair with Francis Heinemann. She ceases, for
                nine months, to appear in the pages of the *New Age.*

November   First exhibition of the Post-Impressionists at the Grafton Gal-
                lery, arranged by Roger Fry.

3 December   *A Fairy Story* published in the *Open Window.*

(In Eastwood, Notts., D. H. Lawrence's mother dies. J. M. Murry is in Paris.)

1911

January   K.M. moves to 69 CLOVELLY MANSIONS, Gray's Inn Road, residing there until September 1912.

April   L.M. leaves for Rhodesia, depositing £60 in a bank account for K.M.'s expected confinement.

May   K.M.'s mother, brother and sisters travel to London for the Coronation of King George V. K.M. and her brother Leslie form a close friendship (to which L.M. is admitted).

18 May   K.M. returns to the *New Age* with *A Birthday.*

29 June   K.M.'s Theocritus pastiche, *The Festival of the Coronation*, published in the *New Age.*

August   K.M. is ill with "pleurisy." She "dashes off to Bruges," and then goes to GENEVA (*chez* Mme. Bieler, rue St. Léger), where L.M. joins her on returning from Rhodesia. "No baby and no bank account."

December   *In a German Pension* published by Stephen Swift. At W. L. George's house, K.M. (aged twenty-three) meets J. M. Murry (aged twenty-two) the editor of *Rhythm.*

1912

February   K.M. again visits GENEVA. Asks Murry to tea on her return.

28 February   K.M. is staying with Orage and Beatrice Hastings at Pease Pottage, near Crawley.

28 March   The *New Age* attacks "The magazine called *Rhythm,*" and K.M.'s poems therein.

11 April   Having decided to come down from Oxford, Murry becomes K.M.'s lodger at 69 CLOVELLY MANSIONS and, after a little delay, her lover. She is now named as Assistant Editor of *Rhythm.* Friendships with Gordon Campbell and Frederick Goodyear.

2 May   In the *New Age*, Orage launches a violent personal attack, over a pseudonym, on K.M. as "Mrs Foisacre."

3 May   (In Nottingham Mrs. Frieda Weekley, formerly Frieda von Richthofen, elopes with D. H. Lawrence to Germany.)

29 May   (In Bloomsbury, Miss Virginia Stephen becomes engaged to marry Leonard Woolf.)

June   With a partner, L.M. sets up in business as "The Parma Rooms" in South Molton Street—brushing hair. The Diaghilev Ballet comes to London.

Summer	Short friendship with Henri Gaudier-Brzeska. Friendship with Edward Marsh begins.
4 September	"The Two Tigers" move to RUNCTON COTTAGE, near Chichester. Floryan Sobieniowski sorns on them.
October	Charles Granville ("Stephen Swift") absconds with Louise Hadgers to Tangier, leaving Murry responsible for *Rhythm*'s debts. K.M. unable to conceive a child.
November	Returning to London, The Tigers take a one-room flat at 57 CHANCERY LANE. Edward Marsh gives financial support so that *Rhythm* can continue. Gilbert Cannan, Rupert Brooke and Frank Swinnerton are also supporters.
December	The Murrys go to Paris for Christmas with the Campbells and the Cannans, meeting Anne Estelle Rice and J. D. Fergusson there.
1913	K.M.'s allowance is probably £120 a year by now. *Georgian Poetry 1911–12,* edited by Edward Marsh, is published from the Poetry Bookshop.
March	The Murrys take "The Gables," at CHOLESBURY, Bucks., a cottage near Gilbert Cannan's windmill. (Chancery Lane retained as an office for *Rhythm.*)
May	*Rhythm* is reorganised as the *Blue Review,* but ends after three issues. K.M.'s published letters to Murry begin at this time, and D. H. Lawrence calls at the office in June.
June	The Murrys visit Lawrence and Frieda at Broadstairs and read *Sons and Lovers.*
1 July	The *Blue Review* having failed, Murry and K.M. move to Chaucer Mansions, BARON'S COURT, and Murry concentrates on literary journalism. Meetings with Lawrence and Frieda.
December	Since Murry is "bursting to write a novel" and believes he will write well in Paris, they move to 31 RUE DE TOURNON, where Murry begins *Still Life* and K.M. writes *Something Childish But Very Natural,* her only story in this year. K.M.'s sister Vera, who is visiting England from Canada, lends her some money for this excursion.
	In Paris, K.M. meets Murry's friend Francis Carco. *Rhythm*'s printers press Murry for debt.
1914	
26 February	Now a declared bankrupt, Murry is forced to return to London and the *Westminster Gazette.* They stay for a time at 119 BEAUFORT MANSIONS, CHELSEA.

27 March	L.M. leaves for Rhodesia for two years.
April	The Murrys move for economy into dingy rooms at 102 EDITH GROVE, where Katherine has an attack of pleurisy. Lawrence and Frieda visit them there.
July	They move into 111 ARTHUR STREET, CHELSEA, although it has vermin.
13 July	Lawrence and Frieda are married, Frieda giving her former wedding ring to Katherine, who wears it for the rest of her life, and to her grave.
August	On the outbreak of World War I Murry enlists in the territorials, but gets a medical exemption on the following day.
September	After a holiday in Cornwall they return to Arthur Street, determined to live cheaply in the country on K.M.'s allowance, and write.
26 October	They move into ROSE TREE COTTAGE, The Lee, near Great Missenden—three miles from the Lawrences' cottage at Chesham. They meet S. S. Koteliansky. Murry is working on *Still Life*.
December	Discontented with Jack, K.M. intends to leave him, and soon is receiving love-letters from Francis Carco in Paris.
	Christmas parties at the Lawrences' and the Cannans'. At the latter, a psychological explosion occurs when K.M., in a play, "leaves" Murry for Mark Gertler.
1915	K.M.'s allowance is now (apparently) £120 a year.
3 January	(James Elroy Flecker, aged thirty-one, a *Blue Review* contributor, dies of tuberculosis in Switzerland.) K.M. suffers from "arthritis." Murry also records in his journal that "her cough" has been very bad. The Lawrences leave Chesham for Greatham, Sussex.
12 February	Leslie Beauchamp, arriving in England to join up, gives K.M. money for a "week in Paris."
15 February	K.M., her cough a little better, leaves for Paris and proceeds to GRAY. Spends four days there with Francis Carco.
25 February	K.M. returns to Rose Tree Cottage and a reconciliation with Murry.
18 March	K.M. goes to Carco's flat on the QUAI AUX FLEURS, this time to write.
26 March	(Publication of Virginia Woolf's *The Voyage Out* is followed by her most violent mental breakdown.)
31 March	K.M. returns to live with Murry in rooms at 95 ELGIN CRESCENT.
23 April	She has begun her New Zealand story, *The Aloe*.
	(Death of Rupert Brooke at Skyros.)

5 May	K.M. goes once more to the QUAI AUX FLEURS to write. *Spring Pictures* and *The Little Governess* are written there.
7 May	(S.S. *Lusitania* torpedoed.)
19 May	K.M. returns to Elgin Crescent.
June	The Murrys move to No. 5 ACACIA ROAD, St. John's Wood. Murry is now established as the *Times Literary Supplement*'s reviewer of French books.
	(Gaudier-Brzeska killed in battle.)
Autumn	Murry and Lawrence begin the *Signature*. Leslie Beauchamp spends his final leave with K.M. at Acacia Road. Their meetings have prompted K.M. to write *The Wind Blows*, which is published in the *Signature*.
7 October	Leslie Beauchamp "blown to bits" in France.
	Lawrence's new novel *The Rainbow* suppressed shortly afterwards.
4 November	Dialogue, *Stay-Laces*, published in the *New Age*.
5 November	Attending party in Dorothy Brett's studio, K.M. meets Lytton Strachey and others of the Garsington set.
Mid-November	K.M. and J.M.M. leave for the South of France. They stay at Cassis, then move to BANDOL.
7 December	Murry returns to London, leaving K.M. at the Hôtel Beau Rivage, Bandol.
31 December	After a Christmas at Garsington, Murry rejoins K.M. at the VILLA PAULINE, Bandol.
1916	K.M.'s allowance from her father is £120 a year.
	(In this year Constance Garnett's translations of Chekhov begin appearing.)
February	Blissfully happy at the Villa Pauline, K.M. rewrites *The Aloe*, while Murry writes his study of Dostoevsky. Corporal Frederick Goodyear is writing to K.M.
	Her father raises her allowance to £156 a year.
21 February	(Battle of Verdun begins.)
7 April	With considerable misgiving, Murry and K.M. join the Lawrences at HIGHER TREGERTHEN, near Zennor, Cornwall, where "everything seems to be made of boulders." Violent rows between Lawrence and Frieda make them decide to leave. Murry has inadvertently rejected Lawrence.
June	They leave for Sunnyside Cottage, MYLOR, near Penrhyn, on the south side of Cornwall. Goodyear visits them there.
July	Once more discontented with Murry, Katherine "leaves" him,

	but after a weekend spent at Garsington (her first visit) she suddenly returns to Mylor.
	(Battle of the Somme, 1 July–13 Nov.)
16–17 July	At Garsington: K.M., J. T. Sheppard, Fredegond Shove, "Carrington," David Garnett, G. F. Short, Lytton Strachey, Evan Morgan, and many others.
August	Threatened with menial duties in the army, Murry goes up to London to seek employment of national importance. Through J. T. Sheppard (at Garsington) he gets a job in Military Intelligence (M.I.7)
26 August	At Garsington: K.M., Mary Hutchinson, Clive Bell, Aldous Huxley, T. W. Earp, Dorothy Brett, J. M. Keynes, J. T. Sheppard.
	The Murrys have now left Mylor. K.M. is staying in Brett's studio at 4 LOGAN PLACE, near Earl's Court.
31 August	In the Café Royal with Koteliansky and Gertler, K.M. snatches Lawrence's *Amores* from persons jeering at the poems.
4 September	Murry starts work with M.I.7 in Watergate House, Adelphi, receiving a regular salary for the first time in his life.
	K.M. visits Garsington again.
20 September	Frieda Lawrence, visiting London, does *not* wish to see Katherine. Koteliansky also is estranged, for the next two years. The Lawrences and Koteliansky now regard K.M. and Murry as liars.
29 September	Murry and Katherine move into J. M. Keynes's house, No. 3 GOWER STREET, BLOOMSBURY, sharing it with Dorothy Brett and Dora Carrington. From there, or from his office, Murry begins writing private letters to Lady Ottoline Morrell.
	L.M. returns from Rhodesia, trains as a machinist, takes lodgings in Hampstead, and works at an aeroplane factory in Putney.
1 November	Brett informs Lady Ottoline that K.M. is "in love with some man."
	About this time, Lytton Strachey arranges the first meeting between K.M. and Virginia Woolf.
3–5 November	K.M. and Murry at Garsington.
23 November	K.M. dines with Bertrand Russell. A private correspondence with him begins. . . . .
26 November	(Murry at Garsington.)
3 December	(At Garsington: K.M., Murry, Augustine Birrell, T. S. Eliot, J. T. Sheppard, Clive Bell, Ethel Sands, Dorothy Brett.)

10 December	. . . . . but Russell is also beginning an affair with Lady Constance Malleson, to whom he sends descriptions of K.M.
25 December	Murry and Katherine, Brett and Carrington, Lytton Strachey, Bertrand Russell, Aldous Huxley and Maria Nys all at Garsington for Christmas, where K.M. writes a playlet, *The Laurels,* in which all of these except Brett and Russell act comic parts.
27 December	Lady Ottoline reads Lawrence's new novel, *Women in Love,* in its original form. Horrified, she seeks comfort from K.M., Brett, Russell, and others.
1917	K.M.'s allowance is £156 a year, and Murry's salary is £260.
1 February	Leaving Gower Street and Bloomsbury, K.M. moves into a studio at 141a CHURCH STREET, CHELSEA. Meetings with Virginia Woolf begin there.
24 February	A cool letter from K.M. appears to end her relation with Bertrand Russell.
Late February	Murry takes rooms at 47 REDCLIFFE ROAD, Fulham, his rent being £35 a year.
16 March	Lt. Frederick Goodyear leaves for France.
19 April	K.M. returns to the *New Age,* publishing several "dialogues" there during the summer. She also has "a play half written."
26 April	Leonard and Virginia Woolf having installed a printing press at Hogarth House, Virginia asks K.M. for a story to publish.
20 May	At Garsington: Murry; Alix Sargant-Florence.
23 May	Near Arras, Lt. Frederick Goodyear dies of wounds.
3 June	At Garsington: K.M., Murry, Alvaro ("Chile") Guevara. Copies of T. S. Eliot's newly published *Prufrock* being produced by Clive Bell, K.M. gives a reading of it to the assembled company.
Summer	K.M. is refashioning *The Aloe* for the Woolfs to print under the new name of *Prelude.*
20 June	Virginia Woolf has "an odd talk with Katherine Mansfield."
21 July	At Garsington: K.M., J.M.M., and Arthur (Richard) Murry.
18 August	At Asheham, in Sussex, Virginia Woolf shows K.M. her story *Kew Gardens,* apparently written upon a suggestion made by her. This is V.W.'s first departure from traditional narrative.
September	Murry at Garsington (date uncertain). A little episode in the moonlight with Lady Ottoline, as described in her *Memoirs.*
4 October	*A Dill Pickle* published in the *New Age.*
8 October	Virginia Woolf starts regularly writing a diary.
9 October	The Woolfs take a proof of the first page of *Prelude.*

10 October	K.M. to dinner with the Woolfs to discuss "delicate matters," and to see the proof. Unfortunately K.M. "stinks like a civet cat."
17 November	(The Woolfs pay their first visit to Garsington.)
23 November	Ill from overwork, Murry goes to stay at Garsington to recuperate. K.M. goes with him for the weekend.
c. 12 December	After being chilled on a visit to Garsington, K.M. succumbs in the studio to her "beastly cough" and sends for a doctor. Finding a "spot" in her left lung, he advises her to go abroad at once.
Christmas	Murry is at Garsington; K.M. goes there a few days later.
1918	K.M.'s allowance is now £208 a year; Murry's salary is about £500.
7 January	K.M. leaves alone for BANDOL (Hôtel Beau Rivage). Exhausting wartime journey makes her ill.
29 January	K.M. begins writing *Je ne parle pas français.*
12 February	Disturbed by news of K.M.'s health, L.M. arrives uninvited at Bandol. *Bliss* begun.
19 February	K.M. has first haemorrhage of the lungs. Develops hatred for L.M.
21 March	K.M. and Ida leave Bandol for PARIS but are not permitted to travel further. They stay at the Select Hôtel, Place de la Sorbonne.
11 April	After three exhausting weeks in Paris under bombardment, they cross the Channel, K.M. joining Murry at 47 REDCLIFFE ROAD.
3 May	The Murrys are married at South Kensington Register Office, with J. D. Fergusson and Dorothy Brett as witnesses. K.M. continues wearing Frieda's ring. (Lytton Strachey's *Eminent Victorians* published.)
17 May	K.M. goes to the Headland Hotel, LOOE, CORNWALL.
22 June	J.M.M. joins K.M. at Looe.
c. 1 July	They return to live at 47 REDCLIFFE ROAD while they prepare a house they have bought in Hampstead.
10 July	First copies of *Prelude* sent out from the Hogarth Press. Murry's review of Siegfried Sassoon's *Counter-Attack and Other Poems* causes a rumpus at Garsington and Brixton Prison.
August	*Bliss* published in the *English Review.*
8 August	K.M.'s mother dies in Wellington.
Late August	The Murrys move into "The Elephant," 2 Portland Villas, East Heath Road, HAMPSTEAD—their own house for the first time. L.M. is to live with them there.

September	K.M. invites Koteliansky to the house (with the Campbells) and contrives a reconciliation.
	On the recommendation of Anne Estelle Rice, K.M. consults Dr. Sorapure, whose wise understanding causes her to trust his advice for the rest of her life.
14 October	Two separate TB specialists examine K.M. at Portland Villas and advise her to enter a sanatorium. Otherwise—"four years at the outside."
October	Lawrence comes to London. Friendly meetings with K.M. at Hampstead.
	Richard Murry is printing his brother's *Poems, 1917–1918* at Portland Villas.
November	Worldwide influenza epidemic. In Wellington, it carries off K.M.'s Uncle Val, and in England, her great-aunt Louie, the mother of "Elizabeth."
December	K.M. learns the cause of her arthritis from Dr. Sorapure. Temporary estrangement from Virginia Woolf.
1919	At some time in this year K.M.'s father raises her annual cash allowance to £300 and, unknown to her, provides the same for her three sisters in the form of capital holdings.
c. 10 January	K.M. begins a "treatment by injections" which causes high fever.
February	Murry, appointed editor of the *Athenaeum* at £800 p.a., leaves his War Office post as Chief Censor.
7–10 March	Murry is at Garsington. In his absence, Koteliansky visits Katherine at Portland Villas.
4 April	Murry's first number of the *Athenaeum*. T. S. Eliot at the last moment decides against leaving Lloyd's Bank to become Murry's assistant. "K.M." begins reviewing novels each week. She also starts helping Koteliansky to translate Chekhov's letters.
12 May	*Kew Gardens* by Virginia Woolf, *The Critic in Judgment* by J. M. Murry, and *Poems* by T. S. Eliot all published by the Hogarth Press.
29 May	The Murrys give an *Athenaeum* party at Portland Villas. In addition to L.M. there are now three servants.
May to July	Seven visits to K.M. at Hampstead by Virginia Woolf, the last being on 12 July.
Early August	K.M. feels so ill that she has decided to enter a sanatorium for the winter.

16 August	Harold Beauchamp comes to London, a widower. Sees K.M. for the first time since March 1912. Offended by Murry.
17 August	Dr. Sorapure having advised K.M. not to enter a sanatorium, she decides to go to the Italian Riviera.
9 September	Preparing to go away, K.M. writes an informal will—a letter to be left at the bank for Murry.
11 September	K.M.'s longest stay in any one place since "Clovelly Mansions" comes to an end as Murry accompanies her and L.M. to San Remo, Italy. After settling them into the CASETTA DEERHOLM, OSPEDALETTI, he returns to Hampstead.
12 November	Harold Beauchamp, with his Roman Catholic cousin Connie Beauchamp (of Menton), visits K.M. at the Casetta.
21 November	K.M. reviews *Night and Day* in the *Athenaeum*.
5 December	Murry ably criticises the Georgian Poets in the *Athenaeum*.
16 December	Disturbed by K.M.'s unhappy letters, Murry joins her at the Casetta (until 2 January 1920).
1920	K.M.'s allowance is now £300 a year.
5 January	(The day after landing at Auckland, Harold Beauchamp marries Annie's closest friend, Mrs. Laura Bright.)
11 January	*The Man Without a Temperament* written.
21 January	K.M. leaves Ospedaletti for MENTON to be near Miss Beauchamp. She stays at first in L'Hermitage, a private nursing home. L.M. takes a nursing job nearby.
7 February	K.M. receives Lawrence's letter: "You revolt me, stewing in your consumption."
15 February	K.M. moves into the VILLA FLORA, MENTON, to live with Miss Beauchamp and Miss Fullerton. She gathers from them that her allowance is grudgingly paid by her father. *Je ne parle pas français* (The Heron Press) published from 2 Portland Villas.
19 February	Murry is at Garsington with [from the visitor's book] Francis Macnamara, Alvaro Guevara, D. E. Brett, M. Gertler, C. H. Douglas, Edith Sitwell, Margaret Morris, Aldous Huxley, J. M. Keynes, T. S. Eliot and Vivien Eliot.
c. 3 March	Influenced by Miss Fullerton, K.M. writes a note informing L.M. (in Menton) that she is "going to become a Roman Catholic." *The Man Without a Temperament* published in *Art and Letters*.
9 April	Sydney and Violet Schiff call on K.M.—the start of a new friendship.
24–26 April	(J.M.M. at Garsington.)

c. 27 April	K.M. leaves Menton for London with L.M., to live at 2 PORT-LAND VILLAS for the summer.
28 May	Virginia Woolf visits K.M. for "2 hours priceless talk."
June	K.M. begins publishing short stories in the *Athenaeum*.
August	As she prepares to go away for the winter, K.M. becomes aware of an intimacy between Murry and Dorothy Brett, who now lives in Thurlow Road, Hampstead.
23 August	Virginia Woolf goes to Hampstead to see K.M.—their last meeting.
	"Elizabeth" (the Countess Russell) also calls to see her there—their first meeting as friends and equals.
c. 11 September	Accompanied by Ida, K.M. leaves Hampstead for the VILLA ISOLA BELLA, Menton—as tenant of Miss Beauchamp and Miss Fullerton, who still hope for her conversion.
16 September	K.M. is obliged to pay Floryan Sobieniowski £40 (= her advance for *Bliss*) for the letters she wrote him in 1909.
2 November	*The Stranger* written (see also July 1909 and 5 Jan. 1920).
11 November	*Miss Brill* published in the *Athenaeum*.
December	*Bliss and Other Stories* published by Constable.
	(In Canada, Vera's husband, "Mac," is now earning £11,000 a year.)
10 December	"K.M." publishes her last review in the *Athenaeum*.
	(On the same day Murry, in London, gives Princess Bibesco a copy of his Heron Press volume of *Poems,* inscribed, "Bless you.")
13 December	*The Daughters of the Late Colonel* completed.
c. 18 December	J.M.M. leaves London for Menton.
19 December	Aware of a relationship between Murry and Elizabeth Bibesco, K.M. writes her "confession" on the subject of human suffering. Ida is at the Villa Isola Bella all this time.
1921	
11 January	Murry takes a trip to London, returning on 19 January.
3 February	Murry back to London to arrange to leave for good.
9 February	K.M. sends A. R. Orage a letter that leads to renewal of their friendship.
c. 16 February	Virginia Woolf, hearing from Murry of Katherine's loneliness, writes to her but receives no answer.
c. 20 February	Having wound up his affairs in London, Murry returns to Menton.
9 March	K.M. learns that her father, on reading *Je ne parle pas français,*

	"chucked the thing behind the fireplace." She is inhibited from writing to him.
c. 13 March	L.M. goes to London to clear out 2 Portland Villas.
24 March	K.M. orders Princess Bibesco to stop writing love letters to her husband.
7 April	J. W. N. Sullivan at Villa Isola Bella.
Mid-April	L.M. returns to Menton.
4 May	Her failure to become a Roman Catholic being a disappointment to Miss Beauchamp, K.M. leaves the Villa Isola Bella for BAUGY, SWITZERLAND, accompanied by L.M., while Murry goes to Oxford to deliver his lectures, "The Problem of Style." She has two rooms at the Hôtel Beau Site, Clarens-Montreux. L.M. stays at Blonay.
14 May	K.M. goes by car to Sierre for the day, to see Dr. Stephani. She decides to move there.
26 May	"I long, above everything, to write about *family love.*"
June	(*Women in Love* published in London.)
21 May	Fearing that her father has stopped her allowance, K.M. asks Murry to open and read a letter from him. (She was mistaken. It continues at £300 a year.) She leaves Montreux for SIERRE (Pension du Lac).
9 June	Murry leaves London to join K.M. at the Hôtel Château Belle Vue, Sierre.
23 June	Rainer Maria Rilke, house-hunting, is at the same hotel.
? 23 June	The Murrys move into the CHALET DES SAPINS, Montana-sur-Sierre (not far from "Elizabeth's" chalet at Randogne), where K.M. begins writing stories for the *Sphere,* to pay her medical bills. L.M. works at a clinic in Montana and sleeps in the village.
25 July	*Women in Love* has arrived to be reviewed by Murry.
8 August	K.M. writing *At the Bay,* in a desire to present *her* view of human love.
11 August	*The Voyage* begun. L.M. visits London.
23 August	K.M. (in fever) working on *A Married Man's Story.*
6 September	L.M. arrives from London, bringing Wingley with her.
September	K.M. plans a "novel" to be called *Karori.*
10 September	She finishes *At the Bay* and sends it to J. C. Squire.
14 October	*The Garden Party* finished, and the name adopted for her new book. Squire has accepted *At the Bay* for the *London Mercury.*
18 October	K.M. asks Koteliansky for the address of Dr. Manoukhin in Paris.
27 October	K.M. lists "Stories for my new book," with alternating "N.Z." and "London" settings.

30 October	*The Doll's House* finished.
1 November	After a pained silence of 21 months, K.M. writes an important letter to her father begging "forgiveness."
29 November	K.M. asks Koteliansky for information about Dr. Manoukhin's treatment. Her letters show a desire for reconciliation with Koteliansky.
4 December	From her bed, she writes to Dr. Manoukhin.
24 December	His reply arrives.
31 December	*Marriage à la Mode* (containing a dig at Aldous Huxley) is published in the *Sphere*.

1922

1 January	K.M. writing *The Doves' Nest* and reading *Cosmic Anatomy*, sent to the Chalet by Orage (who has been seeing Ouspensky).
9 January	"I have £100 saved for this *last chance.*"
11 January	K.M. writes *A Cup of Tea* in 4–5 hours.
24 January	*Taking the Veil* written in "about 3 hours finally."
30 January	With Ida, K.M. leaves Montana for PARIS (Victoria Palace Hotel).
31 January	Sees Manoukhin and decides next day to begin his treatment, at 300 francs a time (about £7 10s).
7 February	She has begun to write *The Fly.*
9 February	Murry leaves Sierre by the night train to join K.M. in Paris. (Rilke finishes his seventh *Duino Elegy* at Château de Muzot and composes the eighth.)
10 February	L.M. returns to Montana to close up the Chalet des Sapins.
23 February	*The Garden Party and Other Stories* published by Constable.
26 February	*The Fly* completed.
18 March	K.M. replies to an affectionate letter from her father. *The Fly* published in the *Nation*.
29 March	James Joyce has tea with the Murrys at their hotel. K.M. "seems to understand his book better than her husband."
April	The Manoukhin treatments continue, leaving K.M. exhausted and unable to write.
3 May	K.M. tells J. B. Pinker she will not agree to a re-issue of *In a German Pension*. She begins a "serial" for the *Sphere*.
c. 28 May	L.M. goes to London, seeing K.M. in Paris on the way. No longer needed, she is to find work in England.
4 June	After a tiring last week of many engagements, K.M. and Murry leave Paris for the Hôtel d'Angleterre, RANDOGNE-SUR-SIERRE. An exhausting journey for K.M.

417

c. 8 June	K.M., "as ill as ever I was," asks Ida to write and offer to return to her.
12 June	Elizabeth arrives at the Chalet Soleil, Randogne.
29 June	Because of a rift between them, K.M. leaves Murry for the Hôtel Château Belle Vue, SIERRE, with L.M., while "J. remains aloft."
5 July	Dorothy Brett is staying with Katherine at Sierre.
7 July	As a gift for Brett, K.M. finishes her last completed story, *The Canary*.
July	Elizabeth lends K.M. £100.
7 August	K.M. privately writes a "farewell letter" to be left for Murry. Rather suddenly, she decides to go to London before returning to Manoukhin in Paris.
14 August	K.M. makes her will at Sierre. (In Wellington on this date, Lawrence sends her a postcard with the one word, "Ricordi.")
16 August	Accompanied by L.M. and Murry, K.M. travels to London— to Dorothy Brett's house, No. 6 POND STREET, HAMPSTEAD.
22 August	She has seen her father in London.
26–28 August	Murry is at Garsington. Meets W.J. Dunning there.
30 August	At Pond Street, K.M. has the first of her conversations with Orage concerning Gurdjieff.
1 September	Murry goes to live in Vivian Locke-Ellis's house at Selsfield. During September, with Murry out of the way, K.M. has further talks with Orage at Pond Street, has Koteliansky to tea three times, and attends lectures by P. D. Ouspensky.
17 September	An unpleasant meeting with Wyndham Lewis at the Schiffs'.
2 October	K.M. to PARIS (Select Hôtel), with L.M.
14 October	Orage arrives in Paris.
16 October	K.M. to Le Prieuré, Avon, FONTAINEBLEAU.
20 October	L.M. leaves K.M. for the last time. She goes to a farm at Lisieux. T. S. Eliot's *The Waste Land* is published in the *Criterion*.
27 October	*Jacob's Room* (Virginia Woolf) is published.
31 December	K.M. repays £100 to Elizabeth and writes to her father. Her allowances since 1908 now amount to about £2,600, to which should be added medical bills in 1910 and 1918.
1923	
9 January	At K.M.'s invitation, Murry goes to Fontainebleau to see her, arriving in the early afternoon. That evening she has a massive haemorrhage, and dies.

Bibliography

In sections II and III the place of publication for books, unless otherwise stated, is London.

I: By Katherine Mansfield

In a German Pension. London, Stephen Swift, December 1911. New York, Knopf, 1926.

Prelude. Richmond, Hogarth Press, July 1918.

Je ne parle pas français. Hampstead, Heron Press, February 1920.

Bliss and Other Stories. London, Constable, December 1920. New York, Knopf, January 1921.

The Garden Party and Other Stories. London, Constable, February 1922. New York, Knopf, May 1922.

The Doves' Nest and Other Stories, ed. J. M. Murry. London, Constable, June 1923. New York, Knopf, August 1923.

Poems, ed. J. M. Murry. London, Constable, November 1923. New York, Knopf, February 1924.

Something Childish and Other Stories, ed. J. M. Murry. London, Constable, August 1924. As *The Little Girl,* New York, Knopf, October 1924.

The Journal of Katherine Mansfield, ed. J. M. Murry. London, Constable, 1927. New York, Knopf, 1927.

The Letters of Katherine Mansfield, ed. J. M. Murry, 2 vols. London, Constable, 1928. 1 vol., New York, Knopf, 1929. (Includes letters to Murry among letters to others. There is much shortening and suppression, but many letters, notably those to Dorothy Brett, are at present known only from the extracts given in this edition.)

Maxim Gorki, *Reminiscences of Leonid Andreyev*, translated from the Russian by Katherine Mansfield and S. S. Koteliansky. New York, Crosby Gaige, 1928.

The Aloe, ed. J. M. Murry. London, Constable, 1930. New York, Knopf, 1930.

Novels and Novelists, ed. J. M. Murry. London, Constable, 1930. (Her *Athenaeum* reviews, with one omission.)

Stories by Katherine Mansfield. New York, Knopf, 1930. (The contents of the five main volumes arranged roughly in order of composition.)

The Scrapbook of Katherine Mansfield, ed. J. M. Murry. London, Constable, 1937, but my references are to the New York edition, 1939. (Nearly all of its contents have since been incorporated in the 1954 *Journal, q.v.* below.)

"To Stanislaw Wyspianski" (poem). Privately printed for Bertram Rota, London, 1938.

Collected Stories of Katherine Mansfield. London, Constable, 1945. (The five main volumes bundled together as an "omnibus," without rearrangement of contents.)

Katherine Mansfield's Letters to John Middleton Murry, 1913–1922, ed. J. M. Murry. London, Constable, 1951.

Journal of Katherine Mansfield, "Definitive Edition," ed. J. M. Murry. London, Constable, 1954.

"The Unpublished Manuscripts of Katherine Mansfield," transcribed and edited by Margaret Scott in six parts, in *Turnbull Library Record* (Wellington). All volume numbers are "new series":

1. "Juliet." Vol. III, 1:4–28, March 1970.

2. Juvenilia from 1906. Vol. III, 3:128–36, November 1970.

3. Juvenilia, *c.* 1907–1908, and fragment of the play, "A Ship in the Harbour" (April 1917). Vol. IV, 1:4–20, May 1971.

4. Wörishofen fragment, "Elena and Peter." Vol. V, 1:19–25, May 1972.

5. "The Laurels," fragment of a Christmas play written and acted at Garsington, 1916. Vol. VI, 2:4–8, October 1973.

6. Two "Maata" fragments (1913). Vol. VII, 1:4–14, May 1974.

Brave Love (1915), transcribed by Margaret Scott, in *Landfall* (Christchurch), XXVI, 1:3–30, March 1972.

Old Tar (from *Westminster Gazette*, 25 October 1913), in I. A. Gordon, ed., *Undiscovered Country, the New Zealand Stories of Katherine Mansfield*. London, 1974.

II: Selected Critical Monographs and Articles, Listed by Date of Publication

Mantz, Ruth Elvish. *The Critical Bibliography of Katherine Mansfield*. 1931.

Schneider, Elisabeth. "Katherine Mansfield and Chekhov," in *Modern Language Notes*, 50:394–96, June 1935.

Bibliography

Sewell, Arthur. *Katherine Mansfield, a Critical Essay.* Auckland, 1936.

Daiches, David. *New Literary Values.* 1936, pp. 83–114.

Porter, Katherine Anne. "The Art of Katherine Mansfield," in the *Nation*, New York, 145:435–36, 23 October 1937.

Berkman, Sylvia. *Katherine Mansfield, a Critical Study.* New Haven, 1951.

Hynes, Sam. "Katherine Mansfield: The Defeat of the Personal," in *South Atlantic Quarterly*, October 1953, pp. 555–60.

Bowen, Elizabeth. "A Living Writer," in *Cornhill Magazine*, no. 1010, pp. 121–34, Winter 1956–57.

Gordon, Ian A. "The Editing of Katherine Mansfield's *Journal* and *Scrapbook*," in *Landfall* (Christchurch), XIII, 1:62–69, March 1959. (Describes the jumble of notebooks, diaries and loose papers now in Wellington, and the relation to these of Murry's three published collections.)

Distel, M. "Katherine Mansfields Erzählung, *Je ne parle pas français*," Frankfurt, 1959; reprint from *Die Neueren Sprachen*, 6:249–63, 1959. (Detailed discussion of the cuts made in the 1920 version.)

Bateson, F. W., and B. Shahevitch. "Katherine Mansfield's 'The Fly,' " in *Essays in Criticism*, 12:39–53, January 1962; and discussion by other contributors in July and October.

Sutherland, Ronald. "Katherine Mansfield: Plagiarist, Disciple, or Ardent Admirer?" in *Critique*, 5:58–76, 1962.

Brophy, Brigid. "Katherine Mansfield," in *London Magazine*, December 1962. Reprinted in Brophy, *Don't Never Forget.* 1966.

Gordon, Ian A. *Katherine Mansfield* (a British Council booklet). 1963.

Daly, Saralyn R. *Katherine Mansfield.* New York, 1965.

Isherwood, Christopher. "Katherine Mansfield," in *Exhumations.* 1966.

Hormasji, Nariman. *Katherine Mansfield, An Appraisal.* Auckland, 1967.

Beachcroft, T. O. *The Modest Art, a Survey of the Short Story in English.* 1968, pp. 162–75.

Mortelier, Christiane. "The Genesis and Development of the Katherine Mansfield Legend in France," in *AUMLA* (Christchurch, N.Z.), 34:252–63, November 1970.

Margalaner, Marvin. *The Fiction of Katherine Mansfield.* Carbondale, Illinois, 1971.

Scott, Margaret. "The Extant Manuscripts of Katherine Mansfield," in *Etudes Anglaises*, XXVI, 4:413–19, 1973.

Beachcroft, T. O. "Katherine Mansfield's Encounter with Theocritus," in *English*, XXIII, 115:13–19, Spring 1974.

O'Sullivan, Vincent. "The Magnetic Chain: Notes and Approaches to K.M.," in *Landfall*, 114:95–131, June 1975. Studies early influences (Pater and Wilde) and their later implications.

Kurylo, Charanne C. "Chekhov and Katherine Mansfield: A Study in Literary

Influence" (unpublished dissertation). University of North Carolina, 1974.

Stead, C. K. "Katherine Mansfield and the Art of Fiction," in *New Review*, 4:42, pp. 27–36, September 1977.

Stone, Jean E. *Katherine Mansfield, Publications in Australia, 1907–1909*. Sydney, 1977.

Beachcroft, T. O., and others. Contributions to a Katherine Mansfield number of *Modern Fiction Studies*, vol. 24, no. 3, Autumn 1978.

III: Biographical and Historical

BOOKS

Alpers, Antony. *Katherine Mansfield, a Biography*. New York, 1953. (Now superseded, but it does contain a little material not repeated in this book.)

Anderson, Margaret. *The Unknowable Gurdjieff*. 1962.

[Baker, Ida]. *Katherine Mansfield, the Memories of L.M.* 1971.

Beauchamp, Sir Harold. *Reminiscences and Recollections*. New Plymouth, N.Z., 1937. (With a chapter on Katherine Mansfield contributed by Guy H. Scholefield.)

Bell, Quentin. *Bloomsbury*. 1974.

———. *Virginia Woolf, a Biography*. 2 vols. 1972.

Blue Review, The, May–July 1913, reprinted in one volume. Frank Cass, 1968.

Bowden, G. C. F. *Mathias Alexander and the Creative Advance of the Individual*. L. N. Fowler, 1965.

Carco, Francis. *Les Innocents*. Paris, 1916.

———. *Montmartre à vingt ans*. Paris, 1938.

———. *Bohème d'artiste*. Paris, 1940.

Carrington, Dora. *Letters and Extracts from Her Diaries*, ed. David Garnett. 1970.

Carswell, John. *Lives and Letters: A. R. Orage, Katherine Mansfield, Beatrice Hastings, John Middleton Murry, S. S. Koteliansky, 1906–1957*. 1978.

Darroch, Sandra Jobson. *Ottoline*. 1976.

Delany, Paul. *D. H. Lawrence's Nightmare*. New York, 1978.

Delavenay, Emile. *D. H. Lawrence, the Man and His Work*. 1972.

Ede, H. S. *Savage Messiah* (a life of Gaudier-Brzeska). 1931.

Fussell, Paul. *The Great War and Modern Memory*. 1975.

Gertler, Mark. *Selected Letters*, ed. Noel Carrington. 1965.

Glenavy, Beatrice Lady. *Today We Will Only Gossip*. 1964.

Gurdjieff, G. I. *All and Everything*. 1950.

———. *Meetings with Remarkable Men*. 1963.

Hassall, Christopher. *Edward Marsh*. 1959.

———. *Rupert Brooke, a Biography.* 1964.

Hastings, Beatrice. *The Old* New Age—*Orage and Others.* Blue Moon Press, 1935.

Holroyd, Michael. *Lytton Strachey, a Biography,* and *Lytton Strachey and the Bloomsbury Group.* 2 vols. Harmondsworth, 1971.

Hynes, Samuel. *The Edwardian Turn of Mind.* 1968.

Kaye, Elaine. *A History of Queen's College, London.* 1972.

Lawrence, D. H. *Letters,* ed. Aldous Huxley. 1932.

———. *Collected Letters,* ed. Harry T. Moore. New York, 1962.

———. "Prologue to *Women in Love,*" in *Phoenix II,* ed. W. Roberts and Harry T. Moore. 1968.

Lawrence, Frieda. *The Memoirs and Correspondence,* ed. E. W. Tedlock Jr. New York, 1964.

Lea, F. A. *John Middleton Murry.* 1959.

Lenoël, Odette. *La Vocation de Katherine Mansfield.* Paris, 1946.

Mairet, Philip. *A. R. Orage, a Memoir.* 1936; and New York (with a new Introduction), 1966.

Mantz, Ruth Elvish, and J. M. Murry. *The Life of Katherine Mansfield.* 1933.

Martin, Wallace. The New Age *Under Orage, Chapters in English Cultural History.* Manchester, 1967.

———. *Orage as Critic,* 1974.

Marwick, Arthur. *The Deluge, British Society in World War I.* Harmondsworth, 1967.

"M.B. Oxon." *Cosmic Anatomy, or the Structure of the Ego.* 1921. (No copy in BL.)

Merlin, Roland. *Le Drame Secret de Katherine Mansfield.* Paris, 1950.

Meyers, Jeffrey. *Katherine Mansfield, a Biography.* 1978.

Morrell, Lady Ottoline. *Ottoline, the Early Memoirs,* and *Ottoline at Garsington 1915–1918,* both ed. Robert Gathorne Hardy. 1963 and 1974. See also Darroch, above.

Murry, Colin Middleton. *One Hand Clapping, a Memoir of Childhood.* 1975.

Murry, John Middleton. *Still Life.* 1916.

———. *God, Being an Introduction to the Science of Metabiology.* 1929.

———. *Son of Woman, the Story of D. H. Lawrence.* 1931.

———. *Between Two Worlds, an Autobiography.* 1935.

———. *Katherine Mansfield and Other Literary Portraits.* 1949.

———. See also Mantz, 1933, above.

Nehls, Edward, ed. *D. H. Lawrence, a Composite Biography.* 3 vols. Madison, Wisconsin, 1957, 1958, 1959.

Noble, Joan Russell, ed. *Recollections of Virginia Woolf.* 1972.

Nott, C. S. *Journey Through This World,* 1969. (Describes meetings with Gurdjieff, Ouspensky, and Orage.)

Nowell-Smith, Simon, ed. *Edwardian England, 1901–1914.* 1964.

Orage, A. R. *Readers and Writers, 1917–1921.* 1922.

O'Sullivan, Vincent. *Katherine Mansfield's New Zealand.* 1975. (Photographs, with captions drawn from K.M.'s writings. Useful pictorial supplement to the early biography.)

Orton, William. *The Last Romantic.* 1937.

Ouspensky, P. D. *In Search of the Miraculous.* 1950.

Peters, Arthur Anderson. *Gurdjieff Remembered.* 1965.

Priestley, J. B. *The Edwardians.* 1970.

Rayfield, Donald. *Chekhov, The Evolution of His Art.* 1975.

Rosenbaum, S. P., ed. *The Bloomsbury Group, a Collection of Memoirs, Commentary and Criticism.* Toronto, 1975.

Schwendimann, Max. *Katherine Mansfield, ihr Leben in Darstellung und Dokumenten.* Munich, 1967.

Selver, Paul. *Orage and the* New Age *Circle.* 1959.

Swinnerton, Frank. *The Georgian Literary Scene.* 1938.

Walker, Kenneth. *Venture with Ideas.* 1951.

———. *A Study of Gurdjieff's Teaching.* 1957.

———. *The Making of Man.* 1963.

Woolf, Virginia. *Letters,* ed. Nigel Nicholson and Joanne Trautmann. Vols. I and II. 1975 and 1976.

———. *The Diary of Virginia Woolf,* ed. Anne Olivier Bell. Vols. I and II. 1977 and 1978.

Zytaruk, George, ed. *The Quest for Rananim, D. H. Lawrence's Letters to S. S. Koteliansky.* Montréal, 1971.

ARTICLES

Anonymous. "A Fashion in the Forest of Fontainebleau," in *Graphic,* CVII: 335, 10 March 1923. (Photographs.)

Bechhofer, C. E. "The Forest Philosophers," in *Century Magazine,* n.s., 86: 66–78, May 1924.

Clarke, Brice. "Katherine Mansfield's Illness," in *Proceedings of the Royal Society of Medicine,* 48:1029–32, April 1955.

Grindea, Miron, ed., *ADAM International Review,* no. 300, 1963–65. (An editorial on K.M. and Beatrice Hastings, forty-six letters by K.M. and other contributions.)

———. *ADAM,* special Mansfield issue, nos. 370–75, 1972–73, containing letters by her to V. Woolf, Richard Murry, and Bertrand Russell, and other contributions.

"Hudson, Stephen" (Sydney Schiff). "First Meetings with Katherine Mansfield," in *Cornhill Magazine,* 1017:202–12, Autumn 1958.

Kafian, Adèle. "The Last Days of Katherine Mansfield," in *Adelphi,* October–December 1946, pp. 36–39.

Leeming, Owen. "Katherine Mansfield's Sisters" (transcription of interviews recorded in London), in *New Zealand Listener,* 1 March, 29 March, 5 April, and 11 April 1963.

Olgivanna (Mrs. Frank Lloyd Wright, *née* Lazovich). "The Last Days of Katherine Mansfield," in *Bookman,* New York, 73:6–13, March 1931.

Orage, A. R. "Talks with Katherine Mansfield," in *Century Magazine,* n.s., 87:36–40, November 1924. Reprinted in his *Selected Essays and Critical Writings,* ed. H. Read and D. Saurat. 1967.

Saurat, Denis. "A Visit to Gourdyev," in *Living Age,* 345:427–33, January 1934.

Young, James Carruthers. "An Experiment at Fontainebleau, a Personal Reminiscence," in *New Adelphi,* n.s., 1:26–40, September 1927.

Notes

To keep down the number of reference figures in the narrative several methods have been used. They include the following:

1. Wherever possible the information needed to find a reference has been unobtrusively slipped into the text, or is implied there. For example, the dates of letters to the editor of the *New Age* cited on page 113 and of the letter to Brett on page 284 can be deduced from their respective contexts.

2. All references to stories and poems by Katherine Mansfield which are in collected editions rely on title only.

3. Reference to letters by Katherine Mansfield which appear in collected editions is usually made by date and recipient only. This will enable them to be located easily in the forthcoming full edition. The same rule has been followed for D. H. Lawrence.

4. Reference to a book that has an index is often made by title only, and sometimes by less than that (as with Beauchamp's *Reminiscences* and Murry's *Between Two Worlds*).

5. Most excerpts from K.M.'s notebooks and diaries have in fact been taken from or checked with the originals in Wellington, but for the reader's convenience I have called them *Journal* entries if they appear in the 1954 edition of *The Journal of Katherine Mansfield* and if Murry's transcription there is accurate. The abbreviation *"Journal"* at all times means that volume (no references at all being drawn from the earlier version), and in later chapters I have occasionally relied on its text, being unable to reconsult the original papers after 1973.

All unpublished material, with one or two deliberate exceptions, is documented in the usual way. Where letters or papers were lent to me but have since gone into an institutional collection I have given that source. Published letters to Richard Murry come under item 3 above, others being distinguished as "p.c.a.," for photocopy lent to author.

Most of K.M.'s letters to persons other than her husband are cited from originals whether published or not, but those to Dorothy Brett and one or two others are at present known to me only through published excerpts. As far as possible, excerpts from letters to Murry have been checked with the originals in Wellington. A special arrangement existing in 1973 denied me access to his own letters to K.M.

For Lawrence's letters I have had to use three published sources, of which the one that is most important here is George Zytaruk's full edition of the letters to Koteliansky, entitled *The Quest for Rananim.*

For K.M.'s *collected* letters—until a new edition is available—the following simple rule will help any reader needing further information: if the letter is to Murry, use his 1951 edition (letters to him alone); if to anyone else, consult the 1928 edition unless my reference shows another source.

ABBREVIATIONS USED IN THE NOTES

ATL Alexander Turnbull Library, Wellington, New Zealand.

BL The British Library (formerly British Museum).

B.T.W. Between Two Worlds, an Autobiography, by J. M. Murry, (London, 1935).

CINCINNATI Special Collections Department, University of Cincinnati Libraries.

CORNELL Rare Books Department, Cornell University Library, Ithaca, New York.

HUNTINGTON The Huntington Library, San Marino, California.

Journal The Journal of Katherine Mansfield (London, 1954).

KING'S The Library, King's College, Cambridge (the Charleston Papers).

MCMASTER Bertrand Russell Archives, Mills Memorial Library, McMaster University, Hamilton, Ontario.

N.A. The *New Age,* London, vols. VI–XXI, November 1909–October 1917 (odd volume numbers, November–April; even numbers, May–October).

n.d. no date.

NYPL The Berg Collection, New York Public Library.

p.c.a. photocopy lent to author.

Scrapbook The Scrapbook of Katherine Mansfield, ed. J. M. Murry, (New York, 1940).

SUSSEX University of Sussex Library (The Monk's House Papers).

TEXAS Humanities Research Center, University of Texas at Austin.

T.L.R. The *Turnbull Library Record,* Wellington, New Zealand.

T.L.S. The Times Literary Supplement, London.

t.s. typescript copy.

UCLA Research Library, University of California, Los Angeles.

v.v. viva voce, in conversation with the author.
WINDSOR Windsor University Library, Windsor, Ontario.

NOTES

The most commonly cited books and articles are referred to in the Notes in an abbreviated form: for full details see the Bibliography.

I: Places of Origin

1. Harold Beauchamp, *Reminiscences and Recollections* (1937) (see Bibliography).
2. *Cyclopaedia of New Zealand* (Wellington, 1897), vol. 1, p. 707.
3. K.M. to Murry, 8 April 1920.
4. R. B. Beckett, ed., *John Constable's Correspondence* (1967), vol. 5, p. 142.
5. See Leslie de Charms, *Elizabeth of the German Garden* (1958).
6. For a full report of the researches made in Sydney by Jean E. Stone, see her "Katherine Mansfield: Australian Family Associations," in *Biblionews* (Sydney), Third Series, 242nd issue, vol. 3, no. 4, 1978.
7. Information about old Karori and life at Chesney Wold from interviews in 1947 with Miss Rose Ridler, Miss Newcomb, and Mrs. Harold Miller.
8. Mrs. A. J. Norie, letter in Mantz papers, TEXAS.
9. *High School Reporter*, Wellington, September 1898.
10. *Journal*, p. 106.
11. *High School Reporter*, December 1899.
12. Marion C. Ruddick, "Incidents in the Life of Katherine Mansfield," unpublished t.s. lent by Mrs. Mackintosh Bell, Ottawa.
13. K.M. to Dorothy Brett, 8 August 1921.
14. Mantz and Murry (1933), pp. 136–37, and J. C. Beaglehole, *Victoria University College, an Essay Towards a History* (Wellington, 1949).
15. Tosti Murray, *Marsden, the History of a New Zealand School for Girls* (Wellington, 1967).
16. Mantz and Murry (1933), p. 152.
17. Miss Eva Butts, v.v., 1947.
18. "Kezia and Tui," in *Scrapbook*, p. 50, and "Sewing Class" in *Journal*, p. 115.
19. From the prayerbook, in TEXAS.
20. Margaret Scott, ed., "The Unpublished Manuscripts of Katherine Mansfield: Text of *Juliet*," *T.L.R.*, March 1970, pp. 4–28.
21. Agreement between the subscribers, recipients and trustees of the Trowell Fund, 9 March 1903, ATL.

II: Queen's College, London

1. Elaine Kaye, *History of Queen's College, London* (1972), p. 13. The next two paragraphs draw freely on this work, but my account is also based on conversations in 1949 with Mrs. M. J. Murphy, and letters from her, as well as conversations with Miss Ida Baker, Miss Ruth Herrick, and Katherine Mansfield's sisters, Vera and Chaddie.
2. Elaine Kaye's history (above), p. 136.
3. K.M. to Sylvia Payne, 23 December 1903, ATL.
4. *His Ideal*, in Notebook No. 40, ATL. There is also a later version in Notebook No. 29.
5. MS poem, "The Old Year and the New Year, 31 xii 03," ATL; and *Journal*, p. 1.
6. K.M. to Sylvia Payne at 78 Wimpole Street, 24 January 1904, ATL.
7. From the unfinished novel, "Juliet," in *T.L.R.*, March 1970, p. 14. (See note 19 below.)
8. Baker (1971), p. 27, and Murry, in a paragraph interpolated in Mantz and Murry (1933), p. 208.
9. *A Fairy Story* in *Open Window*, December 1910, pp. 162–76.
10. Countess von Arnim, *Elizabeth and Her German Garden* (1898).
11. *Die Einsame*, (The Lonely One), in *Queen's College Magazine*, vol. XXII, March 1904, pp. 129–31.
12. E. M. Forster, quoted in Leslie de Charms, *Elizabeth of the German Garden* (1958).
13. Notebook No. 29, ATL.
14. From "Love's Entreaty," in *Two Songs*, Eduard Bote and G. Bock (Berlin, 1904). A copy in ATL is inscribed, "To Tom, from Kathleen, 13.9.04."
15. Mrs. J. W. N. Sullivan (Vere Bartrick-Baker), v.v., 23 August 1949.
16. Miss Baker, v.v., 1948, and Mantz and Murry (1933), pp. 219–20.
17. Miss Herrick, v.v., 1947, and Eileen Palliser, quoted in Mantz and Murry (1933), p. 221.
18. Mrs. J. W. N. Sullivan, v.v., 1949.
19. Margaret Scott, ed., "The Unpublished Manuscripts of Katherine Mansfield: I," in *T.L.R.*, March 1970, pp. 4–28. The fragments are there lettered alphabetically in their order in the notebook. My reconstruction takes them in this order: A (H I) B (Q S) C D E F G, J, LMNOP, R (K) T.
20. Mantz and Murry (1933), p. 224.

III: Wellington After London

1. *Journal*, pp. 5–7, and Notebook No. 1, ATL.
2. J. C. Beaglehole, *Victoria University College, an Essay Towards a History* (Wellington, 1949), p. 29.
3. Chaddie Beauchamp to Sylvia Payne, n.d. [early January 1907]. All of Chaddie's letters in this chapter are cited from copies made from the originals once owned by Mrs. M. J. Murphy.
4. *Weekly Press* (Christchurch), 8 July 1908, p. 72.
5. K.M. to Sylvia Payne, 8 January 1907, ATL.
6. *Journal*, p. 222.
7. *Dominion* (Wellington), 8 November 1907, p. 11.
8. Notebooks No. 39 and No. 1, ATL.
9. Typed copy of "New Zealand Journal by Maata," in Mantz papers, TEXAS.
10. "E.K.B." (Mrs. G. G. S. Robison), v.v., 1947.
11. *Free Lance*, 13 April 1907, p. 1.
12. *Free Lance*, 4 May 1907.
13. Notes of an interview with Miss Putnam, Mantz papers, TEXAS.
14. *Journal*, pp. 12–13; and Notebook No. 39, pp. 15a–17a, ATL.
15. *Journal*, 29 June 1907, completed from Notebook No. 39, p. 17, ATL.
16. Dr. Scholefield in Beauchamp (1937), p. 194.
17. Marie Bashkirtseff, *Journal*, trans. M. Blind (1890).
18. K.M. to Mattie Putnam, 22 July 1907, ATL.
19. Tom L. Mills, "Katherine Mansfield: How Kathleen Beauchamp Came into Her Own," in *New Zealand Railways Magazine* (Wellington), 1 September 1933, pp. 6–7; and Mantz and Murry (1933), pp. 269–71.
20. See Dorothy Landin, "Katherine Mansfield's First Story" (interview with E. J. Brady, giving copies of the letters), in *Newsview* (Auckland), February 1949, pp. 19–21.
21. *Native Companion* (Melbourne), October 1907; reprinted in Jean E. Stone, *Katherine Mansfield: Publications in Australia, 1907–09* (Sydney, 1977).
22. *Native Companion*, December 1907; reprinted in Stone (as preceding).
23. *Journal*, p. 21.
24. *Journal*, p. 22.
25. K.M. to Mrs. Beauchamp, unposted letter, 20 November 1907, MSS. Papers 119:14, ATL.
26. Letter from Elsie D. Webber to H. G. Cook, 20 February 1956, ATL.
27. *Journal*, p. 23.
28. *Journal*, p. 25.
29. *Journal*, p. 29.

30. R. R. Beauchamp, "A Family Affair—or, What Became of Fred?" in the *Press* (Christchurch), 17 May 1975, p. 12.

31. *Journal*, p. 30.

32. *To Stanislaw Wyspiański* (Bertram Rota, London, 1939); also in Curnow, ed., *The Penguin Anthology of New Zealand Verse* (1960).

33. *Journal*, p. 35.

34. K.M. to Sylvia Payne, 4 March 1908, ATL.

35. Miss Baker, v.v., 1948.

36. *Journal*, pp. 35–37.

37. *Dominion* (Wellington), 20 June 1908, p. 11.

38. Original MS. (so punctuated), shown to the author in 1947 by Mr. Siegfried Eichelbaum, Wellington.

39. "Priscilla" in *Evening Post* (Wellington), 4 July 1908, p. 15.

40. Remark well known in the family of Captain Weston.

IV: Beauchamp Lodge, 1908

1. Miss Ruth Herrick, v.v., 1947, and Mrs. Woodhouse, v.v., 1948.

2. Notes of an interview with Ida Baker in Miss Mantz's "Calendar," vol. 3, TEXAS.

3. Mrs. Woodhouse, v.v., 1948–49, and "Notes re K.M." (1948), in author's possession.

4. Margaret Scott, ed., "The Unpublished Manuscripts of Katherine Mansfield: Two Maata Fragments," in *T.L.R.*, May 1974, pp. 4–11.

5. K.M. to Garnet Trowell, n.d. [September 1908], WINDSOR. All letters to Garnet Trowell cited in this chapter are from the same collection.

6. K.M. to G.T. from Beauchamp Lodge, 6 October 1908.

7. K.M. to G.T. from Upper Warlingham, 16 October 1908.

8. Baker (1971), p. 39.

9. Notebook No. 29, p. 37, ATL.

10. K.M. to G.T. from Beauchamp Lodge, 17 September 1908.

11. K.M. to G.T. "Wednesday night" [23 September 1908].

12. K.M. to G.T., 3 October 1908.

13. From "Melrose," Upper Warlingham, 15 October 1908.

14. Notebook No. 8, p. 61a, ATL.

15. Notebook No. 8, pp. 61–50 *(sic)* ff., 21 October 1908, ATL.

16. Notebook No. 8, ATL.

17. K.M. to G.T. from Devonport, 8 November 1908.

18. From a typed copy supplied by G. N. Morris, 1948.

19. *Collected Stories* (1945), p. 524.

20. *The Tiredness of Rosabel* was dated by Murry and Ida Baker jointly, after K.M.'s death, when Murry still had the manuscript. There is a problem,

however: the "electric staircase" at Earl's Court underground station, to which Rosabel refers, was only completed in October 1911, though there was something of the sort at Harrod's in 1908. This implies that the manuscript must have been revised after 1911—how far, one cannot say; the escalator may simply have been moved from Harrod's to Earl's Court. Since it is most unlikely that K.M. could have willingly returned to all the painful associations of Beauchamp Lodge after 1911, I believe the story must have been written approximately as we know it, while she was living there. Some light may be thrown on this problem if the manuscript turns up.

21. "Jacob Tonson" (Arnold Bennett), in the *New Age,* 25 April 1908 and 8 September 1910.
22. Arthur Misener, *The Saddest Story* (1971), p. 154.
23. Mrs. Woodhouse, "Notes re K.M.," in author's possession.
24. Mrs. Woodhouse, "Notes re K.M."
25. Miss Watson to the author, 10 November 1949.

V: "Mss. Bowden," 1909

1. Entry No. 109 in Register Book of Marriages No. 45, Paddington Registration District, 2 March 1909.
2. Baker (1971), p. 46.
3. Mrs. Woodhouse to the author, 31 October 1949.
4. "A Biographical Note on Katherine Mansfield" (1948), unpublished t.s. in author's possession, is the main source of information from Mr. Bowden, but it is supplemented by various letters, 1949–50, and by conversations with him and his wife and son in 1972.
5. "A Little Episode" (excerpts), typed copy, n.d., TEXAS.
6. K.M. to Garnet Trowell, 28 September 1908, WINDSOR.
7. MS. fragment, n.d., photocopied by the author.
8. Murry always believed that Katherine, as is stated in the *Journal,* joined Garnet in Hull in November 1908, and in a letter to the author of 15 September 1953 he mentioned "evidence" for this, and gave the dates, 4 and 5 November. He believed, as well, that that is when she became pregnant. But Kathleen could not have left London then, for there exist no fewer than three of her envelopes, all clearly postmarked Paddington, which were posted on those dates. Two of them went to Garnet in Hull, the contents being unknown. See also the footnote on page 98, which discusses the implications of a pregnancy beginning in November 1908.
9. *Journal,* p. 42, corrected from MSS. Papers 119:12, ATL.
10. "I am in a carriage with vier männe. . . . . At Hereford a man and a woman enter, sit opposite me. . . . ."—Notebook No. 2, p. 72, ATL.

11. *Journal,* pp. 40–41.
12. This is actually Murry's recollection of what K.M. must have told him, given in Mantz and Murry (1933), p. 321. The description otherwise follows Miss Baker's account.
13. Mrs. C. M. Renshaw (Jeanne Beauchamp), v.v., 1949.
14. G. C. Bowden to Andrew Moore, 27 February 1919, copy in author's possession.
15. The will of Annie Burnell Beauchamp, 27 January 1903, filed at the Supreme Court, Wellington.
16. Josef Wolf, Kneipp-Archivar, Bad Wörishofen, to the author, 30 August 1976. All the information about K.M.'s movements in Wörishofen has been supplied from official sources by Herr Wolf. Jeffrey Meyers, in his 1978 biography, states that Mrs. Beauchamp "decided to conceal the scandal by taking her daughter to a convent in Germany and leaving her there," but this is incorrect.
17. Josef Wolf to the author, 1976; and the story, *Frau Fischer,* in *In a German Pension.*
18. *Journal,* p. 42, and MSS. papers 119:12, ATL.
19. *Journal,* p. 43. The original is not in any of K.M.'s notebooks in Wellington. Murry included various marginalia, and notes from flyleaves of K.M.'s books, when compiling the *Journal,* making his own deductions as to appropriate dates.
20. Margaret Scott, ed., "The Unpublished Manuscripts of Katherine Mansfield, Part IV," in *T.L.R.,* May 1972, pp. 19–25.
21. Fräulein Maria Brechenmacher v.v. to Maria Theresia Riley in Wörishofen, 24 February 1977.
22. In Mantz and Murry (1933), p. 325.
23. Jeffrey Meyers, "Katherine Mansfield's 'To Stanislaw Wyspianski [sic],' " in *Modern Fiction Studies,* vol. 24, no. 3, Autumn 1978, pp. 337–41. Professor Meyers makes assertions in this article about K.M.'s physical relations with Sobieniowski, both in Wörishofen and in London later, for which there is, of course, no evidence to be had.
24. Photocopied by the author.
25. Sobieniowski to K.M., 12 December 1909, p.c.a., trans. Anne-Marie Epp.
26. Vera French to K.M., 12 December 1909, p.c.a.
27. Ida Baker to K.M., 21 December 1909, p.c.a.
28. Sobieniowski to K.M., 9 January 1910, p.c.a., trans. Anne-Marie Epp.
29. G. C. Bowden, "A Biographical Note" (see note 4 above).

VI: *The New Age*

1. *New English Weekly*, A. R. Orage memorial number, 15 November 1934, p. 99.
2. Quoted in Wallace Martin, *"The New Age" Under Orage* (1967).
3. Letter to the editor, *N.A.* 12 November 1912.
4. Orage to Middleton Murry, 9 June 1933, TEXAS.
5. Elisabeth Schneider, "Katherine Mansfield and Chekhov," in *Modern Language Notes*, June 1935, pp. 394–97.
6. R. Sutherland, "Katherine Mansfield: Plagiarist, Disciple, or Ardent Admirer?" in *Critique*, vol. 5, no. 2, Fall 1962, pp. 58–76.
7. C. E. Bechhofer Roberts, v.v., 16 November 1949.
8. Beatrice Lady Glenavy, v.v., 1950.
9. Ida Baker to Garnet Trowell, 29 July 1910, WINDSOR.
10. E. B. d'Auvergne to the author, 5 July 1954.
11. Orton, *The Last Romantic* (1937), pp. 269–84. All quotations not taken from a letter to the author, and all the notebook entries given by Orton, will be found there.
12. Baker (1971), p. 62.
13. Huntly Carter, "The Post Savages," *N.A.* 8 December 1910, pp. 140–42; George Calderon, "The Post-Impressionists," *N.A.*, 24 November 1910, pp. 89–90; "Jacob Tonson" (Arnold Bennett), "Books and Persons," *N.A.*, 8 December 1910, p. 135.
14. K.M. to Dorothy Brett, 5 December 1921.
15. J. M. Murry to the author, 18 September 1953.
16. E. B. d'Auvergne to the author, 5 July 1954.
17. Baker (1971), p. 65.
18. Leslie Beauchamp to Ida Baker from 34 Norfolk Square, 20 May and 10 June 1911, ATL.
19. *N.A.*, 29 June 1911, p. 196.
20. Beachcroft, *The Modest Art* (1968), p. 17.
21. Brice Clarke, M.D., "Katherine Mansfield's Illness," in *Proceedings of the Royal Society of Medicine*, vol. 48, April 1955, pp. 1029–32.
22. *Daily Telegraph*, 8 December 1911, and *Morning Post*, n.d., both from typed copies supplied by G. N. Morris; publisher's advertisement, n.d., copy lent by Mrs. C. M. Pickthall; *N.A.*, 21 December 1911, p. 188.

VII: *Rhythm*, 1912

1. Sources, from here on, include F. A. Lea's *John Middleton Murry* (1959), Murry's *Between Two Worlds* (1935), and his contribution to John Lehmann's *Coming to London* (1957).
2. *N.A.*, 30 November 1911, p. 115.
3. Margaret Morris, *The Art of J. D. Fergusson* (1974), p. 64.
4. Notes of an interview with Orage, Mantz papers, TEXAS.
5. *The Breidenbach Family in England* (*N.A.* 17 Aug. 1911, p. 371), which I ascribed to K.M. in my previous book, was unsigned, and was not listed among her contributions in the *N.A.* index for that half-year. It is a very clever imitation of her *Pension* sketches, but its characters talk at times in a Hans Breitman kind of "broken English," which the *Pension* characters never do. If that might seem consistent with the English setting, the game is given away by the Christian names of the Herr Doctor Breidenbach and his wife: they are Carl and Emelie. The piece is clearly a weekend concoction by Beatrice Hastings (*née* Emily Alice Haigh) and her frequent house-guest in 1911, Carl Eric Bechhofer, who was then 17, and a prolific *New Age* parodist. "The Mating of Gwendolen," by "Mouche" (*N.A.*, 2 November 1911), has also been attributed to K.M. by Jack Garlington (*Modern Language Notes*, vol. 71, February 1956, pp. 91–92), but I think mistakenly, if only because "Mouche" was also the author of a later story, "A Flirtation" (*N.A.*, 1 August 1912), not conceivably by K.M.
6. Murry to K.M., 27 January 1912, typed copy, TEXAS.
7. *N.A.*, 7 March 1912, p. 447.
8. *N.A.*, 18 April 1912, p. 589. Beatrice Hastings says in her Blue Moon Press booklet of 1936 that she wrote these articles, but this one contains an obvious interpolation by Orage (a view endorsed by Miss Alice Marks).
9. *Frederick Goodyear, Letters and Remains, 1887–1917*, Foreword by F. W. Leith Ross (1920).
10. H. S. Ede, *Savage Messiah* (1931), p. 140.
11. "A Fourth Tale for Men Only" ran consecutively from 2 May to 6 June 1912.
12. Interview with Orage, Mantz papers, TEXAS.
13. G. C. Bowden to the author, 16 November 1949 and 22 February 1950.
14. G. C. Bowden to W. Somerset Maugham, 23 April 1959 (copy supplied by Mr. Bowden).
15. Lord Glenavy (Gordon Campbell), v.v., 1950.
16. "Books and Persons," *N.A.*, 23 March 1911, p. 492.

17. C. Hassall, *A Biography of Edward Marsh* (1959), pp. 215–20. Statements elsewhere attributed to Murry are from *B.T.W.*
18. H. S. Ede (1931), pp. 138–40; and *B.T.W.*, pp. 221–31.
19. Advertisement of C. W. Daniel, *N.A.*, 5 January 1911.
20. *The Times*, 3 July and 5 July 1913.

VIII: *The Blue Review*

1. Murry to Edward Marsh, 25 October 1912, NYPL.
2. Frank Swinnerton, *Background with Chorus* (1956), pp. 145–53.
3. *Between Two Worlds*, p. 237; and Murry to Marsh, 18 January 1913, NYPL.
4. Murry to Marsh, "Tuesday night" [1912], NYPL.
5. G. Cannan *et al.* to Compton Mackenzie, n.d. [November 1912], TEXAS; and Murry to Thomas Moult, 25 November 1912, NYPL.
6. *Hearth and Home*, 28 November 1912, pp. 233–34.
7. *N.A.*, 2 January 1913, p. 212.
8. Edward Marsh, *A Number of People* (1939).
9. Murry to Marsh, 18 January 1913, NYPL. The loan, at 12 1/2 per cent from the Westminster Loan and Discount Association, was actually needed to pay off recent printing bills and rent due at Runcton. Marsh good-humouredly but inaccurately described the fate of the guarantee in his book, *A Number of People* (1939), but the account given here is based on letters preserved among his own papers. Both men recalled the incident inaccurately.
10. Hassall, *Rupert Brooke* (1964), p. 374.
11. Murry to Walpole, 10 March and 12 March 1913, TEXAS.
12. Murry to K.M., 12 May 1913, typed copy, TEXAS.
13. K.M. to J.M.M., "Tuesday," in *Letters* (1951), p. 6.
14. Murry to Walpole, 18 May 1913, TEXAS.
15. Murry to Marsh, 1 July 1913, NYPL.
16. Murry to Leonard Woolf, 16 July 1913, NYPL.
17. E. Delavenay, *D. H. Lawrence, the Man and His Work* (1972), p. 413.
18. In *Phoenix II* (1968), pp. 92–108.
19. A pencilled note, *c.* 1930, in the margin of Murry's MS. journal for 23 December 1914, beside some early reservations about *The Rainbow*.
20. D.H.L. to J.M.M. from Lerici, n.d., 1913 (Moore edition, p. 238).

IX: Indiscreet Journeys

1. Murry's journal, 27 October 1913.
2. Murry to Marsh, 5 January 1914, NYPL.

3. F. W. Leith-Ross in *Frederick Goodyear, Letters and Remains* (1920); and K.M. to J.M.M., 6 February 1918.

4. *B.T.W.*, p. 275; and Murry to K.M., 10 February 1914, typed copy, TEXAS.

5. *Journal*, p. 51.

6. Miss Baker, v.v., 1949. Murry's date in K.M.'s *Collected Poems* is incorrect.

7. *B.T.W.*, p. 281.

8. Murry to Marsh from Edith Grove, "Friday," NYPL.

9. *Still Life* (1916), pp. 107 and 121.

10. *B.T.W.*, p. 286.

11. K.M. to Sylvia Payne from Rye, 23 September 1914, ATL.

12. Murry to Marsh from 111 Arthur Street, "Saturday" [3 October 1914], NYPL.

13. Mrs. O. Raymond Drey, v.v., 1948.

14. Murry's journal, 18 November 1914.

15. Leonard Woolf, *Beginning Again* (1964), pp. 251–52.

16. John Carswell, *Lives and Letters* (1978), pp. 101–102.

17. *B.T.W.*, pp. 320 and 340.

18. *T.L.R.*, May 1972, pp. 19–20.

19. Murry's journal, 23 December 1914.

20. Cannan to Lady Ottoline Morrell, n.d. [26 December 1914], TEXAS.

21. Quoted in E. W. Tedlock Jr., ed., *Frieda Lawrence, the Memoirs and Correspondence* (New York, 1964), p. 358.

22. D.H.L. to W. E. Hopkin, 18 January 1915.

23. Catherine Carswell, *The Savage Pilgrimage* (1932), p. 22.

24. *Landfall* (New Zealand), vol. 26, no. 1, March 1972, pp. 3–29.

25. Murry's journal records the fact, and uses that phrase, on 12 February 1915.

26. Leslie Beauchamp to his parents, 11 February 1915, ATL.

27. *Journal*, p. 75.

28. *B.T.W.*, p. 340.

29. Two 1914 letters from Beatrice Hastings to Wyndham Lewis (CORNELL) disclose a helpless infatuation for him: "My love is altogether beyond me. . . . . It is always tears now. . . . . I am afraid of being alone."

30. K.M. to J.M.M., 21 March 1915.

31. *Montmartre à vingt ans* (Paris, 1938), pp. 195–96, trans. Stella Wynne-Edwards.

X: Acacia Road and the Villa Pauline

1. Leslie Beauchamp to his parents, 25 August 1915, ATL.

2. D.H.L. to Lady Cynthia Asquith, 5 September 1915.

3. Miss Nathan, v.v., 1973.

4. Edward Shanks to the author, 2 September 1949.

5. Murry, MS. fragment quoted by Carswell (1978), pp. 111–12; Lady Glenavy's

recollections quoted in the next paragraph are from her *Today We Will Only Gossip* (1964), pp. 82–83.

6. From the inscribed copy, NYPL.

7. *B.T.W.*, p. 351.

8. For the *Rainbow* affair and its consequences, see Delavenay, *D. H. Lawrence* (1972), pp. 235–42. Other details are from Nehls's *Composite Biography* of Lawrence, vol. I, 1957.

9. *N.A.*, 4 November 1915, p. 14.

10. Murry to K.M., 6:00 P.M., 20 December 1915, typed copy, TEXAS.

11. Murry to K.M., 10:00 P.M., 20 December 1915, typed copy, TEXAS.

12. Murry to K.M., 26 December 1915, typed copy, TEXAS.

13. K.M. to O.M. [21 January 1916], TEXAS.

14. There are more facts about K.M.'s forebears in Alpers (1953).

15. *The Aloe* (New York, 1930), pp. 126–27.

16. Annie Beauchamp to Clara Palmer, 16 March 1916.

17. D.H.L. to K.M., 7 January 1916, 12 December 1915, and 20 December 1915.

18. K.M. to O.M. (with addition by J.M.M.), 26 February 1916, TEXAS.

19. D.H.L. to the Murrys, 11 March 1916; and Frieda Lawrence to K.M. (with pencilled additions by D.H.L.), written from The Tinner's Arms, Zennor, about the same date, ATL.

20. Goodyear's letters to K.M., 14 February, *c.* 28 February and 9 April 1916, are in ATL. The full text of her unposted "Sunday" letter to him [4 March 1916] is in her Notebook No. 34, ATL.

XI: Cornwall, 1916

1. K.M. to J.M.M., 11 May 1915, ATL.

2. Frieda Lawrence to O.M., n.d. [before 7 April 1916], TEXAS.

3. Murry to O.M., 12 April 1916, TEXAS.

4. In D. H. Lawrence, *Phoenix II* (1968), pp. 92–108.

5. K.M. to Beatrice Campbell [11 May 1916], quoted in Glenavy (1964), p. 94.

6. K.M. to Koteliansky, 11 May 1916, folio 200, BL.

7. K.M. to O.M., "A Tuesday night, No, it's Wednesday" [17 May 1916], TEXAS.

8. K.M. to Beatrice Campbell, as in note 5 above.

9. K.M. to Koteliansky, 24 June, and n.d. [3 July 1916], folios 187 and 191, BL.

10. D.H.L. to Koteliansky, 7 July 1916; and see preceding note.

11. K.M. to J.M.M., "Sunday night" [20 August 1916], ATL.

12. See note 17, below.

13. The description that follows draws upon Lady Ottoline's *Memoirs* (for details, see note 15 below), on conversations with her daughter Mrs. Igor

Vinogradoff, and on many other sources, including Leonard Woolf, *Downhill All the Way* (1967), and Michael Holroyd, *Lytton Strachey, a Biography* (1971).

14. *Virginia Woolf and Lytton Strachey: Letters*, ed. Leonard Woolf and James Strachey (1956), pp. 60–62.

15. *Ottoline at Garsington, Memoirs of Lady Ottoline Morrell, 1915–1918*, ed. R. Gathorne Hardy (1974), p. 49.

16. *In Confidence*, in *N.A.*, 24 May 1917, pp. 88–89.

17. See Gertler, *Selected Letters*, ed. Noel Carrington (1965), pp. 114–15 (where Gertler's letter, as Mr. Carrington agrees, should be dated 20 July 1916), and Glenavy (1964), p. 97. Paul Delany, *D. H. Lawrence's Nightmare* (1978), has the facts as well as the date of this episode wrong. K.M. did not go to Garsington for a rendezvous with Gertler (whom she disliked). His unhappiness there was caused by Carrington's rejection of him.

18. *B.T.W.*, p. 421.

19. Both the verse and the letter are quoted from *Frederick Goodyear, Letters and Remains* (1920).

20. Murry to Edward Marsh, 10 July 1916, NYPL.

21. Clive Bell to Vanessa Bell, "Tuesday" [5 September 1916] (CBVB am I, 20), KING'S. "5£" is not a printer's error.

22. D.H.L. to Koteliansky, 15 December 1916.

23. Murry to O.M., 28 July 1916, TEXAS.

24. D.H.L. to J.M.M., 28 August 1916; and to Koteliansky, 30 August 1916.

XII: Gower Street and Garsington

1. Strachey's letter is among Lady Ottoline's papers in TEXAS. The book was a private edition of the letters of the family of Lady Desborough, mother of the poet Julian Grenfell.

2. Gertler to O.M., n.d. [31 August 1916], TEXAS.

3. Huxley to O.M., "Thursday" [31 August 1916], and K.M. to O.M., "Tuesday" [12 September 1916], TEXAS. The episode occurred on Wednesday 30 August; Gertler and Huxley wrote to O.M. next day, and Lawrence acknowledged Koteliansky's description on 4 September.

4. Murry began the process in his *Reminiscences of D. H. Lawrence* (1933), by implying that Philip Heseltine and Michael Arlen (though he did not name them) were the two who jeered at the poems. Heseltine's biographer, Cecil Gray, tried to exonerate Heseltine, but received no help from Arlen, who gave a lying confirmation some years later. (The relevant passages from Lawrence, Murry and Arlen can be found in E. H. Nehls's *Composite Biography* of Lawrence, vol. I, pp. 399–400.) Meyers (1978) repeats the false allegation against Heseltine.

5. Frieda Lawrence to Koteliansky, 20 September 1916, quoted in E. W. Tedlock Jr., ed., *Frieda Lawrence, the Memoirs and Correspondence* (1964).
6. In Glenavy, *Today We Will Only Gossip* (1964), p. 95.
7. Carrington to Gertler, n.d. [*c.* 10 September 1916], TEXAS. Previous accounts of the lodging arrangements given by Roy Harrod in his life of Keynes (and therefore by Holroyd in his life of Strachey) and, more recently, by Paul Delany, have all put the parties on the wrong floors. Carrington's letter is clear on the point, and is borne out by subsequent events.
8. All of Murry's letters to O.M., quoted here, are in TEXAS.
9. Clive Bell to Vanessa Bell [6 or 13 December 1916] (CBVB am I, 22), KING'S.
10. All of Brett's letters to O.M., quoted here, are in TEXAS. They are mostly undated, but have lent themselves to dating by various means.
11. Brett to O.M. [21 October and 26 October 1916], TEXAS.
12. Brett to O.M. [2 November 1916], TEXAS.
13. B.R. to O.M., June 1917, TEXAS.
14. K.M. to B.R., 1 December 1916, MCMASTER.
15. B.R. to O.M., 3 December 1916, TEXAS.
16. K.M. to B.R., "Thursday evening" [7 or 14 December 1916], MCMASTER.
17. Brett to O.M., 9 December 1916, TEXAS.
18. K.M. to B.R., 17 December 1916, MCMASTER.
19. Baker (1971), p. 100.
20. Strachey to O.M., 31 October 1916, TEXAS.
21. Morrell, *Memoirs*, vol. II (1974), p. 127.
22. Brett to O.M., 7 or 14 December 1916, TEXAS.
23. See Carrington's *Letters* (1970), letter of 30 July 1916.
24. Carrington to Noel Carrington, 26 December 1916, in *Country Life*, 23 December 1971, p. 1794. The same letter is quoted *passim* in this section.
25. Murry to O.M. [24 December 1916], TEXAS.
26. Murry to Brett [24 December 1916], CINCINNATI.
27. K.M. to J.M.M., n.d., in *Letters* (1951), p. 93.
28. In Grover Smith, ed., *The Letters of Aldous Huxley* (1969).
29. For a transcription made by Margaret Scott see *T.L.R.*, October 1973, pp. 5–8.
30. Morrell, *Memoirs*, vol. II (1974), p. 128.
31. K.M. to O.M., "Tuesday" [2 January 1917], and "Sunday night" [14 January 1917), TEXAS.
32. Clive Bell to Vanessa Bell, 20 January 1917 (CBVB am I 24), KING'S.
33. *Letters* (1951), p. 91.
34. K.M. to B.R. [5 January 1917], MCMASTER.
35. K.M. to O.M., 14 January 1917, TEXAS.
36. V.W. to Vanessa Bell, 11 February 1917, NYPL.
37. K.M. to B.R., 24 January 1917, ATL.

38. Russell's *Autobiography, 1914–1944* (1968), p. 27.
39. K.M. to O.M., 6 February 1917, TEXAS.
40. Bertrand Russell, "The World After the War, VI: National Defence," in *Ploughshare*, vol. 1, no. 2, n.s., January 1917; and K.M. to B.R., 24 February 1917, MCMASTER.
41. K.M. to O.M. [*c.* 1 June 1917], handwritten copy, TEXAS.

XIII: A Studio in Chelsea

1. Baker (1971), p. 100.
2. K.M. to O.M., "Tuesday midnight" [? 3 April 1917], TEXAS.
3. Beachcroft, "Katherine Mansfield's Encounter with Theocritus," in *English*, Spring 1974, pp. 13–19.
4. Clive Bell, *Old Friends* (1956), p. 122.
5. K.M. to V.W., n.d. [May 1919], SUSSEX.
6. Untitled MS. fragment of the play, ATL.
7. *N.A.*, 19 April 1917, p. 595.
8. Murry's unpublished journal, in possession of his son Mr. J. M. Murry.
9. Aldous Huxley to Julian Huxley in his *Letters*, ed. Grover Smith, 1969, p. 140.
10. *N.A.*, 19 April 1917, p. 595.
11. A nineteen-page fragment of MS., identified in Murry's hand as a translation from Wyspiański, appears in Notebook No. 32 (which also contains some 1917 material), ATL. Another fragment, the opening of the tragedy *The Judges*, identified in Sobieniowski's hand and dated by him "1917," is in NYPL.
12. K.M. to O.M., "Saturday afternoon—in the garden," TEXAS.
13. Lady Ottoline Morrell, "K.M." in *Katherine Mansfield: An Exhibition* (catalogue), Humanities Research Center, University of Texas at Austin, 1973.
14. K.M. to O.M., "Saturday night" [11 August 1917], TEXAS.
15. L.M. told the author that she used to brush K.M.'s hair by the hour throughout their friendship, but that "she couldn't bear it if I *touched* her."

XIV: Katherine and Virginia, 1917–1923

1. Quentin Bell, *Virginia Woolf*, vol. II (1972), p. 28. Biographical facts about V.W. in this chapter, if not otherwise acknowledged, are owed to Professor Bell's work or to her diary.
2. Leonard Woolf, *Beginning Again* (1964), pp. 203–204.

3. V.W. to Vanessa Bell, 21 June 1917, NYPL. (All V.W./V.B. letters are quoted from that collection); and V.W. to Violet Dickinson, 10 June 1918, NYPL.
4. K.M. to O.M., "Tuesday" [3 July 1917], dated by reference to a letter of Murry's; TEXAS.
5. V.W. to O.M., "Aug. 15th" [1917], TEXAS.
6. K.M. to O.M. "Wednesday," TEXAS. Murry's dating, as of 1928, is clearly correct. The letter was written on 15 August.
7. K.M. to V.W., n.d. (assigned to 21 August by reference to the *Journal*), NYPL.
8. Murry to O.M., "Sunday" [possibly 7 October 1917], TEXAS.
9. Mrs. Alix Strachey in J. R. Noble, ed., *Recollections of Virginia Woolf* (1972); and her letter to Frances Partridge, 11 October 1971, made available by Mr. Stanley Olsen.
10. Murry to O.M., 15 September 1917, and K.M. to O.M., "Sunday night," TEXAS; Clive Bell to Vanessa Bell (CB/VB am I 40), KING'S.
11. The diary passage is in the *Diary*, vol. I, p. 58, and Woolf's comment is from his *Beginning Again*, p. 205. For K.M.'s use of *Genêt fleuri*, see her letters to Murry of 12 December 1915, 19 March 1918, and 13/14 October 1919.
12. Quentin Bell, vol. II (1972), p. 37.
13. Anne Estelle Rice, "Memories of Katherine Mansfield," in *ADAM* 300, 1963, p. 76; Frieda Lawrence's *Memoirs*, ed. E. W. Tedlock Jr. (1964), pp. 425–26; Lady Ottoline Morrell, quoted in *ADAM* nos. 370–75, 1972–73, p. 11; Helen Harris, MS. notes on K.M., n.d., TEXAS; Francis Carco, *Montmartre à vingt ans* (1938), p. 179.
14. K.M. to Brett, 11 October 1917, in *Letters* (1928), vol. I.
15. V.W.'s *Diary*, 2 March 1918.
16. K.M. to O.M., "Friday" ["27 June 1919"—J.M.M.], TEXAS.
17. K.M. to J.M.M., 10 November, 13 November, and 26 November 1919, ATL.
18. K.M. to J.M.M., 10 November 1919, ATL.
19. K.M. to J.M.M., 16 November 1919, ATL.
20. V.W.'s *Diary*, 31 May 1920, and 5 June 1920. The remark, quoted just below, about "some suffering animal," is from the *Diary*, 16 January 1920.
21. K.M. to V.W., 27 December 1920, typed copy, SUSSEX.
22. V.W. to Brett, 2 March 1923, CINCINNATI.
23. V.W.'s *Diary*, 28 January 1923.

XV: Bandol, 1918

1. J.M.M. to Arthur Murry, 9 September 1917, CINCINNATI.
2. *B.T.W.*, p. 444, and K.M. to O.M., n.d. [before 23 November 1917], TEXAS.
3. *N.A.*, 6 September 1917, pp. 411–12.
4. O.M. to Bertrand Russell, 23 November 1917, MCMASTER.
5. Clive Bell's letter to Vanessa Bell, 2 January 1918 (CBVB am I, 43), KING'S,

records the Garsington visit, and Murry's commentary in the 1951 *Letters*, p. iii, gives the date of departure. See also K.M. to J.M.M., 13 January, 23 March, and 2 June 1918, in which "Aunt Martha" refers to her menstrual period.

6. K.M. to J.M.M., 11 January 1918.
7. K.M. to J.M.M., "Sunday night" [3 February 1918].
8. Murry to K.M., 30 March 1918, quoted in F. A. Lea's biography, p. 62.
9. Brigid Brophy, *Don't Never Forget* (1966), pp. 255–63.
10. K.M. to J.M.M., 26 January 1918.
11. K.M. to J.M.M., 12 February, 14 February, 20 February, and 16 February 1918.
12. K.M. to J.M.M., 18 March 1918.
13. K.M. to J.M.M., letter of 10 and 11 February 1918.
14. K.M. to J.M.M., 3 February 1918.
15. Notebook No. 15, ATL, p. 1; and *Journal*, p. 128.
16. *Je ne parle pas français* (Heron Press, Hampstead, 1920), p. 25.
17. K.M. to J.M.M., 6 April, 7 April, and 7 December 1920.
18. K.M. to J.M.M., 28 February 1918, ATL.
19. K.M. to J.M.M., 13 March 1918.
20. Murry to K.M., as in note 8, above.
21. K.M. to J.M.M., 2 April 1918.
22. K.M. to J.M.M., 26 March 1918.
23. K.M. to J.M.M., 23 March 1918.

XVI: Waiting for The Elephant

1. *Journal*, 26 April 1918, and K.M. to Ida Baker, 18 May 1918, quoted in Baker (1971), p. 113.
2. V.W. to O.M., 28 May 1918, TEXAS.
3. K.M. to J.M.M., 27 May 1918.
4. Annie Beauchamp to Clara Palmer, 6 May 1918, ATL.
5. K.M. to J.M.M. (unposted), 9 June 1918.
6. See the items by Elizabeth Bowen, Katherine Anne Porter, T. O. Beachcroft, Frank O'Connor, Christopher Isherwood and David Daiches in Section II of the Bibliography. André Maurois's comment was made in his *Poets and Prophets* (1935).
7. *Nation*, 20 July 1918; O.M. to J.M.M., quoted in his reply to her of 16 July 1918, TEXAS; Murry to O.M., as preceding; O.M. to B.R. in prison, n.d., late July 1918, MCMASTER; B.R. to *Nation* (as "Philalethes"), n.d. [c. 20 July 1918], original in TEXAS; B.R. to O.M. from prison, 25 July [1918], TEXAS; K.M. to O.M., "Tuesday" [23 July 1918], TEXAS; Siegfried Sassoon to O.M., quoted in O.M. to B.R., 30 July 1918, MCMASTER; B.R. to O.M. on *Prelude*,

25 July 1918, TEXAS; K.M. to V.W. ("after the great San Philip's a-running down of the little Revenge in this week's *Nation* I don't think I *can* break crumb in their house again"), 23 July 1918, NYPL; Clive Bell to Vanessa Bell, "Wednesday" [29 July 1918] (CBVB am I, 55/1), KING'S; B.R. to O.M. on the Murrys, 25 July and 26 August 1918, TEXAS; Brett to O.M., n.d., TEXAS.

8. O.M. to B.R., 17 August 1918, MCMASTER.

9. Baker (1971), pp. 55 and 128.

10. Beatrice Lady Glenavy, v.v., 1948.

11. *Journal*, p. 150; and K.M. to Brett, 27 October 1918.

12. *B.T.W.*, p. 490; and V.W. to Vanessa Bell, 6 November 1918, NYPL.

13. Harold Beauchamp to the proprietors of the Bank of New Zealand, 6 December 1918, from the bank's *Reports of Proceedings*, August 1900 to June 1920, p. 401.

14. Beatrice Lady Glenavy (1964), p. 111.

15. Virginia Woolf, *Diary*, vol. I, p. 243.

XVII: The *Athenaeum* and the Casetta

1. He had made the remark in a book review; see *The Evolution of an Intellectual* (1920), p. 98.

2. Strachey to O.M., March 1919, TEXAS; V.W.'s diary, 19 March 1919, NYPL; D.H.L. to Koteliansky, 17 January 1919.

3. V.W.'s diary, 17 April 1919, NYPL; and *Athenaeum*, 2 May 1919.

4. K.M. to J.M.M., 26 November 1919, ATL.

5. See Beachcroft (1968), p. 147.

6. My quotations are all from the U.S. edition (1930).

7. K.M. to O.M., "Wednesday" [18 June 1919], TEXAS; to Anne Estelle Rice, 13 August 1919, in *Letters* (1928), vol. I; and to O.M. [August 1919], TEXAS.

8. K.M. to J.M.M., 9 September 1919, ATL.

9. What follows draws upon K.M.'s letters to J.M.M., on some of his to her, on talks with Miss Baker, 1949–50, and on her book (1971).

10. *Journal*, p. 190, and K.M. to J.M.M., 23 November 1919.

11. K.M. to J.M.M., 20 November 1919, ATL.

12. C. Hassall, *Edward Marsh* (1964), pp. 474–75.

13. *Journal*, pp. 181–82. See especially the bitter poem *Et Après*.

14. *The Aloe* (New York, 1930), p. 130; and in *Prelude*, episode XI.

15. K.M. to J.M.M., 21 January 1920, and 8:00 A.M., 30 November 1919.

16. *Journal*, 12 January 1920, corrected from the diary, ATL.

17. K.M. to J.M.M., 13 January 1920.

18. K.M. to J.M.M., 21 January and 22 January 1920, ATL.

XVIII: Conquest of the Personal

1. *Journal*, p. 195.
2. K.M. to J.M.M., 5 December 1919.
3. *Journal*, 1 February 1920.
4. K.M. to J.M.M., 7 February 1920; and Lea (1959), p. 83.
5. *Journal*, 8 February 1920.
6. K.M. to J.M.M., 10 February 1920.
7. Baker (1971), p. 149.
8. From the book (inscribed "To Katie from Jinnie, St. Joseph's Day 1920"), in ATL.
9. *Journal*, 7 January 1920.
10. Harold Beauchamp, recorded on 9 March 1921 in Murry's journal from K.M.'s conversation, and inserted in her *Journal* under that date. Murry never learned how the remark had reached K.M.
11. K.M. to J.M.M., 10 October 1920.
12. K.M. to Violet Schiff, n.d. [mid-May 1920], BL.
13. K.M. to Violet Schiff, "Monday" [10 May 1920], BL.
14. K.M. to Violet Schiff, "Friday" [14 or 21 May 1920], BL.
15. *Journal*, p. 205. The piece is actually an unused draft for a review of W. Bryher's *Development*.
16. K.M. to Violet Schiff, "Monday" [10 May 1920], BL. If it was published, this must have been the belated anonymous review of *Night and Day*, in *Nation*, 15 May. Mrs. Woolf thought that review was by Sylvia Lynd (*Diary*, 20 May), but it reads very much like a second attempt by K.M. to review the book without constraint. Far more temperate than "smashing," it calls the book a comedy, "witty in phrase, exquisitely 'mounted,' stage-managed so that all its scenes move with a lifelike ease—and wrongly cast." Its anonymous writing would amply explain K.M.'s reluctance to meet with Virginia that week.
17. Thomas Moult, "Katherine Mansfield as I Knew Her," in *T.P.'s Weekly*, 1 December 1928, p. 176.
18. K.M. to J.M.M., 7 November 1920, ATL.
19. J.M.M. to Brett, 8 March 1920, CINCINNATI.
20. Notebook No. 25, p. 2, ATL. Murry suppressed this passage when editing the *Journal* in Brett's lifetime, pencilling a note beside it to the effect that he had done so for her sake, but also "for J.M.M. a little."
21. Lea (1959), p. 81.
22. K.M. to J.M.M., 16 September 1920. The original letter (evidently abridged for publication by J.M.M.) is not in Wellington.
23. Copy of Murry's letter supplied by F. A. Lea; biographical details from

Slownik Wspolczesnych Pisarzy Polskich (Warsaw, 1964). K.M.'s MS. version of a part of Wyspiański's *The Judges,* made in 1917 and so identified in Sobieniowski's hand, is in NYPL.

24. K.M. to J.M.M., 31 October 1920.
25. K.M. to J.M.M., 14 November, 17 November, and 18 November 1920.
26. K.M. to J.M.M., 17 November 1920.
27. Murry to K.M., *c.* 10 December 1920.
28. Telegram to Murry, 12 December 1920, ATL.
29. MSS. Papers 119/10, ATL.
30. Murry to Brett, "Wednesday" [22 December 1920], CINCINNATI.
31. From the original in possession of Mrs. Jessie Orage. The letter is incorrectly dated in Mairet (1936), Carswell (1978), and Meyers (1978), but was correctly dated in Alpers (1953).
32. D.H.L. to Mary Cannan, 12 February 1921, and to Koteliansky, 2 March 1921.
33. K.M. to J.M.M., 25 September 1920.
34. K.M. to Garnet Trowell, 17 September 1908.
35. From the fragment, "Geneva," written in January 1917 and given in *Scrapbook* (1915) under the heading, "The Lost Battle."
36. J.M.M., "On Reading Novels," in *Things to Come* (1928), p. 250.
37. K.M. to W. Gerhardi, 23 June 1921, and to Brett, 11 November 1921. Hardy's message was given personally to Murry at Max Gate.
38. D. Daiches, *New Literary Values* (1936), p. 84.
39. K.M. to L.M., 20 March 1921, quoted in Baker (1971), p. 162.
40. Typed copy, TEXAS.
41. *Journal,* pp. 228 and 229–30. See also *Letters* (1951), p. 604, and Murry's introductory note to the posthumous, *Something Childish but Very Natural.*
42. *Journal,* pp. 241–42.

XIX: The Chalet des Sapins, Montana

1. K.M. to J.M.M., "Monday" [23 May 1921], ATL.
2. Murry to K.M. [26 May and 2 June 1921], ATL.
3. Squire to K.M., 17 May 1921, UCLA.
4. K.M. to Mrs. Belloc-Lowndes, 26 May 1921, TEXAS.
5. J. R. von Salis, *Rainer Maria Rilke: The Years in Switzerland,* trans. N. K. Cruickshank (Berkeley, 1964).
6. K.M. to O.M., 24 July 1921, TEXAS.
7. K.M. to Richard Murry, "Sunday" [24 July 1921], p.c.a.
8. See page 372.
9. *Journal,* p. 256.
10. *Journal,* p. 262 and p. 257.
11. As in note 6 above.

12. H. Coombes, ed., *D. H. Lawrence* (Penguin Critical Anthology) (1973), pp. 138–43.
13. K.M. to Richard Murry, 9 August 1921; and K.M. to Brett, 29 August 1921.
14. Virginia Woolf, *The Waves* (1931).
15. In *New Statesman and Nation*, 2 February 1946.
16. K.M. to Harold Beauchamp, 1 November 1921, ATL. The original of this letter, formerly in the Turnbull Library, is no longer there. My reproduction is from a photocopy made in Canada.
17. K.M. to Koteliansky, n.d. [*c.* 20 December 1921], BL.
18. D.H.L. to Koteliansky, 10 November 1921.

XX: In Search of a Miracle

1. K.M. to Richard Murry, 20 June 1921. In fact the reckless payments which E.J. Brady of the *Native Companion* sent her in 1907 were probably the highest recompense, for the words involved, that she ever received from any magazine.
2. In *Letters* (1951), p. 641.
3. *Sketch* to K.M., 2 January 1922, Pinker Collection, Northwestern University, Evanston, Illinois.
4. Murry understood that the visit was for a consultation only (c.f. K.M. to Violet Schiff, n.d., "I won't stay—just see my man and return in the spring"), but an entry of 14 January in "Elizabeth's" journal (HUNTINGTON) says: "She starts in a fortnight and will be away four months."
5. K.M. to J.M.M., 1 February 1922; K.M. to Mrs. C. M. Pickthall, 5 February 1922; and *Journal*, 9 February 1922.
6. Murry to K.M., 9 February 1922, typed copy, TEXAS. The tipping of the guard is described in J.M.M. to "Elizabeth," 9 May 1922, HUNTINGTON.
7. F. W. Bateson and B. Shahevitch, "Katherine Mansfield's 'The Fly': A Critical Exercise," in *Essays in Criticism*, vol. 12, 1962, pp. 39–53. The other contributions are listed in C. T. Wright, "The Genesis of a Short Story," in *Philological Quarterly*, vol. 34, January 1955, pp. 91–96.
8. Notebook No. 6, p. 3, and Notebook No. 1 ("Juliet"), p. 104a, ATL.
9. K.M. to J.M.M., 7 February, and to Brett, 14 February and 26 February 1922.
10. For detailed citations, see Alpers (1953), p. 376.
11. V. Schiff to Wyndham Lewis (enclosing K.M.'s letter), 4 April 1922, CORNELL.
12. K.M. to Brett, 1 May 1922.
13. Quoted in Baker (1971), p. 193.
14. "Elizabeth" to K.M., "Thursday" [11 May 1922], HUNTINGTON.
15. J.M.M. to "Elizabeth," 9 May 1922, HUNTINGTON.
16. K.M. to Ida Baker, 5 June 1922, quoted in Baker (1971), p. 198.

17. Quoted in Baker (1971), p. 200.
18. K.M. to "Elizabeth" [12 June 1922], BL.
19. K.M. to Harold Beauchamp, 18 March 1922, ATL.
20. K.M. to H.B., n.d. [early June 1922], ATL.
21. *Letters* (1951), p. 656.
22. *Journal,* 4 July 1922.
23. Copies of these undated letters are in HUNTINGTON. The first belongs to 30 July 1922.
24. Quoted in Lea (1959), p. 95.
25. K.M.'s will, Public Record Office, London.
26. K.M. to J.M.M., 20 September 1922, and D.H.L. to J.M.M., 2 February 1923.

XXI: To Fontainebleau

1. P. D. Ouspensky, *In Search of the Miraculous* (New York, 1949), pp. 34–36.
2. C. E. Bechhofer Roberts, "The Forest Philosophers," in *World's Work,* July 1924, pp. 9–16; and J. C. Young, "An Experiment at Fontainebleau," in *New Adelphi,* September 1927, pp. 26–40.
3. K.M. to Harold Beauchamp, 18 August 1922, ATL.
4. K.M. to "Elizabeth" [22 August 1922], BL.
5. In K.M.'s *Letters* (1951), p. 659.
6. K.M. to Koteliansky, *c.* 30 August 1922, BL.
7. Kenneth Walker, *Venture with Ideas* (1951), pp. 19–28.
8. Murry to Violet Schiff, 21 December 1948, BL.
9. Wyndham Lewis to V. Schiff, *c.* 20 September 1922, BL.
10. Lewis to Sydney Schiff, *c.* 20 September 1922, BL.
11. K.M. to Richard Murry, 3 October 1922, p.c.a.
12. Violet Schiff to Lewis, 19 October 1922, CORNELL.
13. Miss Alice Marks, v.v., 1949.
14. J. C. Young (as in note 2, above), and Baker (1971), p. 226.
15. C. S. Nott, *The Teachings of Gurdjieff* (1961), pp. 42–46.
16. K.M. to J.M.M., 11 October, 14 October, and 16 October 1922.
17. K.M. to J.M.M., 18 October and 20 October 1922.
18. Quoted in Baker (1971), pp. 213–18.
19. K.M. to J.M.M., 20 October 1922.
20. K.M. to J.M.M., 27 October 1922.
21. "Olgivanna," "The Last Days of Katherine Mansfield," in *Bookman* (New York), March 1931, pp. 6–13.
22. Walker, *The Making of Man* (1963), p. 150.
23. K.M. to J.M.M., 12 November 1922.
24. K.M. to J.M.M., n.d. [after 19 November] and 9 December 1922.
25. Lea (1959), p. 93.

26. K.M. to J.M.M., 9 December 1922.
27. K.M. to J.M.M., 17 December 1922.
28. Orage, "Talks with Katherine Mansfield," in *Century Magazine,* November 1924, pp. 36–40.
29. "Olgivanna," as in note 21 above.
30. Adèle Kafian, "The Last Days of Katherine Mansfield," in *New Adelphi,* October–December 1946, pp. 36–39.
31. In Baker (1971), p. 227.
32. K.M. to "Elizabeth," 31 December 1922, HUNTINGTON.
33. K.M. to her sisters Chaddie and Jeanne, 31 December 1922, original owned by the late Mrs. C. M. Pickthall.
34. K.M. to Harold Beauchamp, 31 December 1922.
35. In K.M.'s *Letters* (1951), p. 700.
36. "Olgivanna" (1931), pp. 12–13.
37. Kafian (1946).
38. D.H.L. to J.M.M., 2 February 1923.
39. E. M. Forster to J.M.M., "4.i.23" (in error for 4.ii.23), TEXAS.

XXII: Afterwards

1. Sir Harold Beauchamp, *Reminiscences* (1937), pp. 182 and 217; Carswell (1978), p. 197.
2. J.M.M. to O.M., "Monday" [January 1923], TEXAS.
3. J.M.M. to Brett, 1 February 1923, CINCINNATI. The letter which follows is also in that collection.
4. Capt. C. M. Renshaw, v.v., 1949.
5. Quoted in Ernest Griffin, *John Middleton Murry* (New York, 1969), p. 70.
6. To Koteliansky, 4 October 1916, quoted in *Frieda Lawrence, the Memoirs and Correspondence,* ed. E. W. Tedlock Jr. (1964), p. 205.

Index

*denotes fictional character.

Katherine Mansfield's poems and early writings are included in the main Mansfield entry; all other works by Katherine Mansfield are individually listed.

Index

Acknowledgments continued from the copyright page

G. C. BOWDEN: From "Biographical Note on Katherine Mansfield" by permission of C. M. Bowden and A. F. Moore Bowden.

FRANCIS CARCO: From *Montmartre A Vingt Ans.* © Albin Michel 1938, 1965 by Albin Michel. Reprinted by permission of Editions Albin Michel.

DORA CARRINGTON: From Dora Carrington's letter to Noel Carrington published in *Country Life* Magazine, 23 December 1971. Used by permission of Mrs. Frances Partridge.

DAVID DAICHES: From *New Literary Values* by David Daiches and reprinted with his permission.

ELIZABETH: From *Elizabeth and Her German Garden* by Countess Russell. Reprinted by permission of Macmillan Administration (Basingstoke) Ltd.

CONSTANCE GARNETT: From *The Steppe* by Anton Chekhov, translated by Constance Garnett. © by the Estate of Constance Garnett. Reprinted by permission of Chatto & Windus Ltd., and A. P. Watt, Ltd.

EDMUND GOSSE: From *Father and Son* by Edmund Gosse, first published by William Heinemann Ltd. Reprinted by permission of William Heinemann Ltd.

ALDOUS HUXLEY: From *Letters of Aldous Huxley*, edited by Grover Smith. Copyright © 1969 by Laura Huxley, Copyright © 1969 by Grover Smith. Reprinted by permission of Harper & Row and Chatto & Windus Ltd.

D. H. LAWRENCE: From *The Letters of D. H. Lawrence*, edited by Aldous Huxley. Copyright 1932 by the Estate of D. H. Lawrence, Copyright © renewed 1960 by Angelo Ravagli and C. M. Weekley, Executors of the Estate of Frieda Lawrence Ravagli. From *Women in Love* by D. H. Lawrence. Copyright 1920, 1922 by D. H. Lawrence. Copyright renewed 1948, 1950 by Frieda Lawrence. Reprinted by permission of Viking Penguin Inc., and Laurence Pollinger Ltd. All rights reserved.

FRIEDA LAWRENCE: From *Frieda Lawrence: The Memoirs and Correspondence*, edited by E. W. Tedlock. Copyright © 1961, 1964 by the Estate of Frieda Lawrence. Reprinted by permission of Alfred A. Knopf, Inc. and Laurence Pollinger Ltd.

JOHN MIDDLETON MURRY: From *Journal of Katherine Mansfield.* Copyright 1927 by Alfred A. Knopf, Inc. and renewed 1955 by J. Middleton Murry. From *The Letters of Katherine Mansfield*, edited by John Middleton Murry. Copyright 1929 by Alfred A. Knopf, Inc., and renewed 1957 by J. Middleton Murry. From *Katherine Mansfield's Letters to John Middleton Murry 1913–1922.* Copyright 1929, 1951 by Alfred A. Knopf, Inc. and renewed © 1957 by J. Middleton Murry. All reprinted by permission of Alfred A. Knopf, Inc.

A. R. ORAGE: From *Tales for Men Only* by A. R. Orage. Copyright © 1974 by Artemis Press Limited for Mrs. A. R. Orage. Reprinted by permission of Artemis Press Ltd.

RAINER MARIA RILKE: From *Rilke, Europe, and the English-Speaking World*, by E. C. Mason. Copyright © 1969 by Cambridge University Press. Reprinted by permission of Cambridge University Press.

H. G. WELLS: From *Ann Veronica* by H. G. Wells. Copyright 1909 by H. G. Wells. Reprinted by permission of J. M. Dent & Sons Ltd. and A. P. Watt Ltd. and the Estate of the late H. G. Wells.

VIRGINIA WOOLF: From *The Waves* by Virginia Woolf, Copyright 1931 by Harcourt Brace Jovanovich, Inc.; renewed © 1959 by Leonard Woolf. From *The Diary of Virginia Woolf* (Vols. I and II), edited by Anne Oliver Bell, and from *The Letters of Virginia Woolf* (Vols. I, II, III, IV), edited by Nigel Nicolson and Joanne Trautmann. All reprinted by permission of Harcourt Brace Jovanovich, Inc., and The Hogarth Press.